OXFORD SHAKESPEARE CONCORDANCES

OXFORD SHAKESPEARE CONCORDANCES

CORIOLANUS

A CONCORDANCE TO THE TEXT
OF THE FIRST FOLIO

OXFORD
AT THE CLARENDON PRESS
1972

Oxford University Press, Ely House, London W. 1

GLASGOW   NEW YORK   TORONTO   MELBOURNE   WELLINGTON
CAPE TOWN   IBADAN   NAIROBI   DAR ES SALAAM   LUSAKA   ADDIS ABABA
DELHI   BOMBAY   CALCUTTA   MADRAS   KARACHI   LAHORE   DACCA
KUALA LUMPUR   SINGAPORE   HONG KONG   TOKYO

FILMSET BY COMPUTAPRINT LIMITED
AND PRINTED IN GREAT BRITAIN
AT THE UNIVERSITY PRESS, OXFORD
BY VIVIAN RIDLER
PRINTER TO THE UNIVERSITY

GENERAL INTRODUCTION

In this series of Oxford Shakespeare Concordances, a separate
volume is devoted to each of the plays. The text for each concordance
is the one chosen as copy-text by Dr. Alice Walker for the Oxford
Old Spelling Shakespeare now in preparation.

Each concordance takes account of every word in the text, and re-
presents their occurrence by frequency counts, line numbers, and
reference lines, or a selection of these according to the interest of the
particular word. The number of words which have frequency counts
only has been kept as low as possible. The introduction to each
volume records the facsimile copy of the text from which the concordance was prepared, a table of Folio through line numbers and
Globe edition act and scene numbers, a list of the misprints corrected in the text, and an account of the order of printing, and the
proof-reading, abstracted from Professor Charlton Hinman's *The
Printing and Proof-Reading of the First Folio of Shakespeare* (Oxford,
1963).

The following notes on the main features of the concordances may
be helpful.[1]

A. *The Text*

The most obvious misprints have been corrected, on conservative
principles, and have been listed for each play in the introduction to
the corresponding concordance. Wrong-fount letters have been
silently corrected.

Obvious irregularities on the part of the original compositor—
for example the anomalous absence of full stops after speech prefixes—have been normalized and noted. Colons, semicolons, exclama-
tion and interrogation marks after italicized words have been
modernized to roman fount after current practice, since this aspect of

[1] An account of the principles and methods by which the concordances were
edited appears in *Studies in Bibliography*, vol. 22, 1969.

compositorial practice would not normally be studied from a concordance. The spacing of words in the original printed texts, particularly in 'justified' lines, is extremely variable; spacing has been normalized on the basis of the compositor's practice as revealed in the particular column or page.

For ease of reference, the contractions *S.*, *L.*, *M.*, and forms such as *Mist.* and tildes, have been expanded when the compositor's own preferred practice is clear, and the expansion has been noted in the text. For M^r, the superior character has been lowered silently. Superior characters like the circumflex in *baâ* and those in $\overset{t}{y}$, $\overset{e}{y}$, $\overset{u}{y}$, and $\overset{c}{w}$, have been ignored. The reader should find little difficulty in distinguishing the original form of the pronominal contractions when they are encountered in the text. They are listed under Y and W respectively.

B. *Arrangement of entries*

The words in the text are arranged alphabetically, with numerals and & and &c listed at the end. Words starting with I and J, and U and V, will be found together under I and V respectively. The reader should note that the use of U for the medial V (and I for J) leads in some cases to an unfamiliar order of entry. For example, ADUISED is listed before ADULTERY. The reader will usually find the word he wants if he starts his inquiry at the modern spelling, for when the old spelling differs considerably from the modern spelling, a reference such as 'ENFORCE *see* inforce' will direct the reader to the entry in the concordance.

In hyphenated compounds where the hyphen is the second or third character of the heading-word (as in A-BOORD), the hyphenated form may be listed some distance from other occurrences of the same word in un-hyphenated form. In significant cases, references are given to alert the user.

Under the heading-word, the line numbers or lines of context are in the order of the text. The heading-word is followed by a frequency count of the words in short and long (that is, marked with an asterisk) lines, and the reference lines. When a word has been treated as one to have a frequency count only, or a list of the line numbers and count, any further count which follows will refer to the reference lines listed under the same heading. Where there are two counts but no reference lines (as with AN), the first count refers to the speech prefix.

C. *Special Forms*

(*a*) The following words have not been given context lines and line references but are dealt with only by the counting of their frequency:

A AM AND ARE AT BE BY HE I IN IS IT OF ON SHE THE THEY TO WAS WE WITH YOU

These forms occur so often in most texts that the reader can locate them more easily by examining the text of the play than he could by referring to an extensive listing in the concordance.

Homographs of these words (for example I = *ay*) have been listed in full and are given separate counts under the same heading-word.

(*b*) A larger number of words, consisting mainly of variant spellings, have been given line references as well as frequency counts.

These words are: ACTUS AN AR ART ATT AU BEE BEEING BEEN BEENE BEING BENE BIN BUT CAN CANST CE COULD COULDST DE DECIMA DES DID DIDD DIDDEST DIDDST DO DOE DOES DOEST DOETH DONE DOO DOOE DOOES DOOEST DOOING DOON DOONE DOOS DOOST DOOTH DOS DOST DOTH DU E EN EST ET ETC FINIS FOR FROM HA HAD HADST HAH HAS HAST HATH HAUE HEE HEEL HEELE HEL HELL HER HIM HIR HIS IE IF IL ILL ILLE INTO LA LE LES MA MAIE MAIEST MAIST MAY ME MEE MIGHT MIGHTEST MIGHTST MINE MOI MOY MY NE NO NOE NON NONA NOR NOT O OCTAUA OFF OH OR OU OUR OUT PRIMA PRIMUS QUARTA QUARTUS QUE QUINTA QUINTUS SCAENA SCENA SCOENA SECUNDA SECUNDUS SEPTIMA SEPTIMUS SEXTA SHAL SHALL SHALT SHEE SHOLD SHOLDE SHOLDST SHOULD SHOULDE SHOULDST SIR SO SOE TE TERTIA TERTIUS THAT THEE THEIR THEIRE THEM THEN THER THERE THESE THEYR THIS THOSE THOU THY TIS TU VN VNE VOS VOSTRE VOUS VS WAST WEE WER WERE WERT WHAT WHEN WHER WHERE WHICH WHO WHOM WHOME WHY WIL WILL WILT WILTE WOLD WOLDE WOLDST WOULD WOULDE WOULDEST WOULDST YE YEE YF YOUE YOUR YT & &c 1 2 3 4.

Homographs of words on this list (e.g. *bee* = n.) have been listed in full, and also have separate counts.

(*c*) All speech prefixes, other than *All.*, *Both.*, and those which represent the names of actors, have been treated as count-only words. In some cases, however, where a speech prefix corresponds to a form already on the count-only list (e.g. *Is.*), a full entry has been given. In some other cases, when two counts are given for the same heading-word for no apparent reason, the count which does not correspond to the following full references or to the list of line references is that of the speech prefix form (for example AN in *The Tempest*).

(*d*) Hyphenated compounds such as *all-building-law* have been listed under the full form, and also under each main constituent after the first. In this example there are entries under ALL-BUILDING-LAW, BUILDING, and LAW. When, however, one of the constituents of the compound is a word on the count- or location-only list ((*a*) or (*b*) above), it is dealt with in whichever of these two lists applies. References such as 'AT *see also* bemock't-at-stabs' are given to assist the reader in such cases.

Simple or non-hyphenated compounds such as *o'th'King* have been listed only under the constituent parts—in this example under OTH and KING.

(*e*) 'Justified' lines where the spellings *may* have been affected by the compositor's need to fit the text to his measure are distinguished by an asterisk at the beginning of the reference line. If only location is being given, the asterisk occurs before the line reference. If only frequency counts are being given, the number *after* the asterisk records the frequency of forms occurring in 'justified' lines. Lines which do not extend to the full width of the compositor's measure have not been distinguished as 'justified' lines, even though in many cases the shorter line may have affected the spelling.

D. *Line Numbers*

The lines in each text have been numbered from the first *Actus Primus* or stage direction and thereafter in normal reading order, including all stage directions and act and scene divisions. Each typographical line has been counted as a unit when it contains matter for inclusion in the concordance. Catchwords are not included in the count. The only general exception is that turn-overs are regarded as belonging to their base-lines; where a turn-over occurs on a line by itself, it has been reckoned as part of the base-line, and the line containing only the turn-over has not been counted as a separate line. Turn-overs may readily be distinguished by vertical stroke and single bracket after the last word of the base-line; for example *brought with* | (*child,*.

When two or more lines have been joined in order to provide a fuller context, the line-endings are indicated by a vertical stroke |, and the line reference applies to that part of the line before the vertical stroke. For the true line-numbers of words in the following part of the context line, the stated line-number should be increased by one each time a vertical stroke occurs, save when the next word is a turn-over.

The numbering of the quarto texts has been fitted to that of the corresponding Folio texts; lines in the Quarto which do not occur in the Folio are prefixed by +. The line references are similarly specified. The line references of these concordances therefore provide a consistent permanent numbering of each typographical line of text, based on the First Folio.

PROGRAM CHANGES

Preparation of concordances to the first few texts, and the especial complexity of *Wiv.*, have enabled some improvements to be made to the main concordance program. For texts other than *Tmp.*, *TGV*, *MM*, and *Err.*, the concordances have been prepared with the improved program.

Speech-prefixes now have separate entries under the appropriate heading-word and follow any other entry under the same heading-word. Entries under AN in *Wiv.*, AND and TO in *TN*, and AD in *AYL* offer examples. This alteration provides a clearer record of the total number of occurrences of words which occur both as speech-prefixes and also as forms on the 'count only' or 'locations only' lists.

Another modification supplies a more precise reference to the location of words such as BEENE for which line numbers but no full lines are given. When a 'location only' word is encountered to the right of the 'end-of-line' bar (which shows that lines of text have been joined together in order to provide a sufficient context), the line number is now adjusted to supply the exact reference. In the concordances to the texts listed above, users will find that in some instances the particular occurrence of a 'location only' word which they wish to consult in the text is to be found in the line after the one specified in the concordance; this depends on whether lines have been joined in the computer-readable version of the text from which the concordance was made. It is not expected that readers will be seriously inconvenienced by this. Should a concordance to the First Folio be published, it will, of course, incorporate all improvements.

CORIOLANUS

The concordance to *Cor.* was made from the Lee facsimile (Oxford, 1902) of the Chatsworth copy of the First Folio. Professor Charlton Hinman (*Printing and Proof-Reading of the First Folio*. Oxford, 1963, vol. 1, p. 285) records that only aa6^v of *Cor.* shows evidence of proof-correction; the facsimile contains the corrected state. He gives the order of printing of this part of F (vol. 2, p. 516) as follows:

By Ax	By By	By Ax	By Ax	Eyx Ex	By Ax	Ey Eyx	By By
aa3^v:4	aa3:4^v	aa2:5^v	aa2^v:5	$\underline{dd3^v:4}$	aa1^v:6	$\underline{dd3:4^v}$	aa1:6^v

	Ax						
Ex Ex	Bx By	By Ex	By Ex	By By	By Ex	By Ex	By By
$\underline{dd2^v:5}$	bb3^v:4	$\underline{cc1:6^v}$	cc1^v:6	bb3:4^v	cc2:5^v	cc2^v:5	cc3^v:4

							Ax
By Ex	[Continues with *JC* etc. to forme lll:6^v]					By Ex	Bx By
$\underline{cc3:4^v}$						$\underline{ee3:4^v}$	bb2^v:5

By By	Ey Ex	Ax By	Ax By
bb2:5^v	$\underline{ee2^v:5}$	bb1^v:6	bb1:6^v

TABLE OF LINE AND ACT/SCENE NUMBERS

Page	Col.	Comp.	F line nos.	Globe act/scene nos.
aa1	a	B	1–50	1.1.1–1.1.50
	b	B	51–100	1.1.101
aa1^v	a	B	101–66	1.1.162
	b	B	167–231	1.1.221
aa2	a	B	232–95	1.1.269
	b	B	296–359	1.2.38
aa2^v	a	B	360–422	1.3.65
	b	B	423–86	1.4.2
aa3	a	B	487–550	1.4.49
	b	B	551–615	1.6.11
aa3^v	a	B	616–80	1.6.62
	b	B	681–743	1.8.15
aa4	a	A	744–803	1.9.47
	b	A	804–67	1.10.9
aa4^v	a	B	868–926	2.1.33
	b	B	927–92	2.1.106
aa5	a	A	993–1056	2.1.176
	b	A	1057–121	2.1.220
aa5^v	a	A	1122–85	2.1.273
	b	A	1186–246	2.2.43

Page	Col.	Comp.	F line nos.	Globe act/scene nos.
aa6	a	A	1247–312	2.2.102
	b	A	1313–76	2.2.157
aa6ᵛ	a	B	1377–442	2.3.59
	b	B	1443–507	2.3.123
bb1	a	A	1508–71	2.3.179
	b	A	1572–637	2.3.242
bb1ᵛ	a	A	1638–701	3.1.22
	b	A	1702–67	3.1.75
bb2	a	B	1768–833	3.1.136
	b	B	1834–99	3.1.192
bb2ᵛ	a	A	1900–65	3.1.241
	b	A / B	1966–92 / 1993–2031	3.1.294
bb3	a	B	2032–97	3.2.12
	b	B	2098–163	3.2.64
bb3ᵛ	a	A	2164–229	3.2.121
	b	B	2230–93	3.3.28
bb4	a	B	2294–359	3.3.77
	b	B	2360–425	3.3.135
bb4ᵛ	a	B	2426–86	4.1.44
	b	B	2487–552	4.2.40
bb5	a	B	2553–618	4.3.56
	b	B	2619–84	4.5.33
bb5ᵛ	a	B	2685–750	4.5.99
	b	B	2751–816	4.5.164
bb6	a	B	2817–82	4.5.240
	b	B	2883–948	4.6.45
bb6ᵛ	a	B	2949–3014	4.6.97
	b	B	3015–80	4.6.153
cc1	a	B	3081–146	4.7.55
	b	B	3147–207	5.1.49
cc1ᵛ	a	B	3208–73	5.2.38
	b	B	3274–339	5.2.111
cc2	a	B	3340–405	5.3.55
	b	B	3406–71	5.3.116
cc2ᵛ	a	B	3472–537	5.3.160
	b	B	3538–603	5.4.37
cc3	a	B	3604–66	5.6.15
	b	B	3667–732	5.6.69
cc3ᵛ	a	B	3733–85	5.6.115
	b	B	3786–839 (Finis)	5.6.156

The misprints, etc. corrected in the text were:

aa1ᵛ	125	2ˍCit.	aa6ᵛ	1440	tougne
aa2	244	Cominsn,	bb6	2921	Neighbours˙:
	272	you	bb6ᵛ	3063	oue
aa2ᵛ	445	Vlug.	cc1	3148	*exeunt*

In line 1209, the speech-prefix *1.*off*. should be read as *1.*Off*.

June, 1971   T. H. H.

CORIOLANUS

1

ABOUT *cont.*
  Mar. As with a man busied about Decrees: 645
  *helpe will serue: for once we stood vp about the Corne, 1401
  2 *Sen.* Weapons, weapons, weapons: | *They all bustle about Coriolanus.* 1892
  Mene. What is about to be? I am out of Breath, 1897
  Corio. Let them pull all about mine eares, present me 2084
  Volum. He must, and will: | Prythee now say you will, and goe about it. 2203
  Bru. Go about it, | Put him to Choller straite, he hath bene vs'd 2289
  Mine armes about that body, where against 2765
  *1 What an Arme he has, he turn'd me about with his 2813
  Our Tradesmen singing in their shops, and going | About their
  Functions friendly. 2900
  Then when these Fellowes ran about the streets, | Crying Confusion. 2926
  Com. Hee'l shake your Rome about your eares. 3016
  *thee. The glorious Gods sit in hourely Synod about thy 3304
ABRAM = *1
  *heads are some browne, some blacke, some Abram, some 1405
ABSENCE = 2*2
  *I should freelier reioyce in that absence wherein 364
  *the yearne she spun in *Vlisses* absence, did but fill *Athica* 447
  By calmenesse, or by absence: all's in anger. | *Menen.* Onely faire
  speech. 2199
  And loose aduantage, which doth euer coole | Ith'absence of the needer. 2483
ABSOLUTE = 3*1
  Heare you this Triton of the *Minnoues*? Marke you | His absolute Shall? 1782
  Cor. Thogh there the people had more absolute powre 1812
  Volum. You are too absolute, 2134
  Auf. Therefore most absolute Sir, if thou wilt haue 2795
ABUNDANCE = 1*1
  *to particularize their abundance, our sufferance is a 23
  Men. In what enormity is *Martius* poore in, that you | two haue not in
  abundance? 913
ABUNDANTLY = 1
  For though abundantly they lacke discretion 214
ABUSD = 2
  Com. The People are abus'd: set on, this paltring 1746
  He hath abus'd your Powers. 3752
ACCEPT = 2
  And cannot now accept, to grace him onely, 3362
  Sicin. First, the Gods blesse you for your tydings: | Next, accept my
  thankefulnesse. 3633
ACCEPTANCE = *1
  *vs his Noble deeds, we must also tell him our Noble ac-|ceptance 1395
ACCESSE = 1
  *this Varlet heere: This, who like a blocke hath denyed | my accesse to
  thee. 3313
ACCIDENTALLY = *1
  *accidentally to encounter you. You haue ended my Bu-|sinesse, 2607
ACCLAMATIONS = 1
  You shoot me forth in acclamations hyperbolicall, 806
ACCOMPANIED = 1
  Edile. Hee's comming. | *Bru.* How accompanied? 2265
ACCOMPANY = 1
  and I will merrily accompany you home. 2608
ACCOMPLISH = 1
  Out of my Files, his proiects, to accomplish 3687

ACCORDING = *1
 Men. Not according to the prayer of the people, for | they loue not
 Martius. 901
ACCOUNT = 2*3
 2.Cit. What he cannot helpe in his Nature, you ac- | count 42
 Coriol. You should account mee the more Vertuous, 1485
 *of them, 'tis a condition they account gentle: & since 1488
 When he shall come to his account, he knowes not 3109
 When ere we come to our account. 3117
ACCOUNTED = *1
 1.Cit. We are accounted poore Citizens, the Patri- | cians 17
ACCUSATION = 1
 Most Valour spoke not for them. Th'Accusation 1824
ACCUSATIONS = 1*1
 1.Cit. If I must not, I neede not be barren of Accusa- | tions 45
 With Accusations, as I heare more strong | Then are vpon you yet. 2251
ACCUSD = 2
 Or be accus'd of Folly. I shall tell you 90
 Rebell'd against the Belly; thus accus'd it: 99
ACCUSE = 2
 Let them accuse me by inuention: I | Will answer in mine Honor. 2254
 Will vouch the truth of it. Him I accuse: 3654
ACCUSERS = 1
 Not rash like his Accusers, and thus answered. 136
ACHES *see* akes
ACHIEUE *see* atcheeue
ACHIEUED *see* atchieued
ACHIEUING *see* atchieuing
ACQUAINTANCE = 1
 I vrg'd our old acquaintance, and the drops 3162
ACT = 3*1
 *repeale daily any wholsome Act established against 83
 That could be brought to bodily act, ere Rome 319
 He that ha's but effected his good will, | Hath ouerta'ne mine Act. 768
 When he might act the Woman in the Scene, 1310
ACTING = 1
 Corio. It is a part that I shall blush in acting, 1366
ACTION = 12*1
 More then his singularity, he goes | Vpon this present Action. 310
 *had rather had eleuen dye Nobly for their Countrey, then | one
 voluptuously surfet out of Action. 385
 Deny your asking, take your choice of those | That best can ayde your
 action. 683
 action out-done his former deeds doubly. 1033
 In humane Action, and Capacitie, 1176
 Action is eloquence, and the eyes of th'ignorant 2177
 And by my Bodies action, teach my Minde | A most inherent Basenesse. 2230
 *the man I thinke, that shall set them in present Action. So 2616
 And you are darkned in this action Sir, | Euen by your owne. 3095
 The action of your selfe, or else to him, had left it soly. 3107
 Set downe our Hoast. My partner in this Action, 3348
 Of our great Action; therefore shall he dye, 3703
 The charges of the Action. We haue made peace 3744
ACTIONS = 1*2
 *helpes are many, or else your actions would growe won- | drous 932
 *Honors in their Eyes, and his actions in their Hearts, that 1232
 His rougher Actions for malicious sounds: 2332

ACTOR = 1
Corio. Like a dull Actor now, I haue forgot my part,　　3390
ACTS = 1
The booke of his good Acts, whence men haue read　　3253
ACTUS *l*.1　895　1671　2434　3149 = 5
ADDITION = 1 *1
　Marcus Caius Coriolanus. Beare th'addition Nobly euer?　　821
　To vnder-crest your good Addition, | To th'fairenesse of my power.　　828
ADIEU = 2
　begg'd: I haue your Almes, Adieu.　　1472
　Droope not, Adieu: Farewell my Wife, my Mother,　　2458
ADMIRE = 1
　I'th'end admire: where Ladies shall be frighted,　　752
ADMIT = 1
　The People doe admit you, and are summon'd　　1537
ADMITS = 2
　Auf. I know it: | And my pretext to strike at him, admits　　3671
　There was a yeelding; this admits no excuse.　　3732
ADMITTED = *1
　*Neuer admitted a priuat whisper, no not with such frends | That
　thought them sure of you.　　3353
ADMITTING = 1
　A twist of rotten Silke, neuer admitting　　3764
ADOOING *see* dooing
ADOPT = 1
　You adopt your policy: How is it lesse or worse　　2145
ADRIAN = 1
　Rom. I know you well sir, and you know mee: your | name I thinke is
　Adrian.　　2571
ADUANCD = 2
　Filling the aire with Swords aduanc'd) and Darts,　　678
　Which being aduanc'd, declines, and then men dye.　　1058
ADUANCE = 1 *1
　Aduance braue *Titus*, | They do disdaine vs much beyond our Thoughts,　　518
　*haue hearts inclinable to honor and aduance the Theame | of our
　Assembly.　　1264
ADUANTAGE *see also* vantage = 2
　You should haue ta'ne th'aduantage of his Choller, | And pass'd him
　vnelected.　　1600
　And loose aduantage, which doth euer coole | Ith'absence of the needer.　　2483
ADUERSARIES = 1
　their Aduersaries. Haue you an Army ready ʾsay you?　　2611
ADUERSLY = *1
　*aduersly, I make a crooked face at it, I can say, your　　952
ADUISD = 1
　Scicin. Thus to haue said, | As you were fore-aduis'd, had toucht his
　Spirit,　　1592
ADUISE = 1
　What peace you'l make, aduise me: For my part,　　3556
AEDILE see also Edi., Edile. = 3
　Enter an Aedile.　　1874
　Enter an Aedile.　　2938
AEDILE = 1　　2939
AEDILES see also Ediles = 4
　Enter a rabble of Plebeians with the Aediles.　　1886
　Bru. Seize him *Aediles*.　　1890

AEDILES *cont*.
    Brut. Aediles seize him. | *All Ple*. Yeeld *Martius*, yeeld.   1928
    In this Mutinie, the Tribunes, the Aediles, and the | *People are beat in*.   1949
AEDILES = 1
AENIGMA = 1
    Coriol. Your Aenigma.   1481
AFARRE *see* a-farre, farre
AFFAIRES = *1
    *Corio. Wife, Mother, Child, I know not. My affaires | Are Seruanted
    to others: Though I owe   3317
AFFECT = *1
    *to seeme to affect the mallice and displeasure of the Peo-|ple,   1224
AFFECTED = 1
    Thou hast affected the fiue straines of Honor,   3506
AFFECTING = *1
    *Sicin. And affecting one sole Throne, without assista(n)ce   2932
AFFECTION = 2
    Vnto the appetite; and affection common   106
    The Grandchilde to her blood. But out affection,   3373
AFFECTIONS = 2
    Deserues your Hate: and your Affections are   188
    Then as guided by your owne true affections, and that   1634
AFFECTS = 1
    Bru. In this point charge him home, that he affects   2259
AFFIDIOUS = 1
    To endure Friends, that you directly set me | Against *Affidious*, and his
    Antiats,   675
AFFIDIUS = 1
    Com. But I feare | They'l roare him in againe. *Tullus Affidius*,   3047
AFFLICTS = *1
    *that afflicts vs, the obiect of our misery, is as an inuento-|ry   22
AFFRICKE = 1
    Not Affricke ownes a Serpent I abhorre   727
AFFRIGHT *see* fright
AFFRIGHTS = 1
    That like nor Peace, nor Warre? The one affrights you,   180
AFIRE = *1
    *I am husht vntill our City be afire, & then Ile speak a litle | *Holds her
    by the hand silent*.   3538
AFOOT *see* a-foot
AFTER = 10*3
    *I saw him run after a gilded Butterfly, & when   423
    *he caught it, he let it go againe, and after it againe, and o-|uer   424
    And the Gods doome him after.   730
    We doe request your kindest eares: and after   1260
    After the inueterate Hate he beares you.   1629
    Scici. Say you chose him, more after our commandment,   1633
    Who after great *Hostilius* here was King,   1643
    Let vs seeme humbler after it is done, | Then when it was a dooing. 2507
    Conies after Raine) and reuell all with him.   2871
    Sicin. Yet your good will | Must haue that thankes from Rome, after
    the measure | As you intended well.   3202
    He sent in writing after me: what he would not,   3229
    *Mene. Ha's he din'd can'st thou tell? For I would not | speake with
    him, till after dinner.   3271
    After your way. His Tale pronounc'd, shall bury | His Reasons, with his
    Body.   3717

AFTERNOONE = 1*1
  play the idle Huswife with me this afternoone. 433
  *Drum strooke vp this afternoone: 'Tis as it were a parcel 2874
AFTER-MEETING = 1
  As the maine Point of this our after-meeting, 1246
AGAIN = *2
  *and ouer he comes, and vp againe: catcht it again: or 425
  *Cori. That Ile straight do: and knowing my selfe again, | Repayre
  toth'Senate-|house. 1543
AGAINE = 17*6
  *he caught it, he let it go againe, and after it againe, and o-|uer 424
  *and ouer he comes, and vp againe: catcht it again: or 425
  We shall be charg'd againe. Whiles we haue strooke 607
  If ere againe I meet him beard to beard, 869
  Coriol. Your Honors pardon: | I had rather haue my Wounds to heale
  againe, 1279
  2 Cit. And 'twere to giue againe: but 'tis no matter. 1474
  And now againe, of him that did not aske, but mock, 1610
  Readie when time shall prompt them, to make roade | Vpon's againe. 1678
  That we shall hardly in our ages see | Their Banners waue againe. 1681
  And I will speak't againe. 1751
  And therein behold themselues: I say againe, 1758
  Enter Brutus and Sicinius with the rabble againe. 1993
  Be rein'd againe to Temperance, then he speakes 2293
  I am so dishonour'd, that the very houre | You take it off againe. 2338
  *would make it flame againe. For the Nobles receyue so 2590
  *3 But when they shall see sir, his Crest vp againe, and 2869
  *2 Why then wee shall haue a stirring World againe: 2876
  Thrusts forth his hornes againe into the world 2947
  Bru. Rais'd onely, that the weaker sort may wish | Good Martius home
  againe. 2980
  Com. But I feare | They'l roare him in againe. Tullus Affidius, 3047
  You know the way home againe. 3333
  Againe, with Romes Mechanickes. Tell me not 3438
AGAINST see also 'gainst = 32*7
  *2.Cit. Would you proceede especially against Caius | Martius. 27
  *All. Against him first: He's a very dog to the Com-|monalty. 29
  Against the Roman State, whose course will on 70
  *repeale daily any wholsome Act established against 83
  Rebell'd against the Belly; thus accus'd it: 99
  You cry against the Noble Senate, who 197
  *Thus it is: the Volcies haue an Army forth, against who(m) 460
  Against the Winde a mile: you soules of Geese, 529
  To endure Friends, that you directly set me | Against Affidious, and his
  Antiats, 675
  Able to beare against the great Auffidious 700
  Shall say against their hearts, We thanke the Gods 755
  Against the hospitable Canon, would I 885
  *set vp the bloodie Flagge against all Patience, and 971
  He was your Enemie, euer spake against 1580
  Against the Rectorship of Iudgement? 1608
  Then what you should, made you against the graine 1636
  Against the Volces, for they had so vildly 1685
  For they doe pranke them in Authoritie, | Against all Noble sufferance. 1702
  Brut. The People are incens'd against him. 1713
  Coine words till their decay, against those Meazels 1770
  His popular Shall, against a grauer Bench 1800

6

AGAINST *cont.*

Which they haue often made against the Senate,	1825
Against a falling Fabrick. Will you hence,	1972
And throw't against the Winde. Toth' Market place:	2210
Enui'd against the people; seeking meanes	2380
Rom. I am a Roman, and my Seruices are as you are, | against 'em. Know you me yet.	2574
*The people, against the Senatours, Patricians, and | Nobles.	2584
Against my Cankred Countrey, with the Spleene	2748
Mine armes about that body, where against	2765
Contend against thy Valour. Know thou first,	2771
Who am prepar'd against your Territories, | Though not for Rome it selfe.	2792
Whether to knocke against the Gates of Rome,	2800
Against vs Brats, with no lesse Confidence,	3009
That Rome can make against them.	3052
*willingly consented to his Banishment, yet it was against | our will.	3071
What I can vrge against him, although it seemes	3110
Mine eares against your suites, are stronger then	3323
Your gates against my force. Yet for I loued thee,	3324
Stopt your eares against the generall suite of Rome:	3352

AGD = 1

All. Wee'l Surety him. | *Com.* Ag'd sir, hands off.	1881

AGE = 3*1

Was Brow-bound with the Oake. His Pupill age	1312
Within my Age. But reason with the fellow	2956
*with your age. I say to you, as I was said to, Away. *Exit*	3342
To th'insuing Age, abhorr'd. Speake to me Son:	3505

AGED *see also* ag'd = 1

I would be Consull, sayes he: aged Custome,	1568

AGENTS = 1

2.*Cit.* The former Agents, if they did complaine,	128

AGES = 1

That we shall hardly in our ages see | Their Banners waue againe.	1681

AGREED = 1

Lar. My horse to yours, no. | *Mar.* Tis done. | *Lart.* Agreed.	484

AGREEING = 1

With variable Complexions; all agreeing	1131

AGRIPPA = 1*1

Enter Menenius Agrippa.	52
2 Cit. Worthy *Menenius Agrippa*, one that hath al-|wayes lou'd the people.	53

AGUED = 1

With flight and agued feare, mend and charge home,	533

AGURER = *1

Men. The Agurer tels me, wee shall haue Newes to | night.	898

AH = 1

That weep'st to see me triumph? Ah my deare,	1083

AIDE *see* ayd, ayde
AIDELESSE *see* aydelesse
AIME *see* ayme
AIMES *see* aymes
AIRE *see also* ayre = 1

Filling the aire with Swords aduanc'd) and Darts,	678

AKES = 1

It makes the Consuls base; and my Soule akes	1802

AL = *3

  *1 *Cit*. He's one honest enough, wold al the rest wer so.   55
  Vol. Now the Red Pestilence strike al Trades in Rome, | And
  Occupations perish.   2450
  *they are in a ripe aptnesse, to take al power from the peo- | ple,   2592
ALACKE = 2

  Your knees to them (not armes) must helpe. Alacke,   75
  Whereto we are bound: Alacke, or we must loose   3464
ALARUM *see also* larum = 8

  They'le open of themselues. Harke you, farre off | *Alarum farre off*.   508
  Alarum, the Romans are beat back to their Trenches | Enter Martius
  Cursing.   523
  Another Alarum, and Martius followes them to | gates, and is shut in.   538
  1.*Sol*. See they haue shut him in. *Alarum continues*   546
  Alarum continues still a-farre off.   573
  Alarum, as in Battaile. | Enter Martius and Auffidius at seuerall doores.   722
  Flourish. Alarum. A Retreat is sounded. Enter at | one Doore Cominius,
  with the Romanes: At   744
  When the Alarum were strucke, then idly sit   1289
ALAS = 1

  Alas! how can we, for our Country pray?   3462
ALAYING = *1

  *one that loues a cup of hot Wine, with not a drop of alay- | ing   944
ALEXANDER = *1

  *as a thing made for *Alexander*. What he bids bee done, is   3591
ALIAS = *1

  *proud, violent, testie Magistrates (alias Fooles) | as any in Rome.   940
ALIIS *see Cumalijs*

ALIKE = 3*1

  *sincerely, had I a dozen sons each in my loue alike,   383
  Let's fetch him off, or make remaine alike. | *They fight, and all enter*
  the City.   567
  Auffid. We hate alike: 726
  That when the Sea was calme, all Boats alike   2442
ALL *see also* al, all's, all-haile, all-noble = 133*31

  All. Speake, speake.   6
  *1.*Cit*. You are all resolu'd rather to dy then | to famish?   7
  All. Resolu'd, resolu'd.   9
  All. We know't, we know't.   12
  All. No more talking on't; Let it be done, away, away   15
  All. Against him first: He's a very dog to the Com- | monalty.   29
  All. Nay, but speak not maliciously.   36
  why stay we prating heere? To th'Capitoll. | *All*. Come, come.   49
  *not vppe, they will; and there's all the loue they beare | vs.   86
  Men. There was a time, when all the bodies members   98
  Whereby they liue. And though that all at once   147
  Men. Though all at once, cannot | See what I do deliuer out to each,   150
  Yet I can make my Awdit vp, that all   152
  From me do backe receiue the Flowre of all,   153
  Bru. Come: halfe all *Cominius* Honors are to *Martius*   304
  Though *Martius* earn'd them not: and all his faults   305
  All. The Gods assist you. | *Auf*. And keepe your Honors safe.   355
  All. Farewell. *Exeunt omnes*.   359
  *youth with comelinesse pluck'd all gaze his way; when   368
  Like to a Haruest man, that task'd to mowe | Or all, or loose his hyre.   398
  Val. You would be another *Penelope*: yet they say, all   446
  Mar. All the contagion of the South, light on you,   525

ALL *cont.*

All hurt behinde, backes red, and faces pale	532
All. To th'pot I warrant him. *Enter Titus Lartius*	547
Tit. What is become of *Martius?* | *All.* Slaine (Sir) doubtlesse.	548
Clapt to their Gates, he is himselfe alone, | To answer all the City.	552
Let's fetch him off, or make remaine alike. | *They fight, and all enter the City.*	567
Call thither all the Officers a'th'Towne,	601
Mar. I do beseech you, | By all the Battailes wherein we haue fought,	671
They all shout and waue their swords, take him vp in their | Armes, and cast vp their Caps.	695
(Though thankes to all) must I select from all:	702
Make good this ostentation, and you shall | Diuide in all, with vs. *Exeunt*	708
And tent themselues with death: of all the Horses,	783
Whereof we haue ta'ne good, and good store of all,	784
A long flourish. They all cry, Martius, Martius,	794
Made all of false-fac'd soothing:	800
As to vs, to all the World, That *Caius Martius*	815
With all his trim belonging; and from this time,	818
With all th'applause and Clamor of the Hoast,	820
I meane to stride your Steed, and at all times	827
Embarquements all of Fury, shall lift vp	881
Bru. And topping all others in boasting.	917
*set vp the bloodie Flagge against all Patience, and	971
*bleeding, the more intangled by your hearing: All the	973
*worth all your predecessors, since *Deucalion,* though per-|aduenture	986
*fiddious'd, for all the Chests in Carioles, and the Gold	1028
Herauld. Know Rome, that all alone *Martius* did fight	1064
All. Welcome to Rome, renowned *Coriolanus.*	1070
Coriol. Oh! you haue, I know, petition'd all the Gods | for my prosperitie. *Kneeles.*	1074
And y'are welcome all.	1090
Bru. All tongues speake of him, and the bleared sights	1123
With variable Complexions; all agreeing	1131
*without any further deed, to haue them at all into	1230
He had rather venture all his Limbes for Honor,	1294
Whom with all prayse I point at, saw him fight,	1304
He lurcht all Swords of the Garland: for this last,	1315
Our purpose to them, and to our Noble Consull | Wish we all Ioy, and Honor.	1375
Senat. To *Coriolanus* come all ioy and Honor.	1377
*I thinke, if all our wittes were to issue out of one Scull,	1407
*of one direct way, should be at once to all the points | a'th Compasse.	1409
3 Cit. Are you all resolu'd to giue your voyces? But	1422
All. Content, content.	1435
Men. You'l marre all,	1449
Corio. A match Sir, there's in all two worthie voyces	1471
What Custome wills in all things, should we doo't?	1509
All. Amen, Amen. God saue thee, Noble Consull.	1528
All. No, no: no man saw 'em.	1564
All reuoke your ignorant election: Enforce his Pride,	1622
All. We will so: almost all repent in their election. | *Exeunt Plebeians.*	1659
Cornets. Enter Coriolanus, Menenius, all the Gentry, | Cominius, Titus Latius, and other Senators.	1672
That of all things vpon the Earth, he hated	1691
For they doe pranke them in Authoritie, | Against all Noble sufferance.	1702

ALL *cont*.

Scicin. Stop, or all will fall in broyle.	1714
Corio. Why this was knowne before. | *Brut*. Not to them all.	1730
All cause vnborne, could neuer be the Natiue	1826
*Insult without all reason: where Gentry, Title, wisedom	1843
All. Wee'l Surety him. | *Com*. Ag'd sir, hands off.	1881
Sicin. Heere's hee, that would take from you all your | power.	1888
All. Downe with him, downe with him.	1891
2 *Sen*. Weapons, weapons, weapons: | *They all bustle about Coriolanus*.	1892
All. Peace, peace, peace, stay, hold, peace.	1896
All. Let's here our Tribune: peace, speake, speake, | speake.	1901
Martius would haue all from you; *Martius*,	1904
Sena. To vnbuild the Citie, and to lay all flat.	1908
All. True, the People are the Citie.	1910
Brut. By the consent of all, we were establish'd the | Peoples Magistrates.	1911
All. You so remaine. | *Mene*. And so are like to doe.	1913
And burie all, which yet distinctly raunges | In heapes, and piles of Ruine.	1917
Brut. Aediles seize him. | *All Ple*. Yeeld *Martius*, yeeld.	1928
All. Downe with him, downe with him. *Exeunt*.	1948
All will be naught else.	1952
All. He shall sure ont. | *Mene*. Sir, sir. *Sicin*. Peace.	2004
Bru. He Consull. | *All*. No, no, no, no, no.	2014
Were to vs all that doo't, and suffer it	2040
Corio. Let them pull all about mine eares, present me	2084
Now, this no more dishonors you at all,	2157
Then thou of them. Come all to ruine, let	2234
Of all the Trades in Rome. Looke, I am going:	2244
Sicin. Haue you a Catalogue | *Of all the Voices that we haue procur'd, set downe by'th | (Pole?	2269
Must all determine heere?	2316
From Rome all season'd Office, and to winde	2343
All. To'th'Rocke, to'th'Rocke with him.	2356
All. It shall be so, it shall be so: let him away:	2391
It shall bee so. | *All*. It shall be so, it shall be so.	2406
They all shout, and throw vp their Caps.	2425
All. Our enemy is banish'd, he is gone: Hoo, oo.	2427
As he hath follow'd you, with all despight	2429
All. Come, come, lets see him out at gates, come:	2432
That when the Sea was calme, all Boats alike	2442
Sicin. Bid them all home, he's gone: & wee'l no further,	2503
Volum. Bastards, and all. | Good man, the Wounds that he does beare for Rome!	2537
Whom you haue banish'd, does exceed you all.	2554
*strange things from Rome: all tending to the good of	2610
To thee particularly, and to all the Volces	2723
Haue all forsooke me, hath deuour'd the rest:	2733
I had fear'd death, of all the Men i'th'World	2738
Of all the vnder Fiends. But if so be,	2749
Thou art thence Banish'd, we would muster all	2786
3 I would not be a Roman of all Nations; I had as | liue be a condemn'd man.	2835
*will mowe all downe before him, and leaue his passage | poul'd.	2861
Conies after Raine) and reuell all with him.	2871
All. The Gods preserue you both.	2915
Bru. Gooden to you all, gooden to you all.	2917

ALL *cont.*

All. Now the Gods keepe you.	2923
O'recome with Pride, Ambitious, past all thinking | Selfe-louing.	2930
Sicin. We should by this, to all our Lamention,	2934
All to the Senate-house: some newes is comming | That turnes their Countenances.	2965
Before you finde it other. All the Regions	3021
Mene. We are all vndone, vnlesse | The Noble man haue mercy.	3026
Is all the Policy, Strength, and Defence	3051
If he could burne vs all into one coale, | We haue deseru'd it.	3063
2 Cit. So did we all. But come, let's home. *Exit Cit.*	3084
To th'vulgar eye, that he beares all things fairely:	3112
Auf. All places yeelds to him ere he sits downe,	3119
(As he hath spices of them all) not all,	3137
*Thou art poor'st of all; then shortly art thou mine. *Exeunt*	3148
He would not answer too: Forbad all Names,	3164
So that all hope is vaine, vnlesse his Noble Mother,	3231
(Of whom hee's cheefe) with all the size that verity	3256
All bond and priuiledge of Nature breake;	3374
Shew duty as mistaken, all this while, | Betweene the Childe, and Parent.	3405
Which by th'interpretation of full time, | May shew like all your selfe.	3421
How more vnfortunate then all liuing women	3452
That all but we enioy. For how can we?	3461
To haue a Temple built you: All the Swords	3567
shall our poore City finde: and all this is long of you.	3598
And hale him vp and downe; all swearing, if	3606
Mess. Sir, we haue all great cause to giue great thanks.	3635
Call all your Tribes together, praise the Gods,	3642
All. Welcome Ladies, welcome. | *A Flourish with Drummes & Trumpets.*	3647
'Twixt you there's difference: but the fall of either | Makes the Suruiuor heyre of all.	3669
In all his owne desires: Nay, let him choose	3686
Which he did end all his; and tooke some pride	3690
All Lords. You are most welcome home.	3721
All. We haue. | *1.Lord.* And greeue to heare't:	3725
Staine all your edges on me. Boy, false Hound:	3783
All Consp. Let him dye for't.	3792
All People. Teare him to peeces, do it presently:	3793
Auf. Insolent Villaine. | *All Consp.* Kill, kill, kill, kill, kill him.	3803
3.Lord. Tread not vpon him Masters, all be quiet, | Put vp your Swords.	3812

ALLAY = 1

Wherein I seeme vnnaturall: Desire not t'allay	3439

ALLAYING *see* alaying

ALLOW = 1

Allow their Officers, and are content	2319

ALLOWANCE = 1

Of no allowance, to your bosomes truth.	2156

ALLS = 2*1

Carioles like a Planet: now all's his,	1328
By calmenesse, or by absence: all's in anger. | *Menen.* Onely faire speech.	2199
Mene. All's well, and might haue bene much better, | if he could haue temporiz'd.	2909

ALL-HAILE = 1

Giue the All-haile to thee, and cry be Blest	3496

ALL-NOBLE = 1
    Then thee all-Noble *Martius*. Let me twine   2764
ALMES = 3
    begg'd: I haue your Almes, Adieu.   1472
    That hath receiu'd an Almes. I will not doo't,   2228
    Auf. Euen so, as with a man by his owne Almes im- | poyson'd, and with
    his Charity slaine.   3661
ALMOST = 5*2
    Menen. Nay these are almost thoroughly perswaded: 213
    To take in many Townes, ere (almost) Rome | Should know we were
    a-foot.   340
    *1.*Off*. Come, come, they are almost here: how many | stand for
    Consulships?   1205
    All. We will so: almost all repent in their election. | *Exeunt Plebeians*.   1659
    *This lyes glowing I can tell you, and is almost mature for | the violent
    breaking out.   2594
    Haue (almost) stampt the Leasing. Therefore Fellow,   3260
    Mes. Almost at point to enter.   3637
ALONE = 12*2
    Let vs alone to guard *Corioles*   344
    Vol. Let her alone Ladie, as she is now: 468
    Clapt to their Gates, he is himselfe alone, | To answer all the City.   552
    Mar. Let him alone,   654
    Let him alone: Or so many so minded,   692
    Oh me alone, make you a sword of me: 697
    Alone I fought in your *Corioles* walles,   733
    Brut. We do it not alone, sir.   930
    Men. I know you can doe very little alone, for your   931
    *much alone. You talke of Pride: Oh, that you could turn   934
    Herauld. Know Rome, that all alone *Martius* did fight   1064
    Was tim'd with dying Cryes: alone he entred   1324
    Beleeu't not lightly, though I go alone   2467
    Alone I did it, Boy.   3787
ALONG = 6
    Bru. Let's along. *Exeunt*   312
    Prythee *Virgilia* turne thy solemnesse out a doore, | And go along with
    vs.   472
    Mene. Ile keepe you company. Will you along?   1545
    Corio. Come Sir, along with vs.   1961
    Take this along, I writ it for thy sake,   3325
    Which we will second, when he lies along   3716
ALREADY = 5*1
    2 *Cit*. We cannot Sir, we are vndone already.   65
    In whom already he's well grac'd, cannot   294
    Some parcels of their Power are forth already,   350
    *charges distinctly billetted already in th'entertainment,   2613
    Associated with *Auffidius*, Rages | Vpon our Territories, and haue
    already   2989
    Which you deny already: yet we will aske,   3444
ALSO = 1*1
    *vs his Noble deeds, we must also tell him our Noble ac- | ceptance   1395
    Th'art tyr'd, then in a word, I also am   2751
ALTER = *1
    Sicin. Is't possible, that so short a time can alter the | condition of a
    man.   3578
ALTERATION = 1
    1 Heere's a strange alteration?   2809

ALTHOUGH = 2
Volum. Prythee now, | Goe, and be rul'd: although I know thou hadst
rather   2192
What I can vrge against him, although it seemes   3110
ALTITUDE = 1
*his Mother, and to be partly proud, which he is, euen to | the altitude
of his vertue.   40
ALTOGETHER = 1*1
*his behauiour: we are not to stay altogether, but to come   1429
*As the recomforted through th'gates. Why harke you: | *Trumpets,
Hoboyes, Drums beate, altogether*.   3620
ALWAYES = 2*2
*2 *Cit*. Worthy *Menenius Agrippa*, one that hath al-|wayes lou'd the
people.   53
Edile. With old *Menenius*, and those Senators | That alwayes fauour'd
him.   2267
*3 I do not say thwacke our Generall, but he was al-|wayes good
enough for him   2841
alwayes factionary on the party of your Generall.   3267
AM = 31*15
AMAZONIAN = 1
When with his Amazonian Shinne he droue   1305
AMBITIOUS = 2*1
*thing: you are ambitious, for poore knaues cappes and   964
As euer in Ambitious strength, I did   2770
O'recome with Pride, Ambitious, past all thinking | Selfe-louing.   2930
AMEN = 5
All. Amen, Amen. God saue thee, Noble Consull.   1528
2.*Cit*. Amen, Sir: to my poore vnworthy notice,   1556
1 *Sen*. Amen, Amen. | *Mene*. A Noble wish.   2307
AMENDED = 1
In that's no Changeling, and I must excuse | What cannot be amended.   3102
AMONG = 4
Doe presse among the popular Throngs, and puffe   1133
No Heart among you? Or had you Tongues, to cry   1607
There's some among you haue beheld me fighting,   1941
And dye among our Neighbours: Nay, behold's,   3530
AMONGS = 1
Supplied with worthy men, plant loue amongs   2304
AMONGST = 2
There is *Auffidious*. List what worke he makes | Among'st your clouen
Army.   510
2.*Cit*. Not one amongst vs, saue your selfe, but sayes   1560
AMPLIFIED = 1
His Fame vnparalell'd, happely amplified: 3254
AN *l*.*22 155 *370 410 *422 *460 620 622 627 689 802 872 *936 *966 *984
*1011 *1051 1062 1171 1307 1787 1874 2030 2038 2222 2228 2264 2300
*2536 2611 2614 2624 *2647 *2697 *2701 2766 *2813 2831 2938 3002
3230 *3239 *3297 3381 3467 3510 3528 *3586 *3588 3619 3785 = 33*18,
1
They said they were an hungry, sigh'd forth Prouerbes   218
ANCESTOR = 1
And Nobly nam'd, so twice being Censor, | Was his great Ancestor.   1646
ANCIENT = 5
Vpon their ancient mallice, will forget   1150
Where is your ancient Courage? You were vs'd   2439
And they, stand in their ancient strength.   2510

ANCIENT *cont*.
My throat to thee, and to thy Ancient Malice: 2753
A roote of Ancient Enuy. If Iupiter   2761
ANCUS = 1
That *Ancus Martius*, *Numaes* Daughters Sonne: 1642
AND *see also* and't, &. = 572*138, *2
  *that: and he had stay'd by him, I would not haue been so   1027
  *2 And hee had bin Cannibally giuen, hee might haue | boyld and eaten
  him too.   2848
ANDT = 1
But and't please you deliuer.   97
ANGER *see also* anger's = 4
With their refusall, both obserue and answer | The vantage of his anger.   1665
But yet a braine, that leades my vse of Anger | To better vantage.   2121
By calmenesse, or by absence: all's in anger. | *Menen*. Onely faire
speech.   2199
In Anger, *Iuno*-like: Come, come, come. *Exeunt*   2568
ANGERS = 1
Volum. Angers my Meate: I suppe vpon my selfe,   2565
ANGRY = 3*1
  Men. Because you talke of Pride now, will you not | be angry.   922
  *Giue your dispositions the reines, and bee angry at your   927
And being angry, does forget that euer   1987
  *Friends: the Commonwealth doth stand, and so would | do, were he
more angry at it.   2907
ANNALES = 1
If you haue writ your Annales true, 'tis there,   3784
ANNIUS = 1
*Enter Sicinius Velutus, Annius Brutus Cominius, Titus | Lartius, with
other Senatours*.   244
ANON = 2*1
You anon doe meet the Senate. | *Corio*. Is this done?   1534
To meet anon, vpon your approbation.   1538
  *2 *Ser*. Are you so braue: Ile haue you talkt with anon   2672
ANOTHER = 9*6
Would feede on one another? What's their seeking?   199
  Val. You would be another *Penelope*: yet they say, all   446
Farther then seene, and one infect another   528
Another Alarum, and Martius followes them to | gates, and is shut in.
another Doore Martius, with his | Arme in a Scarfe.   746
  *another, his Wife another, and (I thinke) there's one at | home for you.   1006
  *3.*Cit*. Nay your wit will not so soone out as another   1413
One time will owe another.   1966
Enter another Seruingman.   2656
1 I, and it makes men hate one another.   2887
  *3 Reason, because they then lesse neede one another: 2888
And would haue sent it. Another word *Menenius*,   3326
  *not from another: Let your Generall do his worst. For   3340
Enter another Messenger.   3609
ANSWER = 16
2.*Cit*. Well sir, what answer made the Belly.   108
2.*Cit*. Your Bellies answer: What   117
What could the Belly answer?   129
Patience awhile; you'st heare the Bellies answer.   132
2.*Cit*. It was an answer, how apply you this?   155
We neuer yet made doubt but Rome was ready | To answer vs.   333
Clapt to their Gates, he is himselfe alone, | To answer all the City.   552

ANSWER *cont.*

With their refusall, both obserue and answer | The vantage of his anger.	1665
Sicin. Ha's spoken like a Traitor, and shall answer | As Traitors do.	1862
And follow to thine answer.	1879
Where he shall answer by a lawfull Forme | (In peace) to his vtmost perill.	2067
To answer mildely: for they are prepar'd	2250
Let them accuse me by inuention: I | Will answer in mine Honor.	2254
Sicin. Answer to vs. | *Corio*. Say then: 'tis true, I ought so	2340
He would not answer too: Forbad all Names,	3164
For's priuate Friends. His answer to me was	3177

ANSWERD = 1 * ⌐

Of the whole body, the Belly answer'd.	107
*They vented their Complainings, which being answer'd	222

ANSWERED = 1

Not rash like his Accusers, and thus answered.	136

ANSWERING = 1

The benefit of our Leuies, answering vs	3730

ANTIATES = 1

With no lesse Honor to the *Antiates*	3745

ANTIATS = 2

To endure Friends, that you directly set me | Against *Affidious*, and his *Antiats*,	675
And that the Spoile got on the *Antiats*	2262

ANTIENTS = 1

Com. As I guesse *Martius*, | Their Bands i'th Vaward are the Antients	667

ANTIQUE = 1

The Dust on antique Time would lye vnswept,	1510

ANTIUM = 5

Yeelded the Towne: he is retyred to Antium.	1686
Corio. At Antium liues he?	1695
Latius. At Antium.	1696
Corio. A goodly City is this *Antium*. Citty,	2623
Cit. And you. \[**Corio*. Direct me, if it be your will, where great *Auf-* | *fidius* lies: Is he in *Antium*?	2630

ANUILE = 1

The Anuile of my Sword, and do contest	2768

ANY = 12*7

1. *Citizen*. | *Before we proceed any further, heare me speake.	4
*repeale daily any wholsome Act established against	83
And were I any thing but what I am,	251
Mar. Those are they | That most are willing; if any such be heere,	685
Wherein you see me smear'd, if any feare	688
If any thinke, braue death out-weighes bad life,	690
*proud, violent, testie Magistrates (alias Fooles) | as any in Rome.	940
**Menen*. You know neither mee, your selues, nor any	963
*without any further deed, to haue them at all into	1230
*3 *Cit*. You must thinke if we giue you any thing, we | hope to gaine by you.	1463
*1.*Cit*. Hee ha's done Nobly, and cannot goe without | any honest mans Voyce.	1524
Where it is: not poyson any further.	1780
With those that haue but little: this must be patcht | With Cloth of any Colour.	1978
Menen. That's worthily | As any eare can heare. Come, let's not weepe,	2495
*question askt him by any of the Senators, but they stand	2853
2 And he's as like to do't, as any man I can imagine.	2863

ANY *cont.*

    *for such things as you. I can scarse thinke ther's any, y'are   3338

    Volum. Oh no more, no more: | You haue said you will not grant vs any

      thing: 3441

    Shew'd thy deere Mother any curtesie,   3518

ANYTHING *see* thing

APES = 1

    From Slaues, that Apes would beate; *Pluto* and Hell,   531

APOPLEXY = *1

    *of Vent. Peace, is a very Apoplexy, Lethargie, mull'd,   2881

APPARANCE = 1

    Thou hast a Grim apparance, and thy Face   2717

APPARANT = 1

    And so he thinkes, and is no lesse apparant   3111

APPARRELL = 1

    Enter Coriolanus in meane Apparrell, dis-|guisd, and muffled.   2621

APPEAR = *1

    *Then dangerous to me: To *Auffidious* thus, I will appear | (and fight.   592

APPEARANCE *see* apparance

APPEARD = 1*1

    It seem'd appear'd to Rome. By the discouery,   338

    *your Fauour is well appear'd by your Tongue. What's   2579

APPEARE = 6*1

    Appeare in your impediment. For the Dearth,   73

    Com. Whose yonder, | That doe's appeare as he were Flead? O Gods, 629

    Appeare i'th'Market place, nor on him put   1156

    Senat. Call *Coriolanus.* | *Off.* He doth appeare.   1347

    Auffidius will appeare well in these Warres, his great   2603

    The Feast smels well: but I appeare not like a Guest.   2660

    Intends t'appeare before the People, hoping   3656

APPEERE = 1

    To begge of Hob and Dicke, that does appeere   1507

APPETITE = 2

    Vnto the appetite; and affection common   106

    A sickmans Appetite; who desires most that   189

APPLAUSE = 1

    With all th'applause and Clamor of the Hoast,   820

APPLY = 1

    2.Cit. It was an answer, how apply you this?   155

APPLYED = 1

    And Balmes applyed to you, yet dare I neuer   682

APPREHENDED = 1

    Bru. The Ediles hoe: Let him be apprehended: 1875

APPREHENSION = 1

    Th'apprehension of his present portance,   1627

APPROACHES *see also* approches = 1

    Auf. He approaches, you shall heare him.   3733

APPROBATION = 3

    Volum. I, worthy *Menenius,* and with most prosperous | approbation. 1000

    To meet anon, vpon your approbation.   1538

    That hee's your fixed enemie; and reuoke | Your suddaine approbation. 1653

APPROCHES = *1

    Volum. Honorable *Menenius,* my Boy *Martius* appro-|ches: 997

APPROUE = 1

    Corio. I muse my Mother | Do's not approue me further, who was wont 2092

APRON = 1

    You and your Apron men: you, that stood so much   3013

APT = 1
I haue a heart as little apt as yours,   2120
APTNESSE = *1
   *they are in a ripe aptnesse, to take al power from the peo-|ple,   2592
ARABIA = 1
Were in Arabia, and thy Tribe before him, | His good Sword in his
hand.   2533
ARCH = 1
Ne're through an Arch so hurried the blowne Tide,   3619
ARE *see also* y'are = 111*46
ARGUING = 1
Win vpon power, and throw forth greater Theames | For Insurrections
arguing.   234
ARITHMETICK = 1
Com. But now 'tis oddes beyond Arithmetick,   1970
ARM = *1
   Com. Away, the Tribunes do attend you: arm your self   2249
ARMD = 1
Make motion through my Lips, and my Arm'd knees   2226
ARME = 4*2
The Counsailor Heart, the Arme our Souldier,   119
another Doore Martius, with his | Arme in a Scarfe.   746
   Volum. Ith' Shoulder, and ith' left Arme: there will be   1043
Death, that darke Spirit, in's neruie Arme doth lye,   1057
Or loose mine Arme for't: Thou hast beate mee out   2779
   *1 What an Arme he has, he turn'd me about with his   2813
ARMES = 8
Your knees to them (not armes) must helpe. Alacke,   75
Mes. The newes is sir, the Volcies are in Armes.   241
The Volces are in Armes.   247
Mart. Oh! let me clip ye | In Armes as sound, as when I woo'd in heart;   640
*They all shout and waue their swords, take him vp in their | Armes, and
cast vp their Caps.*   695
From these old armes and legges, by the good Gods | I'ld with thee,
euery foot.   2498
Mine armes about that body, where against   2765
In Italy, and her Confederate Armes   3568
ARMIE = 2
What you haue done, before our Armie heare me.   778
More then the instant Armie we can make | Might stop our
Countryman.   3191
ARMIES = 2
1.Sen. Our Armie's in the Field: 332
Mar. How farre off lie these Armies?   493
ARMOUR = 1
For the whole State; I would put mine Armour on,   2126
ARMS = *1
   *strong breaths, they shal know we haue strong arms too.   62
ARMY *see also* armie = 6*1
Bring vp your Army: but (I thinke) you'l finde   346
   *Thus it is: the Volcies haue an Army forth, against who(m)   460
There is *Auffidious.* List what worke he makes | Among'st your clouen
Army.   510
Enter the Army of the Volces.   514
their Aduersaries. Haue you an Army ready say you?   2611
A fearefull Army, led by *Caius Martius,*   2988
1.Con. So he did my Lord: | The Army marueyl'd at it, and in the last,   3695

ARRANT = *1
    Mene. Now you Companion: Ile say an arrant for you: 3297
ARRIUING = 1
    I'th' Body of the Weale: and now arriuing   1582
ART *see also* th'art *l*.167 264 556 557 2182 2486 2786 2798 *3148 *3306
    *3414 3523 3615 = 10*4
ARTICLE = 1
    Which easily endures not Article,   1598
ARTICULATE = 1
    The best, with whom we may articulate, | For their owne good, and
    ours.   834
AS = 183*44
    *that afflicts vs, the obiect of our misery, is as an inuento-|ry   22
    Your suffering in this dearth, you may as well   68
    Strike at the Heauen with your staues, as lift them   69
    When you curse them, as Enemies.   79
    As well as speake, it taintingly replyed   112
    As you maligne our Senators, for that | They are not such as you.   115
    And feebling such as stand not in their liking,   207
    With thousands of these quarter'd slaues, as high   211
    As I could picke my Lance.   212
    As they would hang them on the hornes a'th Moone,   226
    Sicin. Was euer man so proud as is this *Martius*?   280
    (As children from a Beare) the *Volces* shunning him: 393
    *as your finger, that you might leaue pricking it for   449
    Vol. Let her alone Ladie, as she is now: 468
    Enter Martius, Titus Lartius, with Drumme and Co-|lours, with
    Captaines and Souldiers, as   478
    Mess. They lye in view, but haue not spoke as yet.   488
    As they vs to our Trenches followes.   537
    A Carbuncle intire: as big as thou art   557
    Thou mad'st thine enemies shake, as if the World | Were Feauorous,
    and did tremble.   562
    Enter Cominius as it were in retire, with soldiers.   603
    Leade their successes, as we wish our owne,   610
    Com. Whose yonder, | That doe's appeare as he were Flead? O Gods,   629
    Mart. Oh! let me clip ye | In Armes as sound, as when I woo'd in heart;   640
    As merry, as when our Nuptiall day was done, | And Tapers burnt to
    Bedward.   642
    Mar. As with a man busied about Decrees: 645
    The Mouse ne're shunn'd the Cat, as they did budge | From Rascals
    worse then they.   657
    Com. As I guesse *Martius*, | Their Bands i'th Vaward are the Antients   667
    (As it were sinne to doubt) that loue this painting   687
    A Shield, as hard as his. A certaine number   701
    (As cause will be obey'd:) please you to March,   704
    As I haue set them downe. If I do send, dispatch   715
    Alarum, as in Battaile. | Enter Martius and Auffidius at seuerall doores.   722
    I haue done as you haue done, that's what I can,   766
    Induc'd as you haue beene, that's for my Countrey: 767
    When Steele growes soft, as the Parasites Silke,   801
    As if I lou'd my little should be dieted | In prayses, sawc'st with Lyes.   807
    As to vs, to all the World, That *Caius Martius*   815
    Be free, as is the Winde: deliuer him, *Titus*.   849
    As often as we eate. By th'Elements,   868
    Men. I, to deuour him, as the hungry Plebeians would | the Noble
    Martius.   906

AS *cont*.

*pleasures (at the least) if you take it as a pleasure to you, in	928
*proud, violent, testie Magistrates (alias Fooles) | as any in Rome.	940
*Meeting two such Weales men as you are (I cannot call	950
*shall encounter such ridiculous Subiects as you are, when	980
*honourable a graue, as to stuffe a Botchers Cushion, or to	983
*How now (my as faire as Noble) Ladyes, and the Moone	994
Com. On, to the Capitall. *Flourish. Cornets.* | *Exeunt in State, as before*.	1120
As if that whatsoeuer God, who leades him,	1138
Which that he will giue them, make I as little question,	1152
As he is proud to doo't.	1153
Nor shewing (as the manner is) his Wounds	1158
Scicin. It shall be to him then, as our good wills; a | sure destruction.	1168
Scicin. This (as you say) suggested,	1181
If he be put vpon't, and that's as easie,	1184
As to set Dogges on Sheepe, will be his fire	1185
Vpon him as he pass'd: the Nobles bended	1195
As to *Ioues* Statue, and the Commons made	1196
Enter two Officers, to lay Cushions, as it were, | *in the Capitoll*.	1203
*is as bad, as that which he dislikes, to flatter them for | their loue.	1225
*and his assent is not by such easie degrees as those, who	1228
As the maine Point of this our after-meeting,	1246
I loue them as they weigh---	1286
Turne terror into sport: as Weeds before	1319
Runne reeking o're the liues of men, as if 'twere	1333
And look'd vpon things precious, as they were	1341
And take to you, as your Predecessors haue,	1364
As if I had receiu'd them for the hyre | Of their breath onely.	1371
As if he did contemne what he requested, | Should be in them to giue.	1382
*3.*Cit*. Nay your wit will not so soone out as another	1413
As you were lesson'd: When he had no Power,	1578
That as his worthy deeds did clayme no lesse	1587
Scicin. Thus to haue said, | As you were fore-aduis'd, had toucht his Spirit,	1592
As cause had call'd you vp, haue held him to;	1596
Then Dogges, that are as often beat for barking, | As therefore kept to doe so.	1619
Then as guided by your owne true affections, and that	1634
If, as his nature is, he fall in rage	1664
And this shall seeme, as partly 'tis, their owne,	1669
Corio. So then the Volces stand but as at first,	1677
Suffer't, and liue with such as cannot rule, | Nor euer will be ruled.	1723
Let me deserue so ill as you, and make me | Your fellow Tribune.	1737
Or neuer be so Noble as a Consull,	1743
Corio. Now as I liue, I will.	1754
Let them regard me, as I doe not flatter,	1757
As for my Country, I haue shed my blood,	1768
Bru. You speake a'th'people, as if you were a God,	1773
Cor. Choller? Were I as patient as the midnight sleep,	1777
Be not as common Fooles; if you are not,	1794
And such a one as he, who puts his Shall,	1799
The Corne a'th'Store-house gratis, as 'twas vs'd | Sometime in Greece.	1809
Sicin. Ha's spoken like a Traitor, and shall answer | As Traitors do.	1862
Attach thee as a Traitorous Innouator:	1877
Com. Stand fast, we haue as many friends as enemies.	1954
Mene. I would they were Barbarians, as they are,	1962
Though in Rome litter'd: not Romans, as they are not,	1963

AS *cont.*

Mene. Heere me speake? As I do know	2010
Least parties (as he is belou'd) breake out,	2056
Sic. Noble *Menenius*, be you then as the peoples officer:	2073
I haue a heart as little apt as yours,	2120
The violent fit a'th'time craues it as Physicke	2125
With Honour, as in Warre; since that to both | It stands in like request.	2147
Now humble as the ripest Mulberry,	2180
Were fit for thee to vse, as they to clayme,	2184
As thou hast power and person.	2187
Menen. This but done, | Euen as she speakes, why their hearts were yours:	2188
For they haue Pardons, being ask'd, as free, | As words to little purpose.	2190
Volum. I prythee now sweet Son, as thou hast said	2214
Small as an Eunuch, or the Virgin voyce	2222
With as bigge heart as thou. Do as thou list,	2237
With Accusations, as I heare more strong | Then are vpon you yet.	2251
Corio. I, as an Hostler, that fourth poorest peece	2300
To suffer lawfull Censure for such faults | As shall be prou'd vpon you.	2320
But as I say, such as become a Soldier, | Rather then enuy you.	2333
In thy hands clutcht: as many Millions in	2351
Thou lyest vnto thee, with a voice as free, | As I do pray the Gods.	2353
Sicin. For that he ha's | (As much as in him lies) from time to time	2378
To plucke away their power: as now at last,	2381
As Enemy to the people, and his Countrey.	2405
As reeke a'th'rotten Fennes: whose Loues I prize,	2409
As the dead Carkasses of vnburied men,	2410
As most abated Captiues, to some Nation	2420
As he hath follow'd you, with all despight	2429
As 'tis to laugh at 'em. My Mother, as you wot well	2465
Menen. That's worthily | As any eare can heare. Come, let's not weepe,	2495
As he began, and not vnknit himselfe | The Noble knot he made.	2541
Cats, that can iudge as fitly of his worth,	2545
As I can of those Mysteries which heauen | Will not haue earth to know.	2546
As farre as doth the Capitoll exceede	2551
Leaue this faint-puling, and lament as I do,	2567
Rom. I am a Roman, and my Seruices are as you are, | against 'em. Know you me yet.	2574
Are still together: who Twin (as 'twere) in Loue,	2641
*1 A strange one as euer I look'd on: I cannot get him	2675
As Benefits to thee. For I will fight	2747
As hotly, and as Nobly with thy Loue,	2769
As euer in Ambitious strength, I did	2770
As best thou art experienc'd, since thou know'st	2798
finger and his thumbe, as one would set vp a Top.	2814
*1 He had so, looking as it were, would I were hang'd	2818
3 I would not be a Roman of all Nations; I had as | liue be a condemn'd man.	2835
*3 Why he is so made on heere within, as if hee were	2851
2 And he's as like to do't, as any man I can imagine.	2863
*3 Doo't? he will doo't: for look you sir, he has as ma-|ny	2864
*Friends as Enemies: which Friends sir as it were, durst	2865
*not (looke you sir) shew themselues (as we terme it) his | Friends, whilest he's in Directitude.	2866
*Drum strooke vp this afternoone: 'Tis as it were a parcel	2874

AS *cont*.

*1 Let me haue Warre say I, it exceeds peace as farre	2879
*as day do's night: It's sprightly walking, audible, and full	2880
*2 'Tis so, and as warres in some sort may be saide to	2884
*The Warres for my money. I hope to see Romanes as	2889
cheape as Volcians. They are rising, they are rising. | *Both*. In, in, in, in.	
Exeunt	2890
Bru. Farewell kinde Neighbours: | We wisht *Coriolanus* had lou'd you as	
we did.	2921
And vowes Reuenge as spacious, as betweene | The yong'st and oldest	
thing.	2977
**Mene*. As *Hercules* did shake downe Mellow Fruite:	3017
Deserue such pitty of him, as the Wolfe	3030
As those should do that had deseru'd his hate,	3033
Com. You haue brought | A Trembling vpon Rome, such as was neuer	3039
As if he were his Officer: Desperation,	3050
Which will not proue a whip: As many Coxcombes	3060
As you threw Caps vp, will he tumble downe,	3061
Your Soldiers vse him as the Grace 'fore meate,	3093
Fights Dragon-like, and does atcheeue as soone	3114
As draw his Sword: yet he hath left vndone	3115
Will be as rash in the repeale, as hasty	3123
As is the Aspray to the Fish, who takes it	3125
As he controll'd the warre. But one of these	3136
(As he hath spices of them all) not all,	3137
Hath not a Tombe so euident as a Chaire | T'extoll what it hath done.	3143
As *Cominius* is return'd, vnheard: what then?	3199
But as a discontented Friend, greefe-shot | With his vnkindnesse. Say't	
be so?	3200
Sicin. Yet your good will | Must haue that thankes from Rome, after	
the measure | As you intended well.	3202
Red as 'twould burne Rome: and his Iniury	3225
And his Wife, who (as I heare) meane to solicite him	3232
*1 Faith Sir, if you had told as many lies in his behalfe,	3262
*as you haue vttered words in your owne, you should not	3263
*passe heere: no, though it were as vertuous to lye, as to | liue chastly.	
Therefore go backe.	3264
*2 Howsoeuer you haue bin his Lier, as you say you	3268
Mene. I am as thy Generall is.	3274
*1 Then you should hate Rome, as he do's. Can you,	3275
*Dotant as you seeme to be? Can you think to blow	3281
*such weake breath as this? No, you are deceiu'd, therfore	3283
*for such things as you. I can scarse thinke ther's any, y'are	3338
*with your age. I say to you, as I was said to, Away. *Exit*	3342
As if Olympus to a Mole-hill should	3379
*As if a man were Author of himself, & knew no other kin	3385
Long as my Exile, sweet as my Reuenge!	3394
Shew duty as mistaken, all this while, | Betweene the Childe, and	
Parent.	3405
Corio. The Noble Sister of *Publicola*; | The Moone of Rome: Chaste as	
the Isicle	3416
Must as a Forraine Recreant be led	3469
As poysonous of your Honour. No, our suite	3492
*as a thing made for *Alexander*. What he bids bee done, is	3591
Mes. As certaine as I know the Sun is fire:	3617
*As the recomforted through th'gates. Why harke you: | *Trumpets,*	
Hoboyes, Drums beate, altogether.	3620

AS *cont*.

A City full: Of Tribunes such as you,	3628
Auf. Euen so, as with a man by his owne Almes im-|poyson'd, and with his Charity slaine.	3661
We must proceed as we do finde the People.	3667
He wadg'd me with his Countenance, as if | I had bin Mercenary.	3693
As cheape as Lies; he sold the Blood and Labour	3702
Auf. My Lords, | When you shall know (as in this Rage	3814
As the most Noble Coarse, that euer Herald | Did follow to his Vrne.	3824

ASH = 1

My grained Ash an hundred times hath broke,	2766

ASIDE = 2*1

Would the Nobility lay aside their ruth,	209
Val. Come, lay aside your stitchery, I must haue you	432
Bru. and Scic. Aside.	992

ASKD = 1

For they haue Pardons, being ask'd, as free, | As words to little purpose.	2190

ASKE = 6*1

*You two are old men, tell me one thing that I shall aske | you.	910
1 *Cit*. The price is, to aske it kindly.	1466
And now againe, of him that did not aske, but mock,	1610
Com. Who shall aske it?	3028
Corio. I beseech you peace: | Or if you'ld aske, remember this before;	3433
For we haue nothing else to aske, but that	3443
Which you deny already: yet we will aske,	3444

ASKER = 1

Scicin. Haue you, ere now, deny'd the asker:	1609

ASKING = 2

Deny your asking, take your choice of those | That best can ayde your action.	683
In asking their good loues, but thou wilt frame	2185

ASKT = *1

*question askt him by any of the Senators, but they stand	2853

ASLEEPE *see also* a-sleepe = 1

thinke our Fellowes are asleepe.	2655

ASPECT = 1

Hath an Aspect of intercession, which	3381

ASPRAY = 1

As is the Aspray to the Fish, who takes it	3125

ASSAULT = 2

1 I, and for an assault too.	2831
March to assault thy Country, then to treade	3478

ASSAULTED = 1

Enter Martius bleeding, assaulted by the Enemy.	564

ASSE = *2

*the Asse in compound, with the Maior part of your sylla-|bles.	954
*3 I'th City of Kites and Crowes? What an Asse it is,	2697

ASSEMBLE = 2

Scici. Let them assemble: and on a safer Iudgement,	1621
Sicin. Assemble presently the people hither:	2274

ASSEMBLY = 2

You, the great Toe of this Assembly?	163
*haue hearts inclinable to honor and aduance the Theame | of our Assembly.	1264

ASSENT = *1

*and his assent is not by such easie degrees as those, who	1228

ASSES = *1
    *be intomb'd in an Asses Packe-saddle; yet you must bee   984
ASSIST = 2
    All. The Gods assist you. | *Auf*. And keepe your Honors safe.   355
    Yet he shall haue a Noble Memory. Assist.   3836
ASSISTANCE = *1
    Sicin. And affecting one sole Throne, without assista(n)ce   2932
ASSOCIATED = 1
    Associated with *Auffidius*, Rages | Vpon our Territories, and haue
    already   2989
ASSUNDER = 1
    Of more strong linke assunder, then can euer   72
ASSURD = 1
    Was not our recompence, resting well assur'd   1818
ASSURED = *1
    *I was hardly moued to come to thee: but beeing assured   3308
ASSWAGE = *1
    *Gods asswage thy wrath, and turne the dregs of it, vpon   3312
ASUNDER *see* assunder
AT *see also* at's = 69*13
ATCHEEUE = 1
    Fights Dragon-like, and does atcheeue as soone   3114
ATCHIEUED = 1
    The Treasure in this field atchieued, and Citie,   785
ATCHIEUING = 1
    And by deed-atchieuing Honor newly nam'd,   1078
ATH = 24*3
    *What showts are these? The other side a'th City is risen: 48
    Touching the Weale a'th Common, you shall finde   159
    As they would hang them on the hornes a'th Moone,   226
    Call thither all the Officers a'th'Towne,   601
    Where is the enemy? Are you Lords a'th Field?   661
    *you are censured heere in the City, I mean of vs a'th'right | hand File,
    do you?   919
    Then we to stretch it out. Masters a'th' People,   1259
    *of one direct way, should be at once to all the points | a'th Compasse.   1409
    Corio. Well then I pray, your price a'th'Consulship.   1465
    Bru. You speake a'th'people, as if you were a God,   1773
    The Corne a'th'Store-house gratis, as 'twas vs'd | Sometime in Greece.   1809
    Breake ope the Lockes a'th'Senate, and bring in | The Crowes to pecke
    the Eagles.   1835
    A brand to th'end a'th World.   2041
    The violent fit a'th'time craues it as Physicke   2125
    I'th'right and strength a'th'Commons: be it either   2276
    Insisting on the olde prerogatiue | And power i'th Truth a'th Cause.   2279
    That doth distribute it. In the name a'th'people,   2384
    As reeke a'th'rotten Fennes: whose Loues I prize,   2409
    Th'hoorded plague a'th'Gods requit your loue.   2518
    Till he had forg'd himselfe a name a'th'fire | Of burning Rome.   3166
    To teare with Thunder the wide Cheekes a'th'Ayre,   3508
    Mene. See you yon'd Coin a'th Capitol, yon'd corner | (stone?   3571
    Auf. Go tell the Lords a'th'City, I am heere: 3650
    Together with the Seale a'th Senat, what | We haue compounded on.   3748
    You Lords and Heads a'th'State, perfidiously   3759
    Counsaile a'th'warre: But at his Nurses teares   3765
    Helpe three a'th'cheefest Souldiers, Ile be one.   3831

ATHICA = *1
　*the yearne she spun in *Vlisses* absence, did but fill *Athica*　　　447
ATS = 1
　He ha's it now: and by his Lookes, me thinkes, | 'Tis warme at's heart.　1548
ATTACH = 1
　Attach thee as a Traitorous Innouator:　　　1877
ATTAIND = 1
　Better be held, nor more attain'd then by　　　295
ATTEMPT = 1
　But with his last Attempt, he wip'd it out:　　　3503
ATTEMPTED = 1
　That prosperously I haue attempted, and　　　3740
ATTEND = 5*2
　1.*Sen*. Then worthy *Martius*, | Attend vpon *Cominius* to these Warres.　258
　Sen. Your Company to'th'Capitoll, where I know | Our greatest Friends
　attend vs.　　　269
　Where great Patricians shall attend, and shrug,　　　751
　I know they do attend vs.　　　1386
　Sic. Meet on the Market place: wee'l attend you there:　　　2076
　Com. Away, the Tribunes do attend you: arm your self　　　2249
　Giue him deseru'd vexation. Let a guard | Attend vs through the City.　2430
ATTENDANTS = 2
　Enter Virgilia, Volumnia, Valeria, yong Martius, | with Attendants.　3369
　Enter Tullus Auffidius, with Attendants.　　　3649
ATTENDED = *1
　Auf. I am attended at the Cyprus groue. I pray you　　　890
ATTENDS = 1
　Thether, where more attends you, and you slander　　　77
ATTONE = 1
　He, and *Auffidius* can no more attone | Then violent'st Contrariety.　2984
AUDIBLE = *1
　*as day do's night: It's sprightly walking, audible, and full　　　2880
AUDIENCE = 1*1
　*to a second day of Audience. When you are hearing a　　　968
　Edile. List to your Tribunes. Audience: | Peace I say.　　　2311
AUDIT see awdit
AUF = 35*4
AUFF = 1
AUFFI = *1
　of Auffi. Martius fights til they be driuen in breathles.　　　741
AUFFI = 1
AUFFID = 3
AUFFIDIOUS = 5*1
　Tullus Auffidious, is he within your Walles?　　　501
　There is *Auffidious*. List what worke he makes | Among'st your clouen
　Army.　　　510
　There is the man of my soules hate, *Auffidious*,　　　581
　*Then dangerous to me: To *Auffidious* thus, I will appear | (and fight.　592
　Of their best trust: O're them *Auffidious*, | Their very heart of Hope.　669
　Able to beare against the great *Auffidious*　　　700
AUFFIDIUS see also Affidious, Affidius, Auf., Auff., Auffi., Auffid.,
　Auffidious, Aufid. = 33*2
　Tullus Auffidius that will put you too't:　　　249
　Enter Tullus Auffidius with Senators of Coriolus.　　　313
　1.*Sen*. So, your opinion is *Auffidius*, | That they of Rome are entred in
　our Counsailes,　　　314

AUFFIDIUS cont.

2.*Sen.* Noble *Auffidius*, | Take your Commission, hye you to your
Bands,   342
See him plucke *Auffidius* downe by th'haire: 392
Vir. Heauens blesse my Lord from fell *Auffidius.*   407
Vol. Hee'l beat *Auffidius* head below his knee, | And treade vpon his
necke.   408
Alarum, as in Battaile. | *Enter Martius and Auffidius at seueral doores.*   722
But then *Auffidius* was within my view,   844
A flourish. Cornets. Enter Tullus Auffidius | *bloudie, with two or three
Souldiors.*   857
Menen. Ha's he disciplin'd *Auffidius* soundly?   1023
**Volum. Titus Lartius* writes, they fought together, but | *Auffidius* got
off.   1024
Corio. Tullus Auffidius then had made new head.   1674
Corio. Saw you *Auffidius*? | *Latius.* On safegard he came to me, and did
curse   1683
*Auffidius will appeare well in these Warres, his great   2603
Cit. And you. | **Corio.* Direct me, if it be your will, where great *Auf-
| fidius* lies: Is he in *Antium*?   2630
Enter Auffidius with the Seruingman.   2704
Mene. 'Tis *Auffidius*, | Who hearing of our *Martius* Banishment,   2945
Ioyn'd with *Auffidius*, leads a power 'gainst Rome,   2976
He, and *Auffidius* can no more attone | Then violent'st Contrariety.   2984
Associated with *Auffidius*, Rages | Vpon our Territories, and haue
already   2989
And is *Auffidius* with him? You are they   3055
Enter Auffidius with his Lieutenant.   3090
Enter Coriolanus with Auffidius.   3295
I will not heare thee speake. This man *Auffidius*   3327
Enter Coriolanus and Auffidius.   3346
Corio. Auffidius, and you Volces marke, for wee'l   3447
Auffidius, though I cannot make true Warres,   3548
Ile frame conuenient peace. Now good *Auffidius*,   3549
A Mother lesse? or granted lesse *Auffidius*?   3551
Enter Tullus Auffidius, with Attendants.   3649
Enter 3 or 4 Conspirators of Auffidius Faction. | Most Welcome.   3658
Shall haue Iudicious hearing. Stand *Auffidius*, | And trouble not the
peace.   3799
Draw both the Conspirators, and kils Martius, who | *falles, Auffidius
stands on him.*   3805
2.*Lord.* His owne impatience, | Takes from *Auffidius* a great part of
blame: 3826
AUFFIDIUSSES = *1
**Corio.* O that I had him, with six *Auffidiusses*, or more: 3801
AUFID = 1
AUGHT *see* ought
AUGORS = 1
Your Franchises, whereon you stood, confin'd | Into an Augors boare.   3001
AUGURER *see* agurer
AUOID = 1 *1
*3 What haue you to do here fellow? Pray you auoid | the house.   2677
Heere's no place for you, pray you auoid: Come.   2685
AUOIDED *see* voided
AUSTERITY = 1
Euen with the same austerity and garbe,   3135

AUTHOR = *1
   *As if a man were Author of himself, & knew no other kin   3385
AUTHORITIE = 2
   For they doe pranke them in Authoritie, | Against all Noble sufferance.   1702
   Brut. Or let vs stand to our Authoritie,   1920
AUTHORITIES = 2
   Brutus. So it must fall out | To him, or our Authorities, for an end.   1170
   To know, when two Authorities are vp,   1803
AUTHORITY = *1
   *good: what Authority surfets one, would releeue   18
AWAKE = 1
   Then vale your Ignorance: If none, awake   1792
AWAKEN = 1
   Com. I offered to awaken his regard   3176
AWAY = 24*5
   All. No more talking on't; Let it be done, away, away   15
   Citizens steale away. Manet Sicin. & Brutus.   279
   Volum. Away you Foole; it more becomes a man   401
   Where they shall know our minde. Away. *Exeunt*   602
   And then I came away.   617
   Coriolanus rises, and offers to goe away. | Nay, keepe your place.   1275
   *parts melted away with rotten Dewes, the fourth would   1418
   Mene. Goe, get you to our House: be gone, away.   1951
   Com. Nay, come away. *Exeunt Coriolanus and* | *Cominius.*   1980
   Sicin. He's a Disease that must be cut away.   2032
   Away my disposition, and possesse me | Some Harlots spirit: My throat
   of Warre be turn'd,   2219
   Com. Away, the Tribunes do attend you: arm your self   2249
   To plucke away their power: as now at last,   2381
   All. It shall be so, it shall be so: let him away: 2391
   With many heads butts me away. Nay Mother,   2438
   Corio. Away. | 2 *Ser.* Away? Get you away.   2669
   Corio. Follow your Function, go, and batten on colde | bits. *Pushes
   him away from him.*   2686
   *thy Mistris: Thou prat'st, and prat'st, serue with thy tren-|cher:
   Hence. *Beats him away*   2702
   Come let's away: when *Caius* Rome is thine,   3147
   Corio. Away. | *Mene.* How? Away?   3315
   *with your age. I say to you, as I was said to, Away. *Exit*   3342
   Boy. A shall not tread on me: Ile run away | Till I am bigger, but then
   Ile fight.   3483
   To a Mothers part belongs. He turnes away: 3525
   Where he was to begin, and giue away   3729
   He whin'd and roar'd away your Victory,   3766
AWDIT = 1
   Yet I can make my Awdit vp, that all   152
AWE = 1
   (Vnder the Gods) keepe you in awe, which else   198
AWHILE = 2
   Patience awhile; you'st heare the Bellies answer.   132
   With thee awhile: Determine on some course   2474
AWRY = 1
   Sicin. This is cleane kamme. | *Brut.* Meerely awry: 2042
AY *see* I
AYD = 1
   Those Centuries to our ayd, the rest will serue   716

AYDE = 2*1
  Deny your asking, take your choice of those | That best can ayde your
  aetion.   683
  Heere they fight, and certaine Volces come in the ayde   740
  Sicin. Nay, pray be patient: If you refuse your ayde   3187
AYDELESSE = 1
  With shunlesse destinie: aydelesse came off,   1326
AYME = 1
  We shalbe shortned in our ayme, which was   339
AYMES = 1
  Bru. Fame, at the which he aymes,   293
AYRE = 4
  That do corrupt my Ayre: I banish you,   2411
  That made the Ayre vnwholsome, when you cast   3056
  To teare with Thunder the wide Cheekes a'th'Ayre,   3508
  And had no welcomes home, but he returnes | Splitting the Ayre with
  noyse.   3708
A-FARRE = 1
  Alarum continues still a-farre off.   573
A-FOOT = 1
  To take in many Townes, ere (almost) Rome | Should know we were
  a-foot.   340
A-SLEEPE = 1
  That Babies lull a-sleepe: The smiles of Knaues   2223
BABIES = 1
  That Babies lull a-sleepe: The smiles of Knaues   2223
BABY = 1
  Into a rapture lets her Baby crie,   1125
BACK = 2*1
  *Alarum, the Romans are beat back to their Trenches | Enter Martius
  Cursing*.   523
  1 Be it so, go back: the vertue of your name, | Is not heere passable.   3249
  *1 My Generall cares not for you. Back I say, go: least   3291
BACKE = 12*2
  From me do backe receiue the Flowre of all,   153
  Must to *Corioles* backe, send vs to Rome   833
  Sould. 'Twill be deliuer'd backe on good Condition.   860
  For you the City. Thus I turne my backe;   2422
  2.*Wat*. Stand, and go backe.   3237
  *passe heere: no, though it were as vertuous to lye, as to | liue chastly.
  Therefore go backe.   3264
  *haue, I am one that telling true vnder him, must say you | cannot
  passe. Therefore go backe.   3269
  *backe to Rome, and prepare for your execution: you are   3284
  *I let forth your halfe pinte of blood. Backe, that's the vt-|most of your
  hauing, backe.   3292
  *1 Do you heare how wee are shent for keeping your | greatnesse backe?   3334
  And spurne me backe: But, if it be not so   3522
  Ile not to Rome, Ile backe with you, and pray you   3557
  And you shall beare | A better witnesse backe then words, which we   3563
BACKES = 1
  All hurt behinde, backes red, and faces pale   532
BAD = 2*1
  If any thinke, braue death out-weighes bad life,   690
  Bru. Good or bad?   900
  *is as bad, as that which he dislikes, to flatter them for | their loue.   1225

BAES = 1
Bru. He's a Lambe indeed, that baes like a Beare. 908
BAILE = 1
The one side must haue baile. 171
BAITED = 1
Sicin. Why stay we to be baited 2556
BAITS = 1
With cautelous baits and practice. 2471
BALD = 1*2
*bald; but that our wits are so diuersly Coulord; and true- | ly 1406
What should the people do with these bald Tribunes? 1865
*bald before him. Our Generall himselfe makes a Mistris 2854
BALLAD-MAKERS = 1
*This peace is nothing, but to rust Iron, encrease Taylors, | and breed
Ballad-makers. 2877
BALMES = 1
And Balmes applyed to you, yet dare I neuer 682
BANDS = 2
2.*Sen.* Noble *Auffidius*, | Take your Commission, hye you to your
Bands, 342
Com. As I guesse *Martius*, | Their Bands i'th Vaward are the Antients 667
BANISH = 5
(Eu'n from this instant) banish him our Citie 2386
That do corrupt my Ayre: I banish you, 2411
To banish your Defenders, till at length 2416
To banish him that strooke more blowes for Rome | Then thou hast
spoken words. 2527
1 *Cit.* For mine owne part, | When I said banish him, I said 'twas pitty. 3066
BANISHD = 10*2
Hee's banish'd, and it shall be so. 2392
Bru. There's no more to be said, but he is banish'd 2404
All. Our enemy is banish'd, he is gone: Hoo, oo. 2427
Whom we haue banish'd, does exceed you all. 2554
Vol. Coriolanus Banisht? | *Rom.* Banish'd sir. 2596
Thou art thence Banish'd, we would muster all 2786
*home, I euer said we were i'th wrong, when we banish'd | him. 3082
So hated, and so banish'd: but he ha's a Merit 3139
But what o'that? Go you that banish'd him 3155
*vnto vs. When we banish'd him, we respected not them: 3601
Vnshoot the noise that Banish'd *Martius*; 3644
Being banish'd for't, he came vnto my Harth, 3683
BANISHERS = 1
To be full quit of those my Banishers, 2740
BANISHMENT = 2*2
For death, for fine, or Banishment, then let them 2277
*to heart, the Banishment of that worthy *Coriolanus*, that 2591
Mene. 'Tis *Auffidius*, | Who hearing of our *Martius* Banishment, 2945
*willingly consented to his Banishment, yet it was against | our will. 3071
BANISHT = 1
Vol. Coriolanus Banisht? | *Rom.* Banish'd sir. 2596
BANNERS = 1
That we shall hardly in our ages see | Their Banners waue againe. 1681
BARBARIANS = 1
Mene. I would they were Barbarians, as they are, 1962
BARE = 3
cast vp their Caps and Launces: Cominius | and Lartius stand bare. 795
To buy and sell with Groats, to shew bare heads 2095

BARE *cont*.
  It was a bare petition of a State   3173
BARKING = 1
  Then Dogges, that are as often beat for barking, | As therefore kept to
  doe so.   1619
BARRD = 1
  To vnstable Slightnesse. Purpose so barr'd, it followes,   1847
BARREN = *1
  *1.*Cit*. If I must not, I neede not be barren of Accusa-|tions   45
BARRST = 1
  Thine enmities most capitall: Thou barr'st vs   3459
BASE = 4
  Bury with those that wore them. These base slaues,   578
  It makes the Consuls base; and my Soule akes   1802
  Must I with my base Tongue giue to my Noble Heart   2206
  2.*Con*. And patient Fooles, | Whose children he hath slaine, their base
  throats teare   3710
BASENESSE = 1
  And by my Bodies action, teach my Minde | A most inherent Basenesse. 2230
BASEST = 1
  Men. For that being one o'th lowest, basest, poorest   165
BASTARD = *1
  *deafe, sleepe, insensible, a getter of more bastard Chil-|dren, then
  warres a destroyer of men.   2882
BASTARDS = 2
  Though but Bastards, and Syllables   2155
  Volum. Bastards, and all. | Good man, the Wounds that he does beare
  for Rome!   2537
BATE = 1
  Neyther will they bate one iot of Ceremonie.   1361
BATH = 1
  Com. Though I could wish, | You were conducted to a gentle Bath,   680
BATS = 2
  Where go you with Bats and Clubs? The matter | Speake I pray you.   57
  But make you ready your stiffe bats and clubs,   169
BATTAILE = 3
  And giuen to *Lartius* and to *Martius* Battaile: 615
  Alarum, as in Battaile. | *Enter Martius and Auffidius at seuerall doores*. 722
  And to the Battaile came he, where he did   1332
BATTAILES = 3
  Mar. I do beseech you, | By all the Battailes wherein we haue fought, 671
  And in the brunt of seuenteene Battailes since,   1314
  Of Wounds, two dozen odde: Battailes thrice six   1520
BATTELL = 3
  Rome, and her Rats, are at the point of battell,   170
  Mar. How lies their Battell? Know you on w side   665
  In puny Battell slay me. Saue you sir.   2628
BATTEN = *1
  Corio. Follow your Function, go, and batten on colde | bits. *Pushes
  him away from him*.   2686
BATTERY = *1
  *like a knell, and his hum is a Battery. He sits in his State,   3590
BE *see also* bee, shalbe = 157*46
BEACH = 1
  Then let the Pibbles on the hungry beach   3409
BEAME = 1
  Below the beame of sight; yet will I still | Be thus to them.   2088

BEARD = 2*1

If ere againe I meet him beard to beard, 869
*Volce. You had more Beard when I last saw you, but 2578
BEARDS = *2

*wagging of your Beards, and your Beards deserue not so 982
BEARE = 20*5

*not vppe, they will; and there's all the loue they beare | vs. 86
(As children from a Beare) the Volces shunning him: 393
That beare the shapes of men, how haue you run 530
Able to beare against the great Auffidious 700
The rest shall beare the businesse in some other fight 703
*Marcus Caius Coriolanus. Beare th'addition Nobly euer? 821
Bru. He's a Lambe indeed, that baes like a Beare. 908
*Men. Hee's a Beare indeede, that liues like a Lambe. 909
*And though I must be content to beare with those, 955
Watcht for your Voyces: for your Voyces, beare 1519
Your Liberties, and the Charters that you beare 1581
Beare him toth' Rock Tarpeian, and from thence | Into destruction cast him. 1926
And beare him to the Rock. Corio. drawes his Sword. 1939
Like interrupted Waters, and o're-beare | What they are vs'd to beare. 1974
Which I can scarsely beare. 2127
A Lye, that it must beare well? I will doo't: 2207
Will beare the Knaue by'th Volume: 2301
That common chances. Common men could beare, 2441
Volum. Bastards, and all. | Good man, the Wounds that he does beare for Rome! 2537
*Which thou should'st beare me, only that name remains. 2730
And beare the Palme, for hauing brauely shed 3472
And you shall beare | A better witnesse backe then words, which we 3563
Must beare my beating to his Graue, shall ioyne | To thrust the Lye vnto him. 3779
1.Lord. Beare from hence his body, 3822
BEARES = 5

After the inueterate Hate he beares you. 1629
Vpon the wounds his body beares, which shew 2325
Beares a Command in't: Though thy Tackles torne, 2718
Of our designe. He beares himselfe more proudlier, 3099
To th'vulgar eye, that he beares all things fairely: 3112
BEARING = 4

Still cubbording the Viand, neuer bearing 102
Onely for bearing Burthens, and sore blowes | For sinking vnder them. 1179
Skaling his present bearing with his past, 1652
Exeunt bearing the Body of Martius. A dead March | Sounded. 3837
BEAST = *1

*Corio. Come leaue your teares: a brief farwel: the beast 2437
BEASTLY = *1

*the Beastly Plebeans. I will be bold to take my leaue of | you. 990
BEASTS = 2

Sicin. Nature teaches Beasts to know their Friends. 903
But like Beasts, and Cowardly Nobles, 3044
BEAT = 6

Vol. Hee'l beat Auffidius head below his knee, | And treade vpon his necke. 408
Alarum, the Romans are beat back to their Trenches | Enter Martius Cursing. 523
I haue fought with thee; so often hast thou beat me: 866

BEAT *cont*.

Then Dogges, that are as often beat for barking, | As therefore kept to doe so. 1619

In this Mutinie, the Tribunes, the Aediles, and the | People are beat in. 1949

Corio. On faire ground, I could beat fortie of them. 1967

BEATE = 8

From Slaues, that Apes would beate; *Pluto* and Hell, 531

If you'l stand fast, wee'l beate them to their Wiues, 536

Com. Where is that Slaue | Which told me they had beate you to your Trenches? 651

Or loose mine Arme for't: Thou hast beate mee out 2779

Like a bold Flood o're-beate. Oh come, go in, 2789

And beate the Messenger, who bids beware | Of what is to be dreaded. 2959

*As the recomforted through th'gates. Why harke you: | *Trumpets, Hoboyes, Drums beate, altogether*. 3620

Beate thou the Drumme that it speake mournfully: 3832

BEATEN = *1

*2 Here sir, I'de haue beaten him like a dogge, but for | disturbing the Lords within. 2706

BEATING = 2

Beating your Officers, cursing your selues, 2360

Must beare my beating to his Graue, shall ioyne | To thrust the Lye vnto him. 3779

BEATS = 1

*thy Mistris: Thou prat'st, and prat'st, serue with thy tren-|cher: Hence. *Beats him away* 2702

BECAUSE = 2*2

Because I am the Store-house, and the Shop 140

Men. Because you talke of Pride now, will you not | be angry. 922

Volum. Because, that | Now it lyes you on to speake to th'people: 2150

*3 Reason, because they then lesse neede one another: 2888

BECOME = 3*3

*we become Rakes. For the Gods know, I speake this in 25

*would become such a person, that it was no better then 371

Tit. What is become of *Martius*? | *All*. Slaine (Sir) doubtlesse. 548

Men. Our very Priests must become Mockers, if they 979

Victorie in his Pocket? the wounds become him. 1020

But as I say, such as become a Soldier, | Rather then enuy you. 2333

BECOMES = 2

Volum. Away you Foole; it more becomes a man 401

Becomes not Rome: nor ha's *Coriolanus* 1747

BECOMT = 1

Of that Integrity which should becom't: 1858

BED = 2*1

*he wonne Honor, then in the embracements of his Bed, 365

Patri. I would they were a bed. 1990

Whose Houres, whose Bed, whose Meale and Exercise 2640

BEDWARD = 1

As merry, as when our Nuptiall day was done, | And Tapers burnt to Bedward. 642

BED-FELLOW = 1

their Bed-fellow: Worthie *Cominius* speake. 1274

BEE *l*.*33 *927 *969 *976 *984 *1468 *1477 2390 2406 *3081 *3341 *3591 *3600 = 2*11

BEEING *l*.*35 *3308 = *2

BEEN *l*.*1027 1270 = 1*1

BEENE *see also* been, bene, bin *l*.*381 767 *1211 *1229 *1404 *2106 2197
  2455 2466 *2583 2782 2955 3252 3320 = 8*6
BEESOME = *1
  *too? What harme can your beesome Conspectui-|ties   959
BEFORE *see also* fore = 38*9
  1. *Citizen*. | *Before we proceed any further, heare me speake.   4
  *before their Citie *Carioles*, they nothing doubt preuai-|ling,   463
  before the City Corialus: to them | a Messenger.   480
  Now put your Shields before your hearts, and fight   516
  He has the stampe of *Martius*, and I haue | Before time seene him thus.   631
  Yet cam'st thou to a Morsell of this Feast, | Hauing fully din'd before.   757
  What you haue done, before our Armie heare me.   778
  Before the common distribution, | At your onely choyse.   787
  For what he did before *Corioles*, call him,   819
  Volum. Hee had, before this last Expedition, twentie | fiue Wounds
  vpon him.   1049
  Before him, hee carryes Noyse;   1055
  Com. On, to the Capitall. *Flourish*. *Cornets*. | *Exeunt in State, as before*. 1120
  *the People, Lictors before them: Coriolanus, Mene-|nius, Cominius the
  Consul: Scicinius and Brutus*   1240
  The brizled Lippes before him: he bestrid   1306
  Before, and in Corioles, let me say   1316
  Turne terror into sport: as Weeds before   1319
  We will be there before the streame o'th' People: 1668
  Corio. Why this was knowne before. | *Brut*. Not to them all.   1730
  A Noble life, before a Long, and Wish,   1852
  Before the Tagge returne? whose Rage doth rend   1973
  Being once gangren'd, is not then respected | For what before it was.   2046
  Before you had worne it out. | *Corio*. Let go.   2104
  Before he should thus stoope to'th'heart, but that   2124
  To haue my praise for this, performe a part | Thou hast not done
  before.   2216
  More then a wilde exposture, to each chance | That starts i'th'way
  before thee.   2475
  Were in Arabia, and thy Tribe' before him, | His good Sword in his
  hand.   2533
  Corio. Which is his house, beseech you? | *Cit*. This heere before you.   2635
  Stand I before thee heere: Then if thou hast   2741
  *on't before *Corioles*, he scotcht him, and notcht him like a |
  Carbinado.   2846
  *bald before him. Our Generall himselfe makes a Mistris   2854
  *will mowe all downe before him, and leaue his passage | poul'd.   2861
  And quietnesse of the people, which before   2895
  Destroy, what lies before'em.   2944
  Before you punish him, where he heard this,   2957
  O're-borne their way, consum'd with fire, and tooke | What lay before
  them.   2991
  Before you finde it other. All the Regions   3021
  A Mile before his Tent, fall downe, and knee   3156
  The Gaoler to his pitty. I kneel'd before him,   3226
  2 You'l see your Rome embrac'd with fire, before | You'l speake with
  Coriolanus.   3243
  Corio. We will before the walls of Rome to morrow   3347
  I kneele before thee, and vnproperly   3404
  Corio. I beseech you peace: | Or if you'ld aske, remember this before;   3433
  *like an Engine, and the ground shrinkes before his Trea-|ding.   3588
  *And make triumphant fires, strew Flowers before them: 3643

BEFORE *cont.*
    Intends t'appeare before the People, hoping   3656
    He bow'd his Nature, neuer knowne before,   3677
    What faults he made before the last, I thinke   3727
BEFORES = 1
    If they set downe before's: for the remoue   345
BEGAN *see also* gan = 2
    How youngly he began to serue his Countrey,   1639
    As he began, and not vnknit himselfe | The Noble knot he made.   2541
BEGGARS = 1
    The Glasses of my sight: A Beggars Tongue   2225
BEGGD = 3
    Com. Oh well begg'd: 847
    begg'd: I haue your Almes, Adieu.   1472
    He mock'd vs, when he begg'd our Voyces.   1557
BEGGE = 4
    Am bound to begge of my Lord Generall.   839
    Toth' People, begge their stinking Breaths.   1159
    To begge of Hob and Dicke, that does appeere   1507
    To begge of thee, it is my more dis-honor,   2233
BEGGERS = 1
    Which they haue giuen to Beggers.   1764
BEGGING = 1
    Corio. No Sir, 'twas neuer my desire yet to trouble the | poore with
    begging.   1461
BEGIN = 4
    Martius. The Gods begin to mocke me: 837
    A Curse begin at very root on's heart,   1094
    From where he should begin, and end, but will | Lose those he hath
    wonne.   1145
    Where he was to begin, and giue away   3729
BEGINNING = 1
    Will proue to bloody: and the end of it, | Vnknowne to the Beginning.   2071
BEGUN = 1
    Bru. And when such time they haue begun to cry,   2282
BEHALFE = 1*1
    The Nobility are vexed, whom we see haue sided | In his behalfe.   2504
    *1 Faith Sir, if you had told as many lies in his behalfe,   3262
BEHAUIOUR = *1
    *his behauiour: we are not to stay altogether, but to come   1429
BEHELD = 4
    Hadst thou beheld | *Martius.* Pray now, no more: 762
    And stand vpon my common part with those, | That haue beheld the
    doing.   792
    There's some among you haue beheld me fighting,   1941
    I haue seene the Sterne, and thou hast oft beheld   2462
BEHINDE = 3
    Ere stay behinde this Businesse. | *Men.* Oh true-bred.   267
    All hurt behinde, backes red, and faces pale   532
    And behinde him, hee leaues Teares: 1056
BEHOLD = 5*1
    Behold, these are the Tribunes of the People,   1700
    And therein behold themselues: I say againe,   1758
    Though they themselues did suffer by't, behold   2898
    *more long in Spectatorship, and crueller in suffering, be-|hold   3302
    Corio. O Mother, Mother! | What haue you done? Behold, the Heauens
    do ope,   3540

BEHOLD cont.
  Sena. Behold our Patronnesse, the life of Rome: 3641
BEHOLDING = *1
  *an houre from her beholding; I considering how Honour   370
BEHOLDS = 1
  And dye among our Neighbours: Nay, behold's,   3530
BEHOLDST = 1
  Was my belou'd in Rome: yet thou behold'st.   3328
BEING see also beeing l.165 *222 *285 863 879 929 *989 1058 *1398
  *1417 1646 *1718 1788 1819 1822 1987 2046 2050 2182 2190 2292 2337
  *2444 *2604 *2665 3674 3683 3735 = 20*9
BELEEUE = 5
  Nor Cowardly in retyre: Beleeue me Sirs,   606
  Thou't not beleeue thy deeds: but Ile report it,   749
  And say 'tis true; I'de not beleeue them more   2763
  But for your Sonne, beleeue it: Oh beleeue it,   3545
BELEEUT = 1
  Beleeu't not lightly, though I go alone   2467
BELLIES = 2
  2.Cit. Your Bellies answer: What   117
  Patience awhile; you'st heare the Bellies answer.   132
BELLY = 9
  Rebell'd against the Belly; thus accus'd it: 99
  Of the whole body, the Belly answer'd.   107
  2.Cit. Well sir, what answer made the Belly.   108
  For looke you I may make the belly Smile,   111
  2.Cit. Should by the Cormorant belly be restrain'd,   125
  What could the Belly answer?   129
  Your most graue Belly was deliberate,   135
  (You my good Friends, this sayes the Belly) marke me.   148
  Men. The Senators of Rome, are this good Belly,   156
BELONGING = 1
  With all his trim belonging; and from this time,   818
BELONGS see also longs = 1
  To a Mothers part belongs. He turnes away: 3525
BELOUD = 3
  Least parties (as he is belou'd) breake out,   2056
  Cogge their Hearts from them, and come home belou'd   2243
  Was my belou'd in Rome: yet thou behold'st.   3328
BELOW = 4*1
  *Below their cobled Shooes. They say ther's grain enough?   208
  A place below the first: for what miscarries   296
  Vol. Hee'l beat Auffidius head below his knee, | And treade vpon his
  necke.   408
  And fell below his Stem: his Sword, Deaths stampe,   1321
  Below the beame of sight; yet will I still | Be thus to them.   2088
BEMOCKE = 1
  Sicin. Bemocke the modest Moone.   286
BENCH = 2
  His popular Shall, against a grauer Bench   1800
  To'th'greater Bench, in a Rebellion: 1867
BENCHD = 1
  Brutus. Sir, I hope my words dis-bench'd you not? | Coriol. No Sir: yet
  oft,   1282
BENCHER = *1
  *perfecter gyber for the Table, then a necessary Bencher in | the
  Capitoll.   977

BEND = 1
 Who bow'd but in my Stirrop, bend like his   2227
BENDED = 1
 Vpon him as he pass'd: the Nobles bended   1195
BENE *l*.2290 2396 *2909 *3309 = 2*2
BENEATH = *1
 *Beneath abhorring. What would you haue, you Curres,   179
BENEFIT = 3
 No publique benefit which you receiue   160
 That if thou conquer Rome, the benefit   3499
 The benefit of our Leuies, answering vs   3730
BENEFITS = 1
 As Benefits to thee. For I will fight   2747
BENT = 1
 Whether 'tis bent: most likely, 'tis for you: | Consider of it.   330
BEREAUES = 1
 Mangles true iudgement, and bereaues the State   1857
BESEECH = 12*3
 Yet are they passing Cowardly. But I beseech you,   215
 Virg. Beseech you giue me leaue to retire my selfe.   389
 Mar. I do beseech you, | By all the Battailes wherein we haue fought, 671
 Would seeme but modest: therefore I beseech you,   776
 Corio. I doe beseech you, | Let me o're-leape that custome: for I cannot 1355
 *bountifull to the desirers: Therefore beseech you, I may | be Consull. 1493
 Senat. No more words, we beseech you.   1766
 Nothing is done to purpose. Therefore beseech you,   1848
 Mene. Heare me one word, 'beseech you Tribunes,   1930
 You cannot Tent your selfe: be gone, 'beseech you.   1960
 Mene. Calmely, I do beseech you.   2299
 Corio. Which is his house, beseech you? | *Cit.* This heere before you. 2635
 To say, beseech you cease. You haue made faire hands,   3037
 Lieu. Sir, I beseech you, think you he'l carry Rome?   3118
 Corio. I beseech you peace: | Or if you'ld aske, remember this before; 3433
BESIDE = 1
 Sicin. One thus descended, | That hath beside well in his person
 wrought,   1648
BESIDES = 2
 Sicin. Besides, if things go well,   301
 And his old Hate vnto you: besides, forget not   1623
BEST = 12*5
 Our mustie superfluity. See our best Elders.   243
 Of their best trust: O're them *Auffidious,* | Their very heart of Hope. 669
 Deny your asking, take your choice of those | That best can ayde your
 action.   683
 And foure shall quickly draw out my Command, | Which men are best
 inclin'd.   705
 The best, with whom we may articulate, | For their owne good, and
 ours.   834
 *you speake best vnto the purpose. It is not woorth the   981
 *some of the best of 'em were hereditarie hang-|men.   987
 He prou'd best man i'th' field, and for his meed   1311
 That our best Water, brought by Conduits hither,   1645
 Mene. I could my selfe take vp a Brace o'th' best of | them, yea, the
 two Tribunes.   1968
 The same you are not, which for your best ends   2144
 As best thou art experienc'd, since thou know'st   2798
 Doe's of the Shepheards: For his best Friends, if they   3031

BEST *cont*.
   *of vs, that we did we did for the best, and though wee   3070
   *And I am out, euen to a full Disgrace. Best of my Flesh,   3391
   My best and freshest men, seru'd his designements   3688
   Let's make the Best of it.   3828
BESTOW = 2
   Men. I will tell you, | If you'l bestow a small (of what you haue little)   130
   Bestow your su'd-for Tongues?   1611
BESTRID = 1
   The brizled Lippes before him: he bestrid   1306
BESTRIDE = 1
   Bestride my Threshold. Why, thou Mars I tell thee,   2776
BETRAYD = 1
   He ha's betray'd your businesse, and giuen vp   3760
BETTER = 10*7
   Better be held, nor more attain'd then by   295
   *would become such a person, that it was no better then   371
   She will but disease our better mirth.   469
   *better report then a Horse-drench. Is he not wounded?   1015
   Scicin. I wish no better, then haue him hold that pur-|pose, and to put
     it in execution.   1165
   *no better a ground. Therefore, for *Coriolanus* neyther to   1215
   *1.*Cit*. And to make vs no better thought of a little   1400
   Coriol. Most sweet Voyces: | Better it is to dye, better to sterue,   1503
   This Mutinie were better put in hazard,   1662
   Brut. Not vnlike each way to better yours.   1735
   Then were they chosen: in a better houre,   1869
   But yet a braine, that leades my vse of Anger | To better vantage.   2121
   Corio. I haue deseru'd no better entertainment, in be-|ing *Coriolanus*.
   Enter second Seruant.   2664
   Mene. All's well, and might haue bene much better, | if he could haue
     temporiz'd.   2909
   That shapes man Better: and they follow him   3008
   And you shall beare | A better witnesse backe then words, which we   3563
BETWEEN = *1
   Mene. There is differency between a Grub & a But-|terfly,   3580
BETWEENE = 5*3
   'Tis sworne betweene vs, we shall euer strike   353
   *hearing a cause betweene an Orendge wife, and a Forfet-|seller,   966
   *matter betweene party and party, if you chaunce to bee   969
   *Enter Cominius the Generall, and Titus Latius: be-|tweene them
   Coriolanus, crown'd with an Oaken*   1060
   That we labour'd (no impediment betweene)   1631
   Rom. I shall betweene this and Supper, tell you most   2609
   And vowes Reuenge as spacious, as betweene | The yong'st and oldest
   thing.   2977
   Shew duty as mistaken, all this while, | Betweene the Childe, and
   Parent.   3405
BETWIXT *see* 'twixt
BEWAILE = 1
   Which to this houre bewaile the Iniury,   3835
BEWARE = 1
   And beate the Messenger, who bids beware | Of what is to be dreaded.   2959
BEWITCHMENT = *1
   *the bewitchment of some popular man, and giue it   1492
BEWRAY = 1
   And state of Bodies would bewray what life   3450

BEYOND = 3
Aduance braue *Titus*, | They do disdaine vs much beyond our Thoughts, 518
Beyond the marke of others: our then Dictator, 1303
Com. But now 'tis oddes beyond Arithmetick, 1970
BID = 5*2
We are fit to bid her welcome. *Exit Gent*. 406
Corio. Bid them wash their Faces, 1453
Bid me farewell, and smile. I pray you come: 2491
Sicin. Bid them all home, he's gone: & wee'l no further, 2503
Sicin. Bid them home: say their great enemy is gone, 2509
Be held by you denials. Do not bid me 3436
Bid them repayre to th'Market place, where I 3652
BIDDING = *1
*finisht with his bidding. He wants nothing of a God but | Eternity, and
a Heauen to Throne in. 3592
BIDS = 1*1
And beate the Messenger, who bids beware | Of what is to be dreaded. 2959
*as a thing made for *Alexander*. What he bids bee done, is 3591
BIG = 1
A Carbuncle intire: as big as thou art 557
BIGGE = 1
With as bigge heart as thou. Do as thou list, 2237
BIGGER = 1
Boy. A shall not tread on me: Ile run away | Till I am bigger, but then
Ile fight. 3483
BILES *see* byles
BILLETTED = *1
*charges distinctly billetted already in th'entertainment, 2613
BIN *l*.318 587 *1482 *1483 *1486 2062 2107 *2114 *2586 *2848 *3268
3694 = 5*7
BIRTH-PLACE = 1
My Birth-place haue I, and my loues vpon 2649
BITE = 1
Mene. Ile vndertak't: | I thinke hee'l heare me. Yet to bite his lip, 3205
BITS = 1
Corio. Follow your Function, go, and batten on colde | bits. *Pushes
him away from him*. 2686
BITTEREST = 1
To bitterest Enmity: So fellest Foes, 2644
BLACKE = *1
*heads are some browne, some blacke, some Abram, some 1405
BLAME = 4
being so: you blame *Martius* for being proud. 929
And perish constant Fooles: who is't can blame him? 3024
That if you faile in our request, the blame 3445
2.*Lord*. His owne impatience, | Takes from *Auffidius* a great part of
blame: 3826
BLANKES = 1
 And of his Friends there, it is Lots to Blankes, 3247
BLAST = 1
To helpe our fielded Friends. Come, blow thy blast. 498
BLAZE = 1*1
To kindle their dry Stubble: and their Blaze | Shall darken him for euer. 1186
Rom. The maine blaze of it is past, but a small thing 2589
BLEARED = *1
Bru. All tongues speake of him, and the bleared sights 1123

BLED = 2

My Nose that bled, or foyl'd some debile Wretch,   804
That we haue bled together. *Coriolanus*   3163

BLEEDING = 1*1

Enter Martius bleeding, assaulted by the Enemy.   564
*bleeding, the more intangled by your hearing: All the   973

BLEEDST = 1

Lar. Worthy Sir, thou bleed'st,   586

BLENDED = 1

When both your voices blended, the great'st taste   1797

BLESSE = 3

Vir. Heauens blesse my Lord from fell *Auffidius*.   407
Corio. You blesse me Gods.   2794
Sicin. First, the Gods blesse you for your tydings: | Next, accept my
thankefulnesse.   3633

BLESSED = 1

Sicin. Oh blessed Heauens!   2529

BLEST = 2*1

Brutus. Which the rather wee shall be blest to doe, if   1266
Volum. Oh stand vp blest! | Whil'st with no softer Cushion then the
Flint   3402
Giue the All-haile to thee, and cry be Blest   3496

BLIND = *1

*And the blind to heare him speak: Matrons flong Gloues,   1193

BLINDE = 1

Auf. Why Noble Lords, | Will you be put in minde of his blinde
Fortune,   3788

BLOCKE = *1

*this Varlet heere: This, who like a blocke hath denyed | my accesse to
thee.   3313

BLOCKE-HEAD = *1

*mans will, 'tis strongly wadg'd vp in a blocke-head: but   1414

BLOOD *see also* bloud = 19*2

I send it through the Riuers of your blood   142
Thou Rascall, that art worst in blood to run,   167
Virg. His bloody Brow? Oh Iupiter, no blood.   400
Then *Hectors* forhead, when it spit forth blood   404
The blood I drop, is rather Physicall   591
Com. I, if you come not in the blood of others, | But mantled in your
owne.   638
By th'Blood we haue shed together, | By th'Vowes we haue made   673
And made what worke I pleas'd: 'Tis not my blood,   734
He was a thing of Blood, whose euery motion   1323
As for my Country, I haue shed my blood,   1768
Killing our Enemies, the blood he hath lost   2036
Which else would put you to your fortune, and | The hazard of much
blood.   2159
The extreme Dangers, and the droppes of Blood   2726
Drawne Tunnes of Blood out of thy Countries brest,   2756
*the man in blood, they will out of their Burroughes (like   2870
The Veines vnfill'd, our blood is cold, and then   3209
These Pipes, and these Conueyances of our blood   3212
*I let forth your halfe pinte of blood. Backe, that's the vt- | most of your
hauing, backe.   3292
The Grandchilde to her blood. But out affection,   3373
Thy Wife and Childrens blood: For my selfe, Sonne,   3473
As cheape as Lies; he sold the Blood and Labour   3702

BLOODIE = *1
*set vp the bloodie Flagge against all Patience, and   971
BLOODY see also bloodie, bloudie = 4
   Though you were borne in Rome; his bloody brow   396
   Virg. His bloody Brow? Oh Iupiter, no blood.   400
   Will proue to bloody: and the end of it, | Vnknowne to the Beginning. 2071
   With bloody passage led your Warres, euen to   3741
BLOUD = 2
   My Mother, who ha's a Charter to extoll her Bloud,   764
   The bloud vpon your Visage dryes, 'tis time   855
BLOUDIE = 1
   A flourish. Cornets. Enter Tullus Auffidius | bloudie, with two or three Souldiors.   857
BLOW = 1*1
   To helpe our fielded Friends. Come, blow thy blast.   498
   *Dotant as you seeme to be? Can you think to blow   3281
BLOWES = 5*1
   Onely for bearing Burthens, and sore blowes | For sinking vnder them. 1179
   When blowes haue made me stay, I fled from words.   1284
   That wonne you without blowes, despising   2421
   Shew'd Mastership in floating. Fortunes blowes,   2443
   To banish him that strooke more blowes for Rome | Then thou hast spoken words.   2527
   Volum. Moe Noble blowes, then euer y wise words.   2530
BLOWNE = 1*1
   *none but my selfe could moue thee, I haue bene blowne   3309
   Ne're through an Arch so hurried the blowne Tide,   3619
BLUSH = 3
   Whether I blush or no: howbeit, I thanke you,   826
   Corio. It is a part that I shall blush in acting,   1366
   Blush, that the world goes well: who rather had,   2897,
BLUSHD = 1
   That Pages blush'd at him, and men of heart | Look'd wond'ring each at others. 3767
BOARE = 1
   Your Franchises, whereon you stood, confin'd | Into an Augors boare. 3001
BOASTING = 1
   Bru. And topping all others in boasting.   917
BOATS = 1
   That when the Sea was calme, all Boats alike   2442
BODIED = *1
   *tender-bodied, and the onely Sonne of my womb; when   367
BODIES see also bodyes = 2*1
   Men. There was a time, when all the bodies members   98
   And by my Bodies action, teach my Minde | A most inherent Basenesse. 2230
   And state of Bodies would bewray what life   3450
BODILY = 1
   That could be brought to bodily act, ere Rome   319
BODY = 13
   I'th midd'st a th'body, idle and vnactiue,   101
   Of the whole body, the Belly answer'd.   107
   Who is the sinke a th'body.   126
   Of the whole Body. But, if you do remember,   141
   *for his place: he receiued in the repulse of *Tarquin* seuen | hurts ith' Body.   1045
   Your louing motion toward the common Body, | To yeeld what passes here.   1261

BODY *cont.*

I'th' Body of the Weale: and now arriuing	1582
To iumpe a Body with a dangerous Physicke,	1853
Vpon the wounds his body beares, which shew	2325
Mine armes about that body, where against	2765
After your way. His Tale pronounc'd, shall bury | His Reasons, with his Body.	3717
1.*Lord.* Beare from hence his body,	3822
Exeunt bearing the Body of Martius. A dead March | Sounded.	3837

BODYES = 1

When he hath power to crush? Why, had your Bodyes	1606

BOILED *see* boyld

BOLD = 2*2

*And make bold power looke pale, they threw their caps	225
Misguide thy Opposers swords, Bold Gentleman: | Prosperity be thy Page.	595
*the Beastly Plebeans. I will be bold to take my leaue of | you.	990
Like a bold Flood o're-beate. Oh come, go in,	2789

BOLDER = *1

Auf. Bolder, though not so subtle: my valors poison'd,	876

BOLT *see* boult

BOLTED *see* boulted

BOND = 1

All bond and priuiledge of Nature breake;	3374

BONES = 1

Corio. Hence rotten thing, or I shall shake thy bones | Out of thy Garments.	1883

BONNET = 1

Goe to them, with this Bonnet in thy hand,	2174

BONNETTED = *1

*hauing beene supple and courteous to the People, Bon- | netted,	1229

BOOKE = 2

In Ioues owne Booke, like an vnnaturall Dam | Should now eate vp her owne.	2030
The booke of his good Acts, whence men haue read	3253

BORNE = 5

Will then cry out of *Martius:* Oh, if he | Had borne the businesse.	299
Though you were borne in Rome; his bloody brow	396
O're-borne their way, consum'd with fire, and tooke | What lay before them.	2991
Ioyn'd in Commission with him: but either haue borne	3106
I haue borne this Businesse.	3350

BOSOMES = 2

Of no allowance, to your bosomes truth.	2156
Whose double bosomes seemes to weare one heart,	2639

BOSOME-MULTIPLIED = 1

How shall this Bosome-multiplied, digest	1828

BOTCHERS = *1

*honourable a graue, as to stuffe a Botchers Cushion, or to	983

BOTH = 27*3

Val. My Ladies both good day to you. | *Vol.* Sweet Madam.	411
Val. How do you both? You are manifest house-kee- | pers.	414
*That both our powers, with smiling Fronts encountring,	611
Both. Well sir.	912
Both. Why? how are we censur'd?	921
Both. Well, well sir, well.	924
Both. What then sir?	938

BOTH *cont*.

*peace you make in their Cause, is calling both the parties	974
We met here, both to thanke, and to remember, | With Honors like himselfe.	1254
Both Field and Citie ours, he neuer stood	1335
Both. The Gods giue you ioy Sir heartily.	1502
With their refusall, both obserue and answer | The vantage of his anger.	1665
When both your voices blended, the great'st taste	1797
May enter 'twixt the gap of Both, and take | The one by th'other.	1805
What may be sworne by, both Diuine and Humane,	1840
Mene. On both sides more respect.	1887
With Honour, as in Warre; since that to both | It stands in like request.	2147
Corio. First heare me speake. | *Both Tri*. Well, say: Peace hoe.	2313
Thy lying tongue, both numbers. I would say	2352
Both. What, what, what? Let's partake.	2834
Both. Wherefore? Wherefore?	2837
cheape as Volcians. They are rising, they are rising. | *Both*. In, in, in, in. *Exeunt*	2890
Haile Sir. *Mene*. Haile to you both.	2905
All. The Gods preserue you both.	2915
Are bound to pray for you both.	2919
Both Tri. Farewell, farewell. *Exeunt Citizens*	2924
Com. Oh I, what else? *Exeunt both*.	3076
Rather to shew a Noble grace to both parts,	3476
1 *Lord*. Peace both, and heare me speake.	3781
Draw both the Conspirators, and kils Martius, who | falles, Auffidius stands on him.	3805

BOTTOME = *1

*white o'th'eye to his Discourse. But the bottome of the	2856

BOULT = 1

And yet to change thy Sulphure with a Boult	3509

BOULTED = 1

In boulted Language: Meale and Bran together	2064

BOUND = 8*1

*whence he return'd, his browes bound with Oake. I tell	375
Am bound to begge of my Lord Generall.	839
Was Brow-bound with the Oake. His Pupill age	1312
To where you are bound, you must enquire your way,	1741
Are bound to pray for you both.	2919
Bound with an Oath to yeeld to his conditions:	3230
Whereto we are bound, together with thy victory:	3463
Whereto we are bound: Alacke, or we must loose	3464
More bound to's Mother, yet heere he let's me prate	3516

BOUNTIFULL = *1

*bountifull to the desirers: Therefore beseech you, I may | be Consull.	1493

BOUT = 1

Her richest Lockram 'bout her reechie necke,	1127

BOWD = 2

Who bow'd but in my Stirrop, bend like his	2227
He bow'd his Nature, neuer knowne before,	3677

BOWELS = 2

Into the bowels of vngratefull Rome,	2788
His Countries Bowels out; and to poore we	3458

BOWER = 1

Then flatter him in a Bower. *Enter Cominius*.	2195

BOWES = 2

And when it bowes, stand'st vp: Thou art left *Martius*,	556

BOWES *cont.*

Of stronger earth then others: my Mother bowes, 3378

BOWLE = 1

Like to a Bowle vpon a subtle ground 3258

BOY = 9*2

*very pretty boy. A my troth, I look'd vpon him a Wens-|day 421
Volum. Honorable *Menenius*, my Boy *Martius* appro-|ches: 997
In supplication Nod: and my yong Boy 3380
Volum. Your knee, Sirrah. | *Corio*. That's my braue Boy. 3429
Virg. I, and mine, that brought you forth this boy, 3481
He cares not for your weeping. Speake thou Boy, 3513
This Boy that cannot tell what he would haue, 3531
Corio. Hear'st thou Mars? | *Auf*. Name not the God, thou boy of
Teares. 3769
Too great for what containes it. Boy? Oh Slaue, 3774
Staine all your edges on me. Boy, false Hound: 3783
Alone I did it, Boy. 3787

BOY = 1

BOYES = 3

Tent in my cheekes, and Schoole-boyes Teares take vp 2224
Least that thy Wiues with Spits, and Boyes with stones 2627
Then Boyes pursuing Summer Butter-flies, | Or Butchers killing Flyes. 3010

BOYLD = 1

*2 And hee had bin Cannibally giuen, hee might haue | boyld and eaten
him too. 2848

BRACE = 1*2

Men. Why then you should discouer a brace of vn-|meriting, 939
And keepe their teeth cleane: So, heere comes a brace, 1454
Mene. I could my selfe take vp a Brace o'th' best of | them, yea, the
two Tribunes. 1968

BRAG = 1

Corio. To brag vnto them, thus I did, and thus 1369

BRAGGART = 1

Which was your shame, by this vnholy Braggart? 3790

BRAGGD = 1

Auf. Wer't thou the *Hector*, | That was the whip of your bragg'd
Progeny, 737

BRAINE = 2*1

Euen to the Court, the Heart, to th'seate o'th'Braine, 143
*would infect my Braine, being the Heardsmen of 989
But yet a braine, that leades my vse of Anger | To better vantage. 2121

BRAN = 2

And leaue me but the Bran. What say you too't? 154
In boulted Language: Meale and Bran together 2064

BRAND = 1*1

A brand to th'end a'th World. 2041
Me. 'Tis true, if he were putting to my house, the brand 3035

BRATS = 1

Against vs Brats, with no lesse Confidence, 3009

BRAUE = 5*2

Aduance braue *Titus*, | They do disdaine vs much beyond our Thoughts, 518
If any thinke, braue death out-weighes bad life, 690
*1.*off*. That's a braue fellow: but hee's vengeance | prowd, and loues not
the common people. 1209
You haue done a braue deede: Ere you go, heare this: 2550
*2 *Ser*. Are you so braue: Ile haue you talkt with anon 2672
And this braue Fellow too: we are the Graines, 3184

BRAUE *cont.*
  Volum. Your knee, Sirrah. | *Corio.* That's my braue Boy.   3429
BRAUELY = 1
  And beare the Palme, for hauing brauely shed   3472
BRAWNE = 1
  Once more to hew thy Target from thy Brawne,   2778
BREAD = 1
  hunger for Bread, not in thirst for Reuenge.   26
BREAKE = 8*2
  To breake the heart of generosity,   224
  Hearke, our Drummes | *Are bringing forth our youth: Wee'l breake
  our Walles   504
  Breake ope the Lockes a'th'Senate, and bring in | The Crowes to pecke
  the Eagles.   1835
  Least parties (as he is belou'd) breake out,   2056
  With vs to breake his necke.   2295
  On a dissention of a Doit, breake out   2643
  The Volces dare breake with vs.   2952
  That which shall breake his necke, or hazard mine,   3116
  All bond and priuiledge of Nature breake;   3374
  *and he returning to breake our necks, they respect not vs.   3602
BREAKER = 1
  Mar. Ile fight with none but thee, for I do hate thee | Worse then a
  Promise-breaker.   724
BREAKING = 2
  *This lyes glowing I can tell you, and is almost mature for | the violent
  breaking out.   2594
  Breaking his Oath and Resolution, like   3763
BREAST *see* brest
BREASTS *see* brests
BREATH = 4*4
  Com. Breath you my friends, wel fought, we are come | (off,   604
  *What I think, I vtter, and spend my malice in my breath.   949
  As if I had receiu'd them for the hyre | Of their breath onely.   1371
  Mene. What is about to be? I am out of Breath,   1897
  Corio. You common cry of Curs, whose breath I hate,   2408
  Sigh'd truer breath. But that I see thee heere   2773
  Vpon the voyce of occupation, and | The breath of Garlicke-eaters.   3014
  *such weake breath as this? No, you are deceiu'd, therfore   3283
BREATHLES = *1
  of Auffi. Martius fights til they be driuen in breathles.   741
BREATHS = 1*1
  *strong breaths, they shal know we haue strong arms too.   62
  Toth' People, begge their stinking Breaths.   1159
BRED = 3
  Ere stay behinde this Businesse. | *Men.* Oh true-bred.   267
  Mene. Consider this: He ha's bin bred i'th'Warres   2062
  Thou art their Souldier, and being bred in broyles,   2182
BREED = 1
  *This peace is nothing, but to rust Iron, encrease Taylors, | and breed
  Ballad-makers.   2877
BREEFE = *1
  *and to make it breefe Warres. This is true on mine   464
BREEFELY = 1
  Sic. Speake breefely then, | For we are peremptory to dispatch   2021
BREST = 3
  To ease his Brest with panting. | *Menen.* Worthy man.   1336

BREST *cont*.
  What his Brest forges, that his Tongue must vent,   1986
  Drawne Tunnes of Blood out of thy Countries brest,   2756
BRESTS = 2
  Then gilt his Trophe. The brests of *Hecuba*   402
  In Volcean brests. That we haue beene familiar,   3320
BRETHREN = 1
  Some certaine of your Brethren roar'd, and ranne   1442
BRIARS = 1
  Corio. Scratches with Briars, scarres to moue | Laughter onely.   2327
BRIBE = 1
  A Bribe, to pay my Sword: I doe refuse it,   791
BRIEF *see also* breefe = *1
  Corio. Come leaue your teares: a brief farwel: the beast   2437
BRIEFELY *see also* breefely = *1
  Com. 'Tis not a mile: briefely we heard their drummes.   621
BRING = 12*1
  Bring vp your Army: but (I thinke) you'l finde   346
  How could'st thou in a mile confound an houre, | And bring thy Newes
    so late?   622
  ('Tis South the City Mils) bring me word thither   891
  bring our selues to be monstrous members.   1399
  Plague vpon't, I cannot bring | My tongue to such a pace. Looke Sir,
    my wounds,   1439
  Breake ope the Lockes a'th'Senate, and bring in | The Crowes to pecke
    the Eagles.   1835
  To bring the Roofe to the Foundation,   1916
  Ile go to him, and vndertake to bring him in peace,   2066
  Where if you bring not *Martius*, wee'l proceede | In our first way.   2077
  Menen. Ile bring him to you.   2079
  That's yet vnbruis'd: bring me but out at gate.   2488
  *his Mother shall bring from him: There is no more   3596
  The Romane Ladies bring not comfort home   3607
BRINGING = *1
  Hearke, our Drummes | *Are bringing forth our youth: Wee'l breake
    our Walles   504
BRINGS = *1
  Menen. So doe I too, if it be not too much: brings a   1019
BRIZLED = 1
  The brizled Lippes before him: he bestrid   1306
BROILE *see* broyle
BROILES *see* broyles
BROKE = 2*1
  That Hunger-broke stone wals: that dogges must eate   219
  *Whose Passions, and whose Plots haue broke their sleep   2645
  My grained Ash an hundred times hath broke,   2766
BROOD = 1
  When she (poor Hen) fond of no second brood,   3519
BROOKE = *1
  *wonder, his insolence can brooke to be commanded vn- | der *Cominius*?   291
BROTHER = *1
  *my sworne Brother the people to earne a deerer estima- | tion   1487
BROTHERS = 1
  At home, vpon my Brothers Guard, euen there   884
BROUGHT = 8*2
  That could be brought to bodily act, ere Rome   319
  Halfe an houre since brought my report.   627

BROUGHT *cont.*
  3 Cit. We do Sir, tell vs what hath brought you too't.   1456
  That our best Water, brought by Conduits hither,   1645
  Hath brought me to thy Harth, not out of Hope   2736
  Com. You haue brought | A Trembling vpon Rome, such as was neuer   3039
  S'incapeable of helpe. | *Tri.* Say not, we brought it.   3041
  (Trust too't, thou shalt not) on thy Mothers wombe | That brought thee
  to this world.   3479
  Virg. I, and mine, that brought you forth this boy,   3481
  *The gates of Rome: Our spoiles we haue brought home   3742
BROW = 2*1
  Though you were borne in Rome; his bloody brow   396
  Virg. His bloody Brow? Oh Iupiter, no blood.   400
  Corio. Prepare thy brow to frowne: knowst y me yet?   2720
BROWES = *2
  *whence he return'd, his browes bound with Oake. I tell   375
  Volum. On's Browes: *Menenius,* hee comes the third | time home with
  the Oaken Garland.   1021
BROWNE = *1
  *heads are some browne, some blacke, some Abram, some   1405
BROW-BOUND = 1
  Was Brow-bound with the Oake. His Pupill age   1312
BROYLE = 1
  Scicin. Stop, or all will fall in broyle.   1714
BROYLES = 1
  Thou art their Souldier, and being bred in broyles,   2182
BRU = 1
  Bru. and Scic. Aside.   992
BRU = 40*6
BRUNT = 1
  And in the brunt of seuenteene Battailes since,   1314
BRUSING = 1
  That his Contempt shall not be brusing to you,   1605
BRUT = 28*4
BRUTUS see also Bru., Brut. = 15
  Of their owne choice. One's *Iunius Brutus,*   230
  *Enter Sicinius Velutus, Annius Brutus Cominius, Titus | Lartius, with
  other Senatours.*   244
  Citizens steale away. Manet Sicin. & Brutus.   279
  Enter Menenius with the two Tribunes of the | people, Sicinius & Brutus.   896
  Enter Brutus and Scicinius.   1122
  *the People, Lictors before them: Coriolanus, Mene-!nius, Cominius the
  Consul: Scicinius and Brutus*   1240
  Flourish Cornets. | Then Exeunt. Manet Sicinius and Brutus.   1378
  Enter Menenius, with Brutus and Scicinius.   1530
  Enter Scicinius and Brutus.   1699
  Sicinius, Brutus, Coriolanus, Citizens.   1895
  Enter Brutus and Sicinius with the rabble againe.   1993
  Enter Sicinius and Brutus.   2258
  Enter the two Tribunes, Sicinius, and Brutus, | with the Edile.   2501
  Enter the two Tribunes, Sicinius, and Brutus.   2892
  *Enter Menenius, Cominius, Sicinius, Brutus, | the two Tribunes, with
  others.*   3150
BRUTUS = 9*3
BUDGE = 1
  The Mouse ne're shunn'd the Cat, as they did budge | From Rascals
  worse then they.   657

BUDGER = 1
  Mar. Let the first Budger dye the others Slaue,   729
BUILDINGS = 1
  And the Buildings of my Fancie: 1113
BUILT = 1
  To haue a Temple built you: All the Swords   3567
BULKES = 1
  Stalls, Bulkes, Windowes, are smother'd vp,   1129
BURDENS *see* burthens
BURIE = 1
  And burie all, which yet distinctly raunges | In heapes, and piles of
  Ruine.   1917
BURNE = 3
  Corio. Let them hang. | *Volum.* I, and burne too.   2111
  If he could burne vs all into one coale, | We haue deseru'd it.   3063
  Red as 'twould burne Rome: and his Iniury   3225
BURNED = 1
  Com. Your Temples burned in their Ciment, and   3000
BURNING = 2
  Of *Phoebus* burning Kisses: such a poother,   1137
  Till he had forg'd himselfe a name a'th'fire | Of burning Rome.   3166
BURNT = 2
  As merry, as when our Nuptiall day was done, | And Tapers burnt to
  Bedward.   642
  Aboue the Moone. We must be burnt for you.   3186
BURROUGHES = *1
  *the man in blood, they will out of their Burroughes (like   2870
BURTHENS = 1
  Onely for bearing Burthens, and sore blowes | For sinking vnder them.   1179
BURY *see also* burie = 2
  Bury with those that wore them. These base slaues,   578
  After your way. His Tale pronounc'd, shall bury | His Reasons, with his
  Body.   3717
BUSIED = 1
  Mar. As with a man busied about Decrees: .   645
BUSINES = *1
  *2 *Cit.* Our busines is not vnknowne to th'Senat, they   59
BUSINESSE = 7*2
  Ere stay behinde this Businesse. | *Men.* Oh true-bred.   267
  Will then cry out of *Martius:* Oh, if he | Had borne the businesse.   299
  Virg. But had he died in the Businesse Madame, how | then?   379
  The rest shall beare the businesse in some other fight   703
  Com. You are like to doe such businesse.   1734
  Thy Knee bussing the stones: for in such businesse   2176
  *accidentally to encounter you. You haue ended my Bu-|sinesse,   2607
  I haue borne this Businesse.   3350
  He ha's betray'd your businesse, and giuen vp   3760
BUSSING = 1
  Thy Knee bussing the stones: for in such businesse   2176
BUSTLE = 1
  2 Sen. Weapons, weapons, weapons: | *They all bustle about Coriolanus.*   1892
BUT *l.**19 *21 *34 36 92 97 110 141 154 161 169 215 251 284 *290 323
  333 346 *366 *379 443 *447 469 488 507 515 560 639 655 659 677 699
  724 749 768 776 790 844 915 *936 *1014 *1024 1080 1101 1102 1110
  1115 1145 1149 1163 1201 *1207 *1209 *1221 *1231 *1271 *1273 1285
  *1338 *1391 *1406 *1414 *1422 *1429 1459 1473 1474 1560 1569 1579
  1610 1625 1632 1651 1656 1677 1763 *1785 1786 1788 1844 1868 1909

BUT *cont*.
  1931 1970 1978 *2006 2024 2033 2097 2121 2124 2136 2153 2154 2155
  2171 2185 2188 2208 2227 2239 2256 2283 2333 2365 2374 2383 2404
  2418 2488 2494 2497 *2525 2532 2560 2561 *2578 *2589 2660 2679
  *2706 2728 2739 2749 2754 2757 2773 2785 2802 *2819 2822 *2827
  *2841 2850 *2853 *2856 *2857 *2869 2872 *2877 *2885 *2906 2929 2956
  2969 3019 3044 3047 *3084 3092 3106 3127 3134 3136 3139 3155 3189
  3200 3211 *3238 3294 *3300 *3308 *3309 3373 3384 3392 3443 3461
  3484 3498 3503 3510 3522 3532 3545 3547 3555 3562 *3575 *3592 3669
  3678 3704 3708 3723 3728 3738 3751 3765 = 147*45

BUTCHER = 1	
Were he the Butcher of my Sonne, he should	848
BUTCHERS = 1	
Then Boyes pursuing Summer Butter-flies, | Or Butchers killing Flyes.	3010
BUTS = 1	
The Trumpets, Sack-buts, Psalteries, and Fifes,	3622
BUTTERFLY = *3	
*I saw him run after a gilded Butterfly, & when	423
*Mene. There is difference between a Grub & a But-|terfly,	3580
*yet your Butterfly was a Grub: this *Martius*, is	3581
BUTTER-FLIES = 1	
Then Boyes pursuing Summer Butter-flies, | Or Butchers killing Flyes.	3010
BUTTOCKE = *1	
*triuiall motion: One, that conuerses more with the But-|tocke	947
BUTTS *see also* buts = 1	
With many heads butts me away. Nay Mother,	2438
BUY = 4	
Mart. Ile buy him of you.	490
To buy and sell with Groats, to shew bare heads	2095
But with a graine a day, I would not buy	2374
Bru. Let's to the Capitoll: would halfe my wealth | Would buy this for a lye.	3087
BY *see also* by't, by'th = 77*23, 2	
When by and by the dinne of Warre gan pierce	1329
Corio. I by and by; But we will drinke together:	3562
BYLES = *1	
*You Shames of Rome: you Heard of Byles and Plagues	526
BYT = 1	
Though they themselues did suffer by't, behold	2898
BYTH = 4*1	
Not by your owne instruction, nor by'th'matter	2152
Sicin. Haue you a Catalogue | *Of all the Voices that we haue procur'd, set downe by'th | (Pole?	2269
Will beare the Knaue by'th Volume:	2301
And take our friendly Senators by'th'hands	2790
Subscrib'd by'th'Consuls, and Patricians,	3747
CAIUS = 16*4	
*1.*Cit*. First you know, *Caius Martius* is chiefe enemy | to the people.	10
*2.*Cit*. Would you proceede especially against *Caius* | *Martius*.	27
Enter Caius Martius.	172
Mess. Where's *Caius Martius*? | *Mar*. Heere: what's the matter!	239
Tit. No *Caius Martius*, | Ile leane vpon one Crutch, and fight with tother,	265
If we, and *Caius Martius* chance to meete,	352
*Drum and Trumpet toward Cominius, and Caius Mar-|tius,	711
As to vs, to all the World, That *Caius Martius*	815
*Marcus Caius Coriolanus. Beare th'addition Nobly euer?	821

CAIUS *cont.*

Omnes. Marcus Caius Coriolanus.	823
With Fame, a Name to *Martius Caius*:	1066
These in honor followes *Martius Caius Coriolanus.*	1067
My gentle *Martius*, worthy *Caius*,	1077
By *Martius Caius Coriolanus*: whom	1253
Corio. My name is *Caius Martius*, who hath done	2722
*3 Why here's he that was wont to thwacke our Ge-|nerall, *Caius Martius.*	2838
Bru. Caius Martius was | A worthy Officer i'th'Warre, but Insolent,	2928
A fearefull Army, led by *Caius Martius*,	2988
Come let's away: when *Caius* Rome is thine,	3147
Corio. Martius? | *Auf.* I *Martius, Caius Martius*: Do'st thou thinke	3755

CALAMITY = 2

You are transported by Calamity	76
An euident Calamity, though we had	3467

CALL *see also* call't = 16*2

And call him Noble, that was now your Hate:	194
Me thinkes I see him stampe thus, and call thus,	394
Call thither all the Officers a'th'Towne,	601
Where is he? Call him hither.	653
For what he did before *Corioles*, call him,	819
*Meeting two such Weales men as you are (I cannot call	950
What is it (*Coriolanus*) must I call thee?	1079
Wee call a Nettle, but a Nettle;	1101
Senat. Call *Coriolanus.* | *Off.* He doth appeare.	1347
*he himselfe stucke not to call vs the many-headed Multi-|tude.	1402
Call our Cares, Feares; which will in time	1834
Sicin. Go call the people, in whose name my Selfe	1876
To call them Wollen Vassailes, things created	2094
Call me their Traitor, thou iniurious Tribune.	2349
out o'thhouse: Prythee call my Master to him.	2676
Com. Yet one time he did call me by my name:	3161
Call all your Tribes together, praise the Gods,	3642
To call me to your Senate, Ile deliuer	3819

CALLD = 7*1

A perpetuall spoyle: and till we call'd	1334
Menen. Hee's right Noble, let him be call'd for.	1346
3.Cit. We haue beene call'd so of many, not that our	1404
As cause had call'd you vp, haue held him to;	1596
To hopelesse restitution, so he might | Be call'd your Vanquisher.	1693
Scandal'd the Suppliants: for the People, call'd them	1728
And Manhood is call'd Foolerie, when it stands	1971
In a most deere particular. He call'd me Father:	3154

CALLING = *1

*peace you make in their Cause, is calling both the parties	974

CALLS = 1

Their needlesse Vouches: Custome calls me too't.	1508

CALLT = 1

Brut. Call't not a Plot:	1725

CALME = 4

Mene. Be calme, be calme.	1720
Mene. Let's be calme.	1745
That when the Sea was calme, all Boats alike	2442

CALMELY = 1

Mene. Calmely, I do beseech you.	2299

CALMENESSE = 1
By calmenesse, or by absence: all's in anger. | *Menen*. Onely faire
speech.   2199
CALS = *1
*2 *Ser*. Where's *Cotus*: my M.(aster) cals for him: *Cotus*. *Exit*   2657
CALUED = 1
Though calued i'th' Porch o'th' Capitoll: 1964
CALUES = 1
Euen to *Calues* wish, not fierce and terrible   559
CAMBRICK = *1
*full of Mothes. Come, I would your Cambrick were sen-|sible   448
CAME = 7*1
Which ne're came from the Lungs, but euen thus: 110
Val. Verily I do not iest with you: there came newes | from him last
night.   456
And then I came away.   617
With shunlesse destinie: aydelesse came off,   1326
And to the Battaile came he, where he did   1332
The Noble House o'th'*Martians*: from whence came   1641
Corio. Saw you *Auffidius*? | *Latius*. On safegard he came to me, and did
curse   1683
Being banish'd for't, he came vnto my Harth,   3683
CAMMELS = 1
Then Cammels in their Warre, who haue their Prouand   1178
CAMPE = 1*1
*Our Guider come, to th'Roman Campe conduct vs. *Exit*   721
My Noble Steed, knowne to the Campe, I giue him,   817
CAMST = 1
Yet cam'st thou to a Morsell of this Feast, | Hauing fully din'd before.   757
CAN *l*.*38 72 152 *291 354 455 684 766 864 *931 *952 *959 *1222 1292
1716 2011 2127 2135 2166 *2201 2246 2376 2396 2496 2545 2546 *2594
*2833 2863 2954 2984 3024 3052 3110 3191 3196 *3275 *3281 *3338
3377 3461 3462 3515 *3578 = 31*13
CANKRED = 1
Against my Cankred Countrey, with the Spleene   2748
CANNIBALLY = *1
*2 And hee had bin Cannibally giuen, hee might haue | boyld and eaten
him too.   2848
CANNON = 1
Com. 'Twas from the Cannon.   1784
CANNOT = 34*10
*2.*Cit*. What he cannot helpe in his Nature, you ac-|count   42
2 *Cit*. We cannot Sir, we are vndone already.   65
Men. Though all at once, cannot | See what I do deliuer out to each,   150
In whom already he's well grac'd, cannot   294
with my prayers: but I cannot go thither.   443
We cannot keepe the Towne.   718
But cannot make my heart consent to take   790
I would I were a Roman, for I cannot,   862
*Meeting two such Weales men as you are (I cannot call   950
Scicin. He cannot temp'rately transport his Honors,   1144
The man I speake of, cannot in the World   1300
I cannot speake him home: he stopt the flyers,   1317
Senat. He cannot but with measure fit the Honors | which we deuise
him.   1338
Corio. I doe beseech you, | Let me o're-leape that custome: for I cannot   1355

CANNOT *cont.*

Plague vpon't, I cannot bring | My tongue to such a pace. Looke Sir, my wounds, 1439

1.Cit. Hee ha's done Nobly, and cannot goe without | any honest mans Voyce. 1524

Suffer't, and liue with such as cannot rule, | Nor euer will be ruled. 1723

Cannot conclude, but by the yea and no 1844

Confusions neere, I cannot speake. You, Tribunes 1898

You cannot Tent your selfe: be gone, 'beseech you. 1960

Corio. For them, I cannot do it to the Gods, 2132

Of contradiction. Being once chaft, he cannot 2292

Volce. He cannot choose: I am most fortunate, thus 2606

*1 A strange one as euer I look'd on: I cannot get him 2675

And cannot liue but to thy shame, vnlesse | It be to do thee seruice. 2757

*in him. He had sir, a kinde of face me thought, I cannot 2816

*2 Faith looke you, one cannot tell how to say that: for 2829

*be a Rauisher, so it cannot be denied, but peace is a great | maker of Cuckolds. 2885

Bru. Go see this Rumorer whipt, it cannot be, 2951

Mene. Cannot be? | We haue Record, that very well it can, 2953

Sicin. Tell not me: I know this cannot be. | *Bru.* Not possible. 2961

The Tribunes cannot doo't for shame; the people 3029

Auf. I cannot helpe it now, 3097

In that's no Changeling, and I must excuse | What cannot be amended. 3102

Bru. You know the very rode into his kindnesse, | And cannot lose your way. 3217

*haue, I am one that telling true vnder him, must say you | cannot passe. Therefore go backe. 3269

*perceiue, that a Iacke gardant cannot office me from my 3299

And cannot now accept, to grace him onely, 3362

Murd'ring Impossibility, to make | What cannot be, slight worke. 3412

These warres determine: If I cannot perswade thee, 3475

This Boy that cannot tell what he would haue, 3531

Auffidius, though I cannot make true Warres, 3548

Auf. Sir, I cannot tell, 3666

Prouok'd by him, you cannot) the great danger 3816

CANON = 1

Against the hospitable Canon, would I 885

CANOPY = 2

3 Where dwel'st thou? | *Corio.* Vnder the Canopy. 2691

3 Vnder the Canopy | *Corio.* I. 2693

CANST *l.**3271 = *1

CAPACITIE = 1

In humane Action, and Capacitie, 1176

CAPARISON = 1

Titus Lartius. Oh Generall: | Here is the Steed, wee the Caparison: 760

CAPITALL = 3

Com. On, to the Capitall. *Flourish. Cornets.* | *Exeunt in State, as before.* 1120

Euen this so criminall, and in such capitall kinde 2363

Thine enmities most capitall: Thou barr'st vs 3459

CAPITOL = *1

Mene. See you yon'd Coin a'th Capitol, yon'd corner | (stone? 3571

CAPITOLL = 14

why stay we prating heere? To th'Capitoll. | *All.* Come, come. 49

What's done i'th Capitoll: Who's like to rise, 204

Sen. Your Company to'th'Capitoll, where I know | Our greatest Friends attend vs. 269

CAPITOLL cont.

Being naked, sicke; nor Phane, nor Capitoll,	879
*perfecter gyber for the Table, then a necessary Bencher in | the Capitoll.	977
Mess. You are sent for to the Capitoll:	1190
Brutus. Let's to the Capitoll,	1199
Enter two Officers, to lay Cushions, as it were, | in the Capitoll.	1203
And presently, when you haue drawne your number, | Repaire toth' Capitoll.	1657
Scicin. Toth' Capitoll, come:	1667
Though calued i'th' Porch o'th' Capitoll:	1964
As farre as doth the Capitoll exceede	2551
Mene. You haue made good worke | You and your cry. Shal's to the Capitoll?	3074
Bru. Let's to the Capitoll: would halfe my wealth | Would buy this for a lye.	3087

CAPITULATE = 1

Dismisse my Soldiers, or capitulate	3437

CAPPE = 1

Menen. Take my Cappe Iupiter, and I thanke thee:	1002

CAPPES = *1

*thing: you are ambitious, for poore knaues cappes and	964

CAPS = 6*1

*And make bold power looke pale, they threw their caps	225
*They all shout and waue their swords, take him vp in their | Armes, and cast vp their Caps.	695
cast vp their Caps and Launces: Cominius | and Lartius stand bare.	795
A Shower, and Thunder, with their Caps, and Showts:	1197
They all shout, and throw vp their Caps.	2425
Your stinking, greasie Caps, in hooting	3057
As you threw Caps vp, will he tumble downe,	3061

CAPTAINE = 2

Mene. Sirra, if thy Captaine knew I were heere,	3287
1 Come, my Captaine knowes you not. | Mene. I meane thy Generall.	3289

CAPTAINES = 2

*Enter Martius, Titus Lartius, with Drumme and Co-|lours, with Captaines and Souldiers, as	478
Garland, with Captaines and Soul-|diers, and a Herauld.	1062

CAPTIUES = 1

As most abated Captiues, to some Nation	2420

CARBINADO = 1

*on't before Corioles, he scotcht him, and notcht him like a | Carbinado.	2846

CARBUNCLE = 1

A Carbuncle intire: as big as thou art	557

CARD = 1

2 Cit. Care for vs? True indeed, they nere car'd for vs	80

CARE = 4*3

Men. I tell you Friends, most charitable care	66
The Helmes o'th State; who care for you like Fathers,	78
2 Cit. Care for vs? True indeed, they nere car'd for vs	80
Lieu. Feare not our care Sir.	719
*care whether they loue, or hate him, manifests the true	1216
*1.Off. If he did not care whether he had their loue, or	1219
*Menen. I neither care for th'world, nor your General:	3337

CARELESNESSE = 1
   *knowledge he ha's in their disposition, and out of his No-|ble
   carelesnesse lets them plainely see't.   1217
CARES = 2*2
   *Their Counsailes, and their Cares; disgest things rightly,   158
   Call our Cares, Feares; which will in time   1834
   *1 My Generall cares not for you. Back I say, go: least   3291
   He cares not for your weeping. Speake thou Boy,   3513
CARIOLES = 2*3
   *before their Citie *Carioles*, they nothing doubt preuai-|ling,   463
   Titus Lartius, *hauing set a guard vpon Carioles, going with*   710
   *fiddious'd, for all the Chests in Carioles, and the Gold   1028
   Such eyes the Widowes in Carioles were,   1084
   Carioles like a Planet: now all's his,   1328
CARKASSES = 1
   As the dead Carkasses of vnburied men,   2410
CARRIED = 2
   I carried from thee deare; and my true Lippe   3396
   When he had carried Rome, and that we look'd | For no lesse Spoile,
   then Glory.   3697
CARRIES = *1
   *that's no matter, the greater part carries it, I say. If hee   1423
CARRY = 5*1
   1.*Rom*. This will I carry to *Rome*. | 2.*Rom*. And I this.   570
   Oh he would misse it, rather then carry it,   1162
   And carry with vs Eares and Eyes for th' time, | But Hearts for the
   euent.   1200
   Coriolanus will carry it.   1208
   **Lieu*. Sir, I beseech you, think you he'l carry Rome?   3118
   Carry his Honors eeuen: whether 'twas Pride   3128
CARRYES = 1
   Before him, hee carryes Noyse;   1055
CASE = *1
   **Mene*. No, in such a case the Gods will not bee good   3600
CASKE = 1
   From th'Caske to th'Cushion: but commanding peace   3134
CAST = 6
   **They all shout and waue their swords, take him vp in their | Armes, and*
   cast vp their Caps.   695
   cast vp their Caps and Launces: Cominius | and Lartius stand bare.   795
   Which (I doubt not) but our Rome | Will cast vpon thee.   1115
   But that you must cast your Election on him.   1632
   Beare him toth' Rock Tarpeian, and from thence | Into destruction cast
   him.   1926
   That made the Ayre vnwholsome, when you cast   3056
CAT = 1
   The Mouse ne're shunn'd the Cat, as they did budge | From Rascals
   worse then they.   657
CATALOGUE = 1
   Sicin. Haue you a Catalogue | *Of all the Voices that we haue procur'd,
   set downe by'th | (Pole?   2269
CATCH = 1
   The very way to catch them.   1772
CATCHING = 1
   Least his infection being of catching nature, | Spred further.   2050
CATCHT = *1
   *and ouer he comes, and vp againe: catcht it again: or   425

CATS = 1
  Cats, that can iudge as fitly of his worth,   2545
CAUGHT = 1*1
  *he caught it, he let it go againe, and after it againe, and o-|uer   424
  Will or exceed the Common, or be caught   2470
CAUSD = *1
  *Latius. He had, my Lord, and that it was which caus'd | Our swifter
  Composition.   1675
CAUSE = 14*4
  (As cause will be obey'd:) please you to March,   704
  *hearing a cause betweene an Orendge wife, and a Forfet-|seller,   966
  *peace you make in their Cause, is calling both the parties   974
  *is comming home: hee ha's more cause to be prowd: 1041
  With the least cause, these his new Honors,   1151
  You know the cause (Sir) of my standing heere.   1455
  As cause had call'd you vp, haue held him to;   1596
  Corio. I wish I had a cause to seeke him there,   1697
  All cause vnborne, could neuer be the Natiue   1826
  Whereon part do's disdaine with cause, the other   1842
  Leaue vs to cure this Cause.   1958
  Insisting on the olde prerogatiue | And power i'th Truth a'th Cause. 2279
  A cause for thy Repeale, we shall not send   2481
  And by my troth you haue cause: you'l Sup with me.   2564
  *Volce. You take my part from me sir, I haue the most | cause to be
  glad of yours.   2618
  2 What cause do you thinke I haue to swoond?   3336
  Stand to me in this cause. Oh Mother! Wife!   3558
  *Mess. Sir, we haue all great cause to giue great thanks.   3635
CAUTELOUS = 1
  With cautelous baits and practice.   2471
CAUTION = *1
  *Brutus. Most willingly: but yet my Caution was   1271
CEASE = 3
  If not, why cease you till you are so?   662
  Let them not cease, but with a dinne confus'd   2283
  To say, beseech you cease. You haue made faire hands,   3037
CEDARS = 1
  Strike the proud Cedars 'gainst the fiery Sun: 3411
CEMENT see ciment
CENSOR = 1
  And Nobly nam'd, so twice being Censor, | Was his great Ancestor. 1646
CENSURD = 1
  Both. Why? how are we censur'd?   921
CENSURE = 3
  To th'vtmost of a man, and giddy censure   298
  To suffer lawfull Censure for such faults | As shall be prou'd vpon you. 2320
  My selfe your loyall Seruant, or endure | Your heauiest Censure. 3820
CENSURED = *1
  *you are censured heere in the City, I mean of vs a'th'right | hand File,
  do you?   919
CENTURIES = 1
  Those Centuries to our ayd, the rest will serue   716
CENTURIONS = *1
  *Vol. A most Royall one: The Centurions, and their   2612
CEREMONIE = 1
  Neyther will they bate one iot of Ceremonie.   1361

CERTAINE = 10*1

Enter certaine Romanes with spoiles.   569
A Shield, as hard as his. A certaine number   701
*Heere they fight, and certaine Volces come in the ayde   740
Virgil. Yes certaine, there's a Letter for you, I saw't.   1010
Some certaine of your Brethren roar'd, and ranne   1442
Our certaine death: therefore it is decreed,   2025
The end of Warres vncertaine: but this certaine,   3498
Sicin. Friend, art thou certaine this is true?   3615
Is't most certaine.   3616
Mes. As certaine as I know the Sun is fire: 3617
For certaine drops of Salt, your City Rome: 3761

CERTAINELY = 1

3.*Cit.* Certainely, he flowted vs downe-right.   1558

CERTAINTIES = 1

Auf. O doubt not that, | I speake from Certainties. Nay more,   348

CHACE = 1

Mes. Spies of the *Volces* | Held me in chace, that I was forc'd to wheele   624

CHAFFE = 2

Of noysome musty Chaffe. He said, 'twas folly   3179
You are the musty Chaffe, and you are smelt   3185

CHAFT = 1

Of contradiction. Being once chaft, he cannot   2292

CHAINE = *1

*chaine vp and restraine the poore. If the Warres eate vs   85

CHAIRE = 1

Hath not a Tombe so euident as a Chaire | T'extoll what it hath done.   3143

CHAIRES = 1

Th'honor'd Goddes | Keepe Rome in safety, and the Chaires of Iustice   2302

CHAMBER-POT = *1

*in roaring for a Chamber-pot, dismisse the Controuersie   972

CHANCE *see also* chaunce = 6

If we, and *Caius Martius* chance to meete,   352
Inforce the present Execution | Of what we chance to Sentence.   2284
More then a wilde exposture, to each chance | That starts i'th'way
before thee.   2475
To take the one the other, by some chance,   2646
Least you shall chance to whip your Information,   2958
Like him by chance: yet giue vs our dispatch: 3537

CHANCES = 2

That common chances. Common men could beare,   2441
To faile in the disposing of those chances   3131

CHANGD = 1

Virg. The sorrow that deliuers vs thus chang'd, | Makes you thinke so.   3388

CHANGE = 6

With euery Minute you do change a Minde,   193
From whom I haue receiu'd not onely greetings, | But with them,
change of Honors.   1109
Corio. May I change these Garments? | *Scicin.* You may, Sir.   1541
Corio. What makes this change? | *Menen.* The matter?   1707
More then you doubt the change on't: That preferre   1851
And yet to change thy Sulphure with a Boult   3509

CHANGELING = 1

In that's no Changeling, and I must excuse | What cannot be amended.   3102

CHANNELL = 1

And make your Channell his? If he haue power,   1791

CHARACTER *see also* charracter = *1
  Mene. I paint him in the Character. Mark what mer-|cy   3595
CHARGD = 2*1
  We shall be charg'd againe. Whiles we haue strooke   607
  Corio. Shall I be charg'd no further then this present?   2315
  Should say be good to Rome, they charg'd him, euen   3032
CHARGE = 5*1
  With flight and agued feare, mend and charge home,   533
  A Foe to'th'publike Weale. Obey I charge thee,   1878
  Bru. In this point charge him home, that he affects   2259
  Sicin. We charge you, that you haue contriu'd to take   2342
  Sicin. Peace: | We neede not put new matter to his charge: 2357
  With our owne charge: making a Treatie, where   3731
CHARGES = 2*1
  The Charges of our Friends. The Roman Gods,   609
  *charges distinctly billetted already in th'entertainment,   2613
  The charges of the Action. We haue made peace   3744
CHARITABLE = 1
  Men. I tell you Friends, most charitable care   66
CHARITY = 1
  Auf. Euen so, as with a man by his owne Almes im-|poyson'd, and with
  his Charity slaine.   3661
CHARMES = 1
  Fall deepe in loue with thee, and her great charmes   594
CHARRACTER = *1
  *gleane out of this Charracter, if I be knowne well e-|nough too.   960
CHARTER = 1
  My Mother, who ha's a Charter to extoll her Bloud,   764
CHARTERS = 1
  Your Liberties, and the Charters that you beare   1581
CHASE *see* chace
CHASTE = 1
  Corio. The Noble Sister of *Publicola*; | The Moone of Rome: Chaste as
  the Isicle   3416
CHASTLY = 1
  *passe heere: no, though it were as vertuous to lye, as to | liue chastly.
  Therefore go backe.   3264
CHATS = 1
  While she chats him: the Kitchin *Malkin* pinnes   1126
CHAUNCE = *1
  *matter betweene party and party, if you chaunce to bee   969
CHEAPE = 3*1
  *saying, *Martius* is proud: who in a cheape estimation, is   985
  cheape as Volcians. They are rising, they are rising. | *Both*. In, in, in, in.
  Exeunt   2890
  To make Coales cheape: A Noble memory.   3170
  As cheape as Lies; he sold the Blood and Labour   3702
CHECKE = 1
  Nor checke my Courage for what they can giue,   2376
CHEEFE = 1
  (Of whom hee's cheefe) with all the size that verity   3256
CHEEFEST = 1
  Helpe three a'th'cheefest Souldiers, Ile be one.   3831
CHEEKES = 3
  In their nicely gawded Cheekes, toth' wanton spoyle   1136
  Tent in my cheekes, and Schoole-boyes Teares take vp   2224
  To teare with Thunder the wide Cheekes a'th'Ayre,   3508

CHESTS = *1
  *fiddious'd, for all the Chests in Carioles, and the Gold   1028
CHIDE = 1
  Chide me no more. Ile Mountebanke their Loues,   2242
CHIEFE *see also* cheefe = *1
  *1.*Cit.* First you know, *Caius Martius* is chiefe enemy | to the people.   10
CHIEFEST *see also* cheefest = 1
  That Valour is the chiefest Vertue,   1298
CHILD = *2
  *he was a Man-child, then now in first seeing he had pro-|ued himselfe
  a man.   377
  Corio. Wife, Mother, Child, I know not. My affaires | Are Seruanted
  to others: Though I owe   3317
CHILDE = 6
  Val. Indeed la, tis a Noble childe. | *Virg.* A Cracke Madam.   430
  I am one of those: his Mother, Wife, his Childe,   3183
  Shew duty as mistaken, all this while, | Betweene the Childe, and
  Parent.   3405
  Making the Mother, wife, and Childe to see,   3456
  Requires nor Childe, nor womans face to see: | I haue sate too long.   3486
  His Wife is in *Corioles*, and his Childe   3536
CHILDISH = 1
  Or seeing it, of such Childish friendlinesse, | To yeeld your Voyces?   1575
CHILDISHNESSE = 1
  Perhaps thy childishnesse will moue him more   3514
CHILDREN = 4*1
  (As children from a Beare) the *Volces* shunning him: 393
  Towards her deserued Children, is enroll'd   2029
  *deafe, sleepe, insensible, a getter of more bastard Chil-|dren, then
  warres a destroyer of men.   2882
  1 Our selues, our wiues, and children, on our knees,   2918
  2.*Con.* And patient Fooles, | Whose children he hath slaine, their base
  throats teare   3710
CHILDRENS = 2
  Corio. Haue I had Childrens Voyces?   1711
  Thy Wife and Childrens blood: For my selfe, Sonne,   3473
CHINNE *see* shinne
CHOAKE = 1
  To choake it in the vtt'rance: So our Vertue,   3140
CHOICE *see also* choyse = 3*1
  Of their owne choice. One's *Iunius Brutus*,   230
  Deny your asking, take your choice of those | That best can ayde your
  action.   683
  *the wisedome of their choice, is rather to haue my Hat,   1489
  Volum. At thy choice then: 2232
CHOLLER = 3*1
  You should haue ta'ne th'aduantage of his Choller, | And pass'd him
  vnelected.   1600
  Mene. What, what? His Choller?   1776
  Cor. Choller? Were I as patient as the midnight sleep,   1777
  Bru. Go about it, | Put him to Choller straite, he hath bene vs'd   2289
CHOOSE = 3*1
  Giuen Hidra heere to choose an Officer, | That with his peremptory
  Shall, being but   1787
  Most pallates theirs. They choose their Magistrate,   1798
  Volce. He cannot choose: I am most fortunate, thus   2606
  In all his owne desires: Nay, let him choose   3686

CHOSE = 1*2
   Scici. How now, my Masters, haue you chose this man?   1553
   They haue chose a Consull, that will from them take   1617
   Scici. Say you chose him, more after our commandment,   1633
CHOSEN = 1*1
   Sicin. When we were chosen Tribunes for the people.   282
   Then were they chosen: in a better houre,   1869
CHOYSE = 1
   Before the common distribution, | At your onely choyse.   787
CHRONICLE = 1
   Whose Chronicle thus writ, The man was Noble,   3502
CHURCH-YARD = 1
   Like Graues i'th holy Church-yard.   2326
CICATRICES = *1
   *large Cicatrices to shew the People, when hee shall stand   1044
CIMENT = 1
   Com. Your Temples burned in their Ciment, and   3000
CIRCUMUENTION = 1
   Had circumuention: 'tis not foure dayes gone   320
CIT = *1
   *2 *Cit*. So did we all. But come, let's home. *Exit Cit*.   3084
CIT = 15*10
CITIE = 13*1
   That in these seuerall places of the Citie,   196
   The Citie is well stor'd.   201
   *before their Citie *Carioles*, they nothing doubt preuai- | ling,   463
   Mar. They feare vs not, but issue forth their Citie.   515
   The Treasure in this field atchieued, and Citie,   785
   Wash my fierce hand in's heart. Go you to th'Citie,   886
   The mortall Gate of th' Citie, which he painted   1325
   Both Field and Citie ours, he neuer stood   1335
   Sena. To vnbuild the Citie, and to lay all flat.   1908
   Scici. What is the Citie, but the People?   1909
   All. True, the People are the Citie.   1910
   Com. That is the way to lay the Citie flat,   1915
   Vnlesse by not so doing, our good Citie | Cleaue in the midd'st, and
   perish.   2117
   (Eu'n from this instant) banish him our Citie   2386
CITIES = 1
   I'th'field proue flatterers, let Courts and Cities be   799
CITIZEN see also *Cit*., 1., 1.*Cit*., 2., 2.*Cit*., 3.*Cit*. = 3
   Mene. Consider further: | That when he speakes not like a Citizen,   2329
   Enter a Citizen.   2629
   Corio. Thanke you sir, farewell. *Exit Citizen*   2637
CITIZEN = 2
CITIZENS see also *Cit*., *Cittizens* = 14*1
   Enter a Company of Mutinous Citizens, with Staues, | *Clubs, and other*
   weapons.   2
   2.*Cit*. One word, good Citizens.   16
   *1.*Cit*. We are accounted poore Citizens, the Patri- | cians   17
   Citizens steale away. Manet Sicin. & Brutus.   279
   Enter seuen or eight Citizens.   1387
   Enter three of the Citizens.   1452
   Exeunt. Enter two other Citizens.   1475
   Enter three Citizens more.   1516
   Sicin. Helpe ye Citizens.   1885
   Tribunes, Patricians, Citizens: what ho: 1894

CITIZENS cont.
  Sicinius, Brutus, Coriolanus, Citizens.   1895
  Mene. Lo Citizens, he sayes he is Content.   2323
  Enter three or foure Citizens.   2914
  Both Tri. Farewell, farewell. *Exeunt Citizens*   2924
  Enter a Troope of Citizens.   3053
CITTIZENS = 1
  Mess. The Cittizens of *Corioles* haue yssued,   614
CITTY = 3
  Corio. A goodly City is this *Antium.* Citty,   2623
  To melt the Citty Leades vpon your pates,   2997
  Gaue way vnto your Clusters, who did hoote | Him out o'th'Citty.   3045
CITY *see also* citie, citty = 19*6
  *What showts are these? The other side a'th City is risen: 48
  The rabble should haue first vnroo'st the City   232
  before the City Corialus: to them | a Messenger.   480
  Clapt to their Gates, he is himselfe alone, | To answer all the City.   552
  Let's fetch him off, or make remaine alike. | *They fight, and all enter the City.*   567
  Conuenient Numbers to make good the City,   583
  ('Tis South the City Mils) bring me word thither   891
  *you are censured heere in the City, I mean of vs a'th'right | hand File, do you?   919
  *That would depopulate the city, & be euery man himself   1995
  For you the City. Thus I turne my backe;   2422
  Giue him deseru'd vexation. Let a guard | Attend vs through the City.   2430
  Corio. A goodly City is this *Antium.* Citty,   2623
  3 Where's that? | *Corio.* I'th City of Kites and crowes.   2695
  *3 I'th City of Kites and Crowes? What an Asse it is,   2697
  *out the intended fire, your City is ready to flame in, with   3282
  *I am husht vntill our City be afire, & then Ile speak a litle | *Holds her by the hand silent.*   3538
  shall our poore City finde: and all this is long of you.   3598
  A City full: Of Tribunes such as you,   3628
  Sicin. They are neere the City.   3636
  Auf. Go tell the Lords a'th'City, I am heere: 3650
  The City Ports by this hath enter'd, and   3655
  Enter the Lords of the City.   3720
  For certaine drops of Salt, your City Rome: 3761
  I say your City to his Wife and Mother,   3762
  Traile your steele Pikes. Though in this City hee   3833
CLAMBRING = 1
  Clambring the Walls to eye him: 1128
CLAMOR = 1
  With all th'applause and Clamor of the Hoast,   820
CLAPT = 1
  Clapt to their Gates, he is himselfe alone, | To answer all the City.   552
CLAYME = 2
  That as his worthy deeds did clayme no lesse   1587
  Were fit for thee to vse, as they to clayme,   2184
CLEANE = 2
  And keepe their teeth cleane: So, heere comes a brace,   1454
  Sicin. This is cleane kamme. | *Brut.* Meerely awry: 2042
CLEAUE = 1
  Vnlesse by not so doing, our good Citie | Cleaue in the midd'st, and perish.   2117

CLEEP = 1
And scarr'd the Moone with splinters: heere I cleep 2767
CLIP = 1
Mart. Oh! let me clip ye | In Armes as sound, as when I woo'd in heart; 640
CLOATHES = *1
*a Cudgell, and yet my minde gaue me, his cloathes made | a false
report of him. 2811
CLOCKD = 1
Ha's clock'd thee to the Warres: and safelie home 3520
CLOTH = 1
With those that haue but little: this must be patcht | With Cloth of any
Colour. 1978
CLOUD *see* clowd
CLOUDS = *1
Corio. Why then should I be Consull? by yond Clouds 1736
CLOUEN = 1
There is *Auffidious.* List what worke he makes | Among'st your clouen
Army. 510
CLOWD = 1
Should from yond clowd speake diuine things, 2762
CLUBS = 3
*Enter a Company of Mutinous Citizens, with Staues, | Clubs, and other
weapons.* 2
Where go you with Bats and Clubs? The matter | Speake I pray you. 57
But make you ready your stiffe bats and clubs, 169
CLUSTERS = 2
Gaue way vnto your Clusters, who did hoote | Him out o'th'Citty. 3045
Mene. Heere come the Clusters. 3054
CLUTCHT = 1
In thy hands clutcht: as many Millions in 2351
COALE = 2
Then is the coale of fire vpon the Ice, 184
If he could burne vs all into one coale, | We haue deseru'd it. 3063
COALES = 1
To make Coales cheape: A Noble memory. 3170
COARSE = 1
As the most Noble Coarse, that euer Herald | Did follow to his Vrne. 3824
COAT = 1
That like an Eagle in a Doue-coat, I | Flatter'd your Volcians in
Corioles. 3785
COBLED = *1
*Below their cobled Shooes. They say ther's grain enough? 208
COCKLE = 1
The Cockle of Rebellion, Insolence, Sedition, 1760
COFFIND = 1
Would'st thou haue laugh'd, had I come Coffin'd home, 1082
COGGE = 1
Cogge their Hearts from them, and come home belou'd 2243
COIN = *1
Mene. See you yon'd Coin a'th Capitol, yon'd corner | (stone? 3571
COINE = 1
Coine words till their decay, against those Meazels 1770
COLD = 2
Brut. Sir, those cold wayes, | That seeme like prudent helpes, are very
poysonous, 1936
The Veines vnfill'd, our blood is cold, and then 3209

COLDE = *1
*Corio. Follow your Function, go, and batten on colde | bits. *Pushes him away from him.*   2686
COLDER = 1
My Rages and Reuenges, with your colder reasons.   3440
COLLECTED = 1
Sicin. Haue you collected them by Tribes? | *Edile.* I haue.   2272
COLLIKE = *1
*pinch'd with the Collike, you make faces like Mum-|mers,   970
COLOUR = 1
With those that haue but little: this must be patcht | With Cloth of any Colour.   1978
COLOURED *see* coulord
COLOURS = *2
Enter Martius, Titus Lartius, with Drumme and Co-|lours, with Captaines and Souldiers, as   478
Enter Coriolanus marching with Drumme, and Colours. The | Commoners being with him.   3734
COM = *1
*so, they are in a most warlike preparation, & hope to com | vpon them, in the heate of their diuision   2587
COM = 58 *9
COMBINE = 1
That they combine not there?   2140
COME = 61 *21
why stay we prating heere? To th'Capitoll. | *All.* Come, come.   49
Bru. Come: halfe all *Cominius* Honors are to *Martius*   304
Gent. Madam, the lady *Valeria* is come to visit you.   388
Come on you Cowards, you were got in feare   395
Val. Come, lay aside your stitchery, I must haue you   432
Come, you must go visit the good Lady that lies in.   441
*full of Mothes. Come, I would your Cambrick were sen-|sible   448
pitie. Come you shall go with vs.   450
Fare you well then. Come good sweet Ladie.   471
To helpe our fielded Friends. Come, blow thy blast.   498
*which makes me sweat with wrath. Come on my fellows   520
And make my Warres on you: Looke too't: Come on,   535
Com. Breath you my friends, wel fought, we are come | (off,   604
Mar. Come I too late?   633
Martius. Come I too late?   637
Com. I, if you come not in the blood of others, | But mantled in your owne.   638
*Our Guider come, to th'Roman Campe conduct vs. *Exit*   721
Heere they fight, and certaine Volces come in the ayde   740
It should be lookt too: come. *Exeunt.*   856
Bru. Come sir come, we know you well enough.   962
Bru. Come, come, you are well vnderstood to bee a   976
he was wont to come home wounded? | *Virgil.* Oh no, no, no.   1016
Would'st thou haue laugh'd, had I come Coffin'd home,   1082
1.Off. Come, come, they are almost here: how many | stand for Consulships?   1205
Senat. To *Coriolanus* come all ioy and Honor.   1377
Bru. Come, wee'l informe them   1384
*his behauiour: we are not to stay altogether, but to come   1429
Here come moe Voyces.   1517
Scicin. Toth' Capitoll, come: 1667
Mene. Come enough.   1837

COME *cont*.

Come trie vpon your selues, what you haue seene me.	1942
Corio. Come Sir, along with vs.	1961
Com. Nay, come away. *Exeunt Coriolanus and	Cominius*.	1980
Our Ediles smot: our selues resisted: come.	2061
Let me desire your company: he must come,	2080
Men. Come, come, you haue bin too rough, somthing	2114
Menen. Noble Lady,	Come goe with vs, speake faire: you may salue so,	2169
Com. Come, come, wee'le prompt you.	2213
Then thou of them. Come all to ruine, let	2234
Cogge their Hearts from them, and come home belou'd	2243
Was ne're distributed. What, will he come?	2263
All. Come, come, lets see him out at gates, come:	2432
The Gods preserue our Noble Tribunes, come. *Exeunt*.	2433
Corio. Come leaue your teares: a brief farwel: the beast	2437
Come my sweet wife, my deerest Mother, and	2489
Bid me farewell, and smile. I pray you come:	2491
Menen. That's worthily	As any eare can heare. Come, let's not weepe,	2495
Corio. Giue me thy hand, come. *Exeunt*	2500
Menen. Come, come, peace.	2539
And so shall sterue with Feeding: come, let's go,	2566
In Anger, *Iuno*-like: Come, come, come. *Exeunt*	2568
Heere's no place for you, pray you auoid: Come.	2685
Like a bold Flood o're-beate. Oh come, go in,	2789
To fright them, ere destroy. But come in,	2802
*2 Come we are fellowes and friends: he was euer too	2843
Sicin. Come, what talke you of *Martius*.	2950
Mene. Heere come the Clusters.	3054
*1 *Cit*. The Gods bee good to vs: Come Masters let's	3081
*2 *Cit*. So did we all. But come, let's home. *Exit Cit*.	3084
When he shall come to his account, he knowes not	3109
When ere we come to our account.	3117
Come let's away: when *Caius* Rome is thine,	3147
*I am an Officer of State, & come to speak with *Coriolanus*	3239
1 Come, my Captaine knowes you not.	*Mene*. I meane thy Generall.	3289
*now presently, and swoond for what's to come vpon	3303
*I was hardly moued to come to thee: but beeing assured	3308
Are we come hither; since that thy sight, which should	3453
Then thou hast to deny't. Come, let vs go:	3534
If not most mortall to him. But let it come:	3547
Come enter with vs: Ladies you deserue	3566
Auf. Say no more. Heere come the Lords,	3719

COMELINESSE = *1

*youth with comelinesse pluck'd all gaze his way; when	368

COMELY = 1

Sicin. This is a happier and more comely time,	2925

COMES = 6*4

1 *Cit*. Soft, who comes heere?	51
But it proceeds, or comes from them to you,	161
*and ouer he comes, and vp againe: catcht it again: or	425
Martius. Yonder comes Newes:	A Wager they haue met.	482
Volum. On's Browes: *Menenius*, hee comes the third	time home with the Oaken Garland.	1021
*Heere he comes, and in the Gowne of humility, marke	1428
And keepe their teeth cleane: So, heere comes a brace,	1454
Sicin. Well, heere he comes.	2298

COMES *cont.*

*Brut. Dismisse them home. Here comes his Mother.	2511
My wife comes formost, then the honour'd mould	3371

COMFORT = 4

Brutus. In that there's comfort. | *Scici.* Doubt not,	1147
Our prayers to the Gods, which is a comfort	3460
Our comfort in the Country. We must finde	3466
The Romane Ladies bring not comfort home	3607

COMFORTABLE = *1

*in a more comfortable sort: If my Sonne were my Hus-|band,	363

COMFORTS = *1

*Make our eies flow with ioy, harts dance with comforts,	3454

COMING *see* comming

COMINIUS see also Com. = 29*5

Enter Sicinius Velutus, Annius Brutus Cominius, Titus | Lartius, with other Senatours.	244
1.*Sen.* Then worthy *Martius,* | Attend vpon *Cominius* to these Warres.	258
*Tit. Lead you on: Follow *Cominius,* we must followe | you, right worthy your Priority.	271
*wonder, his insolence can brooke to be commanded vn-|der *Cominius?*	291
Opinion that so stickes on *Martius,* shall | Of his demerits rob *Cominius.*	302
*Bru. Come: halfe all *Cominius* Honors are to *Martius*	304
Cominius, Martius your old Enemy | (Who is of Rome worse hated then of you)	326
*Cominius the Generall is gone, with one part of our Ro-|mane	461
Whil'st I with those that haue the spirit, wil haste | To helpe *Cominius.*	584
Enter Cominius as it were in retire, with soldiers.	603
*Drum and Trumpet toward Cominius, and Caius Mar-|tius,	711
Flourish. Alarum. A Retreat is sounded. Enter at | one Doore Cominius, with the Romanes: At	744
cast vp their Caps and Launces: Cominius | and Lartius stand bare.	795
Enter Cominius the Generall, and Titus Latius: be-|tweene them Coriolanus, crown'd with an Oaken	1060
the People, Lictors before them: Coriolanus, Mene-|nius, Cominius the Consul: Scicinius and Brutus	1240
1.*Sen.* Speake, good *Cominius:* | Leaue nothing out for length, and make vs thinke	1256
been silent: Please you to heare *Cominius* speake?	1270
their Bed-fellow: Worthie *Cominius* speake.	1274
Then on ones Eares to heare it. Proceed *Cominius.*	1295
Cornets. Enter Coriolanus, Menenius, all the Gentry, | Cominius, Titus Latius, and other Senators.	1672
*Com. Hath he not pass'd the Noble, and the Common? | *Brut.*	1709
Cominius, no.	
Com. Nay, come away. *Exeunt Coriolanus and | Cominius.*	1980
Then flatter him in a Bower. *Enter Cominius.*	2195
Here is *Cominius.*	2196
Enter Coriolanus, Menenius, and Comi-|nius, with others.	2296
Exeunt Coriolanus, Cominius, with Cumalijs.	2424
*Enter Coriolanus, Volumnia, Virgilia, Menenius, Cominius, | with the yong Nobility of Rome.	2435
Your Husband so much swet. *Cominius,*	2457
Volum. My first sonne, | Whether will thou go? Take good *Cominius*	2472
Enter Cominius.	2993
Enter Menenius, Cominius, Sicinius, Brutus, | the two Tribunes, with others.	3150
To heare *Cominius* speake, Ile keepe at home.	3158

COMINIUS cont.

As *Cominius* is return'd, vnheard: what then?	3199
And humme at good *Cominius*, much vnhearts mee.	3207

COMMAND = 3

And foure shall quickly draw out my Command, | Which men are best inclin'd.	705
Beares a Command in't: Though thy Tackles torne,	2718
Vnder your great Command. You are to know,	3739

COMMANDED = *1

*wonder, his insolence can brooke to be commanded vn- | der *Cominius*?	291

COMMANDING = 1

From th'Caske to th'Cushion: but commanding peace	3134

COMMANDMENT = *1

*Scici. Say you chose him, more after our commandment,	1633

COMMANDS = *1

*me, dost not thinke me for the man I am, necessitie com- | mands me name my selfe.	2711

COMMEND = 3

To be set high in place, we did commend	1650
Commend me to my Wife, Ile returne Consull,	2245
Let me commend thee first, to those that shall	2803

COMMENDABLE = 1

And power vnto it selfe most commendable,	3142

COMMING = 6*1

Menen. Ha? *Martius* comming home?	999
hoo, *Martius* comming home? | 2.*Ladies.* Nay, 'tis true.	1003
*is comming home: hee ha's more cause to be prowd:	1041
*1.*Off.* No more of him, hee's a worthy man: make | way, they are comming.	1237
Edile. Hee's comming. | *Bru.* How accompanied?	2265
All to the Senate-house: some newes is comming | That turnes their Countenances.	2965
At *Coriolanus* Exile. Now he's comming,	3058

COMMISSION = 3

2.*Sen.* Noble *Auffidius,* | Take your Commission, hye you to your Bands,	342
Th'one halfe of my Commission, and set downe	2797
Ioyn'd in Commission with him: but either haue borne	3106

COMMIT = 1

Commit the Warre of White and Damaske	1135

COMMON = 15*4

Vnto the appetite; and affection common	106
Touching the Weale a'th Common, you shall finde	159
The common file, (a plague-Tribunes for them)	656
Before the common distribution, | At your onely choyse.	787
And stand vpon my common part with those, | That haue beheld the doing.	792
*1.*off.* That's a braue fellow: but hee's vengeance | prowd, and loues not the common people.	1209
Your louing motion toward the common Body, | To yeeld what passes here.	1261
The common Muck of the World: he couets lesse	1342
*bin a Rod to her Friends, you haue not indeede loued the | Common people.	1483
*that I haue not bin common in my Loue, I will sir flatter	1486
The Tongues o'th' Common Mouth. I do despise them:	1701

COMMON *cont*.

Com. Hath he not pass'd the Noble, and the Common? | *Brut*.
Cominius, no. 1709
Be not as common Fooles; if you are not, 1794
Com. Heare me my Masters, and my common friends. 2393
Corio. You common cry of Curs, whose breath I hate, 2408
That common chances. Common men could beare, 2441
Will or exceed the Common, or be caught 2470
Of thy deepe duty, more impression shew | Then that of common
Sonnes. 3400
COMMONALTY = *1
All. Against him first: He's a very dog to the Com- | monalty. 29
COMMONERS = 2
The Commoners, for whom we stand, but they 1149
*Enter Coriolanus marching with Drumme, and Colours. The |
Commoners being with him*. 3734
COMMONS = 3
As to *Ioues* Statue, and the Commons made 1196
I'th'right and strength a'th'Commons: be it either 2276
Euen in theirs, and in the Commons eares 3653
COMMONWEALTH = *1
*Friends: the Commonwealth doth stand, and so would | do, were he
more angry at it. 2907
COMPANION = *1
Mene. Now you Companion: Ile say an arrant for you: 3297
COMPANIONS = 1
his head, that he giues entrance to such Companions? 2667
COMPANIONSHIP = 1
That it shall hold Companionship in Peace 2146
COMPANY = 5
*Enter a Company of Mutinous Citizens, with Staues, | Clubs, and other
weapons*. 2
Sen. Your Company to'th'Capitoll, where I know | Our greatest Friends
attend vs. 269
Mene. Ile keepe you company. Will you along? 1545
Let me desire your company: he must come, 2080
sir, heartily well met, and most glad of your Company. 2617
COMPASSE = 1
*of one direct way, should be at once to all the points | a'th Compasse. 1409
COMPASSION = 1
Mine eyes to sweat compassion. But (good sir) 3555
COMPETENCIE = 1
From me receiue that naturall competencie 146
COMPLAINE = 1
2.*Cit*. The former Agents, if they did complaine, 128
COMPLAININGS = *1
*They vented their Complainings, which being answer'd 222
COMPLAINT = *1
*the first complaint, hasty and Tinder-like vppon, to 946
COMPLEXIONS = 1
With variable Complexions; all agreeing 1131
COMPOSITION = 1
Latius. He had, my Lord, and that it was which caus'd | Our swifter
Composition. 1675
COMPOUND = *1
*the Asse in compound, with the Maior part of your sylla- | bles. 954

COMPOUNDED = 1
Together with the Seale a'th Senat, what | We haue compounded on. 3748
COMST = 1*1
Sicin. Sir, how com'st that you haue holpe | To make this rescue? 2008
*Auf. Whence com'st thou? What wouldst y? Thy name? 2708
CONCEALEMENT = 1
'Twere a Concealement worse then a Theft, 772
CONCLUDE = 1
Cannot conclude, but by the yea and no 1844
CONDEMND = 1*1
3 I would not be a Roman of all Nations; I had as | liue be a
condemn'd man. 2835
*condemn'd, our Generall has sworne you out of repreeue | and pardon. 3285
CONDEMNE = 1
The Volces whom you serue, you might condemne vs 3491
CONDEMNED = 1
Officious and not valiant, you haue sham'd me | In your condemned
Seconds. 742
CONDEMNING = 1
Condemning some to death, and some to exile, 646
CONDITION = 5*1
Sould. 'Twill be deliuer'd backe on good Condition. 860
Auffid. Condition? 861
Being a *Volce*, be that I am. Condition? 863
What good Condition can a Treatie finde 864
*of them, 'tis a condition they account gentle: & since 1488
*Sicin. Is't possible, that so short a time can alter the | condition of a
man. 3578
CONDITIONS = 3
Bound with an Oath to yeeld to his conditions: 3230
The first Conditions which they did refuse, 3361
On like conditions, will haue Counter-seal'd. 3565
CONDUCT = *1
*Our Guider come, to th'Roman Campe conduct vs. *Exit* 721
CONDUCTED = 1
Com. Though I could wish, | You were conducted to a gentle Bath, 680
CONDUITS = 1
That our best Water, brought by Conduits hither, 1645
CONFEDERATE = 1
In Italy, and her Confederate Armes 3568
CONFESSE = 2*1
Menen. Either you must | Confesse your selues wondrous Malicious, 88
*for their Tongues to be silent, and not confesse so much, 1233
Hast not the soft way, which thou do'st confesse 2183
CONFIDENCE = 1
Against vs Brats, with no lesse Confidence, 3009
CONFIND = 1
Your Franchises, whereon you stood, confin'd | Into an Augors boare. 3001
CONFINE = *1
*Val. Fye, you confine your selfe most vnreasonably: 440
CONFIRMD = 1*1
*halfe an houre together: ha's such a confirm'd coun- | tenance. 422
3.*Cit.* Hee's not confirm'd, we may deny him yet. 1612
CONFIRME = 1
But to confirme my Cursses. Could I meete 'em 2560

CONFOUND = 1
How could'st thou in a mile confound an houre, | And bring thy Newes
so late? 622
CONFUSD = 1
Let them not cease, but with a dinne confus'd 2283
CONFUSION = 2
Neither Supreame; How soone Confusion 1804
Then when these Fellowes ran about the streets, | Crying Confusion. 2926
CONFUSIONS = 1
Confusions neere, I cannot speake. You, Tribunes 1898
CONGREGATIONS = 1
In Congregations, to yawne, be still, and wonder, 2096
CONIECTURALL = 1
Coniecturall Marriages, making parties strong, 206
CONIES = 1
Conies after Raine) and reuell all with him. 2871
CONIURE = *1
*out of your Gates with sighes: and coniure thee to par-|don 3310
CONND = 1
With Precepts that would make inuincible | The heart that conn'd them. 2446
CONQUER = 2
Euer to conquer, and to haue his worth 2291
That if thou conquer Rome, the benefit 3499
CONSCIENCD = *1
*he did it to that end: though soft conscienc'd men can be 38
CONSCIENCE = *1
*returne for Conscience sake, to helpe to get thee a Wife. 1419
CONSENT = 2*2
But cannot make my heart consent to take 790
*they would flye East, West, North, South, and their con-|sent 1408
*Brut. By the consent of all, we were establish'd the | Peoples
Magistrates. 1911
Corio. The God of Souldiers: | With the consent of supreme Ioue,
informe 3423
CONSENTED = *1
*willingly consented to his Banishment, yet it was against | our will. 3071
CONSIDER = 4*1
*2.Cit. Consider you what Seruices he ha's done for his | Country? 31
Whether 'tis bent: most likely, 'tis for you: | Consider of it. 330
Mene. Consider this: He ha's bin bred i'th'Warres 2062
The warlike Seruice he ha's done, consider: Thinke 2324
Mene. Consider further: | That when he speakes not like a Citizen, 2329
CONSIDERING = *1
*an houre from her beholding; I considering how Honour 370
CONSP = 2
CONSPECTUITIES = *1
*too? What harme can your beesome Conspectui-|ties 959
CONSPIRATOR see 1.Con., 2.Con., 3.Con., 3.Consp.
CONSPIRATORS see also Consp. = 2
Enter 3 or 4 Conspirators of Auffidius Faction. | Most Welcome. 3658
Draw both the Conspirators, and kils Martius, who | falles, Auffidius
stands on him. 3805
CONSTANT = 3
And I am constant: Titus Lucius, thou 262
And perish constant Fooles: who is't can blame him? 3024
Auffid. You keepe a constant temper. Exeunt 3329

CONSTRAINES = *1
  *Constraines them weepe, and shake with feare & sorow,   3455
CONSTRUCTION = 1
  A good construction. I rais'd him, and I pawn'd   3673
CONSUL = 1
  the People, Lictors before them: Coriolanus, Mene-|nius, Cominius the
  Consul: Scicinius and Brutus   1240
CONSULL = 25*3
  Scicin. On the suddaine, I warrant him Consull.   1141
  Were he to stand for Consull, neuer would he   1155
  'Tis thought, that *Martius* shall be Consull: 1191
  The present Consull, and last Generall,   1250
  Menen. The Senate, *Coriolanus*, are well pleas'd to make | thee
  Consull.   1350
  Our purpose to them, and to our Noble Consull | Wish we all Ioy, and
  Honor.   1375
  *of your voices, that I may bee Consull, I haue heere the | Customarie
  Gowne.   1477
  *bountifull to the desirers: Therefore beseech you, I may | be Consull.   1493
  Your Voyces? Indeed I would be Consull.   1523
  2.Cit. Therefore let him be Consull: the Gods giue him | ioy, and make
  him good friend to the People.   1526
  All. Amen, Amen. God saue thee, Noble Consull.   1528
  I would be Consull, sayes he: aged Custome,   1568
  They haue chose a Consull, that will from them take   1617
  To Voyce him Consull. Lay the fault on vs.   1637
  Com. They are worne (Lord Consull) so,   1680
  Corio. Why then should I be Consull? by yond Clouds   1736
  Or neuer be so Noble as a Consull,   1743
  Bru. Manifest Treason. | *Sicin.* This a Consull? No.   1872
  Whom late you haue nam'd for Consull.   1905
  Sicin. Consull? what Consull?   2012
  Mene. The Consull *Coriolanus.*   2013
  Bru. He Consull. | *All.* No, no, no, no, no.   2014
  Commend me to my Wife, Ile returne Consull,   2245
  That being past for Consull with full voyce: 2337
  Com. Let me speake: | I haue bene Consull, and can shew from Rome   2395
  If he had gone forth Consull, found it so.   2935
  3.Consp. Sir, his stoutnesse | When he did stand for Consull, which he
  lost | By lacke of stooping.   3679
CONSULS = 5
  An o're-prest Roman, and i'th' Consuls view   1307
  It makes the Consuls base; and my Soule akes   1802
  The Consuls worthinesse, so can I name his Faults.   2011
  Is worth of Consuls, Senators, Patricians,   3627
  Subscrib'd by'th'Consuls, and Patricians,   3747
CONSULSHIP = 1
  Corio. Well then I pray, your price a'th'Consulship.   1465
CONSULSHIPS = 1
  1.Off. Come, come, they are almost here: how many | stand for
  Consulships?   1205
CONSUMD = 1
  O're-borne their way, consum'd with fire, and tooke | What lay before
  them.   2991
CONSUME = 1
  That should consume it, I haue not the face   3036

CONTAGION = 1
   Mar. All the contagion of the South, light on you,   525
CONTAINES = 1
   Too great for what containes it. Boy? Oh Slaue,   3774
CONTEMNE = 1
   As if he did contemne what he requested, | Should be in them to giue.   1382
CONTEMPT = 3
   Brut. Did you perceiue, | He did sollicite you in free Contempt,   1602
   That his Contempt shall not be brusing to you,   1605
   With what Contempt he wore the humble Weed,   1624
CONTEND = 1
   Contend against thy Valour. Know thou first,   2771
CONTENNING = 1
   At Grecian sword. *Contenning*, tell *Valeria*   405
CONTENT = 7*3
   1.Cit. Very well, and could bee content to giue him   33
   *content to say it was for his Countrey, he did it to please   39
   *And though I must be content to beare with those,   955
   With doing them, and is content | To spend the time, to end it.   1344
   All. Content, content.   1435
   Corio. Pray be content: | Mother, I am going to the Market place: 2240
   Allow their Officers, and are content   2319
   Corio. I am Content.   2322
   Mene. Lo Citizens, he sayes he is Content.   2323
CONTEST = 1
   The Anuile of my Sword, and do contest   2768
CONTINUED = 2
   How long continued, and what stock he springs of,   1640
   Sicin. I would he had continued to his Country   2540
CONTINUES = 2
   1.*Sol*. See they haue shut him in. *Alarum continues*   546
   Alarum continues still a-farre off.   573
CONTRADICTION = 1
   Of contradiction. Being once chaft, he cannot   2292
CONTRARIETY = 1
   He, and *Auffidius* can no more attone | Then violent'st Contrariety.   2984
CONTRIUD = *1
   Sicin. We charge you, that you haue contriu'd to take   2342
CONTROL *see* controul't
CONTROLLD = 1
   As he controll'd the warre. But one of these   3136
CONTROUERSIE = *2
   *and then reiourne the Controuersie of three-pence   967
   *in roaring for a Chamber-pot, dismisse the Controuersie   972
CONTROULT = 1
   For th'ill which doth controul't.   1860
CONUENIENT = 2
   Conuenient Numbers to make good the City,   583
   Ile frame conuenient peace. Now good *Auffidius*,   3549
CONUENTED = *1
   Scicin. We are conuented vpon a pleasing Treatie, and   1263
CONUERSATION = *1
   *Godden to your Worships, more of your conuer-|sation   988
CONUERSES = *1
   *triuiall motion: One, that conuerses more with the But-|tocke   947
CONUEYANCES = 1
   These Pipes, and these Conueyances of our blood   3212

CONUEYING = 1
By Interims and conueying gusts, we haue heard 608
COOLE = 1
And loose aduantage, which doth euer coole | Ith'absence of the needer. 2483
COR = 4*3
CORI = *1
CORIALUS = 2
before the City Corialus: to them | a Messenger. 480
They Sound a Parley: Enter two Senators with others on | the Walles of Corialus. 499
CORIO = 1
And beare him to the Rock. *Corio. drawes his Sword.* 1939
CORIO = 107*18
CORIOL = 1
Scicin. Fare you well. Exeunt Coriol. and Mene. 1547
CORIOL = 5*5
*CORIOLANUS see also Cor., Cori., Corio., Coriol. = 42*11*
Marcus Caius Coriolanus. Beare th'addition Nobly euer? 821
Omnes. Marcus Caius Coriolanus. 823
Enter Cominius the Generall, and Titus Latius: be-|tweene them Coriolanus, crown'd with an Oaken 1060
These in honor followes *Martius Caius Coriolanus.* 1067
Welcome to Rome, renowned *Coriolanus.* | *Sound. Flourish.* 1068
All. Welcome to Rome, renowned *Coriolanus.* 1070
What is it (*Coriolanus*) must I call thee? 1079
Coriolanus will carry it. 1208
*no better a ground. Therefore, for *Coriolanus* neyther to 1215
the People, Lictors before them: Coriolanus, Mene-|nius, Cominius the Consul: Scicinius and Brutus 1240
take their places by themselues: Corio-|lanus stands. 1242
By *Martius Caius Coriolanus*: whom 1253
Coriolanus rises, and offers to goe away. | Nay, keepe your place. 1275
Senat. Sit *Coriolanus*: neuer shame to heare | What you haue Nobly done. 1277
To heare my Nothings monster'd. *Exit Coriolanus* 1290
Com. I shall lacke voyce: the deeds of *Coriolanus* 1296
Senat. Call *Coriolanus.* | *Off.* He doth appeare. 1347
Enter Coriolanus. 1349
Menen. The Senate, *Coriolanus*, are well pleas'd to make | thee Consull. 1350
Senat. To *Coriolanus* come all ioy and Honor. 1377
Enter Coriolanus in a gowne of Humility, with | Menenius. 1426
Corio. Where? at the Senate-house? | *Scicin.* There, *Coriolanus.* 1539
Cornets. Enter Coriolanus, Menenius, all the Gentry, | Cominius, Titus Latius, and other Senators. 1672
Becomes not Rome: nor ha's *Coriolanus* 1747
2 Sen. Weapons, weapons, weapons: | *They all bustle about Coriolanus.* 1892
Sicinius, Brutus, Coriolanus, Citizens. 1895
To'th'people: Coriolanus, patience: Speak good *Sicinius.* 1899
Com. Nay, come away. *Exeunt Coriolanus and | Cominius.* 1980
Mene. The Consull *Coriolanus.* 2013
Enter Coriolanus with Nobles. 2083
Enter Coriolanus, Menenius, and Comi-|nius, with others. 2296
Exeunt Coriolanus, Cominius, with Cumalijs. 2424
Enter Coriolanus, Volumnia, Virgilia, Menenius, Cominius, | with the yong Nobility of Rome. 2435
*to heart, the Banishment of that worthy *Coriolanus*, that 2591

CORIOLANUS cont.
Vol. Coriolanus Banisht? | *Rom.* Banish'd sir.	2596
*Opposer *Coriolanus* being now in no request of his coun-|trey.	2604
Enter Coriolanus in meane Apparrell, dis-|guisd, and muffled.	2621
Enter Coriolanus.	2658
Corio. I haue deseru'd no better entertainment, in be-|ing *Coriolanus.*	
Enter second Seruant.	2664
My Surname *Coriolanus.* The painfull Seruice,	2725
Sicin. Your *Coriolanus* is not much mist, but with his	2906
Bru. Farewell kinde Neighbours: | We wisht *Coriolanus* had lou'd you as we did.	2921
At *Coriolanus* Exile. Now he's comming,	3058
That we haue bled together. *Coriolanus*	3163
*I am an Officer of State, & come to speak with *Coriolanus*	3239
2 You'l see your Rome embrac'd with fire, before | You'l speake with *Coriolanus.*	3243
Enter Coriolanus with Auffidius.	3295
*Son *Coriolanus,* guesse but my entertainment with him: if	3300
Enter Coriolanus and Auffidius.	3346
To his sur-name *Coriolanus* longs more pride	3527
Enter Coriolanus marching with Drumme, and Colours. The | Commoners being with him.	3734
Ile grace thee with that Robbery, thy stolne name | *Coriolanus* in *Corioles?*	3757
The Tragedy of Coriolanus.	3839

*CORIOLES see also Carioles, Corialus, Coriolus = 12*1*
Let vs alone to guard *Corioles*	344
Mess. The Cittizens of *Corioles* haue yssued,	614
Holding *Corioles* in the name of Rome,	648
Alone I fought in your *Corioles* walles,	733
For what he did before *Corioles*, call him,	819
Must to *Corioles* backe, send vs to Rome	833
Martius. I sometime lay here in *Corioles*,	841
Within Corioles Gates: where he hath wonne,	1065
Before, and in Corioles, let me say	1316
*on't before *Corioles*, he scotcht him, and notcht him like a | Carbinado.	2846
His Wife is in *Corioles*, and his Childe	3536
Ile grace thee with that Robbery, thy stolne name | *Coriolanus* in *Corioles?*	3757
That like an Eagle in a Doue-coat, I | Flatter'd your Volcians in *Corioles.*	3785

CORIOLUS = 1
Enter Tullus Auffidius with Senators of Coriolus.	313

CORMORANT = 1
2.*Cit.* Should by the Cormorant belly be restrain'd,	125

CORNE = 6*4
*1.*Cit.* Let vs kill him, and wee'l haue Corne at our own | price. Is't a Verdict?	13
Men. For Corne at their owne rates, wherof they say	200
Corne for the Richmen onely: With these shreds	221
The Volces haue much Corne: take these Rats thither,	276
*helpe will serue: for once we stood vp about the Corne,	1401
When Corne was giuen them *gratis*, you repin'd,	1727
Corio. Tell me of Corne: this was my speech,	1750
The Corne a'th'Store-house gratis, as 'twas vs'd | Sometime in Greece.	1809
*More worthier then their Voyces. They know the Corne	1817

CORNE *cont.*
Did not deserue Corne gratis. Being i'th'Warre,   1822
CORNER = *1
Mene. See you yon'd Coin a'th Capitol, yon'd corner | (stone?   3571
CORNETS = 4
A flourish. Cornets. Enter Tullus Auffidius | bloudie, with two or three
Souldiors.   857
Com. On, to the Capitall. Flourish. Cornets. | Exeunt in State, as before. 1120
Flourish Cornets. | Then Exeunt. Manet Sicinius and Brutus.   1378
Cornets. Enter Coriolanus, Menenius, all the Gentry, | Cominius, Titus
Latius, and other Senators.   1672
CORRECTED = 1
Corio. What's this? your knees to me? | To your Corrected Sonne?   3407
CORRECTING = 1
Which often thus correcting thy stout heart,   2179
CORRUPT = 1*1
That do corrupt my Ayre: I banish you,   2411
*it saide, the fittest time to corrupt a mans Wife, is when   2601
CORSLET = *1
*He is able to pierce a Corslet with his eye: Talkes   3589
COSINE = 1
He kill'd my Sonne, my daughter, he kill'd my Cosine   3794
COTT *see* coat
COTUS = *2
*2 Ser. Where's Cotus: my M.(aster) cals for him: Cotus. Exit   2657
COUETOUS = *1
*a Vice in him: You must in no way say he is co-|uetous.   43
COUETS = 1
The common Muck of the World: he couets lesse   1342
COULD l.*33 129 212 319 680 *934 937 1092 1566 1577 1826 1967 *1968
    1992 2063 2441 2497 *2520 2560 *2819 2910 3063 3127 3175 3178 *3309
    3363 3569 = 23*6
COULDST l.622 = 1
COULORD = *1
*bald; but that our wits are so diuersly Coulord; and true-|ly   1406
COUNSAILD = 1
Volum. Pray be counsail'd;   2119
COUNSAILE = 1
Counsaile a'th'warre: But at his Nurses teares   3765
COUNSAILES = 1*1
*Their Counsailes, and their Cares; disgest things rightly,   158
1.Sen. So, your opinion is Auffidius, | That they of Rome are entred in
our Counsailes,   314
COUNSAILOR = 1
The Counsailor Heart, the Arme our Souldier,   119
COUNSELL = 1
Corio. Who euer gaue that Counsell, to giue forth   1808
COUNTENANCE = 1*1
*halfe an houre together: ha's such a confirm'd coun-|tenance.   422
He wadg'd me with his Countenance, as if | I had bin Mercenary.   3693
COUNTENANCES = 1
All to the Senate-house: some newes is comming | That turnes their
Countenances.   2965
COUNTERFET = *1
*off to them most counterfetly, that is sir, I will counter-|fet   1491
COUNTERFETLY = *1
*off to them most counterfetly, that is sir, I will counter-|fet   1491

COUNTERPOIZE = 1
Doth more then counterpoize a full third part   3743
COUNTER-POYSD = 1
Be singly counter-poys'd. At sixteene yeeres,   1301
COUNTER-SEALD = 1
On like conditions, will haue Counter-seal'd.   3565
COUNTREY = 8*6
*content to say it was for his Countrey, he did it to please   39
*had rather had eleuen dye Nobly for their Countrey, then | one
voluptuously surfet out of Action.   385
Induc'd as you haue beene, that's for my Countrey: 767
*2.*Off.* Hee hath deserued worthily of his Countrey,   1227
Thus stood for his Countrey. Therefore please you,   1248
*1. You haue deserued Nobly of your Countrey, and   1479
*1. You haue receyued many wounds for your Coun- | trey.   1497
His Marks of Merit, Wounds receiu'd for's Countrey.   1562
How youngly he began to serue his Countrey,   1639
And what is left, to loose it by his Countrey,   2039
As Enemy to the people, and his Countrey.   2405
*Opposer *Coriolanus* being now in no request of his coun- | trey.   2604
Against my Cankred Countrey, with the Spleene   2748
For mercy to his Countrey: therefore let's hence,   3233
COUNTRIE = 1
The Countrie our deere Nurse, or else thy person   3465
COUNTRIES = 8*2
And that his Countries deerer then himselfe,   691
I got them in my Countries Seruice, when   1441
*Mene. Be that you seeme, truly your Countries friend,   1933
My Countries good, with a respect more tender,   2398
Drawne Tunnes of Blood out of thy Countries brest,   2756
*Thy Countries strength and weaknesse, thine own waies   2799
Would be your Countries Pleader, your good tongue   3190
His Countries Bowels out; and to poore we   3458
Triumphantly treade on thy Countries ruine,   3471
No more infected with my Countries loue   3737
COUNTRIMEN = 1*1
Men. What work's my Countrimen in hand?   56
*Rome, and thy petitionary Countrimen. The good   3311
COUNTRY *see also* countrie = 11*1
*2.*Cit.* Consider you what Seruices he ha's done for his | Country?   31
As for my Country, I haue shed my blood,   1768
By many an Ounce) he dropp'd it for his Country: 2038
When he did loue his Country, it honour'd him.   2044
Sicin. I would he had continued to his Country   2540
He does faire Iustice: if he giue me way, | Ile do his Country Seruice.
Exit.   2651
Shed for my thanklesse Country, are requitted: 2727
*Of shame seene through thy Country, speed thee straight   2744
Alas! how can we, for our Country pray?   3462
Our comfort in the Country. We must finde   3466
March to assault thy Country, then to treade   3478
Destroy'd his Country, and his name remaines   3504
COUNTRYMAN = 1
More then the instant Armie we can make | Might stop our
Countryman.   3191
COURAGE = 2
Nor checke my Courage for what they can giue,   2376

COURAGE *cont.*
   Where is your ancient Courage? You were vs'd   2439
COURSE = 4
   Against the Roman State, whose course will on   70
   Thy exercise hath bin too violent, | For a second course of Fight.   587
   1.*Sen.* Noble Tribunes, | It is the humane way: the other course   2069
   With thee awhile: Determine on some course   2474
COURT = 1
   Euen to the Court, the Heart, to th'seate o'th'Braine,   143
COURTEOUS = *1
   *hauing beene supple and courteous to the People, Bon-|netted,   1229
COURTESIE *see also* curtesie = 1
   The Senates Courtesie? Let deeds expresse   1829
COURTS = 1
   I'th'field proue flatterers, let Courts and Cities be   799
COUSIN *see* cosine
COWARD = 1
   And by his rare example made the Coward   1318
COWARDLY = 3
   Yet are they passing Cowardly. But I beseech you,   215
   Nor Cowardly in retyre: Beleeue me Sirs,   606
   But like Beasts, and Cowardly Nobles,   3044
COWARDS = 1
   Come on you Cowards, you were got in feare   395
COXCOMBES = 1
   Which will not proue a whip: As many Coxcombes   3060
COYD = 1
   The way into his mercy: Nay, if he coy'd   3157
CRAB-TREES = 1
   Some old Crab-trees here at home,   1098
CRACKD = 2
   At a crack'd Drachme: Cushions, Leaden Spoones,   576
   Corio. This last old man, | Whom with a crack'd heart I haue sent to
   Rome,   3355
CRACKE = 1
   Val. Indeed la, tis a Noble childe. | *Virg.* A Cracke Madam.   430
CRACKING = 1
   The way it takes: cracking ten thousand Curbes   71
CRAFT = 1
   True Sword to Sword: Ile potche at him some way, | Or Wrath, or Craft
   may get him.   873
CRAFTED = 1
   You and your Crafts, you haue crafted faire.   3038
CRAFTS = 1
   You and your Crafts, you haue crafted faire.   3038
CRAMMD = *1
   *yet. Suffer vs to famish, and their Store-houses cramm'd   81
CRANKES = 1
   And through the Crankes and Offices of man,   144
CRAUE = 3
   Then craue the higher, which first we do deserue.   1505
   My Nobler friends, I craue their pardons: 1755
   I may be heard, I would craue a word or two,   2018
CRAUES = 1*1
   The violent fit a'th'time craues it as Physicke   2125
   *When most strooke home, being gentle wounded, craues   2444

CREATED = 1
To call them Wollen Vassailes, things created 2094
CREEPING = 1
*growne from Man to Dragon: He has wings, hee's more | then a
creeping thing. 3582
CREPT = 1
Were slyly crept into his humane powers, 1139
CREST = 1*1
To vnder-crest your good Addition, | To th'fairenesse of my power. 828
*3 But when they shall see sir, his Crest vp againe, and 2869
CRIE = 1
Into a rapture lets her Baby crie, 1125
CRIED see cry'd
CRIES see also cryes = 1
Great Nature cries, Deny not. Let the Volces 3382
CRIMINALL = 1
Euen this so criminall, and in such capitall kinde 2363
CROOKED = *1
*aduersly, I make a crooked face at it, I can say, your 952
CROSSE = 1
Ere they lack'd power to crosse you. 2110
CROWES = 2*1
Breake ope the Lockes a'th'Senate, and bring in | The Crowes to pecke
the Eagles. 1835
3 Where's that? | Corio. I'th City of Kites and crowes. 2695
*3 I'th City of Kites and Crowes? What an Asse it is, 2697
CROWND = 2
The Kingly crown'd head, the vigilant eye, 118
Enter Cominius the Generall, and Titus Latius: be-|tweene them
Coriolanus, crown'd with an Oaken 1060
CROWNE = 1
Mene. Now the Gods Crowne thee. 1086
CRUELL = 1*1
*like to finde fame: To a cruell Warre I sent him, from 374
Com. Too modest are you: | More cruell to your good report, then
gratefull 809
CRUELLER = *1
*more long in Spectatorship, and crueller in suffering, be-|hold 3302
CRUELTY = 1
The Cruelty and Enuy of the people, 2731
CRUSH = 2
I thought to crush him in an equall Force, 872
When he hath power to crush? Why, had your Bodyes 1606
CRUTCH = 1
Tit. No Caius Martius, | Ile leane vpon one Crutch, and fight with
tother, 265
CRY see also crie = 11*2
You cry against the Noble Senate, who 197
Will then cry out of Martius: Oh, if he | Had borne the businesse. 299
A long flourish. They all cry, Martius, Martius, 794
No Heart among you? Or had you Tongues, to cry 1607
The People cry you mockt them: and of late, 1726
*Me. Do not cry hauocke, where you shold but hunt | With modest
warrant, 2006
If I say Fine, cry Fine; if Death, cry Death, 2278
Bru. And when such time they haue begun to cry, 2282
*Corio. You common cry of Curs, whose breath I hate, 2408

CRY *cont*.
   Mene. You haue made good worke | You and your cry. Shal's to the
   Capitoll?   3074
   Giue the All-haile to thee, and cry be Blest   3496
   Cry welcome Ladies, welcome.   3646
CRYD = 1
   He cry'd to me: I saw him Prisoner: 843
CRYES = 1
   Was tim'd with dying Cryes: alone he entred   1324
CRYING = 1
   Then when these Fellowes ran about the streets, | Crying Confusion.   2926
CUBBORDING = 1
   Still cubbording the Viand, neuer bearing   102
CUCKOLDS = 1
   *be a Rauisher, so it cannot be denied, but peace is a great | maker of
   Cuckolds.   2885
CUDGELL = *1
   *a Cudgell, and yet my minde gaue me, his cloathes made | a false
   report of him.   2811
CUMALIJS = 1
   Exeunt Coriolanus, Cominius, with Cumalijs.   2424
CUNNING = 1
   A Noble cunning. You were vs'd to load me   2445
CUP = *1
   *one that loues a cup of hot Wine, with not a drop of alay- | ing   944
CURBE = 1
   To curbe the will of the Nobilitie: 1722
CURBES = 1
   The way it takes: cracking ten thousand Curbes   71
CURDIED = 1
   That's curdied by the Frost, from purest Snow,   3418
CURE = 2
   Leaue vs to cure this Cause.   1958
   Mortall, to cut it off: to cure it, easie.   2034
CURRE = 1
   Must giue this Curre the Lye: and his owne Notion,   3777
CURRENT = 1
   To say, hee'l turne your Current in a ditch,   1790
CURRES = *1
   *Beneath abhorring. What would you haue, you Curres,   179
CURS = *1
   *Corio. You common cry of Curs, whose breath I hate,   2408
CURSE = 4
   When you curse them, as Enemies.   79
   And curse that Iustice did it. Who deserues Greatnes,   187
   A Curse begin at very root on's heart,   1094
   Corio. Saw you *Auffidius*? | *Latius*. On safegard he came to me, and did
   curse   1683
CURSES *see also* cursses = 2
   Be Curses to your selues. You should haue said,   1586
   Whose repetition will be dogg'd with Curses: 3501
CURSING = 2
   *Alarum, the Romans are beat back to their Trenches | Enter Martius
   Cursing*.   523
   Beating your Officers, cursing your selues,   2360

CURSSES = 1
  But to confirme my Cursses. Could I meete 'em   2560
CURTESIE = 1
  Shew'd thy deere Mother any curtesie,   3518
CURTSIE = 1
  What is that Curt'sie worth? Or those Doues eyes,   3376
CUSHION = 2*1
  *honourable a graue, as to stuffe a Botchers Cushion, or to   983
  From th'Caske to th'Cushion: but commanding peace   3134
  Volum. Oh stand vp blest! | Whil'st with no softer Cushion then the
  Flint   3402
CUSHIONS = 3
  At a crack'd Drachme: Cushions, Leaden Spoones,   576
  Enter two Officers, to lay Cushions, as it were, | *in the Capitoll.*   1203
  Let them haue Cushions by you. You are Plebeians,   1795
CUSTOMARIE = 1
  *of your voices, that I may bee Consull, I haue heere the | Customarie
  Gowne.   1477
CUSTOME = 7
  Their rotten Priuiledge, and Custome 'gainst   882
  Corio. I doe beseech you, | Let me o're-leape that custome: for I cannot   1355
  Pray you goe fit you to the Custome,   1363
  Their needlesse Vouches: Custome calls me too't.   1508
  What Custome wills in all things, should we doo't?   1509
  Scicin. The Custome of Request you haue discharg'd: 1536
  I would be Consull, sayes he: aged Custome,   1568
CUT = 5*1
  Sicin. He's a Disease that must be cut away.   2032
  Mortall, to cut it off: to cure it, easie.   2034
  Which not to cut, would shew thee but a Foole,   2754
  *Newes is, our Generall is cut i'th'middle, & but one halfe   2857
  Corio. Cut me to peeces Volces men and Lads,   3782
  That he is thus cut off. Please it your Honours   3818
CYPRUS = *1
  Auf. I am attended at the Cyprus groue. I pray you   890
DAILY *see also* dayly = *2
  *repeale daily any wholsome Act established against   83
  *the rich, and prouide more piercing Statutes daily, to   84
DAM = 1
  In Ioues owne Booke, like an vnnaturall Dam | Should now eate vp her
  owne.   2030
DAMASKE = 1
  Commit the Warre of White and Damaske   1135
DAMES = 1
  To winne a vulgar station: our veyl'd Dames   1134
DANCE = 1*1
  *Make our eies flow with ioy, harts dance with comforts,   3454
  Make the Sunne dance. Hearke you. *A shout within*   3624
DANCES = 1
  Thou Noble thing, more dances my rapt heart,   2774
DANGER = 3*1
  *stirre, was pleas'd to let him seeke danger, where he was   373
  Were but one danger, and to keepe him heere   2024
  Wherein you wisht vs parties: Wee'l deliuer you | Of your great danger.   3664
  Prouok'd by him, you cannot) the great danger   3816

DANGEROUS = 5*1
   *Then dangerous to me: To *Auffidious* thus, I will appear | (and fight.   592
   Brut. It will be dangerous to goe on--- No further.   1706
   Your dangerous Lenity: If you are Learn'd,   1793
   To iumpe a Body with a dangerous Physicke,   1853
   Not what is dangerous present, but the losse | Of what is past.   2171
   Thy dangerous Stoutnesse: for I mocke at death   2236
DANGEROUSLY = 1
   Most dangerously you haue with him preuail'd,   3546
DANGERS = 1
   The extreme Dangers, and the droppes of Blood   2726
DARE = 5
   And Balmes applyed to you, yet dare I neuer   682
   (Which I dare vouch, is more then that he hath   2037
   The Volces dare breake with vs.   2952
   For I dare so farre free him, made him fear'd,   3138
   Corio. I dare be sworne you were: 3553
DARES = 1
   Lar. Oh Noble Fellow! | Who sensibly out-dares his sencelesse Sword,   554
DARKE = 1
   Death, that darke Spirit, in's neruie Arme doth lye,   1057
DARKEN = 1
   To kindle their dry Stubble: and their Blaze | Shall darken him for euer.   1186
DARKNED = 1
   And you are darkned in this action Sir, | Euen by your owne.   3095
DARST = 1
   Thou dar'st not this, and that to proue more Fortunes   2750
DARTS = 1
   Filling the aire with Swords aduanc'd) and Darts,   678
DASTARD = 1
   Permitted by our dastard Nobles, who   2732
DAUGHTER = 2*2
   Volum. I pray you daughter sing, or expresse your selfe   362
   *thee Daughter, I sprang not more in ioy at first hearing   376
   Still to remember wrongs? Daughter, speake you: 3512
   He kill'd my Sonne, my daughter, he kill'd my Cosine   3794
DAUGHTERS = 1*2
   That *Ancus Martius*, *Numaes* Daughters Sonne: 1642
   Com. You haue holp to rauish your owne daughters, &   2996
   *daughters, or with the palsied intercession of such a de- | cay'd   3280
DAWES = 1
   then thou dwel'st with Dawes too?   2698
DAY = 6*5
   *for a day of Kings entreaties, a Mother should not sel him   369
   Val. My Ladies both good day to you. | *Vol*. Sweet Madam.   411
   As merry, as when our Nuptiall day was done, | And Tapers burnt to
   Bedward.   642
   *to a second day of Audience. When you are hearing a   968
   But with a graine a day, I would not buy   2374
   But once a day, it would vnclogge my heart | Of what lyes heauy too't.   2561
   Rom. The day serues well for them now. I haue heard   2600
   *3 To morrow, to day, presently, you shall haue the   2873
   *as day do's night: It's sprightly walking, audible, and full   2880
   A merrier day did neuer yet greet Rome,   3613
   A Sea and Land full: you haue pray'd well to day: 3629

DAYES = 4

Had circumuention: 'tis not foure dayes gone 320
Com. If I should tell thee o're this thy dayes Worke, 748
And strucke him on his Knee: in that dayes feates, 1309
*state to finde you out there. You haue well saued mee a | dayes iourney. 2581

DAYLY = 1

Which out of dayly Fortune euer taints 3129

DEAD = 3

As the dead Carkasses of vnburied men, 2410
And wak'd halfe dead with nothing. Worthy *Martius*, 2784
Exeunt bearing the Body of Martius. A dead March | Sounded. 3837

DEADLY = *1

*that say you are reuerend graue men, yet they lye deadly, 956

DEAFE = *1

*deafe, sleepe, insensible, a getter of more bastard Chil- | dren, then warres a destroyer of men. 2882

DEALE = *1

*of Occasion, will rob you of a great deale of Patience: 926

DEARE *see also* deere = 2

That weep'st to see me triumph? Ah my deare, 1083
I carried from thee deare; and my true Lippe 3396

DEARELY *see* deerely
DEARER *see* deerer
DEAREST *see* deerest

DEARTH = 3

Your suffering in this dearth, you may as well 68
Appeare in your impediment. For the Dearth, 73
Whether for East or West: the Dearth is great, 324

DEATH *see also* sdeath = 19*1

Condemning some to death, and some to exile, 646
If any thinke, braue death out-weighes bad life, 690
And tent themselues with death: of all the Horses, 783
Death, that darke Spirit, in's neruie Arme doth lye, 1057
That's sure of death without it: at once plucke out 1854
Scici. This deserues Death. 1919
We were elected theirs, *Martius* is worthy | Of present Death. 1923
He heard the Name of Death. *A Noise within.* 1988
Our certaine death: therefore it is decreed, 2025
What ha's he done to Rome, that's worthy death? 2035
Death on the Wheele, or at wilde Horses heeles, 2085
Thy dangerous Stoutnesse: for I mocke at death 2236
For death, for fine, or Banishment, then let them 2277
If I say Fine, cry Fine; if Death, cry Death, 2278
Deserues th'extreamest death. 2364
Let them pronounce the steepe Tarpeian death, 2372
I had fear'd death, of all the Men i'th'World 2738
*thou stand'st not i'th state of hanging, or of some death 3301
They'l giue him death by Inches. 3608

DEATHS = 2

And fell below his Stem: his Sword, Deaths stampe, 1321
Within thine eyes sate twenty thousand deaths 2350

DEBASE = 1

They gaue vs our demands. Thus we debase 1832

DEBILE = 1
My Nose that bled, or foyl'd some debile Wretch,   804
DECAY = 1
Coine words till their decay, against those Meazels   1770
DECAYD = *1
*daughters, or with the palsied intercession of such a de-|cay'd   3280
DECEIUD = *1
*such weake breath as this? No, you are deceiu'd, therfore   3283
DECLINES = 2
Who thriues, & who declines: Side factions, & giue out   205
Which being aduanc'd, declines, and then men dye.   1058
DECREED = 1
Our certaine death: therefore it is decreed,   2025
DECREES = 1
Mar. As with a man busied about Decrees: 645
DEED = 1*1
*without any further deed, to haue them at all into   1230
2.*Lord*. Thou hast done a deed, whereat | Valour will weepe.   .   3810
DEEDE = 1
You haue done a braue deede: Ere you go, heare this: 2550
DEEDS = 6*3
*now wee'l shew em in deeds: they say poore Suters haue   61
Thou't not beleeue thy deeds: but Ile report it,   749
action out-done his former deeds doubly.   1033
Com. I shall lacke voyce: the deeds of *Coriolanus*   1296
Then Miserie it selfe would giue, rewards his deeds   1343
*his wounds, and tell vs his deeds, we are to put our ton-|gues   1393
*vs his Noble deeds, we must also tell him our Noble ac-|ceptance   1395
That as his worthy deeds did clayme no lesse   1587
The Senates Courtesie? Let deeds expresse   1829
DEED-ATCHIEUING = 1
And by deed-atchieuing Honor newly nam'd,   1078
DEEPE = 2
Fall deepe in loue with thee, and her great charmes   594
Of thy deepe duty, more impression shew | Then that of common
Sonnes.   3400
DEEPEST = 1
And with the deepest malice of the Warre,   2943
DEERE = 5*3
*But they thinke we are too deere, the leannesse   21
*and none lesse deere then thine, and my good *Martius*, I   384
My deere Wiues estimate, her wombes encrease,   2400
*Some tricke not worth an Egge, shall grow deere friends   2647
In a most deere particular. He call'd me Father: 3154
And hangs on *Dians* Temple: Deere *Valeria*.   3419
The Countrie our deere Nurse, or else thy person   3465
Shew'd thy deere Mother any curtesie,   3518
DEERELY = 1
Sicin. He lou'd his Mother deerely.   3584
DEERER = 1*1
And that his Countries deerer then himselfe,   691
*my sworne Brother the people to earne a deerer estima-|tion   1487
DEEREST = 1
Come my sweet wife, my deerest Mother, and   2489
DEFECTIUE = 1
Rather our states defectiue for requitall,   1258

DEFENCE = 2
the Defence of a Towne, our Generall is excellent. 2830
Is all the Policy, Strength, and Defence 3051
DEFEND = 1*1
*Mar. Fiue Tribunes to defend their vulgar wisdoms 229
You make strong partie, or defend your selfe 2198
DEFENDER = *1
*when you haue pusht out your gates, the very Defender 3276
DEFENDERS = 1
To banish your Defenders, till at length 2416
DEFYING = 1
Opposing Lawes with stroakes, and heere defying 2361
DEGREE = 1
But tell the Traitor in the highest degree 3751
DEGREES = *1
*and his assent is not by such easie degrees as those, who 1228
DEITY = 1
Made by some other Deity then Nature, 3007
DELAY = 1
And that you not delay the present (but 677
DELIBERATE = 1
Your most graue Belly was deliberate, 135
DELIUER = 8
But and't please you deliuer. 97
Men. Though all at once, cannot | See what I do deliuer out to each, 150
Be free, as is the Winde: deliuer him, Titus. 849
Still your owne Foes) deliuer you 2419
Deliuer them this Paper: hauing read it, 3651
Wherein you wisht vs parties: Wee'l deliuer you | Of your great danger. 3664
Then shame to th'Romaines. And we heere deliuer 3746
To call me to your Senate, Ile deliuer 3819
DELIUERD = 2*1
Sould. 'Twill be deliuer'd backe on good Condition. 860
*Worshippes haue deliuer'd the matter well, when I finde 953
More fearfull is deliuer'd. 2972
DELIUERS = 1
Virg. The sorrow that deliuers vs thus chang'd, | Makes you thinke so. 3388
DEMAND = 2
Corio. Tush, tush. | Mene. A good demand. 2141
Sicin. I do demand, | If you submit you to the peoples voices, 2317
DEMANDS = 1
They gaue vs our demands. Thus we debase 1832
DEMERITS = 1
Opinion that so stickes on Martius, shall | Of his demerits rob Cominius. 302
DENIALS = 1
Be held by you denials. Do not bid me 3436
DENIED see also denyed = *1
*be a Rauisher, so it cannot be denied, but peace is a great | maker of
Cuckolds. 2885
DENY see also deny't = 6
Deny your asking, take your choice of those | That best can aydę your
action. 683
*1.Cit. Once if he do require our voyces, wee ought | not to deny him. 1388
3.Cit. Hee's not confirm'd, we may deny him yet. 1612
2.Cit. And will deny him: 1613
Great Nature cries, Deny not. Let the Volces 3382
Which you deny already: yet we will aske, 3444

DENYD = 1
Scicin. Haue you, ere now, deny'd the asker: 1609
DENYED = *1
*this Varlet heere: This, who like a blocke hath denyed | my accesse to
thee. 3313
DENYT = 1
Then thou hast to deny't. Come, let vs go: 3534
DEPENDING = 1
On whom depending, their obedience failes 1866
DEPENDS = 1
Which would encrease his euill. He that depends 190
DEPOPULATE = *1
*That would depopulate the city, & be euery man himself 1995
DESCENDED = 1
Scicin. One thus descended, | That hath beside well in his person
wrought, 1648
DESERT = 2
Corio. Mine owne desert. 1457
2 *Cit.* Your owne desert. 1458
DESERUD = 5*1
Deseru'd this so dishonor'd Rub, layd falsely | I'th' plaine Way of his
Merit. 1748
Giue him deseru'd vexation. Let a guard | Attend vs through the City. 2430
Corio. I haue deseru'd no better entertainment, in be-|ing *Coriolanus.*
Enter second Seruant. 2664
As those should do that had deseru'd his hate, 3033
If he could burne vs all into one coale, | We haue deseru'd it. 3063
Auff. I haue not deseru'd it. 3722
DESERUE = 6*1
*wagging of your Beards, and your Beards deserue not so 982
Then craue the higher, which first we do deserue. 1505
Brut. We pray the Gods, he may deserue your loues. 1555
Let me deserue so ill as you, and make me | Your fellow Tribune. 1737
Did not deserue Corne gratis. Being i'th'Warre, 1822
Deserue such pitty of him, as the Wolfe 3030
Come enter with vs: Ladies you deserue 3566
DESERUED = 2*2
2.Off. Hee hath deserued worthily of his Countrey, 1227
*1. You haue deserued Nobly of your Countrey, and 1479
you haue not deserued Nobly. 1480
Towards her deserued Children, is enroll'd 2029
DESERUES = 4
And curse that Iustice did it. Who deserues Greatnes, 187
Deserues your Hate: and your Affections are 188
Scici. This deserues Death. 1919
Deserues th'extreamest death. 2364
DESERUING = 1
Com. You shall not be the Graue of your deseruing, 770
DESIGNE = 1
Of our designe. He beares himselfe more proudlier, 3099
DESIGNEMENTS = 1
My best and freshest men, seru'd his designements 3688
DESIRE = 7*1
And the desire of the Nobles. 1164
Most reuerend and graue Elders, to desire 1249
You must desire them to thinke vpon you. 1445
Corio. I, but mine owne desire. 1459

DESIRE *cont.*

3 *Cit*. How not your owne desire?	1460
Corio. No Sir, 'twas neuer my desire yet to trouble the | poore with begging.	1461
Let me desire your company: he must come,	2080
Wherein I seeme vnnaturall: Desire not t'allay	3439

DESIRERS = *1

*bountifull to the desirers: Therefore beseech you, I may | be Consull.	1493

DESIRES = 3

A sickmans Appetite; who desires most that	189
Say yea to thy desires. A thousand welcomes,	2804
In all his owne desires: Nay, let him choose	3686

DESPAIRE *see* dispaire

DESPERATION = 1

As if he were his Officer: Desperation,	3050

DESPIGHT = 2

Corio. Thou wretch, despight ore-whelme thee:	1864
As he hath follow'd you, with all despight	2429

DESPISE = 1

The Tongues o'th' Common Mouth. I do despise them:	1701

DESPISING = 1

That wonne you without blowes, despising	2421

DESTINIE = 1

With shunlesse destinie: aydelesse came off,	1326

DESTROY = 3

To fright them, ere destroy. But come in,	2802
Destroy, what lies before'em.	2944
To saue the Romanes, thereby to destroy	3490

DESTROYD = 1

Destroy'd his Country, and his name remaines	3504

DESTROYER = 1

*deafe, sleepe, insensible, a getter of more bastard Chil-|dren, then warres a destroyer of men.	2882

DESTRUCTION = 2

Scicin. It shall be to him then, as our good wills; a | sure destruction.	1168
Beare him toth' Rock Tarpeian, and from thence | Into destruction cast him.	1926

DETECT = 1

The happy man; whether detect of iudgement,	3130

DETERMIND = 1

Menen. Hauing determin'd of the Volces,	1244

DETERMINE = 3

Must all determine heere?	2316
With thee awhile: Determine on some course	2474
These warres determine: If I cannot perswade thee,	3475

DEUCALION = *1

*worth all your predecessors, since *Deucalion*, though per-|aduenture	986

DEUILL *see* diuell

DEUISE = 3

Did see, and heare, deuise, instruct, walke, feele,	104
Senat. He cannot but with measure fit the Honors | which we deuise him.	1338
Com. Ile follow thee a Moneth, deuise with thee	2478

DEUOTION = *1

*deuotion, then they can render it him; and leaues nothing	1222

DEUOUR = *1
  Men. I, to deuour him, as the hungry Plebeians would | the Noble
  Martius.   906
DEUOURD = 1
  Haue all forsooke me, hath deuour'd the rest: 2733
DEUOURE = *1
  Bru. The present Warres deuoure him, he is growne | Too proud to be
  so valiant.   287
DEWES = 1*1
  *parts melted away with rotten Dewes, the fourth would   1418
  He watered his new Plants with dewes of Flattery,   3675
DIANS = 1
  And hangs on *Dians* Temple: Deere *Valeria*.   3419
DICKE = 1
  To begge of Hob and Dicke, that does appeere   1507
DICTATOR = 1
  Beyond the marke of others: our then Dictator,   1303
DID *l*.*38 *39 100 104 105 128 187 335 403 *426 *447 563 655 657 664
  819 1064 *1219 1322 1332 1369 1382 1559 1563 1587 1602 1603 1604
  1610 1628 1650 1684 1688 1819 1822 1830 2044 2099 2770 *2820 2898
  2922 *3017 3045 3068 *3069 *3070 *3084 3101 3161 3361 3489 *3585
  3613 3680 3690 3695 3787 3817 3825 = 49*13
DIE *see also* dy, dye = 1*1
  Corio. No, Ile die here: 1940
  *so slight. He that hath a will to die by himselfe, feares it   3339
DIED = *1
  Virg. But had he died in the Businesse Madame, how | then?   379
DIES *see* dyes
DIETED = 2
  As if I lou'd my little should be dieted | In prayses, sawc'st with Lyes.   807
  Till he be dieted to my request,   3215
DIFFERENCE = 2
  At difference in thee: Out of that Ile worke | My selfe a former
  Fortune.   3560
  'Twixt you there's difference: but the fall of either | Makes the Suruiuor
  heyre of all.   3669
DIFFERENCY = *1
  Mene. There is differency between a Grub & a But-|terfly,   3580
DIGEST = 1
  How shall this Bosome-multiplied, digest   1828
DIGNIFIES = 1
  And most dignifies the hauer: if it be,   1299
DIND = 2*1
  Yet cam'st thou to a Morsell of this Feast, | Hauing fully din'd before.   757
  He was not taken well, he had not din'd,   3208
  Mene. Ha's he din'd can'st thou tell? For I would not | speake with
  him, till after dinner.   3271
DINNE = 2
  When by and by the dinne of Warre gan pierce   1329
  Let them not cease, but with a dinne confus'd   2283
DINNER = 1
  Mene. Ha's he din'd can'st thou tell? For I would not | speake with
  him, till after dinner.   3271
DIRECT = 1*2
  *of one direct way, should be at once to all the points | a'th Compasse.   1409
  direct you how you shall go by him.   1434

DIRECT *cont*.

   Cit. And you. | **Corio*. Direct me, if it be your will, where great *Auf-*
   | *fidius* lies: Is he in *Antium*?   2630
DIRECTITUDE = 2

   *not (looke you sir) shew themselues (as we terme it) his | Friends,
   whilest he's in Directitude.   2866
   1 Directitude? What's that?   2868
DIRECTLY = 1 *1

   To endure Friends, that you directly set me | Against *Affidious*, and his
   Antiats,   675
   *1 He was too hard for him directly, to say the Troth   2845
DISADUANTAGE = 1

   Com. Martius, we haue at disaduantage fought,   663
DISBENCHED *see* dis-bench'd
DISCHARGD = 1

   Scicin. The Custome of Request you haue discharg'd: 1536
DISCHARGE = 1

   I shall discharge toth' Life.   2212
DISCIPLIND = 1

   Menen. Ha's he disciplin'd *Auffidius* soundly?   1023
DISCLAIM = *1

   *And straight disclaim their toungs? what are your Offices?   1717
DISCONTENTED = 2

   To'th'discontented Members, the mutinous parts   113
   But as a discontented Friend, greefe-shot | With his vnkindnesse. Say't
   be so?   3200
DISCOUER = *2

   Men. Why then you should discouer a brace of vn- | meriting,   939
   *vndone, that may fully discouer him their opposite. Now   1223
DISCOUERY = 1

   It seem'd appear'd to Rome. By the discouery,   338
DISCOURSE = *1

   *white o'th'eye to his Discourse. But the bottome of the   2856
DISCREET = 1

   You that will be lesse fearefull, then discreet,   1849
DISCRETION = 1

   For though abundantly they lacke discretion   214
DISDAINE = 3

   Aduance braue *Titus*, | They do disdaine vs much beyond our Thoughts,   518
   Which we disdaine should Tetter vs, yet sought   1771
   Whereon part do's disdaine with cause, the other   1842
DISDAINES = *1

   Sicin. Such a Nature, tickled with good successe, dis- | daines   289
DISEASE = 4

   She will but disease our better mirth.   469
   Where the Disease is violent. Lay hands vpon him,   1938
   Sicin. He's a Disease that must be cut away.   2032
   Mene. Oh he's a Limbe, that ha's but a Disease   2033
DISGEST = *1

   *Their Counsailes, and their Cares; disgest things rightly,   158
DISGRACE = 1 *1

   To fobbe off our disgrace with a tale: 96
   *And I am out, euen to a full Disgrace. Best of my Flesh,   3391
DISGUISD = 1

   Enter Coriolanus in meane Apparrell, dis- | *guisd, and muffled.*   2621
DISHONOR *see also* dis-honor = 1

   The sweet which is their poyson. Your dishonor   1856

DISHONORD = 1
　　Deseru'd this so dishonor'd Rub, layd falsely | I'th' plaine Way of his
　　Merit. 1748
DISHONORS = 1
　　Now, this no more dishonors you at all, 2157
DISHONOURD = 2
　　I am so dishonour'd, that the very houre | You take it off againe. 2338
　　To see your Wiues dishonour'd to your Noses. 2998
DISLIKES = *1
　　*is as bad, as that which he dislikes, to flatter them for | their loue. 1225
DISLODGD = 1
　　The Volcians are dislodg'd, and *Martius* gone: 3612
DISMAID = 1
　　Sicin. Go Masters get you home, be not dismaid, 3077
DISMISSE = 2*2
　　*in roaring for a Chamber-pot, dismisse the Controuersie 972
　　Will you dismisse the People? 1551
　　Brut. Dismisse them home. Here comes his Mother. 2511
　　Dismisse my Soldiers, or capitulate 3437
DISMIST = 1
　　'Twas very faintly he said Rise: dismist me 3227
DISOBEDIENCE = *1
　　*I say they norisht disobedience: fed, the ruin of the State. 1813
DISPAIRE = 1
　　Fan you into dispaire: Haue the power still 2415
DISPATCH *see also* despatch = 5
　　Sicin. Let's hence, and heare | How the dispatch is made, and in what
　　fashion 308
　　As I haue set them downe. If I do send, dispatch 715
　　Sic. Speake breefely then, | For we are peremptory to dispatch 2021
　　Like him by chance: yet giue vs our dispatch: 3537
　　To purge himselfe with words. Dispatch. 3657
DISPLACE = *1
　　Mene. If it be possible for you to displace it with your 3573
DISPLEASURE = 1*1
　　*to seeme to affect the mallice and displeasure of the Peo-|ple, 1224
　　And witnesse of the Malice and Displeasure 2729
DISPOSD = 1
　　You had not shew'd them how ye were dispos'd 2109
DISPOSING = 1
　　To faile in the disposing of those chances 3131
DISPOSITION = 2*1
　　Waue thus to expresse his disposition, | And follow *Martius*. 693
　　*knowledge he ha's in their disposition, and out of his No-|ble
　　carelesnesse lets them plainely see't. 1217
　　Away my disposition, and possesse me | Some Harlots spirit: My throat
　　of Warre be turn'd, 2219
DISPOSITIONS = 1*1
　　*Giue your dispositions the reines, and bee angry at your 927
　　With striuing lesse to be so: Lesser had bin | The things of your
　　dispositions, if 2107
DISPROPERTIED = 1
　　And dispropertied their Freedomes; holding them, 1175
DISSEMBLE = 1
　　I would dissemble with my Nature, where 2161
DISSENTION = 1
　　On a dissention of a Doit, breake out 2643

85

DISSENTIOUS = 1*1
*Mar. Thanks. What's the matter you dissentious rogues   174
Dissentious numbers pestring streets, then see   2899
DISSOLUD = 1
Mar. They are dissolu'd: Hang em;   217
DISTINCTION = 1
He throwes without distinction. Giue me leaue,   2065
DISTINCTLY = 1*1
And burie all, which yet distinctly raunges | In heapes, and piles of
Ruine.   1917
*charges distinctly billetted already in th'entertainment,   2613
DISTRESSE = 1
Vpbraid's with our distresse. But sure if you   3189
DISTRIBUTE = 1
That doth distribute it. In the name a'th'people,   2384
DISTRIBUTED = 1
Was ne're distributed. What, will he come?   2263
DISTRIBUTION = 1
Before the common distribution, | At your onely choyse.   787
DISTURBING = 1
*2 Here sir, I'de haue beaten him like a dogge, but for | disturbing the
Lords within.   2706
DIS-BENCHD = 1
Brutus. Sir, I hope my words dis-bench'd you not? | Coriol. No Sir: yet
oft,   1282
DIS-HONOR = 1
To begge of thee, it is my more dis-honor,   2233
DITCH = 1
To say, hee'l turne your Current in a ditch,   1790
DIUELL = 1
Sol. He's the diuell.   875
DIUERSLY = *1
*bald; but that our wits are so diuersly Coulord; and true- | ly   1406
DIUIDE = 1
Make good this ostentation, and you shall | Diuide in all, with vs.
Exeunt   708
DIUINE = 2
What may be sworne by, both Diuine and Humane,   1840
Should from yond clowd speake diuine things,   2762
DIUINES = 1
Which our Diuines lose by em.   1448
DIUISION = 1
*so, they are in a most warlike preparation, & hope to com | vpon
them, in the heate of their diuision   2587
DO see also doe, doo't, do't l.*60 139 141 151 153 162 193 *290 354 *414
*456 519 542 *575 660 671 715 724 *918 920 930 1386 *1388 *1391
*1392 *1411 *1456 1505 *1543 *1635 1701 1859 1863 1865 *2006 2010
2059 2091 2128 2132 2138 2163 2237 2246 2248 *2249 2299 2317 2331
2354 2359 2366 2397 2411 2459 2553 2559 2567 2652 *2677 2700 2758
2768 2840 *2841 2896 2908 2975 3022 3033 3085 3091 3092 *3146 3160
3188 3195 3196 3228 *3334 3336 *3340 3363 3392 3415 3436 3541 *3663
3667 3691 3793 = 70*21
DOE l.791 831 867 *931 *995 *1019 1107 1133 1260 *1266 1352 *1353
1355 1373 1514 1515 1534 1537 1604 1620 1702 1734 1757 1914
1921 = 20*5
DOES see also do's l.416 630 904 *1071 1507 1987 2538 2554 2651 3031
3114 3224 3533 = 12*1

DOG = *1
   *All. Against him first: He's a very dog to the Com-|monalty.   29
DOGGD = 1
   Whose repetition will be dogg'd with Curses: 3501
DOGGE = *1
   *2 Here sir, I'de haue beaten him like a dogge, but for | disturbing the
   Lords within.   2706
DOGGES = 3
   That Hunger-broke stone wals: that dogges must eate   219
   As to set Dogges on Sheepe, will be his fire   1185
   Then Dogges, that are as often beat for barking, | As therefore kept to
   doe so.   1619
DOING *see also* dooing = 4*1
   And stand vpon my common part with those, | That haue beheld the
   doing.   792
   *no, hee waued indifferently, 'twixt doing them neyther   1220
   With doing them, and is content | To spend the time, to end it.   1344
   Please you that I may passe this doing.   1359
   Vnlesse by not so doing, our good Citie | Cleaue in the midd'st, and
   perish.   2117
DOINGS = 1
   To hide your doings, and to silence that,   774
DOIT = 3
   Irons of a Doit, Dublets that Hangmen would   577
   On a dissention of a Doit, breake out   2643
   I'de not haue giuen a doit. Harke, how they ioy. | *Sound still with the
   Shouts.*   3631
DONATION = 1
   Of our so franke Donation. Well, what then?   1827
DONE *see also* done't, don't *l.**15 *31 *37 204 485 579 642 766 778 805
   1033 1278 1522 *1524 1535 1848 2035 2188 2217 2324 2456 2507 2550
   2722 3144 3541 *3591 3810 = 24*5
DONET = 1
   The worthiest men haue done't?   1437
DONT = 1
   Brut. Say you ne're had don't,   1655
DOOING *l.**933 2508 = 1*1
DOOME = 1
   And the Gods doome him after.   730
DOORE = 4
   Prythee *Virgilia* turne thy solemnesse out a doore, | And go along with
   vs.   472
   *Flourish. Alarum. A Retreat is sounded. Enter at | one Doore Cominius,
   with the Romanes: At*   744
   another Doore Martius, with his | Arme in a Scarfe.   746
   Here's no place for you: pray go to the doore? *Exit*   2663
DOORES = 3
   Virg. No (good Madam) | I will not out of doores.   434
   Val. Not out of doores? | *Volum.* She shall, she shall.   436
   Alarum, as in Battaile. | Enter Martius and Auffidius at seuerall doores.   722
DOOT = 8*2
   As he is prowd to doo't.   1153
   What Custome wills in all things, should we doo't?   1509
   Were to vs all that doo't, and suffer it   2040
   Must I then doo't to them?   2133
   A Lye, that it must beare well? I will doo't: 2207
   Corio. Well, I must doo't: 2218

DOOT *cont*.

  That hath receiu'd an Almes. I will not doo't,   2228
  *3 Doo't? he will doo't: for look you sir, he has as ma-|ny   2864
  The Tribunes cannot doo't for shame; the people   3029
DOS *l*.765 1842 2093 *2880 *3275 *3306 = 3*3
DOST *l*.2183 *2711 3510 3756 = 3*1
DOT = 1
  2 And he's as like to do't, as any man I can imagine.   2863
DOTANT = *1
  *Dotant as you seeme to be? Can you think to blow   3281
DOTE = 1
  You are three, that Rome should dote on: 1096
DOTH *l*.1057 1348 1860 1973 2384 2483 2551 *2907 3743 = 8*1
DOUBLE = 2
  Seale what I end withall. This double worship,   1841
  Whose double bosomes seemes to weare one heart,   2639
DOUBLED = 1
  His readie sence: then straight his doubled spirit   1330
DOUBLETS *see* dublets
DOUBLY = 1
  action out-done his former deeds doubly.   1033
DOUBT = 8*1
  We neuer yet made doubt but Rome was ready | To answer vs.   333
  Auf. O doubt not that, | I speake from Certainties. Nay more,   348
  *before their Citie *Carioles*, they nothing doubt preuai-|ling,   463
  (As it were sinne to doubt) that loue this painting   687
  Which (I doubt not) but our Rome | Will cast vpon thee.   1115
  Brutus. In that there's comfort. | *Scici*. Doubt not,   1147
  Then stay past doubt, for greater: 1663
  More then you doubt the change on't: That preferre   1851
  Where haue you lurk'd that you make doubt of it: 3618
DOUBTLESSE = 1
  Tit. What is become of *Martius*? | *All*. Slaine (Sir) doubtlesse.   548
DOUES = 1
  What is that Curt'sie worth? Or those Doues eyes,   3376
DOUE-COAT = 1
  That like an Eagle in a Doue-coat, I | Flatter'd your Volcians in
  Corioles.   3785
DOWN = *2
  *power. Your Lord, and *Titus Lartius*, are set down   462
  *Down Ladies: let vs shame him with him with our knees   3526
DOWNE *see also* downe-right = 21*6
  *And hewes downe Oakes, with rushes. Hang ye: trust ye?   192
  If they set downe before's: for the remoue   345
  They set them downe on two lowe stooles and sowe.   361
  See him plucke *Auffidius* downe by th'haire: 392
  Ere yet the fight be done, packe vp, downe with them.   579
  As I haue set them downe. If I do send, dispatch   715
  Menen. Pray now sit downe.   1287
  All. Downe with him, downe with him.   1891
  Mene. Downe with that Sword, Tribunes withdraw | a while.   1943
  All. Downe with him, downe with him. *Exeunt*.   1948
  Sicin. He shall be throwne downe the Tarpeian rock   1997
  Masters, lay downe your Weapons.   2074
  That the precipitation might downe stretch   2087
  Sicin. Haue you a Catalogue | *Of all the Voices that we haue procur'd,
  set downe by'th | (Pole?   2269

DOWNE *cont.*
We haue beene downe together in my sleepe, 2782
Th'one halfe of my Commission, and set downe 2797
*will mowe all downe before him, and leaue his passage | poul'd. 2861
Mene. As *Hercules* did shake downe Mellow Fruite: 3017
As you threw Caps vp, will he tumble downe, 3061
Auf. All places yeelds to him ere he sits downe, 3119
A Mile before his Tent, fall downe, and knee 3156
Set downe our Hoast. My partner in this Action, 3348
Then pitty to our Prayers. Downe: an end, 3528
The Gods looke downe, and this vnnaturall Scene 3542
And hale him vp and downe; all swearing, if 3606
DOWNE-RIGHT = 1
3.*Cit.* Certainely, he flowted vs downe-right. 1558
DOZEN = 1*1
*sincerely, had I a dozen sons each in my loue alike, 383
Of Wounds, two dozen odde: Battailes thrice six 1520
DRACHME = 1
At a crack'd Drachme: Cushions, Leaden Spoones, 576
DRAGON = 1*1
Like to a lonely Dragon, that his Fenne 2468
*growne from Man to Dragon: He has wings, hee's more | then a
creeping thing. 3582
DRAGON-LIKE = 1
Fights Dragon-like, and does atcheeue as soone 3114
DRAW = 5
And foure shall quickly draw out my Command, | Which men are best
inclin'd. 705
Since a could draw a Sword, and is ill-school'd 2063
Sicin. Draw neere ye people. 2310
As draw his Sword: yet he hath left vndone 3115
*Draw both the Conspirators, and kils Martius, who | falles, Auffidius
stands on him.* 3805
DRAWES = 1
And beare him to the Rock. *Corio. drawes his Sword.* 1939
DRAWNE = 2
And presently, when you haue drawne your number, | Repaire toth'
Capitoll. 1657
Drawne Tunnes of Blood out of thy Countries brest, 2756
DREADED = 2
Of dreaded Iustice, but on the Ministers 2383
And beate the Messenger, who bids beware | Of what is to be dreaded. 2959
DREAMT = 1
Dreamt of encounters 'twixt thy selfe and me: 2781
DREGS = *1
*Gods asswage thy wrath, and turne the dregs of it, vpon 3312
DRENCH = *1
*better report then a Horse-drench. Is he not wounded? 1015
DRIFT = 1
Sicin. We know your drift. Speake what? 2403
DRINKE = 1*1
*you *Licurgusses,*) if the drinke you giue me, touch my Pa-|lat 951
Corio. I by and by; But we will drinke together: 3562
DRIUEN = 1*1
I saw our party to their Trenches driuen, 616
*of *Auffi. Martius fights til they be driuen in breathles.* 741

DRIUES = 1
  One fire driues out one fire; one Naile, one Naile;   3145
DROOPE = 1
  Droope not, Adieu: Farewell my Wife, my Mother,   2458
DROP = 2*1
  The blood I drop, is rather Physicall   591
  *one that loues a cup of hot Wine, with not a drop of alay-|ing   944
  Haue I heard groane, and drop: Then know me not,   2626
DROPPD = 1
  By many an Ounce) he dropp'd it for his Country: 2038
DROPPES = 1
  The extreme Dangers, and the droppes of Blood   2726
DROPS = 3
  I vrg'd our old acquaintance, and the drops   3162
  At a few drops of Womens rhewme, which are   3701
  For certaine drops of Salt, your City Rome: 3761
DROUE = 1
  When with his Amazonian Shinne he droue   1305
DRUM = 1*3
  *Vol. He had rather see the swords, and heare a Drum, | then looke vpon his Schoolmaster.   418
  That's lesser then a little: *Drum a farre off.*   503
  Drum and Trumpet toward Cominius, and Caius Mar-|tius,   711
  *Drum strooke vp this afternoone: 'Tis as it were a parcel   2874
DRUMME = 3*2
  Me thinkes, I heare hither your Husbands Drumme: 391
  Enter Martius, Titus Lartius, with Drumme and Co-|lours, with Captaines and Souldiers, as   478
  Which quier'd with my Drumme into a Pipe,   2221
  Enter Coriolanus marching with Drumme, and Colours. The | Commoners being with him.   3734
  Beate thou the Drumme that it speake mournfully: 3832
DRUMMES = 4*1
  Hearke, our Drummes | *Are bringing forth our youth: Wee'l breake our Walles   504
  *Com. 'Tis not a mile: briefely we heard their drummes.   621
  From th'noise of our owne Drummes.   1443
  All. Welcome Ladies, welcome. | *A Flourish with Drummes & Trumpets.*   3647
  Drummes and Trumpets sounds, with great | showts of the people.   3705
DRUMS = 3
  Neuer sound more: when Drums and Trumpets shall   798
  Flourish. Trumpets sound, and Drums.   822
  As the recomforted through th'gates. Why harke you: | Trumpets, Hoboyes, Drums beate, altogether.   3620
DRY = 1
  To kindle their dry Stubble: and their Blaze | Shall darken him for euer.   1186
DRYES = 1
  The bloud vpon your Visage dryes, 'tis time   855
DUBLETS = 1
  Irons of a Doit, Dublets that Hangmen would   577
DULL = 1*1
  *And gladly quak'd, heare more: where the dull Tribunes,   753
  Corio. Like a dull Actor now, I haue forgot my part,   3390
DUMBE = 1
  I haue seene the dumbe men throng to see him,   1192
DURING = *1
  Brutus. Then our Office may, during his power, goe | sleepe.   1142

DURST = 1*1
  *Friends as Enemies: which Friends sir as it were, durst   2865
  And durst not once peepe out.   2949
DUST = 3
  The Dust on antique Time would lye vnswept,   1510
  And throw their power i'th'dust.   1871
  This Mould of *Martius*, they to dust should grinde it,   2209
DUTIES = *1
  Lar. So, let the Ports be guarded; keepe your Duties   714
DUTY = 3
  Of thy deepe duty, more impression shew | Then that of common
  Sonnes.   3400
  Shew duty as mistaken, all this while, | Betweene the Childe, and
  Parent.   3405
  That thou restrain'st from me the Duty, which   3524
DWELST = 2
  3 Where dwel'st thou? | *Corio.* Vnder the Canopy.   2691
  then thou dwel'st with Dawes too?   2698
DY = *1
  1.Cit. You are all resolu'd rather to dy then | to famish?   7
DYE = 6*1
  *had rather had eleuen dye Nobly for their Countrey, then | one
  voluptuously surfet out of Action.   385
  Mar. Let the first Budger dye the others Slaue,   729
  Which being aduanc'd, declines, and then men dye.   1058
  Coriol. Most sweet Voyces: | Better it is to dye, better to sterue,   1503
  And dye among our Neighbours: Nay, behold's,   3530
  Of our great Action; therefore shall he dye,   3703
  All Consp. Let him dye for't.   3792
DYES = 1
  He dyes to night.   2026
DYING = 1
  Was tim'd with dying Cryes: alone he entred   1324
EACH = 8*1
  Men. Though all at once, cannot | See what I do deliuer out to each,   150
  *sincerely, had I a dozen sons each in my loue alike,   383
  Brut. Not vnlike each way to better yours.   1735
  In Peace, what each of them by th'other loose,   2139
  More then a wilde exposture, to each chance | That starts i'th'way
  before thee.   2475
  Each word thou hast spoke, hath weeded from my heart   2760
  Vnbuckling Helmes, fisting each others Throat,   2783
  This we receiu'd, and each in either side   3495
  That Pages blush'd at him, and men of heart | Look'd wond'ring each
  at others.   3767
EAGLE = 1
  That like an Eagle in a Doue-coat, I | Flatter'd your Volcians in
  Corioles.   3785
EAGLES = 1
  Breake ope the Lockes a'th'Senate, and bring in | The Crowes to pecke
  the Eagles.   1835
EARE = 2*1
  reproofe and rebuke from euery Eare that heard it.   1236
  Menen. That's worthily | As any eare can heare. Come, let's not weepe,   2495
  *Will I lend eare to. Ha? what shout is this? *Shout within*   3366
EARES = 12*2
  Mar. Were halfe to halfe the world by th'eares, & he   254

EARES *cont*.

And carry with vs Eares and Eyes for th' time, | But Hearts for the euent.	1200
We doe request your kindest eares: and after	1260
Then on ones Eares to heare it. Proceed *Cominius*.	1295
Corio. Let them pull all about mine eares, present me	2084
More learned then the eares, wauing thy head,	2178
Corio. A name vnmusicall to the Volcians eares,	2714
*sayes, and sole the Porter of Rome Gates by th'eares. He	2860
Com. Hee'l shake your Rome about your eares.	3016
My name hath touch't your eares: it is *Menenius*.	3248
Mine eares against your suites, are stronger then	3323
Stopt your eares against the generall suite of Rome:	3352
Euen in theirs, and in the Commons eares	3653
'Fore your owne eyes, and eares?	3791

EARND = 1

Though *Martius* earn'd them not: and all his faults	305

EARNE = *1

*my sworne Brother the people to earne a deerer estima-|tion	1487

EARNEST = *1

*Val. In earnest it's true; I heard a Senatour speake it.	459

EARNESTNESSE = 2

In earnestnesse to see him: seld-showne Flamins	1132
Mes. The Nobles in great earnestnesse are going	2964

EARTH = 5

That of all things vpon the Earth, he hated	1691
As I can of those Mysteries which heauen | Will not haue earth to know.	2546
Of stronger earth then others: my Mother bowes,	3378
Leaue vnsaluted: Sinke my knee i'th'earth, *Kneeles*	3399
This Orbe o'th'earth: His last offences to vs	3798

EARTHLY = *1

*were shee Earthly, no Nobler; whither doe you follow | your Eyes so fast?	995

EASE = 1

To ease his Brest with panting. | *Menen*. Worthy man.	1336

EASIE = 3*2

If he be put vpon't, and that's as easie,	1184
*and his assent is not by such easie degrees as those, who	1228
Mortall, to cut it off: to cure it, easie.	2034
*easie groanes of old women, the Virginall Palms of your	3279
Might haue found easie Fines: But there to end	3728

EASILY = 1

Which easily endures not Article,	1598

EAST = 1*1

Whether for East or West: the Dearth is great,	324
*they would flye East, West, North, South, and their con-|sent	1408

EATE = 3*1

*chaine vp and restraine the poore. If the Warres eate vs	85
That Hunger-broke stone wals: that dogges must eate	219
As often as we eate. By th'Elements,	868
In Ioues owne Booke, like an vnnaturall Dam | Should now eate vp her owne.	2030

EATEN = 1

*2 And hee had bin Cannibally giuen, hee might haue | boyld and eaten him too.	2848

EATERS = 1
Vpon the voyce of occupation, and | The breath of Garlicke-eaters.   3014
EDGE = 1
And he shall feele mine edge.   522
EDGES = 1
Staine all your edges on me. Boy, false Hound: 3783
EDI = 1
EDICTS = *1
*with Graine: Make Edicts for Vsurie, to support Vsu-|rers;   82
EDIFICES = 1
Of these faire Edifices fore my Warres   2625
EDILE see also Edi. = 3
Enter an Edile.   2264
Enter the Edile with the Plebeians.   2309
Enter the two Tribunes, Sicinius, and Brutus, | with the Edile.   2501
EDILE = 7
EDILES = 2
Bru. The Ediles hoe: Let him be apprehended: 1875
Our Ediles smot: our selues resisted: come.   2061
EEUEN = 1
Carry his Honors eeuen: whether 'twas Pride   3128
EFFECTED = 1
He that ha's but effected his good will, | Hath ouerta'ne mine Act.   768
EGGE = *1
*Some tricke not worth an Egge, shall grow deere friends   2647
EIECT = 1
This Viporous Traitor: to eiect him hence   2023
EIES = *1
*Make our eies flow with ioy, harts dance with comforts,   3454
EIGHT = 1*1
Enter seuen or eight Citizens.   1387
*Mother now, then an eight yeare old horse. The tartnesse   3586
EITHER *see also* eyther = 6
Menen. Either you must | Confesse your selues wondrous Malicious,   88
I'th'right and strength a'th'Commons: be it either   2276
Ioyn'd in Commission with him: but either haue borne   3106
Our wish, which side should win. For either thou   3468
This we receiu'd, and each in either side   3495
'Twixt you there's difference: but the fall of either | Makes the Suruiuor
heyre of all.   3669
ELDERS = 2
Our mustie superfluity. See our best Elders.   243
Most reuerend and graue Elders, to desire   1249
ELECTED = 1
We were elected theirs, *Martius* is worthy | Of present Death.   1923
ELECTION = 3
All reuoke your ignorant election: Enforce his Pride,   1622
But that you must cast your Election on him.   1632
All. We will so: almost all repent in their election. | *Exeunt Plebeians.*   1659
ELEMENTS = 1
As often as we eate. By th'Elements,   868
ELEUEN = *1
*had rather had eleuen dye Nobly for their Countrey, then | one
voluptuously surfet out of Action.   385
ELOQUENCE = 1
Action is eloquence, and the eyes of th'ignorant   2177

ELSE = 13*1
(Vnder the Gods) keepe you in awe, which else	198
Three or foure miles about, else had I sir	626
Which without note, here's many else haue done,	805
*helpes are many, or else your actions would growe won- | drous	932
Or else it would haue gall'd his surly nature,	1597
All will be naught else.	1952
Which else would put you to your fortune, and | The hazard of much blood.	2159
I would the Gods had nothing else to do,	2559
Had we no other quarrell else to Rome, but that	2785
Com. Oh I, what else? *Exeunt both.*	3076
The action of your selfe, or else to him, had left it soly.	3107
For we haue nothing else to aske, but that	3443
The Countrie our deere Nurse, or else thy person	3465
With Manacles through our streets, or else	3470

ELSEWHERE = 1
There is a world elsewhere.	2423

EM = 12*3
*now wee'l shew em in deeds: they say poore Suters haue	61
Mar. Hang 'em: They say?	202
Mar. They are dissolu'd: Hang em;	217
*some of the best of 'em were hereditarie hang- | men.	987
Coriol. Thinke vpon me? Hang 'em,	1446
Which our Diuines lose by em.	1448
Ile leaue you: Pray you speake to em, I pray you | In wholsome manner. *Exit*	1450
All. No, no: no man saw 'em.	1564
1.Cit. I twice fiue hundred, & their friends, to piece 'em.	1615
What the vengeance, could he not speake'em faire?	1992
How you can frowne, then spend a fawne vpon'em,	2166
As 'tis to laugh at 'em. My Mother, you wot well	2465
But to confirme my Cursses. Could I meete 'em	2560
Rom. I am a Roman, and my Seruices are as you are, | against 'em. Know you me yet.	2574
Destroy, what lies before'em.	2944

EMBARQUEMENTS = 1
Embarquements all of Fury, shall lift vp	881

EMBASSES = 1
I haue yeelded too. Fresh Embasses, and Suites,	3364

EMBRAC'D = 1
2 You'l see your Rome embrac'd with fire, before | You'l speake with *Coriolanus.*	3243

EMBRACE = 1
When first I did embrace him. Yet his Nature	3101

EMBRACEMENTS = *1
*he wonne Honor, then in the embracements of his Bed,	365

EMPERICKQUTIQUE = *1
*is but Emperickqutique; and to this Preseruatiue, of no	1014

EMULATION = 2
Shooting their Emulation.	227
He's mine, or I am his: Mine Emulation	870

ENCOUNTER = 1*2
And would'st doe so, I thinke, should we encounter	867
*shall encounter such ridiculous Subiects as you are, when	980
*accidentally to encounter you. You haue ended my Bu- | sinesse,	2607

ENCOUNTERS = 1
Dreamt of encounters 'twixt thy selfe and me: 2781
ENCOUNTRING = *1
*That both our powers, with smiling Fronts encountring,   611
ENCREASE = 2*2
Which would encrease his euill. He that depends   190
My deere Wiues estimate, her wombes encrease,   2400
*This peace is nothing, but to rust Iron, encrease Taylors, | and breed
Ballad-makers.   2877
*you, bee that you are, long; and your misery encrease   3341
END = 14*3
*he did it to that end: though soft conscienc'd men can be   38
I'th'end admire: where Ladies shall be frighted,   752
From where he should begin, and end, but will | Lose those he hath
wonne.   1145
Brutus. So it must fall out | To him, or our Authorities, for an end.   1170
With doing them, and is content | To spend the time, to end it.   1344
Seale what I end withall. This double worship,   1841
A brand to th'end a'th World.   2041
Will proue to bloody: and the end of it, | Vnknowne to the Beginning.   2071
Sicin. What then? | *Virg*. When then? Hee'ld make an end of thy
posterity   2535
*Son and Heire to Mars, set at vpper end o'th'Table: No   2852
Their talke at Table, and their Thankes at end,   3094
Then seeke the end of one; thou shalt no sooner   3477
The end of Warres vncertaine: but this certaine,   3498
Then pitty to our Prayers. Downe: an end,   3528
Seducing so my Friends: and to this end,   3676
Which he did end all his; and tooke some pride   3690
Might haue found easie Fines: But there to end   3728
ENDED = *2
Vol. Hath bin; is it ended then? Our State thinks not   2586
*accidentally to encounter you. You haue ended my Bu- | sinesse,   2607
ENDS = 2
The same you are not, which for your best ends   2144
Auf. Onely their ends you haue respected,   3351
ENDUE = 1
And the Tribunes endue you with the Peoples Voyce,   1532
ENDURE = 2
To endure Friends, that you directly set me | Against *Affidious*, and his
Antiats,   675
My selfe your loyall Seruant, or endure | Your heauiest Censure.   3820
ENDURES = 1
Which easily endures not Article,   1598
ENEMIE = 5
He was your Enemie, euer spake against   1580
That hee's your fixed enemie; and reuoke | Your suddaine approbation. 1653
Follow thine Enemie in a fierie Gulfe,   2194
This Enemie Towne: Ile enter, if he slay me   2650
And more a Friend, then ere and Enemie,   2805
ENEMIES = 9*2
When you curse them, as Enemies.   79
Thou mad'st thine enemies shake, as if the World | Were Feauorous,
and did tremble.   562
Mene. Now it's twentie seuen; euery gash was an | Enemies Graue.
Hearke, the Trumpets.   1051
*1. You haue bin a scourge to her enemies, you haue   1482

ENEMIES *cont.*
Com. Stand fast, we haue as many friends as enemies.   1954
Killing our Enemies, the blood he hath lost   2036
Her Enemies markes vpon me. I do loue   2397
Your Enemies, with nodding of their Plumes   2414
*Friends as Enemies: which Friends sir as it were, durst   2865
Your Enemies and his, finde something in him.   3025
And therein shew'd like Enemies.   3034
ENEMY = 7*3
*1.*Cit*. First you know, *Caius Martius* is chiefe enemy | to the people.   10
Cominius, *Martius* your old Enemy | (Who is of Rome worse hated then
of you)   326
Mar. Say, ha's our Generall met the Enemy?   487
Enter Martius bleeding, assaulted by the Enemy.   564
Where is the enemy? Are you Lords a'th Field?   661
As Enemy to the people, and his Countrey.   2405
Edile. The peoples Enemy is gone, is gone.   2426
All. Our enemy is banish'd, he is gone: Hoo, oo.   2427
Sicin. Bid them home: say their great enemy is gone,   2509
*enemy your shield, thinke to front his reuenges with the   3278
ENFORCE *see also* inforce = 1
All reuoke your ignorant election: Enforce his Pride,   1622
ENFORCEMENT *see* inforcement
ENGINE = *1
*like an Engine, and the ground shrinkes before his Trea- | ding.   3588
ENIGMA *see* aenigma
ENIOY = 1
That all but we enioy. For how can we?   3461
ENMITIES = 1
Thine enmities most capitall: Thou barr'st vs   3459
ENMITY = 1
To bitterest Enmity: So fellest Foes,   2644
ENORMITY = *1
Men. In what enormity is *Martius* poore in, that you | two haue not in
abundance?   913
ENOUGH = 6*5
*1 *Cit*. He's one honest enough, wold al the rest wer so.   55
*Below their cobled Shooes. They say ther's grain enough?   208
Sicin. *Menenius*, you are knowne well enough too.   942
*of my Microcosme, followes it that I am knowne well e- | nough   958
*gleane out of this Charracter, if I be knowne well e- | nough too.   960
Bru. Come sir come, we know you well enough.   962
Mene. Come enough.   1837
Bru. Enough, with ouer measure. | *Corio*. No, take more.   1838
Bru. Has said enough.   1861
Vol. You might haue beene enough the man you are,   2106
*3 I do not say thwacke our Generall, but he was al- | wayes good
enough for him   2841
ENQUIRE = 1
To where you are bound, you must enquire your way,   1741
ENRAGD = *1
*whether his fall enrag'd him, or how 'twas, hee did so set   426
ENROLLD = 1
Towards her deserued Children, is enroll'd   2029
ENSHELLED *see* in-shell'd
ENSUING *see* insuing

ENTANGLED *see* intangled
ENTER = 92*4

ENTER *cont.*

Enter a rabble of Plebeians with the Aediles.	1886
Enter Brutus and Sicinius with the rabble againe.	1993
Enter Coriolanus with Nobles.	2083
Enter Volumnia.	2090
Enter Menenius with the Senators.	2113
Then flatter him in a Bower. *Enter Cominius.*	2195
Enter Sicinius and Brutus.	2258
Enter an Edile.	2264
Enter Coriolanus, Menenius, and Comi-|nius, with others.	2296
Enter the Edile with the Plebeians.	2309
To enter our Rome gates. I'th'Peoples name, | I say it shall bee so.	2389
*Enter Coriolanus, Volumnia, Virgilia, Menenius, Cominius, | with the yong Nobility of Rome.	2435
Enter the two Tribunes, Sicinius, and Brutus, | with the Edile.	2501
Enter Volumnia, Virgilia, and Menenius.	2512
Enter a Roman, and a Volce.	2570
Enter Coriolanus in meane Apparrell, dis-|guisd, and muffled.	2621
Enter a Citizen.	2629
This Enemie Towne: Ile enter, if he slay me	2650
Musicke playes. Enter a Seruingman.	2653
Enter another Seruingman.	2656
Enter Coriolanus.	2658
Enter the first Seruingman.	2661
*Corio. I haue deseru'd no better entertainment, in be-|ing *Coriolanus.*	
Enter second Seruant.	2664
Enter 3 Seruingman, the 1 meets him.	2673
Enter Auffidius with the Seruingman.	2704
Enter two of the Seruingmen.	2808
Enter the third Seruingman.	2832
Enter the two Tribunes, Sicinius, and Brutus.	2892
Enter Menenius.	2902
Enter three or foure Citizens.	2914
Enter an Aedile.	2938
Enter a Messenger.	2963
Enter Messenger.	2986
Enter Cominius.	2993
Enter a Troope of Citizens.	3053
Enter Auffidius with his Lieutenant.	3090
Enter Menenius, Cominius, Sicinius, Brutus, | the two Tribunes, with others.	3150
Enter Menenius to the Watch or Guard.	3235
Enter Coriolanus with Auffidius.	3295
Enter Coriolanus and Auffidius.	3346
Enter Virgilia, Volumnia, Valeria, yong Martius, | with Attendants.	3369
Come enter with vs: Ladies you deserue	3566
Enter Menenius and Sicinius.	3570
Enter a Messenger.	3603
Enter another Messenger.	3609
Mes. Almost at point to enter.	3637
Enter two Senators, with Ladies, passing ouer | the Stage, with other Lords.	3639
Enter Tullus Auffidius, with Attendants.	3649
Enter 3 or 4 Conspirators of Auffidius Faction. | Most Welcome.	3658
Enter the Lords of the City.	3720
*Enter Coriolanus marching with Drumme, and Colours. The | Commoners being with him.	3734

ENTERD = 1*1
   The City Ports by this hath enter'd, and   3655
   *1.*Con.* Your Natiue Towne you enter'd like a Poste,   3707
ENTERED *see* enter'd, entred
ENTERS = 1*1
   With them he enters: who vpon the sodaine   551
   Enters with a Lieutenant, other Souldiours, and a | Scout.   712
ENTERTAINMENT = *3
   *charges distinctly billetted already in th'entertainment,   2613
   Corio. I haue deseru'd no better entertainment, in be-|ing *Coriolanus.*
   Enter second Seruant.   2664
   Son Coriolanus, guesse but my entertainment with him: if   3300
ENTIRE *see* intire
ENTOMBD *see* intomb'd
ENTRANCE = 1
   his head, that he giues entrance to such Companions?   2667
ENTREAT = 1
   Put on the Gowne, stand naked, and entreat them   1357
ENTREATIES *see also* intreaties = *1
   *for a day of Kings entreaties, a Mother should not sel him   369
ENTREATY *see* intreaty
ENTRED = 4
   1.*Sen.* So, your opinion is *Auffidius*, | That they of Rome are entred in
   our Counsailes,   314
   Man-entred thus, he waxed like a Sea,   1313
   Was tim'd with dying Cryes: alone he entred   1324
   Are entred in the Roman Territories,   2942
ENUID = 1
   Enui'd against the people; seeking meanes   2380
ENUIED = 1
   That enuied his receite: euen so most fitly,   114
ENUY = 5
   More then thy Fame and Enuy: Fix thy foot.   728
   Inforce him with his enuy to the people,   2261
   But as I say, such as become a Soldier, | Rather then enuy you. 2333
   The Cruelty and Enuy of the people,   2731
   A roote of Ancient Enuy. If Iupiter   2761
ENUYING = 1
   I sinne in enuying his Nobility: 250
EPITOME = 1
   Volum. This is a poore Epitome of yours,   3420
EQUALL = 2
   Bru. He has no equall.   281
   I thought to crush him in an equall Force,   872
ERE = 18*2
   *gaine to them. Let vs reuenge this with our Pikes, ere   24
   Ere so preuayl'd with me; it will in time   233
   Ere stay behinde this Businesse. | *Men.* Oh true-bred.   267
   That could be brought to bodily act, ere Rome   319
   To take in many Townes, ere (almost) Rome | Should know we were
   a-foot.   340
   Ere yet the fight be done, packe vp, downe with them.   579
   Where ere we doe repose vs, we will write   831
   If ere againe I meet him beard to beard,   869
   Ere in our owne house I doe shade my Head,   1107
   Scicin. Haue you, ere now, deny'd the asker: 1609
   Ere they lack'd power to crosse you.   2110

ERE *cont.*

You haue done a braue deede: Ere you go, heare this:	2550
To fright them, ere destroy. But come in,	2802
And more a Friend, then ere and Enemie,	2805
*of their Feast, and to be executed ere they wipe their lips.	2875
When ere we come to our account.	3117
Auf. All places yeelds to him ere he sits downe,	3119
Speed how it will. I shall ere long, haue knowledge	Of my successe.	
Exit.	3220
Hath Virgin'd it ere since. You Gods, I pray,	3397
3.*Con.* Therefore at your vantage,	Ere he expresse himselfe, or moue	
the people	3713

ERRAND *see* arrant

ERROR = 1

And mountainous Error be too highly heapt,	1511

ESCAPE *see* scape

ESPECIALLY = 1*2

*2.*Cit.* Would you proceede especially against *Caius*	*Martius*.	27
Bru. He's poore in no one fault, but stor'd withall.	*Sicin*. Especially in	
Pride.	915
*little finger, there is some hope the Ladies of Rome, espe-|cially	3574

ESTABLISHD = *1

Brut. By the consent of all, we were establish'd the	Peoples	
Magistrates.	1911

ESTABLISHED = *1

*repeale daily any wholsome Act established against	83

ESTATE = *1

Menen. A Letter for me? it giues me an Estate of se-|uen	1011

ESTIMATE = 1

My deere Wiues estimate, her wombes encrease,	2400

ESTIMATION = 1*4

*saying, *Martius* is proud: who in a cheape estimation, is	985
*their estimation, and report: but hee hath so planted his	1231
*my sworne Brother the people to earne a deerer estima-|tion	1487
He would vse me with estimation.	3288
*you shall know now that I am in estimation: you shall	3298

ETERNITY = 1

*finisht with his bidding. He wants nothing of a God but	Eternity, and	
a Heauen to Throne in.	3592

EUADE = 1

Tyrannicall power: If he euade vs there,	2260

EUEN *see also* eeuen, eu'n = 17*2

*his Mother, and to be partly proud, which he is, euen to	the altitude	
of his vertue.	40
Which ne're came from the Lungs, but euen thus:	110
That enuied his receite: euen so most fitly,	114
Euen to the Court, the Heart, to th'seate o'th'Braine,	143
Euen to *Calues* wish, not fierce and terrible	559
Euen like a fawning Grey-hound in the Leash,	To let him slip at will.	649
At home, vpon my Brothers Guard, euen there	884
Euen when the Nauell of the State was touch'd,	1820
Menen. This but done,	Euen as she speakes, why their hearts were	
yours:	2188
Euen this so criminall, and in such capitall kinde	2363
Should say be good to Rome, they charg'd him, euen	3032
And you are darkned in this action Sir,	Euen by your owne.	3095
Euen to my person, then I thought he would	3100

EUEN *cont*.

Euen with the same austerity and garbe,	3135
*And I am out, euen to a full Disgrace. Best of my Flesh,	3391
Volum. Euen he, your wife, this Ladie, and my selfe, | Are Sutors to you.	3431
Euen in theirs, and in the Commons eares	3653
Auf. Euen so, as with a man by his owne Almes im- | poyson'd, and with his Charity slaine.	3661
With bloody passage led your Warres, euen to	3741

EUENT = 1

And carry with vs Eares and Eyes for th' time, | But Hearts for the euent.	1200

EUER = 22*6

Of more strong linke assunder, then can euer	72
2.*Cit*. We haue euer your good word.	177
Sicin. Was euer man so proud as is this *Martius*?	280
What euer haue bin thought one in this State	318
'Tis sworne betweene vs, we shall euer strike	353
Marcus Caius Coriolanus. Beare th'addition Nobly euer?	821
Com. Euer right. | *Cor*. *Menenius*, euer, euer.	1103
To kindle their dry Stubble: and their Blaze | Shall darken him for euer.	1186
He was your Enemie, euer spake against	1580
Suffer't, and liue with such as cannot rule, | Nor euer will be ruled.	1723
Then euer frown'd in Greece. By Ioue himselfe,	1801
Corio. Who euer gaue that Counsell, to giue forth	1808
And being angry, does forget that euer	1987
Euer to conquer, and to haue his worth	2291
And loose aduantage, which doth euer coole | Ith'absence of the needer.	2483
Volum. Moe Noble blowes, then euer y wise words.	2530
*and to plucke from them their Tribunes for euer.	2593
*1 A strange one as euer I look'd on: I cannot get him	2675
Since I haue euer followed thee with hate,	2755
As euer in Ambitious strength, I did	2770
*2 Come we are fellowes and friends: he was euer too	2843
*home, I euer said we were i'th wrong, when we banish'd | him.	3082
Which out of dayly Fortune euer taints	3129
For I haue euer verified my Friends,	3255
Pardon me Lords, 'tis the first time that euer	3775
As the most Noble Coarse, that euer Herald | Did follow to his Vrne.	3824

EUERIE = *1

*He's to make his requests by particulars, wherein euerie	1431

EUERY = 8*3

With euery Minute you do change a Minde,	193
Virg. Giue me excuse good Madame, I will obey you | in euery thing heereafter.	466
More then I know the sound of *Martius* Tongue | From euery meaner man.	635
Mene. Now it's twentie seuen; euery gash was an | Enemies Graue. Hearke, the Trumpets.	1051
*2.*Off*. Three, they say: but 'tis thought of euery one,	1207
reproofe and rebuke from euery Eare that heard it.	1236
He was a thing of Blood, whose euery motion	1323
*That would depopulate the city, & be euery man himself	1995
Let euery feeble Rumor shake your hearts:	2413
From these old armes and legges, by the good Gods | I'ld with thee, euery foot.	2498

EUERY *cont.*
   Like a great Sea-marke standing euery flaw, | And sauing those that eye
   thee.   3427
EUERYONE *see* euerie, euery
EUERYTHING *see* euery
EUIDENT = 2
   Hath not a Tombe so euident as a Chaire | T'extoll what it hath done.   3143
   An euident Calamity, though we had   3467
EUILL = 1
   Which would encrease his euill. He that depends   190
EUN = 1
   (Eu'n from this instant) banish him our Citie   2386
EUNUCH = 1
   Small as an Eunuch, or the Virgin voyce   2222
EXAMINE = 1
   And you the mutinous Members: For examine   157
EXAMPLE = 1
   And by his rare example made the Coward   1318
EXAMPLES = 1
   And three examples of the like, hath beene   2955
EXCEED = 2
   Will or exceed the Common, or be caught   2470
   Whom you haue banish'd, does exceed you all.   2554
EXCEEDE = 1
   As farre as doth the Capitoll exceede   2551
EXCEEDS = *1
   *1 Let me haue Warre say I, it exceeds peace as farre   2879
EXCELLENT = 1*1
   Val. In truth la go with me, and Ile tell you excellent | newes of your
   Husband.   453
   the Defence of a Towne, our Generall is excellent.   2830
EXCUSE = 2*1
   Virg. Giue me excuse good Madame, I will obey you | in euery thing
   heereafter.   466
   In that's no Changeling, and I must excuse | What cannot be amended. 3102
   There was a yeelding; this admits no excuse.   3732
EXECUTED = *1
   *of their Feast, and to be executed ere they wipe their lips.   2875
EXECUTION = 3*1
   Scicin. I wish no better, then haue him hold that pur-|pose, and to put
   it in execution.   1165
   Inforce the present Execution | Of what we chance to Sentence.   2284
   *backe to Rome, and prepare for your execution: you are   3284
   *is no hope in't, our throats are sentenc'd, and stay vppon | execution. 3576
EXERCISE = 2
   Thy exercise hath bin too violent, | For a second course of Fight.   587
   Whose Houres, whose Bed, whose Meale and Exercise   2640
EXEUNT = 33*2
   Your valour puts well forth: Pray follow. *Exeunt*.   278
   Bru. Let's along. *Exeunt*   312
   All. Farewell. *Exeunt omnes*.   359
   Val. Well, then farewell. *Exeunt Ladies*.   477
   3.Rom. A Murrain on't, I tooke this for Siluer. *Exeunt*.   572
   Where they shall know our minde. Away. *Exeunt*   602
   Make good this ostentation, and you shall | Diuide in all, with vs.
   Exeunt   708
   It should be lookt too: come. *Exeunt*.   856

EXEUNT *cont.*

Com. On, to the Capitall. *Flourish. Cornets.* | *Exeunt in State, as before.*	1120
Scicin. Haue with you. *Exeunt.*	1202
Flourish Cornets. | *Then Exeunt. Manet Sicinius and Brutus.*	1378
Exeunt. Enter two other Citizens.	1475
Scicin. Fare you well. *Exeunt Coriol. and Mene.*	1547
All. We will so: almost all repent in their election. | *Exeunt Plebeians.*	1659
Which we haue goaded on-ward. *Exeunt.*	1670
All. Downe with him, downe with him. *Exeunt.*	1948
Com. Nay, come away. *Exeunt Coriolanus and* | *Cominius.*	1980
Sena. Pray you let's to him. *Exeunt Omnes.*	2082
Corio. Well mildely be it then, Mildely. *Exeunt.*	2257
Exeunt Coriolanus, Cominius, with Cumalijs.	2424
The Gods preserue our Noble Tribunes, come. *Exeunt.*	2433
Corio. Giue me thy hand, come. *Exeunt*	2500
In Anger, *Iuno*-like: Come, come, come. *Exeunt*	2568
Rom. Well, let vs go together. *Exeunt.*	2620
Yet *Martius* that was much. Your hand: most welcome. | *Exeunt*	2806
cheape as Volcians. They are rising, they are rising. | *Both.* In, in, in, in. *Exeunt*	2890
Both Tri. Farewell, farewell. *Exeunt Citizens*	2924
Com. Oh I, what else? *Exeunt both.*	3076
Sicin. Pray let's go. *Exeunt Tribunes.*	3089
*Thou art poor'st of all; then shortly art thou mine. *Exeunt*	3148
And with our faire intreaties hast them on. *Exeunt*	3234
Auffid. You keepe a constant temper. *Exeunt*	3329
Could not haue made this peace. *Exeunt.*	3569
Sicin. Wee'l meet them, and helpe the ioy. *Exeunt.*	3638
Exeunt bearing the Body of Martius. A dead March | *Sounded.*	3837

EXILE = 5

Condemning some to death, and some to exile,	646
Vagabond exile, Fleaing, pent to linger	2373
At *Coriolanus* Exile. Now he's comming,	3058
Long as my Exile, sweet as my Reuenge!	3394
We haue led since thy Exile. Thinke with thy selfe,	3451

EXIT = 12*4

We are fit to bid her welcome. *Exit Gent.*	406
*Our Guider come, to th'Roman Campe conduct vs. *Exit*	721
To heare my Nothings monster'd. *Exit Coriolanus*	1290
Ile leaue you: Pray you speake to em, I pray you | In wholsome manner. *Exit*	1450
Volum. Do your will. *Exit Volumnia*	2248
With one that wants her Wits. *Exit Tribunes.*	2557
Mene. Fie, fie, fie. *Exit.*	2569
Corio. Thanke you sir, farewell. *Exit Citizen*	2637
He does faire Iustice: if he giue me way, | Ile do his Country Seruice. *Exit.*	2651
2 Ser. Where's *Cotus*: my M.(aster) cals for him: *Cotus. Exit*	2657
Here's no place for you: pray go to the doore? *Exit*	2663
2 And I shall. *Exit second Seruingman.*	2690
2 Cit. So did we all. But come, let's home. *Exit Cit.*	3084
Speed how it will. I shall ere long, haue knowledge | Of my successe. *Exit.*	3220
*with your age. I say to you, as I was said to, Away. *Exit*	3342
The Oake not to be winde-shaken. *Exit Watch.*	3345

EXPECTED = 1

When it was lesse expected. He replyed	3172

EXPEDITION = *1
Volum. Hee had, before this last Expedition, twentie | fiue Wounds
vpon him.   1049
EXPELL = 1
To expell him thence. I thinke hee'l be to Rome   3124
EXPERIENCD = 1
As best thou art experienc'd, since thou know'st   2798
EXPOSTURE = 1
More then a wilde exposture, to each chance | That starts i'th'way
before thee.   2475
EXPRESSE = 3*1
Volum. I pray you daughter sing, or expresse your selfe   362
Waue thus to expresse his disposition, | And follow *Martius*.   693
The Senates Courtesie? Let deeds expresse   1829
3.*Con*. Therefore at your vantage, | Ere he expresse himselfe, or moue
the people   3713
EXPULSION = 1
No, not th'expulsion of the *Tarquins*.   .   3614
EXTOLL = 2
My Mother, who ha's a Charter to extoll her Bloud,   764
Hath not a Tombe so euident as a Chaire | T'extoll what it hath done.   3143
EXTREAMEST = 1
Deserues th'extreamest death.   2364
EXTREAMITIES = 1
To say, Extreamities was the trier of spirits,   2440
EXTREME = 1
The extreme Dangers, and the droppes of Blood   2726
EXTREMITIES = 1
But when extremities speake. I haue heard you say,   2136
EXTREMITY = 1
Hoop'd out of Rome. Now this extremity,   2735
EYE = 5*2
The Kingly crown'd head, the vigilant eye,   118
Clambring the Walls to eye him: 1128
*white o'th'eye to his Discourse. But the bottome of the   2856
To th'vulgar eye, that he beares all things fairely: 3112
Com. I tell you, he doe's sit in Gold, his eye   3224
Like a great Sea-marke standing euery flaw, | And sauing those that eye
thee.   3427
*He is able to pierce a Corslet with his eye: Talkes   3589
EYES *see also* eies = 11*4
Bru. Mark'd you his lip and eyes. | *Sicin*. Nay, but his taunts.   283
*your eyes toward the Napes of your neckes, and make   935
*were shee Earthly, no Nobler; whither doe you follow | your Eyes so
fast?   995
Such eyes the Widowes in Carioles were,   1084
And carry with vs Eares and Eyes for th' time, | But Hearts for the
euent.   1200
*Honors in their Eyes, and his actions in their Hearts, that   1232
Action is eloquence, and the eyes of th'ignorant   2177
Within thine eyes sate twenty thousand deaths   2350
*And venomous to thine eyes. My (sometime) Generall,   2461
*2 *Ser*. Whence are you sir? Ha's the Porter his eyes in   2666
Go whip him fore the peoples eyes: His raising, | Nothing but his
report.   2968
What is that Curt'sie worth? Or those Doues eyes,   3376
Corio. These eyes are not the same I wore in Rome.   3387

EYES *cont.*

Mine eyes to sweat compassion. But (good sir)	3555
'Fore your owne eyes, and eares?	3791

EYTHER = 2

Scicin. Why eyther were you ignorant to see't?	1574
Eyther his gracious Promise, which you might	1595

FABRICK = 1

Against a falling Fabrick. Will you hence,	1972

FABRICKE = 1

In this our Fabricke, if that they---	122

FACD = 1

Made all of false-fac'd soothing:	800

FACE = 6*4

Shalt see me once more strike at *Tullus* face.	263
And when my Face is faire, you shall perceiue	825
*aduersly, I make a crooked face at it, I can say, your	952
Where it did marke, it tooke from face to foot:	1322
Thou hast a Grim apparance, and thy Face	2717
*2 Nay, I knew by his face that there was some-thing	2815
*in him. He had sir, a kinde of face me thought, I cannot	2816
That should consume it, I haue not the face	3036
Requires nor Childe, nor womans face to see: | I haue sate too long.	3486
*of his face, sowres ripe Grapes. When he walks, he moues	3587

FACES = 2*2

All hurt behinde, backes red, and faces pale	532
*that tell you haue good faces, if you see this in the Map	957
*pinch'd with the Collike, you make faces like Mum-|mers,	970
Corio. Bid them wash their Faces,	1453

FACTION = 1

Enter 3 *or* 4 *Conspirators of Auffidius Faction.* | Most Welcome.	3658

FACTIONARY = 1

always factionary on the party of your Generall.	3267

FACTIONS = 1

Who thriues, & who declines: Side factions, & giue out	205

FAILE = 2*1

To faile in the disposing of those chances	3131
*Rights by rights fouler, strengths by strengths do faile.	3146
That if you faile in our request, the blame	3445

FAILES = 1

On whom depending, their obedience failes	1866

FAINTLY = 1

'Twas very faintly he said Rise: dismist me	3227

FAINT-PULING = 1

Leaue this faint-puling, and lament as I do,	2567

FAIRE = 13*2

Lar. Now the faire Goddesse Fortune,	593
And when my Face is faire, you shall perceiue	825
*How now (my as faire as Noble) Ladyes, and the Moone	994
Corio. On faire ground, I could beat fortie of them.	1967
What the vengeance, could he not speake'em faire?	1992
Menen. Noble Lady, | Come goe with vs, speake faire: you may salue so,	2169
By calmenesse, or by absence: all's in anger. | *Menen.* Onely faire speech.	2199
Their mercie, at the price of one faire word,	2375
Of these faire Edifices fore my Warres	2625

FAIRE *cont.*

He does faire Iustice: if he giue me way, | Ile do his Country Seruice.
Exit. 2651

*You haue made faire worke I feare me: pray your newes, 3004

You haue made faire worke. 3018

To say, beseech you cease. You haue made faire hands, 3037

You and your Crafts, you haue crafted faire. 3038

And with our faire intreaties hast them on. *Exeunt* 3234

FAIRELY = 1

To th'vulgar eye, that he beares all things fairely: 3112

FAIRENESSE = 1

To vnder-crest your good Addition, | To th'fairenesse of my power. 828

FAITH = 4*3

*What are you sowing heere? A fine spotte in good | faith. How does
your little Sonne? 415

Yet by the faith of men, we haue 1097

*2.*Off.* 'Faith, there hath beene many great men that 1211

*2 Faith looke you, one cannot tell how to say that: for 2829

Omnes. Faith, we heare fearfull Newes. 3065

Mene. Good faith Ile proue him, 3219

*1 Faith Sir, if you had told as many lies in his behalfe, 3262

FALL = 7*1

*whether his fall enrag'd him, or how 'twas, hee did so set 426

Fall deepe in loue with thee, and her great charmes 594

Brutus. So it must fall out | To him, or our Authorities, for an end. 1170

If, as his nature is, he fall in rage 1664

Scicin. Stop, or all will fall in broyle. 1714

A Mile before his Tent, fall downe, and knee 3156

'Twixt you there's difference: but the fall of either | Makes the Suruiuor
heyre of all. 3669

And Ile renew me in his fall. But hearke. 3704

FALLES = 1

*Draw both the Conspirators, and kils Martius, who | falles, Auffidius
stands on him.* 3805

FALLING = 1

Against a falling Fabrick. Will you hence, 1972

FALNE = *1

*shee's falne out with her Husband. Your Noble *Tullus* 2602

FALSE = 3

False to my Nature? Rather say, I play | The man I am. 2100

*a Cudgell, and yet my minde gaue me, his cloathes made | a false
report of him. 2811

Staine all your edges on me. Boy, false Hound: 3783

FALSELY = 1

Deseru'd this so dishonor'd Rub, layd falsely | I'th' plaine Way of his
Merit. 1748

FALSE-FACD = 1

Made all of false-fac'd soothing: 800

FAME = 6*1

Bru. Fame, at the which he aymes, 293

*like to finde fame: To a cruell Warre I sent him, from 374

More then thy Fame and Enuy: Fix thy foot. 728

With Fame, a Name to *Martius Caius:* 1066

His Fame vnparalell'd, happely amplified: 3254

In mine owne person: holpe to reape the Fame 3689

The man is Noble, and his Fame folds in 3797

FAMILIAR = 1
  In Volcean brests. That we haue beene familiar,   3320
FAMISH = 1*1
  *1.*Cit*. You are all resolu'd rather to dy then | to famish?   7
  *yet. Suffer vs to famish, and their Store-houses cramm'd   81
FAMOUSLIE = *1
  *1.*Cit*. I say vnto you, what he hath done Famouslie,   37
FAN = 1
  Fan you into dispaire: Haue the power still   2415
FANCIE = 1
  And the Buildings of my Fancie: 1113
FANE *see* phane
FARE = 4
  Fare you well then. Come good sweet Ladie.   471
  My worke hath yet not warm'd me. Fare you well: 590
  Scicin. Fare you well. *Exeunt Coriol. and Mene*.   1547
  Corio. Fare ye well: | Thou hast yeares vpon thee, and thou art too full   2485
FAREWELL = 11
  1.*Sen*. Farewell.   357
  2.*Sen*. Farewell.   358
  All. Farewell. *Exeunt omnes*.   359
  Val. Well, then farewell. *Exeunt Ladies*.   477
  Mar. Thy Friend no lesse, | Then those she placeth highest: So farewell.   597
  Droope not, Adieu: Farewell my Wife, my Mother,   2458
  Bid me farewell, and smile. I pray you come: 2491
  Corio. Thanke you sir, farewell. *Exit Citizen*   2637
  Bru. Farewell kinde Neighbours: | We wisht *Coriolanus* had lou'd you as
  we did.   2921
  Both Tri. Farewell, farewell. *Exeunt Citizens*   2924
FARRE = 10*1
  Mar. How farre off lie these Armies?   493
  That's lesser then a little: *Drum a farre off*.   503
  They'le open of themselues. Harke you, farre off | *Alarum farre off*.   508
  Alarum continues still a-farre off.   573
  And thus farre hauing stretcht it (here be with them)   2175
  Thy selfe (forsooth) hereafter theirs so farre,   2186
  As farre as doth the Capitoll exceede   2551
  The meanest house in Rome; so farre my Sonne   2552
  *1 Let me haue Warre say I, it exceeds peace as farre   2879
  For I dare so farre free him, made him fear'd,   3138
FARTHER = 2
  Farther then seene, and one infect another   528
  *them. I will make much of your voyces, and so trouble | you no
  farther.   1500
FARWEL = *1
  Corio. Come leaue your teares: a brief farwel: the beast   2437
FASHION = 2
  Sicin. Let's hence, and heare | How the dispatch is made, and in what
  fashion   308
  Which most gibingly, vngrauely, he did fashion   1628
FAST = 4*1
  If you'l stand fast, wee'l beate them to their Wiues,   536
  *were shee Earthly, no Nobler; whither doe you follow | your Eyes so
  fast?   995
  Fast Foe toth' *Plebeij*, your Voyces might   1585
  Com. Stand fast, we haue as many friends as enemies.   1954
  *Oh World, thy slippery turnes! Friends now fast sworn,   2638

FASTS = 1
Then in our Priest-like Fasts: therefore Ile watch him   3214
FATHER = 5*1
Was not a man my Father? Had'st thou Foxship   2526
In a most deere particular. He call'd me Father: 3154
*Father *Menenius* do's. O my Son, my Son! thou art pre-|paring   3306
Lou'd me, aboue the measure of a Father,   3357
The Sonne, the Husband, and the Father tearing   3457
Marcus, he kill'd my Father.   3795
FATHERS = 2*1
The Helmes o'th State; who care for you like Fathers,   78
Val. A my word the Fathers Sonne: Ile sweare 'tis a   420
Vol. One on's Fathers moods.   429
FATIGATE = 1
Requickned what in flesh was fatigate,   1331
FAULT = 4
Shall be the Generals fault, though he performe   297
Bru. He's poore in no one fault, but stor'd withall. | *Sicin*. Especially in
Pride.   915
Brut. Lay a fault on vs, your Tribunes,   1630
To Voyce him Consull. Lay the fault on vs.   1637
FAULTS = 6
he hath faults (with surplus) to tyre in repetition. | *Showts within*.   46
Though *Martius* earn'd them not: and all his faults   305
And the faults of fooles, but folly.   1102
The Consuls worthinesse, so can I name his Faults.   2011
To suffer lawfull Censure for such faults | As shall be prou'd vpon you.   2320
What faults he made before the last, I thinke   3727
FAUOUR = *1
*your Fauour is well appear'd by your Tongue. What's   2579
FAUOURD = 1
Edile. With old *Menenius*, and those Senators | That alwayes fauour'd
him.   2267
FAUOURING = *1
*Tiber in't: Said, to be something imperfect in fauou-|ring   945
FAUOURS = 1
Vpon your fauours, swimmes with finnes of Leade,   191
FAWNE = 1
How you can frowne, then spend a fawne vpon'em,   2166
FAWNING = 1
Euen like a fawning Grey-hound in the Leash, | To let him slip at will.   649
FEAR = *1
Sicin. We heare not of him, neither need we fear him,   2893
FEARD = 3
Makes fear'd, and talk'd of more then seene: your Sonne   2469
I had fear'd death, of all the Men i'th'World   2738
For I dare so farre free him, made him fear'd,   3138
FEARE = 10*2
Come on you Cowards, you were got in feare   395
Mar. They feare vs not, but issue forth their Citie.   515
With flight and agued feare, mend and charge home,   533
Wherein you see me smear'd, if any feare   688
Lieu. Feare not our care Sir.   719
We are the greater pole, and in true feare   1831
Thy Mother rather feele thy Pride, then feare   2235
*You haue made faire worke I feare me: pray your newes,   3004
Com. But I feare | They'l roare him in againe. *Tullus Affidius*,   3047

FEARE *cont.*
    This true, which they so seeme to feare. Go home, 3079
    And shew no signe of Feare. 3080
    *Constraines them weepe, and shake with feare & sorow, 3455
FEAREFULL = 3
    You that will be lesse fearefull, then discreet, 1849
    Sicin. What more fearefull? 2973
    A fearefull Army, led by *Caius Martius,* 2988
FEARES = 2*1
    1.*Senat.* No, nor a man that feares you lesse then he, 502
    Call our Cares, Feares; which will in time 1834
    *so slight. He that hath a will to die by himselfe, feares it 3339
FEARFULL = 2
    More fearfull is deliuer'd. 2972
    Omnes. Faith, we heare fearfull Newes. 3065
FEARING = 1
    Not fearing outward force: So shall my Lungs 1769
FEAST = 2*1
    Yet cam'st thou to a Morsell of this Feast, | Hauing fully din'd before. 757
    The Feast smels well: but I appeare not like a Guest. 2660
    *of their Feast, and to be executed ere they wipe their lips. 2875
FEASTS = 1
    Cit. He is, and Feasts the Nobles of the State, at his | house this night. 2633
FEATES = 1
    And strucke him on his Knee: in that dayes feates, 1309
FEAUOROUS = 1
    Thou mad'st thine enemies shake, as if the World | Were Feauorous,
    and did tremble. 562
FED = *1
    *I say they norisht disobedience: fed, the ruin of the State. 1813
FEEBLE = 1
    Let euery feeble Rumor shake your hearts: 2413
FEEBLING = 1
    And feebling such as stand not in their liking, 207
FEEBLY = 1
    Should not be vtter'd feebly: it is held, 1297
FEEDE = 1
    Would feede on one another? What's their seeking? 199
FEEDING = 2
    And so shall sterue with Feeding: come, let's go, 2566
    With Wine and Feeding, we haue suppler Soules 3213
FEELE = 4
    Did see, and heare, deuise, instruct, walke, feele, 104
    And he shall feele mine edge. 522
    Thy Mother rather feele thy Pride, then feare 2235
    With what he would say, let him feele your Sword: 3715
FEELES = 1
    Your ignorance (which findes not till it feeles, 2417
FELL = 2
    Vir. Heauens blesse my Lord from fell *Auffidius.* 407
    And fell below his Stem: his Sword, Deaths stampe, 1321
FELLEST = 1
    To bitterest Enmity: So fellest Foes, 2644
FELLOW = 14*4
    Men. What then? Fore me, this Fellow speakes. | What then? What
    then? 123
    Lar. Oh Noble Fellow! | Who sensibly out-dares his sencelesse Sword, 554

FELLOW *cont.*

*1.*off*. That's a braue fellow: but hee's vengeance | prowd, and loues not the common people.	1209
their Bed-fellow: Worthie *Cominius* speake.	1274
Let me deserue so ill as you, and make me | Your fellow Tribune.	1737
*3 What haue you to do here fellow? Pray you auoid | the house.	2677
Auf. Where is this Fellow?	2705
Within my Age. But reason with the fellow	2956
And this braue Fellow too: we are the Graines,	3184
Mene. I tell thee Fellow, | Thy Generall is my Louer: I haue beene	3251
Haue (almost) stampt the Leasing. Therefore Fellow,	3260
Men. Prythee fellow, remember my name is *Menenius,*	3266
Mene. Nay but Fellow, Fellow.	3294
1 A Noble Fellow I warrant him.	3343
*2 The worthy Fellow is our General. He's the Rock,	3344
This Fellow had a Volcean to his Mother:	3535
The Plebeians haue got your Fellow Tribune,	3605

FELLOWES = 4*1

Com. March on my Fellowes:	707
thinke our Fellowes are asleepe.	2655
3 What Fellowes this?	2674
*2 Come we are fellowes and friends: he was euer too	2843
Then when these Fellowes ran about the streets, | Crying Confusion.	2926

FELLOWS = *1

*which makes me sweat with wrath. Come on my fellows	520

FELLOWSHIP = 1

But kneeles, and holds vp hands for fellowship,	3532

FENNE = 1

Like to a lonely Dragon, that his Fenne	2468

FENNES = 1

As reeke a'th'rotten Fennes: whose Loues I prize,	2409

FESTER = 1

Com. Should they not: | Well might they fester 'gainst Ingratitude,	781

FETCH = 1

Let's fetch him off, or make remaine alike. | *They fight, and all enter the City.*	567

FEW = 1

At a few drops of Womens rhewme, which are	3701

FIDDIOUSD = *1

*fiddious'd, for all the Chests in Carioles, and the Gold	1028

FIE *see also* fye = 3*3

Mene. Fie, fie, fie, this is the way to kindle, not to | quench.	1906
Mene. Fie, fie, fie. *Exit.*	2569

FIELD = 7

1.*Sen.* Our Armie's in the Field:	332
Where is the enemy? Are you Lords a'th Field?	661
For a short holding, if we loose the Field,	717
The Treasure in this field atchieued, and Citie,	785
I'th'field proue flatterers, let Courts and Cities be	799
He prou'd best man i'th' field, and for his meed	1311
Both Field and Citie ours, he neuer stood	1335

FIELDED = 1

To helpe our fielded Friends. Come, blow thy blast.	498

FIENDS = 1

Of all the vnder Fiends. But if so be,	2749

FIERCE = 2

Euen to *Calues* wish, not fierce and terrible	559

FIERCE *cont.*
  Wash my fierce hand in's heart. Go you to th'Citie,   886
FIERIE = 1
  Follow thine Enemie in a fierie Gulfe,   2194
FIERY = 1
  Strike the proud Cedars 'gainst the fiery Sun: 3411
FIFES = 1
  The Trumpets, Sack-buts, Psalteries, and Fifes,   3622
FIGHT = 12*1
  Tit. No *Caius Martius,* | Ile leane vpon one Crutch, and fight with
  tother,   265
  Now put your Shields before your hearts, and fight   516
  Let's fetch him off, or make remaine alike. | *They fight, and all enter*
  the City.   567
  Ere yet the fight be done, packe vp, downe with them.   579
  Thy exercise hath bin too violent, | For a second course of Fight.   587
  *Then dangerous to me: To *Auffidious* thus, I will appear | (and fight.   592
  The rest shall beare the businesse in some other fight   703
  Mar. Ile fight with none but thee, for I do hate thee | Worse then a
  Promise-breaker.   724
  Heere they fight, and certaine Volces come in the ayde   740
  Herauld. Know Rome, that all alone *Martius* did fight   1064
  Whom with all prayse I point at, saw him fight,   1304
  As Benefits to thee. For I will fight   2747
  Boy. A shall not tread on me: Ile run away | Till I am bigger, but then
  Ile fight.   3483
FIGHTING = 1
  There's some among you haue beheld me fighting,   1941
FIGHTS = 1*1
  of Auffi. Martius fights til they be driuen in breathles.   741
  Fights Dragon-like, and does atcheeue as soone   3114
FILE = 2
  The common file, (a plague-Tribunes for them)   656
  *you are censured heere in the City, I mean of vs a'th'right | hand File,
  do you?   919
FILES = 1
  Out of my Files, his proiects, to accomplish   3687
FILL = *1
  *the yearne she spun in *Vlisses* absence, did but fill *Athica*   447
FILLD = 1
  Leades fill'd, and Ridges hors'd   1130
FILLING = 1
  Filling the aire with Swords aduanc'd) and Darts,   678
FILLOP = 1
  Fillop the Starres: Then, let the mutinous windes   3410
FIND = 1
  This Tiger-footed-rage, when it shall find   2053
FINDE = 11*4
  Touching the Weale a'th Common, you shall finde   159
  Where he should finde you Lyons, findes you Hares: 182
  Bring vp your Army: but (I thinke) you'l finde   346
  *like to finde fame: To a cruell Warre I sent him, from   374
  What good Condition can a Treatie finde   864
  My hate to *Martius.* Where I finde him, were it   883
  *Worshippes haue deliuer'd the matter well, when I finde   953
  *2. Wee hope to finde you our friend: and therefore   1495
  You finde him like a Soldier: do not take   2331

FINDE *cont*.

*state to finde you out there. You haue well saued mee a | dayes
iourney. 2581
Before you finde it other. All the Regions 3021
Your Enemies and his, finde something in him. 3025
Our comfort in the Country. We must finde 3466
shall our poore City finde: and all this is long of you. 3598
We must proceed as we do finde the People. 3667
FINDES = 2
Where he should finde you Lyons, findes you Hares: 182
Your ignorance (which findes not till it feeles, 2417
FINE = 3*1
*What are you sowing heere? A fine spotte in good | faith. How does
your little Sonne? 415
For death, for fine, or Banishment, then let them 2277
If I say Fine, cry Fine; if Death, cry Death, 2278
FINES = 1
Might haue found easie Fines: But there to end 3728
FINGER = 1*2
*as your finger, that you might leaue pricking it for 449
finger and his thumbe, as one would set vp a Top. 2814
*little finger, there is some hope the Ladies of Rome, espe- | cially 3574
FINISHT = *1
*finisht with his bidding. He wants nothing of a God but | Eternity, and
a Heauen to Throne in. 3592
FINNES = 1
Vpon your fauours, swimmes with finnes of Leade, 191
FIRE = 9*2
Then is the coale of fire vpon the Ice, 184
They'l sit by th'fire, and presume to know 203
As to set Dogges on Sheepe, will be his fire 1185
O're-borne their way, consum'd with fire, and tooke | What lay before
them. 2991
One fire driues out one fire; one Naile, one Naile; 3145
Till he had forg'd himselfe a name a'th'fire | Of burning Rome. 3166
2 You'l see your Rome embrac'd with fire, before | You'l speake with
Coriolanus. 3243
*out the intended fire, your City is ready to flame in, with 3282
*fire for vs: looke thee, heere's water to quench it. 3307
Mes. As certaine as I know the Sun is fire: 3617
FIRES = 1*2
Or by the fires of heauen, Ile leaue the Foe, 534
Corio. The fires i'th'lowest hell. Fould in the people: 2348
*And make triumphant fires, strew Flowers before them: 3643
FIRST = 20*5
*1.*Cit*. First you know, *Caius Martius* is chiefe enemy | to the people. 10
All. Against him first: He's a very dog to the Com- | monalty. 29
That I receiue the generall Food at first 138
Lead'st first to win some vantage. 168
The rabble should haue first vnroo'st the City 232
A place below the first: for what miscarries 296
*thee Daughter, I sprang not more in ioy at first hearing 376
*he was a Man-child, then now in first seeing he had pro- | ued himselfe
a man. 377
Mar. Let the first Budger dye the others Slaue, 729
*the first complaint, hasty and Tinder-like vppon, to 946
Then craue the higher, which first we do deserue. 1505

FIRST *cont.*

Corio. So then the Volces stand but as at first,	1677
Where if you bring not *Martius*, wee'l proceede | In our first way.	2077
My praises made thee first a Souldier; so	2215
Corio. First heare me speake. | *Both Tri.* Well, say: Peace hoe.	2313
Volum. My first sonne, | Whether will thou go? Take good *Cominius*	2472
Enter the first Seruingman.	2661
Contend against thy Valour. Know thou first,	2771
Then when I first my wedded Mistris saw	2775
Let me commend thee first, to those that shall	2803
When first I did embrace him. Yet his Nature	3101
By Soueraignty of Nature. First, he was	3126
The first Conditions which they did refuse,	3361
Sicin. First, the Gods blesse you for your tydings: | Next, accept my thankefulnesse.	3633
Pardon me Lords, 'tis the first time that euer	3775

FISH = 1

As is the Aspray to the Fish, who takes it	3125

FISTING = 1

Vnbuckling Helmes, fisting each others Throat,	2783

FIT = 6*1

Which you do liue vpon: and fit it is,	139
We are fit to bid her welcome. *Exit Gent.*	406
*Senat. He cannot but with measure fit the Honors | which we deuise him.	1338
Pray you goe fit you to the Custome,	1363
The violent fit a'th'time craues it as Physicke	2125
Were fit for thee to vse, as they to clayme,	2184
Com. I haue beene i'th' Market place: and Sir 'tis fit	2197

FITLY = 2

That enuied his receite: euen so most fitly,	114
Cats, that can iudge as fitly of his worth,	2545

FITNESSE = 1

Of no more Soule, nor fitnesse for the World,	1177

FITTEST = *1

*it saide, the fittest time to corrupt a mans Wife, is when	2601

FIUE = 4*2

*Mar. Fiue Tribunes to defend their vulgar wisdoms	229
I'th'part that is at mercy? fiue times, *Martius*,	865
*Volum. Hee had, before this last Expedition, twentie | fiue Wounds vpon him.	1049
Ile haue fiue hundred Voyces of that sound.	1614
*1.Cit. I twice fiue hundred, & their friends, to piece 'em.	1615
Thou hast affected the fiue straines of Honor,	3506

FIX = 1

More then thy Fame and Enuy: Fix thy foot.	728

FIXED = 1

That hee's your fixed enemie; and reuoke | Your suddaine approbation.	1653

FLAGGE = *1

*set vp the bloodie Flagge against all Patience, and	971

FLAME = *2

*would make it flame againe. For the Nobles receyue so	2590
*out the intended fire, your City is ready to flame in, with	3282

FLAMINS = 1

In earnestnesse to see him: seld-showne Flamins	1132

FLAT = 2

Sena. To vnbuild the Citie, and to lay all flat.	1908

FLAT *cont.*
  Com. That is the way to lay the Citie flat,   1915
FLATTER = 4*3
  Mar. He that will giue good words to thee, wil flatter   178
  *is as bad, as that which he dislikes, to flatter them for | their loue.   1225
  Menen. Masters of the People, | Your multiplying Spawne, how can he
  flatter?   1291
  *that I haue not bin common in my Loue, I will sir flatter   1486
  Let them regard me, as I doe not flatter,   1757
  He would not flatter *Neptune* for his Trident,   1984
  Then flatter him in a Bower. *Enter Cominius.*   2195
FLATTERD = 1*1
  *haue flatter'd the people, who ne're loued them; and there   1212
  That like an Eagle in a Doue-coat, I | Flatter'd your Volcians in
  Corioles.   3785
FLATTERERS = 2
  I'th'field proue flatterers, let Courts and Cities be   799
  Time-pleasers, flatterers, foes to Noblenesse.   1729
FLATTERY = 2
  Or neuer trust to what my Tongue can do | I'th way of Flattery further.   2246
  He watered his new Plants with dewes of Flattery,   3675
FLAW = 1
  Like a great Sea-marke standing euery flaw, | And sauing those that eye
  thee.   3427
FLEAD = 1
  Com. Whose yonder, | That doe's appeare as he were Flead? O Gods,   629
FLEAING = 1
  Vagabond exile, Fleaing, pent to linger   2373
FLED = 1
  When blowes haue made me stay, I fled from words.   1284
FLESH = 1*1
  Requickned what in flesh was fatigate,   1331
  *And I am out, euen to a full Disgrace. Best of my Flesh,   3391
FLEYED *see* flead
FLIES *see* flyes = 1
  Then Boyes pursuing Summer Butter-flies, | Or Butchers killing Flyes.   3010
FLIGHT = 1
  With flight and agued feare, mend and charge home,   533
FLINT = 1
  Volum. Oh stand vp blest! | Whil'st with no softer Cushion then the
  Flint   3402
FLOATING = 1
  Shew'd Mastership in floating. Fortunes blowes,   2443
FLONG = *1
  *And the blind to heare him speak: Matrons flong Gloues,   1193
FLOOD = 1
  Like a bold Flood o're-beate. Oh come, go in,   2789
FLOURISH = 9
  Flourish. Alarum. A Retreat is sounded. Enter at | one Doore Cominius,
  with the Romanes: At   744
  A long flourish. They all cry, Martius, Martius,   794
  Flourish. Trumpets sound, and Drums.   822
  A flourish. Cornets. Enter Tullus Auffidius | bloudie, with two or three
  Souldiors.   857
  A showt, and flourish. | *Volum.* These are the Vshers of *Martius:*   1053
  Welcome to Rome, renowned *Coriolanus.* | *Sound. Flourish.*   1068
  Com. On, to the Capitall. *Flourish. Cornets.* | *Exeunt in State, as before.*   1120

FLOURISH *cont.*
   Flourish Cornets. | Then Exeunt. Manet Sicinius and Brutus.   1378
   All. Welcome Ladies, welcome. | *A Flourish with Drummes & Trumpets.*   3647
FLOUTED *see* flowted
FLOW = *1
   *Make our eies flow with ioy, harts dance with comforts,   3454
FLOWER = *1
   Com. Flower of Warriors, how is't with *Titus Lartius?*   644
FLOWERS = *1
   *And make triumphant fires, strew Flowers before them: 3643
FLOWRE = 1
   From me do backe receiue the Flowre of all,   153
FLOWTED = 1
   3.*Cit.* Certainely, he flowted vs downe-right.   1558
FLUNG *see* flong
FLYE = 5*1
   Auf. If I flye *Martius,* hollow me like a Hare.   731
   Shall flye out of it selfe, nor sleepe, nor sanctuary,   878
   *they would flye East, West, North, South, and their con-|sent   1408
   *2.*Cit.* Thinke you so? Which way do you iudge my | wit would flye.   1411
   Auf. Do they still flye to'th'Roman?   3091
   Mes. Sir, if you'ld saue your life, flye to your House,   3604
FLYERS = 3
   Not for the flyers: Marke me, and do the like.   542
   1.*Sol.* Following the Flyers at the very heeles,   550
   I cannot speake him home: he stopt the flyers,   1317
FLYES = 1
   Then Boyes pursuing Summer Butter-flies, | Or Butchers killing Flyes.   3010
FOBBE = 1
   To fobbe off our disgrace with a tale: 96
FOE = 3
   Or by the fires of heauen, Ile leaue the Foe,   534
   Fast Foe toth' *Plebeij,* your Voyces might   1585
   A Foe to'th'publike Weale. Obey I charge thee,   1878
FOES = 3
   Time-pleasers, flatterers, foes to Noblenesse.   1729
   Still your owne Foes) deliuer you   2419
   To bitterest Enmity: So fellest Foes,   2644
FOGGE = *1
   *3 *Cit.* To loose it selfe in a Fogge, where being three   1417
FOILED *see* foyl'd
FOLD *see* fould
FOLDS = 1
   The man is Noble, and his Fame folds in   3797
FOLLOW = 10*4
   Tit. Lead you on: Follow *Cominius,* we must followe | you, right
worthy your Priority.   271
   Mar. Nay let them follow,   275
   Your valour puts well forth: Pray follow. *Exeunt.*   278
   Waue thus to expresse his disposition, | And follow *Martius.*   693
   *were shee Earthly, no Nobler; whither doe you follow | your Eyes so
fast?   995
   *with our owne tongues, therefore follow me, and Ile   1433
   And follow to thine answer.   1879
   Or what is worst will follow.   2081
   Follow thine Enemie in a fierie Gulfe,   2194
   Sicin. Go see him out at Gates, and follow him   2428

FOLLOW *cont.*

Com. Ile follow thee a Moneth, deuise with thee	2478
*Corio. Follow your Function, go, and batten on colde | bits. *Pushes him away from him.*	2686
That shapes man Better: and they follow him	3008
As the most Noble Coarse, that euer Herald | Did follow to his Vrne.	3824

FOLLOWD = 1

As he hath follow'd you, with all despight	2429

FOLLOWE = *1

*Tit. Lead you on: Follow *Cominius*, we must followe | you, right worthy your Priority.	271

FOLLOWED = 1

Since I haue euer followed thee with hate,	2755

FOLLOWER = 1

I seem'd his Follower, not Partner; and	3692

FOLLOWERS = 1

'Tis for the followers Fortune, widens them,	541

FOLLOWES = 4*1

As they vs to our Trenches followes.	537
Another Alarum, and Martius followes them to | gates, and is shut in.	538
*of my Microcosme, followes it that I am knowne well e-|nough	958
These in honor followes *Martius Caius Coriolanus.*	1067
To vnstable Slightnesse. Purpose so barr'd, it followes,	1847

FOLLOWING = 1

1.*Sol.* Following the Flyers at the very heeles,	550

FOLLY = 4

Or be accus'd of Folly. I shall tell you	90
Auf. Nor did you thinke it folly,	335
And the faults of fooles, but folly.	1102
Of noysome musty Chaffe. He said, 'twas folly	3179

FOND = 2

Tis fond to waile ineuitable strokes,	2464
When she (poor Hen) fond of no second brood,	3519

FOOD = 1

That I receiue the generall Food at first	138

FOOLE = 3*2

Volum. Away you Foole; it more becomes a man	401
For Truth to o're-peere. Rather then foole it so,	1512
Sicin. Are you mankinde? | **Volum.* I foole, is that a shame. Note but this Foole,	2524
Which not to cut, would shew thee but a Foole,	2754

FOOLERIE = 1

And Manhood is call'd Foolerie, when it stands	1971

FOOLES = 4*1

*proud, violent, testie Magistrates (alias Fooles) | as any in Rome.	940
And the faults of fooles, but folly.	1102
Be not as common Fooles; if you are not,	1794
And perish constant Fooles: who is't can blame him?	3024
2.*Con.* And patient Fooles, | Whose children he hath slaine, their base throats teare	3710

FOOLE-HARDINESSE = 1

1.*Sol.* Foole-hardinesse, not I. | 2.*Sol.* Nor I.	544

FOOLISH = 1

Like Romans, neither foolish in our stands,	605

FOORTH = 1

*Vir. No good Madam, pardon me, indeed I will not | foorth.	451

FOOT = 5
To take in many Townes, ere (almost) Rome | Should know we were
a-foot.   340
More then thy Fame and Enuy: Fix thy foot.   728
Where it did marke, it tooke from face to foot: 1322
From these old armes and legges, by the good Gods | I'ld with thee,
euery foot.   2498
and to be on foot at an houres warning.   2614
FOOTE = 3
  Menen. The seruice of the foote   2045
We haue a Power on foote: and I had purpose   2777
Vnlesse by vsing meanes I lame the foote   3098
FOOTED = 1
This Tiger-footed-rage, when it shall find   2053
FOR *see also* for's, for't, su'd-for *l.**25 26 *31 *39 67 73 78 80 *82 111 115
157 165 *200 214 *220 221 235 *282 296 324 330 345 347 *369 *385
*449 492 521 541 542 *572 588 655 656 717 724 735 767 802 803 819
835 862 871 877 888 *901 *925 929 *931 *933 *964 *972 *977 998 1007
1009 1010 *1011 *1026 *1028 *1045 1075 1149 1155 1171 1177 1179
1180 1187 1190 1200 1201 1206 *1215 *1225 *1233 1245 1248 1257 1258
1294 1302 1311 1315 1346 1356 1358 1371 *1392 *1394 *1396 *1401
*1419 *1497 1512 1518 1519 1521 1546 1571 1588 1589 1611 1619 1663
1685 1702 1728 1740 1744 1756 *1761 1768 1824 1860 1905 1959 1983
1984 2022 2038 2047 2126 2132 2144 2167 2176 2184 2190 2216 2236
2250 2277 2287 2320 2332 2337 2345 2365 2376 2378 2422 2481 *2520
2527 2531 2538 *2590 *2593 *2594 *2600 *2657 2663 2685 *2706 *2711
2727 2737 2747 2793 2825 *2829 2831 2843 2844 *2845 *2858 *2864
*2889 2919 2948 2987 3023 3029 3031 3062 3066 *3070 3088 3105 3113
3138 3169 3180 3182 3186 3197 3233 3255 *3271 *3284 *3291 *3297
*3303 *3307 3324 3325 *3334 *3337 *3338 *3340 3359 3393 3443 3447
3461 3462 3468 3472 3473 *3497 3511 3513 3532 3545 3556 *3573 *3591
3630 3633 3674 3680 3698 3700 3761 3774 3823 = 174*59
FORBAD = 1
He would not answer too: Forbad all Names,   3164
FORBID = 2
  Mene. Shall it be put to that? | *Sena.* The Gods forbid: 1955
  Menen. Now the good Gods forbid,   2027
FORCD = 1*1
  Mes. Spies of the *Volces* | Held me in chace, that I was forc'd to wheele 624
  *I was forc'd to scoul'd. Your iudgments my graue Lords   3776
FORCE = 4
I thought to crush him in an equall Force,   872
Not fearing outward force: So shall my Lungs   1769
  Corio. Why force you this?   2149
Your gates against my force. Yet for I loued thee,   3324
FORE = 5
  Men. What then? Fore me, this Fellow speakes. | What then? What
then?   123
Of these faire Edifices fore my Warres   2625
Go whip him fore the peoples eyes: His raising, | Nothing but his
report.   2968
Your Soldiers vse him as the Grace 'fore meate,   3093
'Fore your owne eyes, and eares?   3791
FORENOONE = *1
  *legges: you weare out a good wholesome Forenoone, in   965
FOREUER *see* euer

FOREHEAD *see* forhead

FORE-ADUISD = 1

Scicin. Thus to haue said, | As you were fore-aduis'd, had toucht his
Spirit,   1592

FORFETSELLER = *1

*hearing a cause betweene an Orendge wife, and a Forfet-|seller,   966

FORGD = 1

Till he had forg'd himselfe a name a'th'fire | Of burning Rome.   3166

FORGES = 1

What his Brest forges, that his Tongue must vent,   1986

FORGET = 4

Vpon their ancient mallice, will forget   1150
I would they would forget me, like the Vertues   1447
And his old Hate vnto you: besides, forget not   1623
And being angry, does forget that euer   1987

FORGETFULNESSE = 1

Ingrate forgetfulnesse shall poison rather   3321

FORGIUE = 3

To giue or to forgiue; but when we haue stufft   3211
Forgiue my Tyranny: but do not say,   3392
For that forgiue our Romanes. O a kisse   3393

FORGOT = 3

Lartius. Martius, his Name. | *Martius.* By *Iupiter* forgot: 850
Volce. It is so sir, truly I haue forgot you.   2573
Corio. Like a dull Actor now, I haue forgot my part,   3390

FORHEAD = 1*1

Then *Hectors* forhead, when it spit forth blood   404
*of the night, then with the forhead of the morning.   948

FORME = 2

Your Honor with your forme.   1365
Where he shall answer by a lawfull Forme | (In peace) to his vtmost
perill.   2067

FORMER = 4

2.*Cit.* The former Agents, if they did complaine,   128
Com. It is your former promise. | *Mar.* Sir it is,   260
action out-done his former deeds doubly.   1033
At difference in thee: Out of that Ile worke | My selfe a former
Fortune.   3560

FORMERLY = 1

But what is like me formerly.   2494

FORMOST = 2

Of this most wise Rebellion, thou goest formost: 166
My wife comes formost, then the honour'd mould   3371

FORRAINE = 1

Must as a Forraine Recreant be led   3469

FORS = 3

His Marks of Merit, Wounds receiu'd for's Countrey.   1562
Or *Ioue*, for's power to Thunder: his Heart's his Mouth: 1985
For's priuate Friends. His answer to me was   3177

FORSOOKE = 1

Haue all forsooke me, hath deuour'd the rest: 2733

FORSOOTH = 1

Thy selfe (forsooth) hereafter theirs so farre,   2186

FORSWORNE = 2

Which can make Gods forsworne? I melt, and am not   3377
The thing I haue forsworne to graunt, may neuer   3435

FORT = 5*1
*good report for't, but that hee payes himselfe with bee-|ing proud.   34
Volum. Oh, he is wounded, I thanke the Gods for't.   1018
They ne're did seruice for't; being prest to'th'Warre,   1819
Or loose mine Arme for't: Thou hast beate mee out   2779
Being banish'd for't, he came vnto my Harth,   3683
All Consp. Let him dye for't.   3792
FORTH *see also* foorth = 15*3
They said they were an hungry, sigh'd forth Prouerbes   218
Win vpon power, and throw forth greater Theames | For Insurrections
arguing.   234
Your valour puts well forth: Pray follow. *Exeunt*.   278
Some parcels of their Power are forth already,   350
With his mail'd hand, then wiping, forth he goes   397
Then *Hectors* forhead, when it spit forth blood   404
*Thus it is: the Volcies haue an Army forth, against who(m)   460
Hearke, our Drummes | *Are bringing forth our youth: Wee'l breake
our Walles   504
Mar. They feare vs not, but issue forth their Citie.   515
We render you the Tenth, to be ta'ne forth,   786
You shoot me forth in acclamations hyperbolicall,   806
Corio. Who euer gaue that Counsell, to giue forth   1808
And we of thee. So if the time thrust forth   2480
My Friends of Noble touch: when I am forth,   2490
If he had gone forth Consull, found it so.   2935
Thrusts forth his hornes againe into the world   2947
*I let forth your halfe pinte of blood. Backe, that's the vt-|most of your
hauing, backe.   3292
Virg. I, and mine, that brought you forth this boy,   3481
FORTIE = 1
Corio. On faire ground, I could beat fortie of them.   1967
FORTNIGHT = *1
*haue had inkling this fortnight what we intend to do, w   60
FORTUNATE = *1
Volce. He cannot choose: I am most fortunate, thus   2606
FORTUNE = 8
'Tis for the followers Fortune, widens them,   541
Lar. Now the faire Goddesse Fortune,   593
Patri. This man ha's marr'd his fortune.   1982
Which else would put you to your fortune, and | The hazard of much
blood.   2159
Which out of dayly Fortune euer taints   3129
I purpose not to waite on Fortune, till   3474
At difference in thee: Out of that Ile worke | My selfe a former
Fortune.   3560
Auf. Why Noble Lords, | Will you be put in minde of his blinde
Fortune,   3788
FORTUNES = 4
Your person most: That he would pawne his fortunes   1692
My Fortunes and my Friends at stake, requir'd   2162
Shew'd Mastership in floating. Fortunes blowes,   2443
Thou dar'st not this, and that to proue more Fortunes   2750
FORTY *see* fortie
FORWARD = 1
1 But when goes this forward: 2872
FOUGHT = 6*2
Com. You haue fought together?   253

119

FOUGHT *cont*.
*Com. Breath you my friends, wel fought, we are come | (off,	604
Com. Martius, we haue at disaduantage fought,	663
Mar. I do beseech you, | By all the Battailes wherein we haue fought,	671
Alone I fought in your *Corioles* walles,	733
I haue fought with thee; so often hast thou beat me:	866
*Volum. Titus Lartius writes, they fought together, but | *Auffidius* got off.	1024
When *Tarquin* made a Head for Rome, he fought	1302

FOULD = *1
*Corio. The fires i'th'lowest hell. Fould in the people:	2348

FOULER = *1
**Rights by rights fouler, strengths by strengths do faile.	3146

FOUND = 4*1
**Sonne, I therein would haue found issue. Heare me pro-|fesse	382
In our well-found Successes, to report	1251
To your remembrances: but you haue found,	1651
If he had gone forth Consull, found it so.	2935
Might haue found easie Fines: But there to end	3728

FOUNDATION = 1
To bring the Roofe to the Foundation,	1916

FOURE *see also* 4. = 5
Had circumuention: 'tis not foure dayes gone	320
Three or foure miles about, else had I sir	626
But is foure *Volces*? None of you, but is	699
And foure shall quickly draw out my Command, | Which men are best inclin'd.	705
Enter three or foure Citizens.	2914

FOURTH = 1*1
**parts melted away with rotten Dewes, the fourth would	1418
Corio. I, as an Hostler, that fourth poorest peece	2300

FOXES = 1
Where Foxes, Geese you are: No surer, no,	183

FOXSHIP = 1
Was not a man my Father? Had'st thou Foxship	2526

FOYLD = 1
My Nose that bled, or foyl'd some debile Wretch,	804

FRAGMENTS = 1
Mar. Go get you home you Fragments.	237

FRAMD = 1
Wherein this Trunke was fram'd, and in her hand	3372

FRAME = 2*2
In asking their good loues, but thou wilt frame	2185
*Com. I thinke 'twill serue, if he can thereto frame his | spirit.	2201
*Volum. Thou art my Warriour, I hope to frame thee | Do you know this Lady?	3414
Ile frame conuenient peace. Now good *Auffidius*,	3549

FRANCHISES = 1
Your Franchises, whereon you stood, confin'd | Into an Augors boare.	3001

FRANKE = 1
Of our so franke Donation. Well, what then?	1827

FREE = 6
Be free, as is the Winde: deliuer him, *Titus*.	849
Brut. Did you perceiue, | He did sollicite you in free Contempt,	1602
For they haue Pardons, being ask'd, as free, | As words to little purpose.	2190
Thou lyest vnto thee, with a voice as free, | As I do pray the Gods.	2353

FREE *cont.*
    For I dare so farre free him, made him fear'd,   3138
    But to be rough, vnswayable, and free.   3678
FREEDOME = 1
    To giue my poore Host freedome.   846
FREEDOMES = 1
    And dispropertied their Freedomes; holding them,   1175
FREELIER = *1
    *I should freelier reioyce in that absence wherein   364
FREELY = 1
    Mes. It is spoke freely out of many mouths,   2974
FRENDS = *1
    *Neuer admitted a priuat whisper, no not with such frends | That
    thought them sure of you.   3353
FRESH = 1
    I haue yeelded too. Fresh Embasses, and Suites,   3364
FRESHEST = 1
    My best and freshest men, seru'd his designements   3688
FRIEND = 7*3
    Men. Note me this good Friend;   134
    Mar. Thy Friend no lesse, | Then those she placeth highest: So farewell.   597
    *2. Wee hope to finde you our friend: and therefore   1495
    2.Cit. Therefore let him be Consull: the Gods giue him | ioy, and make
    him good friend to the People.   1526
    Mene. Be that you seeme, truly your Countries friend,   1933
    I prythee noble friend, home to thy House,   1957
    1 Ser. What would you haue Friend? whence are you?   2662
    And more a Friend, then ere and Enemie,   2805
    But as a discontented Friend, greefe-shot | With his vnkindnesse. Say't
    be so?   3200
    Sicin. Friend, art thou certaine this is true?   3615
FRIENDLINESSE = 1
    Or seeing it, of such Childish friendlinesse, | To yeeld your Voyces?   1575
FRIENDLY = 3
    And translate his Mallice towards you, into Loue, | Standing your
    friendly Lord.   1590
    And take our friendly Senators by'th'hands   2790
    Our Tradesmen singing in their shops, and going | About their
    Functions friendly.   2900
FRIENDS *see also* frends = 23*11
    Menen. Why Masters, my good Friends, mine honest   63
    Men. I tell you Friends, most charitable care   66
    True is it my Incorporate Friends (quoth he)   137
    (You my good Friends, this sayes the Belly) marke me.   148
    Sen. Your Company to'th'Capitoll, where I know | Our greatest Friends
    attend vs.   269
    To helpe our fielded Friends. Come, blow thy blast.   498
    Com. Breath you my friends, wel fought, we are come | (off,   604
    The Charges of our Friends. The Roman Gods,   609
    To endure Friends, that you directly set me | Against *Affidious*, and his
    Antiats,   675
    Sicin. Nature teaches Beasts to know their Friends.   903
    *bin a Rod to her Friends, you haue not indeede loued the | Common
    people.   1483
    1.Cit. I twice fiue hundred, & their friends, to piece 'em.   1615
    Brut. Get you hence instantly, and tell those friends,   1616
    My Nobler friends, I craue their pardons: 1755

FRIENDS *cont*.

Com. Stand fast, we haue as many friends as enemies.	1954
Honor and Policy, like vnseuer'd Friends,	2137
My Fortunes and my Friends at stake, requir'd	2162
Com. Heare me my Masters, and my common friends.	2393
My Friends of Noble touch: when I am forth,	2490
*Oh World, thy slippery turnes! Friends now fast sworn,	2638
*Some tricke not worth an Egge, shall grow deere friends	2647
*2 Come we are fellowes and friends: he was euer too	2843
*Friends as Enemies: which Friends sir as it were, durst	2865
*not (looke you sir) shew themselues (as we terme it) his | Friends, whilest he's in Directitude.	2866
Were in wilde hurry. Heere do we make his Friends	2896
*Friends: the Commonwealth doth stand, and so would | do, were he more angry at it.	2907
Doe's of the Shepheards: For his best Friends, if they	3031
For's priuate Friends. His answer to me was	3177
Mene. Good my Friends, | If you haue heard your Generall talke of Rome,	3245
And of his Friends there, it is Lots to Blankes,	3247
For I haue euer verified my Friends,	3255
Nor from the State, nor priuate friends heereafter	3365
Seducing so my Friends: and to this end,	3676

FRIGHT = 1

To fright them, ere destroy. But come in,	2802

FRIGHTED = 1

I'th'end admire: where Ladies shall be frighted,	752

FROM *l*.110 146 153 161 162 349 *370 *374 393 407 439 457 497 531 *634 636 658 702 759 818 *1005 *1031 1109 1145 1236 1284 1322 1367 1443 1594 1617 1626 1641 1784 *1888 1904 1926 2238 2243 2343 2379 2386 2388 2396 2493 2498 *2580 *2592 *2593 *2610 *2618 2687 2760 2762 2778 2787 2913 3134 3203 3240 3242 *3299 *3340 3365 3396 3418 3448 3488 3524 *3582 *3596 3822 3827 = 59*15

FRONT = *1

*enemy your shield, thinke to front his reuenges with the	3278

FRONTS = *1

*That both our powers, with smiling Fronts encountring,	611

FROST = 1

That's curdied by the Frost, from purest Snow,	3418

FROWND = 1

Then euer frown'd in Greece. By Ioue himselfe,	1801

FROWNE = 1*1

How you can frowne, then spend a fawne vpon'em,	2166
Corio. Prepare thy brow to frowne: knowst y me yet?	2720

FRUITE = *1

Mene. As *Hercules* did shake downe Mellow Fruite:	3017

FULL = 7*3

*full of Mothes. Come, I would your Cambrick were sen-|sible	448
That being past for Consull with full voyce:	2337
Corio. Fare ye well: | Thou hast yeares vpon thee, and thou art too full	2485
To be full quit of those my Banishers,	2740
*as day do's night: It's sprightly walking, audible, and full	2880
*And I am out, euen to a full Disgrace. Best of my Flesh,	3391
Which by th'interpretation of full time, | May shew like all your selfe.	3421
A City full: Of Tribunes such as you,	3628
A Sea and Land full: you haue pray'd well to day:	3629
Doth more then counterpoize a full third part	3743

FULLY = 2*1
    Yet cam'st thou to a Morsell of this Feast, | Hauing fully din'd before.   757
    *vndone, that may fully discouer him their opposite. Now   1223
    To oppose his hatred fully. Welcome home.   1698
FUNCTION = *1
    *Corio. Follow your Function, go, and batten on colde | bits. *Pushes
    him away from him.*   2686
FUNCTIONS = 1
    Our Tradesmen singing in their shops, and going | About their
    Functions friendly.   2900
FUNDAMENTALL = 1
    That loue the Fundamentall part of State   1850
FURTHER = 11*4
    1. *Citizen.* | *Before we proceed any further, heare me speake.   4
    *without any further deed, to haue them at all into   1230
    I haue no further with you. Was not this mockerie?   1573
    Scicin. Passe no further. | *Cor.* Hah? what is that?   1704
    Brut. It will be dangerous to goe on--- No further.   1706
    Where it is: not poyson any further.   1780
    And therefore Law shall scorne him further Triall   1999
    The which shall turne you to no further harme, | Then so much losse of
    time.   2019
    Least his infection being of catching nature, | Spred further.   2050
    Corio. I muse my Mother | Do's not approue me further, who was wont   2092
    Or neuer trust to what my Tongue can do | I'th way of Flattery further.   2246
    Corio. Shall I be charg'd no further then this present?   2315
    Mene. Consider further: | That when he speakes not like a Citizen,   2329
    Com. Know, I pray you. | *Corio.* Ile know no further: 2370
    Sicin. Bid them all home, he's gone: & wee'l no further,   2503
FURY = 1
    Embarquements all of Fury, shall lift vp   881
FUSTIE = 1
    That with the fustie Plebeans, hate thine Honors,   754
FYE = *1
    Val. Fye, you confine your selfe most vnreasonably: 440
GAINE = 1*1
    *gaine to them. Let vs reuenge this with our Pikes, ere   24
    *3 *Cit.* You must thinke if we giue you any thing, we | hope to gaine by
    you.   1463
GAINST = 6
    Com. Should they not: | Well might they fester 'gainst Ingratitude,   781
    If 'gainst your selfe you be incens'd, wee'le put you   812
    Their rotten Priuiledge, and Custome 'gainst   882
    In soothing them, we nourish 'gainst our Senate   1759
    Ioyn'd with *Auffidius*, leads a power 'gainst Rome,   2976
    Strike the proud Cedars 'gainst the fiery Sun: 3411
GALEN = *1
    *the Physician: The most soueraigne Prescription in *Galen*,   1013
GALLD = 1
    Or else it would haue gall'd his surly nature,   1597
GAN = 1
    When by and by the dinne of Warre gan pierce   1329
GANGREND = 1
    Being once gangren'd, is not then respected | For what before it was.   2046
GAOLER = 1
    The Gaoler to his pitty. I kneel'd before him,   3226

GAP = 1
May enter 'twixt the gap of Both, and take | The one by th'other.   1805
GARBE = 1
Euen with the same austerity and garbe,   3135
GARDANT = *1
*perceiue, that a Iacke gardant cannot office me from my   3299
GARLAND = 5
Him vilde, that was your Garland. What's the matter,   195
Weares this Warres Garland: in token of the which,   816
*Volum. On's Browes: Menenius, hee comes the third | time home with
the Oaken Garland.   1021
Garland, with Captaines and Soul-|diers, and a Herauld.   1062
He lurcht all Swords of the Garland: for this last,   1315
GARLICKE-EATERS = 1
Vpon the voyce of occupation, and | The breath of Garlicke-eaters.   3014
GARMENTS = 2
Corio. May I change these Garments? | Scicin. You may, Sir.   1541
Corio. Hence rotten thing, or I shall shake thy bones | Out of thy
Garments.   1883
GARNERS = 1
To gnaw their Garners. Worshipfull Mutiners,   277
GASH = *1
*Mene. Now it's twentie seuen; euery gash was an | Enemies Graue.
Hearke, the Trumpets.   1051
GATE = 2
The mortall Gate of th' Citie, which he painted   1325
That's yet vnbruis'd: bring me but out at gate.   2488
GATES = 12*5
Rather then they shall pound vs vp our Gates,   506
Another Alarum, and Martius followes them to | gates, and is shut in.   538
So, now the gates are ope: now proue good Seconds,   540
Clapt to their Gates, he is himselfe alone, | To answer all the City.   552
Lart. Hence; and shut your gates vpon's: 720
Within Corioles Gates: where he hath wonne,   1065
They would not thred the Gates: This kinde of Seruice   1821
To enter our Rome gates. I'th'Peoples name, | I say it shall bee so.   2389
Sicin. Go see him out at Gates, and follow him   2428
All. Come, come, lets see him out at gates, come: 2432
Whether to knocke against the Gates of Rome,   2800
*sayes, and sole the Porter of Rome Gates by th'eares. He   2860
*when you haue pusht out your gates, the very Defender   3276
*out of your Gates with sighes: and coniure thee to par-|don   3310
Your gates against my force. Yet for I loued thee,   3324
*As the recomforted through th'gates. Why harke you: | Trumpets,
Hoboyes, Drums beate, altogether.   3620
*The gates of Rome: Our spoiles we haue brought home   3742
GATI = 1
Enter the Gati.   543
GAUE = 5*1
And gaue him gracefull posture.   1140
Corio. Who euer gaue that Counsell, to giue forth   1808
They gaue vs our demands. Thus we debase   1832
*a Cudgell, and yet my minde gaue me, his cloathes made | a false
report of him.   2811
Gaue way vnto your Clusters, who did hoote | Him out o'th'Citty.   3045
Made him ioynt-seruant with me: Gaue him way   3685

GAWDED = 1
In their nicely gawded Cheekes, toth' wanton spoyle   1136
GAZE = *1
*youth with comelinesse pluck'd all gaze his way; when   368
GEESE = 2
  Where Foxes, Geese you are: No surer, no,   183
Against the Winde a mile: you soules of Geese,   529
GENERAL = *2
*Menen. I neither care for th'world, nor your General: 3337
*2 The worthy Fellow is our General. He's the Rock,   3344
GENERALL = 21*11
That I receiue the generall Food at first   138
*Cominius the Generall is gone, with one part of our Ro-|mane   461
Mar. Say, ha's our Generall met the Enemy?   487
And harke, what noyse the Generall makes: To him   580
Titus Lartius. Oh Generall: | Here is the Steed, wee the Caparison: 760
Martius. I thanke you Generall: 789
Am bound to begge of my Lord Generall.   839
*Senate ha's Letters from the Generall, wherein hee giues   1031
Enter Cominius the Generall, and Titus Latius: be-|tweene them
Coriolanus, crown'd with an Oaken   1060
Oh welcome home: and welcome Generall,   1089
The present Consull, and last Generall,   1250
Of generall Ignorance, it must omit | Reall Necessities, and giue way
the while   1845
And you, will rather shew our generall Lowts,   2165
*And venomous to thine eyes. My (sometime) Generall,   2461
the Defence of a Towne, our Generall is excellent.   2830
*3 Why here's he that was wont to thwacke our Ge-|nerall, Caius
Martius.   2838
1 Why do you say, thwacke our Generall?   2840
*3 I do not say thwacke our Generall, but he was al-|wayes good
enough for him   2841
*bald before him. Our Generall himselfe makes a Mistris   2854
*Newes is, our Generall is cut i'th'middle, & but one halfe   2857
Which was sometime his Generall: who loued him   3153
*I You may not passe, you must returne: our Generall | will no more
heare from thence.   3241
Mene. Good my Friends, | If you haue heard your Generall talke of
Rome,   3245
Mene. I tell thee Fellow, | Thy Generall is my Louer: I haue beene
alwayes factionary on the party of your Generall.   3251
    3267
Mene. I am as thy Generall is.   3274
*condemn'd, our Generall has sworne you out of repreeue | and pardon.   3285
1 Come, my Captaine knowes you not. | Mene. I meane thy Generall.   3289
*1 My Generall cares not for you. Back I say, go: least   3291
*not from another: Let your Generall do his worst. For   3340
Stopt your eares against the generall suite of Rome: 3352
1.Con. How is it with our Generall?   3660
GENERALS = 1
Shall be the Generals fault, though he performe   297
GENEROSITY = 1
To breake the heart of generosity,   224
GENT = 1
We are fit to bid her welcome. Exit Gent.   406
GENT = 1

GENTLE = 3*2
  Com. Though I could wish, | You were conducted to a gentle Bath,   680
  My gentle *Martius*, worthy *Caius*,   1077
  *of them, 'tis a condition they account gentle: & since   1488
  Then to take in a Towne with gentle words,   2158
  *When most strooke home, being gentle wounded, craues   2444
GENTLEMAN *see also Gent.* = 2*1
  Misguide thy Opposers swords, Bold Gentleman: | Prosperity be thy Page.   595
  3 What are you? | *Corio.* A Gentleman.   2680
  *3 Pray you poore Gentleman, take vp some other sta- | tion: 2684
GENTLEMEN = 1
  He did informe the truth: but for our Gentlemen,   655
GENTLER = 1
  Which you are out of, with a gentler spirit,   1742
GENTLEWOMAN see also Gent. = 2
  Enter a Gentlewoman.   387
  Enter Valeria with an Vsher, and a Gentlewoman.   410
GENTRY = 2*1
  But by the suite of the Gentry to him,   1163
  Cornets. Enter Coriolanus, Menenius, all the Gentry, | *Cominius, Titus Latius, and other Senators.*   1672
  *Insult without all reason: where Gentry, Title, wisedom   1843
GET = 9*2
  Mar. Go get you home you Fragments.   237
  True Sword to Sword: Ile potche at him some way, | Or Wrath, or Craft may get him.   873
  *returne for Conscience sake, to helpe to get thee a Wife.   1419
  Brut. Get you hence instantly, and tell those friends,   1616
  Mene. Goe, get you to our House: be gone, away.   1951
  2.*Sena.* Get you gone.   1953
  Volum. Now pray sir get you gone.   2549
  Pray get you out.   2668
  Corio. Away. | *2 Ser.* Away? Get you away.   2669
  *1 A strange one as euer I look'd on: I cannot get him   2675
  Sicin. Go Masters get you home, be not dismaid,   3077
GETTER = *1
  *deafe, sleepe, insensible, a getter of more bastard Chil- | dren, then warres a destroyer of men.   2882
GIBER *see* gyber
GIBINGLY = 1
  Which most gibingly, vngrauely, he did fashion   1628
GIDDY = 1
  To th'vtmost of a man, and giddy censure   298
GIFTS = 1
  I that now refus'd most Princely gifts,   838
GILDED = *1
  *I saw him run after a gilded Butterfly, & when   423
GILT = 1
  Then gilt his Trophe. The brests of *Hecuba*   402
GIRD = *1
  Bru. Being mou'd, he will not spare to gird the Gods.   285
GIUE *see also* giu't = 32*11
  1.Cit. Very well, and could bee content to giue him   33
  Mar. He that will giue good words to thee, wil flatter   178
  Who thriues, & who declines: Side factions, & giue out   205
  Virg. Beseech you giue me leaue to retire my selfe.   389

GIUE *cont*.
*Virg. Giue me excuse good Madame, I will obey you | in euery thing
heereafter.   466
*Lart. No, Ile nor sel, nor giue him: Lend you him I will   491
May giue you thankfull Sacrifice. Thy Newes?   612
To vs, that giue you truly: by your patience,   811
My Noble Steed, knowne to the Campe, I giue him,   817
To giue my poore Host freedome.   846
**Giue your dispositions the reines, and bee angry at your   927
**you *Licurgusses*,) if the drinke you giue me, touch my Pa-|lat   951
Herauld. Giue way there, and goe on.   1105
Which that he will giue them, make I as little question,   1152
more pertinent then the rebuke you giue it.   1272
Then Miserie it selfe would giue, rewards his deeds   1343
For my Wounds sake, to giue their sufferage: 1358
As if he did contemne what he requested, | Should be in them to giue. 1382
**3 *Cit*. Are you all resolu'd to giue your voyces? But   1422
**3 *Cit*. You must thinke if we giue you any thing, we | hope to gaine by
you.   1463
2 *Cit*. And 'twere to giue againe: but 'tis no matter.   1474
**the bewitchment of some popular man, and giue it   1492
giue you our voices heartily.   1496
Both. The Gods giue you ioy Sir heartily.   1502
*2.Cit. Therefore let him be Consull: the Gods giue him | ioy, and make
him good friend to the People.   1526
Senat. Tribunes giue way, he shall toth' Market place.   1712
Corio. Who euer gaue that Counsell, to giue forth   1808
Bru. Why shall the people giue | One that speakes thus, their voyce? 1814
Corio. Ile giue my Reasons,   1816
Of generall Ignorance, it must omit | Reall Necessities, and giue way
the while   1845
He throwes without distinction. Giue me leaue,   2065
Must I with my base Tongue giue to my Noble Heart   2206
Nor checke my Courage for what they can giue,   2376
Giue him deseru'd vexation. Let a guard | Attend vs through the City. 2430
Corio. Giue me thy hand, come. *Exeunt*   2500
He does faire Iustice: if he giue me way, | Ile do his Country Seruice.
Exit.   2651
To giue or to forgiue; but when we haue stufft   3211
Giue the All-haile to thee, and cry be Blest   3496
Like him by chance: yet giue vs our dispatch: 3537
They'l giue him death by Inches.   3608
*Mess. Sir, we haue all great cause to giue great thanks.   3635
Where he was to begin, and giue away   3729
Must giue this Curre the Lye: and his owne Notion,   3777
GIUEN = 7*2
And giuen to *Lartius* and to *Martius* Battaile: 615
When Corne was giuen them *gratis*, you repin'd,   1727
Which they haue giuen to Beggers.   1764
Giuen Hidra heere to choose an Officer, | That with his peremptory
Shall, being but   1787
Giuen Hostile strokes, and that not in the presence   2382
**2 And hee had bin Cannibally giuen, hee might haue | boyld and eaten
him too.   2848
**of them, and in a violent popular ignorance, giuen your   3277
I'de not haue giuen a doit. Harke, how they ioy. | *Sound still with the
Shouts*.   3631

GIUEN *cont*.

He ha's betray'd your businesse, and giuen vp   3760
GIUES = 1*2
    Menen. A Letter for me? it giues me an Estate of se-|uen   1011
    *Senate ha's Letters from the Generall, wherein hee giues   1031
    his head, that he giues entrance to such Companions?   2667
GIUING = 1*2
    *were a Mallice, that giuing it selfe the Lye, would plucke   1235
    *one of vs ha's a single Honor, in giuing him our own voi-|ces   1432
    With giuing him glory.   3712
GIUT = 1
    When we shall hap to giu't them.   2288
GLAD = 5*2
    Mar. I am glad on't, then we shall ha meanes to vent   242
    Vir. I am glad to see your Ladyship.   413
    That is not glad to see thee.   1095
    sir, heartily well met, and most glad of your Company.   2617
    Volce. You take my part from me sir, I haue the most | cause to be
    glad of yours.   2618
    These are a Side, that would be glad to haue   3078
    Auf. I am glad thou hast set thy mercy, & thy Honor   3559
GLADLY = *1
    *And gladly quak'd, heare more: where the dull Tribunes,   753
GLASSES = 1
    The Glasses of my sight: A Beggars Tongue   2225
GLEANE = *1
    *gleane out of this Charracter, if I be knowne well e-|nough too.   960
GLORIOUS = *1
    *thee. The glorious Gods sit in hourely Synod about thy   3304
GLORY = 2
    When he had carried Rome, and that we look'd | For no lesse Spoile,
    then Glory.   3697
    With giuing him glory.   3712
GLOUES = *1
    *And the blind to heare him speak: Matrons flong Gloues,   1193
GLOWING = *1
    *This lyes glowing I can tell you, and is almost mature for | the violent
    breaking out.   2594
GNAW = 1
    To gnaw their Garners. Worshipfull Mutiners,   277
GO *see also* goe = 45*5
    Where go you with Bats and Clubs? The matter | Speake I pray you.   57
    Mar. Go get you home you Fragments.   237
    Sicin. Besides, if things go well,   301
    *he caught it, he let it go againe, and after it againe, and o-|uer   424
    Come, you must go visit the good Lady that lies in.   441
    with my prayers: but I cannot go thither.   443
    pitie. Come you shall go with vs.   450
    Val. In truth la go with me, and Ile tell you excellent | newes of your
    Husband.   453
    Honor, and so I pray go with vs.   465
    Prythee *Virgilia* turne thy solemnesse out a doore, | And go along with
    vs.   472
    Lar. Thou worthiest *Martius*, | Go sound thy Trumpet in the Market
    place,   599
    Wash my fierce hand in's heart. Go you to th'Citie,   886
    Soul. Will not you go?   889

GO *cont.*

direct you how you shall go by him.	1434
Let the high Office and the Honor go	1513
Sicin. Go call the people, in whose name my Selfe	1876
Ile go to him, and vndertake to bring him in peace,	2066
Bru. Go not home.	2075
Before you had worne it out.	*Corio.* Let go.	2104
Corio. The word is, Mildely. Pray you let vs go,	2253
Bru. Go about it,	Put him to Choller straite, he hath bene vs'd	2289
Sicin. Go see him out at Gates, and follow him	2428
Beleeu't not lightly, though I go alone	2467
Volum. My first sonne,	Whether will thou go? Take good *Cominius*	2472
Of the warres surfets, to go roue with one	2487
Brut. Pray let's go.	2548
You haue done a braue deede: Ere you go, heare this:	2550
And so shall sterue with Feeding: come, let's go,	2566
Rom. Well, let vs go together. *Exeunt.*	2620
Here's no place for you: pray go to the doore? *Exit*	2663
Corio. Follow your Function, go, and batten on colde	bits. *Pushes him away from him.*	2686
Like a bold Flood o're-beate. Oh come, go in,	2789
*the intreaty and graunt of the whole Table. Hee'l go he	2859
Bru. Go see this Rumorer whipt, it cannot be,	2951
Go whip him fore the peoples eyes: His raising,	Nothing but his report.	2968
Sicin. Go Masters get you home, be not dismaid,	3077
This true, which they so seeme to feare. Go home,	3079
Sicin. Pray let's go. *Exeunt Tribunes.*	3089
Menen. No, ile not go: you heare what he hath said	3152
But what o'that? Go you that banish'd him	3155
Sicin. Pray you go to him.	*Mene.* What should I do?	3194
2.Wat. Stand, and go backe.	3237
1 Be it so, go back: the vertue of your name,	Is not heere passable.	3249
*passe heere: no, though it were as vertuous to lye, as to	liue chastly. Therefore go backe.	3264
*haue, I am one that telling true vnder him, must say you	cannot passe. Therefore go backe.	3269
*1 My Generall cares not for you. Back I say, go: least	3291
Volum. Nay, go not from vs thus:	3488
Then thou hast to deny't. Come, let vs go:	3534
I will go meete the Ladies. This *Volumnia,*	3626
Auf. Go tell the Lords a'th'City, I am heere:	3650

GOADED = 1

Which we haue goaded on-ward. *Exeunt.*	1670

GOAT = 1

Corio. Hence old Goat.	1880

GOD = 6*3

*hee wounded, God saue your good Worships? *Martius*	1040
As if that whatsoeuer God, who leades him,	1138
All. Amen, Amen. God saue thee, Noble Consull.	1528
Bru. You speake a'th'people, as if you were a God,	1773
Cor. Shall? O God! but most vnwise Patricians: why	1785
Com. If? He is their God, he leads them like a thing	3006
Corio. The God of Souldiers:	With the consent of supreame Ioue, informe	3423
*finisht with his bidding. He wants nothing of a God but	Eternity, and a Heauen to Throne in.	3592

GOD *cont*.

  Corio. Hear'st thou Mars? | *Auf*. Name not the God, thou boy of
Teares.   3769
GODDED = 1
  Nay godded me indeed. Their latest refuge   3358
GODDEN = *1
  *Godden to your Worships, more of your conuer- | sation   988
GODDES = 1
  Th'honor'd Goddes | Keepe Rome in safety, and the Chaires of Iustice   2302
GODDESSE = 1
  Lar. Now the faire Goddesse Fortune,   593
GODS *see also* sdeath = 35*10
  *we become Rakes. For the Gods know, I speake this in   25
  The Gods, not the Patricians make it, and   74
  (Vnder the Gods) keepe you in awe, which else   198
  *That meate was made for mouths. That the gods sent not   220
  Bru. Being mou'd, he will not spare to gird the Gods.   285
  All. The Gods assist you. | *Auf*. And keepe your Honors safe.   355
  The Charges of our Friends. The Roman Gods,   609
  Com. Whose yonder, | That doe's appeare as he were Flead? O Gods,   629
  And the Gods doome him after.   730
  Shall say against their hearts, We thanke the Gods   755
  Martius. The Gods begin to mocke me: 837
  Volum. Oh, he is wounded, I thanke the Gods for't.   1018
  Virgil. The Gods graunt them true.   1037
  Coriol. Oh! you haue, I know, petition'd all the Gods | for my
prosperitie. *Kneeles*.   1074
  Mene. Now the Gods Crowne thee.   1086
  Menen. Oh me the Gods, you must not speak of that,   1444
  Both. The Gods giue you ioy Sir heartily.   1502
  2.Cit. Therefore let him be Consull: the Gods giue him | ioy, and make
him good friend to the People. .   1526
  Brut. We pray the Gods, he may deserue your loues.   1555
  Mene. Shall it be put to that? | *Sena*. The Gods forbid: 1955
  Menen. Now the good Gods forbid,   2027
  Corio. For them, I cannot do it to the Gods,   2132
  Thou lyest vnto thee, with a voice as free, | As I do pray the Gods.   2353
  The Gods preserue our Noble Tribunes, come. *Exeunt*.   2433
  Corio. O the Gods!   2477
  From these old armes and legges, by the good Gods | I'ld with thee,
euery foot.   2498
  Th'hoorded plague a'th'Gods requit your loue.   2518
  I would the Gods had nothing else to do,   2559
  Corio. You blesse me Gods.   2794
  All. The Gods preserue you both.   2915
  All. Now the Gods keepe you.   2923
  Bru. The Gods haue well preuented it, and Rome | Sits safe and still,
without him.   2936
  1 Cit. The Gods bee good to vs: Come Masters let's   3081
  *thee. The glorious Gods sit in hourely Synod about thy   3304
  *Gods asswage thy wrath, and turne the dregs of it, vpon   3312
  Which can make Gods forsworne? I melt, and am not   3377
  Hath Virgin'd it ere since. You Gods, I pray,   3397
  Our prayers to the Gods, which is a comfort   3460
  To imitate the graces of the Gods.   3507
  Thou art not honest, and the Gods will plague thee   3523
  The Gods looke downe, and this vnnaturall Scene   3542

GODS *cont.*

Sicin. The Gods be good vnto vs.	3599
*Mene. No, in such a case the Gods will not bee good	3600
Sicin. First, the Gods blesse you for your tydings: | Next, accept my	
thankefulnesse.	3633
Call all your Tribes together, praise the Gods,	3642

GOE = 15*3

Martius. I will goe wash:	824
Com. Goe we to our Tent:	854
for the loue of *Iuno* let's goe.	998
*Volum. Good Ladies let's goe. Yes, yes, yes: The	1030
Herauld. Giue way there, and goe on.	1105
*Brutus. Then our Office may, during his power, goe | sleepe.	1142
Coriolanus rises, and offers to goe away. | Nay, keepe your place.	1275
Pray you goe fit you to the Custome,	1363
*1.Cit. Hee ha's done Nobly, and cannot goe without | any honest mans	
Voyce.	1524
Brut. Let them goe on:	1661
Brut. It will be dangerous to goe on--- No further.	1706
Mene. Goe, get you to our House: be gone, away.	1951
Menen. Noble Lady, | Come goe with vs, speake faire: you may salue	
so,	2169
Goe to them, with this Bonnet in thy hand,	2174
Volum. Prythee now, | Goe, and be rul'd: although I know thou hadst	
rather	2192
Volum. He must, and will: | Prythee now say you will, and goe about it.	2203
Corio. Must I goe shew them my vnbarb'd Sconce?	2205
And for Romes good, Ile tell thee what: yet goe:	2531

GOES = 5

More then his singularity, he goes | Vpon this present Action.	310
With his mail'd hand, then wiping, forth he goes	397
How the world goes: that to the pace of it	892
1 But when goes this forward:	2872
Blush, that the world goes well: who rather had,	2897

GOEST = 1

Of this most wise Rebellion, thou goest formost:	166

GOING = 4*1

*Titus Lartius, hauing set a guard vpon Carioles, going with	710
Corio. Pray be content: | Mother, I am going to the Market place:	2240
Of all the Trades in Rome. Looke, I am going:	2244
Our Tradesmen singing in their shops, and going | About their	
Functions friendly.	2900
Mes. The Nobles in great earnestnesse are going	2964

GOLD = 1*1

**fiddious'd, for all the Chests in Carioles, and the Gold	1028
Com. I tell you, he doe's sit in Gold, his eye	3224

GONE *see also* begone = 16*3

Com. Noble *Martius.* | *Sen.* Hence to your homes, be gone.	273
Had circumuention: 'tis not foure dayes gone	320
*Cominius the Generall is gone, with one part of our Ro-|mane	461
Mene. Goe, get you to our House: be gone, away.	1951
2.Sena. Get you gone.	1953
You cannot Tent your selfe: be gone, 'beseech you.	1960
Be gone, put not your worthy Rage into your Tongue,	1965
Mene. Pray you be gone:	1976
Edile. The peoples Enemy is gone, is gone.	2426
All. Our enemy is banish'd, he is gone: Hoo, oo.	2427

GONE *cont*.

Sicin. Bid them all home, he's gone: & wee'l no further,	2503
Sicin. Bid them home: say their great enemy is gone,	2509
Nay, and you shall heare some. Will you be gone?	2521
Volum. Now pray sir get you gone.	2549
If he had gone forth Consull, found it so.	2935
Then pitty: Note how much, therefore be gone.	3322
The Volcians are dislodg'd, and *Martius* gone:	3612
Auf. My Rage is gone,	And I am strucke with sorrow. Take him vp:	3829

GOOD = 65*24

2.*Cit*. One word, good Citizens.	16
*good: what Authority surfets one, would releeue	18
*good report for't, but that hee payes himselfe with bee-|ing proud.	34
Menen. Why Masters, my good Friends, mine honest	63
Men. Note me this good Friend;	134
(You my good Friends, this sayes the Belly) marke me.	148
Men. The Senators of Rome, are this good Belly,	156
2.*Cit*. We haue euer your good word.	177
Mar. He that will giue good words to thee, wil flatter	178
Sicin. Such a Nature, tickled with good successe, dis-|daines	289
Volum. Then his good report should haue beene my	381
*and none lesse deere then thine, and my good *Martius*, I	384
Val. My Ladies both good day to you. | *Vol*. Sweet Madam.	411
*What are you sowing heere? A fine spotte in good | faith. How does your little Sonne?	415
Vir. I thanke your Lady-ship: Well good Madam.	417
Virg. No (good Madam) | I will not out of doores.	434
Come, you must go visit the good Lady that lies in.	441
Vir. No good Madam, pardon me, indeed I will not | foorth.	451
Virg. Oh good Madam, there can be none yet.	455
Virg. Giue me excuse good Madame, I will obey you | in euery thing heereafter.	466
Fare you well then. Come good sweet Ladie.	471
Lart. So, the good Horse is mine.	489
So, now the gates are ope: now proue good Seconds,	540
Conuenient Numbers to make good the City,	583
Make good this ostentation, and you shall | Diuide in all, with vs. *Exeunt*	708
He that ha's but effected his good will, | Hath ouerta'ne mine Act.	768
Whereof we haue ta'ne good, and good store of all,	784
Com. Too modest are you: | More cruell to your good report, then gratefull	809
To vnder-crest your good Addition, | To th'fairenesse of my power.	828
The best, with whom we may articulate, | For their owne good, and ours.	834
Sould. 'Twill be deliuer'd backe on good Condition.	860
What good Condition can a Treatie finde	864
Bru. Good or bad?	900
*but an Interiour suruey of your good selues. Oh that you | could.	936
*that tell you haue good faces, if you see this in the Map	957
*legges: you weare out a good wholesome Forenoone, in	965
Volum. Good Ladies let's goe. Yes, yes, yes: The	1030
*hee wounded, God saue your good Worships? *Martius*	1040
Volum. Nay, my good Souldier, vp:	1076
The good Patricians must be visited,	1108
Cor. Know, good Mother, | I had rather be their seruant in my way,	1117
Scicin. It shall be to him then, as our good wills; a | sure destruction.	1168

GOOD *cont.*

*good, nor harme: but hee seekes their hate with greater	1221
1.*Sen.* Speake, good *Cominius*: | Leaue nothing out for length, and make vs thinke	1256
That's thousand to one good one, when you now see	1293
*shew you, which shall bee yours in priuate: your good | voice sir, what say you?	1468
*2.*Cit.* Therefore let him be Consull: the Gods giue him | ioy, and make him good friend to the People.	1526
Not hauing the power to do the good it would	1859
*To'th'people: *Coriolanus*, patience: Speak good *Sicinius*.	1899
Mene. If by the Tribunes leaue, | And yours good people,	2016
Menen. Now the good Gods forbid,	2027
Vnlesse by not so doing, our good Citie | Cleaue in the midd'st, and perish.	2117
Corio. Tush, tush. | *Mene.* A good demand.	2141
In asking their good loues, but thou wilt frame	2185
To haue't with saying, Good morrow.	2377
My Countries good, with a respect more tender,	2398
Volum. My first sonne, | Whether will thou go? Take good *Cominius*	2472
From these old armes and legges, by the good Gods | I'ld with thee, euery foot.	2498
And for Romes good, Ile tell thee what: yet goe:	2531
Were in Arabia, and thy Tribe before him, | His good Sword in his hand.	2533
Volum. Bastards, and all. | Good man, the Wounds that he does beare for Rome!	2537
*strange things from Rome: all tending to the good of	2610
But with that Surname, a good memorie	2728
*3 I do not say thwacke our Generall, but he was al-|wayes good enough for him	2841
Bru. We stood too't in good time. Is this *Menenius*?	2903
Bru. Rais'd onely, that the weaker sort may wish | Good *Martius* home againe.	2980
Com. Oh you haue made good worke.	2994
Mene. You haue made good worke,	3012
Should say be good to Rome, they charg'd him, euen	3032
Mene. You haue made good worke | You and your cry. Shal's to the Capitoll?	3074
*1 *Cit.* The Gods bee good to vs: Come Masters let's	3081
And shewes good Husbandry for the Volcian State,	3113
Menen. Why so: you haue made good worke:	3168
Would be your Countries Pleader, your good tongue	3190
Sicin. Yet your good will | Must haue that thankes from Rome, after the measure | As you intended well.	3202
And humme at good *Cominius*, much vnhearts mee.	3207
Mene. Good faith Ile proue him,	3219
Mene. Good my Friends, | If you haue heard your Generall talke of Rome,	3245
The booke of his good Acts, whence men haue read	3253
*Rome, and thy petitionary Countrimen. The good	3311
Ile frame conuenient peace. Now good *Auffidius*,	3549
Mine eyes to sweat compassion. But (good sir)	3555
Sicin. The Gods be good vnto vs.	3599
Mene. No, in such a case the Gods will not bee good	3600
Mess. Good Newes, good newes, the Ladies haue | (preuayl'd.	3611
Mene. This is good Newes:	3625

GOOD *cont.*
    A good construction. I rais'd him, and I pawn'd   3673
GOODEN = 3
    Sicin. Gooden our Neighbours.   2916
    Bru. Gooden to you all, gooden to you all.   2917
GOODLY = 4
    Here's goodly worke.   1989
    Corio. A goodly City is this *Antium.* Citty,   2623
    Corio. A goodly House: 2659
    Com. Y'are goodly things, you Voyces.   3073
GOSLING = 1
    Be such a Gosling to obey instinct; but stand   3384
GOT = 6
    Come on you Cowards, you were got in feare   395
    Volum. Titus Lartius writes, they fought together, but | *Auffidius* got
    off.   1024
    Then heare say how I got them.   1281
    I got them in my Countries Seruice, when   1441
    And that the Spoile got on the *Antiats*   2262
    The Plebeians haue got your Fellow Tribune,   3605
GOWNE = 3*1
    Put on the Gowne, stand naked, and entreat them   1357
    Enter Coriolanus in a gowne of Humility, with | Menenius.   1426
    *Heere he comes, and in the Gowne of humility, marke   1428
    *of your voices, that I may bee Consull, I haue heere the | Customarie
    Gowne.   1477
GRACD = 1
    In whom already he's well grac'd, cannot   294
GRACE = 4
    Your Soldiers vse him as the Grace 'fore meate,   3093
    And cannot now accept, to grace him onely,   3362
    Rather to shew a Noble grace to both parts,   3476
    Ile grace thee with that Robbery, thy stolne name | *Coriolanus* in
    Corioles?   3757
GRACEFULL = 1
    And gaue him gracefull posture.   1140
GRACES = 1
    To imitate the graces of the Gods.   3507
GRACIOUS = 3
    But oh, thy Wife. | *Corio.* My gracious silence, hayle: 1080
    Then what he stood for: so his gracious nature   1588
    Eyther his gracious Promise, which you might   1595
GRAFTED = 1
    That will not be grafted to your Rallish.   1099
GRAIN = *1
    *Below their cobled Shooes. They say ther's grain enough?   208
GRAINE = 4*1
    *with Graine: Make Edicts for Vsurie, to support Vsu- | rers;   82
    Then what you should, made you against the graine   1636
    But with a graine a day, I would not buy   2374
    For one poore graine or two, to leaue vnburnt | And still to nose
    th'offence.   3180
    Menen. For one poore graine or two?   3182
GRAINED = 1
    My grained Ash an hundred times hath broke,   2766
GRAINES = 1
    And this braue Fellow too: we are the Graines,   3184

GRANDCHILDE = 1
    The Grandchilde to her blood. But out affection,   3373
GRANT *see also* graunt = 2
    I'th'Warre do grow together: Grant that, and tell me   2138
    Volum. Oh no more, no more: | You haue said you will not grant vs any
    thing: 3441
GRANTED *see also* graunted = 2
    And a petition granted them, a strange one,   223
    A Mother lesse? or granted lesse *Auffidius*?   3551
GRAPES = *1
    *of his face, sowres ripe Grapes. When he walks, he moues   3587
GRATEFULL = 1
    Com. Too modest are you: | More cruell to your good report, then
    gratefull   809
GRATIFIE = 1
    To gratifie his Noble seruice, that hath   1247
GRATIS = 3
    When Corne was giuen them *gratis*, you repin'd,   1727
    The Corne a'th'Store-house gratis, as 'twas vs'd | Sometime in Greece.   1809
    Did not deserue Corne gratis. Being i'th'Warre,   1822
GRATITUDE = 1
    That our renowned Rome, whose gratitude   2028
GRAUE = 6*3
    Your most graue Belly was deliberate,   135
    Com. You shall not be the Graue of your deseruing,   770
    *that say you are reuerend graue men, yet they lye deadly,   956
    *honourable a graue, as to stuffe a Botchers Cushion, or to   983
    Mene. Now it's twentie seuen; euery gash was an | Enemies Graue.
    Hearke, the Trumpets.   1051
    Most reuerend and graue Elders, to desire   1249
    You graue, but wreaklesse Senators, haue you thus   1786
    *I was forc'd to scoul'd. Your iudgments my graue Lords   3776
    Must beare my beating to his Graue, shall ioyne | To thrust the Lye
    vnto him.   3779
GRAUER = 1
    His popular Shall, against a grauer Bench   1800
GRAUES = 1
    Like Graues i'th holy Church-yard.   2326
GRAUNT = 2*1
    Virgil. The Gods graunt them true.   1037
    *the intreaty and graunt of the whole Table. Hee'l go he   2859
    The thing I haue forsworne to graunt, may neuer   3435
GRAUNTED = 2
    Menen. What is graunted them?   228
    Your Voyces therefore: when we graunted that,   1570
GREASIE = 1
    Your stinking, greasie Caps, in hooting   3057
GREAT = 23*10
    You, the great Toe of this Assembly?   163
    2.*Cit.* I the great Toe? Why the great Toe?   164
    Whether for East or West: the Dearth is great,   324
    To keepe your great pretences vayl'd, till when   336
    Fall deepe in loue with thee, and her great charmes   594
    Able to beare against the great *Auffidious*   700
    Where great Patricians shall attend, and shrug,   751
    Men. Why 'tis no great matter: for a very little theefe   925
    *of Occasion, will rob you of a great deale of Patience: 926

GREAT *cont*.

*2.*Off*. 'Faith, there hath beene many great men that	1211
Who after great *Hostilius* here was King,	1643
And Nobly nam'd, so twice being Censor, | Was his great Ancestor.	1646
And sacke great Rome with Romanes.	2057
Those whose great power must try him.	2362
Sicin. Bid them home: say their great enemy is gone,	2509
Auffidius will appeare well in these Warres, his great	2603
Cit. And you. | *Corio*. Direct me, if it be your will, where great *Auf-* | *fidius* lies: Is he in *Antium*?	2630
Great hurt and Mischiefe: thereto witnesse my	2724
*be a Rauisher, so it cannot be denied, but peace is a great | maker of Cuckolds.	2885
Mes. The Nobles in great earnestnesse are going	2964
Great Nature cries, Deny not. Let the Volces	3382
Like a great Sea-marke standing euery flaw, | And sauing those that eye thee.	3427
*For making vp this peace. Thou know'st (great Sonne)	3497
Mess. Sir, we haue all great cause to giue great thanks.	3635
Wherein you wisht vs parties: Wee'l deliuer you | Of your great danger.	3664
Of our great Action; therefore shall he dye,	3703
Drummes and Trumpets sounds, with great | showts of the people.	3705
Vnder your great Command. You are to know,	3739
Too great for what containes it. Boy? Oh Slaue,	3774
Prouok'd by him, you cannot) the great danger	3816
2.Lord. His owne impatience, | Takes from *Auffidius* a great part of blame:	3826

GREATER = 5*3

Win vpon power, and throw forth greater Theames | For Insurrections arguing.	234
*good, nor harme: but hee seekes their hate with greater	1221
*that's no matter, the greater part carries it, I say. If hee	1423
Then stay past doubt, for greater:	1663
We are the greater pole, and in true feare	1831
To'th'greater Bench, in a Rebellion:	1867
1 I thinke he is: but a greater soldier then he, | You wot one.	2822
*1 Nay not so neither: but I take him to be the greater | Souldiour.	2827

GREATEST *see also* great'st = 1

Sen. Your Company to'th'Capitoll, where I know | Our greatest Friends attend vs.	269

GREATNES = 1

And curse that Iustice did it. Who deserues Greatnes,	187

GREATNESSE = 1

*1 Do you heare how wee are shent for keeping your | greatnesse backe?	3334

GREATST = 1

When both your voices blended, the great'st taste	1797

GRECIAN = 1

At Grecian sword. *Contenning*, tell *Valeria*	405

GREECE = 2

Then euer frown'd in Greece. By Ioue himselfe,	1801
The Corne a'th'Store-house gratis, as 'twas vs'd | Sometime in Greece.	1809

GREEFE-SHOT = 1

But as a discontented Friend, greefe-shot | With his vnkindnesse. Say't be so?	3200

GREET = 1

A merrier day did neuer yet greet Rome,	3613

GREETINGS = 1
From whom I haue receiu'd not onely greetings, | But with them,
change of Honors.   1109
GREEUE = 1
All. We haue. | 1.*Lord*. And greeue to heare't: 3725
GREY-HOUND = 1
Euen like a fawning Grey-hound in the Leash, | To let him slip at will. 649
GRIEUES = 1
When she do's prayse me, grieues me: 765
GRIM = 2
Onely in strokes, but with thy grim lookes, and   560
Thou hast a Grim apparance, and thy Face   2717
GRINDE = 1
This Mould of *Martius*, they to dust should grinde it,   2209
GROANE = 1
Haue I heard groane, and drop: Then know me not,   2626
GROANES = *1
*easie groanes of old women, the Virginall Palms of your   3279
GROATS = 1
To buy and sell with Groats, to shew bare heads   2095
GROUE = *1
Auf. I am attended at the Cyprus groue. I pray you   890
GROUND = 3*2
*no better a ground. Therefore, for *Coriolanus* neyther to   1215
Corio. On faire ground, I could beat fortie of them.   1967
While I remaine aboue the ground, you shall   2492
Like to a Bowle vpon a subtle ground   3258
*like an Engine, and the ground shrinkes before his Trea-|ding.   3588
GROW = 1*1
I'th'Warre do grow together: Grant that, and tell me   2138
*Some tricke not worth an Egge, shall grow deere friends   2647
GROWE = *1
*helpes are many, or else your actions would growe won-|drous   932
GROWES = 2
When Steele growes soft, as the Parasites Silke,   801
Corio. It is a purpos'd thing, and growes by Plot,   1721
GROWN = *1
Sicin. 'Tis he, 'tis he: O he is grown most kind of late: 2904
GROWNE = *2
Bru. The present Warres deuoure him, he is growne | Too proud to be
so valiant.   287
*growne from Man to Dragon: He has wings, hee's more | then a
creeping thing.   3582
GRUB = *2
Mene. There is differency between a Grub & a But-|terfly,   3580
*yet your Butterfly was a Grub: this *Martius*, is   3581
GUARD = 5*2
Let vs alone to guard *Corioles*   344
Titus Lartius, hauing set a guard vpon Carioles, going with   710
At home, vpon my Brothers Guard, euen there   884
Giue him deseru'd vexation. Let a guard | Attend vs through the City. 2430
Enter Menenius to the Watch or Guard.   3235
Me. You guard like men, 'tis well. But by your leaue,   3238
Manet the Guard and Menenius.   3330
GUARDED = *1
Lar. So, let the Ports be guarded; keepe your Duties   714

GUESSE = 1*2
    *were wholsome, wee might guesse they releeued vs hu-|manely: 20
    Com. As I guesse *Martius*, | Their Bands i'th Vaward are the Antients   667
    *Son *Coriolanus*, guesse but my entertainment with him: if   3300
GUEST = 2
    The Feast smels well: but I appeare not like a Guest.   2660
    *3 What you will not? Prythee tell my Maister what | a strange Guest
    he ha's heere.   2688
GUIDED = 1
    Then as guided by your owne true affections, and that   1634
GUIDER = *1
    *Our Guider come, to th'Roman Campe conduct vs. *Exit*   721
GULFE = 2
    That onely like a Gulfe it did remaine   100
    Follow thine Enemie in a fierie Gulfe,   2194
GUSTS = 1
    By Interims and conueying gusts, we haue heard   608
GYBER = *1
    *perfecter gyber for the Table, then a necessary Bencher in | the
    Capitoll.   977
HA *l*.999 *3366 3771 = 2*1, *1
    Mar. I am glad on't, then we shall ha meanes to vent   242
HAD *l*.*60 300 320 *377 *379 *383 *385 *418 626 652 871 *1027 *1049
    1082 1118 *1219 *1269 1280 *1288 1294 1371 1565 1578 1593 1596 1606
    1607 1655 1674 *1675 1685 *1690 1697 1711 *1812 2060 2103 2104 2107
    2109 2455 2522 2540 2543 *2544 2559 *2578 2738 2777 2785 *2810
    *2816 *2818 2835 *2848 2897 2922 2935 3033 3105 3107 3166 3174 3208
    *3262 3467 3535 3694 3697 3708 *3801 = 49*23
HADST *l*.762 2193 2526 = 3
HAH *see also* ha *l*.1705 = 1
HAILE *see also* hayle = 4
    Haile Sir. *Mene*. Haile to you both.   2905
    Giue the All-haile to thee, and cry be Blest   3496
    Corio. Haile Lords, I am return'd your Souldier: 3736
HAILSTONE = 1
    Or Hailstone in the Sun. Your Vertue is,   185
HAIRE = 2
    See him plucke *Auffidius* downe by th'haire: 392
    And not a haire vpon a Souldiers head   3059
HALE = 1
    And hale him vp and downe; all swearing, if   3606
HALFE = 7*7
    Mar. Were halfe to halfe the world by th'eares, & he   254
    Bru. Come: halfe all *Cominius* Honors are to *Martius*   304
    *halfe an houre together: ha's such a confirm'd coun-|tenance.   422
    For halfe a hundred yeares: Summon the Towne.   492
    Mess. Within this mile and halfe.   494
    Halfe an houre since brought my report.   627
    To one that would doe thus. I am halfe through,   1514
    And wak'd halfe dead with nothing. Worthy *Martius*,   2784
    Th'one halfe of my Commission, and set downe   2797
    *Newes is, our Generall is cut i'th'middle, & but one halfe   2857
    *of what he was yesterday. For the other ha's halfe, by   2858
    Bru. Let's to the Capitoll: would halfe my wealth | Would buy this for
    a lye.   3087
    *I let forth your halfe pinte of blood. Backe, that's the vt-|most of your
    hauing, backe.   3292

HAND = 12*2
Men. What work's my Countrimen in hand?   56
With his mail'd hand, then wiping, forth he goes   397
Wash my fierce hand in's heart. Go you to th'Citie,   886
*you are censured heere in the City, I mean of vs a'th'right | hand File,
do you?   919
Cor. Your Hand, and yours?   1106
Goe to them, with this Bonnet in thy hand,   2174
Corio. Giue me thy hand, come. *Exeunt*   2500
Were in Arabia, and thy Tribe before him, | His good Sword in his
hand.   2533
Yet *Martius* that was much. Your hand: most welcome. | *Exeunt*   2806
*2 By my hand, I had thoght to haue stroken him with   2810
*of him, Sanctifies himselfe with's hand, and turnes vp the   2855
Thus with his speechlesse hand. What he would do   3228
Wherein this Trunke was fram'd, and in her hand   3372
*I am husht vntill our City be afire, & then Ile speak a litle | *Holds her
by the hand silent.*   3538
HANDKERCHERS = 1
Ladies and Maids their Scarffes, and Handkerchers,   1194
HANDLING = 1
That will not hold the handling: or say to them,   2181
HANDS = 9
All. Wee'l Surety him. | *Com.* Ag'd sir, hands off.   1881
Where the Disease is violent. Lay hands vpon him,   1938
Brut. Lay hands vpon him.   1945
With rigorous hands: he hath resisted Law,   1998
The peoples mouths, and we their hands.   2003
In thy hands clutcht: as many Millions in   2351
And take our friendly Senators by'th'hands   2790
To say, beseech you cease. You haue made faire hands,   3037
But kneeles, and holds vp hands for fellowship,   3532
HANG = 6*2
*And hewes downe Oakes, with rushes. Hang ye: trust ye?   192
Mar. Hang 'em: They say?   202
Mar. They are dissolu'd: Hang em;   217
As they would hang them on the hornes a'th Moone,   226
*Picture-like to hang by th'wall, if renowne made it not   372
Coriol. Thinke vpon me? Hang 'em,   1446
Corio. Let them hang. | *Volum.* I, and burne too.   2111
May hang vpon your hardnesse, therefore heare vs.   3446
HANGD = *1
*1 He had so, looking as it were, would I were hang'd   2818
HANGING = *1
*thou stand'st not i'th state of hanging, or of some death   3301
HANGMEN = 1*1
Irons of a Doit, Dublets that Hangmen would   577
*some of the best of 'em were hereditarie hang-|men.   987
HANGS = 1
And hangs on *Dians* Temple: Deere *Valeria*.   3419
HAP = 1
When we shall hap to giu't them.   2288
HAPPELY = 1
His Fame vnparalell'd, happely amplified: 3254
HAPPIER = 1
Sicin. This is a happier and more comely time,   2925

HAPPY = 2

 The happy man; whether detect of iudgement,   3130
 You haue wonne a happy Victory to Rome.   3544

HARD = 2*1

 A Shield, as hard as his. A certaine number   701
 hard for him, I haue heard him say so himselfe.   2844
 *1 He was too hard for him directly, to say the Troth   2845

HARDINESSE = 1

 1.*Sol.* Foole-hardinesse, not I. | 2.*Sol.* Nor I.   544

HARDLY = 1*1

 That we shall hardly in our ages see | Their Banners waue againe. 1681
 *I was hardly moued to come to thee: but beeing assured   3308

HARDNESSE = 1

 May hang vpon your hardnesse, therefore heare vs.   3446

HARDNING = 1

 Heart-hardning spectacles. Tell these sad women,   2463

HARE = 1

 Auf. If I flye *Martius*, hollow me like a Hare.   731

HARES = 1

 Where he should finde you Lyons, findes you Hares: 182

HARKE *see also* hearke = 3*1

 They'le open of themselues. Harke you, farre off | *Alarum farre off.* 508
 And harke, what noyse the Generall makes: To him   580
 *As the recomforted through th'gates. Why harke you: | *Trumpets,*
 Hoboyes, Drums beate, altogether.   3620
 I'de not haue giuen a doit. Harke, how they ioy. | *Sound still with the*
 Shouts.   3631

HARLOTS = 1

 Away my disposition, and possesse me | Some Harlots spirit: My throat
 of Warre be turn'd,   2219

HARME = 3*2

 (Like one that meanes his proper harme) in Manacles,   813
 *too? What harme can your beesome Conspectui-|ties   959
 *good, nor harme: but hee seekes their hate with greater   1221
 The which shall turne you to no further harme, | Then so much losse of
 time.   2019
 The harme of vnskan'd swiftnesse, will (too late)   2054

HARPE = 1

 (Harpe on that still) but by our putting on: 1656

HARROW = 1

 Plough Rome, and harrow Italy, Ile neuer   3383

HARSH = 1

 And harsh in sound to thine.   2715

HARTH = 3

 Corio. Let me but stand, I will not hurt your Harth.   2679
 Hath brought me to thy Harth, not out of Hope   2736
 Being banish'd for't, he came vnto my Harth,   3683

HARTS = *1

 *Make our eies flow with ioy, harts dance with comforts,   3454

HARUEST = 1

 Like to a Haruest man, that task'd to mowe | Or all, or loose his hyre. 398

HAS *l.**31 281 487 631 764 768 1023 *1031 *1041 *1217 *1432 *1524 1548
 1554 1747 1982 2033 2035 2062 2324 2378 *2666 2689 *2813 *2858
 *2864 3139 *3271 *3285 3520 *3582 3760 = 19*13, 2*1

 *halfe an houre together: ha's such a confirm'd coun-|tenance.   422
 Bru. Has said enough.   1861
 Sicin. Ha's spoken like a Traitor, and shall answer | As Traitors do. 1862

HAST *l.*866 2183 2187 2214 2217 2462 2486 2528 2717 2741 2760 2779
3506 3517 3534 *3559 3773 3810 = 17*1, 1
   And with our faire intreaties hast them on. *Exeunt*   3234
HASTE *see also* hast = 1
   Whil'st I with those that haue the spirit, wil haste | To helpe *Cominius.*   584
HASTILY = 1
   Enter a Messenger hastily.   238
HASTY = 1*1
   *the first complaint, hasty and Tinder-like vppon, to   946
   Will be as rash in the repeale, as hasty   3123
HAT = 2*2
   Corio. Kindly sir, I pray let me ha't: I haue wounds to   1467
   2 *Cit.* You shall ha't worthy Sir.   1470
   *the wisedome of their choice, is rather to haue my Hat,   1489
   And with his Hat, thus wauing it in scorne,   1567
HATCHING = *1
   *They needs must shew themselues, which in the hatching   337
HATE = 12*5
   Deserues your Hate: and your Affections are   188
   And call him Noble, that was now your Hate: 194
   There is the man of my soules hate, *Auffidious,*   581
   Mar. Ile fight with none but thee, for I do hate thee | Worse then a
     Promise-breaker.   724
   Auffid. We hate alike: 726
   That with the fustie Plebeans, hate thine Honors,   754
   My hate to *Martius.* Where I finde him, were it   883
   *so that if they loue they know not why, they hate vpon   1214
   *care whether they loue, or hate him, manifests the true   1216
   *good, nor harme: but hee seekes their hate with greater   1221
   And his old Hate vnto you: besides, forget not   1623
   After the inueterate Hate he beares you.   1629
   Corio. You common cry of Curs, whose breath I hate,   2408
   Since I haue euer followed thee with hate,   2755
   1 I, and it makes men hate one another.   2887
   As those should do that had deseru'd his hate,   3033
   *1 Then you should hate Rome, as he do's. Can you,   3275
HATED = 3
   Cominius, Martius your old Enemy | (Who is of Rome worse hated then
     of you)   326
   That of all things vpon the Earth, he hated   1691
   So hated, and so banish'd: but he ha's a Merit   3139
HATH *l.*37 46 *53 587 590 756 769 871 *1005 *1032 1065 1146 1173
*1211 *1227 *1231 1247 *1267 *1456 1606 1649 *1709 1998 2036 2037
2228 2290 2365 2429 *2583 *2586 2722 2733 2736 2760 2766 2955 3115
3137 3143 3144 3152 3248 *3313 *3339 3381 3397 3655 3711 3752
3834 = 37*14
HATRED = 2
   We must suggest the People, in what hatred   1172
   To oppose his hatred fully. Welcome home.   1698
HAUE *see also* ha, ha't, haue't, th'haue *l.*13 *60 *61 *62 67 91 131 171
177 *179 232 *246 248 253 276 318 322 323 *381 *382 *432 *460 483
488 507 530 546 584 607 608 614 631 663 666 672 673 674 715 742 766
767 778 *779 784 793 803 805 853 866 *898 914 *953 *957 *1027 *1074
1082 1097 1109 1111 *1165 1174 1178 1192 1202 *1212 *1213 *1230
*1264 1278 1280 1284 *1288 1360 1364 *1391 *1392 *1404 *1436 1437
*1467 1472 *1477 *1479 1480 *1482 *1483 *1486 *1489 *1497 1518 1521
1522 1531 1536 *1553 1561 *1572 1573 1577 1586 1592 1596 1597 1600

HAUE *cont.*
1609 1614 1617 1651 1657 1670 1711 1716 1719 1732 *1761 1764 1768
1786 1791 1795 1825 1904 1905 1941 1942 1954 1978 2008 2060 2099
2103 *2106 *2114 2120 2131 2136 2190 2197 2211 2216 2269 *2270 2271
2272 2273 2282 2291 *2342 2359 2396 2415 2456 2462 2466 2504 2506
*2516 2547 2550 2554 2563 2564 2573 *2580 *2581 *2600 *2607 2611
*2618 2626 *2645 2649 *2662 *2664 *2672 *2677 *2706 2733 2739 2755
2777 2780 2782 2795 *2810 2844 *2848 *2873 *2876 *2879 *2909 2910
2936 2940 2954 2990 2994 *2996 *3004 3012 3018 3027 3036 3037 3038
3039 3064 3074 3078 3106 3163 3168 3169 3203 3211 3213 3220 3246
3252 3253 3255 3259 3260 3261 *3263 *3268 *3269 *3276 *3309 3320
3326 3336 3350 3351 3356 3359 3364 3390 3435 3442 3443 3451 3487
3494 3531 3541 3544 3546 3550 3565 3567 3569 3605 3611 3618 3629
3631 *3635 3682 3722 3723 3724 3725 3728 3740 *3742 3744 3749 3784
3799 3836 = 204*69

HAUER = 1
And most dignifies the hauer: if it be,   1299
HAUET = 1
To haue't with saying, Good morrow.   2377
HAUING = 7*2
*Titus Lartius, hauing set a guard vpon Carioles, going with   710
Yet cam'st thou to a Morsell of this Feast, | Hauing fully din'd before.   757
*hauing beene supple and courteous to the People, Bon-|netted,   1229
Menen. Hauing determin'd of the Volces,   1244
Not hauing the power to do the good it would   1859
And thus farre hauing stretcht it (here be with them)   2175
*I let forth your halfe pinte of blood. Backe, that's the vt-|most of your
hauing, backe.   3292
And beare the Palme, for hauing brauely shed   3472
Deliuer them this Paper: hauing read it,   3651
HAUOCKE = *1
Me. Do not cry hauocke, where you shold but hunt | With modest
warrant,   2006
HAYLE = 2
Hayle, Noble *Martius*.   173
But oh, thy Wife. | *Corio*. My gracious silence, hayle: 1080
HAZARD = 3
This Mutinie were better put in hazard,   1662
Which else would put you to your fortune, and | The hazard of much
blood.   2159
That which shall breake his necke, or hazard mine,   3116
HAZARDS = 1
My hazards still haue beene your solace, and   2466
HE *see also* a, hee, he'l, he's = 241*83
HEAD = 8*2
The Kingly crown'd head, the vigilant eye,   118
Vol. Hee'l beat *Auffidius* head below his knee, | And treade vpon his
necke.   408
Ere in our owne house I doe shade my Head,   1107
Corio. I had rather haue one scratch my Head i'th' Sun,   1288
When *Tarquin* made a Head for Rome, he fought   1302
*mans will, 'tis strongly wadg'd vp in a blocke-head: but   1414
Corio. Tullus Auffidius then had made new head.   1674
More learned then the eares, wauing thy head,   2178
his head, that he giues entrance to such Companions?   2667
And not a haire vpon a Souldiers head   3059

HEADED = *1
  *he himselfe stucke not to call vs the many-headed Multi-|tude.   1402
HEADS = 3*1
  *heads are some browne, some blacke, some Abram, some   1405
  To buy and sell with Groats, to shew bare heads   2095
  With many heads butts me away. Nay Mother,   2438
  You Lords and Heads a'th'State, perfidiously   3759
HEALE = 1
  Coriol. Your Honors pardon: | I had rather haue my Wounds to heale
  againe,   1279
HEALTH = *1
  *yeeres health; in which time, I will make a Lippe at   1012
HEAPES = 1
  And burie all, which yet distinctly raunges | In heapes, and piles of
  Ruine.   1917
HEAPT = 1
  And mountainous Error be too highly heapt,   1511
HEARD = 16*4
  A pretty Tale, it may be you haue heard it,   91
  Since I heard thence, these are the words, I thinke   321
  Val. In earnest it's true; I heard a Senatour speake it.   459
  *You Shames of Rome: you Heard of Byles and Plagues   526
  By Interims and conueying gusts, we haue heard   608
  Com. 'Tis not a mile: briefely we heard their drummes.   621
  Brutus. I heard him sweare,   1154
  reproofe and rebuke from euery Eare that heard it.   1236
  I haue seene, and heard of: for your Voyces,   1521
  Corio. Are these your Heard?   1715
  He heard the Name of Death. *A Noise within*.   1988
  I may be heard, I would craue a word or two,   2018
  But when extremities speake. I haue heard you say,   2136
  What you haue seene him do, and heard him speake: 2359
  Rom. The day serues well for them now. I haue heard   2600
  Haue I heard groane, and drop: Then know me not,   2626
  hard for him, I haue heard him say so himselfe.   2844
  Before you punish him, where he heard this,   2957
  Mene. Good my Friends, | If you haue heard your Generall talke of
  Rome,   3245
  Were you in my steed, would you haue heard   3550
HEARDSMEN = *1
  *would infect my Braine, being the Heardsmen of   989
HEARE *see also* here, heare't = 41*12
  1. *Citizen*. | *Before we proceed any further, heare me speake.   4
  2 *Citizen*. Well, | Ile heare it Sir: yet you must not thinke   94
  Did see, and heare, deuise, instruct, walke, feele,   104
  Patience awhile; you'st heare the Bellies answer.   132
  Sicin. Let's hence, and heare | How the dispatch is made, and in what
  fashion   308
  *Sonne, I therein would haue found issue. Heare me pro-|fesse   382
  Me thinkes, I heare hither your Husbands Drumme: 391
  Vol. He had rather see the swords, and heare a Drum, | then looke
  vpon his Schoolemaster.   418
  Mar. Then shall we heare their Larum, & they Ours.   495
  *And gladly quak'd, heare more: where the dull Tribunes,   753
  What you haue done, before our Armie heare me.   778
  To heare themselues remembred.   780
  *And the blind to heare him speak: Matrons flong Gloues,   1193

HEARE *cont*.

been silent: Please you to heare *Cominius* speake?	1270
Senat. Sit *Coriolanus*: neuer shame to heare | What you haue Nobly done.	1277
Then heare say how I got them.	1281
To heare my Nothings monster'd. *Exit Coriolanus*	1290
Then on ones Eares to heare it. Proceed *Cominius*.	1295
Heare you this Triton of the *Minnoues*? Marke you | His absolute Shall?	1782
Scici. Heare me, People peace.	1900
*Mene. Heare me one word, 'beseech you Tribunes,	1930
heare me but a word.	1931
Bru. Wee'l heare no more:	2048
With Accusations, as I heare more strong | Then are vpon you yet.	2251
And when they heare me say, it shall be so,	2275
Corio. First heare me speake. | *Both Tri*. Well, say: Peace hoe.	2313
*Com. Heare me my Masters, and my common friends.	2393
Where thou shalt rest, that thou may'st heare of vs,	2479
Heare from me still, and neuer of me ought	2493
Menen. That's worthily | As any eare can heare. Come, let's not weepe,	2495
*Volum. If that I could for weeping, you should heare,	2520
Nay, and you shall heare some. Will you be gone?	2521
You haue done a braue deede: Ere you go, heare this:	2550
*Rom. I am ioyfull to heare of their readinesse, and am	2615
*Sicin. We heare not of him, neither need we fear him,	2893
Sicin. Where is he, heare you? | *Mene*. Nay I heare nothing:	2911
His Mother and his wife, heare nothing from him.	2913
Omnes. Faith, we heare fearfull Newes.	3065
Menen. No, ile not go: you heare what he hath said	3152
To heare *Cominius* speake, Ile keepe at home.	3158
Com. He would not seeme to know me. | *Menen*. Do you heare?	3159
Mene. Ile vndertak't: | I thinke hee'l heare me. Yet to bite his lip,	3205
Com. Hee'l neuer heare him. | *Sicin*. Not.	3222
And his Wife, who (as I heare) meane to solicite him	3232
**I You may not passe, you must returne: our Generall | will no more heare from thence.	3241
I will not heare thee speake. This man *Auffidius*	3327
**I Do you heare how wee are shent for keeping your | greatnesse backe?	3334
May hang vpon your hardnesse, therefore heare vs.	3446
Heare nought from Rome in priuate. Your request?	3448
Auf. He approaches, you shall heare him.	3733
1 *Lord*. Peace both, and heare me speake.	3781
Auf. My Noble Masters, heare me speake. | 1.*Lord*. O *Tullus*.	3808

HEARET = 1

All. We haue. | 1.*Lord*. And greeue to heare't:	3725

HEARING = 3*4

**thee Daughter, I sprang not more in ioy at first hearing	376
**hearing a cause betweene an Orendge wife, and a Forfet-|seller,	966
**to a second day of Audience. When you are hearing a	968
**bleeding, the more intangled by your hearing: All the	973
Sicin. He's sentenc'd: No more hearing.	2394
Mene. 'Tis *Auffidius*, | Who hearing of our *Martius* Banishment,	2945
Shall haue Iudicious hearing. Stand *Auffidius*, | And trouble not the peace.	3799

HEARKE = 4

Hearke, our Drummes | *Are bringing forth our youth: Wee'l breake our Walles	504

HEARKE *cont.*

Mene. Now it's twentie seuen; euery gash was an | Enemies Graue.

Hearke, the Trumpets.   1051

Make the Sunne dance. Hearke you. *A shout within*   3624

And Ile renew me in his fall. But hearke.   3704

HEARST = 1

Corio. Hear'st thou Mars? | *Auf.* Name not the God, thou boy of

Teares.   3769

HEART = 26*4

The Counsailor Heart, the Arme our Souldier,   119

Euen to the Court, the Heart, to th'seate o'th'Braine,   143

To breake the heart of generosity,   224

Mart. Oh! let me clip ye | In Armes as sound, as when I woo'd in heart;   640

Of their best trust: O're them *Auffidious,* | Their very heart of Hope.   669

But cannot make my heart consent to take   790

Wash my fierce hand in's heart. Go you to th'Citie,   886

Coriol. No more of this, it does offend my heart: pray | now no more.   1071

A Curse begin at very root on's heart,   1094

*then my Heart, I will practice the insinuating nod, and be   1490

He ha's it now: and by his Lookes, me thinkes, | 'Tis warme at's heart.   1548

Brut. With a prowd heart he wore his humble Weeds: 1550

No Heart among you? Or had you Tongues, to cry   1607

I haue a heart as little apt as yours,   2120

Before he should thus stoope to'th'heart, but that   2124

Which your heart prompts you, but with such words   2153

Which often thus correcting thy stout heart,   2179

Must I with my base Tongue giue to my Noble Heart   2206

With as bigge heart as thou. Do.as thou list,   2237

What's in his heart, and that is there which lookes   2294

With Precepts that would make inuincible | The heart that conn'd them.   2446

But once a day, it would vnclogge my heart | Of what lyes heauy too't.   2561

*to heart, the Banishment of that worthy *Coriolanus,* that   2591

Whose double bosomes seemes to weare one heart,   2639

A heart of wreake in thee, that wilt reuenge   2742

Each word thou hast spoke, hath weeded from my heart   2760

Thou Noble thing, more dances my rapt heart,   2774

Corio. This last old man, | Whom with a crack'd heart I haue sent to

Rome,   3355

That Pages blush'd at him, and men of heart | Look'd wond'ring each

at others.   3767

Corio. Measurelesse Lyar, thou hast made my heart   3773

HEARTH *see* harth

HEARTILY = 3

giue you our voices heartily.   1496

Both. The Gods giue you ioy Sir heartily.   1502

sir, heartily well met, and most glad of your Company.   2617

HEARTS *see also* harts = 8*2

Now put your Shields before your hearts, and fight   516

With hearts more proofe then Shields.   517

Shall say against their hearts, We thanke the Gods   755

And carry with vs Eares and Eyes for th' time, | But Hearts for the

euent.   1200

*Honors in their Eyes, and his actions in their Hearts, that   1232

*haue hearts inclinable to honor and aduance the Theame | of our

Assembly.   1264

Or *Ioue,* for's power to Thunder: his Heart's his Mouth: 1985

HEARTS *cont*.
   Menen. This but done, | Euen as she speakes, why their hearts were
   yours: 2188
   Cogge their Hearts from them, and come home belou'd 2243
   Let euery feeble Rumor shake your hearts: 2413
HEART-HARDNING = 1
   Heart-hardning spectacles. Tell these sad women, 2463
HEAT = 1
   Senat. Not in this heat, Sir, now. 1753
HEATE = 1
   *so, they are in a most warlike preparation, & hope to com | vpon
   them, in the heate of their diuision 2587
HEAUEN = 5
   Strike at the Heauen with your staues, as lift them 69
   Or by the fires of heauen, Ile leaue the Foe, 534
   As I can of those Mysteries which heauen | Will not haue earth to
   know. 2546
   Now by the iealous Queene of Heauen, that kisse 3395
   *finisht with his bidding. He wants nothing of a God but | Eternity, and
   a Heauen to Throne in. 3592
HEAUENS = 5
   Vir. Heauens blesse my Lord from fell *Auffidius*. 407
   Virg. Oh heauens! O heauens! | *Corio*. Nay, I prythee woman. 2448
   Sicin. Oh blessed Heauens! 2529
   Corio. O Mother, Mother! | What haue you done? Behold, the Heauens
   do ope, 3540
HEAUIE = 1
   I am light, and heauie; welcome: 1093
HEAUIEST = 1
   My selfe your loyall Seruant, or endure | Your heauiest Censure. 3820
HEAUY = 1
   But once a day, it would vnclogge my heart | Of what lyes heauy too't. 2561
HECTOR = 2
   When she did suckle *Hector*, look'd not louelier 403
   Auf. Wer't thou the *Hector*, | That was the whip of your bragg'd
   Progeny, 737
HECTORS = 1
   Then *Hectors* forhead, when it spit forth blood 404
HECUBA = 1
   Then gilt his Trophe. The brests of *Hecuba* 402
HEE *see also* hee'l, hee'ld, hee's *l*.*34 *366 *426 *1021 *1031 *1040 *1041
   *1044 *1049 1055 1056 *1220 *1221 *1227 *1231 *1392 *1423 *1524
   1565 *1888 *2848 *2851 3833 = 5*20
HEEDE = 1
   But worthy Lords, haue you with heede perused | What I haue written
   to you? 3723
HEEL *l*.408 1790 *2859 3016 3124 3206 3222 = 6*1
HEELD = *1
   Sicin. What then? | *Virg*. When then? Hee'ld make an end of thy
   posterity 2535
HEELES = 3
   1.*Sol*. Following the Flyers at the very heeles, 550
   Tye Leaden pounds too's heeles. Proceed by Processe, 2055
   Death on the Wheele, or at wilde Horses heeles, 2085
HEERE = 33*10
   why stay we prating heere? To th'Capitoll. | *All*. Come, come. 49
   1 *Cit*. Soft, who comes heere? 51

HEERE *cont.*

Mess. Where's *Caius Martius?* | *Mar.* Heere: what's the matter!	239
I haue the Letter heere: yes, heere it is;	322
*What are you sowing heere? A fine spotte in good | faith. How does	
your little Sonne?	415
Mar. See heere these mouers, that do prize their hours	575
Mar. Those are they | That most are willing; if any such be heere,	685
Thou should'st not scape me heere.	739
*Heere they fight, and certaine Volces come in the ayde	740
*you are censured heere in the City, I mean of vs a'th'right | hand File,	
do you?	919
Of our proceedings heere on th'Market place,	1385
*Heere he comes, and in the Gowne of humility, marke	1428
And keepe their teeth cleane: So, heere comes a brace,	1454
You know the cause (Sir) of my standing heere.	1455
*of your voices, that I may bee Consull, I haue heere the | Customarie	
Gowne.	1477
Why in this Wooluish tongue should I stand heere,	1506
Giuen Hidra heere to choose an Officer, | That with his peremptory	
Shall, being but	1787
Mene. Heere me speake? As I do know	2010
Were but one danger, and to keepe him heere	2024
Sicin. Well, heere he comes.	2298
Must all determine heere?	2316
Opposing Lawes with stroakes, and heere defying	2361
And heere remaine with your vncertaintie.	2412
This Ladies Husband heere; this (do you see)	2553
Corio. Which is his house, beseech you? | *Cit.* This heere before you.	2635
1 Ser. Wine, Wine, Wine: What seruice is heere? I	2654
*3 What you will not? Prythee tell my Maister what | a strange Guest	
he ha's heere.	2688
Stand I before thee heere: Then if thou hast	2741
And scarr'd the Moone with splinters: heere I cleep	2767
Sigh'd truer breath. But that I see thee heere	2773
Who now are heere, taking their leaues of mee,	2791
*3 Why he is so made on heere within, as if hee were	2851
Were in wilde hurry. Heere do we make his Friends	2896
Mene. Heere come the Clusters.	3054
1 Be it so, go back: the vertue of your name, | Is not heere passable.	3249
*passe heere: no, though it were as vertuous to lye, as to | liue chastly.	
Therefore go backe.	3264
Mene. Sirra, if thy Captaine knew I were heere,	3287
*this Varlet heere: This, who like a blocke hath denyed | my accesse to	
thee.	3313
More bound to's Mother, yet heere he let's me prate	3516
Auf. Go tell the Lords a'th'City, I am heere:	3650
Auf. Say no more. Heere come the Lords,	3719
Then shame to th'Romaines. And we heere deliuer	3746

HEEREAFTER = 2

Virg. Giue me excuse good Madame, I will obey you | in euery thing	
heereafter.	466
Nor from the State, nor priuate friends heereafter	3365

HEERES = 2*2

Sicin. Heere's hee, that would take from you all your | power.	1888
Heere's no place for you, pray you auoid: Come.	2685
1 Heere's a strange alteration?	2809
*fire for vs: looke thee, heere's water to quench it.	3307

HEES = 6*4

Men. Hee's a Beare indeede, that liues like a Lambe. 909

1.off*. That's a braue fellow: but hee's vengeance | prowd, and loues not
the common people. 1209

1.Off*. No more of him, hee's a worthy man: make | way, they are
comming. 1237

Menen. Hee's right Noble, let him be call'd for. 1346

3*.Cit*. Hee's not confirm'd, we may deny him yet. 1612

That hee's your fixed enemie; and reuoke | Your suddaine approbation. 1653

Edile. Hee's comming. | *Bru*. How accompanied? 2265

Hee's banish'd, and it shall be so. 2392

(Of whom hee's cheefe) with all the size that verity 3256

*growne from Man to Dragon: He has wings, hee's more | then a
creeping thing. 3582

HEIGHTEND = 1

Mine Honor for his truth: who being so heighten'd, 3674

HEIRE *see also* heyre = *1

*Son and Heire to Mars, set at vpper end o'th'Table: No 2852

HEL *l*.*3118 = *1

HELD = 7

Better be held, nor more attain'd then by 295

Mes. Spies of the *Volces* | Held me in chace, that I was forc'd to wheele 624

Learne how 'tis held, and what they are that must | Be Hostages for
Rome. 887

He still hath held them: that to's power he would 1173

Should not be vtter'd feebly: it is held, 1297

As cause had call'd you vp, haue held him to; 1596

Be held by you denials. Do not bid me 3436

HELL = 1*1

From Slaues, that Apes would beate; *Pluto* and Hell, 531

Corio. The fires i'th'lowest hell. Fould in the people: 2348

HELMES = 2

The Helmes o'th State; who care for you like Fathers, 78

Vnbuckling Helmes, fisting each others Throat, 2783

HELPE = 9*6

2.Cit*. What he cannot helpe in his Nature, you ac- | count 42

Your knees to them (not armes) must helpe. Alacke, 75

To helpe our fielded Friends. Come, blow thy blast. 498

Whil'st I with those that haue the spirit, wil haste | To helpe *Cominius*. 584

*helpe will serue: for once we stood vp about the Corne, 1401

*returne for Conscience sake, to helpe to get thee a Wife. 1419

Sicin. Helpe ye Citizens. 1885

Mene. Helpe *Martius*, helpe: you that be noble, helpe | him young and
old. 1946

S'incapeable of helpe. | *Tri*. Say not, we brought it. 3041

Auf. I cannot helpe it now, 3097

In this so neuer-needed helpe, yet do not 3188

Sicin. Wee'l meet them, and helpe the ioy. *Exeunt*. 3638

Helpe three a'th'cheefest Souldiers, Ile be one. 3831

HELPES = 2*1

With other Muniments and petty helpes 121

*helpes are many, or else your actions would growe won- | drous 932

Brut. Sir, those cold wayes, | That seeme like prudent helpes, are very
poysonous, 1936

HEN = 1

When she (poor Hen) fond of no second brood, 3519

HENCE = 13
  Com. Noble *Martius*. | *Sen.* Hence to your homes, be gone. 273
  Sicin. Let's hence, and heare | How the dispatch is made, and in what
  fashion 308
  That we with smoaking swords may march from hence 497
  Lart. Hence; and shut your gates vpon's: 720
  Brut. Get you hence instantly, and tell those friends, 1616
  Corio. Hence old Goat. 1880
  Corio. Hence rotten thing, or I shall shake thy bones | Out of thy
  Garments. 1883
  Against a falling Fabrick. Will you hence, 1972
  This Viperous Traitor: to eiect him hence 2023
  *thy Mistris: Thou prat'st, and prat'st, serue with thy tren-|cher:
  Hence. *Beats him away* 2702
  For mercy to his Countrey: therefore let's hence, 3233
  Then when I parted hence: but still subsisting 3738
  1.*Lord.* Beare from hence his body, 3822
HER *l*.170 *370 406 *442 468 594 764 771 1125 1127 *1482 *1483 2029
2031 2397 2400 2513 2557 *2602 3372 3373 3539 3568 = 19*6
HERALD = 1
  As the most Noble Coarse, that euer Herald | Did follow to his Vrne. 3824
HERAULD = 1
  Garland, with Captaines and Soul-|diers, and a Herauld. 1062
HERAULD = 2
HERCULES = 1*1
  If you had beene the Wife of *Hercules*, 2455
  **Mene.* As *Hercules* did shake downe Mellow Fruite: 3017
HERD *see* heard
HERDSMEN *see* heardsmen
HERE *see also* heere, here's, hereto = 14*5
  Titus Lartius. Oh Generall: | Here is the Steed, wee the Caparison: 760
  Martius. I sometime lay here in *Corioles*, 841
  Haue we no Wine here? 853
  Some old Crab-trees here at home, 1098
  *1.*Off.* Come, come, they are almost here: how many | stand for
  Consulships? 1205
  We met here, both to thanke, and to remember, | With Honors like
  himselfe. 1254
  Your louing motion toward the common Body, | To yeeld what passes
  here. 1261
  Here come moe Voyces. 1517
  Brut. We stay here for the People. 1546
  Here was, I thanke you for your Voyces, thanke you 1571
  Who after great *Hostilius* here was King, 1643
  **All.* Let's here our Tribune: peace, speake, speake, | speake. 1901
  Or let vs lose it: we doe here pronounce, 1921
  Corio. No, Ile die here: 1940
  And thus farre hauing stretcht it (here be with them) 2175
  Here is *Cominius*. 2196
  **Brut.* Dismisse them home. Here comes his Mother. 2511
  *3 What haue you to do here fellow? Pray you auoid | the house. 2677
  *2 Here sir, I'de haue beaten him like a dogge, but for | disturbing the
  Lords within. 2706
HEREAFTER *see also* heereafter = 1
  Thy selfe (forsooth) hereafter theirs so farre, 2186
HEREDITARIE = *1
  *some of the best of 'em were hereditarie hang-|men. 987

HERES = 3*2
Which without note, here's many else haue done, 805
*Volum. Looke, here's a Letter from him, the State hath 1005
Here's goodly worke. 1989
Here's no place for you: pray go to the doore? *Exit* 2663
*3 Why here's he that was wont to thwacke our Ge-|nerall, *Caius*
Martius. 2838
HERETO = 1
*he remember a kinder value of the People, then he hath | hereto priz'd
them at. 1267
HES = 11*5
*All. Against him first: He's a very dog to the Com-|monalty. 29
*1 *Cit*. He's one honest enough, wold al the rest wer so. 55
In whom already he's well grac'd, cannot 294
He's mine, or I am his: Mine Emulation 870
Sol. He's the diuell. 875
Bru. He's a Lambe indeed, that baes like a Beare. 908
Bru. He's poore in no one fault, but stor'd withall. | *Sicin*. Especially in
Pride. 915
*He's to make his requests by particulars, wherein euerie 1431
Sicin. He's a Disease that must be cut away. 2032
Mene. Oh he's a Limbe, that ha's but a Disease 2033
Sicin. He's sentenc'd: No more hearing. 2394
*Sicin. Bid them all home, he's gone: & wee'l no further, 2503
2 And he's as like to do't, as any man I can imagine. 2863
*not (looke you sir) shew themselues (as we terme it) his | Friends,
whilest he's in Directitude. 2866
At *Coriolanus* Exile. Now he's comming, 3058
*2 The worthy Fellow is our General. He's the Rock, 3344
HEW = 1
Once more to hew thy Target from thy Brawne, 2778
HEWES = *1
*And hewes downe Oakes, with rushes. Hang ye: trust ye? 192
HEYRE = 2
'Tis I that made thy Widdowes: Many an heyre 2624
'Twixt you there's difference: but the fall of either | Makes the Suruiuor
heyre of all. 3669
HIDE = 2
To hide your doings, and to silence that, 774
Shew them th'vnaking Skarres, which I should hide, 1370
HIDRA = 1
Giuen Hidra heere to choose an Officer, | That with his peremptory
Shall, being but 1787
HIE *see* hye
HIGH = 3
With thousands of these quarter'd slaues, as high 211
Let the high Office and the Honor go 1513
To be set high in place, we did commend 1650
HIGHER = 1
Then craue the higher, which first we do deserue. 1505
HIGHEST = 3
Mar. Thy Friend no lesse, | Then those she placeth highest: So farewell. 597
Wrench vp thy power to th'highest. 736
But tell the Traitor in the highest degree 3751
HIGHLY = 1
And mountainous Error be too highly heapt, 1511

HILL = 1
As if Olympus to a Mole-hill should   3379
HILLES = 1
Or pile ten hilles on the Tarpeian Rocke,   2086
HIM *l.*13 *29 *33 *43 186 194 195 256 *287 *369 *373 *374 392 393 394
*421 *423 *426 457 490 *491 521 546 547 567 580 632 647 650 653 654
692 *695 730 802 817 819 843 849 869 872 873 874 877 883 *906 *1005
1020 *1026 *1027 *1034 1050 1055 1056 *1123 1124 1126 1128 1132
1138 1140 1141 1154 1156 1163 *1165 *1168 1171 1187 1192 *1193 1195
*1216 *1222 *1223 *1237 *1273 1304 1306 1309 1317 1339 1346 1389
*1395 *1430 *1432 1434 *1526 1527 1577 1594 1596 1599 1601 1610
1612 1613 1632 *1633 1637 1697 1713 1744 1875 1881 1890 1891 1925
1926 1927 1928 1938 1939 1945 1947 1948 1999 2023 2024 2044 2049
2066 2079 2082 2195 2259 2261 2268 2290 2331 2356 2359 2362 2379
2386 2391 2428 2430 2432 2527 2533 *2657 2673 *2675 2676 2687 2704
*2706 *2810 2812 *2816 *2819 2826 *2827 2843 2844 *2845 *2846 2849
*2853 *2854 *2855 *2861 2871 *2893 2913 2937 2957 2968 3008 3024
3025 3030 3032 3043 3046 3048 3055 3067 3083 3092 3093 3101 3106
3107 3110 3119 3121 3124 3138 3153 3155 3171 3194 3214 3216 3219
3222 3226 3232 *3269 3272 *3300 3343 3359 3360 3362 3514 *3526 3537
3546 3547 *3575 3594 *3595 *3596 *3597 *3601 3606 3608 3645 3654
3672 3673 3684 3685 3686 3700 3712 3715 3733 3735 3767 3778 3780
3792 3793 *3801 3804 3806 3812 3816 3823 3830 = 204*61
HIMSELF = *2
*That would depopulate the city, & be euery man himself   1995
*As if a man were Author of himself, & knew no other kin   3385
HIMSELFE = 11*5
*good report for't, but that hee payes himselfe with bee-|ing proud.   34
*he was a Man-child, then now in first seeing he had pro-|ued himselfe
a man.   377
Clapt to their Gates, he is himselfe alone, | To answer all the City.   552
And that his Countries deerer then himselfe,   691
We met here, both to thanke, and to remember, | With Honors like
himselfe.   1254
*he himselfe stucke not to call vs the many-headed Multi-|tude.   1402
Then euer frown'd in Greece. By Ioue himselfe,   1801
As he began, and not vnknit himselfe | The Noble knot he made.   2541
hard for him, I haue heard him say so himselfe.   2844
*bald before him. Our Generall himselfe makes a Mistris   2854
*of him, Sanctifies himselfe with's hand, and turnes vp the   2855
Of our designe. He beares himselfe more proudlier,   3099
Till he had forg'd himselfe a name a'th'fire | Of burning Rome.   3166
*so slight. He that hath a will to die by himselfe, feares it   3339
To purge himselfe with words. Dispatch.   3657
3.Con. Therefore at your vantage, | Ere he expresse himself, or moue
the people   3713
HINT = 1
Sicin. Make them be strong, and ready for this hint   2287
HIRE see higher, hyre
HIS see also at's, for's, in's, on's, perceiue's, too's, to's, with's l.*31 *39
*40 41 *42 114 136 190 250 283 284 *291 303 305 310 *365 *368 *375
*381 396 397 399 400 402 408 409 419 *426 *427 555 676 689 691 693
701 746 759 768 813 818 850 870 *1006 1020 1033 1037 *1045 1139
*1142 1144 1151 1158 1161 1182 1185 *1217 *1227 *1228 *1231 *1232
1247 1248 1294 1305 1309 1311 1312 1318 1321 1328 1330 1336 1343
*1393 *1395 *1429 *1431 1548 *1550 1559 1562 1567 1587 1588 1590
1593 1594 1595 1597 1600 1605 1622 1623 1625 1626 1627 1639 1647

HIS *cont*.
1649 1652 1664 1666 1692 1698 1749 1776 1783 1788 1791 1799 1800
1939 1982 1983 1984 1985 1986 2011 2038 2039 2044 2049 2050 2060
2068 *2201 2227 2261 2291 2294 2295 2325 2332 2358 2405 2456 2468
2505 *2511 2534 2540 2545 *2603 *2604 2633 2635 2652 *2666 2667
*2811 *2813 2814 *2815 *2856 *2861 *2866 *2869 2894 2896 *2906 2913
2947 2968 2969 3025 3031 3033 3049 3050 *3071 3090 3101 3109 3115
3116 3120 3128 3153 3156 3157 3176 3177 3183 3201 3206 3217 3224
3225 3226 3228 3230 3231 3232 3233 3247 3253 3254 3259 *3262 *3268
*3278 *3340 3458 3503 3504 3527 3535 3536 *3575 3584 *3585 *3587
*3588 *3589 *3590 *3592 *3596 3645 3661 3663 3674 3675 3677 3679
3684 3686 3687 3688 3690 3692 3693 3704 3717 3718 3762 3763 3765
3777 3779 3789 3797 3798 3802 3822 3825 3826 = 207*52

HITHER = 5

Me thinkes, I heare hither your Husbands Drumme:	391
Where is he? Call him hither.	653
That our best Water, brought by Conduits hither,	1645
Sicin. Assemble presently the people hither:	2274
Are we come hither; since that thy sight, which should	3453

HITHERWARD = 1

And onely hitherward. I leaue your Honors.	351

HO *see also* hoa, hoo, how = 1

Tribunes, Patricians, Citizens: what ho:	1894

HOA = 1

Mart. Oh they are at it. | *Lart*. Their noise be our instruction. Ladders hoa.	512

HOAST = 2

With all th'applause and Clamor of the Hoast,	820
Set downe our Hoast. My partner in this Action,	3348

HOB = 1

To begge of Hob and Dicke, that does appeere	1507

HOBOYES = 1

*As the recomforted through th'gates. Why harke you: | *Trumpets, Hoboyes, Drums beate, altogether*.	3620

HOE = 3

Bru. The Ediles hoe: Let him be apprehended:	1875
Corio. First heare me speake. | *Both Tri*. Well, say: Peace hoe.	2313
2 *Lord*. Peace hoe: no outrage, peace:	3796

HOLD = 8*2

Scicin. I wish no better, then haue him hold that pur-|pose, and to put it in execution.	1165
All. Peace, peace, peace, stay, hold, peace.	1896
Scici. Therefore lay hold of him:	1925
That it shall hold Companionship in Peace	2146
That will not hold the handling: or say to them,	2181
2.Con. Most Noble Sir, If you do hold the same intent	3663
Lords. Hold, hold, hold, hold.	3807

HOLDING = 3

Holding *Corioles* in the name of Rome,	648
For a short holding, if we loose the Field,	717
And dispropertied their Freedomes; holding them,	1175

HOLDS = 2

But kneeles, and holds vp hands for fellowship,	3532
*I am husht vntill our City be afire, & then Ile speak a litle | *Holds her by the hand silent*.	3538

HOLLOW = 1

Auf. If I flye *Martius*, hollow me like a Hare.	731

HOLP = *1
    Com. You haue holp to rauish your owne daughters,   2996
HOLPE = 2
    Sicin. Sir, how com'st that you haue holpe | To make this rescue?   2008
    In mine owne person: holpe to reape the Fame   3689
HOLY = 2
    Like Graues i'th holy Church-yard.   2326
    More holy, and profound, then mine owne life,   2399
HOME = 29*8
    Mar. Go get you home you Fragments.   237
    With flight and agued feare, mend and charge home,   533
    At home, vpon my Brothers Guard, euen there   884
    Menen. Ha? *Martius* comming home?   999
    hoo, *Martius* comming home? | 2.*Ladies*. Nay, 'tis true.   1003
    *another, his Wife another, and (I thinke) there's one at | home for you.   1006
    he was wont to come home wounded? | *Virgil*. Oh no, no, no.   1016
    Volum. On's Browes: *Menenius*, hee comes the third | time home with
    the Oaken Garland.   1021
    *is comming home: hee ha's more cause to be prowd: 1041
    Would'st thou haue laugh'd, had I come Coffin'd home,   1082
    Oh welcome home: and welcome Generall,   1089
    Some old Crab-trees here at home,   1098
    I cannot speake him home: he stopt the flyers,   1317
    To oppose his hatred fully. Welcome home.   1698
    I prythee noble friend, home to thy House,   1957
    Bru. Go not home.   2075
    Cogge their Hearts from them, and come home belou'd   2243
    Bru. In this point charge him home, that he affects   2259
    *When most strooke home, being gentle wounded, craues   2444
    Sicin. Bid them all home, he's gone: & wee'l no further,   2503
    Sicin. Bid them home: say their great enemy is gone,   2509
    Brut. Dismisse them home. Here comes his Mother.   2511
    Mene. You haue told them home,   2563
    and I will merrily accompany you home.   2608
    Bru. Rais'd onely, that the weaker sort may wish | Good *Martius* home
    againe.   2980
    Sicin. Go Masters get you home, be not dismaid,   3077
    This true, which they so seeme to feare. Go home,   3079
    *home, I euer said we were i'th wrong, when we banish'd | him.   3082
    *2 *Cit*. So did we all. But come, let's home. *Exit Cit*.   3084
    To heare *Cominius* speake, Ile keepe at home.   3158
    You know the way home againe.   3333
    Ha's clock'd thee to the Warres: and safelie home   3520
    This is the last. So, we will home to Rome,   3529
    The Romane Ladies bring not comfort home   3607
    And had no welcomes home, but he returnes | Splitting the Ayre with
    noyse.   3708
    All Lords. You are most welcome home.   3721
    *The gates of Rome: Our spoiles we haue brought home   3742
HOMES = 1
    Com. Noble *Martius*. | *Sen*. Hence to your homes, be gone.   273
HONEST = 2*2
    *1 *Cit*. He's one honest enough, wold al the rest wer so.   55
    Menen. Why Masters, my good Friends, mine honest   63
    *1.*Cit*. Hee ha's done Nobly, and cannot goe without | any honest mans
    Voyce.   1524
    Thou art not honest, and the Gods will plague thee   3523

HONESTER = *1
Corio. I, tis an honester seruice, then to meddle with   2701
HONOR = 19*4
  *he wonne Honor, then in the embracements of his Bed,   365
  Honor, and so I pray go with vs.   465
  Hath not that Honor in't it had: For where   871
  These in honor followes *Martius Caius Coriolanus*.   1067
  And by deed-atchieuing Honor newly nam'd,   1078
  *haue hearts inclinable to honor and aduance the Theame | of our
  Assembly.   1264
  He had rather venture all his Limbes for Honor,   1294
  Your Honor with your forme.   1365
  Our purpose to them, and to our Noble Consull | Wish we all Ioy, and
  Honor.   1375
  Senat. To *Coriolanus* come all ioy and Honor.   1377
  *one of vs ha's a single Honor, in giuing him our own voi- | ces   1432
  Let the high Office and the Honor go   1513
  Honor and Policy, like vnseuer'd Friends,   2137
  Volum. If it be Honor in your Warres, to seeme   2143
  I should do so in Honor. I am in this   2163
  Least I surcease to honor mine owne truth,   2229
  To begge of thee, it is my more dis-honor,   2233
  Let them accuse me by inuention: I | Will answer in mine Honor.   2254
  Thou hast affected the fiue straines of Honor,   3506
  Loden with Honor. Say my Request's vniust,   3521
  Auf. I am glad thou hast set thy mercy, & thy Honor   3559
  Mine Honor for his truth: who being so heighten'd,   3674
  With no lesse Honor to the *Antiates*   3745
HONORABLE = *1
  Volum. Honorable *Menenius*, my Boy *Martius* appro- | ches: 997
HONORD = 2
  By mingling them with vs, the honor'd Number,   1762
  Th'honor'd Goddes | Keepe Rome in safety, and the Chaires of Iustice   2302
HONORS = 10*3
  Bru. Come: halfe all *Cominius* Honors are to *Martius*   304
  To *Martius* shall be Honors, though indeed | In ought he merit not.   306
  And onely hitherward. I leaue your Honors.   351
  All. The Gods assist you. | *Auf*. And keepe your Honors safe.   355
  That with the fustie Plebeans, hate thine Honors,   754
  From whom I haue receiu'd not onely greetings, | But with them,
  change of Honors.   1109
  Scicin. He cannot temp'rately transport his Honors,   1144
  With the least cause, these his new Honors,   1151
  *Honors in their Eyes, and his actions in their Hearts, that   1232
  We met here, both to thanke, and to remember, | With Honors like
  himselfe.   1254
  Coriol. Your Honors pardon: | I had rather haue my Wounds to heale
  againe,   1279
  Senat. He cannot but with measure fit the Honors | which we deuise
  him.   1338
  Carry his Honors eeuen: whether 'twas Pride   3128
HONOUR = 2*1
  *an houre from her beholding; I considering how Honour   370
  With Honour, as in Warre; since that to both | It stands in like request.   2147
  As poysonous of your Honour. No, our suite   3492
HONOURABLE = 1*1
  *honourable a graue, as to stuffe a Botchers Cushion, or to   983

HONOURABLE *cont.*
    Think'st thou it Honourable for a Nobleman   3511
HONOURD = 2
    When he did loue his Country, it honour'd him.   2044
    My wife comes formost, then the honour'd mould   3371
HONOURS = 1
    That he is thus cut off. Please it your Honours   3818
HOO = 2
    hoo, *Martius* comming home? | 2.*Ladies.* Nay, 'tis true.   1003
    All. Our enemy is banish'd, he is gone: Hoo, oo.   2427
HOOPD = 1
    Hoop'd out of Rome. Now this extremity,   2735
HOORDED = 1
    Th'hoorded plague a'th'Gods requit your loue.   2518
HOOTE = 1
    Gaue way vnto your Clusters, who did hoote | Him out o'th'Citty.   3045
HOOTING = 1
    Your stinking, greasie Caps, in hooting   3057
HOPE = 5*6
    Of their best trust: O're them *Auffidious*, | Their very heart of Hope. 669
    Brutus. Sir, I hope my words dis-bench'd you not? | *Coriol.* No Sir: yet
    oft,   1282
    3 Cit. You must thinke if we giue you any thing, we | hope to gaine by
    you.   1463
    2. Wee hope to finde you our friend: and therefore   1495
    *so, they are in a most warlike preparation, & hope to com | vpon
    them, in the heate of their diuision   2587
    Hath brought me to thy Harth, not out of Hope   2736
    *The Warres for my money. I hope to see Romanes as   2889
    So that all hope is vaine, vnlesse his Noble Mother,   3231
    Volum. Thou art my Warriour, I hope to frame thee | Do you know
    this Lady?   3414
    *little finger, there is some hope the Ladies of Rome, espe-|cially 3574
    *is no hope in't, our throats are sentenc'd, and stay vppon | execution. 3576
HOPELESSE = 1
    To hopelesse restitution, so he might | Be call'd your Vanquisher.   1693
HOPING = 1
    Intends t'appeare before the People, hoping   3656
HORNE = 1
    The horne, and noise o'th'Monsters, wants not spirit   1789
HORNES = 2
    As they would hang them on the hornes a'th Moone,   226
    Thrusts forth his hornes againe into the world   2947
HORSD = 1
    Leades fill'd, and Ridges hors'd   1130
HORSE = 2*1
    Lar. My horse to yours, no. | *Mar.* Tis done. | *Lart.* Agreed.   484
    Lart. So, the good Horse is mine.   489
    *Mother now, then an eight yeare old horse. The tartnesse   3586
HORSES = 2
    And tent themselues with death: of all the Horses,   783
    Death on the Wheele, or at wilde Horses heeles,   2085
HORSE-DRENCH = *1
    *better report then a Horse-drench. Is he not wounded?   1015
HOSPITABLE = 1
    Against the hospitable Canon, would I   885

HOST *see also* hoast = 1
To giue my poore Host freedome. 846
HOSTAGES = 1
Learne how 'tis held, and what they are that must | Be Hostages for
Rome. 887
HOSTILE = 1
Giuen Hostile strokes, and that not in the presence 2382
HOSTILIUS = 1
Who after great *Hostilius* here was King, 1643
HOSTLER = 1
Corio. I, as an Hostler, that fourth poorest peece 2300
HOT = *1
*one that loues a cup of hot Wine, with not a drop of alay-|ing 944
HOTLY = 1
As hotly, and as Nobly with thy Loue, 2769
HOUND = 2
Euen like a fawning Grey-hound in the Leash, | To let him slip at will. 649
Staine all your edges on me. Boy, false Hound: 3783
HOURE = 8*2
*an houre from her beholding; I considering how Honour 370
*halfe an houre together: ha's such a confirm'd coun-|tenance. 422
Mes. Aboue an houre, my Lord. 620
How could'st thou in a mile confound an houre, | And bring thy Newes
so late? 622
Halfe an houre since brought my report. 627
We proue this very houre. 679
Then were they chosen: in a better houre, 1869
I am so dishonour'd, that the very houre | You take it off againe. 2338
Vnseparable, shall within this houre, 2642
Which to this houre bewaile the Iniury, 3835
HOURELY = *1
*thee. The glorious Gods sit in hourely Synod about thy 3304
HOURES = 3
Mar. Within these three houres *Tullus* 732
and to be on foot at an houres warning. 2614
Whose Houres, whose Bed, whose Meale and Exercise 2640
HOURS = *1
Mar. See heere these mouers, that do prize their hours 575
HOUSE = 18*2
Because I am the Store-house, and the Shop 140
At a poore mans house: he vs'd me kindly, 842
Menen. I will make my very house reele to night: 1008
Ere in our owne house I doe shade my Head, 1107
Corio. Where? at the Senate-house? | *Scicin*. There, *Coriolanus*. 1539
The Noble House o'th'*Martians*: from whence came 1641
Of the same House *Publius* and *Quintus* were, 1644
The Corne a'th'Store-house gratis, as 'twas vs'd | Sometime in Greece. 1809
Mene. Goe, get you to our House: be gone, away. 1951
I prythee noble friend, home to thy House, 1957
Pursue him to his house, and plucke him thence, 2049
The meanest house in Rome; so farre my Sonne 2552
Cit. He is, and Feasts the Nobles of the State, at his | house this night. 2633
Corio. Which is his house, beseech you? | *Cit*. This heere before you. 2635
Corio. A goodly House: 2659
out o'thhouse: Prythee call my Master to him. 2676
*3 What haue you to do here fellow? Pray you auoid | the house. 2677

HOUSE *cont*.
   All to the Senate-house: some newes is comming | That turnes their
   Countenances.   2965
   Me. 'Tis true, if he were putting to my house, the brand   3035
   Mes. Sir, if you 'ld saue your life, flye to your House,   3604
HOUSES = *1
   *yet. Suffer vs to famish, and their Store-houses cramm'd   81
HOUSEWIFE *see* huswife
HOUSE-KEEPERS = 1
   Val. How do you both? You are manifest house-kee-|pers.   414
HOW = 46*14
   2.*Cit*. It was an answer, how apply you this?   155
   Sicin. Let's hence, and heare | How the dispatch is made, and in what
   fashion   308
   And know how we proceede, | *Auf*. Is it not yours?   316
   *an houre from her beholding; I considering how Honour   370
   Virg. But had he died in the Businesse Madame, how | then?   379
   Val. How do you both? You are manifest house-kee-|pers.   414
   *What are you sowing heere? A fine spotte in good | faith. How does
   your little Sonne?   415
   *whether his fall enrag'd him, or how 'twas, hee did so set   426
   *his teeth, and teare it. Oh, I warrant how he mammockt | it.   427
   Mar. How farre off lie these Armies?   493
   That beare the shapes of men, how haue you run   530
   *Me thinkes thou speak'st not well. How long is't since?   619
   How could'st thou in a mile confound an houre, | And bring thy Newes
   so late?   622
   Com. Flower of Warriors, how is't with *Titus Lartius*?   644
   Com. But how preuail'd you?   659
   Mar. How lies their Battell? Know you on w side   665
   Learne how 'tis held, and what they are that must | Be Hostages for
   Rome.   887
   How the world goes: that to the pace of it   892
   Men. This is strange now: Do you two know, how   918
   Both. Why? how are we censur'd?   921
   *How now (my as faire as Noble) Ladyes, and the Moone   994
   *1.*Off*. Come, come, they are almost here: how many | stand for
   Consulships?   1205
   Then heare say how I got them.   1281
   Menen. Masters of the People, | Your multiplying Spawne, how can he
   flatter?   1291
   Bru. You see how he intends to vse the people.   1380
   direct you how you shall go by him.   1434
   3 *Cit*. How not your owne desire?   1460
   Scici. How now, my Masters, haue you chose this man?   1553
   How in his Suit he scorn'd you: but your Loues,   1625
   How youngly he began to serue his Countrey,   1639
   How long continued, and what stock he springs of,   1640
   Corio. Spoke he of me? | *Latius*. He did, my Lord. | *Corio*. How? what? 1687
   Latius. How often he had met you Sword to Sword: 1690
   Brut. How? I informe them?   1733
   Corio. How? no more?   1767
   Neither Supreame; How soone Confusion   1804
   How shall this Bosome-multiplied, digest   1828
   Sicin. Sir, how com'st that you haue holpe | To make this rescue? 2008
   You had not shew'd them how ye were dispos'd   2109
   You adopt your policy: How is it lesse or worse   2145

HOW *cont*.

How you can frowne, then spend a fawne vpon'em,	2166
Edile. Hee's comming. | *Bru*. How accompanied?	2265
For which you are a Traitor to the people. | *Corio*. How? Traytor?	2345
3 How sir? Do you meddle with my Master?	2700
tell how to tearme it.	2817
*2 Faith looke you, one cannot tell how to say that: for	2829
How probable I do not know, that *Martius*	2975
Mene. How? Was't we? We lou'd him,	3043
Com. I minded him, how Royall 'twas to pardon	3171
Speed how it will. I shall ere long, haue knowledge | Of my successe. *Exit*.	3220
Corio. Away. | *Mene*. How? Away?	3315
Then pitty: Note how much, therefore be gone.	3322
*1 Do you heare how wee are shent for keeping your | greatnesse backe?	3334
You must report to th'Volcian Lords, how plainly	3349
How more vnfortunate then all liuing women	3452
That all but we enioy. For how can we?	3461
Alas! how can we, for our Country pray?	3462
I'de not haue giuen a doit. Harke, how they ioy. | *Sound still with the Shouts*.	3631
1.*Con*. How is it with our Generall?	3660
Corio. Traitor? How now? | *Auf*. I Traitor, *Martius*.	3753

HOWBEIT = 1

Whether I blush or no: howbeit, I thanke you,	826

HOWSOEUER = *1

*2 Howsoeuer you haue bin his Lier, as you say you	3268

HUM *see also* humme = *1

*like a knell, and his hum is a Battery. He sits in his State,	3590

HUMANE = 4

Were slyly crept into his humane powers,	1139
In humane Action, and Capacitie,	1176
What may be sworne by, both Diuine and Humane,	1840
1.*Sen*. Noble Tribunes, | It is the humane way: the other course	2069

HUMANELY = *1

*were wholsome, wee might guesse they releeued vs hu-|manely:	20

HUMBLE = 2*1

Brut. With a prowd heart he wore his humble Weeds:	1550
With what Contempt he wore the humble Weed,	1624
Now humble as the ripest Mulberry,	2180

HUMBLER = 1

Let vs seeme humbler after it is done, | Then when it was a dooing.	2507

HUMILITIE = 1

The Naples Vesture of Humilitie,	1157

HUMILITY = 1*1

Enter Coriolanus in a gowne of Humility, with | Menenius.	1426
*Heere he comes, and in the Gowne of humility, marke	1428

HUMME = 1

And humme at good *Cominius*, much vnhearts mee.	3207

HUMOROUS = *1

Men. I am knowne to be a humorous *Patritian*, and	943

HUNDRED = 4*1

For halfe a hundred yeares: Summon the Towne.	492
Mene. A hundred thousand Welcomes!	1091
Ile haue fiue hundred Voyces of that sound.	1614
1.Cit. I twice fiue hundred, & their friends, to piece 'em.	1615
My grained Ash an hundred times hath broke,	2766

HUNGER = 1
  hunger for Bread, not in thirst for Reuenge.   26
HUNGER-BROKE = 1
  That Hunger-broke stone wals: that dogges must eate   219
HUNGRY = 2*1
  They said they were an hungry, sigh'd forth Prouerbes   218
  *Men. I, to deuour him, as the hungry Plebeians would | the Noble
  Martius.   906
  Then let the Pibbles on the hungry beach   3409
HUNT = 1*1
  Onely my warres with him. He is a Lion | That I am proud to hunt.   256
  *Me. Do not cry hauocke, where you shold but hunt | With modest
  warrant,   2006
HURRIED = 1
  Ne're through an Arch so hurried the blowne Tide,   3619
HURRY = 1
  Were in wilde hurry. Heere do we make his Friends   2896
HURT = 4
  All hurt behinde, backes red, and faces pale   532
  You sooth'd not, therefore hurt not: but your People,   1285
  Corio. Let me but stand, I will not hurt your Harth.   2679
  Great hurt and Mischiefe: thereto witnesse my   2724
HURTS = 1
  *for his place: he receiued in the repulse of Tarquin seuen | hurts ith'
  Body.   1045
HUSBAND = 6*2
  *in a more comfortable sort: If my Sonne were my Hus-|band,   363
  *Val. In truth la go with me, and Ile tell you excellent | newes of your
  Husband.   453
  Your Husband so much swet. Cominius,   2457
  Virg. You shall stay too: I would I had the power | To say so to my
  Husband.   2522
  This Ladies Husband heere; this (do you see)   2553
  *shee's falne out with her Husband. Your Noble Tullus   2602
  Virgil. My Lord and Husband.   3386
  The Sonne, the Husband, and the Father tearing   3457
HUSBANDRY = 1
  And shewes good Husbandry for the Volcian State,   3113
HUSBANDS = 1
  Me thinkes, I heare hither your Husbands Drumme: 391
HUSHT = *1
  *I am husht vntill our City be afire, & then Ile speak a litle | Holds her
  by the hand silent.   3538
HUSWIFE = 1
  play the idle Huswife with me this afternoone.   433
HYDRA see Hidra
HYE = 1
  2.Sen. Noble Auffidius, | Take your Commission, hye you to your
  Bands,   342
HYPERBOLICALL = 1
  You shoot me forth in acclamations hyperbolicall,   806
HYRE = 2
  Like to a Haruest man, that task'd to mowe | Or all, or loose his hyre.   398
  As if I had receiu'd them for the hyre | Of their breath onely.   1371
I see also I'de, I'ld, Ile = 388*132, 15*6
  2.Cit. I sir, well, well.   149

I *cont.*

Com. I, if you come not in the blood of others, | But mantled in your owne.   638

*Men. I, to deuour him, as the hungry Plebeians would | the Noble *Martius.*   906

*Volum. I, worthy *Menenius*, and with most prosperous | approbation.   1000

*Menen. Wondrous: I, I warrant you, and not with-|out his true purchasing.   1035

Corio. I, but mine owne desire.   1459

Brut. I, spare vs not: Say, we read Lectures to you,   1638

Corio. Let them hang. | *Volum.* I, and burne too.   2111

Menen. I, but mildely.   2256

Sicin. Are you mankinde? | *Volum. I foole, is that a shame. Note but this Foole,   2524

3 Vnder the Canopy | *Corio.* I.   2693

*Corio. I, tis an honester seruice, then to meddle with   2701

1 I, and for an assault too.   2831

1 I, and it makes men hate one another.   2887

Brut. But is this true sir? | *Com.* I, and you'l looke pale   3019

Com. Oh I, what else? *Exeunt both.*   3076

*I You may not passe, you must returne: our Generall | will no more heare from thence.   3241

Virg. I, and mine, that brought you forth this boy,   3481

Corio. I by and by; But we will drinke together: 3562

Corio. Traitor? How now? | *Auf.* I Traitor, *Martius.*   3753

Corio. Martius? | *Auf.* I *Martius, Caius Martius*: Do'st thou thinke   3755

IACKE = *1

*perceiue, that a Iacke gardant cannot office me from my   3299

ICE = 1

Then is the coale of fire vpon the Ice,   184

ICICLE *see* isicle

IDE = 4*1

And let me vse my Sword, I'de make a Quarrie   210

vpon my partie, I'de reuolt to make   255

*2 Here sir, I'de haue beaten him like a dogge, but for | disturbing the Lords within.   2706

And say 'tis true; I'de not beleeue them more   2763

I'de not haue giuen a doit. Harke, how they ioy. | *Sound still with the Shouts.*   3631

IDLE = 2

I'th midd'st a th'body, idle and vnactiue,   101

play the idle Huswife with me this afternoone.   433

IDLY = 1

When the Alarum were strucke, then idly sit   1289

IEALOUS = 1

Now by the iealous Queene of Heauen, that kisse   3395

IEST = *1

*Val. Verily I do not iest with you: there came newes | from him last night.   456

IEWELL = 1

Weare not so rich a Iewell. Thou was't a Souldier   558

IF *I.**19 *45 *85 122 128 131 141 299 301 345 352 *363 *372 536 562 638 662 686 688 690 698 715 717 731 748 807 812 869 *928 *951 *957 *960 *969 *979 *1019 1138 1184 *1214 *1219 *1266 1299 1333 1371 1382 *1388 1390 *1392 *1394 *1407 1415 *1423 *1463 *1476 1584 1664 1740 1773 1791 1792 1793 1794 1796 2016 2077 2108 2143 *2201 2260 2278 2318 2401 2455 2480 2497 *2520 *2631 2650 2651 *2710 2737 2741 2749

IF *cont*.
    2761 2795 *2851 2910 2935 3005 3006 3031 *3035 3050 3063 3157 3187
    3189 3246 *3262 3287 *3300 3379 *3385 3434 3445 3475 3489 3499 3522
    3547 *3573 3594 3604 3606 *3663 3693 3784 = 84*33

IGNORANCE = 4*1

Then vale your Ignorance: If none, awake	1792
Of generall Ignorance, it must omit | Reall Necessities, and giue way the while	1845
Your ignorance (which findes not till it feeles,	2417
Do smilingly Reuolt, and who resists | Are mock'd for valiant Ignorance,	3022
*of them, and in a violent popular ignorance, giuen your	3277

IGNORANT = 3

Scicin. Why eyther were you ignorant to see't?	1574
All reuoke your ignorant election: Enforce his Pride,	1622
Action is eloquence, and the eyes of th'ignorant	2177

ILD = 1

From these old armes and legges, by the good Gods | I'ld with thee, euery foot.	2498

ILE *l*.95 266 *420 *438 *453 490 *491 521 534 724 749 873 *1026 *1039
    *1433 1450 *1543 1545 1614 1816 1940 1977 2066 2079 2242 2245 2371
    2459 2478 2531 2650 2652 *2672 *2820 3152 3158 3193 3205 3214 3216
    3219 *3297 3383 3483 3484 *3538 3549 3557 3560 3704 3757 3819
    3831 = 42*12

ILL *l*.1860 = 1, 2

Lessen his person, then an ill report:	689
Let me deserue so ill as you, and make me | Your fellow Tribune.	1737

ILL-SCHOOLD = 1

Since a could draw a Sword, and is ill-school'd	2063

IMAGINE = 1

2 And he's as like to do't, as any man I can imagine.	2863

IMITATE = 1

To imitate the graces of the Gods.	3507

IMPATIENCE = 1

2.*Lord*. His owne impatience, | Takes from *Auffidius* a great part of blame:	3826

IMPEDIMENT = 2

Appeare in your impediment. For the Dearth,	73
That we labour'd (no impediment betweene)	1631

IMPERFECT = *1

*Tiber in't: Said, to be something imperfect in fauou-|ring	945

IMPOSSIBILITY = 1

Murd'ring Impossibility, to make | What cannot be, slight worke.	3412

IMPOYSOND = 1

Auf. Euen so, as with a man by his owne Almes im-|poyson'd, and with his Charity slaine.	3661

IMPRESSION = 1

Of thy deepe duty, more impression shew | Then that of common Sonnes.	3400

IMPREST = 1

Who weares my stripes imprest vpon him, that	3778

IN *see also* in's, in't, i'th = 247*81

INCAPEABLE = 1

S'incapeable of helpe. | *Tri*. Say not, we brought it.	3041

INCENSD = 2

If 'gainst your selfe you be incens'd, wee'le put you	812
Brut. The People are incens'd against him.	1713

INCENST = *1
  Bru. I would he had. | *Volum*. I would he had? Twas thou incenst the
  rable.   2543
INCHES = 1
  They'l giue him death by Inches.   3608
INCLINABLE = *1
  *haue hearts inclinable to honor and aduance the Theame | of our
  Assembly.   1264
INCLINATION = 1
  And try'd his Inclination: from him pluckt   1594
INCLIND = 1
  And foure shall quickly draw out my Command, | Which men are best
  inclin'd.   705
INCLINE = *1
  *would incline to the people, there was neuer a worthier | man.   1424
INCORPORATE = 1
  True is it my Incorporate Friends (quoth he)   137
INCREASE *see* encrease
INDEED = 9*2
  2 *Cit*. Care for vs? True indeed, they nere car'd for vs   80
  To *Martius* shall be Honors, though indeed | In ought he merit not.   306
  Volum. Indeed you shall not: 390
  Val. Indeed la, tis a Noble childe. | *Virg*. A Cracke Madam.   430
  Virg. Indeed no, by your patience; Ile not ouer the   438
  Vir. No good Madam, pardon me, indeed I will not | foorth.   451
  Vir. Indeed Madam.   458
  Virgil. No | At a word Madam; Indeed I must not,   474
  Bru. He's a Lambe indeed, that baes like a Beare.   908
  Your Voyces? Indeed I would be Consull.   1523
  Nay godded me indeed. Their latest refuge   3358
INDEEDE = *2
  Men. Hee's a Beare indeede, that liues like a Lambe.   909
  *bin a Rod to her Friends, you haue not indeede loued the | Common
  people.   1483
INDIFFERENTLY = *1
  *no, hee waued indifferently, 'twixt doing them neyther   1220
INDUCD = 1
  Induc'd as you haue beene, that's for my Countrey: 767
INEUITABLE = 1
  Tis fond to waile ineuitable strokes,   2464
INFANT-LIKE = *1
  *single: your abilities are to Infant-like, for dooing   933
INFECT = 1*1
  Farther then seene, and one infect another   528
  *would infect my Braine, being the Heardsmen of   989
INFECTED = 1
  No more infected with my Countries loue   3737
INFECTION = 1
  Least his infection being of catching nature, | Spred further.   2050
INFERIOUR = 1
  The strongest Nerues, and small inferiour Veines   145
INFIRMITY = 1
  To punish; Not a man, of their Infirmity.   1774
INFORCE = 2
  Inforce him with his enuy to the people,   2261
  Inforce the present Execution | Of what we chance to Sentence.   2284

INFORCEMENT = 1
  And with a sudden re-inforcement strucke   1327
INFORMATION = 1
  Least you shall chance to whip your Information,   2958
INFORMD = 1
  Corio. Haue you inform'd them sithence?   1732
INFORME = 5
  He did informe the truth: but for our Gentlemen,   655
  Bru. Come, wee'l informe them   1384
  Brut. How? I informe them?   1733
  Edile. I shall informe them.   2281
  Corio. The God of Souldiers: | With the consent of supreame Ioue,
  informe   3423
INFRINGE = 1
  Shall I be tempted to infringe my vow   3367
INGRATE = 1
  Ingrate forgetfulnesse shall poison rather   3321
INGRATEFULL = *2
  *were a kinde of ingratefull Iniurie: to report otherwise, 1234
  *multitude to be ingratefull, were to make a Monster of 1397
INGRATITUDE = 1*1
  Com. Should they not: | Well might they fester 'gainst Ingratitude, 781
  *of them. Ingratitude is monstrous, and for the   1396
INHERENT = 1
  And by my Bodies action, teach my Minde | A most inherent Basenesse. 2230
INHERITANCE = 1
  For the inheritance of their loues, and safegard   2167
INHERITED = 1
  Volum. I haue liued, | To see inherited my very Wishes, 1111
INIURIE = *1
  *were a kinde of ingratefull Iniurie: to report otherwise, 1234
INIURIOUS = 1
  Call me their Traitor, thou iniurious Tribune.   2349
INIURY = 2
  Red as 'twould burne Rome: and his Iniury   3225
  Which to this houre bewaile the Iniury,   3835
INKLING = *1
  *haue had inkling this fortnight what we intend to do, w 60
INNOUATOR = 1
  Attach thee as a Traitorous Innouator: 1877
INS = 2
  Wash my fierce hand in's heart. Go you to th'Citie, 886
  Death, that darke Spirit, in's neruie Arme doth lye, 1057
INSENSIBLE = *1
  *deafe, sleepe, insensible, a getter of more bastard Chil-|dren, then
  warres a destroyer of men.   2882
INSHELLED *see* in-shell'd
INSINUATING = *1
  *then my Heart, I will practice the insinuating nod, and be 1490
INSISTING = 1
  Insisting on the olde prerogatiue | And power i'th Truth a'th Cause. 2279
INSOLENCE = 2*1
  *wonder, his insolence can brooke to be commanded vn-|der *Cominius*? 291
  At some time, when his soaring Insolence   1182
  The Cockle of Rebellion, Insolence, Sedition,   1760
INSOLENT = 2
  Bru. Caius Martius was | A worthy Officer i'th'Warre, but Insolent, 2928

INSOLENT *cont.*
Auf. Insolent Villaine. | *All Consp.* Kill, kill, kill, kill, kill him.　　3803
INSTANT = 2
(Eu'n from this instant) banish him our Citie　　2386
More then the instant Armie we can make | Might stop our
Countryman.　　3191
INSTANTLY = 1
Brut. Get you hence instantly, and tell those friends,　　1616
INSTINCT = 1
Be such a Gosling to obey instinct; but stand　　3384
INSTRUCT = 1
Did see, and heare, deuise, instruct, walke, feele,　　104
INSTRUCTION = 2
Mart. Oh they are at it. | *Lart.* Their noise be our instruction. Ladders
hoa.　　512
Not by your owne instruction, nor by'th'matter　　2152
INSTRUMENTS = 1 *1
Like labour with the rest, where th'other Instruments　　103
Mar. May these same Instruments, which you prophane,　　797
INSUING = 1
To th'insuing Age, abhorr'd. Speake to me Son:　　3505
INSULT = *1
*Insult without all reason: where Gentry, Title, wisedom　　1843
INSURRECTIONS = 1 *1
Win vpon power, and throw forth greater Theames | For Insurrections
arguing.　　234
Rom. There hath beene in Rome straunge Insurrecti-|ons:　　2583
INT = 2 *2
Hath not that Honor in't it had: For where　　871
*Tiber in't: Said, to be something imperfect in fauou-|ring　　945
Beares a Command in't: Though thy Tackles torne,　　2718
*is no hope in't, our throats are sentenc'd, and stay vppon | execution.　　3576
INTANGLED = *1
*bleeding, the more intangled by your hearing: All the　　973
INTEGRITY = 1
Of that Integrity which should becom't:　　1858
INTELLIGENCE = *1
Vol. You will be welcome with this intelligence *Ni-|canor.*　　2598
INTEND = *1
*haue had inkling this fortnight what we intend to do, w　　60
INTENDED = 1 *1
Sicin. Yet your good will | Must haue that thankes from Rome, after
the measure | As you intended well.　　3202
*out the intended fire, your City is ready to flame in, with　　3282
INTENDS = 2
Bru. You see how he intends to vse the people.　　1380
Intends t'appeare before the People, hoping　　3656
INTENT = *2
Scicin. May they perceiue's intent: he wil require them　　1381
2.Con. Most Noble Sir, If you do hold the same intent　　3663
INTERCESSION = 1 *1
*daughters, or with the palsied intercession of such a de-|cay'd　　3280
Hath an Aspect of intercession, which　　3381
INTERIMS = 1
By Interims and conueying gusts, we haue heard　　608
INTERIOUR = *1
*but an Interiour suruey of your good selues. Oh that you | could.　　936

INTERPRETATION = 2
Lie in th'interpretation of the time,   3141
Which by th'interpretation of full time, | May shew like all your selfe.   3421
INTERRUPTED = 1
Like interrupted Waters, and o're-beare | What they are vs'd to beare.   1974
INTER-IOYNE = 1
And inter-ioyne their yssues. So with me,   2648
INTIRE = 1
A Carbuncle intire: as big as thou art   557
INTO *l*.1125 1139 *1230 1319 *1394 1590 1927 1965 2221 2344 2415 2788
2947 3002 3063 3157 3217 = 15*2
INTOMBD = *1
*be intomb'd in an Asses Packe-saddle; yet you must bee   984
INTREATIES = 1
And with our faire intreaties hast them on. *Exeunt*   3234
INTREATY = *1
*the intreaty and graunt of the whole Table. Hee'l go he   2859
INUENTION = 1
Let them accuse me by inuention: I | Will answer in mine Honor.   2254
INUENTORY = *1
*that afflicts vs, the obiect of our misery, is as an inuento- | ry   22
INUESTED = 1
Remaines, that in th'Officiall Markes inuested,   1533
INUETERATE = 1
After the inueterate Hate he beares you.   1629
INUINCIBLE = 1
With Precepts that would make inuincible | The heart that conn'd them.   2446
IN-SHELLD = 1
Which were In-shell'd, when *Martius* stood for Rome,   2948
IOINE *see* ioyne
IOINED *see* ioyn'd
IOINT *see* ioynt-seruant
IOT = 1
Neyther will they bate one iot of Ceremonie.   1361
IOUE = 4
By Ioue, 'twould be my minde.   1778
Then euer frown'd in Greece. By Ioue himselfe,   1801
Or *Ioue*, for's power to Thunder: his Heart's his Mouth: 1985
Corio. The God of Souldiers: | With the consent of supreame Ioue,
informe   3423
IOUES = 2
As to *Ioues* Statue, and the Commons made   1196
In Ioues owne Booke, like an vnnaturall Dam | Should now eate vp her
owne.   2030
IOURNEY = 2
I may spurre on my iourney. | *Soul*. I shall sir.   893
*state to finde you out there. You haue well saued mee a | dayes
iourney.   2581
IOY = 6*2
*thee Daughter, I sprang not more in ioy at first hearing   376
Our purpose to them, and to our Noble Consull | Wish we all Ioy, and
Honor.   1375
Senat. To *Coriolanus* come all ioy and Honor.   1377
Both. The Gods giue you ioy Sir heartily.   1502
2.Cit. Therefore let him be Consull: the Gods giue him | ioy, and make
him good friend to the People.   1526
*Make our eies flow with ioy, harts dance with comforts,   3454

IOY *cont*.

I'de not haue giuen a doit. Harke, how they ioy. | *Sound still with the*
Shouts.   3631
Sicin. Wee'l meet them, and helpe the ioy. *Exeunt*.   3638

IOYFULL = *1

Rom. I am ioyfull to heare of their readinesse, and am   2615

IOYND = 3

Ioyn'd with *Auffidius*, leads a power 'gainst Rome,   2976
If *Martius* should be ioyn'd with Volceans.   3005
Ioyn'd in Commission with him: but either haue borne   3106

IOYNE = 2

And inter-ioyne their yssues. So with me,   2648
Must beare my beating to his Graue, shall ioyne | To thrust the Lye
vnto him.   3779

IOYNT-SERUANT = 1

Made him ioynt-seruant with me: Gaue him way   3685

IRON = *1

*This peace is nothing, but to rust Iron, encrease Taylors, | and breed
Ballad-makers.   2877

IRONS = 1

Irons of a Doit, Dublets that Hangmen would   577

IS *see also* all's, angers, armie's, confusions, countries, heart's, heere's,
hee's, here's, he's, is't, it's, one's, request's, shee's, she's, tackles, that's,
there's, ther's, 'tis, valors, warres, what's, where's, who's, whose,
witchcraft's, work's = 158*61

ISICLE = 1

Corio. The Noble Sister of *Publicola*; | The Moone of Rome: Chaste as
the Isicle   3416

ISSUE = 1*2

*Sonne, I therein would haue found issue. Heare me pro- |fesse   382
Mar. They feare vs not, but issue forth their Citie.   515
*I thinke, if all our wittes were to issue out of one Scull,   1407

ISSUED *see* yssued

ISSUES *see* yssues

IST = 4*3

*1.*Cit*. Let vs kill him, and wee'l haue Corne at our own | price. Is't a
Verdict?   13
*Me thinkes thou speak'st not well. How long is't since?   619
Com. Flower of Warriors, how is't with *Titus Lartius*?   644
Com. Tak't, 'tis yours: what is't?   840
And perish constant Fooles: who is't can blame him?   3024
Sicin. Is't possible, that so short a time can alter the | condition of a
man.   3578
Is't most certaine.   3616

IT *see also* and't, becom't, beleeu't, by't, call't, controul't, deny't, done't,
don't, doo't, do't, for't, giu't, ha't, haue't, heare't, in't, is't, it's, know't,
on't, saw't, say't, scale't, see't, speak't, suffer't, 't, tak't, throw't, 'tis,
too't, vndertak't, vpon't, was't = 187*53

ITALY = 2

Plough Rome, and harrow Italy, Ile neuer   3383
In Italy, and her Confederate Armes   3568

ITCH = 1

That rubbing the poore Itch of your Opinion, | Make your selues Scabs.   175

ITH = 32*10

I'th midd'st a th'body, idle and vnactiue,   101
What's done i'th Capitoll: Who's like to rise,   204
Com. As I guesse *Martius*, | Their Bands i'th Vaward are the Antients   667

ITH *cont.*

I'th'end admire: where Ladies shall be frighted,	752
I'th'field proue flatterers, let Courts and Cities be	799
I'th'part that is at mercy? fiue times, *Martius*,	865
Volum. Ith' Shoulder, and ith' left Arme: there will be	1043
*for his place: he receiued in the repulse of *Tarquin* seuen | hurts ith' Body.	1045
Mene. One ith' Neck, and two ith'Thigh, there's nine | that I know.	1047
Appeare i'th'Market place, nor on him put	1156
Corio. I had rather haue one scratch my Head i'th' Sun,	1288
An o're-prest Roman, and i'th' Consuls view	1307
He prou'd best man i'th' field, and for his meed	1311
I'th' Body of the Weale: and now arriuing	1582
Deseru'd this so dishonor'd Rub, layd falsely | I'th' plaine Way of his Merit.	1748
Did not deserue Corne gratis. Being i'th'Warre,	1822
And throw their power i'th'dust.	1871
Though calued i'th' Porch o'th' Capitoll:	1964
Mene. Consider this: He ha's bin bred i'th'Warres	2062
I'th'Warre do grow together: Grant that, and tell me	2138
Com. I haue beene i'th' Market place: and Sir 'tis fit	2197
Or neuer trust to what my Tongue can do | I'th way of Flattery further.	2246
I'th'right and strength a'th'Commons: be it either	2276
Insisting on the olde prerogatiue | And power i'th Truth a'th Cause.	2279
Like Graues i'th holy Church-yard.	2326
Corio. The fires i'th'lowest hell. Fould in the people:	2348
To enter our Rome gates. I'th'Peoples name, | I say it shall bee so.	2389
More then a wilde exposture, to each chance | That starts i'th'way before thee.	2475
And loose aduantage, which doth euer coole | Ith'absence of the needer.	2483
3 Where's that? | *Corio.* I'th City of Kites and crowes.	2695
*3 I'th City of Kites and Crowes? What an Asse it is,	2697
I had fear'd death, of all the Men i'th'World	2738
*2 So did I, Ile be sworne: He is simply the rarest man | i'th'world.	2820
*Newes is, our Generall is cut i'th'middle, & but one halfe	2857
Bru. Caius Martius was | A worthy Officer i'th'Warre, but Insolent,	2928
*home, I euer said we were i'th wrong, when we banish'd | him.	3082
*thou stand'st not i'th state of hanging, or of some death	3301
Leaue vnsaluted: Sinke my knee i'th'earth, *Kneeles*	3399
To shame vnvulnerable, and sticke i'th Warres	3426
Like one i'th'Stockes. Thou hast neuer in thy life,	3517

ITHACA *see Athica*

ITS = 1*3

Val. In earnest it's true; I heard a Senatour speake it.	459
Mene. Now it's twentie seuen; euery gash was an | Enemies Graue. Hearke, the Trumpets.	1051
2 Who my Master? | 1 Nay, it's no matter for that.	2824
*as day do's night: It's sprightly walking, audible, and full	2880

ITSELFE *see* selfe

IUDGE = 1*1

2.Cit. Thinke you so? Which way do you iudge my | wit would flye.	1411
Cats, that can iudge as fitly of his worth,	2545

IUDGEMENT = 4

Against the Rectorship of Iudgement?	1608
Scici. Let them assemble: and on a safer Iudgement,	1621
Mangles true iudgement, and bereaues the State	1857
The happy man; whether detect of iudgement,	3130

IUDGMENTS = *1
*I was forc'd to scoul'd. Your iudgments my graue Lords 3776
IUDICIOUS = 1
Shall haue Iudicious hearing. Stand *Auffidius*, | And trouble not the
peace. 3799
IUMPE = 1
To iumpe a Body with a dangerous Physicke, 1853
IUNIUS = 1
Of their owne choice. One's *Iunius Brutus*, 230
IUNO = 1
for the loue of *Iuno* let's goe. 998
IUNO-LIKE = 1
In Anger, *Iuno*-like: Come, come, come. *Exeunt* 2568
IUPITER = 4
Virg. His bloody Brow? Oh Iupiter, no blood. 400
Lartius. *Martius*, his Name. | *Martius*. By *Iupiter* forgot: 850
Menen. Take my Cappe *Iupiter*, and I thanke thee: 1002
A roote of Ancient Enuy. If Iupiter 2761
IUSTICE = 4
And curse that Iustice did it. Who deserues Greatnes, 187
Th'honor'd Goddes | Keepe Rome in safety, and the Chaires of Iustice 2302
Of dreaded Iustice, but on the Ministers 2383
He does faire Iustice: if he giue me way, | Ile do his Country Seruice.
Exit. 2651
KAMME = 1
Sicin. This is cleane kamme. | *Brut*. Meerely awry: 2042
KEEPE = 13*2
(Vnder the Gods) keepe you in awe, which else 198
To keepe your great pretences vayl'd, till when 336
All. The Gods assist you. | *Auf*. And keepe your Honors safe. 355
Lar. So, let the Ports be guarded; keepe your Duties 714
We cannot keepe the Towne. 718
Coriolanus rises, and offers to goe away. | Nay, keepe your place. 1275
And keepe their teeth cleane: So, heere comes a brace, 1454
Mene. Ile keepe you company. Will you along? 1545
Were but one danger, and to keepe him heere 2024
Th'honor'd Goddes | Keepe Rome in safety, and the Chaires of Iustice 2302
Brut. They haue tane note of vs: keepe on your way. 2516
All. Now the Gods keepe you. 2923
To heare *Cominius* speake, Ile keepe at home. 3158
Auffid. You keepe a constant temper. *Exeunt* 3329
To keepe your name liuing to time. 3482
KEEPERS = 1
Val. How do you both? You are manifest house-kee-|pers. 414
KEEPING = *1
*1 Do you heare how wee are shent for keeping your | greatnesse backe? 3334
KEPT = 1
Then Dogges, that are as often beat for barking, | As therefore kept to
doe so. 1619
KICKT = 1
Com. Our spoyles he kickt at, 1340
KILL = 5*1
1.Cit. Let vs kill him, and wee'l haue Corne at our own | price. Is't a
Verdict? 13
Auf. Insolent Villaine. | *All Consp*. Kill, kill, kill, kill, kill him. 3803
KILLD = 3
He kill'd my Sonne, my daughter, he kill'd my Cosine 3794

KILLD *cont.*
  Marcus, he kill'd my Father.   3795
KILLING = 2
  Killing our Enemies, the blood he hath lost   2036
  Then Boyes pursuing Summer Butter-flies, | Or Butchers killing Flyes.   3010
KILS = 1
  Draw both the Conspirators, and kils Martius, who | falles, Auffidius
  stands on him.   3805
KIN = *1
  *As if a man were Author of himself, & knew no other kin   3385
KIND = 1*1
  1.*Cit.* No, 'tis his kind of speech, he did not mock vs.   1559
  Sicin. 'Tis he, 'tis he: O he is grown most kind of late: 2904
KINDE = 5*2
  Men. Sir, I shall tell you with a kinde of Smile,   109
  *were a kinde of ingratefull Iniurie: to report otherwise,   1234
  They would not thred the Gates: This kinde of Seruice   1821
  Euen this so criminall, and in such capitall kinde   2363
  *in him. He had sir, a kinde of face me thought, I cannot   2816
  Bru. Farewell kinde Neighbours: | We wisht *Coriolanus* had lou'd you as
  we did.   2921
  He was a kinde of Nothing, Titlelesse,   3165
KINDER = *1
  *he remember a kinder value of the People, then he hath | hereto priz'd
  them at.   1267
KINDEST = 1
  We doe request your kindest eares: and after   1260
KINDLE = 1*1
  To kindle their dry Stubble: and their Blaze | Shall darken him for euer.   1186
  Mene. Fie, fie, fie, this is the way to kindle, not to | quench.   1906
KINDLY = 2*1
  At a poore mans house: he vs'd me kindly,   842
  1 *Cit.* The price is, to aske it kindly.   1466
  Corio. Kindly sir, I pray let me ha't: I haue wounds to   1467
KINDNESSE = 1
  Bru. You know the very rode into his kindnesse, | And cannot lose your
  way.   3217
KING = 1
  Who after great *Hostilius* here was King,   1643
KINGLY = 1
  The Kingly crown'd head, the vigilant eye,   118
KINGS = *1
  *for a day of Kings entreaties, a Mother should not sel him   369
KISSE = 2
  For that forgiue our Romanes. O a kisse   3393
  Now by the iealous Queene of Heauen, that kisse   3395
KISSES = 1
  Of *Phoebus* burning Kisses: such a poother,   1137
KITCHIN = 1
  While she chats him: the Kitchin *Malkin* pinnes   1126
KITES = 1*1
  3 Where's that? | *Corio.* I'th City of Kites and crowes.   2695
  *3 I'th City of Kites and Crowes? What an Asse it is,   2697
KNAUE = 1
  Will beare the Knaue by'th Volume: 2301
KNAUES = 2*1
  *thing: you are ambitious, for poore knaues cappes and   964

KNAUES *cont*.
 Knaues. You are a payre of strange ones.   975
 That Babies lull a-sleepe: The smiles of Knaues   2223
KNEE = 6
 Vol. Hee'l beat *Auffidius* head below his knee, | And treade vpon his
 necke.   408
 And strucke him on his Knee: in that dayes feates,   1309
 Thy Knee bussing the stones: for in such businesse   2176
 A Mile before his Tent, fall downe, and knee   3156
 Leaue vnsaluted: Sinke my knee i'th'earth, *Kneeles*   3399
 Volum. Your knee, Sirrah. | *Corio*. That's my braue Boy. 3429
KNEELD = 1
 The Gaoler to his pitty. I kneel'd before him,   3226
KNEELE = 1
 I kneele before thee, and vnproperly   3404
KNEELES = 3
 Coriol. Oh! you haue, I know, petition'd all the Gods | for my
 prosperitie. *Kneeles*.   1074
 Leaue vnsaluted: Sinke my knee i'th'earth, *Kneeles*   3399
 But kneeles, and holds vp hands for fellowship,   3532
KNEES = 4*1
 Your knees to them (not armes) must helpe. Alacke,   75
 Make motion through my Lips, and my Arm'd knees   2226
 1 Our selues, our wiues, and children, on our knees,   2918
 Corio. What's this? your knees to me? | To your Corrected Sonne? 3407
 *Down Ladies: let vs shame him with him with our knees 3526
KNELL = *1
 *like a knell, and his hum is a Battery. He sits in his State, 3590
KNEW = 1*2
 *2 Nay, I knew by his face that there was some-thing   2815
 Mene. Sirra, if thy Captaine knew I were heere,   3287
 *As if a man were Author of himself, & knew no other kin 3385
KNIFE = 1
 Presented to my knife his Throat: I tooke him,   3684
KNOCKE = 1
 Whether to knocke against the Gates of Rome,   2800
KNOT = 1
 As he began, and not vnknit himselfe | The Noble knot he made. 2541
KNOW *see also* know't = 41*14
 *1.*Cit*. First you know, *Caius Martius* is chiefe enemy | to the people. 10
 *we become Rakes. For the Gods know, I speake this in   25
 *strong breaths, they shal know we haue strong arms too. 62
 They'l sit by th'fire, and presume to know   203
 Sicinius Velutus, and I know not. Sdeath,   231
 Sen. Your Company to'th'Capitoll, where I know | Our greatest Friends
 attend vs.   269
 And know how we proceede, | *Auf*. Is it not yours?   316
 To take in many Townes, ere (almost) Rome | Should know we were
 a-foot.   340
 Where they shall know our minde. Away. *Exeunt*   602
 More then I know the sound of *Martius* Tongue | From euery meaner
 man.   635
 Mar. How lies their Battell? Know you on w side   665
 Rome must know the value of her owne: 771
 Sicin. Nature teaches Beasts to know their Friends.   903
 Men. This is strange now: Do you two know, how   918
 Men. I know you can doe very little alone, for your   931

KNOW *cont.*

Bru. Come sir come, we know you well enough.	962
*Menen. You know neither mee, your selues, nor any	963
*Mene. One ith' Neck, and two ith'Thigh, there's nine | that I know.	1047
Herauld. Know Rome, that all alone *Martius* did fight	1064
*Coriol. Oh! you haue, I know, petition'd all the Gods | for my prosperitie. *Kneeles.*	1074
Volum. I know not where to turne.	1088
Cor. Know, good Mother, | I had rather be their seruant in my way,	1117
**be many that they haue loued, they know not wherefore:	1213
**so that if they loue they know not why, they hate vpon	1214
I know they do attend vs.	1386
You know the cause (Sir) of my standing heere.	1455
To know, when two Authorities are vp,	1803
**More worthier then their Voyces. They know the Corne	1817
1 *Cit.* He shall well know the Noble Tribunes are	2002
Mene. Heere me speake? As I do know	2010
Volum. Prythee now, | Goe, and be rul'd: although I know thou hadst rather	2192
Brut. I talke of that, that know it. | *Corio.* You?	2367
Com. Know, I pray you. | *Corio.* Ile know no further:	2370
Sicin. We know your drift. Speake what?	2403
As I can of those Mysteries which heauen | Will not haue earth to know.	2546
*Rom. I know you well sir, and you know mee: your | name I thinke is *Adrian.*	2571
*Rom. I am a Roman, and my Seruices are as you are, | against 'em. Know you me yet.	2574
Haue I heard groane, and drop: Then know me not,	2626
Auf. I know thee not? Thy Name:	2721
Contend against thy Valour. Know thou first,	2771
Sicin. Tell not me: I know this cannot be. | *Bru.* Not possible.	2961
How probable I do not know, that *Martius*	2975
Lieu. I do not know what Witchcraft's in him: but	3092
Com. He would not seeme to know me. | *Menen.* Do you heare?	3159
Bru. You know the very rode into his kindnesse, | And cannot lose your way.	3217
**you shall know now that I am in estimation: you shall	3298
*Corio. Wife, Mother, Child, I know not. My affaires | Are Seruanted to others: Though I owe	3317
You know the way home againe.	3333
*Volum. Thou art my Warriour, I hope to frame thee | Do you know this Lady?	3414
Mes. As certaine as I know the Sun is fire:	3617
Auf. I know it: | And my pretext to strike at him, admits	3671
Vnder your great Command. You are to know,	3739
Auf. My Lords, | When you shall know (as in this Rage	3814

KNOWES = 2*1

*Com. The Shepherd knowes not Thunder fro(m) a Taber,	634
When he shall come to his account, he knowes not	3109
1 Come, my Captaine knowes you not. | *Mene.* I meane thy Generall.	3289

KNOWING = *1

*Cori. That Ile straight do: and knowing my selfe again, | Repayre toth'Senate-|house.	1543

KNOWLEDGE = 1*2

**knowledge he ha's in their disposition, and out of his No-|ble carelesnesse lets them plainely see't.	1217

KNOWLEDGE *cont.*

Coriol. I wil not Seale your knowledge with shewing   1499
Speed how it will. I shall ere long, haue knowledge | Of my successe.
Exit.   3220
KNOWNE = 6*4
They haue prest a Power, but it is not knowne   323
Then reason safely with you: Therefore be it knowne,   814
My Noble Steed, knowne to the Campe, I giue him,   817
Sicin. Menenius, you are knowne well enough too.   942
Men. I am knowne to be a humorous *Patritian*, and   943
*of my Microcosme, followes it that I am knowne well e-|nough   958
*gleane out of this Charracter, if I be knowne well e-|nough too.   960
Men. Oh Sir, you are not right: haue you not knowne   1436
Corio. Why this was knowne before. | *Brut*. Not to them all.   1730
He bow'd his Nature, neuer knowne before,   3677
KNOWST = 1*3
Corio. If *Tullus* not yet thou know'st me, and seeing   2710
Corio. Prepare thy brow to frowne: knowst y me yet?   2720
As best thou art experienc'd, since thou know'st   2798
*For making vp this peace. Thou know'st (great Sonne)   3497
KNOWT = 3
All. We know't, we know't.   12
Sicin. 'Twere well we let the people know't.   1775
LA *l*.430 *453 = 1*1
LABOUR = 3
Like labour with the rest, where th'other Instruments   103
Volum. Why I pray you. | *Vulg*. 'Tis not to saue labour, nor that I want
loue.   444
As cheape as Lies; he sold the Blood and Labour   3702
LABOURD = 1
That we labour'd (no impediment betweene)   1631
LABOURS = 1
Six of his Labours youl'd haue done, and sau'd   2456
LACK = 1
Who lack not Vertue, no, nor Power, but that   1763
LACKD = 2
Ere they lack'd power to crosse you.   2110
Corio. What, what, what: | I shall be lou'd when I am lack'd. Nay
Mother,   2452
LACKE = 4
For though abundantly they lacke discretion   214
And Mothers that lacke Sonnes.   1085
Com. I shall lacke voyce: the deeds of *Coriolanus*   1296
3.*Consp*. Sir, his stoutnesse | When he did stand for Consull, which he
lost | By lacke of stooping.   3679
LADDERS = 1
Mart. Oh they are at it. | *Lart*. Their noise be our instruction. Ladders
hoa.   512
LADIE = 3
Vol. Let her alone Ladie, as she is now: 468
Fare you well then. Come good sweet Ladie.   471
Volum. Euen he, your wife, this Ladie, and my selfe, | Are Sutors to
you.   3431
LADIES *see also* ladyes, 2.*Ladies* = 12*3
Val. My Ladies both good day to you. | *Vol*. Sweet Madam.   411
Val. Well, then farewell. *Exeunt Ladies*.   477
I'th'end admire: where Ladies shall be frighted,   752

LARTIUS see also *Lar.*, *Lart.*, *Latius* = 7*5

  Enter Sicinius Velutus, Annius Brutus Cominius, Titus | Lartius, with
other Senatours.   244
  And *Titus Lartius*, a most valiant Roman,   328
  *power. Your Lord, and *Titus Lartius*, are set down   462
  Enter Martius, Titus Lartius, with Drumme and Co-|lours, with
Captaines and Souldiers, as   478
  All. To th'pot I warrant him. *Enter Titus Lartius*   547
  And giuen to *Lartius* and to *Martius* Battaile: 615
  Com. Flower of Warriors, how is't with *Titus Lartius?*   644
  Titus Lartius, hauing set a guard vpon Carioles, going with   710
  cast vp their Caps and Launces: Cominius | and Lartius stand bare.   795
  To Rome of our successe: you *Titus Lartius*   832
  Volum. Titus Lartius writes, they fought together, but | *Auffidius* got
off.   1024
  And to send for *Titus Lartius*: it remaines,   1245
LARTIUS = 3
LARUM = *1
  Mar. Then shall we heare their Larum, & they Ours.   495
LAST = 11*2
  Val. Verily I do not iest with you: there came newes | from him last
night.   456
  Volum. Hee had, before this last Expedition, twentie | fiue Wounds
vpon him.   1049
  The present Consull, and last Generall,   1250
  He lurcht all Swords of the Garland: for this last,   1315
  To plucke away their power: as now at last,   2381
  Volce. You had more Beard when I last saw you, but   2578
  Corio. This last old man, | Whom with a crack'd heart I haue sent to
Rome,   3355
  But with his last Attempt, he wip'd it out: 3503
  This is the last. So, we will home to Rome,   3529
  To do my selfe this wrong: Till at the last   3691
  1.*Con.* So he did my Lord: | The Army marueyl'd at it, and in the last,   3695
  What faults he made before the last, I thinke   3727
  This Orbe o'th'earth: His last offences to vs   3798
LATE = 6*1
  How could'st thou in a mile confound an houre, | And bring thy Newes
so late?   622
  Mar. Come I too late?   633
  Martius. Come I too late?   637
  The People cry you mockt them: and of late,   1726
  Whom late you haue nam'd for Consull.   1905
  The harme of vnskan'd swiftnesse, will (too late)   2054
  Sicin. 'Tis he, 'tis he: O he is grown most kind of late: 2904
LATELY = *1
  1.Sen. Martius 'tis true, that you haue lately told vs,   246
LATEST = 1
  Nay godded me indeed. Their latest refuge   3358
LATIUS = 2
  Enter Cominius the Generall, and Titus Latius: be-|tweene them
Coriolanus, crown'd with an Oaken   1060
  Cornets. Enter Coriolanus, Menenius, all the Gentry, | Cominius, Titus
Latius, and other Senators.   1672
LATIUS = 3*2
LAUGH = 3
  I could weepe, and I could laugh,   1092

LAUGH *cont.*
  As 'tis to laugh at 'em. My Mother, you wot well   2465
  They laugh at. Oh my Mother, Mother: Oh!   3543
LAUGHD = 1
  Would'st thou haue laugh'd, had I come Coffin'd home,   1082
LAUGHTER = 1
  Corio. Scratches with Briars, scarres to moue | Laughter onely.   2327
LAUNCES = 1
  cast vp their Caps and Launces: Cominius | and Lartius stand bare.   795
LAW = 3
  When what's not meet, but what must be, was Law,   1868
  With rigorous hands: he hath resisted Law,   1998
  And therefore Law shall scorne him further Triall   1999
LAWES = 1
  Opposing Lawes with stroakes, and heere defying   2361
LAWFULL = 3
  Where he shall answer by a lawfull Forme | (In peace) to his vtmost perill.   2067
  To suffer lawfull Censure for such faults | As shall be prou'd vpon you.   2320
  His Tribe, to vse my lawfull Sword.   3802
LAY = 12*1
  Would the Nobility lay aside their ruth,   209
  Val. Come, lay aside your stitchery, I must haue you   432
  Martius. I sometime lay here in *Corioles*,   841
  Enter two Officers, to lay Cushions, as it were, | in the Capitoll.   1203
  Brut. Lay a fault on vs, your Tribunes,   1630
  To Voyce him Consull. Lay the fault on vs.   1637
  Sena. To vnbuild the Citie, and to lay all flat.   1908
  Com. That is the way to lay the Citie flat,   1915
  Scici. Therefore lay hold of him: 1925
  Where the Disease is violent. Lay hands vpon him,   1938
  Brut. Lay hands vpon him.   1945
  Masters, lay downe your Weapons.   2074
  O're-borne their way, consum'd with fire, and tooke | What lay before them.   2991
LAYD = 1
  Deseru'd this so dishonor'd Rub, layd falsely | I'th' plaine Way of his Merit.   1748
LEAD = *1
  Tit. Lead you on: Follow *Cominius*, we must followe | you, right worthy your Priority.   271
LEADE = 3
  Vpon your fauours, swimmes with finnes of Leade,   191
  These three leade on this Preparation   329
  Leade their successes, as we wish our owne,   610
LEADEN = 2
  At a crack'd Drachme: Cushions, Leaden Spoones,   576
  Tye Leaden pounds too's heeles. Proceed by Processe,   2055
LEADER = 1
  Mar. They haue a Leader,   248
LEADES = 4
  Leades fill'd, and Ridges hors'd   1130
  As if that whatsoeuer God, who leades him,   1138
  But yet a braine, that leades my vse of Anger | To better vantage.   2121
  To melt the Citty Leades vpon your pates,   2997
LEADING = 1
  The leading of thine owne Reuenges, take   2796

LEADS = 2

Ioyn'd with *Auffidius*, leads a power 'gainst Rome,   2976
Com. If? He is their God, he leads them like a thing   3006

LEADST = 1

Lead'st first to win some vantage.   168

LEANE = 1

Tit. No *Caius Martius*, | Ile leane vpon one Crutch, and fight with
tother,   265

LEANNESSE = *1

*But they thinke we are too deere, the leannesse   21

LEAPE = 1

Corio. I doe beseech you, | Let me o're-leape that custome: for I cannot 1355

LEARND = 1

Your dangerous Lenity: If you are Learn'd,   1793

LEARNE = 1

Learne how 'tis held, and what they are that must | Be Hostages for
Rome.   887

LEARNED = 1

More learned then the eares, wauing thy head,   2178

LEASH = 1

Euen like a fawning Grey-hound in the Leash, | To let him slip at will. 649

LEASING = 1

Haue (almost) stampt the Leasing. Therefore Fellow,   3260

LEAST = 6*2

*pleasures (at the least) if you take it as a pleasure to you, in   928
With the least cause, these his new Honors,   1151
Least his infection being of catching nature, | Spred further.   2050
Least parties (as he is belou'd) breake out,   2056
Least I surcease to honor mine owne truth,   2229
Least that thy Wiues with Spits, and Boyes with stones   2627
Least you shall chance to whip your Information,   2958
*1 My Generall cares not for you. Back I say, go: least   3291

LEAUE = 14*5

And leaue me but the Bran. What say you too't?   154
And onely hitherward. I leaue your Honors.   351
Virg. Beseech you giue me leaue to retire my selfe.   389
*as your finger, that you might leaue pricking it for   449
Or by the fires of heauen, Ile leaue the Foe,   534
*the Beastly Plebeans. I will be bold to take my leaue of | you.   990
1.*Sen*. Speake, good *Cominius*: | Leaue nothing out for length, and
make vs thinke   1256
Ile leaue you: Pray you speake to em, I pray you | In wholsome manner.
Exit   1450
Leaue vs to cure this Cause.   1958
Mene. If by the Tribunes leaue, | And yours good people,   2016
He throwes without distinction. Giue me leaue,   2065
Corio. Come leaue your teares: a brief farwel: the beast   2437
Bru. Well, well, wee'l leaue you.   2555
Leaue this faint-puling, and lament as I do,   2567
*will mowe all downe before him, and leaue his passage | poul'd.   2861
· For one poore graine or two, to leaue vnburnt | And still to nose
th'offence.   3180
Me. You guard like men, 'tis well. But by your leaue,   3238
I must haue leaue to passe.   3261
Leaue vnsaluted: Sinke my knee i'th'earth, *Kneeles*   3399

LEAUES = 2*1

And behinde him, hee leaues Teares: 1056

LEAUES *cont*.

*deuotion, then they can render it him; and leaues nothing	1222
Who now are heere, taking their leaues of mee,	2791

LECTURES = 1

Brut. I, spare vs not: Say, we read Lectures to you,	1638

LED = 4

A fearefull Army, led by *Caius Martius*,	2988
We haue led since thy Exile. Thinke with thy selfe,	3451
Must as a Forraine Recreant be led	3469
With bloody passage led your Warres, euen to	3741

LEFT = 4*2

And when it bowes, stand'st vp: Thou art left *Martius*,	556
Volum. Ith' Shoulder, and ith' left Arme: there will be	1043
*Your most sweet Voyces: now you haue left your Voyces,	1572
And what is left, to loose it by his Countrey,	2039
The action of your selfe, or else to him, had left it soly.	3107
As draw his Sword: yet he hath left vndone	3115

LEGGE = 1

Our Steed the Legge, the Tongue our Trumpeter,	120

LEGGES = 1*1

*legges: you weare out a good wholesome Forenoone, in	965
From these old armes and legges, by the good Gods │ I'ld with thee, euery foot.	2498

LEND = *2

Lart. No, Ile nor sel, nor giue him: Lend you him I will	491
*Will I lend eare to. Ha? what shout is this? *Shout within*	3366

LENGTH = 2

1.*Sen*. Speake, good *Cominius*: │ Leaue nothing out for length, and make vs thinke	1256
To banish your Defenders, till at length	2416

LENITY = 1

Your dangerous Lenity: If you are Learn'd,	1793

LESSE = 18*2

*and none lesse deere then thine, and my good *Martius*, I	384
1.*Senat*. No, nor a man that feares you lesse then he,	502
Mar. Thy Friend no lesse, │ Then those she placeth highest: So farewell.	597
No lesse then a Traducement,	773
The common Muck of the World: he couets lesse	1342
Haue done many things, some lesse, some more:	1522
That as his worthy deeds did clayme no lesse	1587
If they be Senators: and they are no lesse,	1796
You that will be lesse fearefull, then discreet,	1849
With striuing lesse to be so: Lesser had bin │ The things of your dispositions, if	2107
You adopt your policy: How is it lesse or worse	2145
*3 Reason, because they then lesse neede one another:	2888
Against vs Brats, with no lesse Confidence,	3009
And so he thinkes, and is no lesse apparant	3111
When it was lesse expected. He replyed	3172
Menen. Very well, could he say lesse.	3175
A Mother lesse? or granted lesse *Auffidius*?	3551
When he had carried Rome, and that we look'd │ For no lesse Spoile, then Glory.	3697
With no lesse Honor to the *Antiates*	3745

LESSEN = 1

Lessen his person, then an ill report:	689

LESSER = 2
  That's lesser then a little: *Drum a farre off.*   503
  With striuing lesse to be so: Lesser had bin | The things of your
  dispositions, if   2107
LESSOND = 1
  As you were lesson'd: When he had no Power,   1578
LEST *see* least
LET *see also* let's = 56*12
  1.Cit. Let vs kill him, and wee'l haue Corne at our own | price. Is't a
  Verdict?   13
  All. No more talking on't; Let it be done, away, away   15
  *gaine to them. Let vs reuenge this with our Pikes, ere   24
  And let me vse my Sword, I'de make a Quarrie   210
  Mar. Nay let them follow,   275
  Let vs alone to guard *Corioles*   344
  *stirre, was pleas'd to let him seeke danger, where he was   373ˑ
  *he caught it, he let it go againe, and after it againe, and o-|uer   424
  Vol. Let her alone Ladie, as she is now: 468
  Mart. Oh! let me clip ye | In Armes as sound, as when I woo'd in heart;   640
  Euen like a fawning Grey-hound in the Leash, | To let him slip at will.   649
  Mar. Let him alone,   654
  Let him alone: Or so many so minded,   692
  Lar. So, let the Ports be guarded; keepe your Duties   714
  Mar. Let the first Budger dye the others Slaue,   729
  I'th'field proue flatterers, let Courts and Cities be   799
  Let him be made an Ouerture for th' Warres: 802
  Before, and in Corioles, let me say   1316
  Menen. Hee's right Noble, let him be call'd for.   1346
  Corio. I doe beseech you, | Let me o're-leape that custome: for I cannot   1355
  Corio. Kindly sir, I pray let me ha't: I haue wounds to   1467
  Let the high Office and the Honor go   1513
  2.Cit. Therefore let him be Consull: the Gods giue him | ioy, and make
  him good friend to the People.   1526
  Scici. Let them assemble: and on a safer Iudgement,   1621
  Brut. Let them goe on: 1661
  Let me deserue so ill as you, and make me | Your fellow Tribune.   1737
  Let them regard me, as I doe not flatter,   1757
  Sicin. 'Twere well we let the people know't.   1775
  Let them haue Cushions by you. You are Plebeians,   1795
  The Senates Courtesie? Let deeds expresse   1829
  The Multitudinous Tongue, let them not licke   1855
  Let what is meet, be saide it must be meet,   1870
  Bru. The Ediles hoe: Let him be apprehended: 1875
  Brut. Or let vs stand to our Authoritie,   1920
  Or let vs lose it: we doe here pronounce,   1921
  Let me desire your company: he must come,   2080
  Corio. Let them pull all about mine eares, present me   2084
  Before you had worne it out. | *Corio.* Let go.   2104
  Corio. Let them hang. | *Volum.* I, and burne too.   2111
  Then thou of them. Come all to ruine, let   2234
  Corio. The word is, Mildely. Pray you let vs go,   2253
  Let them accuse me by inuention: I | Will answer in mine Honor.   2254
  For death, for fine, or Banishment, then let them   2277
  Let them not cease, but with a dinne confus'd   2283
  Let them pronounce the steepe Tarpeian death,   2372
  All. It shall be so, it shall be so: let him away: 2391
  Com. Let me speake: | I haue bene Consull, and can shew from Rome   2395

LET *cont*.

Let euery feeble Rumor shake your hearts:	2413
Giue him deseru'd vexation. Let a guard | Attend vs through the City.	2430
Let vs seeme humbler after it is done, | Then when it was a dooing.	2507
Rom. Well, let vs go together. *Exeunt*.	2620
Corio. Let me but stand, I will not hurt your Harth.	2679
Then thee all-Noble *Martius*. Let me twine	2764
Let me commend thee first, to those that shall	2803
*1 Let me haue Warre say I, it exceeds peace as farre	2879
*I let forth your halfe pinte of blood. Backe, that's the vt-|most of your hauing, backe.	3292
*not from another: Let your Generall do his worst. For	3340
Let it be Vertuous to be Obstinate.	3375
Great Nature cries, Deny not. Let the Volces	3382
Then let the Pibbles on the hungry beach	3409
Fillop the Starres: Then, let the mutinous windes	3410
*Down Ladies: let vs shame him with him with our knees	3526
Then thou hast to deny't. Come, let vs go:	3534
If not most mortall to him. But let it come:	3547
In all his owne desires: Nay, let him choose	3686
With what he would say, let him feele your Sword:	3715
All Consp. Let him dye for't.	3792
And mourne you for him. Let him be regarded	3823

LETHARGIE = *1

*of Vent. Peace, is a very Apoplexy, Lethargie, mull'd,	2881

LETS = 21*4

Sicin. Let's hence, and heare | How the dispatch is made, and in what fashion	308
Bru. Let's along. *Exeunt*	312
Let's fetch him off, or make remaine alike. | *They fight, and all enter the City*.	567
for the loue of *Iuno* let's goe.	998
Volum. Good Ladies let's goe. Yes, yes, yes: The	1030
Into a rapture lets her Baby crie,	1125
Brutus. Let's to the Capitoll,	1199
*knowledge he ha's in their disposition, and out of his No-|ble carelesnesse lets them plainely see't.	1217
Mene. Let's be calme.	1745
All. Let's here our Tribune: peace, speake, speake, | speake.	1901
Sena. Pray you let's to him. *Exeunt Omnes*.	2082
All. Come, come, lets see him out at gates, come:	2432
Menen. That's worthily | As any eare can heare. Come, let's not weepe,	2495
Sicin. Let's not meet her.	2513
Brut. Pray let's go.	2548
And so shall sterue with Feeding: come, let's go,	2566
Both. What, what, what? Let's partake.	2834
1 Cit. The Gods bee good to vs: Come Masters let's	3081
2 Cit. So did we all. But come, let's home. *Exit Cit*.	3084
Bru. Let's to the Capitoll: would halfe my wealth | Would buy this for a lye.	3087
Sicin. Pray let's go. *Exeunt Tribunes*.	3089
Come let's away: when *Caius* Rome is thine,	3147
For mercy to his Countrey: therefore let's hence,	3233
More bound to's Mother, yet heere he let's me prate	3516
Let's make the Best of it.	3828

LETTER = 3*2

I haue the Letter heere: yes, heere it is;	322

LETTER *cont.*

Volum. Looke, here's a Letter from him, the State hath   1005
A Letter for me?   1009
Virgil. Yes certaine, there's a Letter for you, I saw't.   1010
Menen. A Letter for me? it giues me an Estate of se-|uen   1011
LETTERS = *1
*Senate ha's Letters from the Generall, wherein hee giues   1031
LEUIES = 1
The benefit of our Leuies, answering vs   3730
LIAR *see* lier, lyar
LIBERTIES = 3
Your Liberties, and the Charters that you beare   1581
Their Liberties, make them of no more Voyce   1618
Scici. You are at point to lose your Liberties: 1903
LIBERTY = 1
if it were at liberty, 'twould sure Southward.   1415
LICKE = 1
The Multitudinous Tongue, let them not licke   1855
LICTORS = 1
the People, Lictors before them: Coriolanus, Mene-|nius, Cominius the
Consul: Scicinius and Brutus   1240
LICURGUSSES = *1
*you *Licurgusses*,) if the drinke you giue me, touch my Pa-|lat   951
LIE *see also* lye = 2
Mar. How farre off lie these Armies?   493
Lie in th'interpretation of the time,   3141
LIEFE *see* liue
LIER = *1
*2 Howsoeuer you haue bin his Lier, as you say you   3268
LIES *see also* lyes = 8*1
Come, you must go visit the good Lady that lies in.   441
Mar. How lies their Battell? Know you on w side   665
Sicin. For that he ha's | (As much as in him lies) from time to time   2378
Cit. And you. | *Corio.* Direct me, if it be your will, where great *Auf-*
|*fidius* lies: Is he in *Antium*?   2630
Destroy, what lies before'em.   2944
*1 Faith Sir, if you had told as many lies in his behalfe,   3262
My Reuenge properly, my remission lies   3319
As cheape as Lies; he sold the Blood and Labour   3702
Which we will second, when he lies along   3716
LIEST *see* lyest
LIEU = 3*1
LIEUTENANT *see also* Lieu. = 1*1
Enters with a Lieutenant, other Souldiours, and a | Scout.   712
Enter Auffidius with his Lieutenant.   3090
LIFE = 11
If any thinke, braue death out-weighes bad life,   690
Corio. I doe owe them still my Life, and Seruices.   1352
A Noble life, before a Long, and Wish,   1852
I shall discharge toth' Life.   2212
More holy, and profound, then mine owne life,   2399
(Mistake me not) to saue my life: for if   2737
And state of Bodies would bewray what life   3450
Like one i'th'Stockes. Thou hast neuer in thy life,   3517
Mes. Sir, if you'ld saue your life, flye to your House,   3604
Sena. Behold our Patronnesse, the life of Rome: 3641
Which this mans life did owe you, you'l reioyce   3817

LIFT = 2
Strike at the Heauen with your staues, as lift them 69
Embarquements all of Fury, shall lift vp 881
LIGHT = 2
Mar. All the contagion of the South, light on you, 525
I am light, and heauie; welcome: 1093
LIGHTLY = 1
Beleeu't not lightly, though I go alone 2467
LIKE = 55*14
The Helmes o'th State; who care for you like Fathers, 78
That onely like a Gulfe it did remaine 100
Like labour with the rest, where th'other Instruments 103
Not rash like his Accusers, and thus answered. 136
That like nor Peace, nor Warre? The one affrights you, 180
What's done i'th Capitoll: Who's like to rise, 204
*Picture-like to hang by th'wall, if renowne made it not 372
*like to finde fame: To a cruell Warre I sent him, from 374
Like to a Haruest man, that task'd to mowe | Or all, or loose his hyre. 398
Not for the flyers: Marke me, and do the like. 542
The Thunder-like percussion of thy sounds 561
Like Romans, neither foolish in our stands, 605
Euen like a fawning Grey-hound in the Leash, | To let him slip at will. 649
Auf. If I flye *Martius*, hollow me like a Hare. 731
(Like one that meanes his proper harme) in Manacles, 813
Bru. He's a Lambe indeed, that baes like a Beare. 908
Men. Hee's a Beare indeede, that liues like a Lambe. 909
*single: your abilities are to Infant-like, for dooing 933
*the first complaint, hasty and Tinder-like vppon, to 946
*pinch'd with the Collike, you make faces like Mum-|mers, 970
Brutus. 'Tis most like he will. 1167
I neuer saw the like. 1198
We met here, both to thanke, and to remember, | With Honors like himselfe. 1254
Man-entred thus, he waxed like a Sea, 1313
Carioles like a Planet: now all's his, 1328
I would they would forget me, like the Vertues 1447
Com. You are like to doe such businesse. 1734
What's like to be their words, We did request it, 1830
Sicin. Ha's spoken like a Traitor, and shall answer | As Traitors do. 1862
All. You so remaine. | *Mene*. And so are like to doe. 1913
Brut. Sir, those cold wayes, | That seeme like prudent helpes, are very poysonous, 1936
Like interrupted Waters, and o're-beare | What they are vs'd to beare. 1974
In Ioues owne Booke, like an vnnaturall Dam | Should now eate vp her owne. 2030
Honor and Policy, like vnseuer'd Friends, 2137
With Honour, as in Warre; since that to both | It stands in like request. 2147
Who bow'd but in my Stirrop, bend like his 2227
Like Graues i'th holy Church-yard. 2326
Mene. Consider further: | That when he speakes not like a Citizen, 2329
You finde him like a Soldier: do not take 2331
Like to a lonely Dragon, that his Fenne 2468
But what is like me formerly. 2494
In Anger, *Iuno*-like: Come, come, come. *Exeunt* 2568
The Feast smels well: but I appeare not like a Guest. 2660
*2 Here sir, I'de haue beaten him like a dogge, but for | disturbing the Lords within. 2706

LIKE *cont*.

Like a bold Flood o're-beate. Oh come, go in,	2789
*on't before *Corioles*, he scotcht him, and notcht him like a | Carbinado.	2846
2 And he's as like to do't, as any man I can imagine.	2863
*the man in blood, they will out of their Burroughes (like	2870
And three examples of the like, hath beene	2955
Com. If? He is their God, he leads them like a thing	3006
And therein shew'd like Enemies.	3034
But like Beasts, and Cowardly Nobles,	3044
Bru. I do not like this Newes. | *Sicin*. Nor I.	3085
Fights Dragon-like, and does atcheeue as soone	3114
Then in our Priest-like Fasts: therefore Ile watch him	3214
Me. You guard like men, 'tis well. But by your leaue,	3238
Like to a Bowle vpon a subtle ground	3258
*this Varlet heere: This, who like a blocke hath denyed | my accesse to thee.	3313
Corio. Like a dull Actor now, I haue forgot my part,	3390
Which by th'interpretation of full time, | May shew like all your selfe.	3421
Like a great Sea-marke standing euery flaw, | And sauing those that eye thee.	3427
Like one i'th'Stockes. Thou hast neuer in thy life,	3517
Like him by chance: yet giue vs our dispatch:	3537
On like conditions, will haue Counter-seal'd.	3565
*like an Engine, and the ground shrinkes before his Trea-|ding.	3588
*like a knell, and his hum is a Battery. He sits in his State,	3590
*1.*Con*. Your Natiue Towne you enter'd like a Poste,	3707
Breaking his Oath and Resolution, like	3763
That like an Eagle in a Doue-coat, I | Flatter'd your Volcians in *Corioles*.	3785

LIKELY = 2

Whether 'tis bent: most likely, 'tis for you: | Consider of it.	330
Sicin. This is most likely.	2979

LIKING = 1

And feebling such as stand not in their liking,	207

LIMBE = 1

Mene. Oh he's a Limbe, that ha's but a Disease	2033

LIMBES = 1

He had rather venture all his Limbes for Honor,	1294

LIMITATION = 1

Mene. You haue stood your Limitation:	1531

LINGER = 1

Vagabond exile, Fleaing, pent to linger	2373

LINKE = 1

Of more strong linke assunder, then can euer	72

LION = 1

Onely my warres with him. He is a Lion | That I am proud to hunt.	256

LIONS *see* lyons

LIP = 2

Bru. Mark'd you his lip and eyes. | *Sicin*. Nay, but his taunts.	283
Mene. Ile vndertak't: | I thinke hee'l heare me. Yet to bite his lip,	3205

LIPPE = 1 *1

*yeeres health; in which time, I will make a Lippe at	1012
I carried from thee deare; and my true Lippe	3396

LIPPES = 1

The brizled Lippes before him: he bestrid	1306

LIPS = 1*1
  Make motion through my Lips, and my Arm'd knees   2226
  *of their Feast, and to be executed ere they wipe their lips.   2875
LIST = 3
  There is *Auffidious*. List what worke he makes | Among'st your clouen
  Army.   510
  With as bigge heart as thou. Do as thou list,   2237
  Edile. List to your Tribunes. Audience: | Peace I say.   2311
LITLE = *1
  *I am husht vntill our City be afire, & then Ile speak a litle | *Holds her*
  by the hand silent.   3538
LITTERD = 1
  Though in Rome litter'd: not Romans, as they are not,   1963
LITTLE *see also* litle = 12*4
  But since it serues my purpose, I will venture | To scale't a little more.   92
  Men. I will tell you, | If you'l bestow a small (of what you haue little)   130
  *What are you sowing heere? A fine spotte in good | faith. How does
  your little Sonne?   415
  That's lesser then a little: *Drum a farre off*.   503
  As if I lou'd my little should be dieted | In prayses, sawc'st with Lyes.   807
  Men. Why 'tis no great matter: for a very little theefe   925
  Men. I know you can doe very little alone, for your   931
  Which that he will giue them, make I as little question,   1152
  A little of that worthy Worke, perform'd   1252
  1.Cit. And to make vs no better thought of a little   1400
  With those that haue but little: this must be patcht | With Cloth of any
  Colour.   1978
  I haue a heart as little apt as yours,   2120
  For they haue Pardons, being ask'd, as free, | As words to little
  purpose.   2190
  That thought he could do more: A very little   3363
  And sir, it is no little thing to make   3554
  *little finger, there is some hope the Ladies of Rome, espe- | cially   3574
LIUE = 10
  Which you do liue vpon: and fit it is,   139
  Whereby they liue. And though that all at once   147
  Com. And liue you yet? Oh my sweet Lady, pardon.   1087
  Suffer't, and liue with such as cannot rule, | Nor euer will be ruled.   1723
  Corio. Now as I liue, I will.   1754
  Longer to liue most wearie: and present   2752
  And cannot liue but to thy shame, vnlesse | It be to do thee seruice.   2757
  3 I would not be a Roman of all Nations; I had as | liue be a
  condemn'd man.   2835
  Sicin. Liue, and thriue.   2920
  *passe heere: no, though it were as vertuous to lye, as to | liue chastly.
  Therefore go backe.   3264
LIUED = 1
  Volum. I haue liued, | To see inherited my very Wishes,   1111
LIUES = 2*1
  Men. Hee's a Beare indeede, that liues like a Lambe.   909
  Runne reeking o're the liues of men, as if 'twere   1333
  Corio. At Antium liues he?   1695
LIUING = 2
  How more vnfortunate then all liuing women   3452
  To keepe your name liuing to time.   3482
LO = 1
  Mene. Lo Citizens, he sayes he is Content.   2323

LOAD = 1
A Noble cunning. You were vs'd to load me   2445
LOADEN *see* loden
LOCKES = 1
Breake ope the Lockes a'th'Senate, and bring in | The Crowes to pecke
the Eagles.   1835
LOCKRAM = 1
Her richest Lockram 'bout her reechie necke,   1127
LODEN = 1
Loden with Honor. Say my Request's vniust,   3521
LONELY = 1
Like to a lonely Dragon, that his Fenne   2468
LONG = 8*3
2.*Cit.* Y'are long about it.   133
*Me thinkes thou speak'st not well. How long is't since?   619
A long flourish. They all cry, Martius, *Martius*,   794
How long continued, and what stock he springs of,   1640
A Noble life, before a Long, and Wish,   1852
Speed how it will. I shall ere long, haue knowledge | Of my successe.
Exit.   3220
*more long in Spectatorship, and crueller in suffering, be- | hold   3302
*you, bee that you are, long; and your misery encrease   3341
Long as my Exile, sweet as my Reuenge!   3394
Requires nor Childe, nor womans face to see: | I haue sate too long.   3486
shall our poore City finde: and all this is long of you.   3598
LONGER = 1
Longer to liue most wearie: and present   2752
LONGS = 1
To his sur-name *Coriolanus* longs more pride   3527
LOOK = *1
*3 Doo't? he will doo't: for look you sir, he has as ma- | ny   2864
LOOKD = 4*2
When she did suckle *Hector*, look'd not louelier   403
*very pretty boy. A my troth, I look'd vpon him a Wens- | day   421
And look'd vpon things precious, as they were   1341
*1 A strange one as euer I look'd on: I cannot get him   2675
When he had carried Rome, and that we look'd | For no lesse Spoile,
then Glory.   3697
That Pages blush'd at him, and men of heart | Look'd wond'ring each
at others.   3767
LOOKE = 9*5
For looke you I may make the belly Smile,   111
*And make bold power looke pale, they threw their caps   225
*Vol. He had rather see the swords, and heare a Drum, | then looke
vpon his Schoolmaster.   418
And make my Warres on you: Looke too't: Come on,   535
1.*Sol*. Looke Sir. | *Lar*. O 'tis *Martius*.   565
*Volum. Looke, here's a Letter from him, the State hath   1005
Com. Looke, Sir, your Mother.   1073
Plague vpon't, I cannot bring | My tongue to such a pace. Looke Sir,
my wounds,   1439
Of all the Trades in Rome. Looke, I am going: 2244
*2 Faith looke you, one cannot tell how to say that: for   2829
*not (looke you sir) shew themselues (as we terme it) his | Friends,
whilest he's in Directitude.   2866
Brut. But is this true sir? | *Com*. I, and you'l looke pale   3019
*fire for vs: looke thee, heere's water to quench it.   3307

LOOKE *cont.*
    The Gods looke downe, and this vnnaturall Scene   3542
LOOKES = 3
    Onely in strokes, but with thy grim lookes, and   560
    He ha's it now: and by his Lookes, me thinkes, | 'Tis warme at's heart.   1548
    What's in his heart, and that is there which lookes   2294
LOOKING = *1
    *1 He had so, looking as it were, would I were hang'd   2818
LOOKT = 1
    It should be lookt too: come. *Exeunt.*   856
LOOSE = 8*1
    Like to a Haruest man, that task'd to mowe | Or all, or loose his hyre.   398
    For a short holding, if we loose the Field,   717
    *3 *Cit.* To loose it selfe in a Fogge, where being three   1417
    And what is left, to loose it by his Countrey,   2039
    In Peace, what each of them by th'other loose,   2139
    Yet were there but this single Plot, to loose   2208
    And loose aduantage, which doth euer coole | Ith'absence of the needer.   2483
    Or loose mine Arme for't: Thou hast beate mee out   2779
    Whereto we are bound: Alacke, or we must loose   3464
LORD *see also* 1.*Lord*, 2.*Lord*, 3.*Lord* = 11*2
    Vir. Heauens blesse my Lord from fell *Auffidius.*   407
    threshold, till my Lord returne from the Warres.   439
    *power. Your Lord, and *Titus Lartius*, are set down   462
    Mes. Aboue an houre, my Lord.   620
    Lartius. I shall, my Lord.   836
    Am bound to begge of my Lord Generall.   839
    And translate his Mallice towards you, into Loue, | Standing your
friendly Lord.   1590
    Latius. He had, my Lord, and that it was which caus'd | Our swifter
Composition.   1675
    Com. They are worne (Lord Consull) so,   1680
    Corio. Spoke he of me? | *Latius.* He did, my Lord. | *Corio.* How? what?   1687
    Which he was Lord of: or whether Nature,   3132
    Virgil. My Lord and Husband.   3386
    1.*Con.* So he did my Lord: | The Army marueyl'd at it, and in the last,   3695
  LORD = 2
LORDS = 14*1
    Where is the enemy? Are you Lords a'th Field?   661
    *2 Here sir, I'de haue beaten him like a dogge, but for | disturbing the
Lords within.   2706
    You must report to th'Volcian Lords, how plainly   3349
    *Enter two Senators, with Ladies, passing ouer | the Stage, with other
Lords.*   3639
    Auf. Go tell the Lords a'th'City, I am heere: 3650
    Auf. Say no more. Heere come the Lords,   3719
    Enter the Lords of the City.   3720
    But worthy Lords, haue you with heede perused | What I haue written
to you?   3723
    Corio. Haile Lords, I am return'd your Souldier: 3736
    Auf. Read it not Noble Lords,   3750
    You Lords and Heads a'th'State, perfidiously   3759
    Pardon me Lords, 'tis the first time that euer   3775
    *I was forc'd to scoul'd. Your iudgments my graue Lords   3776
    Auf. Why Noble Lords, | Will you be put in minde of his blinde
Fortune,   3788

LORDS *cont*.

Auf. My Lords, | When you shall know (as in this Rage   3814
LORDS = 2
LOSE *see also* loose = 5
From where he should begin, and end, but will | Lose those he hath
wonne.   1145
Which our Diuines lose by em.   1448
Scici. You are at point to lose your Liberties: 1903
Or let vs lose it: we doe here pronounce,   1921
Bru. You know the very rode into his kindnesse, | And cannot lose your
way.   3217
LOSSE = 2
The which shall turne you to no further harme, | Then so much losse of
time.   2019
Not what is dangerous present, but the losse | Of what is past.   2171
LOST = 2
Killing our Enemies, the blood he hath lost   2036
3.*Consp*. Sir, his stoutnesse | When he did stand for Consull, which he
lost | By lacke of stooping.   3679
LOTS = 1
And of his Friends there, it is Lots to Blankes,   3247
LOUD = 9
*2 *Cit*. Worthy *Menenius Agrippa*, one that hath al-|wayes lou'd the
people.   53
As if I lou'd my little should be dieted | In prayses, sawc'st with Lyes.   807
Corio. What, what, what: | I shall be lou'd when I am lack'd. Nay
Mother,   2452
Menen. Peace, peace, be not so loud.   2519
I lou'd the Maid I married: neuer man   2772
Bru. Farewell kinde Neighbours: | We wisht *Coriolanus* had lou'd you as
we did.   2921
Mene. How? Was't we? We lou'd him,   3043
Lou'd me, aboue the measure of a Father,   3357
Sicin. He lou'd his Mother deerely.   3584
LOUE = 20*8
*not vppe, they will; and there's all the loue they beare | vs.   86
*where he would shew most loue. When yet hee was but   366
*sincerely, had I a dozen sons each in my loue alike,   383
Volum. Why I pray you. | *Vulg*. 'Tis not to saue labour, nor that I want
loue.   444
Fall deepe in loue with thee, and her great charmes   594
(As it were sinne to doubt) that loue this painting   687
*Men. Not according to the prayer of the people, for | they loue not
Martius.   901
Men. Pray you, who does the Wolfe loue? | *Sicin*. The Lambe.   904
for the loue of *Iuno* let's goe.   998
*so that if they loue they know not why, they hate vpon   1214
*care whether they loue, or hate him, manifests the true   1216
*1.*Off*. If he did not care whether he had their loue, or   1219
*is as bad, as that which he dislikes, to flatter them for | their loue.   1225
I loue them as they weigh---   1286
*that I haue not bin common in my Loue, I will sir flatter   1486
And translate his Mallice towards you, into Loue, | Standing your
friendly Lord.   1590
That loue the Fundamentall part of State   1850
When he did loue his Country, it honour'd him.   2044
Supplied with worthy men, plant loue amongs   2304

LOUE *cont*.

Her Enemies markes vpon me. I do loue	2397
Th'hoorded plague a'th'Gods requit your loue.	2518
Are still together: who Twin (as 'twere) in Loue,	2641
As hotly, and as Nobly with thy Loue,	2769
The Senators and Patricians loue him too:	3121
Bru. Onely make triall what your Loue can do, | For Rome, towards	
Martius.	3196
*particular prosperity, and loue thee no worse then thy old	3305
Was to send him: for whose old Loue I haue	3359
No more infected with my Countries loue	3737

LOUED = 2*3

*haue flatter'd the people, who ne're loued them; and there	1212
*be many that they haue loued, they know not wherefore:	1213
*bin a Rod to her Friends, you haue not indeede loued the | Common	
people.	1483
Which was sometime his Generall: who loued him	3153
Your gates against my force. Yet for I loued thee,	3324

LOUELIER = 1

When she did suckle *Hector*, look'd not louelier	403

LOUER = 1

Mene. I tell thee Fellow, | Thy Generall is my Louer: I haue beene	3251

LOUES = 9*2

*one that loues a cup of hot Wine, with not a drop of alay- |ing	944
*1 .*off*. That's a braue fellow: but hee's vengeance | prowd, and loues not	
the common people.	1209
Menen. He loues your People, but tye him not to be	1273
Brut. We pray the Gods, he may deserue your loues.	1555
When he did need your Loues: and doe you thinke,	1604
How in his Suit he scorn'd you: but your Loues,	1625
For the inheritance of their loues, and safegard	2167
In asking their good loues, but thou wilt frame	2185
Chide me no more. Ile Mountebanke their Loues,	2242
As reeke a'th'rotten Fennes: whose Loues I prize,	2409
My Birth-place haue I, and my loues vpon	2649

LOUING = 2

Your louing motion toward the common Body, | To yeeld what passes	
here.	1261
O'recome with Pride, Ambitious, past all thinking | Selfe-louing.	2930

LOWE = 1

They set them downe on two lowe stooles and sowe.	361

LOWEST = 1*1

Men. For that being one o'th lowest, basest, poorest	165
Corio. The fires i'th'lowest hell. Fould in the people:	2348

LOWTS = 1

And you, will rather shew our generall Lowts,	2165

LOYALL = 1

My selfe your loyall Seruant, or endure | Your heauiest Censure.	3820

LOYNES = 1

And treasure of my Loynes: then if I would | Speake that.	2401

LUCIUS = 1

And I am constant: *Titus Lucius*, thou	262

LULL = 1

That Babies lull a-sleepe: The smiles of Knaues	2223

LUNGS = 2

Which ne're came from the Lungs, but euen thus:	110
Not fearing outward force: So shall my Lungs	1769

LURCHT = 1
He lurcht all Swords of the Garland: for this last,   1315
LURKD = 1
Where haue you lurk'd that you make doubt of it: 3618
LYAR = 1
Corio. Measurelesse Lyar, thou hast made my heart   3773
LYCURGUSES see Licurgusses
LYE = 7*3
Mess. They lye in view, but haue not spoke as yet.   488
*that say you are reuerend graue men, yet they lye deadly,   956
Death, that darke Spirit, in's neruie Arme doth lye,   1057
*were a Mallice, that giuing it selfe the Lye, would plucke   1235
The Dust on antique Time would lye vnswept,   1510
A Lye, that it must beare well? I will doo't: 2207
Bru. Let's to the Capitoll: would halfe my wealth | Would buy this for
a lye.   3087
*passe heere: no, though it were as vertuous to lye, as to | liue chastly.
Therefore go backe.   3264
Must giue this Curre the Lye: and his owne Notion,   3777
Must beare my beating to his Graue, shall ioyne | To thrust the Lye
vnto him.   3779
LYES = 3*1
As if I lou'd my little should be dieted | In prayses, sawc'st with Lyes.   807
Volum. Because, that | Now it lyes you on to speake to th'people: 2150
But once a day, it would vnclogge my heart | Of what lyes heauy too't.   2561
*This lyes glowing I can tell you, and is almost mature for | the violent
breaking out.   2594
LYEST = 1
Thou lyest vnto thee, with a voice as free, | As I do pray the Gods.   2353
LYING = 1
Thy lying tongue, both numbers. I would say   2352
LYONS = 1
Where he should finde you Lyons, findes you Hares: 182
MAD = 1
Brut. Why? | *Sicin.* They say she's mad.   2514
MADAM = 8*1
Gent. Madam, the lady *Valeria* is come to visit you.   388
Val. My Ladies both good day to you. | *Vol.* Sweet Madam.   411
Vir. I thanke your Lady-ship: Well good Madam.   417
Val. Indeed la, tis a Noble childe. | *Virg.* A Cracke Madam.   430
Virg. No (good Madam) | I will not out of doores.   434
Vir. No good Madam, pardon me, indeed I will not | foorth.   451
Virg. Oh good Madam, there can be none yet.   455
Vir. Indeed Madam.   458
Virgil. No | At a word Madam; Indeed I must not,   474
MADAME = *2
Virg. But had he died in the Businesse Madame, how | then?   379
Virg. Giue me excuse good Madame, I will obey you | in euery thing
heereafter.   466
MADE = 33*7
2.Cit. Well sir, what answer made the Belly.   108
*That meate was made for mouths. That the gods sent not   220
Sicin. Let's hence, and heare | How the dispatch is made, and in what
fashion   308
We neuer yet made doubt but Rome was ready | To answer vs.   333
*Picture-like to hang by th'wall, if renowne made it not   372
By th'Blood we haue shed together, | By th'Vowes we haue made   673

MADE *cont.*

And made what worke I pleas'd: 'Tis not my blood,	734
Made all of false-fac'd soothing:	800
Let him be made an Ouerture for th' Warres:	802
Haue made them Mules, silenc'd their Pleaders,	1174
As to *Ioues* Statue, and the Commons made	1196
When blowes haue made me stay, I fled from words.	1284
When *Tarquin* made a Head for Rome, he fought	1302
And by his rare example made the Coward	1318
Then what you should, made you against the graine	1636
Corio. Tullus Auffidius then had made new head.	1674
Which they haue often made against the Senate,	1825
My praises made thee first a Souldier; so	2215
Mene. Is this the promise that you made your mother.	2369
As he began, and not vnknit himselfe | The Noble knot he made.	2541
'Tis I that made thy Widdowes: Many an heyre	2624
*a Cudgell, and yet my minde gaue me, his cloathes made | a false report of him.	2811
*3 Why he is so made on heere within, as if hee were	2851
Com. Oh you haue made good worke.	2994
*You haue made faire worke I feare me: pray your newes,	3004
Made by some other Deity then Nature,	3007
Mene. You haue made good worke,	3012
You haue made faire worke.	3018
To say, beseech you cease. You haue made faire hands,	3037
That made the Ayre vnwholsome, when you cast	3056
Mene. You haue made good worke | You and your cry. Shal's to the Capitoll?	3074
For I dare so farre free him, made him fear'd,	3138
Menen. Why so: you haue made good worke:	3168
In the same time 'tis made? I will not.	3368
Could not haue made this peace. *Exeunt.*	3569
*as a thing made for *Alexander.* What he bids bee done, is	3591
Made him ioynt-seruant with me: Gaue him way	3685
What faults he made before the last, I thinke	3727
The charges of the Action. We haue made peace	3744
Corio. Measurelesse Lyar, thou hast made my heart	3773

MADST = 1

Thou mad'st thine enemies shake, as if the World | Were Feauorous, and did tremble.	562

MAGISTRATE = 1

Most pallates theirs. They choose their Magistrate,	1798

MAGISTRATES = 1 *1

*proud, violent, testie Magistrates (alias Fooles) | as any in Rome.	940
Brut. By the consent of all, we were establish'd the | Peoples Magistrates.	1911

MAID = 1

I lou'd the Maid I married: neuer man	2772

MAIDS = 1

Ladies and Maids their Scarffes, and Handkerchers,	1194

MAILD = 1

With his mail'd hand, then wiping, forth he goes	397

MAIMES = 1

Thine owne particular wrongs, and stop those maimes	2743

MAINE = 1 *1

As the maine Point of this our after-meeting,	1246
Rom. The maine blaze of it is past, but a small thing	2589

MAIOR = *1
*the Asse in compound, with the Maior part of your sylla-|bles.   954
MAISTER = *1
*3 What you will not? Prythee tell my Maister what | a strange Guest
he ha's heere.   2688
MAKE = 42*19
The Gods, not the Patricians make it, and   74
*with Graine: Make Edicts for Vsurie, to support Vsu-|rers;   82
For looke you I may make the belly Smile,   111
Yet I can make my Awdit vp, that all   152
But make you ready your stiffe bats and clubs,   169
That rubbing the poore Itch of your Opinion, | Make your selues Scabs.   175
To make him worthy, whose offence subdues him,   186
And let me vse my Sword, I'de make a Quarrie   210
*And make bold power looke pale, they threw their caps   225
vpon my partie, I'de reuolt to make   255
*and to make it breefe Warres. This is true on mine   464
Now Mars, I prythee make vs quicke in worke,   496
And make my Warres on you: Looke too't: Come on,   535
Let's fetch him off, or make remaine alike. | *They fight, and all enter
the City*.   567
Conuenient Numbers to make good the City,   583
Oh me alone, make you a sword of me: 697
Make good this ostentation, and you shall | Diuide in all, with vs.
Exeunt   708
But cannot make my heart consent to take   790
*your eyes toward the Napes of your neckes, and make   935
*aduersly, I make a crooked face at it, I can say, your   952
*pinch'd with the Collike, you make faces like Mum-|mers,   970
*peace you make in their Cause, is calling both the parties   974
Menen. I will make my very house reele to night: 1008
*yeeres health; in which time, I will make a Lippe at   1012
Which that he will giue them, make I as little question,   1152
*1.*Off*. No more of him, hee's a worthy man: make | way, they are
comming.   1237
1.*Sen*. Speake, good *Cominius*: | Leaue nothing out for length, and
make vs thinke   1256
Menen. The Senate, *Coriolanus*, are well pleas'd to make | thee
Consull.   1350
*multitude to be ingratefull, were to make a Monster of   1397
*1.*Cit*. And to make vs no better thought of a little   1400
*He's to make his requests by particulars, wherein euerie   1431
*them. I will make much of your voyces, and so trouble | you no
farther.   1500
*2.*Cit*. Therefore let him be Consull: the Gods giue him | ioy, and make
him good friend to the People.   1526
Their Liberties, make them of no more Voyce   1618
Readie when time shall prompt them, to make roade | Vpon's againe.   1678
Let me deserue so ill as you, and make me | Your fellow Tribune.   1737
And make your Channell his? If he haue power,   1791
The Nature of our Seats, and make the Rabble   1833
Sicin. Sir, how com'st that you haue holpe | To make this rescue?   2008
You make strong partie, or defend your selfe   2198
Make motion through my Lips, and my Arm'd knees   2226
Sicin. Make them be strong, and ready for this hint   2287
With Precepts that would make inuincible | The heart that conn'd them.   2446

MAKE cont.
Sicin. What then? | *Virg. When then? Hee'ld make an end of thy
  posterity   2535
*would make it flame againe. For the Nobles receyue so   2590
And make my misery serue thy turne: So vse it,   2745
Were .in wilde hurry. Heere do we make his Friends   2896
That Rome can make against them.   3052
To make Coales cheape: A Noble memory.   3170
More then the instant Armie we can make | Might stop our
  Countryman.   3191
Bru. Onely make triall what your Loue can do, | For Rome, towards
  Martius.   3196
Which can make Gods forsworne? I melt, and am not   3377
Murd'ring Impossibility, to make | What cannot be, slight worke.   3412
*Make our eies flow with ioy, harts dance with comforts,   3454
Auffidius, though I cannot make true Warres,   3548
And sir, it is no little thing to make   3554
What peace you'l make, aduise me: For my part,   3556
Where haue you lurk'd that you make doubt of it: 3618
Make the Sunne dance. Hearke you. A shout within   3624
*And make triumphant fires, strew Flowers before them: 3643
Let's make the Best of it.   3828
MAKER = 1
*be a Rauisher, so it cannot be denied, but peace is a great | maker of
  Cuckolds.   .   2885
MAKERS = 1
*This peace is nothing, but to rust Iron, encrease Taylors, | and breed
  Ballad-makers.   2877
MAKES = 9*2
The other makes you proud. He that trusts to you,   181
There is Auffidious. List what worke he makes | Among'st your clouen
  Army.   510
*which makes me sweat with wrath. Come on my fellows   520
And harke, what noyse the Generall makes: To him   580
Corio. What makes this change? | Menen. The matter?   1707
It makes the Consuls base; and my Soule akes   1802
Makes fear'd, and talk'd of more then seene: your Sonne   2469
*bald before him. Our Generall himselfe makes a Mistris   2854
1 I, and it makes men hate one another.   2887
Virg. The sorrow that deliuers vs thus chang'd, | Makes you thinke so.   3388
'Twixt you there's difference: but the fall of either | Makes the Suruiuor
  heyre of all.   3669
MAKING = 4*1
Coniecturall Marriages, making parties strong,   206
Making but reseruation of your selues,   2418
Making the Mother, wife, and Childe to see,   3456
*For making vp this peace. Thou know'st (great Sonne)   3497
With our owne charge: making a Treatie, where   3731
MALE-TYGER = *1
*mercy in him, then there is milke in a male-Tyger, that   3597
MALICE see also mallice = 3*1
*What I think, I vtter, and spend my malice in my breath.   949
And witnesse of the Malice and Displeasure   2729
My throat to thee, and to thy Ancient Malice: 2753
And with the deepest malice of the Warre,   2943
MALICIOUS = 2
Menen. Either you must | Confesse your selues wondrous Malicious,   88

MALICIOUS *cont*.
His rougher Actions for malicious sounds: 2332
MALICIOUSLY = 1
All. Nay, but speak not maliciously.   36
MALIGNANTLY = 1
If he should still malignantly remaine   1584
MALIGNE = 1
As you maligne our Senators, for that | They are not such as you.   115
MALKIN = 1
While she chats him: the Kitchin *Malkin* pinnes   1126
MALLICE = 2*2
Vpon their ancient mallice, will forget   1150
*to seeme to affect the mallice and displeasure of the Peo- | ple,   1224
*were a Mallice, that giuing it selfe the Lye, would plucke   1235
And translate his Mallice towards you, into Loue, | Standing your
friendly Lord.   1590
MAMMOCKT = *1
*his teeth, and teare it. Oh, I warrant how he mammockt | it.   427
MAN *see also* man-child, man-entred = 35*11
And through the Crankes and Offices of man,   144
Sicin. Was euer man so proud as is this *Martius*?   280
To th'vtmost of a man, and giddy censure   298
*he was a Man-child, then now in first seeing he had pro- | ued himselfe
a man.   377
Like to a Haruest man, that task'd to mowe | Or all, or loose his hyre. 398
Volum. Away you Foole; it more becomes a man   401
1.*Senat*. No, nor a man that feares you lesse then he,   502
There is the man of my soules hate, *Auffidious*,   581
More then I know the sound of *Martius* Tongue | From euery meaner
man.   635
Mar. As with a man busied about Decrees: 645
*1.*Off*. No more of him, hee's a worthy man: make | way, they are
comming.   1237
The man I speake of, cannot in the World   1300
He prou'd best man i'th' field, and for his meed   1311
To ease his Brest with panting. | *Menen*. Worthy man.   1336
*would incline to the people, there was neuer a worthier | man.   1424
*the bewitchment of some popular man, and giue it   1492
Scici. How now, my Masters, haue you chose this man?   1553
All. No, no: no man saw 'em.   1564
To punish; Not a man, of their Infirmity.   1774
Patri. This man ha's marr'd his fortune.   1982
*That would depopulate the city, & be euery man himself   1995
False to my Nature? Rather say, I play | The man I am.   2100
Vol. You might haue beene enough the man you are,   2106
O're the vast world, to seeke a single man,   2482
Was not a man my Father? Had'st thou Foxship   2526
Volum. Bastards, and all. | Good man, the Wounds that he does beare
for Rome!   2537
*the man I thinke, that shall set them in present Action. So   2616
Why speak'st not? Speake man: What's thy name?   2709
*me, dost not thinke me for the man I am, necessitie com- | mands me
name my selfe.   2711
I lou'd the Maid I married: neuer man   2772
*2 So did I, Ile be sworne: He is simply the rarest man | i'th'world. 2820
3 I would not be a Roman of all Nations; I had as | liue be a
condemn'd man.   2835

MAN *cont.*

2 And he's as like to do't, as any man I can imagine.	2863
*the man in blood, they will out of their Burroughes (like	2870
That shapes man Better: and they follow him	3008
Mene. We are all vndone, vnlesse | The Noble man haue mercy.	3026
The happy man; whether detect of iudgement,	3130
I will not heare thee speake. This man *Auffidius*	3327
Corio. This last old man, | Whom with a crack'd heart I haue sent to Rome,	3355
*As if a man were Author of himself, & knew no other kin	3385
Whose Chronicle thus writ, The man was Noble,	3502
Then can our Reasons. There's no man in the world	3515
Sicin. Is't possible, that so short a time can alter the | condition of a man.	3578
*growne from Man to Dragon: He has wings, hee's more | then a creeping thing.	3582
Auf. Euen so, as with a man by his owne Almes im-|poyson'd, and with his Charity slaine.	3661
The man is Noble, and his Fame folds in	3797

MANACLES = 2

(Like one that meanes his proper harme) in Manacles,	813
With Manacles through our streets, or else	3470

MANET = 3

Citizens steale away. Manet Sicin. & Brutus.	279
Flourish Cornets. | Then Exeunt. Manet Sicinius and Brutus.	1378
Manet the Guard and Menenius.	3330

MANGLES = 1

Mangles true iudgement, and bereaues the State	1857

MANHOOD = 1

And Manhood is call'd Foolerie, when it stands	1971

MANIFEST = 1*1

Val. How do you both? You are manifest house-kee-|pers.	414
Bru. Manifest Treason. | *Sicin.* This a Consull? No.	1872

MANIFESTS = *1

*care whether they loue, or hate him, manifests the true	1216

MANKINDE = 1

Sicin. Are you mankinde? | *Volum.* I foole, is that a shame. Note but this Foole,	2524

MANNER = 2

Nor shewing (as the manner is) his Wounds	1158
Ile leaue you: Pray you speake to em, I pray you | In wholsome manner. *Exit*	1450

MANS = 4*2

At a poore mans house: he vs'd me kindly,	842
*mans will, 'tis strongly wadg'd vp in a blocke-head: but	1414
1.Cit. Hee ha's done Nobly, and cannot goe without | any honest mans Voyce.	1524
Thy teares are salter then a yonger mans,	2460
*it saide, the fittest time to corrupt a mans Wife, is when	2601
Which this mans life did owe you, you'l reioyce	3817

MANTLED = 1

Com. I, if you come not in the blood of others, | But mantled in your owne.	638

MANY = 12*9

To take in many Townes, ere (almost) Rome | Should know we were a-foot.	340
Let him alone: Or so many so minded,	692

MANY *cont*.

Which without note, here's many else haue done,	805
*helpes are many, or else your actions would growe won-|drous	932
*1.*Off*. Come, come, they are almost here: how many | stand for Consulships?	1205
*2.*Off*. 'Faith, there hath beene many great men that	1211
*be many that they haue loued, they know not wherefore:	1213
*3.*Cit*. We haue beene call'd so of many, not that our	1404
*1. You haue receyued many wounds for your Coun-|trey.	1497
Haue done many things, some lesse, some more:	1522
Com. Stand fast, we haue as many friends as enemies.	1954
By many an Ounce) he dropp'd it for his Country:	2038
In thy hands clutcht: as many Millions in	2351
With many heads butts me away. Nay Mother,	2438
'Tis I that made thy Widdowes: Many an heyre	2624
*3 Doo't? he will doo't: for look you sir, he has as ma-|ny	2864
Mes. It is spoke freely out of many mouths,	2974
Which will not proue a whip: As many Coxcombes	3060
2 And so did I. | *3 And so did I: and to say the truth, so did very ma-|ny	3068
*1 Faith Sir, if you had told as many lies in his behalfe,	3262
Hath widdowed and vnchilded many a one,	3834

MANY-HEADED = *1

*he himselfe stucke not to call vs the many-headed Multi-|tude.	1402

MAN-CHILD = *1

*he was a Man-child, then now in first seeing he had pro-|ued himselfe a man.	377

MAN-ENTRED = 1

Man-entred thus, he waxed like a Sea,	1313

MAP = *1

*that tell you haue good faces, if you see this in the Map	957

MAR = 24*8

MARCH = 5

That we with smoaking swords may march from hence	497
(As cause will be obey'd:) please you to March,	704
Com. March on my Fellowes:	707
March to assault thy Country, then to treade	3478
Exeunt bearing the Body of Martius. A dead March | Sounded.	3837

MARCHING = *1

Enter Coriolanus marching with Drumme, and Colours. The | Commoners being with him.	3734

MARCUS = 2*1

Marcus Caius Coriolanus. Beare th'addition Nobly euer?	821
Omnes. Marcus Caius Coriolanus.	823
Marcus, he kill'd my Father.	3795

MARK *see also* marke, marke't = *1

Mene. I paint him in the Character. Mark what mer-|cy	3595

MARKD = 1

Bru. Mark'd you his lip and eyes. | *Sicin*. Nay, but his taunts.	283

MARKE = 9*1

(You my good Friends, this sayes the Belly) marke me.	148
Not for the flyers: Marke me, and do the like.	542
Beyond the marke of others: our then Dictator,	1303
Where it did marke, it tooke from face to foot:	1322
Brutus. Marke you that.	1368
*Heere he comes, and in the Gowne of humility, marke	1428
Heare you this Triton of the *Minnoues*? Marke you | His absolute Shall?	1782

MARKE *cont.*

Sicin. Marke you this people?	2355
Like a great Sea-marke standing euery flaw, | And sauing those that eye thee.	3427
Corio. Auffidius, and you Volces marke, for wee'l	3447

MARKES = 2

Remaines, that in th'Officiall Markes inuested,	1533
Her Enemies markes vpon me. I do loue	2397

MARKET = 9*1

Lar. Thou worthiest *Martius,* | Go sound thy Trumpet in the Market place,	599
Appeare i'th'Market place, nor on him put	1156
Of our proceedings heere on th'Market place,	1385
Senat. Tribunes giue way, he shall toth' Market place.	1712
Com. Well, on to'th'Market place.	1807
Sic. Meet on the Market place: wee'l attend you there:	2076
Com. I haue beene i'th' Market place: and Sir 'tis fit	2197
And throw't against the Winde. Toth' Market place:	2210
Corio. Pray be content: | Mother, I am going to the Market place:	2240
Bid them repayre to th'Market place, where I	3652

MARKS = 1

His Marks of Merit, Wounds receiu'd for's Countrey.	1562

MARRD = 1

Patri. This man ha's marr'd his fortune.	1982

MARRE = 1

Men. You'l marre all,	1449

MARRIAGES = 1

Coniecturall Marriages, making parties strong,	206

MARRIED = 1

I lou'd the Maid I married: neuer man	2772

MARS = 3*1

Now Mars, I prythee make vs quicke in worke,	496
Bestride my Threshold. Why, thou Mars I tell thee,	2776
*Son and Heire to Mars, set at vpper end o'th'Table: No	2852
Corio. Hear'st thou Mars? | *Auf.* Name not the God, thou boy of Teares.	3769

MART = 3

MARTIANS = 1

The Noble House o'th'*Martians*: from whence came	1641

MARTIUS see also Mar., Mart. = 82*14

1.Cit. First you know, *Caius Martius* is chiefe enemy | to the people.	10
2.Cit. Would you proceede especially against *Caius* | *Martius.*	27
Enter Caius Martius.	172
Hayle, Noble *Martius.*	173
Mess. Where's *Caius Martius?* | *Mar.* Heere: what's the matter!	239
1.Sen. Martius 'tis true, that you haue lately told vs,	246
1.*Sen.* Then worthy *Martius,* | Attend vpon *Cominius* to these Warres.	258
Tit. No *Caius Martius,* | Ile leane vpon one Crutch, and fight with tother,	265
Com. Noble *Martius.* | *Sen.* Hence to your homes, be gone.	273
Sicin. Was euer man so proud as is this *Martius?*	280
Will then cry out of *Martius:* Oh, if he | Had borne the businesse.	299
Opinion that so stickes on *Martius,* shall | Of his demerits rob *Cominius.*	302
Bru. Come: halfe all *Cominius* Honors are to *Martius*	304
Though *Martius* earn'd them not: and all his faults	305
To *Martius* shall be Honors, though indeed | In ought he merit not.	306

MARTIUS cont.

MARTIUS cont.

We were elected theirs, *Martius* is worthy │ Of present Death.	1923
Brut. Aediles seize him. │ *All Ple.* Yeeld *Martius*, yeeld.	1928
*Mene. Helpe *Martius*, helpe: you that be noble, helpe │ him young and old.	1946
Where if you bring not *Martius*, wee'l proceede │ In our first way.	2077
This Mould of *Martius*, they to dust should grinde it,	2209
Corio. My name is *Caius Martius*, who hath done	2722
Auf. Oh *Martius*, *Martius*;	2759
Then thee all-Noble *Martius*. Let me twine	2764
And wak'd halfe dead with nothing. Worthy *Martius*,	2784
Yet *Martius* that was much. Your hand: most welcome. │ *Exeunt*	2806
*3 Why here's he that was wont to thwacke our Ge-│nerall, *Caius Martius*.	2838
Bru. *Caius Martius* was │ A worthy Officer i'th'Warre, but Insolent,	2928
Mene. 'Tis *Auffidius*, │ Who hearing of our *Martius* Banishment,	2945
Which were In-shell'd, when *Martius* stood for Rome,	2948
Sicin. Come, what talke you of *Martius*.	2950
How probable I do not know, that *Martius*	2975
Bru. Rais'd onely, that the weaker sort may wish │ Good *Martius* home againe.	2980
A fearefull Army, led by *Caius Martius*,	2988
If *Martius* should be ioyn'd with Volceans.	3005
Bru. Onely make triall what your Loue can do, │ For Rome, towards *Martius*.	3196
Mene. Well, and say that *Martius* returne mee,	3198
Enter Virgilia, Volumnia, Valeria, yong Martius, │ *with Attendants.*	3369
*yet your Butterfly was a Grub: this *Martius*, is	3581
The Volcians are dislodg'd, and *Martius* gone:	3612
Vnshoot the noise that Banish'd *Martius*;	3644
Corio. Traitor? How now? │ *Auf.* I Traitor, *Martius*.	3753
Corio. Martius? │ *Auf.* I *Martius*, *Caius Martius*: Do'st thou thinke	3755
Draw both the Conspirators, and kils Martius, who │ *falles, Auffidius stands on him.*	3805
Exeunt bearing the Body of Martius. A dead March │ *Sounded.*	3837

MARTIUS = 9*1

MARUEYLD = 1

1.*Con.* So he did my Lord: │ The Army marueyl'd at it, and in the last,	3695

MARULLOUS = 1

3 A maru'llous poore one. │ *Corio.* True, so I am.	2682

MASKT = 1

Wherein thou seest me maskt, for thy Reuenge	735

MASTER *see also* maister = 4*1

*2 *Ser.* Where's *Cotus*: my M.(aster) cals for him: *Cotus. Exit*	2657
out o'thhouse: Prythee call my Master to him.	2676
Corio. No, I serue not thy Master.	2699
3 How sir? Do you meddle with my Master?	2700
2 Who my Master? │ 1 Nay, it's no matter for that.	2824

MASTERS = 6*4

*Menen. Why Masters, my good Friends, mine honest	63
Then we to stretch it out. Masters a'th' People,	1259
Menen. Masters of the People, │ Your multiplying Spawne, how can he flatter?	1291
*Scici. How now, my Masters, haue you chose this man?	1553
Masters, lay downe your Weapons.	2074
*Com. Heare me my Masters, and my common friends.	2393
Sicin. Go Masters get you home, be not dismaid,	3077

MASTERS *cont.*
　　*1 *Cit*. The Gods bee good to vs: Come Masters let's　　　　　3081
　　Auf. My Noble Masters, heare me speake. | 1.*Lord*. O *Tullus*.　　3808
　　3.*Lord*. Tread not vpon him Masters, all be quiet, | Put vp your Swords.　3812
MASTERSHIP = 1
　　Shew'd Mastership in floating. Fortunes blowes,　　　　　2443
MATCH = *1
　　Corio. A match Sir, there's in all two worthie voyces　　　1471
MATRONS = *1
　　*And the blind to heare him speak: Matrons flong Gloues,　　1193
MATTER = 12*5
　　Where go you with Bats and Clubs? The matter | Speake I pray you.　57
　　Mar. Thanks. What's the matter you dissentious rogues　　174
　　Him vilde, that was your Garland. What's the matter,　　195
　　Mess. Where's *Caius Martius*? | *Mar*. Heere: what's the matter!　239
　　Men. Why 'tis no great matter: for a very little theefe　925
　　*Worshippes haue deliuer'd the matter well, when I finde　953
　　*matter betweene party and party, if you chaunce to bee　969
　　Brutus. What's the matter?　　　　　1189
　　*that's no matter, the greater part carries it, I say. If hee　1423
　　2 *Cit*. And 'twere to giue againe: but 'tis no matter.　1474
　　Corio. What makes this change? | *Menen*. The matter?　1707
　　Not by your owne instruction, nor by'th'matter　2152
　　Com. Well, well, no more. | *Corio*. What is the matter,　2335
　　Sicin. Peace: | We neede not put new matter to his charge:　2357
　　2 Who my Master? | 1 Nay, it's no matter for that.　2824
　　And pay you for your voyces. 'Tis no matter,　3062
　　Corio. What's the matter?　　　　　3296
MATURE = *1
　　*This lyes glowing I can tell you, and is almost mature for | the violent
　　breaking out.　　　　　2594
MAY *l*.68 91 111 497 527 612 *797 834 874 893 *1142 *1223 1359 *1381
　　1390 *1420 1421 *1476 *1477 *1493 1541 1542 1555 1612 1805 1840
　　2018 2170 2746 *2884 2980 *3241 3422 3435 3446 3494 *3575 = 26*11
MAYST = 2
　　Where thou shalt rest, that thou may'st heare of vs,　　2479
　　Thy thoughts with Noblenesse, that thou mayst proue　3425
ME *see also* mee *l*.*5 123 134 146 148 153 154 210 233 252 263 *382 389
　　391 394 433 *451 *453 *466 *520 542 589 590 *592 606 *619 625 640
　　652 675 688 697 731 735 739 742 765 778 *779 806 837 842 843 866 891
　　*898 *910 *951 1009 *1011 1083 1284 1316 1356 *1433 *1444 1446 1447
　　*1467 1508 1548 1569 1684 1687 1737 1750 1757 1900 *1930 1931 1941
　　1942 2010 2065 2080 2084 2093 2099 2138 2211 2219 2238 2242 2245
　　2254 2275 2313 2349 *2393 2395 2397 2438 2445 2488 2491 2493 2494
　　2500 2564 2575 *2618 2626 2628 *2631 2648 2650 2651 2679 *2710
　　*2711 2713 *2720 *2730 2733 2734 2736 2737 2764 2781 2794 2803
　　*2811 *2813 *2816 *2879 2961 *3004 3154 3159 3161 3177 3206 3227
　　3229 3288 *3299 3357 3358 3407 3436 3438 3483 3505 3516 3522 3524
　　3556 3558 3685 3693 3704 3775 3781 3782 3783 3808 3819 = 132*32
ME = *3
MEALE = 2
　　In boulted Language: Meale and Bran together　　2064
　　Whose Houres, whose Bed, whose Meale and Exercise　2640
MEAN = *1
　　*you are censured heere in the City, I mean of vs a'th'right | hand File,
　　do you?　　　　　919

MEANE = 5
    I meane to stride your Steed, and at all times   827
    Enter Coriolanus in meane Apparrell, dis-|guisd, and muffled.   2621
    Lieu. Yet I wish Sir, | (I meane for your particular) you had not   3104
    And his Wife, who (as I heare) meane to solicite him   3232
    1 Come, my Captaine knowes you not. | *Mene*. I meane thy Generall. 3289
MEANER = 1
    More then I know the sound of *Martius* Tongue | From euery meaner
    man.   635
MEANES = 3*1
    **Mar*. I am glad on't, then we shall ha meanes to vent   242
    (Like one that meanes his proper harme) in Manacles,   813
    Enui'd against the people; seeking meanes   2380
    Vnlesse by vsing meanes I lame the foote   3098
MEANEST = 1
    The meanest house in Rome; so farre my Sonne   2552
MEASURE = 3*1
    **Senat*. He cannot but with measure fit the Honors | which we deuise
    him.   1338
    Bru. Enough, with ouer measure. | *Corio*. No, take more.   1838
    Sicin. Yet your good will | Must haue that thankes from Rome, after
    the measure | As you intended well.   3202
    Lou'd me, aboue the measure of a Father,   3357
MEASURELESSE = 1
    Corio. Measurelesse Lyar, thou hast made my heart   3773
MEATE = 2*1
    *That meate was made for mouths. That the gods sent not   220
    Volum. Angers my Meate: I suppe vpon my selfe,   2565
    Your Soldiers vse him as the Grace 'fore meate,   3093
MEAZELS = 1
    Coine words till their decay, against those Meazels   1770
MECHANICKES = 1
    Againe, with Romes Mechanickes. Tell me not   3438
MEDDLE = 2*1
    3 How sir? Do you meddle with my Master?   2700
    **Corio*. I, tis an honester seruice, then to meddle with   2701
    Mene. No: Ile not meddle.   3193
MEE *l*.*963 *1485 *2571 *2581 2779 2791 3198 3207 *3585 = 4*5
MEED = 1
    He prou'd best man i'th' field, and for his meed   1311
MEERE = 1
    I would haue voided thee. But in meere spight   2739
MEERELY = 1
    Sicin. This is cleane kamme. | *Brut*. Meerely awry: 2042
MEET = 8*1
    If ere againe I meet him beard to beard,   869
    You anon doe meet the Senate. | *Corio*. Is this done?   1534
    To meet anon, vpon your approbation.   1538
    When what's not meet, but what must be, was Law,   1868
    Let what is meet, be saide it must be meet,   1870
    **Sic*. Meet on the Market place: wee'l attend you there: 2076
    Sicin. Let's not meet her.   2513
    Sicin. Wee'l meet them, and helpe the ioy. *Exeunt*.   3638
MEETE = 3
    If we, and *Caius Martius* chance to meete,   352
    But to confirme my Cursses. Could I meete 'em   2560
    I will go meete the Ladies. This *Volumnia*,   3626

MEETING = 1*1
   *Meeting two such Weales men as you are (I cannot call   950
   As the maine Point of this our after-meeting,   1246
MEETS = 1
   Enter 3 Seruingman, the 1 meets him.   2673
MELLOW = *1
   *Mene. As Hercules did shake downe Mellow Fruite: 3017
MELT = 2
   To melt the Citty Leades vpon your pates,   2997
   Which can make Gods forsworne? I melt, and am not   3377
MELTED = *1
   *parts melted away with rotten Dewes, the fourth would   1418
MEMBERS = 3*2
   *Men. There was a time, when all the bodies members   98
   To'th'discontented Members, the mutinous parts   113
   And you the mutinous Members: For examine   157
   *the multitude; of the which, we being members, should   1398
   bring our selues to be monstrous members.   1399
MEMORIE = 2
   I am wearie, yea, my memorie is tyr'd: 852
   But with that Surname, a good memorie   2728
MEMORY = 2
   To make Coales cheape: A Noble memory.   3170
   Yet he shall haue a Noble Memory. Assist.   3836
MEN = 21*6
   *he did it to that end: though soft conscienc'd men can be   38
   That beare the shapes of men, how haue you run   530
   They haue plac'd their men of trust?   666
   And foure shall quickly draw out my Command, | Which men are best
   inclin'd.   705
   *You two are old men, tell me one thing that I shall aske | you.   910
   *Meeting two such Weales men as you are (I cannot call   950
   *that say you are reuerend graue men, yet they lye deadly,   956
   Which being aduanc'd, declines, and then men dye.   1058
   Yet by the faith of men, we haue   1097
   I haue seene the dumbe men throng to see him,   1192
   *2.Off. 'Faith, there hath beene many great men that   1211
   A Vessell vnder sayle, so men obey'd,   1320
   Runne reeking o're the liues of men, as if 'twere   1333
   The worthiest men haue done't?   1437
   Supplied with worthy men, plant loue amongs   2304
   As the dead Carkasses of vnburied men,   2410
   That common chances. Common men could beare,   2441
   I had fear'd death, of all the Men i'th'World   2738
   *deafe, sleepe, insensible, a getter of more bastard Chil- | dren, then
   warres a destroyer of men.   2882
   1 I, and it makes men hate one another.   2887
   You and your Apron men: you, that stood so much   3013
   The second name of men, obeyes his points   3049
   *Me. You guard like men, 'tis well. But by your leaue,   3238
   The booke of his good Acts, whence men haue read   3253
   My best and freshest men, seru'd his designements   3688
   That Pages blush'd at him, and men of heart | Look'd wond'ring each
   at others.   3767
   *Corio. Cut me to peeces Volces men and Lads,   3782
MEN = 13*17

MEND = 2
  With flight and agued feare, mend and charge home,   533
  too rough: you must returne, and mend it.   2115
MENE = 1
  Scicin. Fare you well. *Exeunt Coriol. and Mene.*   1547
MENE = 67*20
MENEN = 31*13
MENENIUS see also Me., Men., Mene., Menen. = 21*9
  Enter Menenius Agrippa.   52
  2 Cit. Worthy *Menenius Agrippa*, one that hath al-|wayes lou'd the
  people.   53
  Enter Menenius with the two Tribunes of the | people, Sicinius & Brutus.   896
  Sicin. Menenius, you are knowne well enough too.   942
  Volum. Honorable *Menenius*, my Boy *Martius* appro-|ches: 997
  Volum. I, worthy *Menenius*, and with most prosperous | approbation.   1000
  Volum. On's Browes: *Menenius*, hee comes the third | time home with
  the Oaken Garland.   1021
  Com. Euer right. | *Cor.* Menenius, euer, euer.   1103
  *the People, Lictors before them: Coriolanus, Mene-|nius, Cominius the
  Consul: Scicinius and Brutus*   1240
  Enter Coriolanus in a gowne of Humility, with | Menenius.   1426
  Enter Menenius, with Brutus and Scicinius.   1530
  *Cornets. Enter Coriolanus, Menenius, all the Gentry, | Cominius, Titus
  Latius, and other Senators.*   1672
  Sic. Noble *Menenius*, be you then as the peoples officer: 2073
  Enter Menenius with the Senators.   2113
  Edile. With old *Menenius*, and those Senators | That alwayes fauour'd
  him.   2267
  Enter Coriolanus, Menenius, and Comi-|nius, with others.   2296
  *Enter Coriolanus, Volumnia, Virgilia, Menenius, Cominius, | with the
  yong Nobility of Rome.*   2435
  Ile do well yet. Thou old and true *Menenius*,   2459
  Enter Volumnia, Virgilia, and Menenius.   2512
  Enter Menenius.   2902
  Bru. We stood too't in good time. Is this *Menenius*?   2903
  *Enter Menenius, Cominius, Sicinius, Brutus, | the two Tribunes, with
  others.*   3150
  Enter Menenius to the Watch or Guard.   3235
  My name hath touch't your eares: it is *Menenius*.   3248
  Men. Prythee fellow, remember my name is *Menenius*,   3266
  *Father *Menenius* do's. O my Son, my Son! thou art pre-|paring   3306
  And would haue sent it. Another word *Menenius*,   3326
  Manet the Guard and Menenius.   3330
  1 Now sir, is your name *Menenius*?   3331
  Enter Menenius and Sicinius.   3570
MERCENARY = 1
  He wadg'd me with his Countenance, as if | I had bin Mercenary.   3693
MERCIE = 1
  Their mercie, at the price of one faire word,   2375
MERCY *see also* mercie = 6*3
  I'th'part that is at mercy? fiue times, *Martius*,   865
  Mene. We are all vndone, vnlesse | The Noble man haue mercy.   3026
  The way into his mercy: Nay, if he coy'd   3157
  For mercy to his Countrey: therefore let's hence,   3233
  May say, this mercy we haue shew'd: the Romanes,   3494
  Auf. I am glad thou hast set thy mercy, & thy Honor   3559
  Sicin. Yes, mercy, if you report him truly.   3594

MERCY *cont.*

*Mene. I paint him in the Character. Mark what mer- |cy	3595
*mercy in him, then there is milke in a male-Tyger, that	3597

MERIT = 4

To *Martius* shall be Honors, though indeed | In ought he merit not.	306
His Marks of Merit, Wounds receiu'd for's Countrey.	1562
Deseru'd this so dishonor'd Rub, layd falsely | I'th' plaine Way of his Merit.	1748
So hated, and so banish'd: but he ha's a Merit	3139

MERRIER = 1

A merrier day did neuer yet greet Rome,	3613

MERRILY = 1

and I will merrily accompany you home.	2608

MERRY = 1

As merry, as when our Nuptiall day was done, | And Tapers burnt to Bedward.	642

MES = 10

MESS = 6*1

MESSENGER see also Mes., Mess. = 9

Enter a Messenger hastily.	238
before the City Corialus: to them | a Messenger.	480
Enter a Messenger.	613
Enter a Messenger.	1188
And beate the Messenger, who bids beware | Of what is to be dreaded.	2959
Enter a Messenger.	2963
Enter Messenger.	2986
Enter a Messenger.	3603
Enter another Messenger.	3609

MET = 6*1

Martius. Yonder comes Newes: | A Wager they haue met.	482
Mar. Say, ha's our Generall met the Enemy?	487
We met here, both to thanke, and to remember, | With Honors like himselfe.	1254
Slew three Opposers: *Tarquins* selfe he met,	1308
*Latius. How often he had met you Sword to Sword:	1690
Volum. Oh y'are well met:	2517
sir, heartily well met, and most glad of your Company.	2617

METHINKES *see* thinkes

METHOUGHT *see* thought

MEYNIE = 1

For the mutable ranke-sented Meynie,	1756

MICROCOSME = *1

*of my Microcosme, followes it that I am knowne well e-|nough	958

MIDDLE = *1

*Newes is, our Generall is cut i'th'middle, & but one halfe	2857

MIDDST = 2

I'th midd'st a th'body, idle and vnactiue,	101
Vnlesse by not so doing, our good Citie | Cleaue in the midd'st, and perish.	2117

MIDNIGHT = *1

*Cor. Choller? Were I as patient as the midnight sleep,	1777

MIGHT *l.**20 *449 782 1310 1367 1585 1595 1693 2087 *2106 2168 *2848
*2909 3192 3491 3728 = 11*5

MILDELY = 5

To answer mildely: for they are prepar'd	2250
Corio. The word is, Mildely. Pray you let vs go,	2253
Menen. I, but mildely.	2256

MILDELY *cont.*
   Corio: Well mildely be it then, Mildely. *Exeunt.*   2257
MILDER = 1
   Why did you wish me milder? Would you haue me   2099
MILE = 4*1
   Mess. Within this mile and halfe.   494
   Against the Winde a mile: you soules of Geese,   529
   Com. 'Tis not a mile: briefely we heard their drummes.   621
   How could'st thou in a mile confound an houre, | And bring thy Newes
   so late?   622
   A Mile before his Tent, fall downe, and knee   3156
MILES = 1
   Three or foure miles about, else had I sir   626
MILKE = *1
   *mercy in him, then there is milke in a male-Tyger, that   3597
MILLIONS = 1
   In thy hands clutcht: as many Millions in   2351
MILS = 1
   ('Tis South the City Mils) bring me word thither   891
MINDE = 6*1
   With euery Minute you do change a Minde,   193
   Where they shall know our minde. Away. *Exeunt*   602
   By Ioue, 'twould be my minde.   1778
   Sicin. It is a minde that shall remain a poison   1779
   And by my Bodies action, teach my Minde | A most inherent Basenesse.   2230
   *a Cudgell, and yet my minde gaue me, his cloathes made | a false
   report of him.   2811
   Auf. Why Noble Lords, | Will you be put in minde of his blinde
   Fortune,   3788
MINDED = 2
   Let him alone: Or so many so minded,   692
   Com. I minded him, how Royall 'twas to pardon   3171
MINDS = *1
   *Your Minds pre-occupy'd with what you rather must do,   1635
MINE *l.*63 *464 489 522 769 870 1457 1459 2084 2126 2229 2238 2255
   2399 2765 2779 3066 3116 *3148 3323 3481 3555 3674 3689 = 22*3
MINGLE = 1
   Where Senators shall mingle teares with smiles,   750
MINGLING = 1
   By mingling them with vs, the honor'd Number,   1762
MINISTER = 1
   And mutually participate, did minister   105
MINISTERS = 1
   Of dreaded Iustice, but on the Ministers   2383
MINNOUES = 1
   Heare you this Triton of the *Minnoues*? Marke you | His absolute Shall?   1782
MINUTE = 1
   With euery Minute you do change a Minde,   193
MIRTH = 2
   She will but disease our better mirth.   469
   I wish you much mirth.   476
MISCARRIES = 1
   A place below the first: for what miscarries   296
MISCHIEFE = 1
   Great hurt and Mischiefe: thereto witnesse my   2724
MISERIE = 1
   Then Miserie it selfe would giue, rewards his deeds   1343

MISERY = 1*2
  *that afflicts vs, the obiect of our misery, is as an inuento-|ry   22
  And make my misery serue thy turne: So vse it,   2745
  *you, bee that you are, long; and your misery encrease   3341
MISGUIDE = 1
  Misguide thy Opposers swords, Bold Gentleman: | Prosperity be thy
  Page.   595
MISSE = 1
  Oh he would misse it, rather then carry it,   1162
MIST = *1
  *Sicin. Your Coriolanus is not much mist, but with his   2906
MISTAKE = 1
  (Mistake me not) to saue my life: for if   2737
MISTAKEN = 1
  Shew duty as mistaken, all this while, | Betweene the Childe, and
  Parent.   3405
MISTRIS = 1*2
  *thy Mistris: Thou prat'st, and prat'st, serue with thy tren-|cher:
  Hence. Beats him away   2702
  Then when I first my wedded Mistris saw   2775
  *bald before him. Our Generall himselfe makes a Mistris   2854
MOCK = 2
  1.Cit. No, 'tis his kind of speech, he did not mock vs.   1559
  And now againe, of him that did not aske, but mock,   1610
MOCKD = 2
  He mock'd vs, when he begg'd our Voyces.   1557
  Do smilingly Reuolt, and who resists | Are mock'd for valiant
  Ignorance,   3022
MOCKE = 2
  Martius. The Gods begin to mocke me: 837
  Thy dangerous Stoutnesse: for I mocke at death   2236
MOCKERIE = 1
  I haue no further with you. Was not this mockerie?   1573
MOCKERS = *1
  *Men. Our very Priests must become Mockers, if they   979
MOCKT = 1
  The People cry you mockt them: and of late,   1726
MODEST = 4
  Sicin. Bemocke the modest Moone.   286
  Would seeme but modest: therefore I beseech you,   776
  Com. Too modest are you: | More cruell to your good report, then
  gratefull   809
  *Me. Do not cry hauocke, where you shold but hunt | With modest
  warrant,   2006
MOE = 1*1
  Here come moe Voyces.   1517
  *Volum. Moe Noble blowes, then euer y wise words.   2530
MOLE-HILL = 1
  As if Olympus to a Mole-hill should   3379
MONETH = 1
  Com. Ile follow thee a Moneth, deuise with thee   2478
MONEY = *1
  *The Warres for my money. I hope to see Romanes as   2889
MONSTER = *1
  *multitude to be ingratefull, were to make a Monster of   1397
MONSTERD = 1
  To heare my Nothings monster'd. Exit Coriolanus   1290

MONSTERS = 1
The horne, and noise o'th'Monsters, wants not spirit   1789
MONSTROUS = 1*1
*of them. Ingratitude is monstrous, and for the   1396
bring our selues to be monstrous members.   1399
MONTH *see* moneth
MOODS = 1
Vol. One on's Fathers moods.   429
MOONE = 5*1
As they would hang them on the hornes a'th Moone,   226
Sicin. Bemocke the modest Moone.   286
*How now (my as faire as Noble) Ladyes, and the Moone   994
And scarr'd the Moone with splinters: heere I cleep   2767
Aboue the Moone. We must be burnt for you.   3186
Corio. The Noble Sister of *Publicola*; | The Moone of Rome: Chaste as
the Isicle   3416
MOOUING = 1
Not to be other then one thing, not moouing   3133
MORE *see also* moe = 75*23
All. No more talking on't; Let it be done, away, away   15
Of more strong linke assunder, then can euer   72
Thether, where more attends you, and you slander   77
*the rich, and prouide more piercing Statutes daily, to   84
But since it serues my purpose, I will venture | To scale't a little more.   92
Shalt see me once more strike at *Tullus* face.   263
Better be held, nor more attain'd then by   295
More then his singularity, he goes | Vpon this present Action.   310
Auf. O doubt not that, | I speake from Certainties. Nay more,   348
Till one can do no more.   354
*in a more comfortable sort: If my Sonne were my Hus- |band,   363
*thee Daughter, I sprang not more in ioy at first hearing   376
Volum. Away you Foole; it more becomes a man   401
With hearts more proofe then Shields.   517
More then I know the sound of *Martius* Tongue | From euery meaner
man.   635
More then thy Fame and Enuy: Fix thy foot.   728
*And gladly quak'd, heare more: where the dull Tribunes,   753
Hadst thou beheld | *Martius*. Pray now, no more: 762
Neuer sound more: when Drums and Trumpets shall   798
No more I say, for that I haue not wash'd   803
Com. Too modest are you: | More cruell to your good report, then
gratefull   809
*triuiall motion: One, that conuerses more with the But- |tocke   947
*bleeding, the more intangled by your hearing: All the   973
*Godden to your Worships, more of your conuer- |sation   988
*is comming home: hee ha's more cause to be prowd: 1041
Coriol. No more of this, it does offend my heart: pray | now no more.   1071
Of no more Soule, nor fitnesse for the World,   1177
1.Off. No more of him, hee's a worthy man: make | way, they are
comming.   1237
more pertinent then the rebuke you giue it.   1272
Coriol. You should account mee the more Vertuous,   1485
Enter three Citizens more.   1516
Haue done many things, some lesse, some more: 1522
Their Liberties, make them of no more Voyce   1618
Scici. Say you chose him, more after our commandment,   1633
Mene. Well, no more.   1765

MORE *cont*.

Senat. No more words, we beseech you.	1766
Corio. How? no more?	1767
Mene. Well, well, no more of that.	1811
*Cor. Thogh there the people had more absolute powre	1812
*More worthier then their Voyces. They know the Corne	1817
Bru. Enough, with ouer measure. | *Corio*. No, take more.	1838
More then you doubt the change on't: That preferre	1851
Mene. On both sides more respect.	1887
(Which I dare vouch, is more then that he hath	2037
Bru. Wee'l heare no more:	2048
Menen. One word more, one word:	2052
Now, this no more dishonors you at all,	2157
More learned then the eares, wauing thy head,	2178
To begge of thee, it is my more dis-honor,	2233
Chide me no more. Ile Mountebanke their Loues,	2242
With Accusations, as I heare more strong | Then are vpon you yet.	2251
Com. Well, well, no more. | *Corio*. What is the matter,	2335
In perill of precipitation | From off the Rocke Tarpeian, neuer more	2387
Sicin. He's sentenc'd: No more hearing.	2394
My Countries good, with a respect more tender,	2398
More holy, and profound, then mine owne life,	2399
Bru. There's no more to be said, but he is banish'd	2404
Makes fear'd, and talk'd of more then seene: your Sonne	2469
More then a wilde exposture, to each chance | That starts i'th'way before thee.	2475
To banish him that strooke more blowes for Rome | Then thou hast spoken words.	2527
Volce. You had more Beard when I last saw you, but	2578
Thou dar'st not this, and that to proue more Fortunes	2750
And say 'tis true; I'de not beleeue them more	2763
Thou Noble thing, more dances my rapt heart,	2774
Once more to hew thy Target from thy Brawne,	2778
And more a Friend, then ere and Enemie,	2805
*but I thought there was more in him, then I could think.	2819
1 But more of thy Newes.	2850
*deafe, sleepe, insensible, a getter of more bastard Chil-|dren, then warres a destroyer of men.	2882
*Friends: the Commonwealth doth stand, and so would | do, were he more angry at it.	2907
Sicin. This is a happier and more comely time,	2925
Mes. Yes worthy Sir, | The Slaues report is seconded, and more	2970
More fearfull is deliuer'd.	2972
Sicin. What more fearefull?	2973
He, and *Auffidius* can no more attone | Then violent'st Contrariety.	2984
Of our designe. He beares himselfe more proudlier,	3099
More then the instant Armie we can make | Might stop our Countryman.	3191
*I You may not passe, you must returne: our Generall | will no more heare from thence.	3241
*more long in Spectatorship, and crueller in suffering, be-|hold	3302
(Though I shew'd sowrely to him) once more offer'd	3360
That thought he could do more: A very little	3363
Of thy deepe duty, more impression shew | Then that of common Sonnes.	3400
Volum. Oh no more, no more: | You haue said you will not grant vs any thing:	3441

MORE *cont.*

How more vnfortunate then all liuing women	3452
Perhaps thy childishnesse will moue him more	3514
More bound to's Mother, yet heere he let's me prate	3516
To his sur-name *Coriolanus* longs more pride	3527
Doe's reason our Petition with more strength	3533
*grovvne from Man to Dragon: He has wings, hee's more | then a creeping thing.	3582
Mene. So did he mee: and he no more remembers his	3585
*his Mother shall bring from him: There is no more	3596
Auf. Say no more. Heere come the Lords,	3719
No more infected with my Countries loue	3737
Doth more then counterpoize a full third part	3743
Corio. Ha? | *Aufid*. No more.	3771
Corio. O that I had him, with six *Auffidiusses*, or more:	3801

MORNING = 2*1

*of the night, then with the forhead of the morning.	948
We powt vpon the Morning, are vnapt	3210
This Morning, for ten thousand of your throates,	3630

MORROW = 1*2

To haue't with saying, Good morrow.	2377
*3 To morrow, to day, presently, you shall haue the	2873
Corio. We will before the walls of Rome to morrow	3347

MORSELL = 1

Yet cam'st thou to a Morsell of this Feast, | Hauing fully din'd before.	757

MORTALL = 3

The mortall Gate of th' Citie, which he painted	1325
Mortall, to cut it off: to cure it, easie.	2034
If not most mortall to him. But let it come:	3547

MOST = 34*16

Men. I tell you Friends, most charitable care	66
That enuied his receite: euen so most fitly,	114
Your most graue Belly was deliberate,	135
Of this most wise Rebellion, thou goest formost:	166
A sickmans Appetite; who desires most that	189
And *Titus Lartius*, a most valiant Roman,	328
Whether 'tis bent: most likely, 'tis for you: | Consider of it.	330
*where he would shew most loue. When yet hee was but	366
Val. Fye, you confine your selfe most vnreasonably:	440
Mar. Those are they | That most are willing; if any such be heere,	685
I that now refus'd most Princely gifts,	838
Volum. I, worthy *Menenius*, and with most prosperous | approbation.	1000
*the Physician: The most soueraigne Prescription in *Galen*,	1013
Brutus. 'Tis most like he will.	1167
Most reuerend and graue Elders, to desire	1249
Brutus. Most willingly: but yet my Caution was	1271
And most dignifies the hauer: if it be,	1299
*off to them most counterfetly, that is sir, I will counter-|fet	1491
Coriol. Most sweet Voyces: | Better it is to dye, better to sterue,	1503
*Your most sweet Voyces: now you haue left your Voyces,	1572
Which most gibingly, vngrauely, he did fashion	1628
Your person most: That he would pawne his fortunes	1692
Cor. Shall? O God! but most vnwise Patricians: why	1785
Most pallates theirs. They choose their Magistrate,	1798
Most Valour spoke not for them. Th'Accusation	1824
And by my Bodies action, teach my Minde | A most inherent Basenesse.	2230
As most abated Captiues, to some Nation	2420

MOST *cont*.

*When most strooke home, being gentle wounded, craues	2444
*so, they are in a most warlike preparation, & hope to com | vpon	
them, in the heate of their diuision	2587
Volce. He cannot choose: I am most fortunate, thus	2606
Rom. I shall betweene this and Supper, tell you most	2609
Vol. A most Royall one: The Centurions, and their	2612
sir, heartily well met, and most glad of your Company.	2617
Volce. You take my part from me sir, I haue the most | cause to be	
glad of yours.	2618
Longer to liue most wearie: and present	2752
Auf. Therefore most absolute Sir, if thou wilt haue	2795
Yet *Martius* that was much. Your hand: most welcome. | *Exeunt*	2806
Sicin. 'Tis he, 'tis he: O he is grown most kind of late:	2904
Sicin. This is most likely.	2979
And power vnto it selfe most commendable,	3142
In a most deere particular. He call'd me Father:	3154
And the most noble Mother of the world	3398
Thine enmities most capitall: Thou barr'st vs	3459
Most dangerously you haue with him preuail'd,	3546
If not most mortall to him. But let it come:	3547
Is't most certaine.	3616
Enter 3 *or* 4 *Conspirators of Auffidius Faction*. | Most Welcome.	3658
2.Con. Most Noble Sir, If you do hold the same intent	3663
All Lords. You are most welcome home.	3721
As the most Noble Coarse, that euer Herald | Did follow to his Vrne.	3824

MOTHER = 29*9

*his Mother, and to be partly proud, which he is, euen to | the altitude	
of his vertue.	40
Enter Volumnia and Virgilia, mother and wife to Martius:	360
*for a day of Kings entreaties, a Mother should not sel him	369
My Mother, who ha's a Charter to extoll her Bloud,	764
Com. Looke, Sir, your Mother.	1073
Cor. Know, good Mother, | I had rather be their seruant in my way,	1117
Corio. I muse my Mother | Do's not approue me further, who was wont	2092
Thy Mother rather feele thy Pride, then feare	2235
Corio. Pray be content: | Mother, I am going to the Market place:	2240
Mene. Is this the promise that you made your mother.	2369
With many heads butts me away. Nay Mother,	2438
Corio. What, what, what: | I shall be lou'd when I am lack'd. Nay	
Mother,	2452
Droope not, Adieu: Farewell my Wife, my Mother,	2458
As 'tis to laugh at 'em. My Mother, you wot well	2465
Come my sweet wife, my deerest Mother, and	2489
Brut. Dismisse them home. Here comes his Mother.	2511
His Mother and his wife, heare nothing from him.	2913
I am one of those: his Mother, Wife, his Childe,	3183
So that all hope is vaine, vnlesse his Noble Mother,	3231
Corio. Wife, Mother, Child, I know not. My affaires | Are Seruanted	
to others: Though I owe	3317
Of stronger earth then others: my Mother bowes,	3378
And the most noble Mother of the world	3398
Making the Mother, wife, and Childe to see,	3456
More bound to's Mother, yet heere he let's me prate	3516
Shew'd thy deere Mother any curtesie,	3518
This Fellow had a Volcean to his Mother:	3535

MOTHER *cont*.
  Corio. O Mother, Mother! | What haue you done? Behold, the Heauens
  do ope,   3540
  They laugh at. Oh my Mother, Mother: Oh!   3543
  A Mother lesse? or granted lesse *Auffidius*?   3551
  Stand to me in this cause. Oh Mother! Wife!   3558
  *his Mother, may preuaile with him. But I say, there   3575
  Sicin. He lou'd his Mother deerely.   3584
  *Mother now, then an eight yeare old horse. The tartnesse   3586
  *his Mother shall bring from him: There is no more   3596
  Repeale him, with the welcome of his Mother: 3645
  I say your City to his Wife and Mother,   3762
MOTHERS = 3
  And Mothers that lacke Sonnes.   1085
  (Trust too't, thou shalt not) on thy Mothers wombe | That brought thee
  to this world.   3479
  To a Mothers part belongs. He turnes away: 3525
MOTHES = *1
  *full of Mothes. Come, I would your Cambrick were sen-|sible   448
MOTION = 3*1
  *triuiall motion: One, that conuerses more with the But-|tocke   947
  Your louing motion toward the common Body, | To yeeld what passes
  here.   1261
  He was a thing of Blood, whose euery motion   1323
  Make motion through my Lips, and my Arm'd knees   2226
MOUD = 1*1
  Bru. Being mou'd, he will not spare to gird the Gods.   285
  Auf. I was mou'd withall.   3552
MOUE = 3*1
  Corio. Scratches with Briars, scarres to moue | Laughter onely.   2327
  *none but my selfe could moue thee, I haue bene blowne   3309
  Perhaps thy childishnesse will moue him more   3514
  3.*Con*. Therefore at your vantage, | Ere he expresse himselfe, or moue
  the people   3713
MOUED *see also* mou'd = *1
  *I was hardly moued to come to thee: but beeing assured   3308
MOUERS = *1
  Mar. See heere these mouers, that do prize their hours   575
MOUES = *1
  *of his face, sowres ripe Grapes. When he walks, he moues   3587
MOUING *see* moouing
MOULD = 2
  This Mould of *Martius*, they to dust should grinde it,   2209
  My wife comes formost, then the honour'd mould   3371
MOUNTAINOUS = 1
  And mountainous Error be too highly heapt,   1511
MOUNTEBANKE = 1
  Chide me no more. Ile Mountebanke their Loues,   2242
MOURNE = 1
  And mourne you for him. Let him be regarded   3823
MOURNFULLY = 1
  Beate thou the Drumme that it speake mournfully: 3832
MOUSE = 1
  The Mouse ne're shunn'd the Cat, as they did budge | From Rascals
  worse then they.   657
MOUTH = 2
  The Tongues o'th' Common Mouth. I do despise them: 1701

MOUTH *cont*.
Or *Ioue*, for's power to Thunder: his Heart's his Mouth: 1985
MOUTHES = *1
*You being their Mouthes, why rule you not their Teeth?   1718
MOUTHS = 2*1
*That meate was made for mouths. That the gods sent not   220
The peoples mouths, and we their hands.   2003
Mes. It is spoke freely out of many mouths,   2974
MOWE = 1*1
Like to a Haruest man, that task'd to mowe | Or all, or loose his hyre. 398
*will mowe all downe before him, and leaue his passage | poul'd.   2861
MUCH = 13*6
The Volces haue much Corne: take these Rats thither,   276
I wish you much mirth.   476
Aduance braue *Titus*, | They do disdaine vs much beyond our Thoughts,   518
*much alone. You talke of Pride: Oh, that you could turne   934
Menen. So doe I too, if it be not too much: brings a   1019
*for their Tongues to be silent, and not confesse so much,   1233
*them. I will make much of your voyces, and so trouble | you no
farther.   1500
Scicin. You shew too much of that,   1739
The which shall turne you to no further harme, | Then so much losse of
time.   2019
Which else would put you to your fortune, and | The hazard of much
blood.   2159
Sicin. For that he ha's | (As much as in him lies) from time to time 2378
Your Husband so much swet. *Cominius*,   2457
Yet *Martius* that was much. Your hand: most welcome. | *Exeunt*   2806
Sicin. Your *Coriolanus* is not much mist, but with his   2906
Mene. All's well, and might haue bene much better, | if he could haue
temporiz'd.   2909
You and your Apron men: you, that stood so much   3013
And humme at good *Cominius*, much vnhearts mee.   3207
Then pitty: Note how much, therefore be gone.   3322
2 'Tis a spell you see of much power: 3332
MUCK = 1
The common Muck of the World: he couets lesse   1342
MUFFLED = 1
Enter Coriolanus in meane Apparrell, dis- | guisd, and muffled.   2621
MULBERRY = 1
Now humble as the ripest Mulberry,   2180
MULES = 1
Haue made them Mules, silenc'd their Pleaders,   1174
MULLD = *1
*of Vent. Peace, is a very Apoplexy, Lethargie, mull'd,   2881
MULTIPLIED = 1
How shall this Bosome-multiplied, digest   1828
MULTIPLYING = 1
Menen. Masters of the People, | Your multiplying Spawne, how can he
flatter?   1291
MULTITUDE = *3
*multitude to be ingratefull, were to make a Monster of   1397
*the multitude; of the which, we being members, should   1398
*he himselfe stucke not to call vs the many-headed Multi- | tude.   1402
MULTITUDINOUS = 1
The Multitudinous Tongue, let them not licke   1855

MUMMERS = *1
 *pinch'd with the Collike, you make faces like Mum-|mers,   970
MUNIMENTS = 1
 With other Muniments and petty helpes   121
MURDRING = 1
 Murd'ring Impossibility, to make | What cannot be, slight worke.   3412
MURRAIN = *1
 *3.*Rom*. A Murrain on't, I tooke this for Siluer. *Exeunt*.   572
MUSE = 1
 Corio. I muse my Mother | Do's not approue me further, who was wont   2092
MUSICKE = 1
 Musicke playes. Enter a Seruingman.   2653
MUST = 49*14
 *a Vice in him: You must in no way say he is co-|uetous.   43
 *1.*Cit*. If I must not, I neede not be barren of Accusa-|tions   45
 Your knees to them (not armes) must helpe. Alacke,   75
 Menen. Either you must | Confesse your selues wondrous Malicious,   88
 2 *Citizen*. Well, | Ile heare it Sir: yet you must not thinke   94
 The one side must haue baile.   171
 That Hunger-broke stone wals: that dogges must eate   219
 Tit. Lead you on: Follow *Cominius*, we must followe | you, right
 worthy your Priority.   271
 *They needs must shew themselues, which in the hatching   337
 Val. Come, lay aside your stitchery, I must haue you   432
 Come, you must go visit the good Lady that lies in.   441
 Virgil. No | At a word Madam; Indeed I must not,   474
 (Though thankes to all) must I select from all: 702
 Rome must know the value of her owne: 771
 Must to *Corioles* backe, send vs to Rome   833
 Learne how 'tis held, and what they are that must | Be Hostages for
 Rome.   887
 *And though I must be content to beare with those,   955
 Men. Our very Priests must become Mockers, if they   979
 *be intomb'd in an Asses Packe-saddle; yet you must bee   984
 What is it (*Coriolanus*) must I call thee?   1079
 The good Patricians must be visited,   1108
 Brutus. So it must fall out | To him, or our Authorities, for an end.   1170
 We must suggest the People, in what hatred   1172
 Scicin. Sir, the People must haue their Voyces,   1360
 *vs his Noble deeds, we must also tell him our Noble ac-|ceptance   1395
 Corio. What must I say, I pray Sir?   1438
 Menen. Oh me the Gods, you must not speak of that,   1444
 You must desire them to thinke vpon you.   1445
 *3 *Cit*. You must thinke if we giue you any thing, we | hope to gaine by
 you.   1463
 But that you must cast your Election on him.   1632
 *Your Minds pre-occupy'd with what you rather must do,   1635
 Must these haue Voyces, that can yeeld them now,   1716
 To where you are bound, you must enquire your way,   1741
 Of generall Ignorance, it must omit | Reall Necessities, and giue way
 the while   1845
 When what's not meet, but what must be, was Law,   1868
 Let what is meet, be saide it must be meet,   1870
 With those that haue but little: this must be patcht | With Cloth of any
 Colour.   1978
 What his Brest forges, that his Tongue must vent,   1986
 Sicin. He's a Disease that must be cut away.   2032

MUST *cont*.

Let me desire your company: he must come,	2080
too rough: you must returne, and mend it.	2115
Corio. What must I do? | *Mene*. Returne to th'Tribunes.	2128
Must I then doo't to them?	2133
Volum. He must, and will: | Prythee now say you will, and goe about it.	2203
Corio. Must I goe shew them my vnbarb'd Sconce?	2205
Must I with my base Tongue giue to my Noble Heart	2206
A Lye, that it must beare well? I will doo't:	2207
Corio. Well, I must doo't:	2218
Must all determine heere?	2316
Those whose great power must try him.	2362
In that's no Changeling, and I must excuse | What cannot be amended.	3102
Aboue the Moone. We must be burnt for you.	3186
Sicin. Yet your good will | Must haue that thankes from Rome, after the measure | As you intended well.	3202
*I You may not passe, you must returne: our Generall | will no more heare from thence.	3241
I must haue leaue to passe.	3261
*haue, I am one that telling true vnder him, must say you | cannot passe. Therefore go backe.	3269
You must report to th'Volcian Lords, how plainly	3349
Whereto we are bound: Alacke, or we must loose	3464
Our comfort in the Country. We must finde	3466
Must as a Forraine Recreant be led	3469
We must proceed as we do finde the People.	3667
Must giue this Curre the Lye: and his owne Notion,	3777
Must beare my beating to his Graue, shall ioyne | To thrust the Lye vnto him.	3779

MUSTER = 1

Thou art thence Banish'd, we would muster all	2786

MUSTIE = 1

Our mustie superfluity. See our best Elders.	243

MUSTY = 2

Of noysome musty Chaffe. He said, 'twas folly	3179
You are the musty Chaffe, and you are smelt	3185

MUTABLE = 1

For the mutable ranke-sented Meynie,	1756

MUTINERS = 1

To gnaw their Garners. Worshipfull Mutiners,	277

MUTINIE = 2

This Mutinie were better put in hazard,	1662
In this Mutinie, the Tribunes, the Aediles, and the | People are beat in.	1949

MUTINIES = 1

There Mutinies and Reuolts, wherein they shew'd	1823

MUTINOUS = 5

Enter a Company of Mutinous Citizens, with Staues, | Clubs, and other weapons.	2
To'th'discontented Members, the mutinous parts	113
And you the mutinous Members: For examine	157
The people Mutinous: And it is rumour'd,	325
Fillop the Starres: Then, let the mutinous windes	3410

MUTUALLY = 1

And mutually participate, did minister	105

MY *l*.56 *63 92 137 148 152 210 212 255 256 *363 *367 *381 *383 *384
389 407 411 *420 *421 439 443 484 *520 535 581 590 *604 620 627 705
707 734 764 767 790 791 792 804 807 817 825 829 836 839 844 845 846

MY *cont*.

848 852 *876 883 884 886 893 *949 *951 *958 *989 *990 *994 *997 1002
*1008 *1032 *1071 1075 1076 1077 1081 1083 1087 1107 1112 1113 1118
*1271 1280 1282 *1288 1290 1352 1358 *1411 1440 1441 1455 *1461
*1486 *1487 *1489 *1490 *1543 *1553 1556 *1675 1688 1750 1755 1768
1769 1778 1802 1816 1876 *1968 1977 2092 2097 2100 2121 2161 2162
2173 2205 2206 2215 2216 2219 2220 2221 2224 2225 2226 2227 2230
2233 2245 2246 2376 *2393 2398 2400 2401 2411 2422 2458 *2461 2465
2466 2472 2489 2490 2523 2526 2532 2552 2558 2560 2561 2564 2565
*2574 *2607 *2618 2625 2649 *2657 2676 *2688 2700 2713 2722 2724
2725 2727 2737 2740 2745 2746 2748 2753 2760 2766 2768 2774 2775
2776 2782 2797 *2810 *2811 2824 *2889 2956 *3035 3087 3100 3161
3215 3221 3245 3248 3252 3255 *3266 3289 *3291 *3299 *3300 *3306
*3309 3314 *3317 3319 3324 3328 3348 3367 3371 3378 3380 3386 3390
*3391 3392 3394 3396 3399 *3414 3430 3431 3437 3440 3473 3521 3543
3550 3556 3561 3634 3672 3676 3683 3684 3687 3688 3691 3695 3700
3737 3773 *3776 3778 3779 3794 3795 3802 3808 3814 3820
3829 = 212*58

MYSELFE *see* selfe

MYSTERIES = 1

As I can of those Mysteries which heauen | Will not haue earth to know.	2546

NAILE = 2

One fire driues out one fire; one Naile, one Naile;	3145

NAKED = 2

Being naked, sicke; nor Phane, nor Capitoll,	879
Put on the Gowne, stand naked, and entreat them	1357

NAMD = 3

And by deed-atchieuing Honor newly nam'd,	1078
And Nobly nam'd, so twice being Censor, | Was his great Ancestor.	1646
Whom late you haue nam'd for Consull.	1905

NAME = 29*4

Holding *Corioles* in the name of Rome,	648
Lartius. Martius, his Name. | *Martius*. By *Iupiter* forgot:	850
*my Sonne the whole Name of the Warre: he hath in this	1032
With Fame, a Name to *Martius Caius*:	1066
Sicin. Go call the people, in whose name my Selfe	1876
He heard the Name of Death. *A Noise within.*	1988
The Consuls worthinesse, so can I name his Faults.	2011
That doth distribute it. In the name a'th'people,	2384
To enter our Rome gates. I'th'Peoples name, | I say it shall bee so.	2389
Rom. I know you well sir, and you know mee: your | name I thinke is *Adrian*.	2571
Auf. Whence com'st thou? What wouldst y? Thy name?	2708
Why speak'st not? Speake man: What's thy name?	2709
*me, dost not thinke me for the man I am, necessitie com- |mands me name my selfe.	2711
Auf. What is thy name?	2713
Corio. A name vnmusicall to the Volcians eares,	2714
Auf. Say, what's thy name?	2716
Thou shew'st a Noble Vessell: What's thy name?	2719
Auf. I know thee not? Thy Name:	2721
Corio. My name is *Caius Martius*, who hath done	2722
*Which thou should'st beare me, only that name remains.	2730
The second name of men, obeyes his points	3049
Com. Yet one time he did call me by my name:	3161
Till he had forg'd himselfe a name a'th'fire | Of burning Rome.	3166

NAME *cont.*

My name hath touch't your eares: it is *Menenius*.	3248
1 Be it so, go back: the vertue of your name, | Is not heere passable.	3249
Men. Prythee fellow, remember my name is *Menenius*,	3266
1 Now sir, is your name *Menenius*?	3331
To keepe your name liuing to time.	3482
Which thou shalt thereby reape, is such a name	3500
Destroy'd his Country, and his name remaines	3504
To his sur-name *Coriolanus* longs more pride	3527
Ile grace thee with that Robbery, thy stolne name | *Coriolanus* in *Coriolus*?	3757
Corio. Hear'st thou Mars? | *Auf*. Name not the God, thou boy of Teares.	3769

NAMES = 1

He would not answer too: Forbad all Names,	3164

NAPES = *1

*your eyes toward the Napes of your neckes, and make	935

NAPLES = 1

The Naples Vesture of Humilitie,	1157

NATION = 1

As most abated Captiues, to some Nation	2420

NATIONS = 1

3 I would not be a Roman of all Nations; I had as | liue be a condemn'd man.	2835

NATIUE = 1*1

All cause vnborne, could neuer be the Natiue	1826
*1.*Con*. Your Natiue Towne you enter'd like a Poste,	3707

NATURALL = 1

From me receiue that naturall competencie	146

NATURE = 16*2

*2.*Cit*. What he cannot helpe in his Nature, you ac-|count	42
Sicin. Such a Nature, tickled with good successe, dis-|daines	289
Sicin. Nature teaches Beasts to know their Friends.	903
Then what he stood for: so his gracious nature	1588
Or else it would haue gall'd his surly nature,	1597
If, as his nature is, he fall in rage	1664
The Nature of our Seats, and make the Rabble	1833
Mene. His nature is too noble for the World:	1983
Least his infection being of catching nature, | Spred further.	2050
False to my Nature? Rather say, I play | The man I am.	2100
I would dissemble with my Nature, where	2161
Made by some other Deity then Nature,	3007
When first I did embrace him. Yet his Nature	3101
By Soueraignty of Nature. First, he was	3126
Which he was Lord of: or whether Nature,	3132
All bond and priuiledge of Nature breake;	3374
Great Nature cries, Deny not. Let the Volces	3382
He bow'd his Nature, neuer knowne before,	3677

NAUELL = 1

Euen when the Nauell of the State was touch'd,	1820

NAUGHT *see also* nought = 2

All will be naught else.	1952
Then the seuerity of the publike Power, | Which he so sets at naught.	2000

NAY = 25*3

All. Nay, but speak not maliciously.	36
Menen. Nay these are almost thoroughly perswaded:	213
Mar. Nay let them follow,	275

NAY *cont.*

Bru. Mark'd you his lip and eyes. | *Sicin.* Nay, but his taunts.	283
Auf. O doubt not that, | I speake from Certainties. Nay more,	348
hoo, *Martius* comming home? | 2.*Ladies.* Nay, 'tis true.	1003
Volum. Nay, my good Souldier, vp:	1076
Coriolanus rises, and offers to goe away. | Nay, keepe your place.	1275
*3.*Cit.* Nay your wit will not so soone out as another	1413
Com. Nay, come away. *Exeunt Coriolanus and* | *Cominius.*	1980
Mene. Nay temperately: your promise.	2347
With many heads butts me away. Nay Mother,	2438
Virg. Oh heauens! O heauens! | *Corio.* Nay, I prythee woman.	2448
Corio. What, what, what: | I shall be lou'd when I am lack'd. Nay Mother,	2452
Nay, and you shall heare some. Will you be gone?	2521
Nay but thou shalt stay too: I would my Sonne	2532
*2 Nay, I knew by his face that there was some-thing	2815
2 Who my Master? | 1 Nay, it's no matter for that.	2824
*1 Nay not so neither: but I take him to be the greater | Souldiour.	2827
Sicin. Where is he, heare you? | *Mene.* Nay I heare nothing:	2911
The way into his mercy: Nay, if he coy'd	3157
Sicin. Nay, pray be patient: If you refuse your ayde	3187
Would without lapsing suffer: Nay, sometimes,	3257
Mene. Nay but Fellow, Fellow.	3294
Nay godded me indeed. Their latest refuge	3358
Volum. Nay, go not from vs thus:	3488
And dye among our Neighbours: Nay, behold's,	3530
In all his owne desires: Nay, let him choose	3686

NEAR *see* neere

NECESSARY = *1

*perfecter gyber for the Table, then a necessary Bencher in | the Capitoll.	977

NECESSITIE = *1

*me, dost not thinke me for the man I am, necessitie com- |mands me name my selfe.	2711

NECESSITIES = 1

Of generall Ignorance, it must omit | Reall Necessities, and giue way the while	1845

NECK = *1

Mene. One ith' Neck, and two ith'Thigh, there's nine | that I know.	1047

NECKE = 4

Vol. Hee'l beat *Auffidius* head below his knee, | And treade vpon his necke.	408
Her richest Lockram 'bout her reechie necke,	1127
With vs to breake his necke.	2295
That which shall breake his necke, or hazard mine,	3116

NECKES = *1

*your eyes toward the Napes of your neckes, and make	935

NECKS = *1

*and he returning to breake our necks, they respect not vs.	3602

NEED = 1*1

When he did need your Loues: and doe you thinke,	1604
Sicin. We heare not of him, neither need we fear him,	2893

NEEDE = 1*2

*1.*Cit.* If I must not, I neede not be barren of Accusa- |tions	45
Sicin. Peace: | We neede not put new matter to his charge:	2357
*3 Reason, because they then lesse neede one another:	2888

NEEDED = 1
In this so neuer-needed helpe, yet do not 3188
NEEDER = 1
And loose aduantage, which doth euer coole | Ith'absence of the needer. 2483
NEEDLESSE = 1
Their needlesse Vouches: Custome calls me too't. 1508
NEEDS = *1
*They needs must shew themselues, which in the hatching 337
NEERE = 3
Confusions neere, I cannot speake. You, Tribunes 1898
Sicin. Draw neere ye people. 2310
Sicin. They are neere the City. 3636
NEIGHBOURS = 4
Neighbours, will you vndo your selues? 64
Sicin. Gooden our Neighbours. 2916
Bru. Farewell kinde Neighbours: | We wisht *Coriolanus* had lou'd you as
we did. 2921
And dye among our Neighbours: Nay, behold's, 3530
NEITHER *see also* neyther = 2*4
Like Romans, neither foolish in our stands, 605
Menen. You know neither mee, your selues, nor any 963
Neither Supreame; How soone Confusion 1804
*1 Nay not so neither: but I take him to be the greater | Souldiour. 2827
Sicin. We heare not of him, neither need we fear him, 2893
Menen. I neither care for th'world, nor your General: 3337
NEPTUNE = 1
He would not flatter *Neptune* for his Trident, 1984
NERE = 7*1
2 *Cit.* Care for vs? True indeed, they nere car'd for vs 80
Which ne're came from the Lungs, but euen thus: 110
The Mouse ne're shunn'd the Cat, as they did budge | From Rascals
worse then they. 657
*haue flatter'd the people, who ne're loued them; and there 1212
Brut. Say you ne're had don't, 1655
They ne're did seruice for't; being prest to'th'Warre, 1819
Was ne're distributed. What, will he come? 2263
Ne're through an Arch so hurried the blowne Tide, 3619
NERUES = 1
The strongest Nerues, and small inferiour Veines 145
NERUIE = 1
Death, that darke Spirit, in's neruie Arme doth lye, 1057
NETTLE = 2
Wee call a Nettle, but a Nettle; 1101
NEUER *see also* ne're = 24*4
Still cubbording the Viand, neuer bearing 102
We neuer yet made doubt but Rome was ready | To answer vs. 333
And Balmes applyed to you, yet dare I neuer 682
Neuer sound more: when Drums and Trumpets shall 798
Were he to stand for Consull, neuer would he 1155
I neuer saw the like. 1198
Senat. Sit *Coriolanus*: neuer shame to heare | What you haue Nobly
done. 1277
Both Field and Citie ours, he neuer stood 1335
*2 *Cit.* You are neuer without your trickes, you may, | you may. 1420
*would incline to the people, there was neuer a worthier | man. 1424
Corio. No Sir, 'twas neuer my desire yet to trouble the | poore with
begging. 1461

NEUER *cont*.

Or neuer be so Noble as a Consull,	1743
All cause vnborne, could neuer be the Natiue	1826
Though therein you can neuer be too Noble,	2135
You haue put me now to such a part, which neuer	2211
Or neuer trust to what my Tongue can do | I'th way of Flattery further.	2246
In perill of precipitation | From off the Rocke Tarpeian, neuer more	2387
Heare from me still, and neuer of me ought	2493
I lou'd the Maid I married: neuer man	2772
Com. You haue brought | A Trembling vpon Rome, such as was neuer	3039
Com. Hee'l neuer heare him. | *Sicin*. Not.	3222
*Neuer admitted a priuat whisper, no not with such frends | That thought them sure of you.	3353
Plough Rome, and harrow Italy, Ile neuer	3383
The thing I haue forsworne to graunt, may neuer	3435
Like one i'th'Stockes. Thou hast neuer in thy life,	3517
A merrier day did neuer yet greet Rome,	3613
He bow'd his Nature, neuer knowne before,	3677
A twist of rotten Silke, neuer admitting	3764

NEUER-NEEDED = 1

In this so neuer-needed helpe, yet do not	3188

NEW = 4

With the least cause, these his new Honors,	1151
Corio. Tullus Auffidius then had made new head.	1674
Sicin. Peace: | We neede not put new matter to his charge:	2357
He watered his new Plants with dewes of Flattery,	3675

NEWES = 18*6

Mes. The newes is sir, the Volcies are in Armes.	241
Val. In truth la go with me, and Ile tell you excellent | newes of your Husband.	453
Val. Verily I do not iest with you: there came newes | from him last night.	456
Martius. Yonder comes Newes: | A Wager they haue met.	482
May giue you thankfull Sacrifice. Thy Newes?	612
How could'st thou in a mile confound an houre, | And bring thy Newes so late?	622
Men. The Agurer tels me, wee shall haue Newes to | night.	898
*the Newes in Rome: I haue a Note from the Volcean	2580
*3 Oh Slaues, I can tell you Newes, News you Rascals	2833
1 But more of thy Newes.	2850
*Newes is, our Generall is cut i'th'middle, & but one halfe	2857
All to the Senate-house: some newes is comming | That turnes their Countenances.	2965
Mene. What newes? What newes?	2995
Mene. What's the newes? What's the newes?	2999
Mene. Pray now, your Newes:	3003
*You haue made faire worke I feare me: pray your newes,	3004
Omnes. Faith, we heare fearfull Newes.	3065
Bru. I do not like this Newes. | *Sicin*. Nor I.	3085
Sicin. What's the Newes?	3610
Mess. Good Newes, good newes, the Ladies haue | (preuayl'd.	3611
Mene. This is good Newes:	3625

NEWLY = 1

And by deed-atchieuing Honor newly nam'd,	1078

NEWS = *1

*3 Oh Slaues, I can tell you Newes, News you Rascals	2833

NEXT = 1
   Sicin. First, the Gods blesse you for your tydings: | Next, accept my
   thankefulnesse.   3633
NEYTHER = 1*2
   *no better a ground. Therefore, for *Coriolanus* neyther to   1215
   *no, hee waued indifferently, 'twixt doing them neyther   1220
   Neyther will they bate one iot of Ceremonie.   1361
NICANOR = 1*1
   Volce. *Nicanor*: no. | *Rom*. The same sir.   2576
   Vol. You will be welcome with this intelligence *Ni-*|*canor*.   2598
NICELY = 1
   In their nicely gawded Cheekes, toth' wanton spoyle   1136
NIGHT = 4*3
   Val. Verily I do not iest with you: there came newes | from him last
   night.   456
   Men. The Agurer tels me, wee shall haue Newes to | night.   898
   *of the night, then with the forhead of the morning.   948
   Menen. I will make my very house reele to night: 1008
   He dyes to night.   2026
   Cit. He is, and Feasts the Nobles of the State, at his | house this night.   2633
   *as day do's night: It's sprightly walking, audible, and full   2880
NIGHTLY = 1
   Twelue seuerall times, and I haue nightly since   2780
NINE = *1
   Mene. One ith' Neck, and two ith'Thigh, there's nine | that I know.   1047
NO *l*.*15 *43 160 162 183 265 281 354 *371 400 434 *438 *451 474 484
   *491 502 597 763 773 803 826 853 915 *925 *995 *1014 1017 *1071 1072
   *1165 1177 *1215 *1220 *1237 1283 *1392 *1400 *1423 *1461 1474 1501
   1559 1564 1573 1578 1587 1607 1618 1631 1704 1706 1710 1763 1765
   1766 1767 1796 1811 1839 1844 1873 1940 2015 2019 2048 2116 2156
   2157 2242 *2315 2335 2371 2394 2404 *2503 2576 *2604 2663 *2664
   2685 2699 2785 2825 *2852 2984 3009 3062 3080 3102 3111 3122 3152
   3193 3242 *3264 *3283 *3305 *3353 *3385 3403 3441 3477 3492 3515
   3519 3554 *3576 *3585 *3596 *3600 3614 3698 3708 3719 3732 3737
   3745 3772 3796 = 98*32
NOBILITIE = 1
   To curbe the will of the Nobilitie: 1722
NOBILITY = 5
   Would the Nobility lay aside their ruth,   209
   I sinne in enuying his Nobility: 250
   Enter Coriolanus, Volumnia, Virgilia, Menenius, Cominius, | *with the*
   yong Nobility of Rome.   2435
   The Nobility are vexed, whom we see haue sided | In his behalfe.   2504
   And the Nobility of Rome are his: 3120
NOBLE = 48*10
   Hayle, Noble *Martius*.   173
   And call him Noble, that was now your Hate: 194
   You cry against the Noble Senate, who   197
   Com. Noble *Martius*. | *Sen*. Hence to your homes, be gone.   273
   2.*Sen*. Noble *Auffidius*, | Take your Commission, hye you to your
   Bands,   342
   Val. Indeed la, tis a Noble childe. | *Virg*. A Cracke Madam.   430
   Lar. Oh Noble Fellow! | Who sensibly out-dares his sencelesse Sword,   554
   My Noble Steed, knowne to the Campe, I giue him,   817
   Men. I, to deuour him, as the hungry Plebeians would | the Noble
   Martius.   906
   *How now (my as faire as Noble) Ladyes, and the Moone   994

NOBLE *cont.*

*knowledge he ha's in their disposition, and out of his No-|ble	
carelesnesse lets them plainely see't.	1217
To gratifie his Noble seruice, that hath	1247
Menen. Hee's right Noble, let him be call'd for.	1346
Our purpose to them, and to our Noble Consull | Wish we all Ioy, and	
Honor.	1375
*vs his Noble deeds, we must also tell him our Noble ac-|ceptance	1395
All. Amen, Amen. God saue thee, Noble Consull.	1528
The Noble House o'th'*Martians*: from whence came	1641
For they doe pranke them in Authoritie, | Against all Noble sufferance.	1702
Com. Hath he not pass'd the Noble, and the Common? | *Brut.*	
Cominius, no.	1709
Or neuer be so Noble as a Consull,	1743
A Noble life, before a Long, and Wish,	1852
Mene. Helpe *Martius*, helpe: you that be noble, helpe | him young and	
old.	1946
I prythee noble friend, home to thy House,	1957
Mene. His nature is too noble for the World:	1983
1 *Cit.* He shall well know the Noble Tribunes are	2002
1.*Sen.* Noble Tribunes, | It is the humane way: the other course	2069
Sic. Noble *Menenius*, be you then as the peoples officer:	2073
Mene. Well said, Noble woman:	2123
Though therein you can neuer be too Noble,	2135
Menen. Noble Lady, | Come goe with vs, speake faire: you may salue	
so,	2169
Must I with my base Tongue giue to my Noble Heart	2206
1 *Sen.* Amen, Amen. | *Mene.* A Noble wish.	2307
The Gods preserue our Noble Tribunes, come. *Exeunt.*	2433
A Noble cunning. You were vs'd to load me	2445
My Friends of Noble touch: when I am forth,	2490
Volum. Moe Noble blowes, then euer y wise words.	2530
As he began, and not vnknit himselfe | The Noble knot he made.	2541
*shee's falne out with her Husband. Your Noble *Tullus*	2602
Thou shew'st a Noble Vessell: What's thy name?	2719
Then thee all-Noble *Martius*. Let me twine	2764
Thou Noble thing, more dances my rapt heart,	2774
Mene. We are all vndone, vnlesse | The Noble man haue mercy.	3026
A Noble seruant to them, but he could not	3127
To make Coales cheape: A Noble memory.	3170
So that all hope is vaine, vnlesse his Noble Mother,	3231
1 A Noble Fellow I warrant him.	3343
And the most noble Mother of the world	3398
Corio. The Noble Sister of *Publicola*; | The Moone of Rome: Chaste as	
the Isicle	3416
Rather to shew a Noble grace to both parts,	3476
Whose Chronicle thus writ, The man was Noble,	3502
2.Con. Most Noble Sir, If you do hold the same intent	3663
Auf. Read it not Noble Lords,	3750
Auf. Why Noble Lords, | Will you be put in minde of his blinde	
Fortune,	3788
The man is Noble, and his Fame folds in	3797
Auf. My Noble Masters, heare me speake. | 1.*Lord.* O *Tullus*.	3808
As the most Noble Coarse, that euer Herald | Did follow to his Vrne.	3824
Yet he shall haue a Noble Memory. Assist.	3836

NOBLE = 1

NOBLEMAN = 1
Think'st thou it Honourable for a Nobleman   3511
NOBLENESSE = 2
Time-pleasers, flatterers, foes to Noblenesse.   1729
Thy thoughts with Noblenesse, that thou mayst proue   3425
NOBLER = 2*1
*were shee Earthly, no Nobler; whither doe you follow | your Eyes so
fast?   995
My Nobler friends, I craue their pardons: 1755
Noble. You do the Nobler.   2091
NOBLES = 9*1
And the desire of the Nobles.   1164
Vpon him as he pass'd: the Nobles bended   1195
Enter Coriolanus with Nobles.   2083
Your Wife, your Sonne: These Senators, the Nobles,   2164
*The people, against the Senatours, Patricians, and | Nobles.   2584
*would make it flame againe. For the Nobles receyue so   2590
Cit. He is, and Feasts the Nobles of the State, at his | house this night.   2633
Permitted by our dastard Nobles, who   2732
Mes. The Nobles in great earnestnesse are going   2964
But like Beasts, and Cowardly Nobles,   3044
NOBLY = 4*4
*had rather had eleuen dye Nobly for their Countrey, then | one
voluptuously surfet out of Action.   385
Marcus Caius Coriolanus. Beare th'addition Nobly euer?   821
Senat. Sit *Coriolanus*: neuer shame to heare | What you haue Nobly
done.   1277
*1. You haue deserued Nobly of your Countrey, and   1479
you haue not deserued Nobly.   1480
*1.*Cit*. Hee ha's done Nobly, and cannot goe without | any honest mans
Voyce.   1524
And Nobly nam'd, so twice being Censor, | Was his great Ancestor.   1646
As hotly, and as Nobly with thy Loue,   2769
NOD = 1*1
*then my Heart, I will practice the insinuating nod, and be   1490
In supplication Nod: and my yong Boy   3380
NODDING = 1
Your Enemies, with nodding of their Plumes   2414
NOISE *see also* noyse = 5
Mart. Oh they are at it. | *Lart*. Their noise be our instruction. Ladders
hoa.   512
From th'noise of our owne Drummes.   1443
The horne, and noise o'th'Monsters, wants not spirit   1789
He heard the Name of Death. *A Noise within.*   1988
Vnshoot the noise that Banish'd *Martius*;   3644
NOISOME *see* noysome
NONE = 4*2
*and none lesse deere then thine, and my good *Martius*, I   384
Virg. Oh good Madam, there can be none yet.   455
But is foure *Volces*? None of you, but is   699
Mar. Ile fight with none but thee, for I do hate thee | Worse then a
Promise-breaker.   724
Then vale your Ignorance: If none, awake   1792
*none but my selfe could moue thee, I haue bene blowne   3309
NOONE = *1
*the shadow which he treads on at noone, but I do   290

NOR *l.*180 295 335 445 *491 502 545 606 878 879 880 *963 1156 1158
1177 *1221 1724 1744 1747 1763 2152 2376 3086 *3337 3365
3486 = 27*5
NORISHT = *1
*I say they norisht disobedience: fed, the ruin of the State.   1813
NORTH = *1
*they would flye East, West, North, South, and their con-|sent   1408
NOSE = 2
My Nose that bled, or foyl'd some debile Wretch,   804
For one poore graine or two, to leaue vnburnt | And still to nose
th'offence.   3180
NOSES = 1
To see your Wiues dishonour'd to your Noses.   2998
NOT *l.*26 36 *45 *59 74 75 *86 95 116 136 207 *220 231 *285 305 307 317
320 323 347 348 *369 *372 *376 390 403 435 436 *438 445 *451 *456
475 488 515 542 544 558 559 589 590 *619 *621 *634 638 660 662 677
698 719 727 734 739 742 749 770 777 781 803 871 *876 889 *901 902
914 *922 930 *944 *981 *982 *1015 *1019 *1027 *1035 1088 1095 1099
1109 1115 1148 1183 1210 *1213 *1214 *1219 *1228 *1233 *1273 1282
1285 1297 1362 1373 1389 *1402 *1404 *1413 *1429 *1436 *1444 1460
1480 *1483 *1486 *1499 1559 1560 1569 1573 1577 1598 1605 1610 1612
1623 1638 *1709 *1718 1719 1725 1731 1735 1747 1752 1753 1757 1763
1769 1774 1780 1789 1794 1818 1821 1822 1824 1855 1859 1868 *1906
1963 1965 1984 1992 *2006 2046 2060 2075 2077 2093 2109 2117 2140
2144 2152 2171 2181 2183 2217 2228 2283 2306 2330 2331 2358 2374
2382 2417 2458 2467 2481 2496 2513 2519 2526 2541 2547 *2586 2626
*2647 2660 2679 *2688 2699 2709 *2710 *2711 2721 2736 2737 2750
2754 2763 2793 *2827 2835 *2841 *2866 *2893 *2906 2933 2949 2961
2962 2975 3036 3042 3059 3060 3077 3085 3092 3105 3109 3127 3133
3137 3143 3152 3159 3164 3178 3188 3193 3208 3223 3229 *3241 3250
*3263 *3271 3289 *3291 *3301 *3317 3327 *3340 3345 *3353 3368 3377
3382 3387 3392 3436 3438 3439 3442 *3449 3474 3479 3483 3485 3488
3510 3513 3522 3523 3547 3557 3569 *3600 *3601 *3602 3607 3614 3631
3692 3722 3750 3770 3800 3812 = 214*67
NOTCHT = *1
*on't before *Corioles,* he scotcht him, and notcht him like a |
Carbinado.   2846
NOTE = 3*3
Men. Note me this good Friend;   134
Which without note, here's many else haue done,   805
Brut. They haue tane note of vs: keepe on your way.   2516
Sicin. Are you mankinde? | *Volum.* I foole, is that a shame. Note but
this Foole,   2524
*the Newes in Rome: I haue a Note from the Volcean   2580
Then pitty: Note how much, therefore be gone.   3322
NOTHING = 9*4
*before their Citie *Carioles,* they nothing doubt preuai-|ling,   463
*deuotion, then they can render it him; and leaues nothing   1222
1.*Sen.* Speake, good *Cominius:* | Leaue nothing out for length, and
make vs thinke   1256
Nothing is done to purpose. Therefore beseech you,   1848
I would the Gods had nothing else to do,   2559
And wak'd halfe dead with nothing. Worthy *Martius,*   2784
*This peace is nothing, but to rust Iron, encrease Taylors, | and breed
Ballad-makers.   2877
Sicin. Where is he, heare you? | *Mene.* Nay I heare nothing: 2911
His Mother and his wife, heare nothing from him.   2913

NOTHING *cont*.

  Go whip him fore the peoples eyes: His raising, | Nothing but his
report.   2968
  He was a kinde of Nothing, Titlelesse,   3165
  For we haue nothing else to aske, but that   3443
  *finisht with his bidding. He wants nothing of a God but | Eternity, and
a Heauen to Throne in.   3592
NOTHINGS = 1
  To heare my Nothings monster'd. *Exit Coriolanus*   1290
NOTICE = 1
  2.Cit. Amen, Sir: to my poore vnworthy notice,   1556
NOTION = 1
  Must giue this Curre the Lye: and his owne Notion,   3777
NOUGHT = 1
  Heare nought from Rome in priuate. Your request?   3448
NOURISH = 1
  In soothing them, we nourish 'gainst our Senate   1759
NOURISHED *see* norisht
NOW = 50*18
  *now wee'l shew em in deeds: they say poore Suters haue   61
  And call him Noble, that was now your Hate: 194
  *he was a Man-child, then now in first seeing he had pro-|ued himselfe
a man.   377
  Vol. Let her alone Ladie, as she is now: 468
  Now Mars, I prythee make vs quicke in worke,   496
  Now put your Shields before your hearts, and fight   516
  So, now the gates are ope: now proue good Seconds,   540
  Lar. Now the faire Goddesse Fortune,   593
  Hadst thou beheld | *Martius*. Pray now, no more: 762
  I that now refus'd most Princely gifts,   838
  Men. This is strange now: Do you two know, how   918
  Men. Because you talke of Pride now, will you not | be angry.   922
  *How now (my as faire as Noble) Ladyes, and the Moone   994
  Mene. Now it's twentie seuen; euery gash was an | Enemies Graue.
Hearke, the Trumpets.   1051
  Coriol. No more of this, it does offend my heart: pray | now no more.   1071
  Mene. Now the Gods Crowne thee.   1086
  *vndone, that may fully discouer him their opposite. Now   1223
  Menen. Pray now sit downe.   1287
  That's thousand to one good one, when you now see   1293
  Carioles like a Planet: now all's his,   1328
  Coriol. Pray you now, if it may stand with the tune   1476
  He ha's it now: and by his Lookes, me thinkes, | 'Tis warme at's heart.   1548
  Scici. How now, my Masters, haue you chose this man?   1553
  *Your most sweet Voyces: now you haue left your Voyces,   1572
  I'th' Body of the Weale: and now arriuing   1582
  Scicin. Haue you, ere now, deny'd the asker: 1609
  And now againe, of him that did not aske, but mock,   1610
  Must these haue Voyces, that can yeeld them now,   1716
  Mene. Not now, not now.   1752
  Senat. Not in this heat, Sir, now.   1753
  Corio. Now as I liue, I will.   1754
  Com. But now 'tis oddes beyond Arithmetick,   1970
  Menen. Now the good Gods forbid,   2027
  In Ioues owne Booke, like an vnnaturall Dam | Should now eate vp her
owne.   2030
  Volum. Because, that | Now it lyes you on to speake to th'people: 2150

NOW *cont.*

Now, this no more dishonors you at all,	2157
Volum. I prythee now, my Sonne,	2173
Now humble as the ripest Mulberry,	2180
Volum. Prythee now, | Goe, and be rul'd: although I know thou hadst rather	2192
Volum. He must, and will: | Prythee now say you will, and goe about it.	2203
You haue put me now to such a part, which neuer	2211
Volum. I prythee now sweet Son, as thou hast said	2214
To plucke away their power: as now at last,	2381
*Vol. Now the Red Pestilence strike al Trades in Rome, | And Occupations perish.	2450
Brut. Now we haue shewne our power,	2506
Volum. Now pray sir get you gone.	2549
*Rom. The day serues well for them now. I haue heard	2600
*Opposer Coriolanus being now in no request of his coun-|trey.	2604
*Oh World, thy slippery turnes! Friends now fast sworn,	2638
Corio. Now th'art troublesome.	2671
Hoop'd out of Rome. Now this extremity,	2735
Who now are heere, taking their leaues of mee,	2791
All. Now the Gods keepe you.	2923
Mene. Pray now, your Newes:	3003
At *Coriolanus* Exile. Now he's comming,	3058
Auf. I cannot helpe it now,	3097
*Mene. Now you Companion: Ile say an arrant for you:	3297
*you shall know now that I am in estimation: you shall	3298
*now presently, and swoond for what's to come vpon	3303
1 Now sir, is your name *Menenius?*	3331
And cannot now accept, to grace him onely,	3362
Corio. Like a dull Actor now, I haue forgot my part,	3390
Now by the iealous Queene of Heauen, that kisse	3395
Ile frame conuenient peace. Now good *Auffidius,*	3549
*Mother now, then an eight yeare old horse. The tartnesse	3586
Corio. Traitor? How now? | *Auf.* I Traitor, *Martius.*	3753

NOYSE = 3

And harke, what noyse the Generall makes: To him	580
Before him, hee carryes Noyse;	1055
And had no welcomes home, but he returnes | Splitting the Ayre with noyse.	3708

NOYSOME = 1

Of noysome musty Chaffe. He said, 'twas folly	3179

NUMAES = 1

That *Ancus Martius, Numaes* Daughters Sonne:	1642

NUMBER = 3

A Shield, as hard as his. A certaine number	701
And presently, when you haue drawne your number, | Repaire toth' Capitoll.	1657
By mingling them with vs, the honor'd Number,	1762

NUMBERS = 3

Conuenient Numbers to make good the City,	583
Thy lying tongue, both numbers. I would say	2352
Dissentious numbers pestring streets, then see	2899

NUPTIALL = 1

As merry, as when our Nuptiall day was done, | And Tapers burnt to Bedward.	642

NURSE = 2

Are spectacled to see him. Your pratling Nurse	1124

NURSE *cont.*
The Countrie our deere Nurse, or else thy person   3465
NURSES = 1
Counsaile a'th'warre: But at his Nurses teares   3765
O *l.*348 566 630 *1785 2448 2477 *2904 *3306 3393 3540 *3801 3809 = 8*4
OAKE = 3*1
*whence he return'd, his browes bound with Oake. I tell   375
Was Brow-bound with the Oake. His Pupill age   1312
The Oake not to be winde-shaken. *Exit Watch.*   3345
That should but riue an Oake. Why do'st not speake?   3510
OAKEN = 2
Volum. On's Browes: *Menenius*, hee comes the third | time home with
the Oaken Garland.   1021
Enter Cominius the Generall, and Titus Latius: be-|tweene them
Coriolanus, crown'd with an Oaken   1060
OAKES = *1
*And hewes downe Oakes, with rushes. Hang ye: trust ye?   192
OATH = 2
Bound with an Oath to yeeld to his conditions: 3230
Breaking his Oath and Resolution, like   3763
OBEDIENCE = 2
On whom depending, their obedience failes   1866
Haue we not had a taste of his Obedience?   2060
OBEY = 2*1
Virg. Giue me excuse good Madame, I will obey you | in euery thing
heereafter.   466
A Foe to'th'publike Weale. Obey I charge thee,   1878
Be such a Gosling to obey instinct; but stand   3384
OBEYD = 2
(As cause will be obey'd:) please you to March,   704
A Vessell vnder sayle, so men obey'd,   1320
OBEYES = 1
The second name of men, obeyes his points   3049
OBIECT = *1
*that afflicts vs, the obiect of our misery, is as an inuento-|ry   22
OBSERUE = 1
With their refusall, both obserue and answer | The vantage of his anger.   1665
OBSTINATE = 1
Let it be Vertuous to be Obstinate.   3375
OCCASION = *1
*of Occasion, will rob you of a great deale of Patience: 926
OCCUPATION = 1
Vpon the voyce of occupation, and | The breath of Garlicke-eaters.   3014
OCCUPATIONS = 1
Vol. Now the Red Pestilence strike al Trades in Rome, | And
Occupations perish.   2450
OCCUPYD = *1
*Your Minds pre-occupy'd with what you rather must do,   1635
ODDE = 2
3 *Cit.* But this is something odde.   1473
Of Wounds, two dozen odde: Battailes thrice six   1520
ODDES = 1
Com. But now 'tis oddes beyond Arithmetick,   1970
OF *see also* a, on's, o'th, o'that = 364*113
OFF *l.*96 493 503 508 509 567 573 605 1025 *1269 1326 *1491 1882 2034
2339 2388 2497 3818 = 16*3

OFF = 1
OFFENCE = 2
  To make him worthy, whose offence subdues him,   186
  For one poore graine or two, to leaue vnburnt | And still to nose
  th'offence.   3180
OFFENCES = 1
  This Orbe o'th'earth: His last offences to vs   3798
OFFEND = *1
  Coriol. No more of this, it does offend my heart: pray | now no more.   1071
OFFERD = 1
  (Though I shew'd sowrely to him) once more offer'd   3360
OFFERED = 1
  Com. I offered to awaken his regard   3176
OFFERS = 1
  Coriolanus rises, and offers to goe away. | Nay, keepe your place.   1275
OFFICE = 2*2
  Brutus. Then our Office may, during his power, goe | sleepe.   1142
  Let the high Office and the Honor go   1513
  From Rome all season'd Office, and to winde   2343
  *perceiue, that a Iacke gardant cannot office me from my   3299
OFFICER *see also Off*., 1.*Off*., 2.*Off*. = 3*2
  Giuen Hidra heere to choose an Officer, | That with his peremptory
  Shall, being but   1787
  Sic. Noble *Menenius*, be you then as the peoples officer: 2073
  Bru. Caius Martius was | A worthy Officer i'th'Warre, but Insolent,   2928
  As if he were his Officer: Desperation,   3050
  *I am an Officer of State, & come to speak with *Coriolanus*   3239
OFFICERS = 4
  Call thither all the Officers a'th'Towne,   601
  Enter two Officers, to lay Cushions, as it were, | *in the Capitoll*.   1203
  Allow their Officers, and are content   2319
  Beating your Officers, cursing your selues,   2360
OFFICES = 1*1
  And through the Crankes and Offices of man,   144
  *And straight disclaim their toungs? what are your Offices?   1717
OFFICIALL = 1
  Remaines, that in th'Officiall Markes inuested,   1533
OFFICIOUS = 1
  Officious and not valiant, you haue sham'd me | In your condemned
  Seconds.   742
OFT = 2
  Brutus. Sir, I hope my words dis-bench'd you not? | *Coriol*. No Sir: yet
  oft,   1282
  I haue seene the Sterne, and thou hast oft beheld   2462
OFTEN = 5*1
  I haue fought with thee; so often hast thou beat me: 866
  As often as we eate. By th'Elements,   868
  Then Dogges, that are as often beat for barking, | As therefore kept to
  doe so.   1619
  Latius. How often he had met you Sword to Sword: 1690
  Which they haue often made against the Senate,   1825
  Which often thus correcting thy stout heart,   2179
OH *see also* O *l*.268 299 400 *427 455 512 554 640 697 760 847 *934 *936
  1017 1018 *1074 1080 1087 1089 1162 *1436 *1444 2033 2102 2448 2517
  2529 *2638 2759 2789 *2833 2994 3076 3402 3441 3543 3545 3558
  3774 = 32*8

OLD = 12*4

Cominius, Martius your old Enemy | (Who is of Rome worse hated then
of you)   326
*You two are old men, tell me one thing that I shall aske | you.   910
Some old Crab-trees here at home,   1098
And his old Hate vnto you: besides, forget not   1623
Corio. Hence old Goat.   1880
*Mene. Helpe Martius, helpe: you that be noble, helpe | him young and
old.   1946
Ile trie whether my old Wit be in request   1977
Edile. With old Menenius, and those Senators | That alwayes fauour'd
him.   2267
Ile do well yet. Thou old and true Menenius,   2459
From these old armes and legges, by the good Gods | I'ld with thee,
euery foot.   2498
I vrg'd our old acquaintance, and the drops   3162
*easie groanes of old women, the Virginall Palms of your   3279
*particular prosperity, and loue thee no worse then thy old   3305
Corio. This last old man, | Whom with a crack'd heart I haue sent to
Rome,   3355
Was to send him: for whose old Loue I haue   3359
*Mother now, then an eight yeare old horse. The tartnesse   3586

OLDE = 1

Insisting on the olde prerogatiue | And power i'th Truth a'th Cause. 2279

OLDEST = 1

And vowes Reuenge as spacious, as betweene | The yong'st and oldest
thing.   2977

OLYMPUS = 1

As if Olympus to a Mole-hill should   3379

OMIT = 1

Of generall Ignorance, it must omit | Reall Necessities, and giue way
the while   1845

OMNES = 4

All. Farewell. Exeunt omnes.   359
Omnes. Marcus Caius Coriolanus.   823
Sena. Pray you let's to him. Exeunt Omnes.   2082
Omnes. Faith, we heare fearfull Newes.   3065

ON see also a, on's, on't = 67*9

ONCE = 10*3

Whereby they liue. And though that all at once   147
Men. Though all at once, cannot | See what I do deliuer out to each, 150
Shalt see me once more strike at Tullus face.   263
*1.Cit. Once if he do require our voyces, wee ought | not to deny him. 1388
*helpe will serue: for once we stood vp about the Corne,   1401
*of one direct way, should be at once to all the points | a'th Compasse. 1409
That's sure of death without it: at once plucke out   1854
Being once gangren'd, is not then respected | For what before it was. 2046
Of contradiction. Being once chaft, he cannot   2292
But once a day, it would vnclogge my heart | Of what lyes heauy too't. 2561
Once more to hew thy Target from thy Brawne,   2778
And durst not once peepe out.   2949
(Though I shew'd sowrely to him) once more offer'd   3360

ONE see also one's, 1. = 58*22

2.Cit. One word, good Citizens.   16
*good: what Authority surfets one, would releeue   18
*2 Cit. Worthy Menenius Agrippa, one that hath al-|wayes lou'd the
people.   53

ONE *cont.*

*1 *Cit.* He's one honest enough, wold al the rest wer so.	55
Men. For that being one o'th lowest, basest, poorest	165
The one side must haue baile.	171
That like nor Peace, nor Warre? The one affrights you,	180
Would feede on one another? What's their seeking?	199
And a petition granted them, a strange one,	223
Tit. No *Caius Martius,*	Ile leane vpon one Crutch, and fight with	
tother,	265
What euer haue bin thought one in this State	318
Till one can do no more.	354
*had rather had eleuen dye Nobly for their Countrey, then	one	
voluptuously surfet out of Action.	385
Vol. One on's Fathers moods.	429
Cominius the Generall is gone, with one part of our Ro- |mane	461
Farther then seene, and one infect another	528
*Flourish. Alarum. A Retreat is sounded. Enter at	one Doore Cominius,*	
with the Romanes: At	744
(Like one that meanes his proper harme) in Manacles,	813
*You two are old men, tell me one thing that I shall aske	you.	910
Bru. He's poore in no one fault, but stor'd withall.	*Sicin.* Especially in	
Pride.	915
*one that loues a cup of hot Wine, with not a drop of alay- |ing	944
*triuiall motion: One, that conuerses more with the But- |tocke	947
*another, his Wife another, and (I thinke) there's one at	home for you.	1006
Mene. One ith' Neck, and two ith'Thigh, there's nine	that I know.	1047
Onely there's one thing wanting,	1114
2.Off. Three, they say: but 'tis thought of euery one,	1207
Corio. I had rather haue one scratch my Head i'th' Sun,	1288
That's thousand to one good one, when you now see	1293
Neyther will they bate one iot of Ceremonie.	1361
*I thinke, if all our wittes were to issue out of one Scull,	1407
*of one direct way, should be at once to all the points	a'th Compasse.	1409
*one of vs ha's a single Honor, in giuing him our own voi- |ces	1432
To one that would doe thus. I am halfe through,	1514
The one part suffered, the other will I doe.	1515
2.Cit. Not one amongst vs, saue your selfe, but sayes	1560
Sicin. One thus descended,	That hath beside well in his person	
wrought,	1648
And such a one as he, who puts his Shall,	1799
May enter 'twixt the gap of Both, and take	The one by th'other.	1805
Bru. Why shall the people giue	One that speakes thus, their voyce?	1814
Mene. Heare me one word, 'beseech you Tribunes,	1930
One time will owe another.	1966
Were but one danger, and to keepe him heere	2024
Menen. One word more, one word:	2052
When one but of my ordinance stood vp	2097
Their mercie, at the price of one faire word,	2375
Of the warres surfets, to go roue with one	2487
If I could shake off but one seuen teeres	2497
With one that wants her Wits. *Exit Tribunes.*	2557
Vol. A most Royall one: The Centurions, and their	2612
Whose double bosomes seemes to weare one heart,	2639
To take the one the other, by some chance,	2646
*1 A strange one as euer I look'd on: I cannot get him	2675
3 A maru'llous poore one.	*Corio.* True, so I am.	2682
Th'one halfe of my Commission, and set downe	2797

ONE *cont*.

finger and his thumbe, as one would set vp a Top.	2814
1 I thinke he is: but a greater soldier then he, | You wot one.	2822
*2 Faith looke you, one cannot tell how to say that: for	2829
*Newes is, our Generall is cut i'th'middle, & but one halfe	2857
1 I, and it makes men hate one another.	2887
*3 Reason, because they then lesse neede one another:	2888
*Sicin. And affecting one sole Throne, without assista(n)ce	2932
If he could burne vs all into one coale, | We haue deseru'd it.	3063
Not to be other then one thing, not moouing	3133
As he controll'd the warre. But one of these	3136
One fire driues out one fire; one Naile, one Naile;	3145
Com. Yet one time he did call me by my name:	3161
To one whom they had punish'd.	3174
For one poore graine or two, to leaue vnburnt | And still to nose th'offence.	3180
Menen. For one poore graine or two?	3182
I am one of those: his Mother, Wife, his Childe,	3183
*haue, I am one that telling true vnder him, must say you | cannot passe. Therefore go backe.	3269
Then seeke the end of one; thou shalt no sooner	3477
Like one i'th'Stockes. Thou hast neuer in thy life,	3517
Helpe three a'th'cheefest Souldiers, Ile be one.	3831
Hath widdowed and vnchilded many a one,	3834

ONELY = 18*1

That onely like a Gulfe it did remaine	100
Corne for the Richmen onely: With these shreds	221
I would wish me onely he.	252
Onely my warres with him. He is a Lion | That I am proud to hunt.	256
And onely hitherward. I leaue your Honors.	351
*tender-bodied, and the onely Sonne of my womb; when	367
Onely in strokes, but with thy grim lookes, and	560
Before the common distribution, | At your onely choyse.	787
With onely suff'ring staine by him: for him	877
From whom I haue receiu'd not onely greetings, | But with them, change of Honors.	1109
Onely there's one thing wanting,	1114
Onely for bearing Burthens, and sore blowes | For sinking ·vnder them.	1179
As if I had receiu'd them for the hyre | Of their breath onely.	1371
By calmenesse, or by absence: all's in anger. | Menen. Onely faire speech.	2199
Corio. Scratches with Briars, scarres to moue | Laughter onely.	2327
Bru. Rais'd onely, that the weaker sort may wish | Good Martius home againe.	2980
Bru. Onely make triall what your Loue can do, | For Rome, towards Martius.	3196
Auf. Onely their ends you haue respected,	3351
And cannot now accept, to grace him onely,	3362

ONES = 3*1

Of their owne choice. One's Iunius Brutus,	230
Knaues. You are a payre of strange ones.	975
Then on ones Eares to heare it. Proceed Cominius.	1295
*by him where he stands, by ones, by twoes, & by threes.	1430

ONLY = *1

*Which thou should'st beare me, only that name remains.	2730

ONS = 2*1

Vol. One on's Fathers moods.	429

ONS *cont*.
   *Volum. On's Browes: *Menenius*, hee comes the third | time home with
    the Oaken Garland.   1021
   A Curse begin at very root on's heart,   1094
ONT = 3*4
   *All. No more talking on't; Let it be done, away, away   15
   *Mar. I am glad on't, then we shall ha meanes to vent   242
   *3.Rom. A Murrain on't, I tooke this for Siluer. *Exeunt*.   572
   More then you doubt the change on't: That preferre   1851
   All. He shall sure ont. | *Mene*. Sir, sir. *Sicin*. Peace.   2004
   *on't before Corioles, he scotcht him, and notcht him like a |
    Carbinado.   2846
   Sicin. The very tricke on't. | *Mene*. This is vnlikely,   2982
ON-WARD = 1
   Which we haue goaded on-ward. *Exeunt*.   1670
OO = 1
   All. Our enemy is banish'd, he is gone: Hòo, oo.   2427
OPE = 3
   So, now the gates are ope: now proue good Seconds,   540
   Breake ope the Lockes a'th'Senate, and bring in | The Crowes to pecke
    the Eagles.   1835
   Corio. O Mother, Mother! | What haue you done? Behold, the Heauens
    do ope,   3540
OPEN = 1
   They'le open of themselues. Harke you, farre off | *Alarum farre off*.   508
OPINION = 3
   That rubbing the poore Itch of your Opinion, | Make your selues Scabs.   175
   Opinion that so stickes on *Martius*, shall | Of his demerits rob *Cominius*.   302
   1.Sen. So, your opinion is *Auffidius*, | That they of Rome are entred in
    our Counsailes,   314
OPPOSE = 1
   To oppose his hatred fully. Welcome home.   1698
OPPOSER = *1
   *Opposer Coriolanus being now in no request of his coun-|trey.   2604
OPPOSERS = 2
   Misguide thy Opposers swords, Bold Gentleman: | Prosperity be thy
    Page.   595
   Slew three Opposers: *Tarquins* selfe he met,   1308
OPPOSING = 1
   Opposing Lawes with stroakes, and heere defying   2361
OPPOSITE = *1
   *vndone, that may fully discouer him their opposite. Now   1223
OR *l*.90 161 185 324 *362 399 *425 *426 534 567 626 647 692 804 826 858
   870 874 900 *932 *983 1171 *1216 *1219 1387 1575 1597 1607 1714
   1743 1883 1920 1921 1985 2018 2081 2085 2086 2098 2145 2181 2198
   2199 2222 2246 2277 2470 2779 2801 2914 3011 3107 3116 3132 3180
   3182 3211 3235 *3280 *3301 3376 3434 3437 3464 3465 3470 3551 3658
   3714 *3801 3820 = 64*10
ORBE = 1
   This Orbe o'th'earth: His last offences to vs   3798
ORDINANCE = 1
   When one but of my ordinance stood vp   2097
ORE = 5
   Plaister you o're, that you may be abhorr'd   527
   Of their best trust: O're them *Auffidious*, | Their very heart of Hope.   669
   Com. If I should tell thee o're this thy dayes Worke,   748
   Runne reeking o're the liues of men, as if 'twere   1333

ORE *cont.*

O're the vast world, to seeke a single man,	2482

ORECOME = 1

O'recome with Pride, Ambitious, past all thinking | Selfe-louing.	2930

ORENDGE = *1

*hearing a cause betweene an Orendge wife, and a Forfet-|seller,	966

ORE-BEARE = 1

Like interrupted Waters, and o're-beare | What they are vs'd to beare.	1974

ORE-BEATE = 1

Like a bold Flood o're-beate. Oh come, go in,	2789

ORE-BORNE = 1

O're-borne their way, consum'd with fire, and tooke | What lay before them.	2991

ORE-LEAPE = 1

Corio. I doe beseech you, | Let me o're-leape that custome: for I cannot	1355

ORE-PEERE = 1

For Truth to o're-peere. Rather then foole it so,	1512

ORE-PREST = 1

An o're-prest Roman, and i'th' Consuls view	1307

ORE-WHELMD = 1

And Wrath o're-whelm'd my pittie: I request you	845

ORE-WHELME = 1

Corio. Thou wretch, despight ore-whelme thee:	1864

OSTENTATION = 1

Make good this ostentation, and you shall | Diuide in all, with vs. *Exeunt*	708

OTH = 13*3

The Helmes o'th State; who care for you like Fathers,	78
Euen to the Court, the Heart, to th'seate o'th'Braine,	143
Men. For that being one o'th lowest, basest, poorest	165
A place of Potencie, and sway o'th' State,	1583
The Noble House o'th'*Martians*: from whence came	1641
We will be there before the streame o'th' People:	1668
The Tongues o'th' Common Mouth. I do despise them:	1701
The horne, and noise o'th'Monsters, wants not spirit	1789
Vpon the part o'th' People, in whose power	1922
Though calued i'th' Porch o'th' Capitoll:	1964
Mene. I could my selfe take vp a Brace o'th' best of | them, yea, the two Tribunes.	1968
out o'thhouse: Prythee call my Master to him.	2676
*Son and Heire to Mars, set at vpper end o'th'Table: No	2852
*white o'th'eye to his Discourse. But the bottome of the	2856
Gaue way vnto your Clusters, who did hoote | Him out o'th'Citty.	3045
This Orbe o'th'earth: His last offences to vs	3798

OTHAT = 1

But what o'that? Go you that banish'd him	3155

OTHER *see also* tother = 21*5

Enter a Company of Mutinous Citizens, with Staues, | Clubs, and other weapons.	2
*What showts are these? The other side a'th City is risen:	48
Like labour with the rest, where th'other Instruments	103
With other Muniments and petty helpes	121
The other makes you proud. He that trusts to you,	181
What sayes the other Troope?	216
Enter Sicinius Velutus, Annius Brutus Cominius, Titus | Lartius, with other Senatours.	244
Ransoming him, or pittying, threatning th'other;	647

OTHER *cont*.

The rest shall beare the businesse in some other fight	703
Enters with a Lieutenant, other Souldiours, and a ⌈ Scout.	712
Exeunt. Enter two other Citizens.	1475
The one part suffered, the other will I doe.	1515
Cornets. Enter Coriolanus, Menenius, all the Gentry, | Cominius, Titus	
Latius, and other Senators.	1672
May enter 'twixt the gap of Both, and take | The one by th'other.	1805
Whereon part do's disdaine with cause, the other	1842
1.*Sen.* Noble Tribunes, | It is the humane way: the other course	2069
In Peace, what each of them by th'other loose,	2139
To take the one the other, by some chance,	2646
*3 Pray you poore Gentleman, take vp some other sta- | tion:	2684
Had we no other quarrell else to Rome, but that	2785
*of what he was yesterday. For the other ha's halfe, by	2858
Made by some other Deity then Nature,	3007
Before you finde it other. All the Regions	3021
Not to be other then one thing, not moouing	3133
*As if a man were Author of himself, & knew no other kin	3385
Enter two Senators, with Ladies, passing ouer | the Stage, with other	
Lords.	3639

OTHERS = 11

They Sound a Parley: Enter two Senators with others on | the Walles of	
Corialus.	499
Com. I, if you come not in the blood of others, | But mantled in your	
owne.	638
Mar. Let the first Budger dye the others Slaue,	729
Bru. And topping all others in boasting.	917
Beyond the marke of others: our then Dictator,	1303
Enter Coriolanus, Menenius, and Comi- |nius, with others.	2296
Vnbuckling Helmes, fisting each others Throat,	2783
Enter Menenius, Cominius, Sicinius, Brutus, | the two Tribunes, with	
others.	3150
Corio. Wife, Mother, Child, I know not. My affaires | Are Seruanted	
to others: Though I owe	3317
Of stronger earth then others: my Mother bowes,	3378
That Pages blush'd at him, and men of heart | Look'd wond'ring each	
at others.	3767

OTHERWISE = *1

*were a kinde of ingratefull Iniurie: to report otherwise,	1234

OUER *see also* o're = 2*3

*he caught it, he let it go againe, and after it againe, and o- |uer	424
*and ouer he comes, and vp againe: catcht it again: or	425
Virg. Indeed no, by your patience; Ile not ouer the	438
Bru. Enough, with ouer measure. | *Corio.* No, take more.	1838
Enter two Senators, with Ladies, passing ouer | the Stage, with other	
Lords.	3639

OUERTANE = 1

He that ha's but effected his good will, | Hath ouerta'ne mine Act.	768

OUERTURE = 1

Let him be made an Ouerture for th' Warres:	802

OUGHT = 4*1

To *Martius* shall be Honors, though indeed | In ought he merit not.	306
*1.*Cit.* Once if he do require our voyces, wee ought | not to deny him.	1388
Tying him to ought, so putting him to Rage,	1599
Sicin. Answer to vs. | *Corio.* Say then: 'tis true, I ought so	2340
Heare from me still, and neuer of me ought	2493

OUNCE = 1
By many an Ounce) he dropp'd it for his Country: 2038
OUR *l*.*13 *22 *23 *24 *59 96 115 119 120 122 243 270 315 332 339 *461
469 487 498 504 *505 506 513 519 537 582 602 605 609 610 *611 616
642 655 664 716 719 *721 756 778 830 832 854 *979 1107 1115 1134
*1142 *1168 1171 1246 1251 1258 1265 1303 1340 1375 1385 *1388
*1391 *1393 *1395 1399 *1404 *1406 *1407 *1432 *1433 1443 1448
*1495 1496 1554 1557 *1633 1645 1656 1676 1681 1759 *1761 1818 1827
1832 1833 1834 *1901 1920 1951 2025 2028 2036 2061 2078 2117 2165
2305 2306 2386 2389 2427 2433 2506 *2586 2655 2732 2790 2830 *2838
2840 *2841 *2854 *2857 2900 2916 2918 2934 2946 2990 3072 3099 3117
3140 3162 3189 3192 3209 3212 3214 3234 *3241 *3285 *3344 3348 3393
3445 *3449 *3454 3460 3462 3465 3466 3468 3470 3489 3492 3515 *3526
3528 3530 3533 3537 *3538 *3576 3598 *3602 3641 3660 3703 3730 3731
*3742 = 128*41
OURS = 2*1
Mar. Then shall we heare their Larum, & they Ours.   495
The best, with whom we may articulate, | For their owne good, and
ours.   834
Both Field and Citie ours, he neuer stood   1335
OURSELUES *see* selues
OUT *l*.151 205 264 299 386 435 436 472 705 878 *960 *965 1170 *1217
1257 1259 *1407 *1413 1742 1854 1884 1897 2056 2104 2428 2432 2488
*2581 2595 *2602 2643 2668 2676 2735 2736 2756 2779 *2870 2949 2974
3046 3129 3145 *3276 *3282 *3285 *3310 3373 *3391 3458 3503 3560
3687 = 40*13
OUTRAGE = 1
2 *Lord*. Peace hoe: no outrage, peace: 3796
OUTWARD = 2
If these shewes be not outward, which of you   698
Not fearing outward force: So shall my Lungs   1769
OUT-DARES = 1
Lar. Oh Noble Fellow! | Who sensibly out-dares his sencelesse Sword,   554
OUT-DONE = 1
action out-done his former deeds doubly.   1033
OUT-WEIGHES = 1
If any thinke, braue death out-weighes bad life,   690
OWE = 5
Corio. I doe owe them still my Life, and Seruices.   1352
One time will owe another.   1966
But owe thy Pride thy selfe.   2239
Corio. Wife, Mother, Child, I know not. My affaires | Are Seruanted
to others: Though I owe   3317
Which this mans life did owe you, you'l reioyce   3817
OWN = *3
1.Cit. Let vs kill him, and wee'l haue Corne at our own | price. Is't a
Verdict?   13
*one of vs ha's a single Honor, in giuing him our own voi-|ces   1432
*Thy Countries strength and weaknesse, thine own waies   2799
OWNE *see also* owe = 30*4
Men. For Corne at their owne rates, wherof they say   200
Of their owne choice. One's *Iunius Brutus*,   230
Leade their successes, as we wish our owne,   610
Com. I, if you come not in the blood of others, | But mantled in your
owne.   638
Rome must know the value of her owne: 771

OWNE *cont.*

The best, with whom we may articulate, | For their owne good, and ours.	834
Ere in our owne house I doe shade my Head,	1107
*with our owne tongues, therefore follow me, and Ile	1433
From th'noise of our owne Drummes.	1443
Corio. Mine owne desert.	1457
2 *Cit.* Your owne desert.	1458
Corio. I, but mine owne desire.	1459
3 *Cit.* How not your owne desire?	1460
Then as guided by your owne true affections, and that	1634
And this shall seeme, as partly 'tis, their owne,	1669
In Ioues owne Booke, like an vnnaturall Dam | Should now eate vp her owne.	2030
Not by your owne instruction, nor by'th'matter	2152
Least I surcease to honor mine owne truth,	2229
More holy, and profound, then mine owne life,	2399
Still your owne Foes) deliuer you	2419
Thine owne particular wrongs, and stop those maimes	2743
The leading of thine owne Reuenges, take	2796
Com. You haue holp to rauish your owne daughters, &	2996
1 *Cit.* For mine owne part, | When I said banish him, I said 'twas pitty.	3066
And you are darkned in this action Sir, | Euen by your owne.	3095
*as you haue vttered words in your owne, you should not	3263
Auf. Euen so, as with a man by his owne Almes im-|poyson'd, and with his Charity slaine.	3661
In all his owne desires: Nay, let him choose	3686
In mine owne person: holpe to reape the Fame	3689
With our owne charge: making a Treatie, where	3731
Must giue this Curre the Lye: and his owne Notion,	3777
'Fore your owne eyes, and eares?	3791
2.*Lord.* His owne impatience, | Takes from *Auffidius* a great part of blame:	3826

OWNES = 1

Not Affricke ownes a Serpent I abhorre	727

PACE = 2

How the world goes: that to the pace of it	892
Plague vpon't, I cannot bring | My tongue to such a pace. Looke Sir, my wounds,	1439

PACKE = 1

Ere yet the fight be done, packe vp, downe with them.	579

PACKE-SADDLE = *1

*be intomb'd in an Asses Packe-saddle; yet you must bee	984

PAGE = 1

Misguide thy Opposers swords, Bold Gentleman: | Prosperity be thy Page.	595

PAGES = 1

That Pages blush'd at him, and men of heart | Look'd wond'ring each at others.	3767

PAINFULL = 1

My Surname *Coriolanus.* The painfull Seruice,	2725

PAINT = *1

Mene. I paint him in the Character. Mark what mer-|cy	3595

PAINTED = 1

The mortall Gate of th' Citie, which he painted	1325

PAINTING = 1

(As it were sinne to doubt) that loue this painting	687

PAIRE *see also* payre = 1
   A paire of Tribunes, that haue wrack'd for Rome,   3169
PALAT = *1
   *you *Licurgusses*,) if the drinke you giue me, touch my Pa-|lat   951
PALE = 2*1
   *And make bold power looke pale, they threw their caps   225
   All hurt behinde, backes red, and faces pale   532
   Brut. But is this true sir? | *Com*. I, and you'l looke pale   3019
PALLATES = 1
   Most pallates theirs. They choose their Magistrate,   1798
PALME = 1
   And beare the Palme, for hauing brauely shed   3472
PALMS = *1
   *easie groanes of old women, the Virginall Palms of your   3279
PALSIED = *1
   *daughters, or with the palsied intercession of such a de-|cay'd   3280
PALTRING = 1
   Com. The People are abus'd: set on, this paltring   1746
PANTING = 1
   To ease his Brest with panting. | *Menen*. Worthy man.   1336
PAPER = 1
   Deliuer them this Paper: hauing read it,   3651
PARASITES = 1
   When Steele growes soft, as the Parasites Silke,   801
PARCEL = *1
   *Drum strooke vp this afternoone: 'Tis as it were a parcel   2874
PARCELS = 1
   Some parcels of their Power are forth already,   350
PARDON = 5*2
   Vir. No good Madam, pardon me, indeed I will not | foorth.   451
   Com. And liue you yet? Oh my sweet Lady, pardon.   1087
   Coriol. Your Honors pardon: | I had rather haue my Wounds to heale
againe,   1279
   Com. I minded him, how Royall 'twas to pardon   3171
   *condemn'd, our Generall has sworne you out of repreeue | and pardon.   3285
   *out of your Gates with sighes: and coniure thee to par-|don   3310
   Pardon me Lords, 'tis the first time that euer   3775
PARDONS = 2
   My Nobler friends, I craue their pardons: 1755
   For they haue Pardons, being ask'd, as free, | As words to little
purpose.   2190
PARENT = 1
   Shew duty as mistaken, all this while, | Betweene the Childe, and
Parent.   3405
PARLEY = 1
   *They Sound a Parley: Enter two Senators with others on | the Walles of
Corialus*.   499
PART = 15*4
   Cominius the Generall is gone, with one part of our Ro-|mane   461
   And stand vpon my common part with those, | That haue beheld the
doing.   792
   I'th'part that is at mercy? fiue times, *Martius*,   865
   *the Asse in compound, with the Maior part of your sylla-|bles.   954
   Corio. It is a part that I shall blush in acting,   1366
   *that's no matter, the greater part carries it, I say. If hee   1423
   The one part suffered, the other will I doe.   1515
   Whereon part do's disdaine with cause, the other   1842

PART *cont.*

That loue the Fundamentall part of State	1850
Vpon the part o'th' People, in whose power	1922
You haue put me now to such a part, which neuer	2211
To haue my praise for this, performe a part | Thou hast not done before.	2216
*Volce. You take my part from me sir, I haue the most | cause to be glad of yours.	2618
1 *Cit.* For mine owne part, | When I said banish him, I said 'twas pitty.	3066
Corio. Like a dull Actor now, I haue forgot my part,	3390
To a Mothers part belongs. He turnes away:	3525
What peace you'l make, aduise me: For my part,	3556
Doth more then counterpoize a full third part	3743
2.*Lord.* His owne impatience, | Takes from *Auffidius* a great part of blame:	3826

PARTAKE = 1

Both. What, what, what? Let's partake.	2834

PARTED = 1

Then when I parted hence: but still subsisting	3738

PARTICIPATE = 1

And mutually participate, did minister	105

PARTICULAR = 3*1

Thine owne particular wrongs, and stop those maimes	2743
Lieu. Yet I wish Sir, | (I meane for your particular) you had not	3104
In a most deere particular. He call'd me Father:	3154
*particular prosperity, and loue thee no worse then thy old	3305

PARTICULARIZE = *1

*to particularize their abundance, our sufferance is a	23

PARTICULARLY = 1

To thee particularly, and to all the Volces	2723

PARTICULARS = *1

*He's to make his requests by particulars, wherein euerie	1431

PARTIE = 2

vpon my partie, I'de reuolt to make	255
You make strong partie, or defend your selfe	2198

PARTIES = 3*1

Coniecturall Marriages, making parties strong,	206
*peace you make in their Cause, is calling both the parties	974
Least parties (as he is belou'd) breake out,	2056
Wherein you wisht vs parties: Wee'l deliuer you | Of your great danger.	3664

PARTLY = 1*1

*his Mother, and to be partly proud, which he is, euen to | the altitude of his vertue.	40
And this shall seeme, as partly 'tis, their owne,	1669

PARTNER = 2

Set downe our Hoast. My partner in this Action,	3348
I seem'd his Follower, not Partner; and	3692

PARTS = 3*1

To'th'discontented Members, the mutinous parts	113
*parts melted away with rotten Dewes, the fourth would	1418
Or rudely visit them in parts remote,	2801
Rather to shew a Noble grace to both parts,	3476

PARTY *see also* partie = 2*2

I saw our party to their Trenches driuen,	616
*matter betweene party and party, if you chaunce to bee	969
alwayes factionary on the party of your Generall.	3267

PASSABLE = 1
1 Be it so, go back: the vertue of your name, | Is not heere passable.   3249
PASSAGE = 1*1
*will mowe all downe before him, and leaue his passage | poul'd.   2861
With bloody passage led your Warres, euen to   3741
PASSD = 2*1
Vpon him as he pass'd: the Nobles bended   1195
You should haue ta'ne th'aduantage of his Choller, | And pass'd him
vnelected.   1600
*Com. Hath he not pass'd the Noble, and the Common? | Brut.
Cominius, no.   1709
PASSE = 5*2
Please you that I may passe this doing.   1359
Scicin. Passe no further. | Cor. Hah? what is that?   1704
For which the People stirre: if you will passe   1740
*I You may not passe, you must returne: our Generall | will no more
heare from thence.   3241
I must haue leaue to passe.   3261
*passe heere: no, though it were as vertuous to lye, as to | liue chastly.
Therefore go backe.   3264
*haue, I am one that telling true vnder him, must say you | cannot
passe. Therefore go backe.   3269
PASSED see past
PASSES = 1
Your louing motion toward the common Body, | To yeeld what passes
here.   1261
PASSING = 2
Yet are they passing Cowardly. But I beseech you,   215
Enter two Senators, with Ladies, passing ouer | the Stage, with other
Lords.   3639
PASSIONS = *1
*Whose Passions, and whose Plots haue broke their sleep   2645
PAST = 6*1
Skaling his present bearing with his past,   1652
Then stay past doubt, for greater: 1663
Not what is dangerous present, but the losse | Of what is past.   2171
That being past for Consull with full voyce: 2337
*Rom. The maine blaze of it is past, but a small thing   2589
O'recome with Pride, Ambitious, past all thinking | Selfe-louing.   2930
I haue tumbled past the throw: and in his praise   3259
PATCHT = 1
With those that haue but little: this must be patcht | With Cloth of any
Colour.   1978
PATES = 1
To melt the Citty Leades vpon your pates,   2997
PATIENCE = 2*4
Patience awhile; you'st heare the Bellies answer.   132
*Virg. Indeed no, by your patience; Ile not ouer the   438
To vs, that giue you truly: by your patience,   811
*of Occasion, will rob you of a great deale of Patience: 926
*set vp the bloodie Flagge against all Patience, and   971
*To'th'people: Coriolanus, patience: Speak good Sicinius.   1899
PATIENT = 2*1
*Cor. Choller? Were I as patient as the midnight sleep,   1777
Sicin. Nay, pray be patient: If you refuse your ayde   3187
2.Con. And patient Fooles, | Whose children he hath slaine, their base
throats teare   3710

PATRI = 2
PATRICIAN *see Patri., Patritian*
PATRICIANS = 9*3

*1.*Cit.* We are accounted poore Citizens, the Patri-|cians	17
Haue the Patricians of you for your wants.	67
The Gods, not the Patricians make it, and	74
Where great Patricians shall attend, and shrug,	751
The good Patricians must be visited,	1108
A Sennet. Enter the Patricians, and the Tribunes of	1239
Cor. Shall? O God! but most vnwise Patricians: why	1785
Tribunes, Patricians, Citizens: what ho:	1894
*The people, against the Senatours, Patricians, and | Nobles.	2584
The Senators and Patricians loue him too:	3121
Is worth of Consuls, Senators, Patricians,	3627
Subscrib'd by'th'Consuls, and Patricians,	3747

PATRITIAN = *1

Men. I am knowne to be a humorous *Patritian*, and	943

PATRONNESSE = 1

Sena. Behold our Patronnesse, the life of Rome:	3641

PAWND = 1

A good construction. I rais'd him, and I pawn'd	3673

PAWNE = 1

Your person most: That he would pawne his fortunes	1692

PAY = 2

A Bribe, to pay my Sword: I doe refuse it,	791
And pay you for your voyces. 'Tis no matter,	3062

PAYES = *1

*good report for't, but that hee payes himselfe with bee-|ing proud.	34

PAYRE = 1

Knaues. You are a payre of strange ones.	975

PEACE = 32*7

That like nor Peace, nor Warre? The one affrights you,	180
*peace you make in their Cause, is calling both the parties	974
All. Peace, peace, peace, stay, hold, peace.	1896
Scici. Heare me, People peace.	1900
All. Let's here our Tribune: peace, speake, speake, | speake.	1901
Aediles. Peace, peace.	1932
All. He shall sure ont. | *Mene.* Sir, sir. *Sicin.* Peace.	2004
Ile go to him, and vndertake to bring him in peace,	2066
Where he shall answer by a lawfull Forme | (In peace) to his vtmost perill.	2067
To speake of Peace, or Warre. I talke of you,	2098
In Peace, what each of them by th'other loose,	2139
That it shall hold Companionship in Peace	2146
Through our large Temples with y shewes of peace	2305
Edile. List to your Tribunes. Audience: | Peace I say.	2311
Corio. First heare me speake. | *Both Tri.* Well, say: Peace hoe.	2313
Sicin. Peace: | We neede not put new matter to his charge:	2357
Menen. Peace, peace, be not so loud.	2519
Menen. Come, come, peace.	2539
*This peace is nothing, but to rust Iron, encrease Taylors, | and breed Ballad-makers.	2877
*1 Let me haue Warre say I, it exceeds peace as farre	2879
*of Vent. Peace, is a very Apoplexy, Lethargie, mull'd,	2881
*be a Rauisher, so it cannot be denied, but peace is a great | maker of Cuckolds.	2885
His remedies are tame, the present peace,	2894

PEACE *cont.*

From th'Caske to th'Cushion: but commanding peace	3134
Corio. I beseech you peace: | Or if you'ld aske, remember this before;	3433
*For making vp this peace. Thou know'st (great Sonne)	3497
Ile frame conuenient peace. Now good *Auffidius*,	3549
What peace you'l make, aduise me: For my part,	3556
Could not haue made this peace. *Exeunt.*	3569
The charges of the Action. We haue made peace	3744
1 *Lord.* Peace both, and heare me speake.	3781
2 *Lord.* Peace hoe: no outrage, peace:	3796
Shall haue Iudicious hearing. Stand *Auffidius*, | And trouble not the peace.	3799

PEBBLES *see* pibbles

PECKE = 1

Breake ope the Lockes a'th'Senate, and bring in | The Crowes to pecke the Eagles.	1835

PEECE = 1

Corio. I, as an Hostler, that fourth poorest peece	2300

PEECES = 2

Corio. Cut me to peeces Volces men and Lads,	3782
All People. Teare him to peeces, do it presently:	3793

PEEPE = 1

And durst not once peepe out.	2949

PEERE = 1

For Truth to o're-peere. Rather then foole it so,	1512

PENCE = *1

*and then reiourne the Controuersie of three-pence	967

PENELOPE = *1

Val. You would be another *Penelope*: yet they say, all	446

PENT = 1

Vagabond exile, Fleaing, pent to linger	2373

PEOPLE = 59*15

*1.*Cit.* First you know, *Caius Martius* is chiefe enemy | to the people.	10
*2 *Cit.* Worthy *Menenius Agrippa*, one that hath al-|wayes lou'd the people.	53
Sicin. When we were chosen Tribunes for the people.	282
The people Mutinous: And it is rumour'd,	325
Enter Menenius with the two Tribunes of the | people, Sicinius & Brutus.	896
Men. Not according to the prayer of the people, for | they loue not *Martius*.	901
*large Cicatrices to shew the People, when hee shall stand	1044
Toth' People, begge their stinking Breaths.	1159
We must suggest the People, in what hatred	1172
Shall teach the People, which time shall not want,	1183
*1.*off.* That's a braue fellow: but hee's vengeance | prowd, and loues not the common people.	1209
*haue flatter'd the people, who ne're loued them; and there	1212
*to seeme to affect the mallice and displeasure of the Peo-|ple,	1224
*hauing beene supple and courteous to the People, Bon-|netted,	1229
the People, Lictors before them: Coriolanus, Mene-|nius, Cominius the Consul: Scicinius and Brutus	1240
Then we to stretch it out. Masters a'th' People,	1259
*he remember a kinder value of the People, then he hath | hereto priz'd them at.	1267
Menen. He loues your People, but tye him not to be	1273
You sooth'd not, therefore hurt not: but your People,	1285

PEOPLE *cont*.

Menen. Masters of the People, | Your multiplying Spawne, how can he flatter?	1291
*Menen. It then remaines, that you doe speake to the | People.	1353
Scicin. Sir, the People must haue their Voyces,	1360
And might well be taken from the People.	1367
We recommend to you Tribunes of the People	1374
Bru. You see how he intends to vse the people.	1380
*would incline to the people, there was neuer a worthier | man.	1424
*bin a Rod to her Friends, you haue not indeede loued the | Common people.	1483
*my sworne Brother the people to earne a deerer estima-|tion	1487
*2.*Cit*. Therefore let him be Consull: the Gods giue him | ioy, and make him good friend to the People.	1526
The People doe admit you, and are summon'd	1537
Brut. We stay here for the People.	1546
Will you dismisse the People?	1551
We will be there before the streame o'th' People:	1668
Behold, these are the Tribunes of the People,	1700
Brut. The People are incens'd against him.	1713
The People cry you mockt them: and of late,	1726
Scandal'd the Suppliants: for the People, call'd them	1728
For which the People stirre: if you will passe	1740
Com. The People are abus'd: set on, this paltring	1746
Bru. You speake a'th'people, as if you were a God,	1773
Sicin. 'Twere well we let the people know't.	1775
*Cor. Thogh there the people had more absolute powre	1812
Bru. Why shall the people giue | One that speakes thus, their voyce?	1814
What should the people do with these bald Tribunes?	1865
Sicin. Go call the people, in whose name my Selfe	1876
*To'th'people: *Coriolanus*, patience: Speak good *Sicinius*.	1899
Scici. Heare me, People peace.	1900
Scici. What is the Citie, but the People?	1909
All. True, the People are the Citie.	1910
Vpon the part o'th' People, in whose power	1922
In this Mutinie, the Tribunes, the Aediles, and the | People are beat in.	1949
Mene. If by the Tribunes leaue, | And yours good people,	2016
Volum. Because, that | Now it lyes you on to speake to th'people:	2150
Inforce him with his enuy to the people,	2261
Sicin. Assemble presently the people hither:	2274
Sicin. Draw neere ye people.	2310
For which you are a Traitor to the people. | *Corio*. How? Traytor?	2345
*Corio. The fires i'th'lowest hell. Fould in the people:	2348
Sicin. Marke you this people?	2355
Enui'd against the people; seeking meanes	2380
That doth distribute it. In the name a'th'people,	2384
As Enemy to the people, and his Countrey.	2405
*The people, against the Senatours, Patricians, and | Nobles.	2584
*they are in a ripe aptnesse, to take al power from the peo-|ple,	2592
The Cruelty and Enuy of the people,	2731
And quietnesse of the people, which before	2895
The Tribunes cannot doo't for shame; the people	3029
The Tribunes are no Soldiers: and their people	3122
Intends t'appeare before the People, hoping	3656
We must proceed as we do finde the People.	3667
3.*Con*. The People will remaine vncertaine, whil'st	3668
Drummes and Trumpets sounds, with great | showts of the people.	3705

PEOPLE *cont*.

3.*Con*. Therefore at your vantage, | Ere he expresse himselfe, or moue
the people 3713
All People. Teare him to peeces, do it presently: 3793
PEOPLES = 7*1
And the Tribunes endue you with the Peoples Voyce, 1532
Brut. By the consent of all, we were establish'd the | Peoples
Magistrates. 1911
The peoples mouths, and we their hands. 2003
Sic. Noble *Menenius*, be you then as the peoples officer: 2073
Sicin. I do demand, | If you submit you to the peoples voices, 2317
To enter our Rome gates. I'th'Peoples name, | I say it shall bee so. 2389
Edile. The peoples Enemy is gone, is gone. 2426
Go whip him fore the peoples eyes: His raising, | Nothing but his
report. 2968
PERADUENTURE = *1
*worth all your predecessors, since *Deucalion*, though per- | aduenture 986
PERCEIUE = 2*1
And when my Face is faire, you shall perceiue 825
Brut. Did you perceiue, | He did sollicite you in free Contempt, 1602
*perceiue, that a Iacke gardant cannot office me from my 3299
PERCEIUES = *1
Scicin. May they perceiue's intent: he wil require them 1381
PERCUSSION = 1
The Thunder-like percussion of thy sounds 561
PEREMPTORY = 2
Giuen Hidra heere to choose an Officer, | That with his peremptory
Shall, being but 1787
Sic. Speake breefely then, | For we are peremptory to dispatch 2021
PERFECTER = *1
*perfecter gyber for the Table, then a necessary Bencher in | the
Capitoll. 977
PERFIDIOUSLY = 1
You Lords and Heads a'th'State, perfidiously 3759
PERFORMD = 1
A little of that worthy Worke, perform'd 1252
PERFORME = 2
Shall be the Generals fault, though he performe 297
To haue my praise for this, performe a part | Thou hast not done
before. 2216
PERHAPS = 1
Perhaps thy childishnesse will moue him more 3514
PERILL = 2
Where he shall answer by a lawfull Forme | (In peace) to his vtmost
perill. 2067
In perill of precipitation | From off the Rocke Tarpeian, neuer more 2387
PERISH = 3
Vnlesse by not so doing, our good Citie | Cleaue in the midd'st, and
perish. 2117
Vol. Now the Red Pestilence strike al Trades in Rome, | And
Occupations perish. 2450
And perish constant Fooles: who is't can blame him? 3024
PERMIT = 1
But by your Voyces, will not so permit me. 1569
PERMITTED = 1
Permitted by our dastard Nobles, who 2732

PERPETUALL = 1
A perpetuall spoyle: and till we call'd   1334
PERSON = 7*1
*would become such a person, that it was no better then   371
Lessen his person, then an ill report: 689
Scicin. One thus descended, | That hath beside well in his person
wrought,   1648
Your person most: That he would pawne his fortunes   1692
As thou hast power and person.   2187
Euen to my person, then I thought he would   3100
The Countrie our deere Nurse, or else thy person   3465
In mine owne person: holpe to reape the Fame   3689
PERSWADE = 1
These warres determine: If I cannot perswade thee,   3475
PERSWADED = 1
Menen. Nay these are almost thoroughly perswaded: 213
PERTINENT = 1
more pertinent then the rebuke you giue it.   1272
PERUSED = 1
But worthy Lords, haue you with heede perused | What I haue written
to you?   3723
PESTILENCE = *1
Vol. Now the Red Pestilence strike al Trades in Rome, | And
Occupations perish.   2450
PESTRING = 1
Dissentious numbers pestring streets, then see   2899
PETITION = 3
And a petition granted them, a strange one,   223
It was a bare petition of a State   3173
Doe's reason our Petition with more strength   3533
PETITIONARY = *1
*Rome, and thy petitionary Countrimen. The good   3311
PETITIOND = *1
Coriol. Oh! you haue, I know, petition'd all the Gods | for my
prosperitie. *Kneeles*.   1074
PETTIE = 1
But was a pettie seruant to the State,   1579
PETTY = 1
With other Muniments and petty helpes   121
PHANE = 1
Being naked, sicke; nor Phane, nor Capitoll,   879
PHOEBUS = 1
Of *Phoebus* burning Kisses: such a poother,   1137
PHYSICALL = 1
The blood I drop, is rather Physicall   591
PHYSICIAN = *1
*the Physician: The most soueraigne Prescription in *Galen*,   1013
PHYSICKE = 2
To iumpe a Body with a dangerous Physicke,   1853
The violent fit a'th'time craues it as Physicke   2125
PIBBLES = 1
Then let the Pibbles on the hungry beach   3409
PICKE = 2
As I could picke my Lance.   212
He could not stay to picke them, in a pile   3178
PICTURE-LIKE = *1
*Picture-like to hang by th'wall, if renowne made it not   372

PIECE *see also* peece = *1
  *1.*Cit.* I twice fiue hundred, & their friends, to piece 'em.   1615
PIECES *see* peeces
PIERCE = 1*1
  When by and by the dinne of Warre gan pierce   1329
  *He is able to pierce a Corslet with his eye: Talkes   3589
PIERCING = 1*1
  *the rich, and prouide more piercing Statutes daily, to   84
  Piercing our Romanes: Then Valiant *Titus* take   582
PIKES = 1*1
  *gaine to them. Let vs reuenge this with our Pikes, ere   24
  Traile your steele Pikes. Though in this City hee   3833
PILE = 2
  Or pile ten hilles on the Tarpeian Rocke,   2086
  He could not stay to picke them, in a pile   3178
PILES = 1
  And burie all, which yet distinctly raunges | In heapes, and piles of
  Ruine.   1917
PINCHD = *1
  *pinch'd with the Collike, you make faces like Mum-|mers,   970
PIND = 1
  Which yet seeme shut, we haue but pin'd with Rushes,   507
PINNES = 1
  While she chats him: the Kitchin *Malkin* pinnes   1126
PINTE = *1
  *I let forth your halfe pinte of blood. Backe, that's the vt-|most of your
  hauing, backe.   3292
PIPE = 1
  Which quier'd with my Drumme into a Pipe,   2221
PIPES = 1
  These Pipes, and these Conueyances of our blood   3212
PITIE = 1
  pitie. Come you shall go with vs.   450
PITTIE = 1
  And Wrath o're-whelm'd my pittie: I request you   845
PITTY = 5
  Deserue such pitty of him, as the Wolfe   3030
  1 *Cit.* For mine owne part, | When I said banish him, I said 'twas pitty.   3066
  The Gaoler to his pitty. I kneel'd before him,   3226
  Then pitty: Note how much, therefore be gone.   3322
  Then pitty to our Prayers. Downe: an end,   3528
PITTYING = 1
  Ransoming him, or pittying, threatning th'other;   647
PITY *see* pitie, pittie, pitty
PLACD = 1
  They haue plac'd their men of trust?   666
PLACE = 16*2
  A place below the first: for what miscarries   296
  Lar. Thou worthiest *Martius,* | Go sound thy Trumpet in the Market
  place,   599
  *for his place: he receiued in the repulse of *Tarquin* seuen | hurts ith'
  Body.   1045
  Appeare i'th'Market place, nor on him put   1156
  Coriolanus rises, and offers to goe away. | Nay, keepe your place.   1275
  Of our proceedings heere on th'Market place,   1385
  A place of Potencie, and sway o'th' State,   1583
  To be set high in place, we did commend   1650

PLACE *cont*.
Senat. Tribunes giue way, he shall toth' Market place.	1712
Com. Well, on to'th'Market place.	1807
*Sic. Meet on the Market place: wee'l attend you there:	2076
Com. I haue beene i'th' Market place: and Sir 'tis fit	2197
And throw't against the Winde. Toth' Market place:	2210
Corio. Pray be content: | Mother, I am going to the Market place:	2240
My Birth-place haue I, and my loues vpon	2649
Here's no place for you: pray go to the doore? *Exit*	2663
Heere's no place for you, pray you auoid: Come.	2685
Bid them repayre to th'Market place, where I	3652

PLACES = 3
That in these seuerall places of the Citie,	196
take their places by themselues: Corio-|lanus stands.	1242
Auf. All places yeelds to him ere he sits downe,	3119

PLACETH = 1
Mar. Thy Friend no lesse, | Then those she placeth highest: So farewell.	597

PLAGUE = 3
Plague vpon't, I cannot bring | My tongue to such a pace. Looke Sir, my wounds,	1439
Th'hoorded plague a'th'Gods requit your loue.	2518
Thou art not honest, and the Gods will plague thee	3523

PLAGUES = *1
*You Shames of Rome: you Heard of Byles and Plagues	526

PLAGUE-TRIBUNES = 1
The common file, (a plague-Tribunes for them)	656

PLAINE = 1
Deseru'd this so dishonor'd Rub, layd falsely | I'th' plaine Way of his Merit.	1748

PLAINELY = 1
*knowledge he ha's in their disposition, and out of his No-|ble carelesnesse lets them plainely see't.	1217

PLAINLY = 1
You must report to th'Volcian Lords, how plainly	3349

PLAISTER = 1
Plaister you o're, that you may be abhorr'd	527

PLANET = 1
Carioles like a Planet: now all's his,	1328

PLANT = 1
Supplied with worthy men, plant loue amongs	2304

PLANTED = *1
*their estimation, and report: but hee hath so planted his	1231

PLANTS = 1
He watered his new Plants with dewes of Flattery,	3675

PLASTER *see* plaister

PLAY = 2
play the idle Huswife with me this afternoone.	433
False to my Nature? Rather say, I play | The man I am.	2100

PLAYES = 1
Musicke playes. Enter a Seruingman.	2653

PLE = 1

PLEADER = 1
Would be your Countries Pleader, your good tongue	3190

PLEADERS = 1
Haue made them Mules, silenc'd their Pleaders,	1174

PLEASD = 1 *2
*stirre, was pleas'd to let him seeke danger, where he was	373

PLEASD *cont*.

    And made what worke I pleas'd: 'Tis not my blood,   734

    *Menen. The Senate, *Coriolanus*, are well pleas'd to make | thee

    Consull.   1350

PLEASE = 6*1

    *content to say it was for his Countrey, he did it to please   39

    But and't please you deliuer.   97

    (As cause will be obey'd:) please you to March,   704

    Thus stood for his Countrey. Therefore please you,   1248

    been silent: Please you to heare *Cominius* speake?   1270

    Please you that I may passe this doing.   1359

    That he is thus cut off. Please it your Honours   3818

PLEASERS = 1

    Time-pleasers, flatterers, foes to Noblenesse.   1729

PLEASING = *1

    *Scicin. We are conuented vpon a pleasing Treatie, and   1263

PLEASURE = *1

    *pleasures (at the least) if you take it as a pleasure to you, in   928

PLEASURES = *1

    *pleasures (at the least) if you take it as a pleasure to you, in   928

PLEBEANS = 1*1

    That with the fustie Plebeans, hate thine Honors,   754

    *the Beastly Plebeans. I will be bold to take my leaue of | you.   990

PLEBEIANS see also Ple. = 6*1

    *Men. I, to deuour him, as the hungry Plebeians would | the Noble

    Martius.   906

    Enter the Plebeians.   1552

    All. We will so: almost all repent in their election. | *Exeunt Plebeians*.   1659

    Let them haue 'Cushions by you. You are Plebeians,   1795

    Enter a rabble of Plebeians with the Aediles.   1886

    Enter the Edile with the Plebeians.   2309

    The Plebeians haue got your Fellow Tribune,   3605

PLEBEIJ = 1

    Fast Foe toth' *Plebeij*, your Voyces might   1585

PLOT = 3

    Corio. It is a purpos'd thing, and growes by Plot,   1721

    Brut. Call't not a Plot: 1725

    Yet were there but this single Plot, to loose   2208

PLOTS = *1

    *Whose Passions, and whose Plots haue broke their sleep   2645

PLOUGH = 1

    Plough Rome, and harrow Italy, Ile neuer   3383

PLOWED = *1

    *Which we our selues haue plowed for, sow'd, & scatter'd,   1761

PLUCKD = *1

    *youth with comelinesse pluck'd all gaze his way; when   368

PLUCKE = 4*2

    See him plucke *Auffidius* downe by th'haire: 392

    *were a Mallice, that giuing it selfe the Lye, would plucke   1235

    That's sure of death without it: at once plucke out   1854

    Pursue him to his house, and plucke him thence,   2049

    To plucke away their power: as now at last,   2381

    *and to plucke from them their Tribunes for euer.   2593

PLUCKT = 1

    And try'd his Inclination: from him pluckt   1594

PLUMES = 1

    Your Enemies, with nodding of their Plumes   2414

PLUTO = 1
    From Slaues, that Apes would beate; *Pluto* and Hell,   531
POCKET = 1
    Victorie in his Pocket? the wounds become him.   1020
POINT = 6
    Rome, and her Rats, are at the point of battell,   170
    As the maine Point of this our after-meeting,   1246
    Whom with all prayse I point at, saw him fight,   1304
    Scici. You are at point to lose your Liberties: 1903
    Bru. In this point charge him home, that he affects   2259
    Mes. Almost at point to enter.   3637
POINTS = 1 *1
    *of one direct way, should be at once to all the points | a'th Compasse.   1409
    The second name of men, obeyes his points   3049
POISED *see* poys'd
POISON *see also* poyson = 2
    Sicin. It is a minde that shall remain a poison   1779
    Ingrate forgetfulnesse shall poison rather   3321
POISOND = *1
    Auf. Bolder, though not so subtle: my valors poison'd,   876
POISONOUS *see* poysonous
POLE = 2
    We are the greater pole, and in true feare   1831
    Sicin. Haue you a Catalogue | *Of all the Voices that we haue procur'd,
    set downe by'th | (Pole?   2269
POLICY = 3
    Honor and Policy, like vnseuer'd Friends,   2137
    You adopt your policy: How is it lesse or worse   2145
    Is all the Policy, Strength, and Defence   3051
POOR = 1
    When she (poor Hen) fond of no second brood,   3519
POORE = 12 *6
    *1.*Cit*. We are accounted poore Citizens, the Patri- | cians   17
    *now wee'l shew em in deeds: they say poore Suters haue   61
    *chaine vp and restraine the poore. If the Warres eate vs   85
    That rubbing the poore Itch of your Opinion, | Make your selues Scabs.   175
    At a poore mans house: he vs'd me kindly,   842
    To giue my poore Host freedome.   846
    Men. In what enormity is *Martius* poore in, that you | two haue not in
    abundance?   913
    Bru. He's poore in no one fault, but stor'd withall. | *Sicin*. Especially in
    Pride.   915
    *thing: you are ambitious, for poore knaues cappes and   964
    Corio. No Sir, 'twas neuer my desire yet to trouble the | poore with
    begging.   1461
    2.*Cit*. Amen, Sir: to my poore vnworthy notice,   1556
    3 A maru'llous poore one. | *Corio*. True, so I am.   2682
    *3 Pray you poore Gentleman, take vp some other sta- | tion: 2684
    For one poore graine or two, to leaue vnburnt | And still to nose
    th'offence.   3180
    Menen. For one poore graine or two?   3182
    Volum. This is a poore Epitome of yours,   3420
    His Countries Bowels out; and to poore we   3458
    shall our poore City finde: and all this is long of you.   3598
POOREST = 2
    Men. For that being one o'th lowest, basest, poorest   165
    Corio. I, as an Hostler, that fourth poorest peece   2300

POORST = *1
*Thou art poor'st of all; then shortly art thou mine. *Exeunt*   3148
POOTHER = 1
Of *Phoebus* burning Kisses: such a poother,   1137
POPULAR = 2*2
Doe presse among the popular Throngs, and puffe   1133
*the bewitchment of some popular man, and giue it   1492
His popular Shall, against a grauer Bench   1800
*of them, and in a violent popular ignorance, giuen your   3277
PORCH = 1
Though calued i'th' Porch o'th' Capitoll: 1964
PORTANCE = 1
Th'apprehension of his present portance,   1627
PORTER = *2
*2 *Ser*. Whence are you sir? Ha's the Porter his eyes in   2666
*sayes, and sole the Porter of Rome Gates by th'eares. He   2860
PORTS = 1*1
Lar. So, let the Ports be guarded; keepe your Duties   714
The City Ports by this hath enter'd, and   3655
POSSESSE = 1
Away my disposition, and possesse me | Some Harlots spirit: My throat
of Warre be turn'd,   2219
POSSEST = 1
that's in them. Is the Senate possest of this?   1029
POSSIBLE = 1*2
Sicin. Tell not me: I know this cannot be. | *Bru*. Not possible.   2961
Mene. If it be possible for you to displace it with your   3573
Sicin. Is't possible, that so short a time can alter the | condition of a
man.   3578
POSTE = *1
*1.*Con*. Your Natiue Towne you enter'd like a Poste,   3707
POSTERITY = *1
Sicin. What then? | *Virg*. When then? Hee'ld make an end of thy
posterity   2535
POSTURE = 1
And gaue him gracefull posture.   1140
POT = 1*1
All. To th'pot I warrant him. *Enter Titus Lartius*   547
*in roaring for a Chamber-pot, dismisse the Controuersie   972
POTCHE = 1
True Sword to Sword: Ile potche at him some way, | Or Wrath, or Craft
may get him.   873
POTENCIE = 1
A place of Potencie, and sway o'th' State,   1583
POULD = 1
*will mowe all downe before him, and leaue his passage | poul'd.   2861
POUND = 1
Rather then they shall pound vs vp our Gates,   506
POUNDS = 1
Tye Leaden pounds too's heeles. Proceed by Processe,   2055
POUT *see* powt
POW = 1
Volum. True? pow waw.   1038
POWER = 33*7
*And make bold power looke pale, they threw their caps   225
Win vpon power, and throw forth greater Theames | For Insurrections
arguing.   234

POWER *cont*.

They haue prest a Power, but it is not knowne	323
Some parcels of their Power are forth already,	350
*power. Your Lord, and *Titus Lartius*, are set down	462
Wrench vp thy power to th'highest.	736
Enter Titus with his Power, from the Pursuit.	759
To vnder-crest your good Addition, | To th'fairenesse of my power.	828
Brutus. Then our Office may, during his power, goe | sleepe.	1142
He still hath held them: that to's power he would	1173
3.Cit. We haue power in our selues to do it, but it is	1391
*a power that we haue no power to do: For, if hee shew vs	1392
As you were lesson'd: When he had no Power,	1578
When he hath power to crush? Why, had your Bodyes	1606
Who lack not Vertue, no, nor Power, but that	1763
And make your Channell his? If he haue power,	1791
Not hauing the power to do the good it would	1859
And throw their power i'th'dust.	1871
Sicin. Heere's hee, that would take from you all your | power.	1888
Vpon the part o'th' People, in whose power	1922
Or *Ioue*, for's power to Thunder: his Heart's his Mouth:	1985
Then the seuerity of the publike Power, | Which he so sets at naught.	2000
Volum. Oh sir, sir, sir, | I would haue had you put your power well on	2102
Ere they lack'd power to crosse you.	2110
As thou hast power and person.	2187
Tyrannicall power: If he euade vs there,	2260
Insisting on the olde prerogatiue | And power i'th Truth a'th Cause.	2279
Your selfe into a power tyrannicall,	2344
Those whose great power must try him.	2362
To plucke away their power: as now at last,	2381
And in the power of vs the Tribunes, wee	2385
Fan you into dispaire: Haue the power still	2415
Brut. Now we haue shewne our power,	2506
Virg. You shall stay too: I would I had the power | To say so to my Husband.	2522
*they are in a ripe aptnesse, to take al power from the peo-|ple,	2592
We haue a Power on foote: and I had purpose	2777
Ioyn'd with *Auffidius*, leads a power 'gainst Rome,	2976
And power vnto it selfe most commendable,	3142
2 'Tis a spell you see of much power:	3332

POWERS = 3*1

*That both our powers, with smiling Fronts encountring,	611
Were slyly crept into his humane powers,	1139
Reports the Volces with two seuerall Powers	2941
He hath abus'd your Powers.	3752

POWRE = *1

Cor. Thogh there the people had more absolute powre	1812

POWRING = 1

From twelue, to seuentie: and powring Warre	2787

POWT = 1

We powt vpon the Morning, are vnapt	3210

POYSD = 1

Be singly counter-poys'd. At sixteene yeeres,	1301

POYSON = 2

Where it is: not poyson any further.	1780
The sweet which is their poyson. Your dishonor	1856

247

POYSONOUS = 2
Brut. Sir, those cold wayes, | That seeme like prudent helpes, are very
poysonous,   1936
As poysonous of your Honour. No, our suite   3492
PRACTICE = 1*1
*then my Heart, I will practice the insinuating nod, and be   1490
With cautelous baits and practice.   2471
PRAISE *see also* prayse = 4
Mar. Sir, praise me not: 589
To haue my praise for this, performe a part | Thou hast not done
before.   2216
I haue tumbled past the throw: and in his praise   3259
Call all your Tribes together, praise the Gods,   3642
PRAISES *see also* prayses = 1
My praises made thee first a Souldier; so   2215
PRANKE = 1
For they doe pranke them in Authoritie, | Against all Noble sufferance.   1702
PRATE = 2
Corio. What do you prate of Seruice.   2366
More bound to's Mother, yet heere he let's me prate   3516
PRATING = 1
why stay we prating heere? To th'Capitoll. | *All*. Come, come.   49
PRATLING = 1
Are spectacled to see him. Your pratling Nurse   1124
PRATST = *2
*thy Mistris: Thou prat'st, and prat'st, serue with thy tren- | cher:
Hence. *Beats him away*   2702
PRAY = 34*8
Where go you with Bats and Clubs? The matter | Speake I pray you.   57
Your valour puts well forth: Pray follow. *Exeunt*.   278
Volum. I pray you daughter sing, or expresse your selfe   362
Volum. Why I pray you. | *Vulg*. 'Tis not to saue labour, nor that I want
loue.   444
Honor, and so I pray go with vs.   465
Hadst thou beheld | *Martius*. Pray now, no more: 762
Auf. I am attended at the Cyprus groue. I pray you   890
Men. Pray you, who does the Wolfe loue? | *Sicin*. The Lambe.   904
Coriol. No more of this, it does offend my heart: pray | now no more.   1071
Menen. Pray now sit downe.   1287
Pray you goe fit you to the Custome,   1363
Corio. What must I say, I pray Sir?   1438
Ile leaue you: Pray you speake to em, I pray you | In wholsome manner.
Exit   1450
Corio. Well then I pray, your price a'th'Consulship.   1465
Corio. Kindly sir, I pray let me ha't: I haue wounds to   1467
Coriol. Pray you now, if it may stand with the tune   1476
Brut. We pray the Gods, he may deserue your loues.   1555
Mene. Pray you be gone: 1976
Sena. Pray you let's to him. *Exeunt Omnes*.   2082
Volum. Pray be counsail'd;   2119
Corio. Pray be content: | Mother, I am going to the Market place: 2240
Corio. The word is, Mildely. Pray you let vs go,   2253
Thou lyest vnto thee, with a voice as free, | As I do pray the Gods.   2353
Com. Know, I pray you. | *Corio*. Ile know no further: 2370
Bid me farewell, and smile. I pray you come: 2491
Brut. Pray let's go.   2548
Volum. Now pray sir get you gone.   2549

PRAY *cont*.

Here's no place for you: pray go to the doore? *Exit*	2663
Pray get you out.	2668
*3 What haue you to do here fellow? Pray you auoid | the house.	2677
*3 Pray you poore Gentleman, take vp some other sta-|tion:	2684
Heere's no place for you, pray you auoid: Come.	2685
Are bound to pray for you both.	2919
Mene. Pray now, your Newes:	3003
*You haue made faire worke I feare me: pray your newes,	3004
Sicin. Pray let's go. *Exeunt Tribunes.*	3089
Sicin. Nay, pray be patient: If you refuse your ayde	3187
Sicin. Pray you go to him. | *Mene.* What should I do?	3194
Hath Virgin'd it ere since. You Gods, I pray,	3397
Alas! how can we, for our Country pray?	3462
Ile not to Rome, Ile backe with you, and pray you	3557

PRAYD = 1

A Sea and Land full: you haue pray'd well to day:	3629

PRAYER = *1

Men. Not according to the prayer of the people, for | they loue not *Martius*.	901

PRAYERS = 5

with my prayers: but I cannot go thither.	443
The Prayers of Priests, nor times of Sacrifice:	880
Volum. Take my Prayers with you.	2558
Our prayers to the Gods, which is a comfort	3460
Then pitty to our Prayers. Downe: an end,	3528

PRAYSE = 2

When she do's prayse me, grieues me:	765
Whom with all prayse I point at, saw him fight,	1304

PRAYSES = 2

Which to the spire, and top of prayses vouch'd,	775
As if I lou'd my little should be dieted | In prayses, sawc'st with Lyes.	807

PRECEPTS = 1

With Precepts that would make inuincible | The heart that conn'd them.	2446

PRECIOUS = 1

And look'd vpon things precious, as they were	1341

PRECIPITATION = 2

That the precipitation might downe stretch	2087
In perill of precipitation | From off the Rocke Tarpeian, neuer more	2387

PREDECESSORS = 1*1

*worth all your predecessors, since *Deucalion*, though per-|aduenture	986
And take to you, as your Predecessors haue,	1364

PREFERRE = 1

More then you doubt the change on't: That preferre	1851

PREOCCUPIED *see* pre-occupy'd

PREPARATION = 1*1

These three leade on this Preparation	329
*so, they are in a most warlike preparation, & hope to com | vpon them, in the heate of their diuision	2587

PREPARD = 3

Th'haue not prepar'd for vs.	347
To answer mildely: for they are prepar'd	2250
Who am prepar'd against your Territories, | Though not for Rome it selfe.	2792

PREPARE = *2

Corio. Prepare thy brow to frowne: knowst y me yet?	2720
*backe to Rome, and prepare for your execution: you are	3284

PREPARING = *1
*Father *Menenius* do's. O my Son, my Son! thou art pre-|paring   3306
PREROGATIUE = 1
Insisting on the olde prerogatiue | And power i'th Truth a'th Cause.   2279
PRESCRIPTION = *1
*the Physician: The most soueraigne Prescription in *Galen*,   1013
PRESENCE = 1
Giuen Hostile strokes, and that not in the presence   2382
PRESENT = 11*3
Bru. The present Warres deuoure him, he is growne | Too proud to be
so valiant.   287
More then his singularity, he goes | Vpon this present Action.   310
And that you not delay the present (but   677
The present Consull, and last Generall,   1250
Th'apprehension of his present portance,   1627
Skaling his present bearing with his past,   1652
We were elected theirs, *Martius* is worthy | Of present Death.   1923
Corio. Let them pull all about mine eares, present me   2084
Not what is dangerous present, but the losse | Of what is past.   2171
Inforce the present Execution | Of what we chance to Sentence.   2284
Corio. Shall I be charg'd no further then this present?   2315
*the man I thinke, that shall set them in present Action. So   2616
Longer to liue most wearie: and present   2752
His remedies are tame, the present peace,   2894
PRESENTED = 1
Presented to my knife his Throat: I tooke him,   3684
PRESENTLY = 3*2
And presently, when you haue drawne your number, | Repaire toth'
Capitoll.   1657
Sicin. Assemble presently the people hither: 2274
*3 To morrow, to day, presently, you shall haue the   2873
*now presently, and swoond for what's to come vpon   3303
All People. Teare him to peeces, do it presently: 3793
PRESERUATIUE = *1
*is but Emperickqutique; and to this Preseruatiue, of no   1014
PRESERUE = 2
The Gods preserue our Noble Tribunes, come. *Exeunt*.   2433
All. The Gods preserue you both.   2915
PRESSE = 1
Doe presse among the popular Throngs, and puffe   1133
PREST = 3
They haue prest a Power, but it is not knowne   323
An o're-prest Roman, and i'th' Consuls view   1307
They ne're did seruice for't; being prest to'th'Warre,   1819
PRESUME = 1
They'l sit by th'fire, and presume to know   203
PRETENCES = 1
To keepe your great pretences vayl'd, till when   336
PRETEXT = 1
Auf. I know it: | And my pretext to strike at him, admits   3671
PRETTY = 1*1
A pretty Tale, it may be you haue heard it,   91
*very pretty boy. A my troth, I look'd vpon him a Wens-|day   421
PREUAILD *see also* preuayl'd = 2
Com. But how preuail'd you?   659
Most dangerously you haue with him preuail'd,   3546

PREUAILE = *1
  *his Mother, may preuaile with him. But I say, there   3575
PREUAILING = *1
  *before their Citie *Carioles*, they nothing doubt preuai-|ling,   463
PREUAYLD = 2
  Ere so preuayl'd with me; it will in time   233
  Mess. Good Newes, good newes, the Ladies haue | (preuayl'd. 3611
PREUENTED = 1
  Bru. The Gods haue well preuented it, and Rome | Sits safe and still,
  without him.   2936
PRE-OCCUPYD = *1
  *Your Minds pre-occupy'd with what you rather must do,   1635
PRICE = 4
  *1.*Cit.* Let vs kill him, and wee'l haue Corne at our own | price. Is't a
  Verdict?   13
  Corio. Well then I pray, your price a'th'Consulship.   1465
  1 *Cit.* The price is, to aske it kindly.   1466
  Their mercie, at the price of one faire word,   2375
PRICKING = *1
  *as your finger, that you might leaue pricking it for   449
PRIDE = 8*2
  Bru. He's poore in no one fault, but stor'd withall. | *Sicin.* Especially in
  Pride.   915
  Men. Because you talke of Pride now, will you not | be angry. 922
  *much alone. You talke of Pride: Oh, that you could turn   934
  All reuoke your ignorant election: Enforce his Pride,   1622
  Thy Mother rather feele thy Pride, then feare   2235
  But owe thy Pride thy selfe.   2239
  O'recome with Pride, Ambitious, past all thinking | Selfe-louing. 2930
  Carry his Honors eeuen: whether 'twas Pride   3128
  To his sur-name *Coriolanus* longs more pride   3527
  Which he did end all his; and tooke some pride   3690
PRIESTS = 1*1
  The Prayers of Priests, nor times of Sacrifice: 880
  Men. Our very Priests must become Mockers, if they   979
PRIEST-LIKE = 1
  Then in our Priest-like Fasts: therefore Ile watch him   3214
PRIMA *l*.1 = 1
PRIMUS *l*.1 = 1
PRINCELY = 1
  I that now refus'd most Princely gifts,   838
PRIORITY = 1
  Tit. Lead you on: Follow *Cominius*, we must followe | you, right
  worthy your Priority.   271
PRISON = 1
  Aedile. Worthy Tribunes, | There is a Slaue whom we haue put in
  prison,   2939
PRISONER = 1
  He cry'd to me: I saw him Prisoner: 843
PRITHEE *see* prythee
PRIUAT = *1
  *Neuer admitted a priuat whisper, no not with such frends | That
  thought them sure of you.   3353
PRIUATE = 4*1
  *shew you, which shall bee yours in priuate: your good | voice sir, what
  say you?   1468
  Which he could shew in priuate: 1566

PRIUATE *cont*.

For's priuate Friends. His answer to me was	3177
Nor from the State, nor priuate friends heereafter	3365
Heare nought from Rome in priuate. Your request?	3448

PRIUILEDGE = 2

Their rotten Priuiledge, and Custome 'gainst	882
All bond and priuiledge of Nature breake;	3374

PRIZD = 1

*he remember a kinder value of the People, then he hath | hereto priz'd them at.	1267

PRIZE = 1*1

Mar. See heere these mouers, that do prize their hours	575
As reeke a'th'rotten Fennes: whose Loues I prize,	2409

PROBABLE = 1

How probable I do not know, that *Martius*	2975

PROCEED = 4*1

1. *Citizen*. | *Before we proceed any further, heare me speake.	4
Then on ones Eares to heare it. Proceed *Cominius*.	1295
And temp'rately proceed to what you would | Thus violently redresse.	1934
Tye Leaden pounds too's heeles. Proceed by Processe,	2055
We must proceed as we do finde the People.	3667

PROCEEDE = 2*1

2.Cit. Would you proceede especially against *Caius* | *Martius*.	27
And know how we proceede, | *Auf*. Is it not yours?	316
Where if you bring not *Martius*, wee'l proceede | In our first way.	2077

PROCEEDINGS = 1

Of our proceedings heere on th'Market place,	1385

PROCEEDS = 1

But it proceeds, or comes from them to you,	161

PROCESSE = 1

Tye Leaden pounds too's heeles. Proceed by Processe,	2055

PROCURD = *1

Sicin. Haue you a Catalogue | *Of all the Voices that we haue procur'd, set downe by'th | (Pole?	2269

PROFESSE = *1

*Sonne, I therein would haue found issue. Heare me pro- |fesse	382

PROFOUND = 1

More holy, and profound, then mine owne life,	2399

PROGENY = 1

Auf. Wer't thou the *Hector*, | That was the whip of your bragg'd Progeny,	737

PROIECTS = 1

Out of my Files, his proiects, to accomplish	3687

PROMISE = 3*1

Com. It is your former promise. | *Mar*. Sir it is,	260
Eyther his gracious Promise, which you might	1595
Mene. Nay temperately: your promise.	2347
Mene. Is this the promise that you made your mother.	2369

PROMISE-BREAKER = 1

Mar. Ile fight with none but thee, for I do hate thee | Worse then a Promise-breaker.	724

PROMPT = 2

Readie when time shall prompt them, to make roade | Vpon's againe.	1678
Com. Come, come, wee'le prompt you.	2213

PROMPTS = 1

Which your heart prompts you, but with such words	2153

PRONOUNCD = 1
After your way. His Tale pronounc'd, shall bury | His Reasons, with his
Body.   3717
PRONOUNCE = 2
Or let vs lose it: we doe here pronounce,   1921
Let them pronounce the steepe Tarpeian death,   2372
PROOFE = 1
With hearts more proofe then Shields.   517
PROPER = 1
(Like one that meanes his proper harme) in Manacles,   813
PROPERLY = 1
My Reuenge properly, my remission lies   3319
PROPHANE = *1
*Mar. May these same Instruments, which you prophane,   797
PROSPERITIE = 1
*Coriol. Oh! you haue, I know, petition'd all the Gods | for my
prosperitie. Kneeles.   1074
PROSPERITY = 1*1
Misguide thy Opposers swords, Bold Gentleman: | Prosperity be thy
Page.   595
*particular prosperity, and loue thee no worse then thy old   3305
PROSPEROUS = *1
*Volum. I, worthy Menenius, and with most prosperous | approbation.   1000
PROSPEROUSLY = 1
That prosperously I haue attempted, and   3740
PROUAND = 1
Then Cammels in their Warre, who haue their Prouand   1178
PROUD see also prowd = 9*3
*good report for't, but that hee payes himselfe with bee-|ing proud.   34
*his Mother, and to be partly proud, which he is, euen to | the altitude
of his vertue.   40
The other makes you proud. He that trusts to you,   181
Onely my warres with him. He is a Lion | That I am proud to hunt.   256
Sicin. Was euer man so proud as is this Martius?   280
*Bru. The present Warres deuoure him, he is growne | Too proud to be
so valiant.   287
being so: you blame Martius for being proud.   929
*proud, violent, testie Magistrates (alias Fooles) | as any in Rome.   940
*saying, Martius is proud: who in a cheape estimation, is   985
He prou'd best man i'th' field, and for his meed   1311
To suffer lawfull Censure for such faults | As shall be prou'd vpon you. 2320
Strike the proud Cedars 'gainst the fiery Sun: 3411
PROUDLIER = 1
Of our designe. He beares himselfe more proudlier,   3099
PROUE = 9
So, now the gates are ope: now proue good Seconds,   540
We proue this very houre.   679
I'th'field proue flatterers, let Courts and Cities be   799
Will proue to bloody: and the end of it, | Vnknowne to the Beginning.   2071
That my reuengefull Seruices may proue   2746
Thou dar'st not this, and that to proue more Fortunes   2750
Which will not proue a whip: As many Coxcombes   3060
Mene. Good faith Ile proue him,   3219
Thy thoughts with Noblenesse, that thou mayst proue   3425
PROUED see also prou'd = *1
*he was a Man-child, then now in first seeing he had pro-|ued himselfe
a man.   377

253

PROUERBES = 1
They said they were an hungry, sigh'd forth Prouerbes   218
PROUIDE = *1
*the rich, and prouide more piercing Statutes daily, to   84
PROUOKD = 1
Prouok'd by him, you cannot) the great danger   3816
PROWD = 2*2
*is comming home: hee ha's more cause to be prowd: 1041
As he is prowd to doo't.   1153
*1 .off. That's a braue fellow: but hee's vengeance | prowd, and loues not
the common people.   1209
*Brut. With a prowd heart he wore his humble Weeds: 1550
PRUDENT = 1
Brut. Sir, those cold wayes, | That seeme like prudent helpes, are very
poysonous,   1936
PRYTHEE = 9*2
Prythee Virgilia turne thy solemnesse out a doore, | And go along with
vs.   472
Now Mars, I prythee make vs quicke in worke,   496
I prythee noble friend, home to thy House,   1957
Volum. I prythee now, my Sonne,   2173
Volum. Prythee now, | Goe, and be rul'd: although I know thou hadst
rather   2192
Volum. He must, and will: | Prythee now say you will, and goe about it. 2203
Volum. I prythee now sweet Son, as thou hast said   2214
Virg. Oh heauens! O heauens! | Corio. Nay, I prythee woman.   2448
out o'thhouse: Prythee call my Master to him.   2676
*3 What you will not? Prythee tell my Maister what | a strange Guest
he ha's heere.   2688
*Men. Prythee fellow, remember my name is Menenius,   3266
PSALTERIES = 1
The Trumpets, Sack-buts, Psalteries, and Fifes,   3622
PUBLICOLA = 1
Corio. The Noble Sister of Publicola; | The Moone of Rome: Chaste as
the Isicle   3416
PUBLIKE = 2
A Foe to'th'publike Weale. Obey I charge thee,   1878
Then the seuerity of the publike Power, | Which he so sets at naught. 2000
PUBLIQUE = 1
No publique benefit which you receiue   160
PUBLIUS = 1
Of the same House Publius and Quintus were,   1644
PUFFE = 1
Doe presse among the popular Throngs, and puffe   1133
PULING = 1
Leaue this faint-puling, and lament as I do,   2567
PULL = 1
Corio. Let them pull all about mine eares, present me   2084
PUNISH = 2
To punish; Not a man, of their Infirmity.   1774
Before you punish him, where he heard this,   2957
PUNISHD = 1
To one whom they had punish'd.   3174
PUNY = 1
In puny Battell slay me. Saue you sir.   2628
PUPILL = 1
Was Brow-bound with the Oake. His Pupill age   1312

PURCHASING = 1
  Menen. Wondrous: I, I warrant you, and not with-|out his true
purchasing.   1035
PUREST = 1
  That's curdied by the Frost, from purest Snow,   3418
PURGE = 1
  To purge himselfe with words. Dispatch.   3657
PURPOSD = 1
  Corio. It is a purpos'd thing, and growes by Plot,   1721
PURPOSE = 8*2
  But since it serues my purpose, I will venture | To scale't a little more.   92
  And did retyre to win our purpose.   664
  *you speake best vnto the purpose. It is not woorth the   981
  Scicin. I wish no better, then haue him hold that pur-|pose, and to put
it in execution.   1165
  Our purpose to them, and to our Noble Consull | Wish we all Ioy, and
Honor.   1375
  To vnstable Slightnesse. Purpose so barr'd, it followes,   1847
  Nothing is done to purpose. Therefore beseech you,   1848
  For they haue Pardons, being ask'd, as free, | As words to little
purpose.   2190
  We haue a Power on foote: and I had purpose   2777
  I purpose not to waite on Fortune, till   3474
PURSUE = 1
  Pursue him to his house, and plucke him thence,   2049
PURSUING = 1
  Then Boyes pursuing Summer Butter-flies, | Or Butchers killing Flyes. 3010
PURSUIT = 1
  Enter Titus with his Power, from the Pursuit.   759
PUSHES = 1
  Corio. Follow your Function, go, and batten on colde | bits. *Pushes
him away from him.*   2686
PUSHT = *1
  *when you haue pusht out your gates, the very Defender   3276
PUT = 20*1
  Tullus Auffidius that will put you too't: 249
  Now put your Shields before your hearts, and fight   516
  If 'gainst your selfe you be incens'd, wee'le put you   812
  Appeare i'th'Market place, nor on him put   1156
  Scicin. I wish no better, then haue him hold that pur-|pose, and to put
it in execution.   1165
  If he be put vpon't, and that's as easie,   1184
  Put on the Gowne, stand naked, and entreat them   1357
  Menen. Put them not too't: 1362
  *his wounds, and tell vs his deeds, we are to put our ton-|gues   1393
  This Mutinie were better put in hazard,   1662
  Mene. Shall it be put to that? | *Sena*. The Gods forbid: 1955
  Be gone, put not your worthy Rage into your Tongue,   1965
  Volum. Oh sir, sir, sir, | I would haue had you put your power well on 2102
  For the whole State; I would put mine Armour on,   2126
  Which else would put you to your fortune, and | The hazard of much
blood.   2159
  You haue put me now to such a part, which neuer   2211
  Bru. Go about it, | Put him to Choller straite, he hath bene vs'd 2289
  Sicin. Peace: | We neede not put new matter to his charge: 2357
  Aedile. Worthy Tribunes, | There is a Slaue whom we haue put in
prison,   2939

PUT *cont*.

Auf. Why Noble Lords, | Will you be put in minde of his blinde
Fortune, 3788
3.*Lord*. Tread not vpon him Masters, all be quiet, | Put vp your Swords. 3812
PUTS = 2
Your valour puts well forth: Pray follow. *Exeunt*. 278
And such a one as he, who puts his Shall, 1799
PUTTING = 2*1
Tying him to ought, so putting him to Rage, 1599
(Harpe on that still) but by our putting on: 1656
Me. 'Tis true, if he were putting to my house, the brand 3035
QUAKD = *1
*And gladly quak'd, heare more: where the dull Tribunes, 753
QUARRELL = 1
Had we no other quarrell else to Rome, but that 2785
QUARRIE = 1
And let me vse my Sword, I'de make a Quarrie 210
QUARTERD = 1
With thousands of these quarter'd slaues, as high 211
QUARTUS *l*.2434 = 1
QUEENE = 1
Now by the iealous Queene of Heauen, that kisse 3395
QUENCH = 1*1
Mene. Fie, fie, fie, this is the way to kindle, not to | quench. 1906
*fire for vs: looke thee, heere's water to quench it. 3307
QUESTION = 1*1
Which that he will giue them, make I as little question, 1152
*question askt him by any of the Senators, but they stand 2853
QUICKE = 1
Now Mars, I prythee make vs quicke in worke, 496
QUICKLY = 1
And foure shall quickly draw out my Command, | Which men are best
inclin'd. 705
QUIERD = 1
Which quier'd with my Drumme into a Pipe, 2221
QUIET = 1
3.*Lord*. Tread not vpon him Masters, all be quiet, | Put vp your Swords. 3812
QUIETNESSE = 1
And quietnesse of the people, which before 2895
QUINTUS *l*.1644 3149 = 2
QUIT = 1
To be full quit of those my Banishers, 2740
QUOTH = 1
True is it my Incorporate Friends (quoth he) 137
RABBLE = 4
The rabble should haue first vnroo'st the City 232
The Nature of our Seats, and make the Rabble 1833
Enter a rabble of Plebeians with the Aediles. 1886
Enter Brutus and Sicinius with the rabble againe. 1993
RABLE = *1
Bru. I would he had. | *Volum*. I would he had? Twas thou incenst the
rable. 2543
RAGE = 7
Tying him to ought, so putting him to Rage, 1599
If, as his nature is, he fall in rage 1664
Be gone, put not your worthy Rage into your Tongue, 1965
Before the Tagge returne? whose Rage doth rend 1973

RAGE *cont.*

This Tiger-footed-rage, when it shall find	2053
Auf. My Lords, | When you shall know (as in this Rage	3814
Auf. My Rage is gone, | And I am strucke with sorrow. Take him vp:	3829

RAGES = 2

Associated with *Auffidius*, Rages | Vpon our Territories, and haue already	2989
My Rages and Reuenges, with your colder reasons.	3440

RAIMENT = *1

Volum. Should we be silent & not speak, our Raiment	3449

RAINE = 1

Conies after Raine) and reuell all with him.	2871

RAISD = 2

Bru. Rais'd onely, that the weaker sort may wish | Good *Martius* home againe.	2980
A good construction. I rais'd him, and I pawn'd	3673

RAISING = 1

Go whip him fore the peoples eyes: His raising, | Nothing but his report.	2968

RAKES = *1

*we become Rakes. For the Gods know, I speake this in	25

RALLISH = 1

That will not be grafted to your Rallish.	1099

RAN = 1

Then when these Fellowes ran about the streets, | Crying Confusion.	2926

RANGES *see* raunges

RANKE-SENTED = 1

For the mutable ranke-sented Meynie,	1756

RANNE = 1

Some certaine of your Brethren roar'd, and ranne	1442

RANSOMING = 1

Ransoming him, or pittying, threatning th'other;	647

RAPT = 1

Thou Noble thing, more dances my rapt heart,	2774

RAPTURE = 1

Into a rapture lets her Baby crie,	1125

RARE = 1

And by his rare example made the Coward	1318

RAREST = *1

*2 So did I, Ile be sworne: He is simply the rarest man | i'th'world.	2820

RASCALL = 1

Thou Rascall, that art worst in blood to run,	167

RASCALS = 1*1

The Mouse ne're shunn'd the Cat, as they did budge | From Rascals worse then they.	657
*3 Oh Slaues, I can tell you Newes, News you Rascals	2833

RASH = 2

Not rash like his Accusers, and thus answered.	136
Will be as rash in the repeale, as hasty	3123

RATES = *1

Men. For Corne at their owne rates, wherof they say	200

RATHER = 16*8

*1.*Cit.* You are all resolu'd rather to dy then | to famish?	7
*had rather had eleuen dye Nobly for their Countrey, then | one voluptuously surfet out of Action.	385
Vol. He had rather see the swords, and heare a Drum, | then looke vpon his Schoolmaster.	418

RATHER *cont*.
Rather then they shall pound vs vp our Gates,   506
The blood I drop, is rather Physicall   591
Cor. Know, good Mother, | I had rather be their seruant in my way,   1117
Oh he would misse it, rather then carry it,   1162
Rather our states defectiue for requitall,   1258
Brutus. Which the rather wee shall be blest to doe, if   1266
Menen. That's off, that's off: I would you rather had   1269
Coriol. Your Honors pardon: | I had rather haue my Wounds to heale
againe,   1279
Corio. I had rather haue one scratch my Head i'th' Sun,   1288
He had rather venture all his Limbes for Honor,   1294
*the wisedome of their choice, is rather to haue my Hat,   1489
For Truth to o're-peere. Rather then foole it so,   1512
*Your Minds pre-occupy'd with what you rather must do,   1635
False to my Nature? Rather say, I play | The man I am.   2100
And you, will rather shew our generall Lowts,   2165
Volum. Prythee now, | Goe, and be rul'd: although I know thou hadst
rather   2192
Thy Mother rather feele thy Pride, then feare   2235
But as I say, such as become a Soldier, | Rather then enuy you.   2333
Blush, that the world goes well: who rather had,   2897
Ingrate forgetfulnesse shall poison rather   3321
Rather to shew a Noble grace to both parts,   3476
RATS = 2
Rome, and her Rats, are at the point of battell,   170
The Volces haue much Corne: take these Rats thither,   276
RAUISH = *1
Com. You haue holp to rauish your owne daughters, &   2996
RAUISHER = *1
*be a Rauisher, so it cannot be denied, but peace is a great | maker of
Cuckolds.   2885
RAUNGES = 1
And burie all, which yet distinctly raunges | In heapes, and piles of
Ruine.   1917
READ = 4
Brut. I, spare vs not: Say, we read Lectures to you,   1638
The booke of his good Acts, whence men haue read   3253
Deliuer them this Paper: hauing read it,   3651
Auf. Read it not Noble Lords,   3750
READIE = 2
His readie sence: then straight his doubled spirit   1330
Readie when time shall prompt them, to make roade | Vpon's againe.   1678
READINESSE = *1
Rom. I am ioyfull to heare of their readinesse, and am   2615
READY = 5*1
But make you ready your stiffe bats and clubs,   169
We neuer yet made doubt but Rome was ready | To answer vs.   333
Edile. I haue: 'tis ready.   2271
Sicin. Make them be strong, and ready for this hint   2287
their Aduersaries. Haue you an Army ready say you?   2611
*out the intended fire, your City is ready to flame in, with   3282
REALL = 1
Of generall Ignorance, it must omit | Reall Necessities, and giue way
the while   1845
REAPE = 2
Which thou shalt thereby reape, is such a name   3500

REAPE *cont.*
In mine owne person: holpe to reape the Fame   3689
REASON = 3*2
Then reason safely with you: Therefore be it knowne,   814
*Insult without all reason: where Gentry, Title, wisedom   1843
*3 Reason, because they then lesse neede one another: 2888
Within my Age. But reason with the fellow   2956
Doe's reason our Petition with more strength   3533
REASONS = 4
Corio. Ile giue my Reasons,   1816
My Rages and Reuenges, with your colder reasons.   3440
Then can our Reasons. There's no man in the world   3515
After your way. His Tale pronounc'd, shall bury | His Reasons, with his
Body.   3717
REBELLD = 1
Rebell'd against the Belly; thus accus'd it: 99
REBELLION = 3
Of this most wise Rebellion, thou goest formost: 166
The Cockle of Rebellion, Insolence, Sedition,   1760
To'th'greater Bench, in a Rebellion: 1867
REBUKE = 2
reproofe and rebuke from euery Eare that heard it.   1236
more pertinent then the rebuke you giue it.   1272
RECEITE = 1
That enuied his receite: euen so most fitly,   114
RECEIUD = 5
From whom I haue receiu'd not onely greetings, | But with them,
change of Honors.   1109
As if I had receiu'd them for the hyre | Of their breath onely.   1371
His Marks of Merit, Wounds receiu'd for's Countrey.   1562
That hath receiu'd an Almes. I will not doo't,   2228
This we receiu'd, and each in either side   3495
RECEIUE *see also* receyue = 4
That I receiue the generall Food at first   138
From me receiue that naturall competencie   146
From me do backe receiue the Flowre of all,   153
No publique benefit which you receiue   160
RECEIUED *see also* receiu'd, receyued = *1
*for his place: he receiued in the repulse of *Tarquin* seuen | hurts ith'
Body.   1045
RECEYUE = *1
*would make it flame againe. For the Nobles receyue so   2590
RECEYUED = *1
*1. You haue receyued many wounds for your Coun-|trey.   1497
RECKLESS *see* wreaklesse
RECOMFORTED = *1
*As the recomforted through th'gates. Why harke you: | *Trumpets,
Hoboyes, Drums beate, altogether.*   3620
RECOMMEND = 1
We recommend to you Tribunes of the People   1374
RECOMPENCE = 1
Was not our recompence, resting well assur'd   1818
RECONCILE = 1
Is that you reconcile them: While the Volces   3493
RECORD = 1
Mene. Cannot be? | We haue Record, that very well it can,   2953

RECREANT = 1
Must as a Forraine Recreant be led   3469
RECTORSHIP = 1
Against the Rectorship of Iudgement?   1608
RED = 2*1
All hurt behinde, backes red, and faces pale   532
*Vol. Now the Red Pestilence strike al Trades in Rome, | And
Occupations perish.   2450
Red as 'twould burne Rome: and his Iniury   3225
REDRESSE = 1
And temp'rately proceed to what you would | Thus violently redresse. 1934
REECHIE = 1
Her richest Lockram 'bout her reechie necke,   1127
REEKE = 1
As reeke a'th'rotten Fennes: whose Loues I prize,   2409
REEKING = 1
Runne reeking o're the liues of men, as if 'twere   1333
REELE = *1
*Menen. I will make my very house reele to night: 1008
REFUGE = 1
Nay godded me indeed. Their latest refuge   3358
REFUSALL = 1
With their refusall, both obserue and answer | The vantage of his anger. 1665
REFUSD = 1
I that now refus'd most Princely gifts,   838
REFUSE = 3
A Bribe, to pay my Sword: I doe refuse it,   791
Sicin. Nay, pray be patient: If you refuse your ayde   3187
The first Conditions which they did refuse,   3361
REGARD = 2
Let them regard me, as I doe not flatter,   1757
Com. I offered to awaken his regard   3176
REGARDED = 1
And mourne you for him. Let him be regarded   3823
REGIONS = 1
Before you finde it other. All the Regions   3021
REIND = 1
Be rein'd againe to Temperance, then he speakes   2293
REINES = *1
*Giue your dispositions the reines, and bee angry at your   927
REINFORCEMENT see re-inforcement
REIOURNE = *1
*and then reiourne the Controuersie of three-pence   967
REIOYCE = 1*1
*I should freelier reioyce in that absence wherein   364
Which this mans life did owe you, you'l reioyce   3817
RELEEUE = *1
*good: what Authority surfets one, would releeue   18
RELEEUED = *1
*were wholsome, wee might guesse they releeued vs hu- | manely: 20
RELISH see rallish
REMAIN = 1
Sicin. It is a minde that shall remain a poison   1779
REMAINE = 8
That onely like a Gulfe it did remaine   100
Let's fetch him off, or make remaine alike. | They fight, and all enter
the City.   567

REMAINE *cont.*
If he should still malignantly remaine	1584
Corio. Shall remaine?	1781
All. You so remaine. | *Mene.* And so are like to doe.	1913
And heere remaine with your vncertaintie.	2412
While I remaine aboue the ground, you shall	2492
3.*Con.* The People will remaine vncertaine, whil'st	3668

REMAINES = 3*1
And to send for *Titus Lartius*: it remaines,	1245
Menen. It then remaines, that you doe speake to the | People.	1353
Remaines, that in th'Officiall Markes inuested,	1533
Destroy'd his Country, and his name remaines	3504

REMAINS = *1
*Which thou should'st beare me, only that name remains.	2730

REMEDIES = 1
His remedies are tame, the present peace,	2894

REMEDY = 1
Sen. There's no remedy,	2116

REMEMBER = 4*2
Of the whole Body. But, if you do remember,	141
We met here, both to thanke, and to remember, | With Honors like himselfe.	1254
*he remember a kinder value of the People, then he hath | hereto priz'd them at.	1267
Men. Prythee fellow, remember my name is *Menenius*,	3266
Corio. I beseech you peace: | Or if you'ld aske, remember this before;	3433
Still to remember wrongs? Daughter, speake you:	3512

REMEMBERS = *1
Mene. So did he mee: and he no more remembers his	3585

REMEMBRANCES = 1
To your remembrances: but you haue found,	1651

REMEMBRED = 1
To heare themselues remembred.	780

REMISSION = 1
My Reuenge properly, my remission lies	3319

REMOTE = 1
Or rudely visit them in parts remote,	2801

REMOUE = 1
If they set downe before's: for the remoue	345

REND = 1
Before the Tagge returne? whose Rage doth rend	1973

RENDER = 1*1
We render you the Tenth, to be ta'ne forth,	786
*deuotion, then they can render it him; and leaues nothing	1222

RENEW = 1
And Ile renew me in his fall. But hearke.	3704

RENOWNE = *1
*Picture-like to hang by th'wall, if renowne made it not	372

RENOWNED = 3
Welcome to Rome, renowned *Coriolanus*. | *Sound. Flourish.*	1068
All. Welcome to Rome, renowned *Coriolanus*.	1070
That our renowned Rome, whose gratitude	2028

REPAIRE = 1
And presently, when you haue drawne your number, | Repaire toth' Capitoll.	1657

REPAYRE = 2
Cori. That Ile straight do: and knowing my selfe again, | Repayre
toth'Senate- |house.   1543
Bid them repayre to th'Market place, where I   3652
REPEALE = 3*1
*repeale daily any wholsome Act established against   83
A cause for thy Repeale, we shall not send   2481
Will be as rash in the repeale, as hasty   3123
Repeale him, with the welcome of his Mother: 3645
REPENT = 2
All. We will so: almost all repent in their election. | *Exeunt Plebeians.* 1659
Mene. Repent, what you haue spoke.   2131
REPETITION = 2
he hath faults (with surplus) to tyre in repetition. | *Showts within.*   46
Whose repetition will be dogg'd with Curses: 3501
REPIND = 1
When Corne was giuen them *gratis*, you repin'd,   1727
REPLYED = 2
As well as speake, it taintingly replyed   112
When it was lesse expected. He replyed   3172
REPORT = 10*5
*good report for't, but that hee payes himselfe with bee-|ing proud.   34
Volum. Then his good report should haue beene my   381
Halfe an houre since brought my report.   627
Lessen his person, then an ill report: 689
Thou't not beleeue thy deeds: but Ile report it,   749
Com. Too modest are you: | More cruell to your good report, then
gratefull   809
*better report then a Horse-drench. Is he not wounded?   1015
*their estimation, and report: but hee hath so planted his   1231
*were a kinde of ingratefull Iniurie: to report otherwise,   1234
In our well-found Successes, to report   1251
*a Cudgell, and yet my minde gaue me, his cloathes made | a false
report of him.   2811
Go whip him fore the peoples eyes: His raising, | Nothing but his
report.   2968
Mes. Yes worthy Sir, | The Slaues report is seconded, and more   2970
You must report to th'Volcian Lords, how plainly   3349
Sicin. Yes, mercy, if you report him truly.   3594
REPORTS = 1
Reports the Volces with two seuerall Powers   2941
REPOSE = 1
Where ere we doe repose vs, we will write   831
REPREEUE = *1
*condemn'd, our Generall has sworne you out of repreeue | and pardon.   3285
REPROOFE = 1
reproofe and rebuke from euery Eare that heard it.   1236
REPULSE = *1
*for his place: he receiued in the repulse of *Tarquin* seuen | hurts ith'
Body.   1045
REQUEST = 10*1
And Wrath o're-whelm'd my pittie: I request you   845
We doe request your kindest eares: and after   1260
Scicin. The Custome of Request you haue discharg'd: 1536
What's like to be their words, We did request it,   1830
Ile trie whether my old Wit be in request   1977
With Honour, as in Warre; since that to both | It stands in like request.   2147

REQUEST *cont*.

*Opposer *Coriolanus* being now in no request of his coun- |trey.	2604
Till he be dieted to my request,	3215
That if you faile in our request, the blame	3445
Heare nought from Rome in priuate. Your request?	3448
If it were so, that our request did tend	3489

REQUESTED = 1

As if he did contemne what he requested, | Should be in them to giue.	1382

REQUESTS = 1*1

*He's to make his requests by particulars, wherein euerie	1431
Loden with Honor. Say my Request's vniust,	3521

REQUICKNED = 1

Requickned what in flesh was fatigate,	1331

REQUIRD = 1

My Fortunes and my Friends at stake, requir'd	2162

REQUIRE = *2

*Scicin. May they perceiue's intent: he wil require them	1381
*1.Cit. Once if he do require our voyces, wee ought | not to deny him.	1388

REQUIRES = 1

Requires nor Childe, nor womans face to see: | I haue sate too long.	3486

REQUIT = 1

Th'hoorded plague a'th'Gods requit your loue.	2518

REQUITALL = 1

Rather our states defectiue for requitall,	1258

REQUITTED = 1

Shed for my thanklesse Country, are requitted:	2727

RESCUE = 1

Sicin. Sir, how com'st that you haue holpe | To make this rescue?	2008

RESERUATION = 1

Making but reseruation of your selues,	2418

RESISTED = 2

With rigorous hands: he hath resisted Law,	1998
Our Ediles smot: our selues resisted: come.	2061

RESISTS = 1

Do smilingly Reuolt, and who resists | Are mock'd for valiant Ignorance,	3022

RESOLUD = 2*2

*1.Cit. You are all resolu'd rather to dy then | to famish?	7
All. Resolu'd, resolu'd.	9
3 Cit. Are you all resolu'd to giue your voyces? But	1422

RESOLUTION = 1

Breaking his Oath and Resolution, like	3763

RESPECT = 2*1

Mene. On both sides more respect.	1887
My Countries good, with a respect more tender, .	2398
*and he returning to breake our necks, they respect not vs.	3602

RESPECTED = 2*1

Being once gangren'd, is not then respected | For what before it was.	2046
Auf. Onely their ends you haue respected,	3351
*vnto vs. When we banish'd him, we respected not them:	3601

REST = 5*1

1 Cit. He's one honest enough, wold al the rest wer so.	55
Like labour with the rest, where th'other Instruments	103
The rest shall beare the businesse in some other fight	703
Those Centuries to our ayd, the rest will serue	716
Where thou shalt rest, that thou may'st heare of vs,	2479
Haue all forsooke me, hath deuour'd the rest:	2733

RESTING = 1
Was not our recompence, resting well assur'd   1818
RESTITUTION = 1
To hopelesse restitution, so he might | Be call'd your Vanquisher.   1693
RESTRAIND = 1
2.Cit. Should by the Cormorant belly be restrain'd,   125
RESTRAINE = *1
*chaine vp and restraine the poore. If the Warres eate vs   85
RESTRAINST = 1
That thou restrain'st from me the Duty, which   3524
RESUME = 1
Resume that Spirit, when you were wont to say,   2454
RETIRE see also retyre = 2
Virg. Beseech you giue me leaue to retire my selfe.   389
Enter Cominius as it were in retire, with soldiers.   603
RETIRED see retyred
RETIRES = 1
He that retires, Ile take him for a *Volce*,   521
RETREAT = 1
Flourish. Alarum. A Retreat is sounded. Enter at | one Doore Cominius,
with the Romanes: At   744
RETURND = 2*1
*whence he return'd, his browes bound with Oake. I tell   375
As *Cominius* is return'd, vnheard: what then?   3199
Corio. Haile Lords, I am return'd your Souldier: 3736
RETURNE = 6*2
threshold, till my Lord returne from the Warres.   439
*returne for Conscience sake, to helpe to get thee a Wife.   1419
Before the Tagge returne? whose Rage doth rend   1973
too rough: you must returne, and mend it.   2115
Corio. What must I do? | *Mene.* Returne to th'Tribunes.   2128
Commend me to my Wife, Ile returne Consull,   2245
Mene. Well, and say that *Martius* returne mee,   3198
*I You may not passe, you must returne: our Generall | will no more
heare from thence.   3241
RETURNES = 1
And had no welcomes home, but he returnes | Splitting the Ayre with
noyse.   3708
RETURNING = *1
*and he returning to breake our necks, they respect not vs.   3602
RETYRE = 2
Nor Cowardly in retyre: Beleeue me Sirs,   606
And did retyre to win our purpose.   664
RETYRED = 1
Yeelded the Towne: he is retyred to Antium.   1686
REUELL = 1
Conies after Raine) and reuell all with him.   2871
REUENGE = 6*1
*gaine to them. Let vs reuenge this with our Pikes, ere   24
hunger for Bread, not in thirst for Reuenge.   26
Wherein thou seest me maskt, for thy Reuenge   735
A heart of wreake in thee, that wilt reuenge   2742
And vowes Reuenge as spacious, as betweene | The yong'st and oldest
thing.   2977
My Reuenge properly, my remission lies   3319
Long as my Exile, sweet as my Reuenge!   3394

REUENGEFULL = 1
    That my reuengefull Seruices may proue   2746
REUENGES = 2*1
    The leading of thine owne Reuenges, take   2796
    *enemy your shield, thinke to front his reuenges with the   3278
    My Rages and Reuenges, with your colder reasons.   3440
REUEREND = 1*1
    *that say you are reuerend graue men, yet they lye deadly,   956
    Most reuerend and graue Elders, to desire   1249
REUOKE = 2
    All reuoke your ignorant election: Enforce his Pride,   1622
    That hee's your fixed enemie; and reuoke | Your suddaine approbation. 1653
REUOLT = 2
    vpon my partie, I'de reuolt to make   255
    Do smilingly Reuolt, and who resists | Are mock'd for valiant
    Ignorance,   3022
REUOLTS = 1
    There Mutinies and Reuolts, wherein they shew'd   1823
REWARD = 1
    In signe of what you are, not to reward   777
REWARDS = 1
    Then Miserie it selfe would giue, rewards his deeds   1343
RE-INFORCEMENT = 1
    And with a sudden re-inforcement strucke   1327
RHEWME = 1
    At a few drops of Womens rhewme, which are   3701
RICH = 1*1
    *the rich, and prouide more piercing Statutes daily, to   84
    Weare not so rich a Iewell. Thou was't a Souldier   558
RICHEST = 1
    Her richest Lockram 'bout her reechie necke,   1127
RICHMEN = 1
    Corne for the Richmen onely: With these shreds   221
RIDGES = 1
    Leades fill'd, and Ridges hors'd   1130
RIDICULOUS = *1
    *shall encounter such ridiculous Subiects as you are, when   980
RIGHT = 6*2
    *Tit. Lead you on: Follow Cominius, we must followe | you, right
    worthy your Priority.   271
    *you are censured heere in the City, I mean of vs a'th'right | hand File,
    do you?   919
    Com. Euer right. | Cor. Menenius, euer, euer.   1103
    Scicin. 'Tis right. | Brutus. It was his word: 1160
    Menen. Hee's right Noble, let him be call'd for.   1346
    *Men. Oh Sir, you are not right: haue you not knowne   1436
    3.Cit. Certainely, he flowted vs downe-right.   1558
    I'th'right and strength a'th'Commons: be it either   2276
RIGHTLY = *1
    *Their Counsailes, and their Cares; disgest things rightly,   158
RIGHTS = *2
    *Rights by rights fouler, strengths by strengths do faile.   3146
RIGOROUS = 1
    With rigorous hands: he hath resisted Law,   1998
RIPE = *2
    *they are in a ripe aptnesse, to take al power from the peo- | ple,   2592
    *of his face, sowres ripe Grapes. When he walks, he moues   3587

RIPEST = 1
Now humble as the ripest Mulberry,   2180
RISE = 2
What's done i'th Capitoll: Who's like to rise,   204
'Twas very faintly he said Rise: dismist me   3227
RISEN = *1
*What showts are these? The other side a'th City is risen: 48
RISES = 1
Coriolanus rises, and offers to goe away. | Nay, keepe your place.   1275
RISING = 2
cheape as Volcians. They are rising, they are rising. | *Both.* In, in, in, in.
Exeunt   2890
RIUE = 1
That should but riue an Oake. Why do'st not speake?   3510
RIUERS = 1
I send it through the Riuers of your blood   142
ROADE = 1
Readie when time shall prompt them, to make roade | Vpon's againe.   1678
ROARD = 2
Some certaine of your Brethren roar'd, and ranne   1442
He whin'd and roar'd away your Victory,   3766
ROARE = 1
Com. But I feare | They'l roare him in againe. *Tullus Affidius,*   3047
ROARING = *1
*in roaring for a Chamber-pot, dismisse the Controuersie   972
ROATED = 1
That are but roated in your Tongue;   2154
ROB = 1*1
Opinion that so stickes on *Martius*, shall | Of his demerits rob *Cominius*.   302
*of Occasion, will rob you of a great deale of Patience: 926
ROBBERY = 1
Ile grace thee with that Robbery, thy stolne name | *Coriolanus* in
Corioles?   3757
ROCK = 2*2
Beare him toth' Rock Tarpeian, and from thence | Into destruction cast
him.   1926
And beare him to the Rock. *Corio. drawes his Sword.*   1939
Sicin. He shall be throwne downe the Tarpeian rock   1997
*2 The worthy Fellow is our General. He's the Rock,   3344
ROCKE = 4
Or pile ten hilles on the Tarpeian Rocke,   2086
All. To'th'Rocke, to'th'Rocke with him.   2356
In perill of precipitation | From off the Rocke Tarpeian, neuer more   2387
ROD = *1
*bin a Rod to her Friends, you haue not indeede loued the | Common
people.   1483
RODE = 1
Bru. You know the very rode into his kindnesse, | And cannot lose your
way.   3217
ROGUES = *1
Mar. Thanks. What's the matter you dissentious rogues   174
ROM = 3*7
ROMAINES = 1
Then shame to th'Romaines. And we heere deliuer   3746
ROMAN see also Rom., 1.Rom., 2.Rom., 3.Rom. = 10*2
Against the Roman State, whose course will on   70
And *Titus Lartius*, a most valiant Roman,   328

ROMAN cont.

The Charges of our Friends. The Roman Gods,	609
*Our Guider come, to th'Roman Campe conduct vs. *Exit*	721
I would I were a Roman, for I cannot,	862
An o're-prest Roman, and i'th' Consuls view	1307
Enter a Roman, and a Volce.	2570
Rom. I am a Roman, and my Seruices are as you are, | against 'em. Know you me yet.	2574
3 I would not be a Roman of all Nations; I had as | liue be a condemn'd man.	2835
Are entred in the Roman Territories,	2942
Auf. Do they still flye to'th'Roman?	3091
1 You are a Roman, are you?	3273

ROMANE = 1*1

*Cominius the Generall is gone, with one part of our Ro-|mane	461
The Romane Ladies bring not comfort home	3607

ROMANES = 7*1

Enter certaine Romanes with spoiles.	569
Piercing our Romanes: Then Valiant *Titus* take	582
Flourish. Alarum. A Retreat is sounded. Enter at | one Doore Cominius, with the Romanes: At	744
And sacke great Rome with Romanes.	2057
*The Warres for my money. I hope to see Romanes as	2889
For that forgiue our Romanes. O a kisse	3393
To saue the Romanes, thereby to destroy	3490
May say, this mercy we haue shew'd: the Romanes,	3494

ROMANS = 4

Alarum, the Romans are beat back to their Trenches | Enter Martius Cursing.	523
Like Romans, neither foolish in our stands,	605
Though in Rome litter'd: not Romans, as they are not,	1963
Tabors, and Symboles, and the showting Romans,	3623

ROME = 76*13

Men. The Senators of Rome, are this good Belly,	156
Rome, and her Rats, are at the point of battell,	170
1.*Sen.* So, your opinion is *Auffidius*, | That they of Rome are entred in our Counsailes,	314
That could be brought to bodily act, ere Rome	319
Cominius, Martius your old Enemy | (Who is of Rome worse hated then of you)	326
We neuer yet made doubt but Rome was ready | To answer vs.	333
It seem'd appear'd to Rome. By the discouery,	338
To take in many Townes, ere (almost) Rome | Should know we were a-foot.	340
Though you were borne in Rome; his bloody brow	396
*You Shames of Rome: you Heard of Byles and Plagues	526
1.*Rom.* This will I carry to *Rome*. | 2.*Rom.* And I this.	570
Holding *Corioles* in the name of Rome,	648
Our Rome hath such a Souldier.	756
Rome must know the value of her owne:	771
To Rome of our successe: you *Titus Lartius*	832
Must to *Corioles* backe, send vs to Rome	833
Learne how 'tis held, and what they are that must | Be Hostages for Rome.	887
*proud, violent, testie Magistrates (alias Fooles) | as any in Rome.	940
Herauld. Know Rome, that all alone *Martius* did fight	1064
Welcome to Rome, renowned *Coriolanus*. | *Sound. Flourish.*	1068

ROME *cont.*

All. Welcome to Rome, renowned *Coriolanus*.	1070
You are three, that Rome should dote on:	1096
Which (I doubt not) but our Rome | Will cast vpon thee.	1115
When *Tarquin* made a Head for Rome, he fought	1302
Becomes not Rome: nor ha's *Coriolanus*	1747
Though in Rome litter'd: not Romans, as they are not,	1963
That our renowned Rome, whose gratitude	2028
What ha's he done to Rome, that's worthy death?	2035
And sacke great Rome with Romanes.	2057
Of all the Trades in Rome. Looke, I am going:	2244
Th'honor'd Goddes | Keepe Rome in safety, and the Chaires of Iustice	2302
From Rome all season'd Office, and to winde	2343
Bru. But since he hath seru'd well for Rome.	2365
To enter our Rome gates. I'th'Peoples name, | I say it shall bee so.	2389
Com. Let me speake: | I haue bene Consull, and can shew from Rome	2395
Enter Coriolanus, Volumnia, Virgilia, Menenius, Cominius, | with the yong Nobility of Rome.	2435
Vol. Now the Red Pestilence strike al Trades in Rome, | And Occupations perish.	2450
To banish him that strooke more blowes for Rome | Then thou hast spoken words.	2527
Volum. Bastards, and all. | Good man, the Wounds that he does beare for Rome!	2537
The meanest house in Rome; so farre my Sonne	2552
*the Newes in Rome: I haue a Note from the Volcean	2580
Rom. There hath beene in Rome straunge Insurrecti- |ons:	2583
*strange things from Rome: all tending to the good of	2610
Hoop'd out of Rome. Now this extremity,	2735
Had we no other quarrell else to Rome, but that	2785
Into the bowels of vngratefull Rome,	2788
Who am prepar'd against your Territories, | Though not for Rome it selfe.	2792
Whether to knocke against the Gates of Rome,	2800
*sayes, and sole the Porter of Rome Gates by th'eares. He	2860
Bru. The Gods haue well preuented it, and Rome | Sits safe and still, without him.	2936
Which were In-shell'd, when *Martius* stood for Rome,	2948
Ioyn'd with *Auffidius*, leads a power 'gainst Rome,	2976
Com. Hee'l shake your Rome about your eares.	3016
Should say be good to Rome, they charg'd him, euen	3032
Com. You haue brought | A Trembling vpon Rome, such as was neuer	3039
That Rome can make against them.	3052
Lieu. Sir, I beseech you, think you he'l carry Rome?	3118
And the Nobility of Rome are his:	3120
To expell him thence. I thinke hee'l be to Rome	3124
Come let's away: when *Caius* Rome is thine,	3147
Till he had forg'd himselfe a name a'th'fire | Of burning Rome.	3166
A paire of Tribunes, that haue wrack'd for Rome,	3169
Bru. Onely make triall what your Loue can do, | For Rome, towards *Martius*.	3196
Sicin. Yet your good will | Must haue that thankes from Rome, after the measure | As you intended well.	3202
Red as 'twould burne Rome: and his Iniury	3225
1 From whence? *Mene.* From Rome.	3240
2 You'l see your Rome embrac'd with fire, before | You'l speake with *Coriolanus*.	3243

ROME *cont.*
 Mene. Good my Friends, | If you haue heard your Generall talke of
 Rome,   3245
 *1 Then you should hate Rome, as he do's. Can you,   3275
 *backe to Rome, and prepare for your execution: you are   3284
 *Rome, and thy petitionary Countrimen. The good   3311
 Was my belou'd in Rome: yet thou behold'st.   3328
 Corio. We will before the walls of Rome to morrow   3347
 Stopt your eares against the generall suite of Rome: 3352
 Corio. This last old man, | Whom with a crack'd heart I haue sent to
 Rome,   3355
 Plough Rome, and harrow Italy, Ile neuer   3383
 Corio. These eyes are not the same I wore in Rome.   3387
 Corio. The Noble Sister of *Publicola*; | The Moone of Rome: Chaste as
 the Isicle   3416
 Heare nought from Rome in priuate. Your request?   3448
 That if thou conquer Rome, the benefit   3499
 This is the last. So, we will home to Rome,   3529
 You haue wonne a happy Victory to Rome.   3544
 Ile not to Rome, Ile backe with you, and pray you   3557
 *little finger, there is some hope the Ladies·of Rome, espe- |cially 3574
 A merrier day did neuer yet greet Rome,   3613
 Sena. Behold our Patronnesse, the life of Rome: 3641
 When he had carried Rome, and that we look'd | For no lesse Spoile,
 then Glory.   3697
 *The gates of Rome: Our spoiles we haue brought home   3742
 For certaine drops of Salt, your City Rome: 3761
ROMES = 2
 And for Romes good, Ile tell thee what: yet goe: 2531
 Againe, with Romes Mechanickes. Tell me not   3438
ROOFE = 1
 To bring the Roofe to the Foundation,   1916
ROOT = 1
 A Curse begin at very root on's heart,   1094
ROOTE = 1
 A roote of Ancient Enuy. If Iupiter   2761
ROTTEN = 4*1
 Their rotten Priuiledge, and Custome 'gainst   882
 *parts melted away with rotten Dewes, the fourth would   1418
 Corio. Hence rotten thing, or I shall shake thy bones | Out of thy
 Garments.   1883
 As reeke a'th'rotten Fennes: whose Loues I prize,   2409
 A twist of rotten Silke, neuer admitting   3764
ROUE = 1
 Of the warres surfets, to go roue with one   2487
ROUGH = 2*1
 Men. Come, come, you haue bin too rough, somthing   2114
 too rough: you must returne, and mend it.   2115
 But to be rough, vnswayable, and free.   3678
ROUGHER = 1
 His rougher Actions for malicious sounds: 2332
ROYALL = 1*1
 Vol. A most Royall one: The Centurions, and their   2612
 Com. I minded him, how Royall 'twas to pardon   3171
RUB = 1
 Deseru'd this so dishonor'd Rub, layd falsely | I'th' plaine Way of his
 Merit.   1748

RUBBING = 1
That rubbing the poore Itch of your Opinion, | Make your selues Scabs.   175
RUDELY = 1
Or rudely visit them in parts remote,   2801
RUIN = *1
*I say they norisht disobedience: fed, the ruin of the State.   1813
RUINE = 4
And burie all, which yet distinctly raunges | In heapes, and piles of
Ruine.   1917
Of what that want might ruine.   2168
Then thou of them. Come all to ruine, let   2234
Triumphantly treade on thy Countries ruine,   3471
RULD = 1
Volum. Prethee now, | Goe, and be rul'd: although I know thou hadst
rather   2192
RULE = 1*1
*You being their Mouthes, why rule you not their Teeth?   1718
Suffer't, and liue with such as cannot rule, | Nor euer will be ruled.   1723
RULED = 1
Suffer't, and liue with such as cannot rule, | Nor euer will be ruled.   1723
RUMOR = 1
Let euery feeble Rumor shake your hearts: 2413
RUMORER = 1
Bru. Go see this Rumorer whipt, it cannot be,   2951
RUMOURD = 1
The people Mutinous: And it is rumour'd,   325
RUN = 3*1
Thou Rascall, that art worst in blood to run,   167
*I saw him run after a gilded Butterfly, & when   423
That beare the shapes of men, how haue you run   530
Boy. A shall not tread on me: Ile run away | Till I am bigger, but then
Ile fight.   3483
RUNNE = 1
Runne reeking o're the liues of men, as if 'twere   1333
RUSHES = 1*1
*And hewes downe Oakes, with rushes. Hang ye: trust ye?   192
Which yet seeme shut, we haue but pin'd with Rushes,   507
RUST = *1
*This peace is nothing, but to rust Iron, encrease Taylors, | and breed
Ballad-makers.   2877
RUTH = 1
Would the Nobility lay aside their ruth,   209
S = 1
S'incapeable of helpe. | *Tri.* Say not, we brought it.   3041
SACKE = 1
And sacke great Rome with Romanes.   2057
SACK-BUTS = 1
The Trumpets, Sack-buts, Psalteries, and Fifes,   3622
SACRIFICE = 2
May giue you thankfull Sacrifice. Thy Newes?   612
The Prayers of Priests, nor times of Sacrifice: 880
SAD = 1
Heart-hardning spectacles. Tell these sad women,   2463
SADDLE = *1
*be intomb'd in an Asses Packe-saddle; yet you must bee   984
SAFE = 2
All. The Gods assist you. | *Auf.* And keepe your Honors safe.   355

270

SAFE *cont.*
  Bru. The Gods haue well preuented it, and Rome | Sits safe and still,
without him.   2936
SAFEGARD = 2
  Corio. Saw you *Auffidius?* | *Latius.* On safegard he came to me, and did
curse   1683
  For the inheritance of their loues, and safegard   2167
SAFELIE = 1
  Ha's clock'd thee to the Warres: and safelie home   3520
SAFELY = 1
  Then reason safely with you: Therefore be it knowne,   814
SAFER = 1
  Scici. Let them assemble: and on a safer Iudgement,   1621
SAFETY = 1
  Th'honor'd Goddes | Keepe Rome in safety, and the Chaires of Iustice   2302
SAID = 14*3
  They said they were an hungry, sigh'd forth Prouerbes   218
  *Tiber in't: Said, to be something imperfect in fauou- | ring   945
  3.*Cit.* Hee said hee had Wounds,   1565
  Be Curses to your selues. You should haue said,   1586
  Scicin. Thus to haue said, | As you were fore-aduis'd, had toucht his
Spirit,   1592
  Bru. Has said enough.   1861
  Mene. Well said, Noble woman: 2123
  Volum. I prythee now sweet Son, as thou hast said   2214
  Bru. There's no more to be said, but he is banish'd   2404
  1 *Cit.* For mine owne part, | When I said banish him, I said 'twas pitty.   3066
  *home, I euer said we were i'th wrong, when we banish'd | him.   3082
  Menen. No, ile not go: you heare what he hath said   3152
  Of noysome musty Chaffe. He said, 'twas folly   3179
  'Twas very faintly he said Rise: dismist me   3227
  *with your age. I say to you, as I was said to, Away. *Exit*   3342
  Volum. Oh no more, no more: | You haue said you will not grant vs any
thing: 3441
SAIDE = 1*2
  Let what is meet, be saide it must be meet,   1870
  *it saide, the fittest time to corrupt a mans Wife, is when   2601
  *2 'Tis so, and as warres in some sort may be saide to   2884
SAIL *see* sayle
SAKE = 2*1
  For my Wounds sake, to giue their sufferage: 1358
  *returne for Conscience sake, to helpe to get thee a Wife.   1419
  Take this along, I writ it for thy sake,   3325
SALT = 1
  For certaine drops of Salt, your City Rome: 3761
SALTER = 1
  Thy teares are salter then a yonger mans,   2460
SALUE = 1
  Menen. Noble Lady, | Come goe with vs, speake faire: you may salue
so,   2169
SAME = 6*2
  Mar. May these same Instruments, which you prophane,   797
  Of the same House *Publius* and *Quintus* were,   1644
  The same you are not, which for your best ends   2144
  Volce. Nicanor: no. | *Rom.* The same sir.   2576
  Euen with the same austerity and garbe,   3135
  In the same time 'tis made? I will not.   3368

SAME *cont.*

Corio. These eyes are not the same I wore in Rome.	3387
2.Con. Most Noble Sir, If you do hold the same intent	3663

SANCTIFIES = *1

*of him, Sanctifies himselfe with's hand, and turnes vp the	2855

SANCTUARY = 1

Shall flye out of it selfe, nor sleepe, nor sanctuary,	878

SATE = 2

Within thine eyes sate twenty thousand deaths	2350
Requires nor Childe, nor womans face to see: | I haue sate too long.	3486

SAUD = 1

Six of his Labours youl'd haue done, and sau'd	2456

SAUE = 7*1

Volum. Why I pray you. | *Vulg.* 'Tis not to saue labour, nor that I want loue.	444
*hee wounded, God saue your good Worships? *Martius*	1040
All. Amen, Amen. God saue thee, Noble Consull.	1528
2.Cit. Not one amongst vs, saue your selfe, but sayes	1560
In puny Battell slay me. Saue you sir.	2628
(Mistake me not) to saue my life: for if	2737
To saue the Romanes, thereby to destroy	3490
Mes. Sir, if you'ld saue your life, flye to your House,	3604

SAUED = *1

*state to finde you out there. You haue well saued mee a | dayes iourney.	2581

SAUING = 1

Like a great Sea-marke standing euery flaw, | And sauing those that eye thee.	3427

SAW = 7*2

*I saw him run after a gilded Butterfly, & when	423
I saw our party to their Trenches driuen,	616
He cry'd to me: I saw him Prisoner:	843
I neuer saw the like.	1198
Whom with all prayse I point at, saw him fight,	1304
All. No, no: no man saw 'em.	1564
Corio. Saw you *Auffidius*? | *Latius.* On safegard he came to me, and did curse	1683
Volce. You had more Beard when I last saw you, but	2578
Then when I first my wedded Mistris saw	2775

SAWCST = 1

As if I lou'd my little should be dieted | In prayses, sawc'st with Lyes.	807

SAWT = 1

Virgil. Yes certaine, there's a Letter for you, I saw't.	1010

SAY *see also* say't = 47*25

1.Cit. I say vnto you, what he hath done Famouslie,	37
*content to say it was for his Countrey, he did it to please	39
*a Vice in him: You must in no way say he is co-|uetous.	43
*now wee'l shew em in deeds: they say poore Suters haue	61
And leaue me but the Bran. What say you too't?	154
Men. For Corne at their owne rates, wherof they say	200
Mar. Hang 'em: They say?	202
*Below their cobled Shooes. They say ther's grain enough?	208
Val. You would be another *Penelope*: yet they say, all	446
Mar. Say, ha's our Generall met the Enemy?	487
Shall say against their hearts, We thanke the Gods	755
No more I say, for that I haue not wash'd	803
*aduersly, I make a crooked face at it, I can say, your	952

SAY *cont.*

*that say you are reuerend graue men, yet they lye deadly,	956
Scicin. This (as you say) suggested,	1181
2.Off..Three, they say: but 'tis thought of euery one,	1207
Then heare say how I got them.	1281
Before, and in Corioles, let me say	1316
*that's no matter, the greater part carries it, I say. If hee	1423
Corio. What must I say, I pray Sir?	1438
*shew you, which shall bee yours in priuate: your good | voice sir, what say you?	1468
Scici. Say you chose him, more after our commandment,	1633
Brut. I, spare vs not: Say, we read Lectures to you,	1638
Brut. Say you ne're had don't,	1655
And therein behold themselues: I say againe,	1758
To say, hee'l turne your Current in a ditch,	1790
*I say they norisht disobedience: fed, the ruin of the State.	1813
False to my Nature? Rather say, I play | The man I am.	2100
But when extremities speake. I haue heard you say,	2136
That will not hold the handling: or say to them,	2181
Volum. He must, and will: | Prythee now say you will, and goe about it.	2203
And when they heare me say, it shall be so,	2275
If I say Fine, cry Fine; if Death, cry Death,	2278
Edile. List to your Tribunes. Audience: | Peace I say.	2311
Corio. First heare me speake. | *Both Tri.* Well, say: Peace hoe.	2313
But as I say, such as become a Soldier, | Rather then enuy you.	2333
Sicin. Answer to vs. | *Corio.* Say then: 'tis true, I ought so	2340
Thy lying tongue, both numbers. I would say	2352
To enter our Rome gates. I'th'Peoples name, | I say it shall bee so.	2389
To say, Extreamities was the trier of spirits,	2440
Resume that Spirit, when you were wont to say,	2454
Sicin. Bid them home: say their great enemy is gone,	2509
Brut. Why? | *Sicin.* They say she's mad.	2514
Virg. You shall stay too: I would I had the power | To say so to my Husband.	2522
their Aduersaries. Haue you an Army ready say you?	2611
Auf. Say, what's thy name?	2716
And say 'tis true; I'de not beleeue them more	2763
Say yea to thy desires. A thousand welcomes,	2804
*2 Faith looke you, one cannot tell how to say that: for	2829
1 Why do you say, thwacke our Generall?	2840
*3 I do not say thwacke our Generall, but he was al-|wayes good enough for him	2841
hard for him, I haue heard him say so himselfe.	2844
*1 He was too hard for him directly, to say the Troth	2845
*1 Let me haue Warre say I, it exceeds peace as farre	2879
Should say be good to Rome, they charg'd him, euen	3032
To say, beseech you cease. You haue made faire hands,	3037
S'incapeable of helpe. | *Tri.* Say not, we brought it.	3041
2 And so did I. | *3 And so did I: and to say the truth, so did very ma-|ny	3068
Menen. Very well, could he say lesse.	3175
Mene. Well, and say that *Martius* returne mee,	3198
*2 Howsoeuer you haue bin his Lier, as you say you	3268
*haue, I am one that telling true vnder him, must say you | cannot passe. Therefore go backe.	3269
*1 My Generall cares not for you. Back I say, go: least	3291
Mene. Now you Companion: Ile say an arrant for you:	3297

SAY *cont.*

*with your age. I say to you, as I was said to, Away. *Exit*	3342
Forgiue my Tyranny: but do not say,	3392
May say, this mercy we haue shew'd: the Romanes,	3494
Loden with Honor. Say my Request's vniust,	3521
*his Mother, may preuaile with him. But I say, there	3575
With what he would say, let him feele your Sword:	3715
Auf. Say no more. Heere come the Lords,	3719
I say your City to his Wife and Mother,	3762

SAYES = 5*1

(You my good Friends, this sayes the Belly) marke me.	148
What sayes the other Troope?	216
2.*Cit.* Not one amongst vs, saue your selfe, but sayes	1560
I would be Consull, sayes he: aged Custome,	1568
Mene. Lo Citizens, he sayes he is Content.	2323
*sayes, and sole the Porter of Rome Gates by th'eares. He	2860

SAYING = 1*1

*saying, *Martius* is proud: who in a cheape estimation, is	985
To haue't with saying, Good morrow.	2377

SAYLE = 1

A Vessell vnder sayle, so men obey'd,	1320

SAYT = 1

But as a discontented Friend, greefe-shot │ With his vnkindnesse. Say't	
be so?	3200

SCABS = 1

That rubbing the poore Itch of your Opinion, │ Make your selues Scabs.	175

SCALET = 1

But since it serues my purpose, I will venture │ To scale't a little more.	92

SCALING *see* skaling

SCANDALD = 1

Scandal'd the Suppliants: for the People, call'd them	1728

SCAPE = 1

Thou should'st not scape me heere.	739

SCARFE = 1

another Doore Martius, with his │ Arme in a Scarfe.	746

SCARFFES = 1

Ladies and Maids their Scarffes, and Handkerchers,	1194

SCARRD = 1

And scarr'd the Moone with splinters: heere I cleep	2767

SCARRES *see also* skarres = 1

Corio. Scratches with Briars, scarres to moue │ Laughter onely.	2327

SCARSE = *1

*for such things as you. I can scarse thinke ther's any, y'are	3338

SCARSELY = 1

Which I can scarsely beare.	2127

SCATTERD = *1

*Which we our selues haue plowed for, sow'd, & scatter'd,	1761

SCENE *see also* scoena = 2

When he might act the Woman in the Scene,	1310
The Gods looke downe, and this vnnaturall Scene	3542

SCENTED *see* sented

SCHOOLD = 1

Since a could draw a Sword, and is ill-school'd	2063

SCHOOLE-BOYES = 1

Tent in my cheekes, and Schoole-boyes Teares take vp	2224

SCHOOLMASTER = 1
Vol. He had rather see the swords, and heare a Drum, | then looke
vpon his Schoolmaster.   418
SCIC = 1
Bru. and Scic. Aside.   992
SCICI = 7*2
SCICIN = 19*4
SCICINIUS = 4
Enter Brutus and Sicinius.   1122
the People, Lictors before them: Coriolanus, Mene-|nius, Cominius the
Consul: Scicinius and Brutus   1240
Enter Menenius, with Brutus and Scicinius.   1530
Enter Scicinius and Brutus.   1699
SCOENA *l.*1 = 1
SCOLD *see* scoul'd
SCONCE = 1
Corio. Must I goe shew them my vnbarb'd Sconce?   2205
SCORND = 1
How in his Suit he scorn'd you: but your Loues,   1625
SCORNE = 2
And with his Hat, thus wauing it in scorne,   1567
And therefore Law shall scorne him further Triall   1999
SCORNEFULLY = 1
He vs'd vs scornefully: he should haue shew'd vs   1561
SCOTCHT = *1
*on't before *Corioles*, he scotcht him, and notcht him like a |
Carbinado.   2846
SCOULD = *1
*I was forc'd to scoul'd. Your iudgments my graue Lords   3776
SCOURGE = *1
*1. You haue bin a scourge to her enemies, you haue   1482
SCOUT = 1
Enters with a Lieutenant, other Souldiours, and a | Scout.   712
SCRATCH = *1
Corio. I had rather haue one scratch my Head i'th' Sun,   1288
SCRATCHES = 1
Corio. Scratches with Briars, scarres to moue | Laughter onely. 2327
SCULL = *1
*I thinke, if all our wittes were to issue out of one Scull,   1407
SDEATH = 1
Sicinius Velutus, and I know not. Sdeath,   231
SEA = 3
Man-entred thus, he waxed like a Sea,   1313
That when the Sea was calme, all Boats alike   2442
A Sea and Land full: you haue pray'd well to day: 3629
SEALD = 1
On like conditions, will haue Counter-seal'd.   3565
SEALE = 2*1
Coriol. I wil not Seale your knowledge with shewing   1499
Seale what I end withall. This double worship,   1841
Together with the Seale a'th Senat, what | We haue compounded on. 3748
SEASOND = 1
From Rome all season'd Office, and to winde   2343
SEATE = 1
Euen to the Court, the Heart, to th'seate o'th'Braine,   143
SEATS = 1
The Nature of our Seats, and make the Rabble   1833

SEA-MARKE = 1
    Like a great Sea-marke standing euery flaw, | And sauing those that eye
    thee.   3427
SECOND = 6*1
    Thy exercise hath bin too violent, | For a second course of Fight.   587
    *to a second day of Audience. When you are hearing a   968
    *Corio. I haue deseru'd no better entertainment, in be- | ing Coriolanus.
    Enter second Seruant.   2664
    2 And I shall. Exit second Seruingman.   2690
    The second name of men, obeyes his points   3049
    When she (poor Hen) fond of no second brood,   3519
    Which we will second, when he lies along   3716
SECONDED = 1
    Mes. Yes worthy Sir, | The Slaues report is seconded, and more   2970
SECONDS = 2
    So, now the gates are ope: now proue good Seconds,   540
    Officious and not valiant, you haue sham'd me | In your condemned
    Seconds.   742
SECUNDUS l.895 = 1
SEDITION = 1
    The Cockle of Rebellion, Insolence, Sedition,   1760
SEDUCING = 1
    Seducing so my Friends: and to this end,   3676
SEE see also see't = 30*6
    Did see, and heare, deuise, instruct, walke, feele,   104
    Men. Though all at once, cannot | See what I do deliuer out to each,   150
    Our mustie superfluity. See our best Elders.   243
    Shalt see me once more strike at Tullus face.   263
    See him plucke Auffidius downe by th'haire: 392
    Me thinkes I see him stampe thus, and call thus,   394
    Vir. I am glad to see your Ladyship.   413
    *Vol. He had rather see the swords, and heare a Drum, | then looke
    vpon his Schoolmaster.   418
    1.Sol. See they haue shut him in. Alarum continues   546
    *Mar. See heere these mouers, that do prize their hours   575
    Wherein you see me smear'd, if any feare   688
    *that tell you haue good faces, if you see this in the Map   957
    That' weep'st to see me triumph? Ah my deare,   1083
    That is not glad to see thee.   1095
    Volum. I haue liued, | To see inherited my very Wishes,   1111
    Are spectacled to see him. Your pratling Nurse   1124
    In earnestnesse to see him: seld-showne Flamins   1132
    I haue seene the dumbe men throng to see him,   1192
    That's thousand to one good one, when you now see   1293
    Bru. You see how he intends to vse the people.   1380
    That we shall hardly in our ages see | Their Banners waue againe.   1681
    Sicin. Go see him out at Gates, and follow him   2428
    All. Come, come, lets see him out at gates, come: 2432
    The Nobility are vexed, whom we see haue sided | In his behalfe.   2504
    This Ladies Husband heere; this (do you see)   2553
    Sigh'd truer breath. But that I see thee heere   2773
    *3 But when they shall see sir, his Crest vp againe, and   2869
    *The Warres for my money. I hope to see Romanes as   2889
    Dissentious numbers pestring streets, then see   2899
    Bru. Go see this Rumorer whipt, it cannot be,   2951
    To see your Wiues dishonour'd to your Noses.   2998

SEE *cont.*
2 You'l see your Rome embrac'd with fire, before | You'l speake with
  Coriolanus.   3243
2 'Tis a spell you see of much power: 3332
Making the Mother, wife, and Childe to see,   3456
Requires nor Childe, nor womans face to see: | I haue sate too long. 3486
Mene. See you yon'd Coin a'th Capitol, yon'd corner | (stone?   3571
SEEING = 1 *2
  *he was a Man-child, then now in first seeing he had pro-|ued himselfe
  a man.   377
Or seeing it, of such Childish friendlinesse, | To yeeld your Voyces? 1575
Corio. If *Tullus* not yet thou know'st me, and seeing   2710
SEEKE = 3 *1
  *stirre, was pleas'd to let him seeke danger, where he was   373
Corio. I wish I had a cause to seeke him there,   1697
O're the vast world, to seeke a single man,   2482
Then seeke the end of one; thou shalt no sooner   3477
SEEKES = *1
  *good, nor harme: but hee seekes their hate with greater   1221
SEEKING = 2
Would feede on one another? What's their seeking?   199
Enui'd against the people; seeking meanes   2380
SEEMD = 2
It seem'd appear'd to Rome. By the discouery,   338
I seem'd his Follower, not Partner; and   3692
SEEME = 9 *3
Which yet seeme shut, we haue but pin'd with Rushes,   507
Would seeme but modest: therefore I beseech you,   776
*to seeme to affect the mallice and displeasure of the Peo-|ple, 1224
And this shall seeme, as partly 'tis, their owne,   1669
Mene. Be that you seeme, truly your Countries friend,   1933
Brut. Sir, those cold wayes, | That seeme like prudent helpes, are very
  poysonous,   1936
Volum. If it be Honor in your Warres, to seeme   2143
Let vs seeme humbler after it is done, | Then when it was a dooing. 2507
This true, which they so seeme to feare. Go home,   3079
Com. He would not seeme to know me. | *Menen.* Do you heare? 3159
*Dotant as you seeme to be? Can you think to blow   3281
Wherein I seeme vnnaturall: Desire not t'allay   3439
SEEMES = 2
Whose double bosomes seemes to weare one heart,   2639
What I can vrge against him, although it seemes   3110
SEENE = 8 *1
Farther then seene, and one infect another   528
He has the stampe of *Martius,* and I haue | Before time seene him thus. 631
I haue seene the dumbe men throng to see him,   1192
I haue seene, and heard of: for your Voyces,   1521
Come trie vpon your selues, what you haue seene me.   1942
What you haue seene him do, and heard him speake: 2359
I haue seene the Sterne, and thou hast oft beheld   2462
Makes fear'd, and talk'd of more then seene: your Sonne 2469
*Of shame seene through thy Country, speed thee straight 2744
SEEST = 1
Wherein thou seest me maskt, for thy Reuenge   735
SEET = 2
  *knowledge he ha's in their disposition, and out of his No-|ble
  carelesnesse lets them plainely see't.   1217

SEET *cont.*

Scicin. Why eyther were you ignorant to see't?   1574
SEIZE = 2
  Bru. Seize him *Aediles*.   1890
  Brut. Aediles seize him. | *All Ple.* Yeeld *Martius*, yeeld.   1928
SEL = *2
  *for a day of Kings entreaties, a Mother should not sel him   369
  Lart. No, Ile nor sel, nor giue him: Lend you him I will   491
SELD-SHOWNE = 1
  In earnestnesse to see him: seld-showne Flamins   1132
SELECT = 1
  (Though thankes to all) must I select from all: 702
SELF = *1
  Com. Away, the Tribunes do attend you: arm your self   2249
SELFE = 25*7
  Volum. I pray you daughter sing, or expresse your selfe   362
  Virg. Beseech you giue me leaue to retire my selfe.   389
  Val. Fye, you confine your selfe most vnreasonably: 440
  If 'gainst your selfe you be incens'd, wee'le put you   812
  Shall flye out of it selfe, nor sleepe, nor sanctuary,   878
  *were a Mallice, that giuing it selfe the Lye, would plucke   1235
  Slew three Opposers: *Tarquins* selfe he met,   1308
  Then Miserie it selfe would giue, rewards his deeds   1343
  *3 *Cit.* To loose it selfe in a Fogge, where being three   1417
  Cori. That Ile straight do: and knowing my selfe again, | Repayre
  toth'Senate- | house.   1543
  2.*Cit.* Not one amongst vs, saue your selfe, but sayes   1560
  Sicin. Go call the people, in whose name my Selfe   1876
  You cannot Tent your selfe: be gone, 'beseech you.   1960
  Mene. I could my selfe take vp a Brace o'th' best of | them, yea, the
  two Tribunes.   1968
  Thy selfe (forsooth) hereafter theirs so farre,   2186
  You make strong partie, or defend your selfe   2198
  But owe thy Pride thy selfe.   2239
  Your selfe into a power tyrannicall,   2344
  Volum. Angers my Meate: I suppe vpon my selfe,   2565
  *me, dost not thinke me for the man I am, necessitie com- | mands me
  name my selfe.   2711
  Dreamt of encounters 'twixt thy selfe and me: 2781
  Who am prepar'd against your Territories, | Though not for Rome it
  selfe.   2792
  The action of your selfe, or else to him, had left it soly.   3107
  And power vnto it selfe most commendable,   3142
  *none but my selfe could moue thee, I haue bene blowne   3309
  Which by th'interpretation of full time, | May shew like all your selfe.   3421
  Volum. Euen he, your wife, this Ladie, and my selfe, | Are Sutors to
  you.   3431
  We haue led since thy Exile. Thinke with thy selfe,   3451
  Thy Wife and Childrens blood: For my selfe, Sonne,   3473
  At difference in thee: Out of that Ile worke | My selfe a former
  Fortune.   3560
  To do my selfe this wrong: Till at the last   3691
  My selfe your loyall Seruant, or endure | Your heauiest Censure.   3820
SELFE-LOUING = 1
  O'recome with Pride, Ambitious, past all thinking | Selfe-louing.   2930
SELL = 1
  To buy and sell with Groats, to shew bare heads   2095

SELUES = 11*4
Neighbours, will you vndo your selues?   64
Menen. Either you must | Confesse your selues wondrous Malicious,   88
And no way from your selues. What do you thinke?   162
That rubbing the poore Itch of your Opinion, | Make your selues Scabs.   175
*but an Interiour suruey of your good selues. Oh that you | could.   936
Menen. You know neither mee, your selues, nor any   963
3.Cit. We haue power in our selues to do it, but it is   1391
bring our selues to be monstrous members.   1399
Be Curses to your selues. You should haue said,   1586
*Which we our selues haue plowed for, sow'd, & scatter'd,   1761
Come trie vpon your selues, what you haue seene me.   1942
Our Ediles smot: our selues resisted: come.   2061
Beating your Officers, cursing your selues,   2360
Making but reseruation of your selues,   2418
1 Our selues, our wiues, and children, on our knees,   2918
SEN = 5
SENA = 4
SENAT = 1*1
2 Cit. Our busines is not vnknowne to th'Senat, they   59
Together with the Seale a'th Senat, what | We haue compounded on.   3748
SENAT = 6*1
SENATE = 8*2
You cry against the Noble Senate, who   197
that's in them. Is the Senate possest of this?   1029
*Senate ha's Letters from the Generall, wherein hee giues   1031
Menen. The Senate, *Coriolanus*, are well pleas'd to make | thee
Consull.   1350
You anon doe meet the Senate. | *Corio.* Is this done?   1534
In soothing them, we nourish 'gainst our Senate   1759
Which they haue often made against the Senate,   1825
Breake ope the Lockes a'th'Senate, and bring in | The Crowes to pecke
the Eagles.   1835
Mes. You are sent for to the Senate: 2987
To call me to your Senate, Ile deliuer   3819
SENATEHOUSE *see also* senate-house = 1
Cori. That Ile straight do: and knowing my selfe again, | Repayre
toth'Senate- | house.   1543
SENATES = 1
The Senates Courtesie? Let deeds expresse   1829
SENATE-HOUSE = 2
Corio. Where? at the Senate-house? | *Scicin.* There, *Coriolanus.*   1539
All to the Senate-house: some newes is comming | That turnes their
Countenances.   2965
*SENATOR see Sen., Sena., Senat., 1.Sen., 1.Senat., 2.Sen.,
2.Sena.*
SENATORS = 15*1
As you maligne our Senators, for that | They are not such as you.   115
Men. The Senators of Rome, are this good Belly,   156
Enter Tullus Auffidius with Senators of Coriolus.   313
*They Sound a Parley: Enter two Senators with others on | the Walles of
Corialus.*   499
Where Senators shall mingle teares with smiles,   750
*Cornets. Enter Coriolanus, Menenius, all the Gentry, | Cominius, Titus
Latius, and other Senators.*   1672
You graue, but wreaklesse Senators, haue you thus   1786
If they be Senators: and they are no lesse,   1796
Enter Menenius with the Senators.   2113

SENATORS cont.
Your Wife, your Sonne: These Senators, the Nobles, 2164
Edile. With old *Menenius*, and those Senators | That always fauour'd
him. 2267
And take our friendly Senators by'th'hands 2790
*question askt him by any of the Senators, but they stand 2853
The Senators and Patricians loue him too: 3121
Is worth of Consuls, Senators, Patricians, 3627
*Enter two Senators, with Ladies, passing ouer | the Stage, with other
Lords.* 3639
SENATOUR = *1
Val. In earnest it's true; I heard a Senatour speake it. 459
SENATOURS = 1*1
*Enter Sicinius Velutus, Annius Brutus Cominius, Titus | Lartius, with
other Senatours.* 244
*The people, against the Senatours, Patricians, and | Nobles. 2584
SENCE = 1
His readie sence: then straight his doubled spirit 1330
SENCELESSE = 1
Lar. Oh Noble Fellow! | Who sensibly out-dares his sencelesse Sword, 554
SEND = 6
I send it through the Riuers of your blood 142
As I haue set them downe. If I do send, dispatch 715
Must to *Corioles* backe, send vs to Rome 833
And to send for *Titus Lartius*: it remaines, 1245
A cause for thy Repeale, we shall not send 2481
Was to send him: for whose old Loue I haue 3359
SENNET = 2
A Sennet. Trumpets sound. 1059
A Sennet. Enter the Patricians, and the Tribunes of 1239
SENSE *see* sence
SENSIBLE = *1
*full of Mothes. Come, I would your Cambrick were sen-|sible 448
SENSIBLY = 1
Lar. Oh Noble Fellow! | Who sensibly out-dares his sencelesse Sword, 554
SENT = 5*2
*That meate was made for mouths. That the gods sent not 220
*like to finde fame: To a cruell Warre I sent him, from 374
Mess. You are sent for to the Capitoll: 1190
Mes. You are sent for to the Senate: 2987
He sent in writing after me: what he would not, 3229
And would haue sent it. Another word *Menenius*, 3326
Corio. This last old man, | Whom with a crack'd heart I haue sent to
Rome, 3355
SENTED = 1
For the mutable ranke-sented Meynie, 1756
SENTENCD = 1*1
Sicin. He's sentenc'd: No more hearing. 2394
*is no hope in't, our throats are sentenc'd, and stay vppon | execution. 3576
SENTENCE = 1
Inforce the present Execution | Of what we chance to Sentence. 2284
SER = 1*5
SERPENT = 1
Not Affricke ownes a Serpent I abhorre 727
SERUANT = 6
Cor. Know, good Mother, | I had rather be their seruant in my way, 1117
But was a pettie seruant to the State, 1579

SERUANT *cont.*
*Corio. I haue deseru'd no better entertainment, in be-|ing *Coriolanus.*
Enter second Seruant. 2664
A Noble seruant to them, but he could not 3127
Made him ioynt-seruant with me: Gaue him way 3685
My selfe your loyall Seruant, or endure | Your heauiest Censure. 3820
SERUANTED = 1
*Corio. Wife, Mother, Child, I know not. My affaires | Are Seruanted
to others: Though I owe 3317
SERUD = 2
Bru. But since he hath seru'd well for Rome. 2365
My best and freshest men, seru'd his designements 3688
SERUE = 6*3
Mar. Will the time serue to tell, I do not thinke: 660
Those Centuries to our ayd, the rest will serue 716
**helpe will serue: for once we stood vp about the Corne, 1401
How youngly he began to serue his Countrey, 1639
*Com. I thinke 'twill serue, if he can thereto frame his | spirit. 2201
Corio. No, I serue not thy Master. 2699
**thy Mistris: Thou prat'st, and prat'st, serue with thy tren-|cher:
Hence. *Beats him away* 2702
And make my misery serue thy turne: So vse it, 2745
The Volces whom you serue, you might condemne vs 3491
SERUES = 1*1
But since it serues my purpose, I will venture | To scale't a little more. 92
*Rom. The day serues well for them now. I haue heard 2600
SERUICE = 10*2
To gratifie his Noble seruice, that hath 1247
I got them in my Countries Seruice, when 1441
They ne're did seruice for't; being prest to'th'Warre, 1819
They would not thred the Gates: This kinde of Seruice 1821
Menen. The seruice of the foote 2045
The warlike Seruice he ha's done, consider: Thinke 2324
Corio. What do you prate of Seruice. 2366
He does faire Iustice: if he giue me way, | Ile do his Country Seruice.
Exit. 2651
*1 Ser. Wine, Wine, Wine: What seruice is heere? I 2654
*Corio. I, tis an honester seruice, then to meddle with 2701
My Surname *Coriolanus.* The painfull Seruice, 2725
And cannot liue but to thy shame, vnlesse | It be to do thee seruice. 2757
SERUICES = 3*2
*2.Cit. Consider you what Seruices he ha's done for his | Country? 31
Corio. I doe owe them still my Life, and Seruices. 1352
Thinking vpon his Seruices, tooke from you 1626
*Rom. I am a Roman, and my Seruices are as you are, | against 'em.
Know you me yet. 2574
That my reuengefull Seruices may proue 2746
SERUINGMAN see also 1., 1.*Ser.*, 2., 2.*Ser.*, 3. = 7
Musicke playes. Enter a Seruingman. 2653
Enter another Seruingman. 2656
Enter the first Seruingman. 2661
Enter 3 Seruingman, the 1 *meets him.* 2673
2 And I shall. *Exit second Seruingman.* 2690
Enter Auffidius with the Seruingman. 2704
Enter the third Seruingman. 2832
SERUINGMEN = 1
Enter two of the Seruingmen. 2808

SET = 12*8
If they set downe before's: for the remoue	345
They set them downe on two lowe stooles and sowe.	361
*whether his fall enrag'd him, or how 'twas, hee did so set	426
*power. Your Lord, and *Titus Lartius*, are set down	462
To endure Friends, that you directly set me | Against *Affidious*, and his	
Antiats,	675
Titus Lartius, *hauing set a guard vpon Carioles, going with*	710
As I haue set them downe. If I do send, dispatch	715
*set vp the bloodie Flagge against all Patience, and	971
As to set Dogges on Sheepe, will be his fire	1185
To be set high in place, we did commend	1650
Haue you not set them on?	1719
Com. The People are abus'd: set on, this paltring	1746
Sicin. Haue you a Catalogue | *Of all the Voices that we haue procur'd,	
set downe by'th | (Pole?	2269
*the man I thinke, that shall set them in present Action. So	2616
Th'one halfe of my Commission, and set downe	2797
finger and his thumbe, as one would set vp a Top.	2814
*Son and Heire to Mars, set at vpper end o'th'Table: No	2852
And then Ile set vpon him.	3216
Set downe our Hoast. My partner in this Action,	3348
Auf. I am glad thou hast set thy mercy, & thy Honor	3559

SETS = 1
Then the seuerity of the publike Power, | Which he so sets at naught.	2000

SEUEN = 2*3
Menen. A Letter for me? it giues me an Estate of se-|uen	1011
*for his place: he receiued in the repulse of *Tarquin* seuen | hurts ith'	
Body.	1045
Mene. Now it's twentie seuen; euery gash was an | Enemies Graue.	
Hearke, the Trumpets.	1051
Enter seuen or eight Citizens.	1387
If I could shake off but one seuen teeres	2497

SEUENTEENE = 1
And in the brunt of seuenteene Battailes since,	1314

SEUENTIE = 1
From twelue, to seuentie: and powring Warre	2787

SEUERAL = 1
Alarum, as in Battaile. | *Enter Martius and Auffidius at seueral doores.*	722

SEUERALL = 3
That in these seuerall places of the Citie,	196
Twelue seuerall times, and I haue nightly since	2780
Reports the Volces with two seuerall Powers	2941

SEUERITY = 1
Then the seuerity of the publike Power, | Which he so sets at naught.	2000

SEWE *see* sowe
SEWING *see* sowing

SHADE = 1
Ere in our owne house I doe shade my Head,	1107

SHADOW = *1
*the shadow which he treads on at noone, but I do	290

SHAKE = 5*2
Thou mad'st thine enemies shake, as if the World | Were Feauorous,	
and did tremble.	562
Corio. Hence rotten thing, or I shall shake thy bones | Out of thy	
Garments.	1883
Let euery feeble Rumor shake your hearts:	2413

SHAKE *cont.*

If I could shake off but one seuen teeres	2497
Com. Hee'l shake your Rome about your eares.	3016
*Mene. As *Hercules* did shake downe Mellow Fruite:	3017
*Constraines them weepe, and shake with feare & sorow,	3455

SHAKEN = 1

The Oake not to be winde-shaken. *Exit Watch.*	3345

SHAL *l.**62 = *1

SHALBE = 1

We shalbe shortned in our ayme, which was	339

SHALL *see also* shal, shalbe, shal's, shalt *l.*90 109 159 *242 297 302 306 353 390 437 450 *495 506 522 602 607 703 705 708 750 751 752 755 770 798 825 836 878 881 894 *898 *910 *980 *1044 *1168 1183 1187 1191 *1266 1296 1366 1434 *1468 1470 1605 1669 1678 1681 1712 1769 1814 1828 1862 1883 1955 *1997 1999 2002 2004 2019 2053 2067 2146 2212 2275 2281 2288 *2315 2321 2390 2391 2392 2406 2407 2453 2481 2492 2521 2522 2566 *2609 *2616 2642 *2647 2690 2803 *2869 *2873 *2876 2958 3028 3109 3116 3220 *3298 3321 3367 3483 3563 *3596 3598 3700 3703 3717 3733 3779 3799 3815 3836 = 94*20, 6*1

Sicin. It is a minde that shall remain a poison	1779
Corio. Shall remaine?	1781
Heare you this Triton of the *Minnoues*? Marke you | His absolute Shall?	1782
*Cor. Shall? O God! but most vnwise Patricians: why	1785
Giuen Hidra heere to choose an Officer, | That with his peremptory Shall, being but	1787
And such a one as he, who puts his Shall,	1799
His popular Shall, against a grauer Bench	1800

SHALS = 1

Mene. You haue made good worke | You and your cry. Shal's to the Capitoll?	3074

SHALT *l.*263 2479 2532 3477 3479 3500 = 6

SHAMD = 1

Officious and not valiant, you haue sham'd me | In your condemned Seconds.	742

SHAME = 6*3

Senat. Sit *Coriolanus*: neuer shame to heare | What you haue Nobly done.	1277
Sicin. Are you mankinde? | **Volum.* I foole, is that a shame. Note but this Foole,	2524
*Of shame seene through thy Country, speed thee straight	2744
And cannot liue but to thy shame, vnlesse | It be to do thee seruice.	2757
The Tribunes cannot doo't for shame; the people	3029
To shame vnvulnerable, and sticke i'th Warres	3426
*Down Ladies: let vs shame him with him with our knees	3526
Then shame to th'Romaines. And we heere deliuer	3746
Which was your shame, by this vnholy Braggart?	3790

SHAMES = *1

*You Shames of Rome: you Heard of Byles and Plagues	526

SHAPES = 2

That beare the shapes of men, how haue you run	530
That shapes man Better: and they follow him	3008

SHE *see also* shee, she's = 11*1

SHED = 4

By th'Blood we haue shed together, | By th'Vowes we haue made	673
As for my Country, I haue shed my blood,	1768
Shed for my thanklesse Country, are requitted:	2727
And beare the Palme, for hauing brauely shed	3472

SHEE *see also* shee's *l.**995 = *1
SHEEPE = 1

   As to set Dogges on Sheepe, will be his fire   1185
SHEES = *1

   *shee's falne out with her Husband. Your Noble *Tullus*   2602
SHELLD = 1

   Which were In-shell'd, when *Martius* stood for Rome,   2948
SHENT = *1

   *1 Do you heare how wee are shent for keeping your | greatnesse backe?   3334
SHEPHEARDS = 1

   Doe's of the Shepheards: For his best Friends, if they   3031
SHEPHERD = *1

   *Com. The Shepherd knowes not Thunder fro(m) a Taber,   634
SHES = 1

   Brut. Why? | *Sicin.* They say she's mad.   2514
SHEW = 14*7

   *now wee'l shew em in deeds: they say poore Suters haue   61
   *They needs must shew themselues, which in the hatching   337
   *where he would shew most loue. When yet hee was but   366
   *large Cicatrices to shew the People, when hee shall stand   1044
   Shew them th'vnaking Skarres, which I should hide,   1370
   *a power that we haue no power to do: For, if hee shew vs   1392
   *shew you, which shall bee yours in priuate: your good | voice sir, what
   say you?   1468
   Which he could shew in priuate: 1566
   Scicin. You shew too much of that,   1739
   To buy and sell with Groats, to shew bare heads   2095
   And you, will rather shew our generall Lowts,   2165
   Corio. Must I goe shew them my vnbarb'd Sconce?   2205
   Vpon the wounds his body beares, which shew   2325
   Com. Let me speake: | I haue bene Consull, and can shew from Rome   2395
   Which not to cut, would shew thee but a Foole,   2754
   *not (looke you sir) shew themselues (as we terme it) his | Friends,
   whilest he's in Directitude.   2866
   And shew no signe of Feare.   3080
   Of thy deepe duty, more impression shew | Then that of common
   Sonnes.   3400
   Shew duty as mistaken, all this while, | Betweene the Childe, and
   Parent.   3405
   Which by th'interpretation of full time, | May shew like all your selfe.   3421
   Rather to shew a Noble grace to both parts,   3476
SHEWD = 8

   He vs'd vs scornefully: he should haue shew'd vs   1561
   There Mutinies and Reuolts, wherein they shew'd   1823
   You had not shew'd them how ye were dispos'd   2109
   Shew'd Mastership in floating. Fortunes blowes,   2443
   And therein shew'd like Enemies.   3034
   (Though I shew'd sowrely to him) once more offer'd   3360
   May say, this mercy we haue shew'd: the Romanes,   3494
   Shew'd thy deere Mother any curtesie,   3518
SHEWES = 3

   If these shewes be not outward, which of you   698
   Through our large Temples with y shewes of peace   2305
   And shewes good Husbandry for the Volcian State,   3113
SHEWING = 1*1

   Nor shewing (as the manner is) his Wounds   1158
   *Coriol. I wil not Seale your knowledge with shewing   1499

SHEWNE = 1
  Brut. Now we haue shewne our power,   2506
SHEWST = 1
  Thou shew'st a Noble Vessell: What's thy name?   2719
SHIELD = 1*1
  A Shield, as hard as his. A certaine number   701
  *enemy your shield, thinke to front his reuenges with the   3278
SHIELDS = 2
  Now put your Shields before your hearts, and fight   516
  With hearts more proofe then Shields.   517
SHINNE = 1
  When with his Amazonian Shinne he droue   1305
SHIP = 1
  Vir. I thanke your Lady-ship: Well good Madam.   417
SHOLD *l*.*2006 = *1
SHOOES = *1
  *Below their cobled Shooes. They say ther's grain enough?   208
SHOOT = 1
  You shoot me forth in acclamations hyperbolicall,   806
SHOOTING = 1
  Shooting their Emulation.   227
SHOP = 1
  Because I am the Store-house, and the Shop   140
SHOPS = 1
  Our Tradesmen singing in their shops, and going | About their
  Functions friendly.   2900
SHORT = 1*1
  For a short holding, if we loose the Field,   717
  Sicin. Is't possible, that so short a time can alter the | condition of a
  man.   3578
SHORTLY = *1
  *Thou art poor'st of all; then shortly art thou mine. *Exeunt*   3148
SHORTNED = 1
  We shalbe shortned in our ayme, which was   339
SHOT = 1
  But as a discontented Friend, greefe-shot | With his vnkindnesse. Say't
  be so?   3200
SHOULD *see also* shold *l*.125 182 232 341 *364 *369 *381 748 781 807
  848 856 867 *939 1096 1145 1297 1370 1383 *1398 *1409 *1485 1506
  1509 1561 1584 1586 1600 1636 *1736 1771 1858 1865 2031 2124 2163
  2209 *2520 2762 2934 3005 3032 3033 3036 3195 *3263 *3275 3379
  *3449 3453 3468 3510 = 40*12
SHOULDER = *1
  Volum. Ith' Shoulder, and ith' left Arme: there will be   1043
SHOULDST *l*.739 *2730 = 1*1
SHOUT *see also* showt = 2*3
  They all shout and waue their swords, take him vp in their | Armes, and
  cast vp their Caps.   695
  They all shout, and throw vp their Caps.   2425
  *Will I lend eare to. Ha? what shout is this? *Shout within*   3366
  Make the Sunne dance. Hearke you. *A shout within*   3624
SHOUTING *see* showting
SHOUTS = 1
  I'de not haue giuen a doit. Harke, how they ioy. | *Sound still with the*
  Shouts.   3631
SHOW *see* shew

SHOWD *see* shew'd
SHOWER = 1
   A Shower, and Thunder, with their Caps, and Showts: 1197
SHOWES *see* shewes
SHOWING *see* shewing
SHOWNE *see also* shewne = 1
   In earnestnesse to see him: seld-showne Flamins   1132
SHOWST *see* shew'st
SHOWT = 1
   A showt, and flourish. | *Volum*. These are the Vshers of *Martius*:   1053
SHOWTING = 1
   Tabors, and Symboles, and the showting Romans,   3623
SHOWTS = 3*1
   he hath faults (with surplus) to tyre in repetition. | *Showts within.*   46
   *What showts are these? The other side a'th City is risen: 48
   A Shower, and Thunder, with their Caps, and Showts: 1197
   Drummes and Trumpets sounds, with great | *showts of the people.*   3705
SHREDS = 1
   Corne for the Richmen onely: With these shreds   221
SHRINKES = *1
   *like an Engine, and the ground shrinkes before his Trea- | ding.   3588
SHRUG = 1
   Where great Patricians shall attend, and shrug,   751
SHUNLESSE = 1
   With shunlesse destinie: aydelesse came off,   1326
SHUNND = 1
   The Mouse ne're shunn'd the Cat, as they did budge | From Rascals
worse then they.   657
SHUNNING = 1
   (As children from a Beare) the *Volces* shunning him: 393
SHUT = 4
   Which yet seeme shut, we haue but pin'd with Rushes,   507
   Another Alarum, and Martius followes them to | *gates, and is shut in.* 538
   1.*Sol*. See they haue shut him in. *Alarum continues*   546
   Lart. Hence; and shut your gates vpon's: 720
SIC = 1*2
SICIN = 1
   Citizens steale away. Manet Sicin. & Brutus.   279
SICIN = 70*12
SICINIUS see also Scici., Scinin., Scicinius, Sic., Sicin. = 11*1
   Sicinius Velutus, and I know not. Sdeath,   231
   Enter Sicinius Velutus, Annius Brutus Cominius, Titus | *Lartius, with
other Senatours.*   244
   Enter Menenius with the two Tribunes of the | *people, Sicinius & Brutus.* 896
   Flourish Cornets. | *Then Exeunt. Manet Sicinius and Brutus.*   1378
   Sicinius, Brutus, Coriolanus, Citizens.   1895
   To'th'people: Coriolanus, patience: Speak good *Sicinius*.   1899
   Enter Brutus and Sicinius with the rabble againe.   1993
   Enter Sicinius and Brutus.   2258
   Enter the two Tribunes, Sicinius, and Brutus, | *with the Edile.*   2501
   Enter the two Tribunes, Sicinius, and Brutus.   2892
   Enter Menenius, Cominius, Sicinius, Brutus, | *the two Tribunes, with
others.*   3150
   Enter Menenius and Sicinius.   3570
SICKE = 1
   Being naked, sicke; nor Phane, nor Capitoll,   879

SICKMANS = 1
 A sickmans Appetite; who desires most that   189
SIDE = 6*1
 *What showts are these? The other side a'th City is risen: 48
 The one side must haue baile.   171
 Who thriues, & who declines: Side factions, & giue out   205
 Mar. How lies their Battell? Know you on w side   665
 These are a Side, that would be glad to haue   3078
 Our wish, which side should win. For either thou   3468
 This we receiu'd, and each in either side   3495
SIDED = 1
 The Nobility are vexed, whom we see haue sided | In his behalfe.   2504
SIDES = 1
 Mene. On both sides more respect.   1887
SIGHD = 2
 They said they were an hungry, sigh'd forth Prouerbes   218
 Sigh'd truer breath. But that I see thee heere   2773
SIGHES = *1
 *out of your Gates with sighes: and coniure thee to par- | don   3310
SIGHT = 3
 Below the beame of sight; yet will I still | Be thus to them.   2088
 The Glasses of my sight: A Beggars Tongue   2225
 Are we come hither; since that thy sight, which should   3453
SIGHTS = *1
 Bru. All tongues speake of him, and the bleared sights   1123
SIGNE = 2
 In signe of what you are, not to reward   777
 And shew no signe of Feare.   3080
SILENCD = 1
 Haue made them Mules, silenc'd their Pleaders,   1174
SILENCE = 2
 To hide your doings, and to silence that,   774
 But oh, thy Wife. | *Corio*. My gracious silence, hayle: 1080
SILENT = 2*2
 *for their Tongues to be silent, and not confesse so much,   1233
 been silent: Please you to heare *Cominius* speake?   1270
 Volum. Should we be silent & not speak, our Raiment   3449
 *I am husht vntill our City be afire, & then Ile speak a litle | *Holds her
 by the hand silent*.   3538
SILKE = 2
 When Steele growes soft, as the Parasites Silke,   801
 A twist of rotten Silke, neuer admitting   3764
SILUER = *1
 *3.*Rom*. A Murrain on't, I tooke this for Siluer. *Exeunt*.   572
SIMPLY = *1
 *2 So did I, Ile be sworne: He is simply the rarest man | i'th'world.   2820
SINCE = 13*3
 But since it serues my purpose, I will venture | To scale't a little more.   92
 Since I heard thence, these are the words, I thinke   321
 *Me thinkes thou speak'st not well. How long is't since?   619
 Halfe an houre since brought my report.   627
 *worth all your predecessors, since *Deucalion*, though per- | aduenture   986
 And in the brunt of seuenteene Battailes since,   1314
 *of them, 'tis a condition they account gentle: & since   1488
 Since a could draw a Sword, and is ill-school'd   2063
 With Honour, as in Warre; since that to both | It stands in like request.   2147
 Bru. But since he hath seru'd well for Rome.   2365

SINCE *cont*.

Since I haue euer followed thee with hate,	2755
Twelue seuerall times, and I haue nightly since	2780
As best thou art experienc'd, since thou know'st	2798
Hath Virgin'd it ere since. You Gods, I pray,	3397
We haue led since thy Exile. Thinke with thy selfe,	3451
Are we come hither; since that thy sight, which should	3453

SINCERELY = *1

*sincerely, had I a dozen sons each in my loue alike,	383

SINEWES = 1

Auf. There was it:	For which my sinewes shall be stretcht vpon him,	3699

SING = *1

Volum. I pray you daughter sing, or expresse your selfe	362

SINGING = 1

Our Tradesmen singing in their shops, and going	About their Functions friendly.	2900

SINGLE = 2*2

*single: your abilities are to Infant-like, for dooing	933
*one of vs ha's a single Honor, in giuing him our own voi-|ces	1432
Yet were there but this single Plot, to loose	2208
O're the vast world, to seeke a single man,	2482

SINGLY = 1

Be singly counter-poys'd. At sixteene yeeres,	1301

SINGULARITY = 1

More then his singularity, he goes	Vpon this present Action.	310

SINKE = 2

Who is the sinke a th'body.	126
Leaue vnsaluted: Sinke my knee i'th'earth, *Kneeles*	3399

SINKING = 1

Onely for bearing Burthens, and sore blowes	For sinking vnder them.	1179

SINNE = 2

I sinne in enuying his Nobility:	250
(As it were sinne to doubt) that loue this painting	687

SIR *l*.65 95 108 109 149 241 261 549 565 586 589 626 719 894 912 924 930
938 962 1073 1282 1283 1360 1390 *1436 1438 1440 1455 *1456 *1461
*1467 1469 1470 *1471 *1486 *1491 1502 1542 1554 1556 1753 1882
1936 1961 2005 2008 2102 2197 2549 *2571 2573 2577 2597 2617 *2618
2628 2637 *2666 2700 *2706 2795 *2816 *2864 *2865 *2866 *2869 2905
2970 3019 3095 3104 *3118 *3262 3331 3554 3555 3604 *3635 *3663
3666 3679 = 64*20

SIRRA = 1

Mene. Sirra, if thy Captaine knew I were heere,	3287

SIRRAH = 1

Volum. Your knee, Sirrah.	*Corio*. That's my braue Boy.	3429

SIRS = 1

Nor Cowardly in retyre: Beleeue me Sirs,	606

SISTER = 1

Corio. The Noble Sister of *Publicola*;	The Moone of Rome: Chaste as the Isicle	3416

SIT = 5*1

They'l sit by th'fire, and presume to know	203
Senat. Sit *Coriolanus*: neuer shame to heare	What you haue Nobly done.	1277
Menen. Pray now sit downe.	1287
When the Alarum were strucke, then idly sit	1289
Com. I tell you, he doe's sit in Gold, his eye	3224
*thee. The glorious Gods sit in hourely Synod about thy	3304

SITHENCE = 1
   Corio. Haue you inform'd them sithence?   1732
SITS = 2*1
   Bru. The Gods haue well preuented it, and Rome | Sits safe and still,
   without him.   2936
   Auf. All places yeelds to him ere he sits downe,   3119
   *like a knell, and his hum is a Battery. He sits in his State,   3590
SIX = 3*1
   Of Wounds, two dozen odde: Battailes thrice six   1520
   Six of his Labours youl'd haue done, and sau'd   2456
   2 Worth six on him.   2826
   Corio. O that I had him, with six *Auffidiusses*, or more: 3801
SIXTEENE = 1
   Be singly counter-poys'd. At sixteene yeeres,   1301
SIZE = 1
   (Of whom hee's cheefe) with all the size that verity   3256
SKALING = 1
   Skaling his present bearing with his past,   1652
SKARRES = 1
   Shew them th'vnaking Skarres, which I should hide,   1370
SKULL *see* scull
SLAINE = 3
   Tit. What is become of *Martius*? | *All*. Slaine (Sir) doubtlesse.   548
   Auf. Euen so, as with a man by his owne Almes im- | poyson'd, and with
   his Charity slaine.   3661
   2.Con. And patient Fooles, | Whose children he hath slaine, their base
   throats teare   3710
SLANDER = 1
   Thether, where more attends you, and you slander   77
SLAUE = 5
   Com. Where is that Slaue | Which told me they had beate you to your
   Trenches?   651
   Mar. Let the first Budger dye the others Slaue,   729
   Aedile. Worthy Tribunes, | There is a Slaue whom we haue put in
   prison,   2939
   Sicin. 'Tis this Slaue: 2967
   Too great for what containes it. Boy? Oh Slaue,   3774
SLAUES = 5*1
   With thousands of these quarter'd slaues, as high   211
   From Slaues, that Apes would beate; *Pluto* and Hell,   531
   Bury with those that wore them. These base slaues,   578
   And suffer'd me by th'voyce of Slaues to be   2734
   *3 Oh Slaues, I can tell you Newes, News you Rascals   2833
   Mes. Yes worthy Sir, | The Slaues report is seconded, and more   2970
SLAY = 2
   In puny Battell slay me. Saue you sir.   2628
   This Enemie Towne: Ile enter, if he slay me   2650
SLEEP = *2
   Cor. Choller? Were I as patient as the midnight sleep,   1777
   *Whose Passions, and whose Plots haue broke their sleep   2645
SLEEPE = 4*1
   Shall flye out of it selfe, nor sleepe, nor sanctuary,   878
   Brutus. Then our Office may, during his power, goe | sleepe.   1142
   That Babies lull a-sleepe: The smiles of Knaues   2223
   We haue beene downe together in my sleepe,   2782
   *deafe, sleepe, insensible, a getter of more bastard Chil- | dren, then
   warres a destroyer of men.   2882

SLEW = 1
  Slew three Opposers: *Tarquins* selfe he met,   1308
SLIGHT = 1*1
  *so slight. He that hath a will to die by himselfe, feares it   3339
  Murd'ring Impossibility, to make | What cannot be, slight worke.   3412
SLIGHTNESSE = 1
  To vnstable Slightnesse. Purpose so barr'd, it followes,   1847
SLIP = 1
  Euen like a fawning Grey-hound in the Leash, | To let him slip at will.   649
SLIPPERY = *1
  *Oh World, thy slippery turnes! Friends now fast sworn,   2638
SLYLY = 1
  Were slyly crept into his humane powers,   1139
SMALL = 3*1
  Men. I will tell you, | If you'l bestow a small (of what you haue little)   130
  The strongest Nerues, and small inferiour Veines   145
  Small as an Eunuch, or the Virgin voyce   2222
  Rom. The maine blaze of it is past, but a small thing   2589
SMART = *1
  Martius. I haue some Wounds vpon me, and they smart   779
SMEARD = 1
  Wherein you see me smear'd, if any feare   688
SMELS = 1
  The Feast smels well: but I appeare not like a Guest.   2660
SMELT = 1
  You are the musty Chaffe, and you are smelt   3185
SMILE = 3
  Men. Sir, I shall tell you with a kinde of Smile,   109
  For looke you I may make the belly Smile,   111
  Bid me farewell, and smile. I pray you come: 2491
SMILES = 2
  Where Senators shall mingle teares with smiles,   750
  That Babies lull a-sleepe: The smiles of Knaues   2223
SMILING = *1
  *That both our powers, with smiling Fronts encountring,   611
SMILINGLY = 1
  Do smilingly Reuolt, and who resists | Are mock'd for valiant
  Ignorance,   3022
SMOAKING = 1
  That we with smoaking swords may march from hence   497
SMOT = 1
  Our Ediles smot: our selues resisted: come.   2061
SMOTHERD = 1
  Stalls, Bulkes, Windowes, are smother'd vp,   1129
SNOW = 1
  That's curdied by the Frost, from purest Snow,   3418
SO *see also* s', soe *l.**55 114 233 280 288 302 314 *426 465 489 540 558
  598 623 662 692 *714 830 866 867 *876 929 *982 996 *1019 *1027 1170
  *1214 *1231 *1233 1320 *1394 *1404 *1406 *1411 *1413 1454 *1500
  1512 1563 1569 1588 1599 1620 1646 1659 1677 1680 1685 1693 1737
  1743 1748 1769 1827 1847 1913 1914 2001 2011 2020 2058 2107 2117
  2163 2170 2186 2215 2275 2338 2341 2363 2390 2391 2392 2406 2407
  2457 2480 2519 2523 2552 2566 2573 *2587 *2590 *2616 2644 2648
  *2672 2683 2745 2749 *2818 *2820 *2827 2844 *2851 *2884 *2885 *2907
  2933 2935 3013 3068 *3069 3079 *3084 3111 3138 3139 3140 3143 3168
  3188 3201 3231 3249 *3339 3389 3489 3522 3529 *3578 *3585 3619 3661
  3674 3676 3695 = 102*33

SOARING = 1
    At some time, when his soaring Insolence   1182
SODAINE = 1
    With them he enters: who vpon the sodaine   551
SOFT = 3*1
    *he did it to that end: though soft conscienc'd men can be   38
    1 *Cit.* Soft, who comes heere?   51
    When Steele growes soft, as the Parasites Silke,   801
    Hast not the soft way, which thou do'st confesse   2183
SOFTER = 1
    Volum. Oh stand vp blest! | Whil'st with no softer Cushion then the
    Flint   3402
SOL = 1
SOLACE = 1
    My hazards still haue beene your solace, and   2466
SOLD = 1
    As cheape as Lies; he sold the Blood and Labour   3702
SOLDIER *see also Sol.,* 1.*Sol.,* 2.*Sol.,* souldier, souldiour = 3
    You finde him like a Soldier: do not take   2331
    But as I say, such as become a Soldier, | Rather then enuy you. 2333
    1 I thinke he is: but a greater soldier then he, | You wot one. 2822
SOLDIERS *see also* souldiers, souldiours = 4
    Enter Cominius as it were in retire, with soldiers.   603
    Your Soldiers vse him as the Grace 'fore meate,   3093
    The Tribunes are no Soldiers: and their people   3122
    Dismisse my Soldiers, or capitulate   3437
SOLE = *2
    *sayes, and sole the Porter of Rome Gates by th'eares. He 2860
    Sicin. And affecting one sole Throne, without assista(n)ce 2932
SOLELY *see* soly
SOLEMNESSE = 1
    Prythee *Virgilia* turne thy solemnesse out a doore, | And go along with
    vs.   472
SOLICITE = 1
    And his Wife, who (as I heare) meane to solicite him   3232
SOLLICITE = 1
    Brut. Did you perceiue, | He did sollicite you in free Contempt, 1602
SOLY = 1
    The action of your selfe, or else to him, had left it soly.   3107
SOME = 21*12
    Lead'st first to win some vantage.   168
    Some parcels of their Power are forth already,   350
    Condemning some to death, and some to exile,   646
    The rest shall beare the businesse in some other fight   703
    Martius. I haue some Wounds vpon me, and they smart   779
    My Nose that bled, or foyl'd some debile Wretch,   804
    True Sword to Sword: Ile potche at him some way, | Or Wrath, or Craft
    may get him.   873
    *some of the best of 'em were hereditarie hang-|men.   987
    Some old Crab-trees here at home,   1098
    At some time, when his soaring Insolence   1182
    *heads are some browne, some blacke, some Abram, some 1405
    Some certaine of your Brethren roar'd, and ranne   1442
    *the bewitchment of some popular man, and giue it   1492
    Haue done many things, some lesse, some more: 1522
    There's some among you haue beheld me fighting,   1941

SOME *cont.*

Away my disposition, and possesse me | Some Harlots spirit: My throat
of Warre be turn'd,   2219
As most abated Captiues, to some Nation   2420
With thee awhile: Determine on some course   2474
Nay, and you shall heare some. Will you be gone?   2521
To take the one the other, by some chance,   2646
*Some tricke not worth an Egge, shall grow deere friends   2647
*3 Pray you poore Gentleman, take vp some other sta- | tion: 2684
*2 'Tis so, and as warres in some sort may be saide to   2884
All to the Senate-house: some newes is comming | That turnes their
Countenances.   2965
Made by some other Deity then Nature,   3007
*thou stand'st not i'th state of hanging, or of some death   3301
*little finger, there is some hope the Ladies of Rome, espe- | cially 3574
Which he did end all his; and tooke some pride   3690
SOMETHING *see also* some-thing = 2*1
*Tiber in't: Said, to be something imperfect in fauou- | ring   945
3 *Cit.* But this is something odde.   1473
Your Enemies and his, finde something in him.   3025
SOMETIME = 3*1
Martius. I sometime lay here in *Corioles*,   841
The Corne a'th'Store-house gratis, as 'twas vs'd | Sometime in Greece. 1809
*And venomous to thine eyes. My (sometime) Generall,   2461
Which was sometime his Generall: who loued him   3153
SOMETIMES = 1
Would without lapsing suffer: Nay, sometimes,   3257
SOME-THING = *1
*2 Nay, I knew by his face that there was some-thing   2815
SOMTHING = *1
Men. Come, come, you haue bin too rough, somthing   2114
SON = 2*4
Volum. I prythee now sweet Son, as thou hast said   2214
*Son and Heire to Mars, set at vpper end o'th'Table: No   2852
*Son *Coriolanus*, guesse but my entertainment with him: if   3300
*Father *Menenius* do's. O my Son, my Son! thou art pre- | paring 3306
To th'insuing Age, abhorr'd. Speake to me Son: 3505
SONNE = 14*6
*in a more comfortable sort: If my Sonne were my Hus- | band, 363
*tender-bodied, and the onely Sonne of my womb; when   367
*Sonne, I therein would haue found issue. Heare me pro- | fesse 382
*What are you sowing heere? A fine spotte in good | faith. How does
your little Sonne?   415
Val. A my word the Fathers Sonne: Ile sweare 'tis a   420
Were he the Butcher of my Sonne, he should   848
*my Sonne the whole Name of the Warre: he hath in this   1032
That *Ancus Martius*, *Numaes* Daughters Sonne: 1642
Your Wife, your Sonne: These Senators, the Nobles,   2164
Volum. I prythee now, my Sonne,   2173
Makes fear'd, and talk'd of more then seene: your Sonne   2469
Volum. My first sonne, | Whether will thou go? Take good *Cominius* 2472
Nay but thou shalt stay too: I would my Sonne   2532
The meanest house in Rome; so farre my Sonne   2552
Corio. What's this? your knees to me? | To your Corrected Sonne? 3407
The Sonne, the Husband, and the Father tearing   3457
Thy Wife and Childrens blood: For my selfe, Sonne,   3473
*For making vp this peace. Thou know'st (great Sonne)   3497

SONNE *cont.*
    But for your Sonne, beleeue it: Oh beleeue it,   3545
    He kill'd my Sonne, my daughter, he kill'd my Cosine   3794
SONNES = 2
    And Mothers that lacke Sonnes.   1085
    Of thy deepe duty, more impression shew | Then that of common
    Sonnes.   3400
SONS = *1
    *sincerely, had I a dozen sons each in my loue alike,   383
SOONE = 2*1
    *3.*Cit.* Nay your wit will not so soone out as another   1413
    Neither Supreame; How soone Confusion   1804
    Fights Dragon-like, and does atcheeue as soone   3114
SOONER = 1
    Then seeke the end of one; thou shalt no sooner   3477
SOOTHD = 1
    You sooth'd not, therefore hurt not: but your People,   1285
SOOTHING = 2
    Made all of false-fac'd soothing: 800
    In soothing them, we nourish 'gainst our Senate   1759
SORE = 2
    Onely for bearing Burthens, and sore blowes | For sinking vnder them.   1179
    Mene. For 'tis a Sore vpon vs,   1959
SOROW = *1
    *Constraines them weepe, and shake with feare & sorow,   3455
SORROW = 2
    Virg. The sorrow that deliuers vs thus chang'd, | Makes you thinke so.   3388
    Auf. My Rage is gone, | And I am strucke with sorrow. Take him vp: 3829
SORT = 1*2
    *in a more comfortable sort: If my Sonne were my Hus-|band,   363
    *2 'Tis so, and as warres in some sort may be saide to   2884
    Bru. Rais'd onely, that the weaker sort may wish | Good *Martius* home
    againe.   2980
SOUERAIGNE = *1
    *the Physician: The most soueraigne Prescription in *Galen,*   1013
SOUERAIGNTY = 1
    By Soueraignty of Nature. First, he was   3126
SOUGHT = 2
    Your Voyces? for your Voyces I haue sought,   1518
    Which we disdaine should Tetter vs, yet sought   1771
SOUL = 2
SOULD = 1
SOULDIER *see also Soul., Sould.* = 7
    The Counsailor Heart, the Arme our Souldier,   119
    Weare not so rich a Iewell. Thou was't a Souldier   558
    Our Rome hath such a Souldier.   756
    Volum. Nay, my good Souldier, vp: 1076
    Thou art their Souldier, and being bred in broyles,   2182
    My praises made thee first a Souldier; so   2215
    Corio. Haile Lords, I am return'd your Souldier: 3736
SOULDIERS = 5
    *Enter Martius, Titus Lartius, with Drumme and Co-|lours, with
    Captaines and Souldiers, as*   478
    Garland, with Captaines and Soul-|diers, and a Herauld.   1062
    And not a haire vpon a Souldiers head   3059
    Corio. The God of Souldiers: | With the consent of supreme Ioue,
    informe   3423

SOULDIERS *cont.*
  Helpe three a'th'cheefest Souldiers, Ile be one.   3831
SOULDIORS = 1
  A flourish. Cornets. Enter Tullus Auffidius | bloudie, with two or three
  Souldiors.   857
SOULDIOUR = 1
  *1 Nay not so neither: but I take him to be the greater | Souldiour.   2827
SOULDIOURS = *1
  *Enters with a Lieutenant, other Souldiours, and a | Scout.   712
SOULE = 2
  Of no more Soule, nor fitnesse for the World,   1177
  It makes the Consuls base; and my Soule akes   1802
SOULES = 3
  Against the Winde a mile: you soules of Geese,   529
  There is the man of my soules hate, *Auffidious*,   581
  With Wine and Feeding, we haue suppler Soules   3213
SOUND = 11
  They Sound a Parley: Enter two Senators with others on | the Walles of
  Corialus.   499
  Lar. Thou worthiest *Martius*, | Go sound thy Trumpet in the Market
  place,   599
  More then I know the sound of *Martius* Tongue | From euery meaner
  man.   635
  Mart. Oh! let me clip ye | In Armes as sound, as when I woo'd in heart;   640
  Neuer sound more: when Drums and Trumpets shall   798
  Flourish. Trumpets sound, and Drums.   822
  A Sennet. Trumpets sound.   1059
  Welcome to Rome, renowned *Coriolanus.* | *Sound. Flourish.*   1068
  Ile haue fiue hundred Voyces of that sound.   1614
  And harsh in sound to thine.   2715
  I'de not haue giuen a doit. Harke, how they ioy. | *Sound still with the*
  Shouts.   3631
SOUNDED = 2
  Flourish. Alarum. A Retreat is sounded. Enter at | one Doore Cominius,
  with the Romanes: At   744
  Exeunt bearing the Body of Martius. A dead March | Sounded.   3837
SOUNDLY = 1
  Menen. Ha's he disciplin'd *Auffidius* soundly?   1023
SOUNDS = 3
  The Thunder-like percussion of thy sounds   561
  His rougher Actions for malicious sounds: 2332
  Drummes and Trumpets sounds, with great | showts of the people.   3705
SOURLY *see* sowrely
SOURS *see* sowres
SOUTH = 2*1
  Mar. All the contagion of the South, light on you,   525
  ('Tis South the City Mils) bring me word thither   891
  *they would flye East, West, North, South, and their con- | sent   1408
SOUTHWARD = 1
  if it were at liberty, 'twould sure Southward.   1415
SOWD = *1
  *Which we our selues haue plowed for, sow'd, & scatter'd,   1761
SOWE = 1
  They set them downe on two lowe stooles and sowe.   361
SOWING = *1
  *What are you sowing heere? A fine spotte in good | faith. How does
  your little Sonne?   415

SOWRELY = 1
  (Though I shew'd sowrely to him) once more offer'd   3360
SOWRES = *1
  *of his face, sowres ripe Grapes. When he walks, he moues   3587
SPACIOUS = 1
  And vowes Reuenge as spacious, as betweene | The yong'st and oldest
  thing.   2977
SPAKE = 1
  He was your Enemie, euer spake against   1580
SPARE = 1*1
  *Bru. Being mou'd, he will not spare to gird the Gods.   285
  Brut. I, spare vs not: Say, we read Lectures to you,   1638
SPAWNE = 1
  Menen. Masters of the People, | Your multiplying Spawne, how can he
  flatter?   1291
SPEAK see also speak't = 1*6
  All. Nay, but speak not maliciously.   36
  *And the blind to heare him speak: Matrons flong Gloues,   1193
  *Menen. Oh me the Gods, you must not speak of that,   1444
  *To'th'people: Coriolanus, patience: Speak good Sicinius.   1899
  *I am an Officer of State, & come to speak with Coriolanus   3239
  *Volum. Should we be silent & not speak, our Raiment   3449
  *I am husht vntill our City be afire, & then Ile speak a litle | Holds her
  by the hand silent.   3538
SPEAKE = 39*9
  1. Citizen. | *Before we proceed any further, heare me speake.   4
  All. Speake, speake.   6
  *we become Rakes. For the Gods know, I speake this in   25
  Where go you with Bats and Clubs? The matter | Speake I pray you. 57
  As well as speake, it taintingly replyed   112
  Auf. O doubt not that, | I speake from Certainties. Nay more, 348
  *Val. In earnest it's true; I heard a Senatour speake it.   459
  *you speake best vnto the purpose. It is not woorth the   981
  *Bru. All tongues speake of him, and the bleared sights   1123
  1.Sen. Speake, good Cominius: | Leaue nothing out for length, and
  make vs thinke   1256
  been silent: Please you to heare Cominius speake?   1270
  their Bed-fellow: Worthie Cominius speake.   1274
  The man I speake of, cannot in the World   1300
  I cannot speake him home: he stopt the flyers,   1317
  *Menen. It then remaines, that you doe speake to the | People. 1353
  *into those wounds, and speake for them: So if he tel   1394
  Ile leaue you: Pray you speake to em, I pray you | In wholsome manner.
  Exit   1450
  Bru. You speake a'th'people, as if you were a God,   1773
  Confusions neere, I cannot speake. You, Tribunes   1898
  *All. Let's here our Tribune: peace, speake, speake, | speake. 1901
  What the vengeance, could he not speake'em faire?   1992
  Mene. Heere me speake? As I do know   2010
  Sic. Speake breefely then, | For we are peremptory to dispatch 2021
  To speake of Peace, or Warre. I talke of you,   2098
  But when extremities speake. I haue heard you say,   2136
  Volum. Because, that | Now it lyes you on to speake to th'people: 2150
  Menen. Noble Lady, | Come goe with vs, speake faire: you may salue
  so,   2169
  Corio. First heare me speake. | Both Tri. Well, say: Peace hoe. 2313
  What you haue seene him do, and heard him speake: 2359

SPEAKE *cont.*

Com. Let me speake: | I haue bene Consull, and can shew from Rome 2395
And treasure of my Loynes: then if I would | Speake that. 2401
Sicin. We know your drift. Speake what? 2403
Why speak'st not? Speake man: What's thy name? 2709
Should from yond clowd speake diuine things, 2762
To heare *Cominius* speake, Ile keepe at home. 3158
2 You'l see your Rome embrac'd with fire, before | You'l speake with
Coriolanus. 3243
*Mene. Ha's he din'd can'st thou tell? For I would not | speake with
him, till after dinner. 3271
I will not heare thee speake. This man *Auffidius* 3327
To th'insuing Age, abhorr'd. Speake to me Son: 3505
That should but riue an Oake. Why do'st not speake? 3510
Still to remember wrongs? Daughter, speake you: 3512
He cares not for your weeping. Speake thou Boy, 3513
1 *Lord.* Peace both, and heare me speake. 3781
Auf. My Noble Masters, heare me speake. | 1.*Lord.* O *Tullus.* 3808
Beate thou the Drumme that it speake mournfully: 3832
SPEAKES = 5
Men. What then? Fore me, this Fellow speakes. | What then? What
then? 123
Bru. Why shall the people giue | One that speakes thus, their voyce? 1814
Menen. This but done, | Euen as she speakes, why their hearts were
yours: 2188
Be rein'd againe to Temperance, then he speakes 2293
Mene. Consider further: | That when he speakes not like a Citizen, 2329
SPEAKEST = 1
Com. Though thou speakest truth, 618
SPEAKST = 1*1
**Me thinkes thou speak'st not well. How long is't since? 619
Why speak'st not? Speake man: What's thy name? 2709
SPEAKT = 1
And I will speak't againe. 1751
SPECTACLED = 1
Are spectacled to see him. Your pratling Nurse 1124
SPECTACLES = 1
Heart-hardning spectacles. Tell these sad women, 2463
SPECTATORSHIP = *1
**more long in Spectatorship, and crueller in suffering, be-|hold 3302
SPEECH = 3
1.*Cit.* No, 'tis his kind of speech, he did not mock vs. 1559
Corio. Tell me of Corne: this was my speech, 1750
By calmenesse, or by absence: all's in anger. | *Menen.* Onely faire
speech. 2199
SPEECHLESSE = 1
Thus with his speechlesse hand. What he would do 3228
SPEED = 1*1
**Of shame seene through thy Country, speed thee straight 2744
Speed how it will. I shall ere long, haue knowledge | Of my successe.
Exit. 3220
SPEEDY = *1
*Virg. I will wish her speedy strength, and visite her 442
SPELL = 1
2 'Tis a spell you see of much power: 3332
SPEND = 2*1
**What I think, I vtter, and spend my malice in my breath. 949

SPEND *cont.*
  With doing them, and is content | To spend the time, to end it. 1344
  How you can frowne, then spend a fawne vpon'em, 2166
SPICES = 1
  (As he hath spices of them all) not all, 3137
SPIES = 1
  Mes. Spies of the *Volces* | Held me in chace, that I was forc'd to wheele 624
SPIGHT = 1
  I would haue voided thee. But in meere spight 2739
SPIRE = 1
  Which to the spire, and top of prayses vouch'd, 775
SPIRIT = 9
  Whil'st I with those that haue the spirit, wil haste | To helpe *Cominius*. 584
  Death, that darke Spirit, in's neruie Arme doth lye, 1057
  His readie sence: then straight his doubled spirit 1330
  Scicin. Thus to haue said, | As you were fore-aduis'd, had toucht his
  Spirit, 1592
  Which you are out of, with a gentler spirit, 1742
  The horne, and noise o'th'Monsters, wants not spirit 1789
  Com. I thinke 'twill serue, if he can thereto frame his | spirit. 2201
  Away my disposition, and possesse me | Some Harlots spirit: My throat
  of Warre be turn'd, 2219
  Resume that Spirit, when you were wont to say, 2454
SPIRITS = 1
  To say, Extreamities was the trier of spirits, 2440
SPIT = 1
  Then *Hectors* forhead, when it spit forth blood 404
SPITS = 1
  Least that thy Wiues with Spits, and Boyes with stones 2627
SPLEENE = 1
  Against my Cankred Countrey, with the Spleene 2748
SPLINTERS = 1
  And scarr'd the Moone with splinters: heere I cleep 2767
SPLITTING = 1
  And had no welcomes home, but he returnes | Splitting the Ayre with
  noyse. 3708
SPOILE *see also* spoyle = 2
  And that the Spoile got on the *Antiats* 2262
  When he had carried Rome, and that we look'd | For no lesse Spoile,
  then Glory. 3697
SPOILES *see also* spoyles = 1*1
  Enter certaine Romanes with spoiles. 569
  *The gates of Rome: Our spoiles we haue brought home 3742
SPOKE = 7*1
  Mess. They lye in view, but haue not spoke as yet. 488
  Valer. In troth, there's wondrous things spoke of him. 1034
  Corio. Spoke he of me? | *Latius.* He did, my Lord. | *Corio.* How? what? 1687
  Most Valour spoke not for them. Th'Accusation 1824
  Mene. Repent, what you haue spoke. 2131
  Each word thou hast spoke, hath weeded from my heart 2760
  Mes. It is spoke freely out of many mouths, 2974
  Auf. That I would haue spoke of: 3682
SPOKEN = 2
  Sicin. Ha's spoken like a Traitor, and shall answer | As Traitors do. 1862
  To banish him that strooke more blowes for Rome | Then thou hast
  spoken words. 2527

SPOONES = 1
At a crack'd Drachme: Cushions, Leaden Spoones,   576
SPORT = 1
Turne terror into sport: as Weeds before   1319
SPOTTE = *1
*What are you sowing heere? A fine spotte in good | faith. How does
your little Sonne?   415
SPOYLE = 2
In their nicely gawded Cheekes, toth' wanton spoyle   1136
A perpetuall spoyle: and till we call'd   1334
SPOYLES = 1
Com. Our spoyles he kickt at,   1340
SPRANG = *1
*thee Daughter, I sprang not more in ioy at first hearing   376
SPRED = 1
Least his infection being of catching nature, | Spred further.   2050
SPRIGHTLY = *1
*as day do's night: It's sprightly walking, audible, and full   2880
SPRINGS = 1
How long continued, and what stock he springs of,   1640
SPUN = *1
*the yearne she spun in *Vlisses* absence, did but fill *Athica*   447
SPURNE = 1
And spurne me backe: But, if it be not so   3522
SPURRE = 1
I may spurre on my iourney. | *Soul*. I shall sir.   893
STAGE = 1
*Enter two Senators, with Ladies, passing ouer | the Stage, with other
Lords*.   3639
STAINE = 2
With onely suff'ring staine by him: for him   877
Staine all your edges on me. Boy, false Hound: 3783
STAKE = 1
My Fortunes and my Friends at stake, requir'd   2162
STALLS = 1
Stalls, Bulkes, Windowes, are smother'd vp,   1129
STAMPE = 3
Me thinkes I see him stampe thus, and call thus,   394
He has the stampe of *Martius*, and I haue | Before time seene him thus.   631
And fell below his Stem: his Sword, Deaths stampe,   1321
STAMPT = 1
Haue (almost) stampt the Leasing. Therefore Fellow,   3260
STAND = 22*4
And feebling such as stand not in their liking,   207
If you'l stand fast, wee'l beate them to their Wiues,   536
And stand vpon my common part with those, | That haue beheld the
doing.   792
cast vp their Caps and Launces: Cominius | and Lartius stand bare.   795
*large Cicatrices to shew the People, when hee shall stand   1044
The Commoners, for whom we stand, but they   1149
Were he to stand for Consull, neuer would he   1155
*1.*Off*. Come, come, they are almost here: how many | stand for
Consulships?   1205
Put on the Gowne, stand naked, and entreat them   1357
Menen. Doe not stand vpon't: 1373
Coriol. Pray you now, if it may stand with the tune   1476
Why in this Wooluish tongue should I stand heere,   1506

STAND *cont*.

Corio. So then the Volces stand but as at first,	1677
Brut. Or let vs stand to our Authoritie,	1920
Com. Stand fast, we haue as many friends as enemies.	1954
And they, stand in their ancient strength.	2510
Corio. Let me but stand, I will not hurt your Harth.	2679
Stand I before thee heere: Then if thou hast	2741
*question askt him by any of the Senators, but they stand	2853
*Friends: the Commonwealth doth stand, and so would | do, were he	
more angry at it.	2907
2.*Wat*. Stand, and go backe.	3237
Be such a Gosling to obey instinct; but stand	3384
Volum. Oh stand vp blest! | Whil'st with no softer Cushion then the	
Flint	3402
Stand to me in this cause. Oh Mother! Wife!	3558
3.*Consp*. Sir, his stoutnesse | When he did stand for Consull, which he	
lost | By lacke of stooping.	3679
Shall haue Iudicious hearing. Stand *Auffidius*, | And trouble not the	
peace.	3799

STANDING = 3

You know the cause (Sir) of my standing heere.	1455
And translate his Mallice towards you, into Loue, | Standing your	
friendly Lord.	1590
Like a great Sea-marke standing euery flaw, | And sauing those that eye	
thee.	3427

STANDS = 5*1

Like Romans, neither foolish in our stands,	605
take their places by themselues: Corio-|lanus stands.	1242
*by him where he stands, by ones, by twoes, & by threes.	1430
And Manhood is call'd Foolerie, when it stands	1971
With Honour, as in Warre; since that to both | It stands in like request.	2147
Draw both the Conspirators, and kils Martius, who | falles, Auffidius	
stands on him.	3805

STANDST = 2*1

What art thou stiffe? Stand'st out?	264
And when it bowes, stand'st vp: Thou art left *Martius*,	556
*thou stand'st not i'th state of hanging, or of some death	3301

STARRES = 1

Fillop the Starres: Then, let the mutinous windes	3410

STARTS = 1

More then a wilde exposure, to each chance | That starts i'th'way	
before thee.	2475

STARUE *see* sterue

STATE = 16*7

Against the Roman State, whose course will on	70
The Helmes o'th State; who care for you like Fathers,	78
What euer haue bin thought one in this State	318
Volum. Looke, here's a Letter from him, the State hath	1005
Com. On, to the Capitall. *Flourish. Cornets*. | *Exeunt in State, as before*.	1120
But was a pettie seruant to the State,	1579
A place of Potencie, and sway o'th' State,	1583
*I say they norish disobedience: fed, the ruin of the State.	1813
Euen when the Nauell of the State was touch'd,	1820
That loue the Fundamentall part of State	1850
Mangles true iudgement, and bereaues the State	1857
For the whole State; I would put mine Armour on,	2126

STATE *cont*.

*state to finde you out there. You haue well saued mee a | dayes
iourney. 2581
*Vol. Hath bin; is it ended then? Our State thinks not 2586
Cit. He is, and Feasts the Nobles of the State, at his | house this night. 2633
And shewes good Husbandry for the Volcian State, 3113
It was a bare petition of a State 3173
*I am an Officer of State, & come to speak with *Coriolanus* 3239
*thou stand'st not i'th state of hanging, or of some death 3301
Nor from the State, nor priuate friends heereafter 3365
And state of Bodies would bewray what life 3450
*like a knell, and his hum is a Battery. He sits in his State, 3590
You Lords and Heads a'th'State, perfidiously 3759
STATES = 1
Rather our states defectiue for requitall, 1258
STATION = 1*1
To winne a vulgar station: our veyl'd Dames 1134
*3 Pray you poore Gentleman, take vp some other sta- | tion: 2684
STATUE = 1
As to *Ioues* Statue, and the Commons made 1196
STATUTES = *1
*the rich, and prouide more piercing Statutes daily, to 84
STAUES = 2
*Enter a Company of Mutinous Citizens, with Staues, | Clubs, and other
weapons.* 2
Strike at the Heauen with your staues, as lift them 69
STAY = 11*2
why stay we prating heere? To th'Capitoll. | *All*. Come, come. 49
Ere stay behinde this Businesse. | *Men*. Oh true-bred. 267
When blowes haue made me stay, I fled from words. 1284
*his behauiour: we are not to stay altogether, but to come 1429
Brut. We stay here for the People. 1546
Then stay past doubt, for greater: 1663
All. Peace, peace, peace, stay, hold, peace. 1896
Virg. You shall stay too: I would I had the power | To say so to my
Husband. 2522
Nay but thou shalt stay too: I would my Sonne 2532
Sicin. Why stay we to be baited 2556
He could not stay to picke them, in a pile 3178
1.Wat. Stay: whence are you. 3236
*is no hope in't, our throats are sentenc'd, and stay vppon | execution. 3576
STAYD = *1
*that: and he had stay'd by him, I would not haue been so 1027
STEALE = 1
Citizens steale away. Manet Sicin. & Brutus. 279
STEED = 5
Our Steed the Legge, the Tongue our Trumpeter, 120
Titus Lartius. Oh Generall: | Here is the Steed, wee the Caparison: 760
My Noble Steed, knowne to the Campe, I giue him, 817
I meane to stride your Steed, and at all times 827
Were you in my steed, would you haue heard 3550
STEELE = 2
When Steele growes soft, as the Parasites Silke, 801
Traile your steele Pikes. Though in this City hee 3833
STEEPE = 1
Let them pronounce the steepe Tarpeian death, 2372

STEM = 1
And fell below his Stem: his Sword, Deaths stampe,   1321
STERNE = 1
I haue seene the Sterne, and thou hast oft beheld   2462
STERUE = 2
  Coriol. Most sweet Voyces: | Better it is to dye, better to sterue,   1503
And so shall sterue with Feeding: come, let's go,   2566
STICKE = 1
To shame vnvulnerable, and sticke i'th Warres   3426
STICKES = 1
Opinion that so stickes on *Martius*, shall | Of his demerits rob *Cominius*.   302
STIFFE = 2
But make you ready your stiffe bats and clubs,   169
What art thou stiffe? Stand'st out?   264
STILL = 19
Still cubbording the Viand, neuer bearing   102
Alarum continues still a-farre off.   573
He still hath held them: that to's power he would   1173
Corio. I doe owe them still my Life, and Seruices.   1352
If he should still malignantly remaine   1584
(Harpe on that still) but by our putting on: 1656
Below the beame of sight; yet will I still | Be thus to them.   2088
In Congregations, to yawne, be still, and wonder,   2096
Fan you into dispaire: Haue the power still   2415
Still your owne Foes) deliuer you   2419
My hazards still haue beene your solace, and   2466
Heare from me still, and neuer of me ought   2493
Are still together: who Twin (as 'twere) in Loue,   2641
Bru. The Gods haue well preuented it, and Rome | Sits safe and still,
without him.   2936
Auf. Do they still flye to'th'Roman?   3091
For one poore graine or two, to leaue vnburnt | And still to nose
th'offence.   3180
Still to remember wrongs? Daughter, speake you: 3512
I'de not haue giuen a doit. Harke, how they ioy. | *Sound still with the
Shouts.*   3631
Then when I parted hence: but still subsisting   3738
STINKING = 2
Toth' People, begge their stinking Breaths.   1159
Your stinking, greasie Caps, in hooting   3057
STIRRE = 1 *1
*stirre, was pleas'd to let him seeke danger, where he was   373
For which the People stirre: if you will passe   1740
STIRRING = *1
*2 Why then wee shall haue a stirring World againe: 2876
STIRROP = 1
Who bow'd but in my Stirrop, bend like his   2227
STITCHERY = *1
Val. Come, lay aside your stitchery, I must haue you   432
STOCK = 1
How long continued, and what stock he springs of,   1640
STOCKES = 1
Like one i'th'Stockes. Thou hast neuer in thy life,   3517
STOLNE = 1
Ile grace thee with that Robbery, thy stolne name | *Coriolanus* in
Corioles?   3757

STONE = 2
    That Hunger-broke stone wals: that dogges must eate   219
    Mene. See you yon'd Coin a'th Capitol, yon'd corner | (stone?   3571
STONES = 2
    Thy Knee bussing the stones: for in such businesse   2176
    Least that thy Wiues with Spits, and Boyes with stones   2627
STOOD = 8*2
    Thus stood for his Countrey. Therefore please you,   1248
    Both Field and Citie ours, he neuer stood   1335
    *helpe will serue: for once we stood vp about the Corne,   1401
    Mene. You haue stood your Limitation: 1531
    Then what he stood for: so his gracious nature   1588
    When one but of my ordinance stood vp   2097
    Bru. We stood too't in good time. Is this *Menenius*?   2903
    Which were In-shell'd, when *Martius* stood for Rome,   2948
    Your Franchises, whereon you stood, confin'd | Into an Augors boare.   3001
    You and your Apron men: you, that stood so much   3013
STOOLES = 1
    They set them downe on two lowe stooles and sowe.   361
STOOPE = 1
    Before he should thus stoope to'th'heart, but that   2124
STOOPING = 1
    3.*Consp*. Sir, his stoutnesse | When he did stand for Consull, which he
    lost | By lacke of stooping.   3679
STOP = 3
    Scicin. Stop, or all will fall in broyle.   1714
    Thine owne particular wrongs, and stop those maimes   2743
    More then the instant Armie we can make | Might stop our
    Countryman.   3191
STOPT = 2
    I cannot speake him home: he stopt the flyers,   1317
    Stopt your eares against the generall suite of Rome: 3352
STORD = 2
    The Citie is well stor'd.   201
    Bru. He's poore in no one fault, but stor'd withall. | *Sicin*. Especially in
    Pride.   915
STORE = 2
    Whereof we haue ta'ne good, and good store of all,   784
    The Corne a'th'Store-house gratis, as 'twas vs'd | Sometime in Greece.   1809
STORE-HOUSE = 1
    Because I am the Store-house, and the Shop   140
STORE-HOUSES = *1
    *yet. Suffer vs to famish, and their Store-houses cramm'd   81
STOUT = 1
    Which often thus correcting thy stout heart,   2179
STOUTNESSE = 2
    Thy dangerous Stoutnesse: for I mocke at death   2236
    3.*Consp*. Sir, his stoutnesse | When he did stand for Consull, which he
    lost | By lacke of stooping.   3679
STRAIGHT = 1*3
    His readie sence: then straight his doubled spirit   1330
    Cori. That Ile straight do: and knowing my selfe again, | Repayre
    toth'Senate-|house.   1543
    *And straight disclaim their toungs? what are your Offices?   1717
    *Of shame seene through thy Country, speed thee straight   2744
STRAINES = 1
    Thou hast affected the fiue straines of Honor,   3506

STRAITE = 1
Bru. Go about it, | Put him to Choller straite, he hath bene vs'd 2289
STRANGE *see also* straunge = 5*3
And a petition granted them, a strange one, 223
Menen. This is strange. 236
Men. This is strange now: Do you two know, how 918
Knaues. You are a payre of strange ones. 975
*strange things from Rome: all tending to the good of 2610
*1 A strange one as euer I look'd on: I cannot get him 2675
*3 What you will not? Prythee tell my Maister what | a strange Guest
he ha's heere. 2688
1 Heere's a strange alteration? 2809
STRAUNGE = *1
Rom. There hath beene in Rome straunge Insurrecti-|ons: 2583
STREAME = 1
We will be there before the streame o'th' People: 1668
STREETS = 4
And not our streets with Warre. 2306
Dissentious numbers pestring streets, then see 2899
Then when these Fellowes ran about the streets, | Crying Confusion. 2926
With Manacles through our streets, or else 3470
STRENGTH = 5*2
Virg. I will wish her speedy strength, and visite her 442
I'th'right and strength a'th'Commons: be it either 2276
And they, stand in their ancient strength. 2510
As euer in Ambitious strength, I did 2770
*Thy Countries strength and weaknesse, thine own waies 2799
Is all the Policy, Strength, and Defence 3051
Doe's reason our Petition with more strength 3533
STRENGTHS = *2
*Rights by rights fouler, strengths by strengths do faile. 3146
STRETCH = 2
Then we to stretch it out. Masters a'th' People, 1259
That the precipitation might downe stretch 2087
STRETCHT = 2
And thus farre hauing stretcht it (here be with them) 2175
Auf. There was it: | For which my sinewes shall be stretcht vpon him, 3699
STREW = *1
*And make triumphant fires, strew Flowers before them: 3643
STRIDE = 1
I meane to stride your Steed, and at all times 827
STRIKE = 5*1
Strike at the Heauen with your staues, as lift them 69
Shalt see me once more strike at *Tullus* face. 263
'Tis sworne betweene vs, we shall euer strike 353
Vol. Now the Red Pestilence strike al Trades in Rome, | And
Occupations perish. 2450
Strike the proud Cedars 'gainst the fiery Sun: 3411
Auf. I know it: | And my pretext to strike at him, admits 3671
STRIPES = 1
Who weares my stripes imprest vpon him, that 3778
STRIUING = 1
With striuing lesse to be so: Lesser had bin | The things of your
dispositions, if 2107
STROAKES = 1
Opposing Lawes with stroakes, and heere defying 2361

STROKEN = *1
*2 By my hand, I had thoght to haue stroken him with   2810
STROKES *see also* stroakes = 3
  Onely in strokes, but with thy grim lookes, and   560
  Giuen Hostile strokes, and that not in the presence   2382
  Tis fond to waile ineuitable strokes,   2464
STRONG = 5*2
  *strong breaths, they shal know we haue strong arms too.   62
  Of more strong linke assunder, then can euer   72
  Coniecturall Marriages, making parties strong,   206
  You make strong partie, or defend your selfe   2198
  With Accusations, as I heare more strong | Then are vpon you yet.   2251
  Sicin. Make them be strong, and ready for this hint   2287
STRONGER = 2
  Mine eares against your suites, are stronger then   3323
  Of stronger earth then others: my Mother bowes,   3378
STRONGEST = 1
  The strongest Nerues, and small inferiour Veines   145
STRONGLY = *1
  *mans will, 'tis strongly wadg'd vp in a blocke-head: but   1414
STROOKE = 2*2
  We shall be charg'd againe. Whiles we haue strooke   607
  *When most strooke home, being gentle wounded, craues   2444
  To banish him that strooke more blowes for Rome | Then thou hast
  spoken words.   2527
  *Drum strooke vp this afternoone: 'Tis as it were a parcel   2874
STRUCKE = 4
  When the Alarum were strucke, then idly sit   1289
  And strucke him on his Knee: in that dayes feates,   1309
  And with a sudden re-inforcement strucke   1327
  Auf. My Rage is gone, | And I am strucke with sorrow. Take him vp: 3829
STUBBLE = 1
  To kindle their dry Stubble: and their Blaze | Shall darken him for euer.   1186
STUCKE = *1
  *he himselfe stucke not to call vs the many-headed Multi- | tude.   1402
STUFFE = *1
  *honourable a graue, as to stuffe a Botchers Cushion, or to   983
STUFFT = 1
  To giue or to forgiue; but when we haue stufft   3211
SUBDUES = 1
  To make him worthy, whose offence subdues him,   186
SUBIECTS = *1
  *shall encounter such ridiculous Subiects as you are, when   980
SUBMIT = 1
  Sicin. I do demand, | If you submit you to the peoples voices,   2317
SUBSCRIBD = 1
  Subscrib'd by'th'Consuls, and Patricians,   3747
SUBSISTING = 1
  Then when I parted hence: but still subsisting   3738
SUBTLE = 1*1
  Auf. Bolder, though not so subtle: my valors poison'd,   876
  Like to a Bowle vpon a subtle ground   3258
SUCCESSE = 2*1
  Sicin. Such a Nature, tickled with good successe, dis- | daines   289
  To Rome of our successe: you *Titus Lartius*   832
  Speed how it will. I shall ere long, haue knowledge | Of my successe.
  Exit.   3220

SUCCESSES = 2

Leade their successes, as we wish our owne,   610
In our well-found Successes, to report   1251

SUCH = 24*11

As you maligne our Senators, for that | They are not such as you.   115
And feebling such as stand not in their liking,   207
*Sicin. Such a Nature, tickled with good successe, dis- | daines   289
*would become such a person, that it was no better then   371
*halfe an houre together: ha's such a confirm'd coun- | tenance.   422
Mar. Those are they | That most are willing; if any such be heere,   685
Our Rome hath such a Souldier.   756
*Meeting two such Weales men as you are (I cannot call   950
*shall encounter such ridiculous Subiects as you are, when   980
Such eyes the Widowes in Carioles were,   1084
Of Phoebus burning Kisses: such a poother,   1137
*and his assent is not by such easie degrees as those, who   1228
Plague vpon't, I cannot bring | My tongue to such a pace. Looke Sir, my wounds,   1439
Or seeing it, of such Childish friendlinesse, | To yeeld your Voyces?   1575
Suffer't, and liue with such as cannot rule, | Nor euer will be ruled.   1723
Com. You are like to doe such businesse.   1734
And such a one as he, who puts his Shall,   1799
Which your heart prompts you, but with such words   2153
Thy Knee bussing the stones: for in such businesse   2176
You haue put me now to such a part, which neuer   2211
Bru. And when such time they haue begun to cry,   2282
To suffer lawfull Censure for such faults | As shall be prou'd vpon you.   2320
But as I say, such as become a Soldier, | Rather then enuy you.   2333
Euen this so criminall, and in such capitall kinde   2363
his head, that he giues entrance to such Companions?   2667
Deserue such pitty of him, as the Wolfe   3030
Com. You haue brought | A Trembling vpon Rome, such as was neuer   3039
*daughters, or with the palsied intercession of such a de- | cay'd   3280
*such weake breath as this? No, you are deceiu'd, therfore   3283
*for such things as you. I can scarse thinke ther's any, y'are   3338
*Neuer admitted a priuat whisper, no not with such frends | That thought them sure of you.   3353
Be such a Gosling to obey instinct; but stand   3384
Which thou shalt thereby reape, is such a name   3500
*Mene. No, in such a case the Gods will not bee good   3600
A City full: Of Tribunes such as you,   3628

SUCKLE = 1

When she did suckle Hector, look'd not louelier   403

SUCKST = 1

Thy Valiantnesse was mine, thou suck'st it from me: 2238

SUDDAINE see also sodaine = 2

Scicin. On the suddaine, I warrant him Consull.   1141
That hee's your fixed enemie; and reuoke | Your suddaine approbation.   1653

SUDDEN = 1

And with a sudden re-inforcement strucke   1327

SUD-FOR = 1

Bestow your su'd-for Tongues?   1611

SUFFER see also suffer't = 4*1

*yet. Suffer vs to famish, and their Store-houses cramm'd   81
Were to vs all that doo't, and suffer it   2040
To suffer lawfull Censure for such faults | As shall be prou'd vpon you.   2320
Though they themselues did suffer by't, behold   2898

SUFFER *cont.*
Would without lapsing suffer: Nay, sometimes,   3257
SUFFERAGE = 1
For my Wounds sake, to giue their sufferage: 1358
SUFFERANCE = 1*1
  *to particularize their abundance, our sufferance is a   23
For they doe pranke them in Authoritie, | Against all Noble sufferance.   1702
SUFFERD = 1
And suffer'd me by th'voyce of Slaues to be   2734
SUFFERED = 1
The one part suffered, the other will I doe.   1515
SUFFERING = 1*1
Your suffering in this dearth, you may as well   68
  *more long in Spectatorship, and crueller in suffering, be-|hold   3302
SUFFERT = 1
Suffer't, and liue with such as cannot rule, | Nor euer will be ruled.   1723
SUFFRING = 1
With onely suff'ring staine by him: for him   877
SUGGEST = 1
We must suggest the People, in what hatred   1172
SUGGESTED = 1
Scicin. This (as you say) suggested,   1181
SUIT = 1
How in his Suit he scorn'd you: but your Loues,   1625
SUITE = 3
But by the suite of the Gentry to him,   1163
Stopt your eares against the generall suite of Rome: 3352
As poysonous of your Honour. No, our suite   3492
SUITES = 2
Mine eares against your suites, are stronger then   3323
I haue yeelded too. Fresh Embasses, and Suites,   3364
SUITORS *see* suters
SULPHURE = 1
And yet to change thy Sulphure with a Boult   3509
SUMMER = 1
Then Boyes pursuing Summer Butter-flies, | Or Butchers killing Flyes.   3010
SUMMON = 1
For halfe a hundred yeares: Summon the Towne.   492
SUMMOND = 1
The People doe admit you, and are summon'd   1537
SUN = 3*1
Or Hailstone in the Sun. Your Vertue is,   185
  Corio. I had rather haue one scratch my Head i'th' Sun,   1288
Strike the proud Cedars 'gainst the fiery Sun: 3411
Mes. As certaine as I know the Sun is fire: 3617
SUNNE = 1
Make the Sunne dance. Hearke you. *A shout within*   3624
SUP *see also* suppe = 1
And by my troth you haue cause: you'l Sup with me.   2564
SUPERFLUITIE = *1
  *vs. If they would yeelde vs but the superfluitie while it   19
SUPERFLUITY = 1
Our mustie superfluity. See our best Elders.   243
SUPPE = 1
Volum. Angers my Meate: I suppe vpon my selfe,   2565
SUPPER = *1
  Rom. I shall betweene this and Supper, tell you most   2609

SUPPLE = *1
  *hauing beene supple and courteous to the People, Bon-|netted,   1229
SUPPLER = 1
  With Wine and Feeding, we haue suppler Soules   3213
SUPPLIANTS = 1
  Scandal'd the Suppliants: for the People, call'd them   1728
SUPPLICATION = 1
  In supplication Nod: and my yong Boy   3380
SUPPLIED = 1
  Supplied with worthy men, plant loue amongs   2304
SUPPORT = *1
  *with Graine: Make Edicts for Vsurie, to support Vsu-|rers;   82
SUPREAME = 2
  Neither Supreame; How soone Confusion   1804
  Corio. The God of Souldiers: | With the consent of supreame Ioue, informe   3423
SURCEASE = 1
  Least I surcease to honor mine owne truth,   2229
SURE = 8
  Scicin. It shall be to him then, as our good wills; a | sure destruction.   1168
  if it were at liberty, 'twould sure Southward.   1415
  Scicin. Why so he did, I am sure.   1563
  That's sure of death without it: at once plucke out   1854
  All. He shall sure ont. | *Mene*. Sir, sir. *Sicin*. Peace.   2004
  Auf. I vnderstand thee well, and be thou sure   3108
  Vpbraid's with our distresse. But sure if you   3189
  *Neuer admitted a priuat whisper, no not with such frends | That thought them sure of you.   3353
SURER = 1
  Where Foxes, Geese you are: No surer, no,   183
SURETY = 1
  All. Wee'l Surety him. | *Com*. Ag'd sir, hands off.   1881
SURFET = 1
  *had rather had eleuen dye Nobly for their Countrey, then | one voluptuously surfet out of Action.   385
SURFETS = 1*1
  *good: what Authority surfets one, would releeue   18
  Of the warres surfets, to go roue with one   2487
SURLY = 1
  Or else it would haue gall'd his surly nature,   1597
SURNAME *see also* sur-name = 2
  My Surname *Coriolanus*. The painfull Seruice,   2725
  But with that Surname, a good memorie   2728
SURPLUS = 1
  he hath faults (with surplus) to tyre in repetition. | *Showts within*.   46
SURUEY = *1
  *but an Interiour suruey of your good selues. Oh that you | could.   936
SURUIUOR = 1
  'Twixt you there's difference: but the fall of either | Makes the Suruiuor heyre of all.   3669
SUR-NAME = 1
  To his sur-name *Coriolanus* longs more pride   3527
SUTERS = *1
  *now wee'l shew em in deeds: they say poore Suters haue   61
SUTORS = 1
  Volum. Euen he, your wife, this Ladie, and my selfe, | Are Sutors to you.   3431

SWAY = 2
Then sway with them in theirs. 1119
A place of Potencie, and sway o'th' State, 1583
SWEARE = 1*1
*Val. A my word the Fathers Sonne: Ile sweare 'tis a 420
Brutus. I heard him sweare, 1154
SWEARING = 1
And hale him vp and downe; all swearing, if 3606
SWEAT see also swet = 1*1
*which makes me sweat with wrath. Come on my fellows 520
Mine eyes to sweat compassion. But (good sir) 3555
SWEET = 8*1
Val. My Ladies both good day to you. | Vol. Sweet Madam. 411
Fare you well then. Come good sweet Ladie. 471
Com. And liue you yet? Oh my sweet Lady, pardon. 1087
Coriol. Most sweet Voyces: | Better it is to dye, better to sterue, 1503
*Your most sweet Voyces: now you haue left your Voyces, 1572
The sweet which is their poyson. Your dishonor 1856
Volum. I prythee now sweet Son, as thou hast said 2214
Come my sweet wife, my deerest Mother, and 2489
Long as my Exile, sweet as my Reuenge! 3394
SWET = 1
Your Husband so much swet. Cominius, 2457
SWIFTER = 1
*Latius. He had, my Lord, and that it was which caus'd | Our swifter
Composition. 1675
SWIFTNESSE = 1
The harme of vnskan'd swiftnesse, will (too late) 2054
SWIMMES = 1
Vpon your fauours, swimmes with finnes of Leade, 191
SWOOND = 1*1
*now presently, and swoond for what's to come vpon 3303
2 What cause do you thinke I haue to swoond? 3336
SWORD = 15*3
And let me vse my Sword, I'de make a Quarrie 210
At Grecian sword. Contenning, tell Valeria 405
Lar. Oh Noble Fellow! | Who sensibly out-dares his sencelesse Sword, 554
Oh me alone, make you a sword of me: 697
A Bribe, to pay my Sword: I doe refuse it, 791
True Sword to Sword: Ile potche at him some way, | Or Wrath, or Craft
may get him. 873
And fell below his Stem: his Sword, Deaths stampe, 1321
*Latius. How often he had met you Sword to Sword: 1690
And beare him to the Rock. Corio. drawes his Sword. 1939
*Mene. Downe with that Sword, Tribunes withdraw | a while. 1943
Since a could draw a Sword, and is ill-school'd 2063
Were in Arabia, and thy Tribe before him, | His good Sword in his
hand. 2533
The Anuile of my Sword, and do contest 2768
As draw his Sword: yet he hath left vndone 3115
With what he would say, let him feele your Sword: 3715
His Tribe, to vse my lawfull Sword. 3802
SWORDS = 6*2
*Vol. He had rather see the swords, and heare a Drum, | then looke
vpon his Schoolmaster. 418
That we with smoaking swords may march from hence 497

SWORDS *cont.*

Misguide thy Opposers swords, Bold Gentleman: | Prosperity be thy Page.	595
Filling the aire with Swords aduanc'd) and Darts,	678
They all shout and waue their swords, take him vp in their | Armes, and cast vp their Caps.	695
He lurcht all Swords of the Garland: for this last,	1315
To haue a Temple built you: All the Swords	3567
3.*Lord.* Tread not vpon him Masters, all be quiet, | Put vp your Swords.	3812

SWORN = *1

*Oh World, thy slippery turnes! Friends now fast sworn,	2638

SWORNE = 3*4

'Tis sworne betweene vs, we shall euer strike	353
Mene. True? Ile be sworne they are true: where is	1039
*my sworne Brother the people to earne a deerer estima-|tion	1487
What may be sworne by, both Diuine and Humane,	1840
*2 So did I, Ile be sworne: He is simply the rarest man | i'th'world.	2820
*condemn'd, our Generall has sworne you out of repreeue | and pardon.	3285
Corio. I dare be sworne you were:	3553

SYLLABLES = 1*1

*the Asse in compound, with the Maior part of you͏̈ sylla-|bles.	954
Though but Bastards, and Syllables	2155

SYMBOLES = 1

Tabors, and Symboles, and the showting Romans,	3623

SYNOD = *1

*thee. The glorious Gods sit in hourely Synod about thy	3304 ·

T = 3

Hath not a Tombe so euident as a Chaire | T'extoll what it hath done.	3143
Wherein I seeme vnnaturall: Desire not t'allay	3439
Intends t'appeare before the People, hoping	3656

TABER = *1

Com. The Shepherd knowes not Thunder fro(m) a Taber,	634

TABLE = 1*3

*perfecter gyber for the Table, then a necessary Bencher in | the Capitoll.	977
*Son and Heire to Mars, set at vpper end o'th'Table: No	2852
*the intreaty and graunt of the whole Table. Hee'l go he	2859
Their talke at Table, and their Thankes at end,	3094

TABORS = 1

Tabors, and Symboles, and the showting Romans,	3623

TACKLES = 1

Beares a Command in't: Though thy Tackles torne,	2718

TAGGE = 1

Before the Tagge returne? whose Rage doth rend	1973

TAILORS *see* taylors

TAINTINGLY = 1

As well as speake, it taintingly replyed	112

TAINTS = 1

Which out of dayly Fortune euer taints	3129

TAKE = 24*10

The Volces haue much Corne: take these Rats thither,	276
To take in many Townes, ere (almost) Rome | Should know we were a-foot.	340
2.*Sen.* Noble *Auffidius,* | Take your Commission, hye you to your Bands,	342
He that retires, Ile take him for a *Volce,*	521
Piercing our Romanes: Then Valiant *Titus* take	582

TAKE *cont*.

Deny your asking, take your choice of those | That best can ayde your
action.   683

*They all shout and waue their swords, take him vp in their | Armes, and
cast vp their Caps.*   695

But cannot make my heart consent to take   790

*pleasures (at the least) if you take it as a pleasure to you, in   928

*the Beastly Plebeans. I will be bold to take my leaue of | you.   990

Menen. Take my Cappe *Iupiter*, and I thanke thee: 1002

take their places by themselues: Corio- |lanus stands.   1242

And take to you, as your Predecessors haue,   1364

They haue chose a Consull, that will from them take   1617

May enter 'twixt the gap of Both, and take | The one by th'other.   1805

Bru. Enough, with ouer measure. | *Corio*. No, take more.   1838

Sicin. Heere's hee, that would take from you all your | power.   1888

Mene. I could my selfe take vp a Brace o'th' best of | them, yea, the
two Tribunes.   1968

Then to take in a Towne with gentle words,   2158

Tent in my cheekes, and Schoole-boyes Teares take vp   2224

You finde him like a Soldier: do not take   2331

I am so dishonour'd, that the very houre | You take it off againe.   2338

Sicin. We charge you, that you haue contriu'd to take   2342

Volum. My first sonne, | Whether will thou go? Take good *Cominius*   2472

Volum. Take my Prayers with you.   2558

*they are in a ripe aptnesse, to take al power from the peo-|ple,   2592

Volce. You take my part from me sir, I haue the most | cause to be
glad of yours.   2618

To take the one the other, by some chance,   2646

*3 Pray you poore Gentleman, take vp some other sta-|tion: 2684

And take our friendly Senators by'th'hands   2790

The leading of thine owne Reuenges, take   2796

*1 Nay not so neither: but I take him to be the greater | Souldiour.   2827

Take this along, I writ it for thy sake,   3325

Auf. My Rage is gone, | And I am strucke with sorrow. Take him vp: 3829

TAKEN *see also* ta'ne = 2

And might well be taken from the People.   1367

He was not taken well, he had not din'd,   3208

TAKES = 3

The way it takes: cracking ten thousand Curbes   71

As is the Aspray to the Fish, who takes it   3125

2.*Lord*. His owne impatience, | Takes from *Auffidius* a great part of
blame: 3826

TAKING = 1

Who now are heere, taking their leaues of mee,   2791

TAKT = 1

Com. Tak't, 'tis yours: what is't?   840

TALE = 3

A pretty Tale, it may be you haue heard it,   91

To fobbe off our disgrace with a tale: 96

After your way. His Tale pronounc'd, shall bury | His Reasons, with his
Body.   3717

TALKD = 1

Makes fear'd, and talk'd of more then seene: your Sonne   2469

TALKE = 6*2

Men. Because you talke of Pride now, will you not | be angry.   922

*much alone. You talke of Pride: Oh, that you could turn   934

Brut. It it were so? | *Sicin*. What do ye talke?   2058

TALKE *cont.*

To speake of Peace, or Warre. I talke of you,	2098
Brut. I talke of that, that know it. | *Corio.* You?	2367
Sicin. Come, what talke you of *Martius.*	2950
Their talke at Table, and their Thankes at end,	3094

Mene. Good my Friends, \| If you haue heard your Generall talke of
Rome,   3245

TALKES = *1

*He is able to pierce a Corslet with his eye: Talkes   3589

TALKING = *1

**All.* No more talking on't; Let it be done, away, away   15

TALKT = *1

**2 Ser.* Are you so braue: Ile haue you talkt with anon   2672

TAME = 1

His remedies are tame, the present peace,   2894

TANE = 4*1

Whereof we haue ta'ne good, and good store of all,	784
We render you the Tenth, to be ta'ne forth,	786
Auffi. The Towne is ta'ne.	859

You should haue ta'ne th'aduantage of his Choller, \| And pass'd him
vnelected.   1600

**Brut.* They haue tane note of vs: keepe on your way.   2516

TAPERS = 1

As merry, as when our Nuptiall day was done, \| And Tapers burnt to
Bedward.   642

TARGET = 1

Once more to hew thy Target from thy Brawne,   2778

TARPEIAN = 4*1

Beare him toth' Rock Tarpeian, and from thence \| Into destruction cast
him.   1926

**Sicin.* He shall be throwne downe the Tarpeian rock	1997
Or pile ten hilles on the Tarpeian Rocke,	2086
Let them pronounce the steepe Tarpeian death,	2372
In perill of precipitation | From off the Rocke Tarpeian, neuer more	2387

TARQUIN = 1*1

*for his place: he receiued in the repulse of *Tarquin* seuen \| hurts ith'
Body.   1045

When *Tarquin* made a Head for Rome, he fought   1302

TARQUINS = 2

Slew three Opposers: *Tarquins* selfe he met,	1308
No, not th'expulsion of the *Tarquins.*	3614

TARTNESSE = *1

*Mother now, then an eight yeare old horse. The tartnesse   3586

TASKD = 1

Like to a Haruest man, that task'd to mowe \| Or all, or loose his hyre.   398

TASTE = 2

When both your voices blended, the great'st taste	1797
Haue we not had a taste of his Obedience?	2060

TAUNTS = 1

Bru. Mark'd you his lip and eyes. \| *Sicin.* Nay, but his taunts.   283

TAYLORS = *1

*This peace is nothing, but to rust Iron, encrease Taylors, \| and breed
Ballad-makers.   2877

TEACH = 2

Shall teach the People, which time shall not want,	1183
And by my Bodies action, teach my Minde | A most inherent Basenesse.	2230

TEACHES = 1
Sicin. Nature teaches Beasts to know their Friends.   903
TEARE = 3*1
  *his teeth, and teare it. Oh, I warrant how he mammockt | it.   427
  To teare with Thunder the wide Cheekes a'th'Ayre,   3508
  2.*Con.* And patient Fooles, | Whose children he hath slaine, their base
  throats teare   3710
  All People. Teare him to peeces, do it presently: 3793
TEARES *see also* teeres = 6*1 ✐
  Where Senators shall mingle teares with smiles,   750
  And behinde him, hee leaues Teares: 1056
  Tent in my cheekes, and Schoole-boyes Teares take vp   2224
  Corio. Come leaue your teares: a brief farwel: the beast   2437
  Thy teares are salter then a yonger mans,   2460
  Counsaile a'th'warre: But at his Nurses teares   3765
  Corio. Hear'st thou Mars? | *Auf.* Name not the God, thou boy of
  Teares.   3769
TEARING = 1
  The Sonne, the Husband, and the Father tearing   3457
TEARME = 1
  tell how to tearme it.   2817
TEERES = 1
  If I could shake off but one seuen teeres   2497
TEETH = 1*2
  *his teeth, and teare it. Oh, I warrant how he mammockt | it.   427
  And keepe their teeth cleane: So, heere comes a brace,   1454
  *You being their Mouthes, why rule you not their Teeth?   1718
TEL = *1
  *into those wounds, and speake for them: So if he tel   1394
TELL = 22*13
  Men. I tell you Friends, most charitable care   66
  Or be accus'd of Folly. I shall tell you   90
  Men. Sir, I shall tell you with a kinde of Smile,   109
  Men. I will tell you, | If you'l bestow a small (of what you haue little)   130
  *whence he return'd, his browes bound with Oake. I tell   375
  At Grecian sword. *Contenning*, tell *Valeria*   405
  Val. In truth la go with me, and Ile tell you excellent | newes of your
  Husband.   453
  Mar. Will the time serue to tell, I do not thinke: 660
  Com. If I should tell thee o're this thy dayes Worke,   748
  *You two are old men, tell me one thing that I shall aske | you.   910
  *that tell you haue good faces, if you see this in the Map   957
  *his wounds, and tell vs his deeds, we are to put our ton-|gues   1393
  *vs his Noble deeds, we must also tell him our Noble ac-|ceptance   1395
  *3 *Cit.* We do Sir, tell vs what hath brought you too't.   1456
  Brut. Get you hence instantly, and tell those friends,   1616
  Corio. Tell me of Corne: this was my speech,   1750
  I'th'Warre do grow together: Grant that, and tell me   2138
  Heart-hardning spectacles. Tell these sad women,   2463
  And for Romes good, Ile tell thee what: yet goe: 2531
  *This lyes glowing I can tell you, and is almost mature for | the violent
  breaking out.   2594
  Rom. I shall betweene this and Supper, tell you most   2609
  *3 What you will not? Prythee tell my Maister what | a strange Guest
  he ha's heere.   2688
  Bestride my Threshold. Why, thou Mars I tell thee,   2776
  tell how to tearme it.   2817

TELL _cont_.
    *2 Faith looke you, one cannot tell how to say that: for   2829
    *3 Oh Slaues, I can tell you Newes, News you Rascals   2833
    Sicin. Tell not me: I know this cannot be. | _Bru_. Not possible.   2961
    Com. I tell you, he doe's sit in Gold, his eye   3224
    Mene. I tell thee Fellow, | Thy Generall is my Louer: I haue beene   3251
    *_Mene_. Ha's he din'd can'st thou tell? For I would not | speake with
    him, till after dinner.   3271
    Againe, with Romes Mechanickes. Tell me not   3438
    This Boy that cannot tell what he would haue,   3531
    Auf. Go tell the Lords a'th'City, I am heere: 3650
    Auf. Sir, I cannot tell,   3666
    But tell the Traitor in the highest degree   3751
TELLING = *1
    *haue, I am one that telling true vnder him, must say you | cannot
    passe. Therefore go backe.   3269
TELS = *1
    *_Men_. The Agurer tels me, wee shall haue Newes to | night.   898
TEMPER = 1
    Auffid. You keepe a constant temper. _Exeunt_   3329
TEMPERANCE = 1
    Be rein'd againe to Temperance, then he speakes   2293
TEMPERATELY = 1
    Mene. Nay temperately: your promise.   2347
TEMPLE = 2
    And hangs on _Dians_ Temple: Deere _Valeria_.   3419
    To haue a Temple built you: All the Swords   3567
TEMPLES = 2
    Through our large Temples with y shewes of peace   2305
    Com. Your Temples burned in their Ciment, and   3000
TEMPORIZD = 1
    *_Mene_. All's well, and might haue bene much better, | if he could haue
    temporiz'd.   2909
TEMPRATELY = 2
    Scicin. He cannot temp'rately transport his Honors,   1144
    And temp'rately proceed to what you would | Thus violently redresse.   1934
TEMPTED = 1
    Shall I be tempted to infringe my vow   3367
TEN = 3
    The way it takes: cracking ten thousand Curbes   71
    Or pile ten hilles on the Tarpeian Rocke,   2086
    This Morning, for ten thousand of your throates,   3630
TEND = 1
    If it were so, that our request did tend   3489
TENDER = 1
    My Countries good, with a respect more tender,   2398
TENDERNESSE = 1
    Corio. Not of a womans tendernesse to be,   3485
TENDER-BODIED = *1
    *tender-bodied, and the onely Sonne of my womb; when   367
TENDING = *1
    *strange things from Rome: all tending to the good of   2610
TENT = 6
    And tent themselues with death: of all the Horses,   783
    Com. So, to our Tent: 830
    Com. Goe we to our Tent: 854
    You cannot Tent your selfe: be gone, 'beseech you.   1960

TENT *cont*.
Tent in my cheekes, and Schoole-boyes Teares take vp	2224
A Mile before his Tent, fall downe, and knee	3156

TENTH = 1
We render you the Tenth, to be ta'ne forth,	786

TERME *see also* tearme = *1
*not (looke you sir) shew themselues (as we terme it) his | Friends, whilest he's in Directitude.	2866

TERRIBLE = 1
Euen to *Calues* wish, not fierce and terrible	559

TERRITORIES = 3
Who am prepar'd against your Territories, | Though not for Rome it selfe.	2792
Are entred in the Roman Territories,	2942
Associated with *Auffidius*, Rages | Vpon our Territories, and haue already	2989

TERROR = 1
Turne terror into sport: as Weeds before	1319

TERTIUS *l*.1671 = 1
TESTIE = *1
*proud, violent, testie Magistrates (alias Fooles) | as any in Rome.	940

TETTER = 1
Which we disdaine should Tetter vs, yet sought	1771

TH *see also* a'th, by'th, i'th, o'th, to'th = 50*9
why stay we prating heere? To th'Capitoll. | *All*. Come, come.	49
*2 *Cit*. Our busines is not vnknowne to th'Senat, they	59
I'th midd'st a th'body, idle and vnactiue,	101
Like labour with the rest, where th'other Instruments	103
Who is the sinke a th'body.	126
Euen to the Court, the Heart, to th'seate o'th'Braine,	143
They'l sit by th'fire, and presume to know	203
Mar. Were halfe to halfe the world by th'eares, & he	254
To th'vtmost of a man, and giddy censure	298
*Picture-like to hang by th'wall, if renowne made it not	372
See him plucke *Auffidius* downe by th'haire:	392
All. To th'pot I warrant him. *Enter Titus Lartius*	547
Ransoming him, or pittying, threatning th'other;	647
By th'Blood we haue shed together, | By th'Vowes we haue made	673
*Our Guider come, to th'Roman Campe conduct vs. *Exit*	721
Wrench vp thy power to th'highest.	736
Let him be made an Ouerture for th' Warres:	802
With all th'applause and Clamor of the Hoast,	820
Marcus Caius Coriolanus. Beare th'addition Nobly euer?	821
To vnder-crest your good Addition, | To th'fairenesse of my power.	828
As often as we eate. By th'Elements,	868
Wash my fierce hand in's heart. Go you to th'Citie,	886
And carry with vs Eares and Eyes for th' time, | But Hearts for the euent.	1200
The mortall Gate of th' Citie, which he painted	1325
Shew them th'vnaking Skarres, which I should hide,	1370
Of our proceedings heere on th'Market place,	1385
From th'noise of our owne Drummes.	1443
Remaines, that in th'Officiall Markes inuested,	1533
You should haue ta'ne th'aduantage of his Choller, | And pass'd him vnelected.	1600
Th'apprehension of his present portance,	1627
May enter 'twixt the gap of Both, and take | The one by th'other.	1805

TH *cont*.

Most Valour spoke not for them. Th'Accusation	1824
For th'ill which doth controul't.	1860
A brand to th'end a'th World.	2041
Corio. What must I do? | *Mene*. Returne to th'Tribunes.	2128
In Peace, what each of them by th'other loose,	2139
Volum. Because, that | Now it lyes you on to speake to th'people:	2150
Action is eloquence, and the eyes of th'ignorant	2177
Th'honor'd Goddes | Keepe Rome in safety, and the Chaires of Iustice	2302
Deserues th'extreamest death.	2364
Th'hoorded plague a'th'Gods requit your loue.	2518
*charges distinctly billetted already in th'entertainment,	2613
And suffer'd me by th'voyce of Slaues to be	2734
Th'one halfe of my Commission, and set downe	2797
*sayes, and sole the Porter of Rome Gates by th'eares. He	2860
To th'vulgar eye, that he beares all things fairely:	3112
From th'Caske to th'Cushion: but commanding peace	3134
Lie in th'interpretation of the time,	3141
For one poore graine or two, to leaue vnburnt | And still to nose	
th'offence.	3180
Menen. I neither care for th'world, nor your General:	3337
You must report to th'Volcian Lords, how plainly	3349
Which by th'interpretation of full time, | May shew like all your selfe.	3421
To th'insuing Age, abhorr'd. Speake to me Son:	3505
No, not th'expulsion of the *Tarquins*.	3614
*As the recomforted through th'gates. Why harke you: | *Trumpets*,	
Hoboyes, Drums beate, altogether.	3620
Bid them repayre to th'Market place, where I	3652
Then shame to th'Romaines. And we heere deliuer	3746

THAN *see* then

THANKE = 10

Vir. I thanke your Lady-ship: Well good Madam.	417
Shall say against their hearts, We thanke the Gods	755
Martius. I thanke you Generall:	789
Whether I blush or no: howbeit, I thanke you,	826
Menen. Take my Cappe *Iupiter*, and I thanke thee:	1002
Volum. Oh, he is wounded, I thanke the Gods for't.	1018
We met here, both to thanke, and to remember, | With Honors like	
himselfe.	1254
Here was, I thanke you for your Voyces, thanke you	1571
Corio. Thanke you sir, farewell. *Exit Citizen*	2637

THANKEFULNESSE = 1

Sicin. First, the Gods blesse you for your tydings: | Next, accept my	
thankefulnesse.	3633

THANKES = 3

(Though thankes to all) must I select from all:	702
Their talke at Table, and their Thankes at end,	3094
Sicin. Yet your good will | Must haue that thankes from Rome, after	
the measure | As you intended well.	3202

THANKFULL = 1

May giue you thankfull Sacrifice. Thy Newes?	612

THANKLESSE = 1

Shed for my thanklesse Country, are requitted:	2727

THANKS = *2

Mar. Thanks. What's the matter you dissentious rogues	174
Mess. Sir, we haue all great cause to giue great thanks.	3635

THART = 2
Corio. Now th'art troublesome. 2671
Th'art tyr'd, then in a word, I also am 2751
THAT *see also* o'that, that's *l*.*22 *34 *38 *53 100 114 115 122 138 146
147 152 165 167 175 *178 180 181 187 189 190 194 195 196 219 *220
*246 249 257 302 315 319 348 *364 *371 398 441 445 *449 497 502 521
527 530 531 *575 577 578 584 *611 625 630 651 675 677 684 686 687
691 738 754 768 774 793 803 804 811 813 815 838 863 865 871 887 892
908 *909 *910 *913 *934 *936 *944 *947 *956 *957 *958 *1027 1048
1057 1064 1083 1085 1095 1096 1099 1138 1147 1152 *1165 1173 1191
*1211 *1213 *1214 *1223 *1225 *1232 *1235 1236 1247 1252 1298 1309
*1353 1356 1359 1366 1368 *1392 *1404 *1406 1416 *1444 *1477 *1486
*1491 1507 1514 1533 *1543 1570 1581 1587 1605 1610 1614 1617 1619
1631 1632 1634 1642 1645 1649 1653 1656 *1675 1681 1691 1692 1705
1716 1739 1763 1779 1788 1808 1811 1815 1849 1850 1851 1858 *1888
1915 *1933 1937 *1943 1946 1955 1978 1986 1987 *1995 2008 2028
2032 2033 2037 2040 2087 2121 2124 2138 2140 2146 2147 2150 2154
2168 2181 2207 2223 2228 2259 2262 2268 *2270 2294 2300 2330 2337
2338 *2342 2367 *2369 2378 2382 2384 2402 2411 2421 2441 2442 2446
2447 2454 2468 2476 2479 *2520 *2525 2527 2538 2545 2557 *2591
*2616 2624 2627 2667 2695 2728 *2730 2742 2746 2750 2765 2773 2785
2803 2806 *2815 2825 *2829 *2838 2868 2897 2954 2966 2975 2980 3008
3013 3033 3036 3052 3056 *3070 3078 3112 3116 3155 3163 3169 3198
3203 3231 3256 *3269 *3298 *3299 3320 *3339 *3341 3354 3363 3376
3388 3393 3395 3401 3425 3428 3443 3445 3453 3461 3480 3481 3489
3493 3499 3510 3524 3531 3560 3572 *3578 *3597 3618 3644 3682 3697
3740 3757 3767 3775 3778 3785 *3801 3818 3824 3832 = 250*68
THATS = 13*5
That's lesser then a little: *Drum a farre off*. 503
I haue done as you haue done, that's what I can, 766
Induc'd as you haue beene, that's for my Countrey: 767
that's in them. Is the Senate possest of this? 1029
If he be put vpon't, and that's as easie, 1184
1 off. That's a braue fellow: but hee's vengeance | prowd, and loues not
the common people. 1209
Menen. That's off, that's off: I would you rather had 1269
That's thousand to one good one, when you now see 1293
*that's no matter, the greater part carries it, I say. If hee 1423
That's sure of death without it: at once plucke out 1854
What ha's he done to Rome, that's worthy death? 2035
That's yet vnbruis'd: bring me but out at gate. 2488
Menen. That's worthily | As any eare can heare. Come, let's not weepe, 2495
In that's no Changeling, and I must excuse | What cannot be amended. 3102
*I let forth your halfe pinte of blood. Backe, that's the vt-|most of your
hauing, backe. 3292
That's curdied by the Frost, from purest Snow, 3418
Volum. Your knee, Sirrah. | *Corio*. That's my braue Boy. 3429
THE *see also* 'th, tother, y = 739*196, 1
I haue seene the Sterne, and thou hast oft beheld 2462
THEAME = *1
*haue hearts inclinable to honor and aduance the Theame | of our
Assembly. 1264
THEAMES = 1
Win vpon power, and throw forth greater Theames | For Insurrections
arguing. 234
THEE *see also* the *l*.*178 *376 594 724 748 866 1002 1079 1086 1095 1116
1351 *1419 1528 1864 1877 1878 2184 2215 2233 2353 2474 2476 2478

THEE *cont*.
2480 2486 2499 2531 2721 2723 2739 2741 2742 *2744 2747 2753 2754
2755 2758 2764 2773 2776 2803 3108 3251 *3304 *3305 *3307 *3308
*3309 *3310 3314 3324 3327 3396 3404 *3414 3428 3475 3480 3496 3520
3523 3560 3757 = 56*11
THEEFE = *1
Men. Why 'tis no great matter: for a very little theefe   925
THEFT = 1
'Twere a Concealement worse then a Theft,   772
THEIR *see also* there *l*.*23 *81 *158 199 *200 207 *208 209 *222 *225 227
*229 230 277 350 *385 *463 *495 513 515 523 536 552 *575 610 616
*621 665 666 668 669 670 *695 696 755 795 835 882 903 *974 1118 1136
1150 1159 1174 1175 1178 1186 1194 1197 *1217 *1219 *1221 *1223
1226 *1231 *1232 *1233 1242 1274 1358 1360 1372 *1408 1453 1454
*1489 1508 *1615 1618 1659 1665 1669 1682 *1717 *1718 1755 1770
1774 1798 1815 *1817 1830 1856 1866 1871 2003 2167 2182 2185 2189
2242 2243 2319 2349 2375 2381 2414 2425 *2509 2510 2588 *2593 2611
*2612 *2615 *2645 2648 2791 *2870 *2875 2900 2901 2966 2991 3000
3006 3094 3122 3351 3358 3711 = 90*40
THEIRS = 5
Then sway with them in theirs.   1119
Most pallates theirs. They choose their Magistrate,   1798
We were elected theirs, *Martius* is worthy | Of present Death.   1923
Thy selfe (forsooth) hereafter theirs so farre,   2186
Euen in theirs, and in the Commons eares   3653
THEM *see also* 'em *l*.*24 69 75 79 161 223 226 228 275 305 361 480 536
538 541 551 578 579 656 669 715 1029 1037 1062 1110 1119 1152 1173
1174 1175 1180 *1212 1219 *1220 *1225 *1230 1240 1268 1281 1286
1344 1352 1357 1362 1369 1370 1371 1375 *1381 1383 1384 *1394 *1396
1441 1445 1453 *1488 *1491 *1500 1617 1618 1621 1661 1678 1701 1702
1716 1719 1726 1727 1728 1731 1732 1733 1757 1759 1762 1772 1795
1824 1855 1967 1969 2084 2089 2094 2109 2111 2132 2133 2139 2174
2175 2181 2205 2234 2243 2254 2272 2277 2281 2283 2287 2288 2372
2447 *2503 *2509 *2511 2563 2588 *2593 *2600 *2616 2763 2801 2802
2992 3006 3052 3127 3137 3178 3234 *3277 3354 *3455 3493 *3601 3638
*3643 3651 3652 = 112*21
THEME *see* theame
THEMSELUES = 6*2
*They needs must shew themselues, which in the hatching   337
They'le open of themselues. Harke you, farre off | *Alarum farre off*.   508
To heare themselues remembred.   780
And tent themselues with death: of all the Horses,   783
take their places by themselues: Corio-|*lanus stands*.   1242
And therein behold themselues: I say againe,   1758
*not (looke you sir) shew themselues (as we terme it) his | Friends,
whilest he's in Directitude.   2866
Though they themselues did suffer by't, behold   2898
THEN *l*.*7 72 123 124 127 184 *242 258 295 299 310 327 *365 *371 *377
380 *381 *384 *385 397 402 404 419 471 477 *495 502 503 506 517 528
582 *592 598 617 635 658 689 691 725 728 772 773 810 814 844 938
*939 *948 *967 *977 *1015 1058 1119 *1142 1162 *1165 *1168 1178
*1222 1259 *1267 1272 1281 1289 1295 1303 1330 1343 *1353 1379 1465
*1490 1505 1512 1588 1619 1634 1636 1663 1674 1677 *1736 1792 1801
*1817 1827 1849 1851 1869 2000 2020 2021 2037 2046 *2073 2130 2133
2158 2166 2178 2195 2232 2234 2235 2252 2257 2277 2293 *2315 2334
2341 2399 2401 2460 2469 2475 2508 2528 *2530 2535 *2536 *2586 2626
2698 *2701 2741 2751 2764 2775 2805 *2819 2822 *2876 2884 *2888

THEN *cont*.
2899 2926 2985 3007 3010 3100 3133 *3148 3191 3199 3209 3214 3216
*3275 *3305 3322 3323 3371 3378 3401 3403 3409 3410 3452 3477 3478
3484 3515 3528 3534 *3538 3564 3583 *3586 *3597 3698 3738 3743
3746 = 138*39
THENCE = 6
Since I heard thence, these are the words, I thinke   321
Beare him toth' Rock Tarpeian, and from thence | Into destruction cast
him.   1926
Pursue him to his house, and plucke him thence,   2049
Thou art thence Banish'd, we would muster all   2786
To expell him thence. I thinke hee'l be to Rome   3124
*I You may not passe, you must returne: our Generall | will no more
heare from thence.   3241
THERE *see also* there's, ther's *l*.*98 455 *456 510 581 884 *1043 1105
*1211 *1212 *1424 1540 1668 1697 *1812 *2076 2140 2208 2260 2294
2423 *2581 *2583 *2815 *2819 2940 3247 *3574 *3575 *3580 *3596
*3597 3699 3728 3732 3784 = 19*17, 1
There Mutinies and Reuolts, wherein they shew'd   1823
THEREBY = 2
To saue the Romanes, thereby to destroy   3490
Which thou shalt thereby reape, is such a name   3500
THEREFORE = 20*5
Would seeme but modest: therefore I beseech you,   776
Then reason safely with you: Therefore be it knowne,   814
*no better a ground. Therefore, for *Coriolanus* neyther to   1215
Thus stood for his Countrey. Therefore please you,   1248
You sooth'd not, therefore hurt not: but your People,   1285
*with our owne tongues, therefore follow me, and Ile   1433
*bountifull to the desirers: Therefore beseech you, I may | be Consull. 1493
*2. Wee hope to finde you our friend: and therefore   1495
*2.*Cit*. Therefore let him be Consull: the Gods giue him | ioy, and make
him good friend to the People.   1526
Your Voyces therefore: when we graunted that,   1570
Then Dogges, that are as often beat for barking, | As therefore kept to
doe so.   1619
Nothing is done to purpose. Therefore beseech you,   1848
Scici. Therefore lay hold of him: 1925
And therefore Law shall scorne him further Triall   1999
Our certaine death: therefore it is decreed,   2025
Auf. Therefore most absolute Sir, if thou wilt haue   2795
Then in our Priest-like Fasts: therefore Ile watch him   3214
For mercy to his Countrey: therefore let's hence,   3233
Haue (almost) stampt the Leasing. Therefore Fellow,   3260
*passe heere: no, though it were as vertuous to lye, as to | liue chastly.
Therefore go backe.   3264
*haue, I am one that telling true vnder him, must say you | cannot
passe. Therefore go backe.   3269
Then pitty: Note how much, therefore be gone.   3322
May hang vpon your hardnesse, therefore heare vs.   3446
Of our great Action; therefore shall he dye,   3703
3.*Con*. Therefore at your vantage, | Ere he expresse himselfe, or moue
the people   3713
THEREIN = 3*1
*Sonne, I therein would haue found issue. Heare me pro-|fesse   382
And therein behold themselues: I say againe,   1758
Though therein you can neuer be too Noble,   2135

THEREIN *cont*.
    And therein shew'd like Enemies. 3034
THERES = 8*5
    *not vppe, they will; and there's all the loue they beare | vs. 86
    *another, his Wife another, and (I thinke) there's one at | home for you. 1006
    Virgil. Yes certaine, there's a Letter for you, I saw't. 1010
    Valer. In troth, there's wondrous things spoke of him. 1034
    Mene. One ith' Neck, and two ith'Thigh, there's nine | that I know. 1047
    Onely there's one thing wanting, 1114
    Brutus. In that there's comfort. | *Scici*. Doubt not, 1147
    Corio. A match Sir, there's in all two worthie voyces 1471
    There's some among you haue beheld me fighting, 1941
    Sen. There's no remedy, 2116
    Bru. There's no more to be said, but he is banish'd 2404
    Then can our Reasons. There's no man in the world 3515
    'Twixt you there's difference: but the fall of either | Makes the Suruiuor
    heyre of all. 3669
THERETO = 1*1
    Com. I thinke 'twill serue, if he can thereto frame his | spirit. 2201
    Great hurt and Mischiefe: thereto witnesse my 2724
THERFORE = *1
    *such weake breath as this? No, you are deceiu'd, therfore 3283
THERS = *2
    *Below their cobled Shooes. They say ther's grain enough? 208
    *for such things as you. I can scarse thinke ther's any, y'are 3338
THESE *l*.*48 196 211 213 221 259 276 321 329 493 *575 578 698 732 *797
    1054 1067 1151 1541 1700 1715 1716 1865 2164 2463 2498 *2603 2625
    2926 3078 3136 3212 3387 3475 = 31*4
THETHER = 1
    Thether, where more attends you, and you slander 77
THEY *see also* they'l, they'le, th'haue = 92*47
THEYL = 3
    They'l sit by th'fire, and presume to know 203
    Com. But I feare | They'l roare him in againe. *Tullus Affidius*, 3047
    They'l giue him death by Inches. 3608
THEYLE = 1
    They'le open of themselues. Harke you, farre off | *Alarum farre off*. 508
THHAUE = 1
    Th'haue not prepar'd for vs. 347
THIEF *see* theefe
THIGH = *1
    Mene. One ith' Neck, and two ith'Thigh, there's nine | that I know. 1047
THINE = 10*3
    *and none lesse deere then thine, and my good *Martius*, I 384
    Thou mad'st thine enemies shake, as if the World | Were Feauorous,
    and did tremble. 562
    That with the fustie Plebeans, hate thine Honors, 754
    And follow to thine answer. 1879
    Follow thine Enemie in a fierie Gulfe, 2194
    Within thine eyes sate twenty thousand deaths 2350
    *And venomous to thine eyes. My (sometime) Generall, 2461
    And harsh in sound to thine. 2715
    Thine owne particular wrongs, and stop those maimes 2743
    The leading of thine owne Reuenges, take 2796
    *Thy Countries strength and weaknesse, thine own waies 2799
    Come let's away: when *Caius* Rome is thine, 3147
    Thine enmities most capitall: Thou barr'st vs 3459

THING = 14*6

And were I any thing but what I am, 251
*Virg. Giue me excuse good Madame, I will obey you | in euery thing
heereafter. 466
*You two are old men, tell me one thing that I shall aske | you. 910
*thing: you are ambitious, for poore knaues cappes and 964
Onely there's one thing wanting, 1114
He was a thing of Blood, whose euery motion 1323
*3 Cit. You must thinke if we giue you any thing, we | hope to gaine by
you. 1463
Corio. It is a purpos'd thing, and growes by Plot, 1721
Corio. Hence rotten thing, or I shall shake thy bones | Out of thy
Garments. 1883
*Rom. The maine blaze of it is past, but a small thing 2589
Thou Noble thing, more dances my rapt heart, 2774
*2 Nay, I knew by his face that there was some-thing 2815
And vowes Reuenge as spacious, as betweene | The yong'st and oldest
thing. 2977
Com. If? He is their God, he leads them like a thing 3006
Not to be other then one thing, not moouing 3133
The thing I haue forsworne to graunt, may neuer 3435
Volum. Oh no more, no more: | You haue said you will not grant vs any
thing: 3441
And sir, it is no little thing to make 3554
*growne from Man to Dragon: He has wings, hee's more | then a
creeping thing. 3582
*as a thing made for Alexander. What he bids bee done, is 3591

THINGS = 10*4

*Their Counsailes, and their Cares; disgest things rightly, 158
Sicin. Besides, if things go well, 301
*Valer. In troth, there's wondrous things spoke of him. 1034
And look'd vpon things precious, as they were 1341
What Custome wills in all things, should we doo't? 1509
Haue done many things, some lesse, some more: 1522
That of all things vpon the Earth, he hated 1691
To call them Wollen Vassailes, things created 2094
With striuing lesse to be so: Lesser had bin | The things of your
dispositions, if 2107
*strange things from Rome: all tending to the good of 2610
Should from yond clowd speake diuine things, 2762
Com. Y'are goodly things, you Voyces. 3073
To th'vulgar eye, that he beares all things fairely: 3112
*for such things as you. I can scarse thinke ther's any, y'are 3338

THINK = *4

*What I think, I vtter, and spend my malice in my breath. 949
*but I thought there was more in him, then I could think. 2819
*Lieu. Sir, I beseech you, think you he'l carry Rome? 3118
*Dotant as you seeme to be? Can you think to blow 3281

THINKE = 26*10

*But they thinke we are too deere, the leannesse 21
2 Citizen. Well, | Ile heare it Sir: yet you must not thinke 94
And no way from your selues. What do you thinke? 162
Since I heard thence, these are the words, I thinke 321
Auf. Nor did you thinke it folly, 335
Bring vp your Army: but (I thinke) you'l finde 346
Valeria. In troth I thinke she would: 470
Mar. Will the time serue to tell, I do not thinke: 660

THINKE *cont*.

If any thinke, braue death out-weighes bad life,	690
And would'st doe so, I thinke, should we encounter	867
*another, his Wife another, and (I thinke) there's one at | home for you.	1006
1.*Sen*. Speake, good *Cominius*: | Leaue nothing out for length, and make vs thinke	1256
*I thinke, if all our wittes were to issue out of one Scull,	1407
*2.*Cit*. Thinke you so? Which way do you iudge my | wit would flye.	1411
You must desire them to thinke vpon you.	1445
Coriol. Thinke vpon me? Hang 'em,	1446
*3 *Cit*. You must thinke if we giue we any thing, we | hope to gaine by you.	1463
Would thinke vpon you, for your Voyces,	1589
When he did need your Loues: and doe you thinke,	1604
Com. I thinke 'twill serue, if he can thereto frame his | spirit.	2201
The warlike Seruice he ha's done, consider: Thinke	2324
Rom. I know you well sir, and you know mee: your | name I thinke is *Adrian*.	2571
*the man I thinke, that shall set them in present Action. So	2616
thinke our Fellowes are asleepe.	2655
*me, dost not thinke me for the man I am, necessitie com-|mands me name my selfe.	2711
1 I thinke he is: but a greater soldier then he, | You wot one.	2822
Mene. I thinke not so.	2933
To expell him thence. I thinke hee'l be to Rome	3124
Mene. Ile vndertak't: | I thinke hee'l heare me. Yet to bite his lip,	3205
*enemy your shield, thinke to front his reuenges with the	3278
2 What cause do you thinke I haue to swoond?	3336
*for such things as you. I can scarse thinke ther's any, y'are	3338
Virg. The sorrow that deliuers vs thus chang'd, | Makes you thinke so.	3388
We haue led since thy Exile. Thinke with thy selfe,	3451
What faults he made before the last, I thinke	3727
Corio. *Martius*? | *Auf*. I *Martius*, *Caius Martius*: Do'st thou thinke	3755

THINKES = 4*1

Me thinkes, I heare hither your Husbands Drumme:	391
Me thinkes I see him stampe thus, and call thus,	394
*Me thinkes thou speak'st not well. How long is't since?	619
He ha's it now: and by his Lookes, me thinkes, | 'Tis warme at's heart.	1548
And so he thinkes, and is no lesse apparant	3111

THINKING = 2

Thinking vpon his Seruices, tooke from you	1626
O'recome with Pride, Ambitious, past all thinking | Selfe-louing.	2930

THINKS = *1

Vol. Hath bin; is it ended then? Our State thinks not	2586

THINKST = 1

Think'st thou it Honourable for a Nobleman	3511

THIRD = 2*1

Volum. On's Browes: *Menenius*, hee comes the third | time home with the Oaken Garland.	1021
Enter the third Seruingman.	2832
Doth more then counterpoize a full third part	3743

THIRST = 1

hunger for Bread, not in thirst for Reuenge.	26

THIS *l*.*24 *25 *60 68 122 123 134 148 155 156 163 166 236 267 280 311 318 329 433 *464 494 570 571 *572 679 687 708 748 757 785 816 818 *918 *957 *960 *1014 1029 *1032 *1049 *1071 1181 1246 1315 1359 1473 1506 1535 *1553 1573 1662 1669 1707 1730 1746 1748 1750 1753

THIS *cont.*
1782 1821 1828 1841 1873 *1906 1919 1949 1958 1978 1982 1994 2009
2023 2042 2053 2062 2149 2157 2163 2174 2188 2208 2209 2216 2259
2287 *2315 2355 2363 *2369 2386 *2525 2550 2553 2567 *2594 *2598
*2609 2623 2634 2636 2642 2650 2674 2705 2735 2750 2872 *2874 *2877
*2903 2925 2934 2951 2957 2961 2967 2979 2983 3019 3079 3085 3088
3095 3184 3188 *3283 *3313 3325 3327 3348 3350 3355 *3366 3372 3405
3407 3415 3420 3431 3434 3480 3481 3494 3495 *3497 3498 3529 3531
3535 3542 3558 3569 *3581 3598 3615 3625 3626 3630 3651 3655 3676
3691 3732 3777 3790 3798 3815 3817 3833 3835 = 142*29

THITHER *see also* thether = 4
The Volces haue much Corne: take these Rats thither,   276
with my prayers: but I cannot go thither.   443
Call thither all the Officers a'th'Towne,   601
('Tis South the City Mils) bring me word thither   891

THOGH = *1
*Cor. Thogh there the people had more absolute powre   1812

THOGHT = *1
*2 By my hand, I had thoght to haue stroken him with   2810

THOROUGHLY = 1
Menen. Nay these are almost thoroughly perswaded: 213

THOSE *l.*578 584 598 683 685 716 792 *955 1146 *1228 *1394 1616 1770
1936 1978 2267 2362 2546 2740 2743 2803 3033 3131 3183 3376
3428 = 23*3

THOU *see also* thou't, y *l.*166 167 262 264 556 557 558 562 586 599 618
*619 622 735 737 739 757 762 866 1082 1864 2182 2183 2185 2187 2193
2214 2217 2234 2237 2238 2349 2353 2459 2462 2473 2479 2486 2526
2528 2532 *2544 2691 2698 *2702 *2708 *2710 2717 2719 *2730 2741
2750 2760 2771 2774 2776 2779 2786 2795 2798 3108 *3148 *3271 *3301
*3306 3328 *3414 3425 3459 3468 3477 3479 *3497 3499 3500 3506 3511
3513 3517 3523 3524 3534 *3559 3615 3756 3769 3770 3773 3810
3832 = 81*14

THOUGH *see also* thogh = 23*6
*he did it to that end: though sóft conscienc'd men can be   38
Whereby they liue. And though that all at once   147
Men. Though all at once, cannot | See what I do deliuer out to each, 150
For though abundantly they lacke discretion   214
Shall be the Generals fault, though he performe   297
Though *Martius* earn'd them not: and all his faults   305
To *Martius* shall be Honors, though indeed | In ought he merit not. 306
Though you were borne in Rome; his bloody brow   396
Com. Though thou speakest truth,   618
Com. Though I could wish, | You were conducted to a gentle Bath,   680
(Though thankes to all) must I select from all: 702
Auf. Bolder, though not so subtle: my valors poison'd,   876
*And though I must be content to beare with those,   955
*worth all your predecessors, since *Deucalion*, though per-|aduenture 986
Though in Rome litter'd: not Romans, as they are not,   1963
Though calued i'th' Porch o'th' Capitoll: 1964
Though therein you can neuer be too Noble,   2135
Though but Bastards, and Syllables   2155
Beleeu't not lightly, though I go alone   2467
Beares a Command in't: Though thy Tackles torne,   2718
Who am prepar'd against your Territories, | Though not for Rome it
selfe.   2792
Though they themselues did suffer by't, behold   2898
*of vs, that we did we did for the best, and though wee   3070

THOUGH *cont.*
*passe heere: no, though it were as vertuous to lye, as to | liue chastly.
Therefore go backe. 3264
Corio. Wife, Mother, Child, I know not. My affaires | Are Seruanted
to others: Though I owe 3317
(Though I shew'd sowrely to him) once more offer'd 3360
An euident Calamity, though we had 3467
Auffidius, though I cannot make true Warres, 3548
Traile your steele Pikes. Though in this City hee 3833
THOUGHT *see also* thoght = 6*4
What euer haue bin thought one in this State 318
I thought to crush him in an equall Force, 872
'Tis thought, that *Martius* shall be Consull: 1191
2.Off. Three, they say: but 'tis thought of euery one, 1207
1.Cit. And to make vs no better thought of a little 1400
*in him. He had sir, a kinde of face me thought, I cannot 2816
*but I thought there was more in him, then I could think. 2819
Euen to my person, then I thought he would 3100
*Neuer admitted a priuat whisper, no not with such frends | That
thought them sure of you. 3353
That thought he could do more: A very little 3363
THOUGHTS = 2
Aduance braue *Titus*, | They do disdaine vs much beyond our Thoughts, 518
Thy thoughts with Noblenesse, that thou mayst proue 3425
THOUSAND = 6
The way it takes: cracking ten thousand Curbes 71
Mene. A hundred thousand Welcomes: 1091
That's thousand to one good one, when you now see 1293
Within thine eyes sate twenty thousand deaths 2350
Say yea to thy desires. A thousand welcomes, 2804
This Morning, for ten thousand of your throates, 3630
THOUSANDS = 1
With thousands of these quarter'd slaues, as high 211
THOUT = 1
Thou't not beleeue thy deeds: but Ile report it, 749
THREATNING = 1
Ransoming him, or pittying, threatning th'other; 647
THRED = 1
They would not thred the Gates: This kinde of Seruice 1821
THREE *see also* 3. = 11*2
These three leade on this Preparation 329
Three or foure miles about, else had I sir 626
Mar. Within these three houres *Tullus* 732
A flourish. Cornets. Enter Tullus Auffidius | bloudie, with two or three
Souldiors. 857
You are three, that Rome should dote on: 1096
2.Off. Three, they say: but 'tis thought of euery one, 1207
Slew three Opposers: *Tarquins* selfe he met, 1308
3 Cit. To loose it selfe in a Fogge, where being three 1417
Enter three of the Citizens. 1452
Enter three Citizens more. 1516
Enter three or foure Citizens. 2914
And three examples of the like, hath beene 2955
Helpe three a'th'cheefest Souldiers, Ile be one. 3831
THREES = *1
*by him where he stands, by ones, by twoes, & by threes. 1430

THREE-PENCE = *1
    *and then reiourne the Controuersie of three-pence   967
THRESHOLD = 2
    threshold, till my Lord returne from the Warres.   439
    Bestride my Threshold. Why, thou Mars I tell thee,   2776
THREW = 1*1
    *And make bold power looke pale, they threw their caps   225
    As you threw Caps vp, will he tumble downe,   3061
THRICE = 1
    Of Wounds, two dozen odde: Battailes thrice six   1520
THRIUE = 1
    Sicin. Liue, and thriue.   2920
THRIUES = 1
    Who thriues, & who declines: Side factions, & giue out   205
THROAT = 4
    Away my disposition, and possesse me | Some Harlots spirit: My throat
    of Warre be turn'd,   2219
    My throat to thee, and to thy Ancient Malice: 2753
    Vnbuckling Helmes, fisting each others Throat,   2783
    Presented to my knife his Throat: I tooke him,   3684
THROATES = 1
    This Morning, for ten thousand of your throates,   3630
THROATS = 1*1
    *is no hope in't, our throats are sentenc'd, and stay vppon | execution.   3576
    2.*Con.* And patient Fooles, | Whose children he hath slaine, their base
    throats teare   3710
THRONE = 1*1
    Sicin. And affecting one sole Throne, without assista(n)ce   2932
    *finisht with his bidding. He wants nothing of a God but | Eternity, and
    a Heauen to Throne in.   3592
THRONG = 1
    I haue seene the dumbe men throng to see him,   1192
THRONGS = 1
    Doe presse among the popular Throngs, and puffe   1133
THROUGH = 8*2
    I send it through the Riuers of your blood   142
    And through the Crankes and Offices of man,   144
    To one that would doe thus. I am halfe through,   1514
    Make motion through my Lips, and my Arm'd knees   2226
    Through our large Temples with y shewes of peace   2305
    Giue him deseru'd vexation. Let a guard | Attend vs through the City.   2430
    *Of shame seene through thy Country, speed thee straight   2744
    With Manacles through our streets, or else   3470
    Ne're through an Arch so hurried the blowne Tide,   3619
    *As the recomforted through th'gates. Why harke you: | *Trumpets,*
    Hoboyes, Drums beate, altogether.   3620
THROW *see also* throw't = 4
    Win vpon power, and throw forth greater Theames | For Insurrections
    arguing.   234
    And throw their power i'th'dust.   1871
    They all shout, and throw vp their Caps.   2425
    I haue tumbled past the throw: and in his praise   3259
THROWES = 1
    He throwes without distinction. Giue me leaue,   2065
THROWNE = *1
    Sicin. He shall be throwne downe the Tarpeian rock   1997

THROWT = 1
And throw't against the Winde. Toth' Market place: 2210
THRUST = 2
And we of thee. So if the time thrust forth   2480
Must beare my beating to his Graue, shall ioyne | To thrust the Lye
vnto him.   3779
THRUSTS = 1
Thrusts forth his hornes againe into the world   2947
THUMBE = 1
finger and his thumbe, as one would set vp a Top.   2814
THUNDER = 3*1
*Com. The Shepherd knowes not Thunder fro(m) a Taber,   634
A Shower, and Thunder, with their Caps, and Showts: 1197
Or *Ioue*, for's power to Thunder: his Heart's his Mouth: 1985
To teare with Thunder the wide Cheekes a'th'Ayre,   3508
THUNDER-LIKE = 1
The Thunder-like percussion of thy sounds   561
THUS = 29*3
Rebell'd against the Belly; thus accus'd it: 99
Which ne're came from the Lungs, but euen thus: 110
Not rash like his Accusers, and thus answered.   136
Me thinkes I see him stampe thus, and call thus,   394
*Thus it is: the Volcies haue an Army forth, against who(m)   460
*Then dangerous to me: To *Auffidious* thus, I will appear | (and fight.   592
He has the stampe of *Martius*, and I haue | Before time seene him thus.   631
Waue thus to expresse his disposition, | And follow *Martius*.   693
Thus stood for his Countrey. Therefore please you,   1248
Man-entred thus, he waxed like a Sea,   1313
Corio. To brag vnto them, thus I did, and thus   1369
To one that would doe thus. I am halfe through,   1514
And with his Hat, thus wauing it in scorne,   1567
Scicin. Thus to haue said, | As you were fore-aduis'd, had toucht his
Spirit,   1592
Scicin. One thus descended, | That hath beside well in his person
wrought,   1648
You graue, but wreaklesse Senators, haue you thus   1786
Bru. Why shall the people giue | One that speakes thus, their voyce?   1814
They gaue vs our demands. Thus we debase   1832
And temp'rately proceed to what you would | Thus violently redresse.   1934
Below the beame of sight; yet will I still | Be thus to them.   2088
Before he should thus stoope to'th'heart, but that   2124
And thus farre hauing stretcht it (here be with them)   2175
Which often thus correcting thy stout heart,   2179
For you the City. Thus I turne my backe;   2422
Volce. He cannot choose: I am most fortunate, thus   2606
Thus with his speechlesse hand. What he would do   3228
Virg. The sorrow that deliuers vs thus chang'd, | Makes you thinke so.   3388
Volum. Nay, go not from vs thus: 3488
Whose Chronicle thus writ, The man was Noble,   3502
That he is thus cut off. Please it your Honours   3818
THWACKE = 1*2
*3 Why here's he that was wont to thwacke our Ge-|nerall, *Caius
Martius*.   2838
1 Why do you say, thwacke our Generall?   2840
*3 I do not say thwacke our Generall, but he was al-|wayes good
enough for him   2841

THY *l*.472 498 560 561 587 595 596 597 600 612 623 728 735 736 748 749
   1080 1883 1884 1957 2174 2176 2178 2179 2186 2232 2235 2236 2238
   2239 2351 2352 2460 2481 2500 2533 *2536 2624 2627 *2638 2699 *2702
   *2708 2709 2713 2716 2717 2718 2719 *2720 2721 2736 *2744 2745 2753
   2756 2757 2769 2771 2778 2781 *2799 2804 2850 3252 3274 3287 3290
   *3304 *3305 *3311 *3312 3325 3400 3425 3451 3453 3463 3465 3471
   3473 3478 3479 3509 3514 3517 3518 *3559 3757 = 82*14

THYSELFE *see* selfe

TIBER *see also* Tyber = *1

  *Tiber in't: Said, to be something imperfect in fauou- | ring   945

TICKLED = *1

  Sicin. Such a Nature, tickled with good successe, dis- | daines   289

TIDE = 1

  Ne're through an Arch so hurried the blowne Tide,   3619

TIDINGS *see* tydings

TIE *see* tye

TIGER *see* tyger

TIGER-FOOTED-RAGE = 1

  This Tiger-footed-rage, when it shall find   2053

TIL = *1

  of Auffi. Martius fights til they be driuen in breathles.   741

TILL = 14

  To keepe your great pretences vayl'd, till when   336
  Till one can do no more.   354
  threshold, till my Lord returne from the Warres.   439
  If not, why cease you till you are so?   662
  A perpetuall spoyle: and till we call'd   1334
  Coine words till their decay, against those Meazels   1770
  To banish your Defenders, till at length   2416
  Your ignorance (which findes not till it feeles,   2417
  Till he had forg'd himselfe a name a'th'fire | Of burning Rome.   3166
  Till he be dieted to my request,   3215
  Mene. Ha's he din'd can'st thou tell? For I would not | speake with
  him, till after dinner.   3271
  I purpose not to waite on Fortune, till   3474
  Boy. A shall not tread on me: Ile run away | Till I am bigger, but then
  Ile fight.   3483
  To do my selfe this wrong: Till at the last   3691

TIMD = 1

  Was tim'd with dying Cryes: alone he entred   1324

TIME = 27*6

  Men. There was a time, when all the bodies members   98
  Ere so preuayl'd with me; it will in time   233
  He has the stampe of *Martius*, and I haue | Before time seene him thus.   631
  Mar. Will the time serue to tell, I do not thinke: 660
  With all his trim belonging; and from this time,   818
  The bloud vpon your Visage dryes, 'tis time   855
  *yeeres health; in which time, I will make a Lippe at   1012
  Volum. On's Browes: Menenius, hee comes the third | time home with
  the Oaken Garland.   1021
  Menen. And 'twas time for him too, Ile warrant him   1026
  At some time, when his soaring Insolence   1182
  Shall teach the People, which time shall not want,   1183
  And carry with vs Eares and Eyes for th' time, | But Hearts for the
  euent.   1200
  With doing them, and is content | To spend the time, to end it.   1344
  The Dust on antique Time would lye vnswept,   1510

TIME *cont*.

TIMES = 5

TIME-PLEASERS = 1

TINDER-LIKE = *1

TIRD *see* tyr'd

TIRE *see* tyre

TIS *1*.*246 320 330 353 *420 430 445 485 541 566 *621 734 840 855 887 891 *925 1004 1160 1167 1191 *1207 *1414 1474 *1488 1549 1559 1669 1959 1970 2197 2271 2341 2464 2465 2624 *2701 2763 *2874 *2884 *2904 2945 2967 *3035 3062 *3238 3332 3368 3775 3784 = 38*14

TIT = 2*1

TITLE = *1

TITLELESSE = 1

TITUS see also Tit. = 13*5

TITUS cont.

To Rome of our successe: you *Titus Lartius*	832
Be free, as is the Winde: deliuer him, *Titus*.	849
*Volum. Titus Lartius writes, they fought together, but	*Auffidius* got off.	1024
Enter Cominius the Generall, and Titus Latius: be-|tweene them Coriolanus, crown'd with an Oaken	1060
And to send for *Titus Lartius*: it remaines,	1245
Cornets. Enter Coriolanus, Menenius, all the Gentry, | *Cominius, Titus Latius, and other Senators.*	1672

TITUS = 1

TO *see also* t', too, to's, to't, to'th = 522*152, 1*2

*single: your abilities are to Infant-like, for dooing	933
*the first complaint, hasty and Tinder-like vppon, to	946
Will proue to bloody: and the end of it, | Vnknowne to the Beginning.	2071

TODAY *see* day

TOE = 3

You, the great Toe of this Assembly?	163
2.*Cit.* I the great Toe? Why the great Toe?	164

TOGETHER = 12*2

Com. You haue fought together?	253
*halfe an houre together: ha's such a confirm'd coun-|tenance.	422
By th'Blood we haue shed together, | By th'Vowes we haue made	673
*Volum. Titus Lartius writes, they fought together, but | *Auffidius* got off.	1024
In boulted Language: Meale and Bran together	2064
I'th'Warre do grow together: Grant that, and tell me	2138
Rom. Well, let vs go together. *Exeunt.*	2620
Are still together: who Twin (as 'twere) in Loue,	2641
We haue beene downe together in my sleepe,	2782
That we haue bled together. *Coriolanus*	3163
Whereto we are bound, together with thy victory:	3463
Corio. I by and by; But we will drinke together:	3562
Call all your Tribes together, praise the Gods,	3642
Together with the Seale a'th Senat, what | We haue compounded on.	3748

TOKEN = 1

Weares this Warres Garland: in token of the which,	816

TOLD = 3*2

*1.*Sen. Martius* 'tis true, that you haue lately told vs,	246
Com. Where is that Slaue | Which told me they had beate you to your Trenches?	651
Brut. Could you not haue told him,	1577
Mene. You haue told them home,	2563
*1 Faith Sir, if you had told as many lies in his behalfe,	3262

TOMBE = 1

Hath not a Tombe so euident as a Chaire | T'extoll what it hath done.	3143

TOMORROW *see* morrow

TONGUE = 13*1

Our Steed the Legge, the Tongue our Trumpeter,	120
More then I know the sound of *Martius* Tongue | From euery meaner man.	635
Plague vpon't, I cannot bring | My tongue to such a pace. Looke Sir, my wounds,	1439
Why in this Wooluish tongue should I stand heere,	1506
The Multitudinous Tongue, let them not licke	1855
Be gone, put not your worthy Rage into your Tongue,	1965
What his Brest forges, that his Tongue must vent,	1986

TONGUE *cont.*

That are but roated in your Tongue;	2154
Must I with my base Tongue giue to my Noble Heart	2206
The Glasses of my sight: A Beggars Tongue	2225
Or neuer trust to what my Tongue can do | I'th way of Flattery further.	2246
Thy lying tongue, both numbers. I would say	2352
*your Fauour is well appear'd by your Tongue. What's	2579
Would be your Countries Pleader, your good tongue	3190

TONGUES = 3*4

*Bru. All tongues speake of him, and the bleared sights	1123
*for their Tongues to be silent, and not confesse so much,	1233
*his wounds, and tell vs his deeds, we are to put our ton- |gues	1393
*with our owne tongues, therefore follow me, and Ile	1433
No Heart among you? Or had you Tongues, to cry	1607
Bestow your su'd-for Tongues?	1611
The Tongues o'th' Common Mouth. I do despise them:	1701

TONIGHT *see* night

TOO *see also* to, too's, too't = 28*9

*But they thinke we are too deere, the leannesse	21
*strong breaths, they shal know we haue strong arms too.	62
*Bru. The present Warres deuoure him, he is growne | Too proud to be so valiant.	287
Thy exercise hath bin too violent, | For a second course of Fight.	587
Mar. Come I too late?	633
Martius. Come I too late?	637
Com. Too modest are you: | More cruell to your good report, then gratefull	809
It should be lookt too: come. *Exeunt.*	856
Sicin. *Menenius*, you are knowne well enough too.	942
*too? What harme can your beesome Conspectui- |ties	959
*gleane out of this Charracter, if I be knowne well e- |nough too.	960
*Menen. So doe I too, if it be not too much: brings a	1019
*Menen. And 'twas time for him too, Ile warrant him	1026
And mountainous Error be too highly heapt,	1511
Scicin. You shew too much of that,	1739
Mene. His nature is too noble for the World:	1983
The harme of vnskan'd swiftnesse, will (too late)	2054
Corio. Let them hang. | *Volum.* I, and burne too.	2111
*Men. Come, come, you haue bin too rough, somthing	2114
too rough: you must returne, and mend it.	2115
Volum. You are too absolute,	2134
Though therein you can neuer be too Noble,	2135
Corio. Fare ye well: | Thou hast yeares vpon thee, and thou art too full	2485
Virg. You shall stay too: I would I had the power | To say so to my Husband.	2522
Nay but thou shalt stay too: I would my Sonne	2532
then thou dwel'st with Dawes too?	2698
1 I, and for an assault too.	2831
*2 Come we are fellowes and friends: he was euer too	2843
*1 He was too hard for him directly, to say the Troth	2845
*2 And hee had bin Cannibally giuen, hee might haue | boyld and eaten him too.	2848
The Senators and Patricians loue him too:	3121
He would not answer too: Forbad all Names,	3164
And this braue Fellow too: we are the Graines,	3184
I haue yeelded too. Fresh Embasses, and Suites,	3364
Requires nor Childe, nor womans face to see: | I haue sate too long.	3486

TOO *cont*.

Too great for what containes it. Boy? Oh Slaue,	3774

TOOKE = 5*1

*3.*Rom*. A Murraine on't, I tooke this for Siluer. *Exeunt*.	572
Where it did marke, it tooke from face to foot:	1322
Thinking vpon his Seruices, tooke from you	1626
O're-borne their way, consum'd with fire, and tooke	What lay before them.	2991
Presented to my knife his Throat: I tooke him,	3684
Which he did end all his; and tooke some pride	3690

TOOS = 1

Tye Leaden pounds too's heeles. Proceed by Processe,	2055

TOOT = 7*2

And leaue me but the Bran. What say you too't?	154
Tullus Auffidius that will put you too't:	249
And make my Warres on you: Looke too't: Come on,	535
Menen. Put them not too't:	1362
*3 *Cit*. We do Sir, tell vs what hath brought you too't.	1456
Their needlesse Vouches: Custome calls me too't.	1508
But once a day, it would vnclogge my heart	Of what lyes heauy too't.	2561
Bru. We stood too't in good time. Is this *Menenius*?	2903
(Trust too't, thou shalt not) on thy Mothers wombe	That brought thee to this world.	3479

TOP = 2

Which to the spire, and top of prayses vouch'd,	775
finger and his thumbe, as one would set vp a Top.	2814

TOPPING = 1

Bru. And topping all others in boasting.	917

TORNE = 1

Beares a Command in't: Though thy Tackles torne,	2718

TOS = 2

He still hath held them: that to's power he would	1173
More bound to's Mother, yet heere he let's me prate	3516

TOTH = 20*1

To'th'discontented Members, the mutinous parts	113
Sen. Your Company to'th'Capitoll, where I know	Our greatest Friends attend vs.	269
In their nicely gawded Cheekes, toth' wanton spoyle	1136
Toth' People, begge their stinking Breaths.	1159
Cori. That Ile straight do: and knowing my selfe again,	Repayre toth'Senate-	house.	1543
Fast Foe toth' *Plebeij*, your Voyces might	1585
And presently, when you haue drawne your number,	Repaire toth' Capitoll.	1657
Scicin. Toth' Capitoll, come:	1667
Senat. Tribunes giue way, he shall toth' Market place.	1712
Com. Well, on to'th'Market place.	1807
They ne're did seruice for't; being prest to'th'Warre,	1819
To'th'greater Bench, in a Rebellion:	1867
A Foe to'th'publike Weale. Obey I charge thee,	1878
*To'th'people: *Coriolanus*, patience: Speak good *Sicinius*.	1899
Beare him toth' Rock Tarpeian, and from thence	Into destruction cast him.	1926
Before he should thus stoope to'th'heart, but that	2124
And throw't against the Winde. Toth' Market place:	2210
I shall discharge toth' Life.	2212
All. To'th'Rocke, to'th'Rocke with him.	2356

TOTH *cont*.
 Auf. Do they still flye to'th'Roman? 3091
TOTHER = 1
 Tit. No *Caius Martius*, | Ile leane vpon one Crutch, and fight with
 tother, 265
TOUCH = 1*1
 *you *Licurgusses*,) if the drinke you giue me, touch my Pa- | lat 951
 My Friends of Noble touch: when I am forth, 2490
TOUCHD = 1
 Euen when the Nauell of the State was touch'd, 1820
TOUCHING = 1
 Touching the Weale a'th Common, you shall finde 159
TOUCHT = 2
 Scicin. Thus to haue said, | As you were fore-aduis'd, had toucht his
 Spirit, 1592
 My name hath touch't your eares: it is *Menenius*. 3248
TOUNGS = *1
 *And straight disclaim their toungs? what are your Offices? 1717
TOWARD = 1*2
 Drum and Trumpet toward Cominius, and Caius Mar- | tius, 711
 *your eyes toward the Napes of your neckes, and make 935
 Your louing motion toward the common Body, | To yeeld what passes
 here. 1261
TOWARDS = 3
 And translate his Mallice towards you, into Loue, | Standing your
 friendly Lord. 1590
 Towards her deserued Children, is enroll'd 2029
 Bru. Onely make triall what your Loue can do, | For Rome, towards
 Martius. 3196
TOWNE = 8*1
 For halfe a hundred yeares: Summon the Towne. 492
 Call thither all the Officers a'th'Towne, 601
 We cannot keepe the Towne. 718
 Auffi. The Towne is ta'ne. 859
 Yeelded the Towne: he is retyred to Antium. 1686
 Then to take in a Towne with gentle words, 2158
 This Enemie Towne: Ile enter, if he slay me 2650
 the Defence of a Towne, our Generall is excellent. 2830
 *1.*Con*. Your Natiue Towne you enter'd like a Poste, 3707
TOWNES = 1
 To take in many Townes, ere (almost) Rome | Should know we were
 a-foot. 340
TRADES = 1*1
 Of all the Trades in Rome. Looke, I am going: 2244
 Vol. Now the Red Pestilence strike al Trades in Rome, | And
 Occupations perish. 2450
TRADESMEN = 1
 Our Tradesmen singing in their shops, and going | About their
 Functions friendly. 2900
TRADUCEMENT = 1
 No lesse then a Traducement, 773
TRAGEDY = 1
 The Tragedy of Coriolanus. 3839
TRAILE = 1
 Traile your steele Pikes. Though in this City hee 3833
TRAITOR *see also* traytor = 7
 Sicin. Ha's spoken like a Traitor, and shall answer | As Traitors do. 1862

TRAITOR *cont*.

 This Viporous Traitor: to eiect him hence 2023
 For which you are a Traitor to the people. | *Corio*. How? Traytor? 2345
 Call me their Traitor, thou iniurious Tribune. 2349
 But tell the Traitor in the highest degree 3751
 Corio. Traitor? How now? | *Auf*. I Traitor, *Martius*. 3753
TRAITOROUS = 1
 Attach thee as a Traitorous Innouator: 1877
TRAITORS = 1
 Sicin. Ha's spoken like a Traitor, and shall answer | As Traitors do. 1862
TRANSLATE = 1
 And translate his Mallice towards you, into Loue, | Standing your
 friendly Lord. 1590
TRANSPORT = 1
 Scicin. He cannot temp'rately transport his Honors, 1144
TRANSPORTED = 1
 You are transported by Calamity 76
TRAYTOR = 1
 For which you are a Traitor to the people. | *Corio*. How? Traytor? 2345
TREAD = 2
 Boy. A shall not tread on me: Ile run away | Till I am bigger, but then
 Ile fight. 3483
 3.*Lord*. Tread not vpon him Masters, all be quiet, | Put vp your Swords. 3812
TREADE = 3
 Vol. Hee'l beat *Auffidius* head below his knee, | And treade vpon his
 necke. 408
 Triumphantly treade on thy Countries ruine, 3471
 March to assault thy Country, then to treade 3478
TREADING = *1
 *like an Engine, and the ground shrinkes before his Trea- |ding. 3588
TREADS = *1
 *the shadow which he treads on at noone, but I do 290
TREASON = 1
 Bru. Manifest Treason. | *Sicin*. This a Consull? No. 1872
TREASURE = 2
 The Treasure in this field atchieued, and Citie, 785
 And treasure of my Loynes: then if I would | Speake that. 2401
TREATIE = 2*1
 What good Condition can a Treatie finde 864
 Scicin. We are conuented vpon a pleasing Treatie, and 1263
 With our owne charge: making a Treatie, where 3731
TREES = 1
 Some old Crab-trees here at home, 1098
TREMBLE = 1
 Thou mad'st thine enemies shake, as if the World | Were Feauorous,
 and did tremble. 562
TREMBLING = 1
 Com. You haue brought | A Trembling vpon Rome, such as was neuer 3039
TRENCHER = *1
 *thy Mistris: Thou prat'st, and prat'st, serue with thy tren- |cher:
 Hence. *Beats him away* 2702
TRENCHES = 4
 *Alarum, the Romans are beat back to their Trenches | Enter Martius
 Cursing*. 523
 As they vs to our Trenches followes. 537
 I saw our party to their Trenches driuen, 616

TRENCHES *cont.*
 Com. Where is that Slaue | Which told me they had beate you to your
 Trenches?   651
TRI = 3
TRIALL = 2
 And therefore Law shall scorne him further Triall   1999
 Bru. Onely make triall what your Loue can do, | For Rome, towards
 Martius.   3196
TRIBE = 2
 Were in Arabia, and thy Tribe before him, | His good Sword in his
 hand.   2533
 His Tribe, to vse my lawfull Sword.   3802
TRIBES = 2
 Sicin. Haue you collected them by Tribes? | *Edile.* I haue.   2272
 Call all your Tribes together, praise the Gods,   3642
TRIBUNE *see also Tri.* = 4*1
 Let me deserue so ill as you, and make me | Your fellow Tribune.   1737
 Nor yoake with him for Tribune.   1744
 *All. Let's here our Tribune: peace, speake, speake, | speake.   1901
 Call me their Traitor, thou iniurious Tribune.   2349
 The Plebeians haue got your Fellow Tribune,   3605
TRIBUNES *see also Tri.* = 31*7
 *Mar. Fiue Tribunes to defend their vulgar wisdoms   229
 *Sicin. When we were chosen Tribunes for the people.   282
 The common file, (a plague-Tribunes for them)   656
 **And gladly quak'd, heare more: where the dull Tribunes,   753
 Enter Menenius with the two Tribunes of the | people, Sicinius & Brutus.   896
 A Sennet. Enter the Patricians, and the Tribunes of   1239
 We recommend to you Tribunes of the People   1374
 And the Tribunes endue you with the Peoples Voyce,   1532
 Brut. Lay a fault on vs, your Tribunes,   1630
 Behold, these are the Tribunes of the People,   1700
 Senat. Tribunes giue way, he shall toth' Market place.   1712
 What should the people do with these bald Tribunes?   1865
 Tribunes, Patricians, Citizens: what ho: 1894
 Confusions neere, I cannot speake. You, Tribunes   1898
 *Mene. Heare me one word, 'beseech you Tribunes,   1930
 *Mene. Downe with that Sword, Tribunes withdraw | a while.   1943
 In this Mutinie, the Tribunes, the Aediles, and the | People are beat in.   1949
 *Mene. I could my selfe take vp a Brace o'th' best of | them, yea, the
 two Tribunes.   1968
 Mene. You worthy Tribunes.   1996
 1 *Cit.* He shall well know the Noble Tribunes are   2002
 Mene. If by the Tribunes leaue, | And yours good people,   2016
 1 *.Sen.* Noble Tribunes, | It is the humane way: the other course   2069
 Corio. What must I do? | *Mene.* Returne to th'Tribunes.   2128
 *Com. Away, the Tribunes do attend you: arm your self   2249
 Edile. List to your Tribunes. Audience: | Peace I say.   2311
 And in the power of vs the Tribunes, wee   2385
 The Gods preserue our Noble Tribunes, come. *Exeunt.*   2433
 Enter the two Tribunes, Sicinius, and Brutus, | with the Edile.   2501
 With one that wants her Wits. *Exit Tribunes.*   2557
 **and to plucke from them their Tribunes for euer.   2593
 Enter the two Tribunes, Sicinius, and Brutus.   2892
 Aedile. Worthy Tribunes, | There is a Slaue whom we haue put in
 prison,   2939
 The Tribunes cannot doo't for shame; the people   3029

TRIBUNES cont.
TRICKE = 1*1
TRICKES = *1
TRIDENT = 1
TRIE = 2
TRIED see try'd
TRIER = 1
TRIM = 1
TRITON = 1
TRIUIALL = *1
TRIUMPH = 1
TRIUMPHANT = *1
TRIUMPHANTLY = 1
TROOPE = 2
TROPHE = 1
TROTH = 2*3
TROUBLE = 1*2
TROUBLESOME = 1
TRUE = 21*8

TRUE *cont*.

*and to make it breefe Warres. This is true on mine	464
True Sword to Sword: Ile potche at him some way, | Or Wrath, or Craft	
may get him.	873
hoo, *Martius* comming home? | 2 *Ladies*. Nay, 'tis true.	1003
Menen. Wondrous: I, I warrant you, and not with- |out his true	
purchasing.	1035
Virgil. The Gods graunt them true.	1037
Volum. True? pow waw.	1038
Mene. True? Ile be sworne they are true: where is	1039
*care whether they loue, or hate him, manifests the true	1216
Then as guided by your owne true affections, and that	1634
We are the greater pole, and in true feare	1831
Mangles true iudgement, and bereaues the State	1857
All. True, the People are the Citie.	1910
Sicin. Answer to vs. | *Corio*. Say then: 'tis true, I ought so	2340
Ile do well yet. Thou old and true *Menenius*,	2459
3 A maru'llous poore one. | *Corio*. True, so I am.	2682
And say 'tis true; I'de not beleeue them more	2763
Brut. But is this true sir? | *Com*. I, and you'l looke pale	3019
Me. 'Tis true, if he were putting to my house, the brand	3035
This true, which they so seeme to feare. Go home,	3079
*haue, I am one that telling true vnder him, must say you | cannot	
passe. Therefore go backe.	3269
I carried from thee deare; and my true Lippe	3396
Auffidius, though I cannot make true Warres,	3548
Sicin. Friend, art thou certaine this is true?	3615
If you haue writ your Annales true, 'tis there,	3784

TRUELY = *1

*bald; but that our wits are so diuersly Coulord; and true- |ly	1406

TRUER = 1

Sigh'd truer breath. But that I see thee heere	2773

TRUE-BRED = 1

Ere stay behinde this Businesse. | *Men*. Oh true-bred.	267

TRULY *see* truely = 3 *1

To vs, that giue you truly: by your patience,	811
Mene. Be that you seeme, truly your Countries friend,	1933
Volce. It is so sir, truly I haue forgot you.	2573
Sicin. Yes, mercy, if you report him truly.	3594

TRUMPET = 2 *1

Enter Martius, and Titus with a Trumpet.	574
Lar. Thou worthiest *Martius*, | Go sound thy Trumpet in the Market	
place,	599
Drum and Trumpet toward Cominius, and Caius Mar- |tius,	711

TRUMPETER = 1

Our Steed the Legge, the Tongue our Trumpeter,	120

TRUMPETS = 8

Neuer sound more: when Drums and Trumpets shall	798
Flourish. Trumpets sound, and Drums.	822
Mene. Now it's twentie seuen; euery gash was an | Enemies Graue.	
Hearke, the Trumpets.	1051
A Sennet. Trumpets sound.	1059
*As the recomforted through th'gates. Why harke you: | *Trumpets*,	
Hoboyes, Drums beate, altogether.	3620
The Trumpets, Sack-buts, Psalteries, and Fifes,	3622
All. Welcome Ladies, welcome. | *A Flourish with Drummes & Trumpets*.	3647
Drummes and Trumpets sounds, with great | showts of the people.	3705

TRUNKE = 1
Wherein this Trunke was fram'd, and in her hand 3372
TRUST = 4*1
*And hewes downe Oakes, with rushes. Hang ye: trust ye? 192
They haue plac'd their men of trust? 666
Of their best trust: O're them *Auffidious*, | Their very heart of Hope. 669
Or neuer trust to what my Tongue can do | I'th way of Flattery further. 2246
(Trust too't, thou shalt not) on thy Mothers wombe | That brought thee
to this world. 3479
TRUSTS = 1
The other makes you proud. He that trusts to you, 181
TRUTH = 8*2
Val. In truth la go with me, and Ile tell you excellent | newes of your
Husband. 453
Com. Though thou speakest truth, 618
He did informe the truth: but for our Gentlemen, 655
For Truth to o're-peere. Rather then foole it so, 1512
Of no allowance, to your bosomes truth. 2156
Least I surcease to honor mine owne truth, 2229
Insisting on the olde prerogatiue | And power i'th Truth a'th Cause. 2279
2 And so did I. | *3 And so did I: and to say the truth, so did very
ma-|ny 3068
Will vouch the truth of it. Him I accuse: 3654
Mine Honor for his truth: who being so heighten'd, 3674
TRY *see also* trie = 1
Those whose great power must try him. 2362
TRYD = 1
And try'd his Inclination: from him pluckt 1594
TULLUS = 10*2
Tullus Auffidius that will put you too't: 249
Shalt see me once more strike at *Tullus* face. 263
Enter Tullus Auffidius with Senators of Coriolus. 313
Tullus Auffidious, is he within your Walles? 501
Mar. Within these three houres *Tullus* 732
*A flourish. Cornets. Enter Tullus Auffidius | bloudie, with two or three
Souldiors*. 857
Corio. Tullus Auffidius then had made new head. 1674
*shee's falne out with her Husband. Your Noble *Tullus* 2602
Corio. If *Tullus* not yet thou know'st me, and seeing 2710
Com. But I feare | They'l roare him in againe. *Tullus Affidius*, 3047
Enter Tullus Auffidius, with Attendants. 3649
Auf. My Noble Masters, heare me speake. | 1.*Lord*. O *Tullus*. 3808
TUMBLE = 1
As you threw Caps vp, will he tumble downe, 3061
TUMBLED = 1
I haue tumbled past the throw: and in his praise 3259
TUNE = *1
Coriol. Pray you now, if it may stand with the tune 1476
TUNNES = 1
Drawne Tunnes of Blood out of thy Countries brest, 2756
TURN = *1
*much alone. You talke of Pride: Oh, that you could turn 934
TURND = 1*1
Away my disposition, and possesse me | Some Harlots spirit: My throat
of Warre be turn'd, 2219
*1 What an Arme he has, he turn'd me about with his 2813

TURNE = 7*1
  Prythee *Virgilia* turne thy solemnesse out a doore, | And go along with
  vs.   472
Volum. I know not where to turne.   1088
Turne terror into sport: as Weeds before   1319
To say, hee'l turne your Current in a ditch,   1790
The which shall turne you to no further harme, | Then so much losse of
  time.   2019
For you the City. Thus I turne my backe;   2422
And make my misery serue thy turne: So vse it,   2745
*Gods asswage thy wrath, and turne the dregs of it, vpon   3312
TURNES = 2*2
*Oh World, thy slippery turnes! Friends now fast sworn,   2638
*of him, Sanctifies himselfe with's hand, and turnes vp the   2855
All to the Senate-house: some newes is comming | That turnes their
  Countenances.   2965
To a Mothers part belongs. He turnes away: 3525
TUSH = 2
Corio. Tush, tush. | *Mene*. A good demand.   2141
TWAS = 7*4
*whether his fall enrag'd him, or how 'twas, hee did so set   426
Menen. And 'twas time for him too, Ile warrant him   1026
Corio. No Sir, 'twas neuer my desire yet to trouble the | poore with
  begging.   1461
Com. 'Twas from the Cannon.   1784
The Corne a'th'Store-house gratis, as 'twas vs'd | Sometime in Greece.   1809
Bru. I would he had. | *Volum*. I would he had? Twas thou incenst the
  rable.   2543
1 *Cit*. For mine owne part, | When I said banish him, I said 'twas pitty. 3066
Carry his Honors eeuen: whether 'twas Pride   3128
Com. I minded him, how Royall 'twas to pardon   3171
Of noysome musty Chaffe. He said, 'twas folly   3179
'Twas very faintly he said Rise: dismist me   3227
TWELUE = 2
Twelue seuerall times, and I haue nightly since   2780
From twelue, to seuentie: and powring Warre   2787
TWENTIE = *2
Volum. Hee had, before this last Expedition, twentie | fiue Wounds
  vpon him.   1049
Mene. Now it's twentie seuen; euery gash was an | Enemies Graue.
  Hearke, the Trumpets.   1051
TWENTY = 1
Within thine eyes sate twenty thousand deaths   2350
TWERE = 5
'Twere a Concealement worse then a Theft,   772
Runne reeking o're the liues of men, as if 'twere   1333
2 *Cit*. And 'twere to giue againe: but 'tis no matter.   1474
Sicin. 'Twere well we let the people know't.   1775
Are still together: who Twin (as 'twere) in Loue,   2641
TWICE = 1*1
*1.*Cit*. I twice fiue hundred, & their friends, to piece 'em.   1615
And Nobly nam'd, so twice being Censor, | Was his great Ancestor.   1646
TWILL = 1*1
Sould. 'Twill be deliuer'd backe on good Condition.   860
Com. I thinke 'twill serue, if he can thereto frame his | spirit.   2201
TWIN = 1
Are still together: who Twin (as 'twere) in Loue,   2641

TWINE = 1
Then thee all-Noble *Martius*. Let me twine   2764
TWIST = 1
A twist of rotten Silke, neuer admitting   3764
TWIXT = 3*1
*no, hee waued indifferently, 'twixt doing them neyther   1220
May enter 'twixt the gap of Both, and take | The one by th'other.   1805
Dreamt of encounters 'twixt thy selfe and me: 2781
'Twixt you there's difference: but the fall of either | Makes the Suruiuor
heyre of all.   3669
TWO = 19*5
They set them downe on two lowe stooles and sowe.   361
*They Sound a Parley: Enter two Senators with others on | the Walles of
Corialus.*   499
*A flourish. Cornets. Enter Tullus Auffidius | bloudie, with two or three
Souldiors.*   857
Enter Menenius with the two Tribunes of the | people, Sicinius & Brutus. 896
*You two are old men, tell me one thing that I shall aske | you.   910
Men. In what enormity is *Martius* poore in, that you | two haue not in
abundance?   913
Men. This is strange now: Do you two know, how   918
*Meeting two such Weales men as you are (I cannot call   950
Mene. One ith' Neck, and two ith'Thigh, there's nine | that I know.   1047
Enter two Officers, to lay Cushions, as it were, | in the Capitoll.   1203
Corio. A match Sir, there's in all two worthie voyces   1471
Exeunt. Enter two other Citizens.   1475
Of Wounds, two dozen odde: Battailes thrice six   1520
To know, when two Authorities are vp,   1803
Mene. I could my selfe take vp a Brace o'th' best of | them, yea, the
two Tribunes.   1968
I may be heard, I would craue a word or two,   2018
Enter the two Tribunes, Sicinius, and Brutus, | with the Edile.   2501
Enter two of the Seruingmen.   2808
Enter the two Tribunes, Sicinius, and Brutus.   2892
Reports the Volces with two seuerall Powers   2941
*Enter Menenius, Cominius, Sicinius, Brutus, | the two Tribunes, with
others.*   3150
For one poore graine or two, to leaue vnburnt | And still to nose
th'offence.   3180
Menen. For one poore graine or two?   3182
*Enter two Senators, with Ladies, passing ouer | the Stage, with other
Lords.*   3639
TWOES = *1
*by him where he stands, by ones, by twoes, & by threes.   1430
TWOULD = 3
if it were at liberty, 'twould sure Southward.   1415
By Ioue, 'twould be my minde.   1778
Red as 'twould burne Rome: and his Iniury   3225
TYBER = 1
Mene. I would they were in Tyber.   1991
TYDINGS = 1
Sicin. First, the Gods blesse you for your tydings: | Next, accept my
thankefulnesse.   3633
TYE = 1*1
Menen. He loues your People, but tye him not to be   1273
Tye Leaden pounds too's heeles. Proceed by Processe,   2055

```
TYGER = *1
    *mercy in him, then there is milke in a male-Tyger, that              3597
TYING = 1
    Tying him to ought, so putting him to Rage,                           1599
TYRANNICALL = 2
    Tyrannicall power: If he euade vs there,                              2260
    Your selfe into a power tyrannicall,                                  2344
TYRANNY = 1
    Forgiue my Tyranny: but do not say,                                   3392
TYRD = 2
    I am wearie, yea, my memorie is tyr'd:                                 852
    Th'art tyr'd, then in a word, I also am                              2751
TYRE = 1
    he hath faults (with surplus) to tyre in repetition. | Showts within.   46
VAGABOND = 1
    Vagabond exile, Fleaing, pent to linger                              2373
VAINE = 1
    So that all hope is vaine, vnlesse his Noble Mother,                  3231
VAL = 4*8
VALE = 1
    Then vale your Ignorance: If none, awake                             1792
VALER = *1
VALERIA see also Val., Valer. = 6
    Gent. Madam, the lady Valeria is come to visit you.                   388
    At Grecian sword. Contenning, tell Valeria                            405
    Enter Valeria with an Vsher, and a Gentlewoman.                       410
    Enter Volumnia, Virgilia, and Valeria.                                993
    Enter Virgilia, Volumnia, Valeria, yong Martius, | with Attendants.  3369
    And hangs on Dians Temple: Deere Valeria.                            3419
VALERIA = 1
VALIANT = 5
    *Bru. The present Warres deuoure him, he is growne | Too proud to be
    so valiant.                                                           287
    And Titus Lartius, a most valiant Roman,                              328
    Piercing our Romanes: Then Valiant Titus take                         582
    Officious and not valiant, you haue sham'd me | In your condemned
    Seconds.                                                              742
    Do smilingly Reuolt, and who resists | Are mock'd for valiant
    Ignorance,                                                           3022
VALIANTNESSE = 1
    Thy Valiantnesse was mine, thou suck'st it from me:                  2238
VALORS = *1
    *Auf. Bolder, though not so subtle: my valors poison'd,               876
VALOUR = 5
    Your valour puts well forth: Pray follow. Exeunt.                     278
    That Valour is the chiefest Vertue,                                  1298
    Most Valour spoke not for them. Th'Accusation                        1824
    Contend against thy Valour. Know thou first,                        2771
    2.Lord. Thou hast done a deed, whereat | Valour will weepe.          3810
VALUE = 1*1
    Rome must know the value of her owne:                                 771
    *he remember a kinder value of the People, then he hath | hereto priz'd
    them at.                                                             1267
VANQUISHER = 1
    To hopelesse restitution, so he might | Be call'd your Vanquisher.   1693
VANTAGE = 4
    Lead'st first to win some vantage.                                    168
```

VANTAGE *cont*.

With their refusall, both obserue and answer | The vantage of his anger. 1665

But yet a braine, that leades my vse of Anger | To better vantage. 2121

3.*Con*. Therefore at your vantage, | Ere he expresse himselfe, or moue the people 3713

VARIABLE = 1

With variable Complexions; all agreeing 1131

VARLET = *1

*this Varlet heere: This, who like a blocke hath denyed | my accesse to thee. 3313

VASSAILES = 1

To call them Wollen Vassailes, things created 2094

VAST = 1

O're the vast world, to seeke a single man, 2482

VAWARD = 1

Com. As I guesse *Martius*, | Their Bands i'th Vaward are the Antients 667

VAYLD = 1

To keepe your great pretences vayl'd, till when 336

VEINES = 2

The strongest Nerues, and small inferiour Veines 145

The Veines vnfill'd, our blood is cold, and then 3209

VELUTUS = 2

Sicinius Velutus, and I know not. Sdeath, 231

Enter Sicinius Velutus, Annius Brutus Cominius, Titus | Lartius, with other Senatours. 244

VENGEANCE = 1*1

*1.*off*. That's a braue fellow: but hee's vengeance | prowd, and loues not the common people. 1209

What the vengeance, could he not speake'em faire? 1992

VENOMOUS = *1

*And venomous to thine eyes. My (sometime) Generall, 2461

VENT = 1*2

Mar. I am glad on't, then we shall ha meanes to vent 242

What his Brest forges, that his Tongue must vent, 1986

*of Vent. Peace, is a very Apoplexy, Lethargie, mull'd, 2881

VENTED = *1

*They vented their Complainings, which being answer'd 222

VENTURE = 2

But since it serues my purpose, I will venture | To scale't a little more. 92

He had rather venture all his Limbes for Honor, 1294

VERDICT = 1

*1.*Cit*. Let vs kill him, and wee'l haue Corne at our own | price. Is't a Verdict? 13

VERIFIED = 1

For I haue euer verified my Friends, 3255

VERILY = *1

Val. Verily I do not iest with you: there came newes | from him last night. 456

VERITY = 1

(Of whom hee's cheefe) with all the size that verity 3256

VERTUE = 6

*his Mother, and to be partly proud, which he is, euen to | the altitude of his vertue. 40

Or Hailstone in the Sun. Your Vertue is, 185

That Valour is the chiefest Vertue, 1298

Who lack not Vertue, no, nor Power, but that 1763

To choake it in the vtt'rance: So our Vertue, 3140

VERTUE *cont*.
1 Be it so, go back: the vertue of your name, | Is not heere passable. 3249
VERTUES = 1
I would they would forget me, like the Vertues 1447
VERTUOUS = 1*2
   Coriol. You should account mee the more Vertuous, 1485
   *passe heere: no, though it were as vertuous to lye, as to | liue chastly.
Therefore go backe. 3264
Let it be Vertuous to be Obstinate. 3375
VERY = 15*10
   All. Against him first: He's a very dog to the Com-|monalty. 29
   1.Cit. Very well, and could bee content to giue him 33
   *very pretty boy. A my troth, I look'd vpon him a Wens-|day 421
1.*Sol*. Following the Flyers at the very heeles, 550
Of their best trust: O're them *Auffidious*, | Their very heart of Hope. 669
We proue this very houre. 679
   Men. Why 'tis no great matter: for a very little theefe 925
   Men. I know you can doe very little alone, for your 931
   Men. Our very Priests must become Mockers, if they 979
   Menen. I will make my very house reele to night: 1008
A Curse begin at very root on's heart, 1094
Volum. I haue liued, | To see inherited my very Wishes, 1111
The very way to catch them. 1772
Brut. Sir, those cold wayes, | That seeme like prudent helpes, are very
poysonous, 1936
Edi. Very well. 2286
I am so dishonour'd, that the very houre | You take it off againe. 2338
   *of Vent. Peace, is a very Apoplexy, Lethargie, mull'd, 2881
Mene. Cannot be? | We haue Record, that very well it can, 2953
Sicin. The very tricke on't. | *Mene*. This is vnlikely, 2982
2 And so did I. | *3 And so did I: and to say the truth, so did very
ma-|ny 3068
Menen. Very well, could he say lesse. 3175
Bru. You know the very rode into his kindnesse, | And cannot lose your
way. 3217
'Twas very faintly he said Rise: dismist me 3227
   *when you haue pusht out your gates, the very Defender 3276
That thought he could do more: A very little 3363
VESSELL = 2
A Vessell vnder sayle, so men obey'd, 1320
Thou shew'st a Noble Vessell: What's thy name? 2719
VESTURE = 1
The Naples Vesture of Humilitie, 1157
VEXATION = 1
Giue him deseru'd vexation. Let a guard | Attend vs through the City. 2430
VEXED = 1
The Nobility are vexed, whom we see haue sided | In his behalfe. 2504
VEYLD *see also* vayl'd = 1
To winne a vulgar station: our veyl'd Dames 1134
VIAND = 1
Still cubbording the Viand, neuer bearing 102
VICE = *1
   *a Vice in him: You must in no way say he is co-|uetous. 43
VICTORIE = 1
Victorie in his Pocket? the wounds become him. 1020
VICTORY = 3
Whereto we are bound, together with thy victory: 3463

VICTORY *cont.*
You haue wonne a happy Victory to Rome. 3544
He whin'd and roar'd away your Victory, 3766
VIEW = 3
Mess. They lye in view, but haue not spoke as yet. 488
But then *Auffidius* was within my view, 844
An o're-prest Roman, and i'th' Consuls view 1307
VIGILANT = 1
The Kingly crown'd head, the vigilant eye, 118
VILDE = 1
Him vilde, that was your Garland. What's the matter, 195
VILDLY = 1
Against the Volces, for they had so vildly 1685
VILLAINE = 1
Auf. Insolent Villaine. | *All Consp.* Kill, kill, kill, kill, kill him. 3803
VIOLENT = 4*2
Thy exercise hath bin too violent, | For a second course of Fight. 587
*proud, violent, testie Magistrates (alias Fooles) | as any in Rome. 940
Where the Disease is violent. Lay hands vpon him, 1938
The violent fit a'th'time craues it as Physicke 2125
*This lyes glowing I can tell you, and is almost mature for | the violent
breaking out. 2594
*of them, and in a violent popular ignorance, giuen your 3277
VIOLENTLY = 1
And temp'rately proceed to what you would | Thus violently redresse. 1934
VIOLENTST = 1
He, and *Auffidius* can no more attone | Then violent'st Contrariety. 2984
VIPER = 1
Sicin. Where is this Viper, 1994
VIPOROUS = 1
This Viporous Traitor: to eiect him hence 2023
VIR = 4*1
VIRG = 9*5
VIRGIL = 5
VIRGILIA see also Vir., Virg., Virgil. = 4*2
Enter Volumnia and Virgilia, mother and wife to Martius: 360
Prythee *Virgilia* turne thy solemnesse out a doore, | And go along with
vs. 472
Enter Volumnia, Virgilia, and Valeria. 993
*Enter Coriolanus, Volumnia, Virgilia, Menenius, Cominius, | with the
yong Nobility of Rome.* 2435
Enter Volumnia, Virgilia, and Menenius. 2512
Enter Virgilia, Volumnia, Valeria, yong Martius, | with Attendants. 3369
VIRGIN = 1
Small as an Eunuch, or the Virgin voyce 2222
VIRGINALL = *1
*easie groanes of old women, the Virginall Palms of your 3279
VIRGIND = 1
Hath Virgin'd it ere since. You Gods, I pray, 3397
VIRTUE *see* vertue
VIRTUES *see* vertues
VIRTUOUS *see* vertuous
VISAGE = 1
The bloud vpon your Visage dryes, 'tis time 855
VISIT = 3
Gent. Madam, the lady *Valeria* is come to visit you. 388
Come, you must go visit the good Lady that lies in. 441

VISIT *cont.*
  Or rudely visit them in parts remote,   2801
VISITE = *1
  Virg. I will wish her speedy strength, and visite her   442
VISITED = 1
  The good Patricians must be visited,   1108
VLISSES = *1
  *the yearne she spun in *Vlisses* absence, did but fill *Athica*   447
VNACTIUE = 1
  I'th midd'st a th'body, idle and vnactiue,   101
VNAKING = 1
  Shew them th'vnaking Skarres, which I should hide,   1370
VNAPT = 1
  We powt vpon the Morning, are vnapt   3210
VNBARBD = 1
  Corio. Must I goe shew them my vnbarb'd Sconce?   2205
VNBORNE = 1
  All cause vnborne, could neuer be the Natiue   1826
VNBRUISD = 1
  That's yet vnbruis'd: bring me but out at gate.   2488
VNBUCKLING = 1
  Vnbuckling Helmes, fisting each others Throat,   2783
VNBUILD = 1
  Sena. To vnbuild the Citie, and to lay all flat.   1908
VNBURIED = 1
  As the dead Carkasses of vnburied men,   2410
VNBURNT = 1
  For one poore graine or two, to leaue vnburnt | And still to nose
  th'offence.   3180
VNCERTAINE = 2
  The end of Warres vncertaine: but this certaine,   3498
  3.Con. The People will remaine vncertaine, whil'st   3668
VNCERTAINTIE = 1
  And heere remaine with your vncertaintie.   2412
VNCHILDED = 1
  Hath widdowed and vnchilded many a one,   3834
VNCLOGGE = 1
  But once a day, it would vnclogge my heart | Of what lyes heauy too't.   2561
VNDER = 7*2
  (Vnder the Gods) keepe you in awe, which else   198
  *wonder, his insolence can brooke to be commanded vn- | der *Cominius?*   291
  Onely for bearing Burthens, and sore blowes | For sinking vnder them.   1179
  A Vessell vnder sayle, so men obey'd,   1320
  3 Where dwel'st thou? | *Corio.* Vnder the Canopy.   2691
  3 Vnder the Canopy | *Corio.* I.   2693
  Of all the vnder Fiends. But if so be,   2749
  *haue, I am one that telling true vnder him, must say you | cannot
  passe. Therefore go backe.   3269
  Vnder your great Command. You are to know,   3739
VNDERSTAND = 1
  Auf. I vnderstand thee well, and be thou sure   3108
VNDERSTOOD = *1
  Bru. Come, come, you are well vnderstood to bee a   976
VNDERTAKE = 1
  Ile go to him, and vndertake to bring him in peace,   2066
VNDERTAKT = 1
  Mene. Ile vndertak't: | I thinke hee'l heare me. Yet to bite his lip,   3205

VNDER-CREST = 1
  To vnder-crest your good Addition, | To th'fairenesse of my power.   828
VNDO = 1
  Neighbours, will you vndo your selues?   64
VNDONE = 3*1
  2 *Cit*. We cannot Sir, we are vndone already.   65
  *vndone, that may fully discouer him their opposite. Now   1223
  Mene. We are all vndone, vnlesse | The Noble man haue mercy.   3026
  As draw his Sword: yet he hath left vndone   3115
VNELECTED = 1
  You should haue ta'ne th'aduantage of his Choller, | And pass'd him
  vnelected.   1600
VNFILLD = 1
  The Veines vnfill'd, our blood is cold, and then   3209
VNFORTUNATE = 1
  How more vnfortunate then all liuing women   3452
VNGRATEFULL *see also* ingratefull = 1
  Into the bowels of vngratefull Rome,   2788
VNGRAUELY = 1
  Which most gibingly, vngrauely, he did fashion   1628
VNHEARD = 1
  As *Cominius* is return'd, vnheard: what then?   3199
VNHEARTS = 1
  And humme at good *Cominius*, much vnhearts mee.   3207
VNHOLY = 1
  Which was your shame, by this vnholy Braggart?   3790
VNIUST = 1
  Loden with Honor. Say my Request's vniust,   3521
VNKINDNESSE = 1
  But as a discontented Friend, greefe-shot | With his vnkindnesse. Say't
  be so?   3200
VNKNIT = 1
  As he began, and not vnknit himselfe | The Noble knot he made.   2541
VNKNOWNE = 1*1
  *2 *Cit*. Our busines is not vnknowne to th'Senat, they   59
  Will proue to bloody: and the end of it, | Vnknowne to the Beginning.   2071
VNLESSE = 5
  Vnlesse by not so doing, our good Citie | Cleaue in the midd'st, and
  perish.   2117
  And cannot liue but to thy shame, vnlesse | It be to do thee seruice.   2757
  Mene. We are all vndone, vnlesse | The Noble man haue mercy.   3026
  Vnlesse by vsing meanes I lame the foote   3098
  So that all hope is vaine, vnlesse his Noble Mother,   3231
VNLIKE = 1
  Brut. Not vnlike each way to better yours.   1735
VNLIKELY = 1
  Sicin. The very tricke on't. | *Mene*. This is vnlikely,   2982
VNMERITING = *1
  Men. Why then you should discouer a brace of vn- | meriting,   939
VNMUSICALL = 1
  Corio. A name vnmusicall to the Volcians eares,   2714
VNNATURALL = 3
  In Ioues owne Booke, like an vnnaturall Dam | Should now eate vp her
  owne.   2030
  Wherein I seeme vnnaturall: Desire not t'allay   3439
  The Gods looke downe, and this vnnaturall Scene   3542

VOICES *cont.*

giue you our voices heartily.	1496
When both your voices blended, the great'st taste	1797
Sicin. Haue you a Catalogue | *Of all the Voices that we haue procur'd, set downe by'th | (Pole?	2269
Sicin. I do demand, | If you submit you to the peoples voices,	2317

VOIDED = 1

I would haue voided thee. But in meere spight	2739

VOL = 5*6

VOLCE see also Vol. = 3

He that retires, Ile take him for a *Volce,*	521
Being a *Volce,* be that I am. Condition?	863
Enter a Roman, and a Volce.	2570

VOLCE = 2*3

VOLCEAN = 2*1

*the Newes in Rome: I haue a Note from the Volcean	2580
In Volcean brests. That we haue beene familiar,	3320
This Fellow had a Volcean to his Mother:	3535

VOLCEANS = 1

If *Martius* should be ioyn'd with Volceans.	3005

VOLCES = 17*1

The Volces are in Armes.	247
The Volces haue much Corne: take these Rats thither,	276
(As children from a Beare) the *Volces* shunning him:	393
Enter the Army of the Volces.	514
Mes. Spies of the *Volces* | Held me in chace, that I was forc'd to wheele	624
But is foure *Volces*? None of you, but is	699
Heere they fight, and certaine Volces come in the ayde	740
Menen. Hauing determin'd of the Volces,	1244
Corio. So then the Volces stand but as at first,	1677
Against the Volces, for they had so vildly	1685
To thee particularly, and to all the Volces	2723
Reports the Volces with two seuerall Powers	2941
The Volces dare breake with vs.	2952
Great Nature cries, Deny not. Let the Volces	3382
Corio. Auffidius, and you Volces marke, for wee'l	3447
The Volces whom you serue, you might condemne vs	3491
Is that you reconcile them: While the Volces	3493
Corio. Cut me to peeces Volces men and Lads,	3782

VOLCIAN = 2

And shewes good Husbandry for the Volcian State,	3113
You must report to th'Volcian Lords, how plainly	3349

VOLCIANS = 4

Corio. A name vnmusicall to the Volcians eares,	2714
cheape as Volcians. They are rising, they are rising. | *Both.* In, in, in, in. *Exeunt*	2890
The Volcians are dislodg'd, and *Martius* gone:	3612
That like an Eagle in a Doue-coat, I | Flatter'd your Volcians in *Corioles.*	3785

VOLCIES = 1*1

Mes. The newes is sir, the Volcies are in Armes.	241
*Thus it is: the Volcies haue an Army forth, against who(m)	460

VOLUM = 34*16

VOLUME = 1

Will beare the Knaue by'th Volume:	2301

VOLUMNIA see also Vol., Volum. = 6*2

*Enter Volumnia and Virgilia, mother and wife to Martius:	360

VOLUMNIA cont.
Enter Volumnia, Virgilia, and Valeria.	993
Enter Volumnia.	2090
Volum. Do your will. *Exit Volumnia*	2248
*Enter Coriolanus, Volumnia, Virgilia, Menenius, Cominius, | *with the*	
yong Nobility of Rome.	2435
Enter Volumnia, Virgilia, and Menenius.	2512
Enter Virgilia, Volumnia, Valeria, yong Martius, | *with Attendants.*	3369
I will go meete the Ladies. This *Volumnia,*	3626

VOLUPTUOUSLY = 1
*had rather had eleuen dye Nobly for their Countrey, then | one	
voluptuously surfet out of Action.	385

VOUCH = 2
(Which I dare vouch, is more then that he hath	2037
Will vouch the truth of it. Him I accuse:	3654

VOUCHD = 1
Which to the spire, and top of prayses vouch'd,	775

VOUCHES = 1
Their needlesse Vouches: Custome calls me too't.	1508

VOW = 1
Shall I be tempted to infringe my vow	3367

VOWES = 2
By th'Blood we haue shed together, | By th'Vowes we haue made	673
And vowes Reuenge as spacious, as betweene | The yong'st and oldest	
thing.	2977

VOYCE = 10
Com. I shall lacke voyce: the deeds of *Coriolanus*	1296
*1.Cit. Hee ha's done Nobly, and cannot goe without | any honest mans	
Voyce.	1524
And the Tribunes endue you with the Peoples Voyce,	1532
Their Liberties, make them of no more Voyce	1618
To Voyce him Consull. Lay the fault on vs.	1637
Bru. Why shall the people giue | One that speakes thus, their voyce?	1814
Small as an Eunuch, or the Virgin voyce	2222
That being past for Consull with full voyce:	2337
And suffer'd me by th'voyce of Slaues to be	2734
Vpon the voyce of occupation, and | The breath of Garlicke-eaters.	3014

VOYCES = 23*7
Scicin. Sir, the People must haue their Voyces,	1360
*1.Cit. Once if he do require our voyces, wee ought | not to deny him.	1388
*3 Cit. Are you all resolu'd to giue your voyces? But	1422
*Corio. A match Sir, there's in all two worthie voyces	1471
*them. I will make much of your voyces, and so trouble | you no	
farther.	1500
Coriol. Most sweet Voyces: | Better it is to dye, better to sterue,	1503
Here come moe Voyces.	1517
Your Voyces? for your Voyces I haue sought,	1518
Watcht for your Voyces: for your Voyces, beare	1519
I haue seene, and heard of: for your Voyces,	1521
Your Voyces? Indeed I would be Consull.	1523
Corio. Worthy Voyces.	1529
1.Cit. He ha's our Voyces, Sir.	1554
He mock'd vs, when he begg'd our Voyces.	1557
But by your Voyces, will not so permit me.	1569
Your Voyces therefore: when we graunted that,	1570
Here was, I thanke you for your Voyces, thanke you	1571
*Your most sweet Voyces: now you haue left your Voyces,	1572

VOYCES *cont.*

Or seeing it, of such Childish friendlinesse, | To yeeld your Voyces?	1575
Fast Foe toth' *Plebeij*, your Voyces might	1585
Would thinke vpon you, for your Voyces,	1589
Ile haue fiue hundred Voyces of that sound.	1614
Corio. Haue I had Childrens Voyces?	1711
Must these haue Voyces, that can yeeld them now,	1716
*More worthier then their Voyces. They know the Corne	1817
And pay you for your voyces. 'Tis no matter,	3062
Com. Y'are goodly things, you Voyces.	3073

VP *see also* vppe = 25*12

*chaine vp and restraine the poore. If the Warres eate vs	85
Yet I can make my Awdit vp, that all	152
Bring vp your Army: but (I thinke) you'l finde	346
*and ouer he comes, and vp againe: catcht it again: or	425
Rather then they shall pound vs vp our Gates,	506
And when it bowes, stand'st vp: Thou art left *Martius*,	556
Ere yet the fight be done, packe vp, downe with them.	579
They all shout and waue their swords, take him vp in their | Armes, and cast vp their Caps.	695
Wrench vp thy power to th'highest.	736
cast vp their Caps and Launces: Cominius | and Lartius stand bare.	795
Embarquements all of Fury, shall lift vp	881
*set vp the bloodie Flagge against all Patience, and	971
Volum. Nay, my good Souldier, vp:	1076
Stalls, Bulkes, Windowes, are smother'd vp,	1129
*helpe will serue: for once we stood vp about the Corne,	1401
*mans will, 'tis strongly wadg'd vp in a blocke-head: but	1414
As cause had call'd you vp, haue held him to;	1596
To know, when two Authorities are vp,	1803
Mene. I could my selfe take vp a Brace o'th' best of | them, yea, the two Tribunes.	1968
In Ioues owne Booke, like an vnnaturall Dam | Should now eate vp her owne.	2030
When one but of my ordinance stood vp	2097
Tent in my cheekes, and Schoole-boyes Teares take vp	2224
They all shout, and throw vp their Caps.	2425
*3 Pray you poore Gentleman, take vp some other sta-|tion:	2684
finger and his thumbe, as one would set vp a Top.	2814
*of him, Sanctifies himselfe with's hand, and turnes vp the	2855
*3 But when they shall see sir, his Crest vp againe, and	2869
*Drum strooke vp this afternoone: 'Tis as it were a parcel	2874
As you threw Caps vp, will he tumble downe,	3061
Volum. Oh stand vp blest! | Whil'st with no softer Cushion then the Flint	3402
*For making vp this peace. Thou know'st (great Sonne)	3497
But kneeles, and holds vp hands for fellowship,	3532
And hale him vp and downe; all swearing, if	3606
He ha's betray'd your businesse, and giuen vp	3760
3.Lord. Tread not vpon him Masters, all be quiet, | Put vp your Swords.	3812
Auf. My Rage is gone, | And I am strucke with sorrow. Take him vp:	3829

VPBRAIDS = 1

Vpbraid's with our distresse. But sure if you	3189

VPON *see also* vpon's, vpon't, vppon = 51*7

Which you do liue vpon: and fit it is,	139
Then is the coale of fire vpon the Ice,	184
Vpon your fauours, swimmes with finnes of Leade,	191

VPON *cont*.

Win vpon power, and throw forth greater Theames | For Insurrections

arguing.   234

vpon my partie, I'de reuolt to make   255

1.*Sen*. Then worthy *Martius*, | Attend vpon *Cominius* to these Warres.   258

Tit. No *Caius Martius*, | Ile leane vpon one Crutch, and fight with

tother,   265

More then his singularity, he goes | Vpon this present Action.   310

Vol. Hee'l beat *Auffidius* head below his knee, | And treade vpon his

necke.   408

*Vol. He had rather see the swords, and heare a Drum, | then looke

vpon his Schoolmaster.   418

*very pretty boy. A my troth, I look'd vpon him a Wens- | day   421

With them he enters: who vpon the sodaine   551

*Titus Lartius, hauing set a guard vpon Carioles, going with   710

*Martius. I haue some Wounds vpon me, and they smart   779

And stand vpon my common part with those, | That haue beheld the

doing.   792

The bloud vpon your Visage dryes, 'tis time   855

At home, vpon my Brothers Guard, euen there   884

*Volum. Hee had, before this last Expedition, twentie | fiue Wounds

vpon him.   1049

Which (I doubt not) but our Rome | Will cast vpon thee.   1115

Vpon their ancient mallice, will forget   1150

Vpon him as he pass'd: the Nobles bended   1195

*so that if they loue they know not why, they hate vpon   1214

*Scicin. We are conuented vpon a pleasing Treatie, and   1263

And look'd vpon things precious, as they were   1341

You must desire them to thinke vpon you.   1445

Coriol. Thinke vpon me? Hang 'em,   1446

To meet anon, vpon your approbation.   1538

Would thinke vpon you, for your Voyces,   1589

Thinking vpon his Seruices, tooke from you   1626

That of all things vpon the Earth, he hated   1691

Vpon the part o'th' People, in whose power   1922

Where the Disease is violent. Lay hands vpon him,   1938

Come trie vpon your selues, what you haue seene me.   1942

Brut. Lay hands vpon him.   1945

Mene. For 'tis a Sore vpon vs,   1959

How you can frowne, then spend a fawne vpon'em,   2166

With Accusations, as I heare more strong | Then are vpon you yet.   2251

To suffer lawfull Censure for such faults | As shall be prou'd vpon you.   2320

Vpon the wounds his body beares, which shew   2325

Her Enemies markes vpon me. I do loue   2397

Corio. Fare ye well: | Thou hast yeares vpon thee, and thou art too full   2485

Volum. Angers my Meate: I suppe vpon my selfe,   2565

*so, they are in a most warlike preparation, & hope to com | vpon

them, in the heate of their diuision   2587

My Birth-place haue I, and my loues vpon   2649

Associated with *Auffidius*, Rages | Vpon our Territories, and haue

already   2989

To melt the Citty Leades vpon your pates,   2997

Vpon the voyce of occupation, and | The breath of Garlicke-eaters.   3014

Com. You haue brought | A Trembling vpon Rome, such as was neuer   3039

And not a haire vpon a Souldiers head   3059

We powt vpon the Morning, are vnapt   3210

And then Ile set vpon him.   3216

VPON *cont*.

Like to a Bowle vpon a subtle ground	3258
*now presently, and swoond for what's to come vpon	3303
*Gods asswage thy wrath, and turne the dregs of it, vpon	3312
May hang vpon your hardnesse, therefore heare vs.	3446
Auf. There was it:	For which my sinewes shall be stretcht vpon him,	3699
Who weares my stripes imprest vpon him, that	3778
3.*Lord*. Tread not vpon him Masters, all be quiet,	Put vp your Swords.	3812

VPONS = 2

Lart. Hence; and shut your gates vpon's:	720
Readie when time shall prompt them, to make roade	Vpon's againe.	1678

VPONT = 3

If he be put vpon't, and that's as easie,	1184
Menen. Doe not stand vpon't:	1373
Plague vpon't, I cannot bring	My tongue to such a pace. Looke Sir, my wounds,	1439

VPPE = *1

*not vppe, they will; and there's all the loue they beare	vs.	86

VPPER = *1

*Son and Heire to Mars, set at vpper end o'th'Table: No	2852

VPPON = *2

*the first complaint, hasty and Tinder-like vppon, to	946
*is no hope in't, our throats are sentenc'd, and stay vppon	execution.	3576

VRGD = 1

I vrg'd our old acquaintance, and the drops	3162

VRGE = 1

What I can vrge against him, although it seemes	3110

VRNE = 1

As the most Noble Coarse, that euer Herald	Did follow to his Vrne.	3824

VS *see also* before's, behold's, let's, shal's, vpbraid's, vpon's *l*.*13 *19 *20 *22 *24 80 *81 *85 87 *246 270 334 344 347 353 450 465 473 496 506 515 519 537 709 *721 811 815 831 833 *919 1200 1257 1386 *1392 *1393 *1395 *1400 *1402 *1432 *1456 1557 1558 1559 1560 1561 1630 1637 1638 1762 1771 1832 1920 1921 1958 1959 1961 2040 2170 2253 2260 2295 2340 2385 2431 2479 2507 *2516 2620 2952 3009 3063 *3070 *3081 *3307 3388 3442 3446 3459 3488 3491 *3526 3534 3537 3566 3599 *3601 *3602 3664 3730 3798 = 68*25

VSD = 7

At a poore mans house: he vs'd me kindly,	842
He vs'd vs scornefully: he should haue shew'd vs	1561
The Corne a'th'Store-house gratis, as 'twas vs'd	Sometime in Greece.	1809
Like interrupted Waters, and o're-beare	What they are vs'd to beare.	1974
Bru. Go about it,	Put him to Choller straite, he hath bene vs'd	2289
Where is your ancient Courage? You were vs'd	2439
A Noble cunning. You were vs'd to load me	2445

VSE = 8

And let me vse my Sword, I'de make a Quarrie	210
Bru. You see how he intends to vse the people.	1380
But yet a braine, that leades my vse of Anger	To better vantage.	2121
Were fit for thee to vse, as they to clayme,	2184
And make my misery serue thy turne: So vse it,	2745
Your Soldiers vse him as the Grace 'fore meate,	3093
He would vse me with estimation.	3288
His Tribe, to vse my lawfull Sword.	3802

VSHER = 1

Enter Valeria with an Vsher, and a Gentlewoman.	410

VSHERS = 1
A showt, and flourish. | *Volum.* These are the Vshers of *Martius*:   1053
VSING = 1
Vnlesse by vsing meanes I lame the foote   3098
VSURERS = *1
*with Graine: Make Edicts for Vsurie, to support Vsu-|rers;   82
VSURIE = *1
*with Graine: Make Edicts for Vsurie, to support Vsu-|rers;   82
VTMOST = 2*1
To th'vtmost of a man, and giddy censure   298
Where he shall answer by a lawfull Forme | (In peace) to his vtmost
perill.   2067
*I let forth your halfe pinte of blood. Backe, that's the vt-|most of your
hauing, backe.   3292
VTTER = *1
*What I think, I vtter, and spend my malice in my breath.   949
VTTERD = 1
Should not be vtter'd feebly: it is held,   1297
VTTERED = *1
*as you haue vttered words in your owne, you should not   3263
VTTRANCE = 1
To choake it in the vtt'rance: So our Vertue,   3140
VULG = 1
Volum. Why I pray you. | *Vulg.* 'Tis not to saue labour, nor that I want
loue.   444
VULGAR = 2*1
Mar. Fiue Tribunes to defend their vulgar wisdoms   229
To winne a vulgar station: our veyl'd Dames   1134
To th'vulgar eye, that he beares all things fairely: 3112
W = 1*1
*haue had inkling this fortnight what we intend to do, w   60
Mar. How lies their Battell? Know you on w side   665
WADGD = 1*1
*mans will, 'tis strongly wadg'd vp in a blocke-head: but   1414
He wadg'd me with his Countenance, as if | I had bin Mercenary.   3693
WAGER = 1
Martius. Yonder comes Newes: | A Wager they haue met.   482
WAGGING = *1
*wagging of your Beards, and your Beards deserue not so   982
WAIES = *1
*Thy Countries strength and weaknesse, thine own waies   2799
WAILE = 1
Tis fond to waile ineuitable strokes,   2464
WAITE = 1
I purpose not to waite on Fortune, till   3474
WAKD = 1
And wak'd halfe dead with nothing. Worthy *Martius*,   2784
WALKE = 1
Did see, and heare, deuise, instruct, walke, feele,   104
WALKING = *1
*as day do's night: It's sprightly walking, audible, and full   2880
WALKS = *1
*of his face, sowres ripe Grapes. When he walks, he moues   3587
WALL = *1
*Picture-like to hang by th'wall, if renowne made it not   372

WALLES = 3*1
  They Sound a Parley: Enter two Senators with others on | the Walles of
  Corialus.   499
  Tullus Auffidious, is he within your Walles?   501
  Hearke, our Drummes | *Are bringing forth our youth: Wee'l breake
  our Walles   504
  Alone I fought in your *Corioles* walles,   733
WALLS = 1*1
  Clambring the Walls to eye him: 1128
  *Corio. We will before the walls of Rome to morrow   3347
WALS = 1
  That Hunger-broke stone wals: that dogges must eate   219
WANT = 3
  Volum. Why I pray you. | *Vulg*. 'Tis not to saue labour, nor that I want
  loue.   444
  Shall teach the People, which time shall not want,   1183
  Of what that want might ruine.   2168
WANTING = 1
  Onely there's one thing wanting,   1114
WANTON = 1
  In their nicely gawded Cheekes, toth' wanton spoyle   1136
WANTS = 3*1
  Haue the Patricians of you for your wants.   67
  The horne, and noise o'th'Monsters, wants not spirit   1789
  With one that wants her Wits. *Exit Tribunes*.   2557
  *finisht with his bidding. He wants nothing of a God but | Eternity, and
  a Heauen to Throne in.   3592
WARD = 1
  Which we haue goaded on-ward. *Exeunt*.   1670
WARLIKE = 1*1
  The warlike Seruice he ha's done, consider: Thinke   2324
  *so, they are in a most warlike preparation, & hope to com | vpon
  them, in the heate of their diuision   2587
WARMD = 1
  My worke hath yet not warm'd me. Fare you well: 590
WARME = 1
  He ha's it now: and by his Lookes, me thinkes, | 'Tis warme at's heart. 1548
WARNING = 1
  and to be on foot at an houres warning.   2614
WARRANT = 4*3
  *his teeth, and teare it. Oh, I warrant how he mammockt | it.   427
  All. To th'pot I warrant him. *Enter Titus Lartius*   547
  *Menen. And 'twas time for him too, Ile warrant him   1026
  *Menen. Wondrous: I, I warrant you, and not with-|out his true
  purchasing.   1035
  Scicin. On the suddaine, I warrant him Consull.   1141
  *Me. Do not cry hauocke, where you shold but hunt | With modest
  warrant,   2006
  1 A Noble Fellow I warrant him.   3343
WARRE = 16*3
  That like nor Peace, nor Warre? The one affrights you,   180
  *like to finde fame: To a cruell Warre I sent him, from   374
  *my Sonne the whole Name of the Warre: he hath in this   1032
  Commit the Warre of White and Damaske   1135
  Then Cammels in their Warre, who haue their Prouand   1178
  When by and by the dinne of Warre gan pierce   1329
  They ne're did seruice for't; being prest to'th'Warre,   1819

WARRE *cont*.

Did not deserue Corne gratis. Being i'th'Warre,	1822
To speake of Peace, or Warre. I talke of you,	2098
I'th'Warre do grow together: Grant that, and tell me	2138
With Honour, as in Warre; since that to both | It stands in like request.	2147
Away my disposition, and possesse me | Some Harlots spirit: My throat of Warre be turn'd,	2219
And not our streets with Warre.	2306
From twelue, to seuentie: and powring Warre	2787
*1 Let me haue Warre say I, it exceeds peace as farre	2879
Bru. *Caius Martius* was | A worthy Officer i'th'Warre, but Insolent,	2928
And with the deepest malice of the Warre,	2943
As he controll'd the warre. But one of them	3136
Counsaile a'th'warre: But at his Nurses teares	3765

WARRES = 17*6

*chaine vp and restraine the poore. If the Warres eate vs	85
Onely my warres with him. He is a Lion | That I am proud to hunt.	256
1.*Sen*. Then worthy *Martius*, | Attend vpon *Cominius* to these Warres.	258
Bru. The present Warres deuoure him, he is growne | Too proud to be so valiant.	287
threshold, till my Lord returne from the Warres.	439
*and to make it breefe Warres. This is true on mine	464
And make my Warres on you: Looke too't: Come on,	535
Let him be made an Ouerture for th' Warres:	802
Weares this Warres Garland: in token of the which,	816
Mene. Consider this: He ha's bin bred i'th'Warres	2062
Volum. If it be Honor in your Warres, to seeme	2143
Of the warres surfets, to go roue with one	2487
Auffidius will appeare well in these Warres, his great	2603
Of these faire Edifices fore my Warres	2625
*deafe, sleepe, insensible, a getter of more bastard Chil-|dren, then warres a destroyer of men.	2882
*2 'Tis so, and as warres in some sort may be saide to	2884
*The Warres for my money. I hope to see Romanes as	2889
To shame vnvulnerable, and sticke i'th Warres	3426
These warres determine: If I cannot perswade thee,	3475
The end of Warres vncertaine: but this certaine,	3498
Ha's clock'd thee to the Warres: and safelie home	3520
Auffidius, though I cannot make true Warres,	3548
With bloody passage led your Warres, euen to	3741

WARRIORS = 1*1

Com. Flower of Warriors, how is't with *Titus Lartius*?	644
Yet welcome Warriors:	1100

WARRIOUR = *1

Volum. Thou art my Warriour, I hope to frame thee | Do you know this Lady?	3414

WAS *see also* 'twas = 57*24

WASH = 3

Martius. I will goe wash:	824
Wash my fierce hand in's heart. Go you to th'Citie,	886
Corio. Bid them wash their Faces,	1453

WASHD = 1

No more I say, for that I haue not wash'd	803

WAST *l*.558 = 1, 1

Mene. How? Was't we? We lou'd him,	3043

WATCH *see also* 1., 1.*Wat*., 2., 2.*Wat*. = 3

Then in our Priest-like Fasts: therefore Ile watch him	3214

WATCH cont.
  Enter Menenius to the Watch or Guard. 3235
  The Oake not to be winde-shaken. *Exit Watch*. 3345
WATCHT = 1
  Watcht for your Voyces: for your Voyces, beare 1519
WATER = 1 *1
  That our best Water, brought by Conduits hither, 1645
  *fire for vs: looke thee, heere's water to quench it. 3307
WATERED = 1
  He watered his new Plants with dewes of Flattery, 3675
WATERS = 1
  Like interrupted Waters, and o're-beare | What they are vs'd to beare. 1974
WAUE = 2 *1
  Waue thus to expresse his disposition, | And follow *Martius*. 693
  *They all shout and waue their swords, take him vp in their | Armes, and
  cast vp their Caps.* 695
  That we shall hardly in our ages see | Their Banners waue againe. 1681
WAUED = *1
  *no, hee waued indifferently, 'twixt doing them neyther 1220
WAUING = 2
  And with his Hat, thus wauing it in scorne, 1567
  More learned then the eares, wauing thy head, 2178
WAW = 1
  Volum. True? pow waw. 1038
WAXED = 1
  Man-entred thus, he waxed like a Sea, 1313
WAY = 27 *6
  *a Vice in him: You must in no way say he is co- |uetous. 43
  The way it takes: cracking ten thousand Curbes 71
  And no way from your selues. What do you thinke? 162
  *youth with comelinesse pluck'd all gaze his way; when 368
  True Sword to Sword: Ile potche at him some way, | Or Wrath, or Craft
  may get him. 873
  Herauld. Giue way there, and goe on. 1105
  Cor. Know, good Mother, | I had rather be their seruant in my way, 1117
  1 .Off. No more of him, hee's a worthy man: make | way, they are
  comming. 1237
  *of one direct way, should be at once to all the points | a'th Compasse. 1409
  2 .Cit. Thinke, you so? Which way do you iudge my | wit would flye. 1411
  2 *Cit*. Why that way? 1416
  Senat. Tribunes giue way, he shall toth' Market place. 1712
  Brut. Not vnlike each way to better yours. 1735
  To where you are bound, you must enquire your way, 1741
  Deseru'd this so dishonor'd Rub, layd falsely | I'th' plaine Way of his
  Merit. 1748
  The very way to catch them. 1772
  Of generall Ignorance, it must omit | Reall Necessities, and giue way
  the while 1845
  Mene. Fie, fie, fie, this is the way to kindle, not to | quench. 1906
  Com. That is the way to lay the Citie flat, 1915
  1 *Sen*. Noble Tribunes, | It is the humane way: the other course 2069
  Where if you bring not *Martius*, wee'l proceede | In our first way. 2077
  Hast not the soft way, which thou do'st confesse 2183
  Or neuer trust to what my Tongue can do | I'th way of Flattery further. 2246
  More then a wilde exposture, to each chance | That starts i'th'way
  before thee. 2475
  Brut. They haue tane note of vs: keepe on your way. 2516

WAY *cont*.

He does faire Iustice: if he giue me way, | Ile do his Country Seruice. *Exit*. 2651

O're-borne their way, consum'd with fire, and tooke | What lay before them. 2991

Gaue way vnto your Clusters, who did hoote | Him out o'th'Citty. 3045

The way into his mercy: Nay, if he coy'd 3157

Bru. You know the very rode into his kindnesse, | And cannot lose your way. 3217

You know the way home againe. 3333

Made him ioynt-seruant with me: Gaue him way 3685

After your way. His Tale pronounc'd, shall bury | His Reasons, with his Body. 3717

WAYES *see also* waies = 1

Brut. Sir, those cold wayes, | That seeme like prudent helpes, are very poysonous, 1936

WE *see also* wee = 138*44

WEAKE = *1

*such weake breath as this? No, you are deceiu'd, therfore 3283

WEAKER = 1

Bru. Rais'd onely, that the weaker sort may wish | Good *Martius* home againe. 2980

WEAKNESSE = *1

*Thy Countries strength and weaknesse, thine own waies 2799

WEALE = 3

Touching the Weale a'th Common, you shall finde 159

I'th' Body of the Weale: and now arriuing 1582

A Foe to'th'publike Weale. Obey I charge thee, 1878

WEALES = *1

*Meeting two such Weales men as you are (I cannot call 950

WEALTH = 1

Bru. Let's to the Capitoll: would halfe my wealth | Would buy this for a lye. 3087

WEAPONS = 5

Enter a Company of Mutinous Citizens, with Staues, | Clubs, and other weapons. 2

2 *Sen*. Weapons, weapons, weapons: | *They all bustle about Coriolanus*. 1892

Masters, lay downe your Weapons. 2074

WEARE *see also* were = 2*1

Weare not so rich a Iewell. Thou was't a Souldier 558

*legges: you weare out a good wholesome Forenoone, in 965

Whose double bosomes seemes to weare one heart, 2639

WEARES = 2

Weares this Warres Garland: in token of the which, 816

Who weares my stripes imprest vpon him, that 3778

WEARIE = 2

I am wearie, yea, my memorie is tyr'd: 852

Longer to liue most wearie: and present 2752

WEDDED = 1

Then when I first my wedded Mistris saw 2775

WEDGD *see* wadg'd

WEE *see also* wee'l, wee'le *l*.*20 761 *898 1101 *1266 *1388 *1495 2385 *2876 *3070 *3334 = 3*8

WEED = 1

With what Contempt he wore the humble Weed, 1624

WEEDED = 1

Each word thou hast spoke, hath weeded from my heart 2760

WEEDS = 1*1

Turne terror into sport: as Weeds before 1319
*Brut. With a prowd heart he wore his humble Weeds: 1550

WEEL = 9*5

*1.Cit. Let vs kill him, and wee'l haue Corne at our own | price. Is't a
Verdict? 13
*now wee'l shew em in deeds: they say poore Suters haue 61
Hearke, our Drummes | *Are bringing forth our youth: Wee'l breake
our Walles 504
If you'l stand fast, wee'l beate them to their Wiues, 536
Bru. Come, wee'l informe them 1384
All. Wee'l Surety him. | Com. Ag'd sir, hands off. 1881
Bru. Wee'l heare no more: 2048
*Sic. Meet on the Market place: wee'l attend you there: 2076
Where if you bring not Martius, wee'l proceede | In our first way. 2077
*Sicin. Bid them all home, he's gone: & wee'l no further, 2503
Bru. Well, well, wee'l leaue you. 2555
Corio. Auffidius, and you Volces marke, for wee'l 3447
Sicin. Wee'l meet them, and helpe the ioy. Exeunt. 3638
Wherein you wisht vs parties: Wee'l deliuer you | Of your great danger. 3664

WEELE = 2

If 'gainst your selfe you be incens'd, wee'le put you 812
Com. Come, come, wee'le prompt you. 2213

WEEPE = 3*1

I could weepe, and I could laugh, 1092
Menen. That's worthily | As any eare can heare. Come, let's not weepe, 2495
*Constraines them weepe, and shake with feare & sorow, 3455
2.Lord. Thou hast done a deed, whereat | Valour will weepe. 3810

WEEPING = 1*1

*Volum. If that I could for weeping, you should heare, 2520
He cares not for your weeping. Speake thou Boy, 3513

WEEPST = 1

That weep'st to see me triumph? Ah my deare, 1083

WEIGH = 1

I loue them as they weigh--- 1286

WEIGHES = 1

If any thinke, braue death out-weighes bad life, 690

WEL = *1

*Com. Breath you my friends, wel fought, we are come | (off, 604

WELCOME = 17*1

We are fit to bid her welcome. Exit Gent. 406
Welcome to Rome, renowned Coriolanus. | Sound. Flourish. 1068
All. Welcome to Rome, renowned Coriolanus. 1070
Oh welcome home: and welcome Generall, 1089
And y'are welcome all. 1090
I am light, and heauie; welcome: 1093
Yet welcome Warriors: 1100
To oppose his hatred fully. Welcome home. 1698
*Vol. You will be welcome with this intelligence Ni-|canor. 2598
Yet Martius that was much. Your hand: most welcome. | Exeunt 2806
Repeale him, with the welcome of his Mother: 3645
Cry welcome Ladies, welcome. 3646
All. Welcome Ladies, welcome. | A Flourish with Drummes & Trumpets. 3647
Enter 3 or 4 Conspirators of Auffidius Faction. | Most Welcome. 3658
All Lords. You are most welcome home. 3721

WELCOMES = 3

Mene. A hundred thousand Welcomes: 1091

WELCOMES *cont.*

Say yea to thy desires. A thousand welcomes,	2804
And had no welcomes home, but he returnes | Splitting the Ayre with noyse.	3708

WELL *see also* wel = 65*14

*1.*Cit.* Very well, and could bee content to giue him	33
Your suffering in this dearth, you may as well	68
2 *Citizen.* Well, | Ile heare it Sir: yet you must not thinke	94
2.*Cit.* Well sir, what answer made the Belly.	108
As well as speake, it taintingly replyed	112
Men. Well, what then?	127
2.*Cit.* I sir, well, well.	149
The Citie is well stor'd.	201
Your valour puts well forth: Pray follow. *Exeunt.*	278
In whom already he's well grac'd, cannot	294
Sicin. Besides, if things go well,	301
Vir. I thanke your Lady-ship: Well good Madam.	417
Fare you well then. Come good sweet Ladie.	471
Val. Well, then farewell. *Exeunt Ladies.*	477
My worke hath yet not warm'd me. Fare you well:	590
*Me thinkes thou speak'st not well. How long is't since?	619
Com. Should they not: | Well might they fester 'gainst Ingratitude,	781
Com. Oh well begg'd:	847
Both. Well sir.	912
Both. Well, well sir, well.	924
Sicin. Menenius, you are knowne well enough too.	942
*Worshippes haue deliuer'd the matter well, when I finde	953
*of my Microcosme, followes it that I am knowne well e-|nough	958
*gleane out of this Charracter, if I be knowne well e-|nough too.	960
Bru. Come sir come, we know you well enough.	962
Bru. Come, come, you are well vnderstood to bee a	976
Menen. The Senate, *Coriolanus,* are well pleas'd to make | thee Consull.	1350
And might well be taken from the People.	1367
Corio. Well then I pray, your price a'th'Consulship.	1465
Scicin. Fare you well. *Exeunt Coriol. and Mene.*	1547
Scicin. One thus descended, | That hath beside well in his person wrought,	1648
Mene. Well, no more.	1765
Sicin. 'Twere well we let the people know't.	1775
Com. Well, on to'th'Market place.	1807
Mene. Well, well, no more of that.	1811
Was not our recompence, resting well assur'd	1818
Of our so franke Donation. Well, what then?	1827
1 *Cit.* He shall well know the Noble Tribunes are	2002
Volum. Oh sir, sir, sir, | I would haue had you put your power well on	2102
Mene. Well said, Noble woman:	2123
Corio. Well, what then? what then?	2130
A Lye, that it must beare well? I will doo't:	2207
Corio. Well, I must doo't:	2218
Corio. Well mildely be it then, Mildely. *Exeunt.*	2257
Edi. Very well.	2286
Sicin. Well, heere he comes.	2298
Corio. First heare me speake. | *Both Tri.* Well, say: Peace hoe.	2313
Com. Well, well, no more. | *Corio.* What is the matter,	2335
Bru. But since he hath seru'd well for Rome.	2365
Ile do well yet. Thou old and true *Menenius,*	2459

WELL *cont.*

As 'tis to laugh at 'em. My Mother, you wot well   2465
Corio. Fare ye well: | Thou hast yeares vpon thee, and thou art too full   2485
Volum. Oh y'are well met: 2517
Bru. Well, well, wee'l leaue you.   2555
*Rom. I know you well sir, and you know mee: your | name I thinke is
Adrian.   2571
**your Fauour is well appear'd by your Tongue. What's   2579
**state to finde you out there. You haue well saued mee a | dayes
iourney.   2581
*Rom. The day serues well for them now. I haue heard   2600
*Auffidius will appeare well in these Warres, his great   2603
sir, heartily well met, and most glad of your Company.   2617
Rom. Well, let vs go together. *Exeunt.*   2620
The Feast smels well: but I appeare not like a Guest.   2660
Blush, that the world goes well: who rather had,   2897
*Mene. All's well, and might haue bene much better, | if he could haue
temporiz'd.   2909
Bru. The Gods haue well preuented it, and Rome | Sits safe and still,
without him.   2936
Mene. Cannot be? | We haue Record, that very well it can,   2953
Auf. I vnderstand thee well, and be thou sure   3108
Menen. Very well, could he say lesse.   3175
Mene. Well, and say that *Martius* returne mee,   3198
Sicin. Yet your good will | Must haue that thankes from Rome, after
the measure | As you intended well.   3202
He was not taken well, he had not din'd,   3208
*Me. You guard like men, 'tis well. But by your leaue,   3238
A Sea and Land full: you haue pray'd well to day: 3629
WELL-FOUND = 1
In our well-found Successes, to report   1251
WENSDAY = *1
**very pretty boy. A my troth, I look'd vpon him a Wens- | day   421
WER *l.**55 = *1
WERE *see also* 'twere *l.**20 218 251 *254 *282 341 *363 395 396 *448 563
603 630 681 687 848 862 883 *987 *995 1139 1155 1203 *1234 *1235
1289 1341 *1397 *1407 1415 1574 1578 1593 1644 1662 1773 *1777 1869
*1911 1923 1962 1990 1991 2024 2040 2058 2109 2184 2189 2208 2439
2445 2454 2533 *2818 *2851 *2865 *2874 2896 2908 2948 *3035 3050
*3082 *3264 3287 *3385 3489 3550 3553 = 49*22, 1
Such eyes the Widowes in Carioles were,   1084
WERT *l.*737 = 1
WEST = 1 *1
Whether for East or West: the Dearth is great,   324
**they would flye East, West, North, South, and their con- | sent   1408
WHAT *l.**18 *31 *37 *42 *48 56 *60 108 117 123 124 127 129 131 151 154
162 *179 216 228 251 264 296 309 318 *415 510 548 580 734 766 777
778 819 840 864 887 *913 938 *949 *959 1079 1172 1262 1278 1331 1382
1438 *1456 1469 1509 1588 1624 *1635 1636 1640 1689 1705 1707 *1717
1776 1827 1840 1841 1865 1868 1870 1894 1897 1909 1934 1942 1975
1986 1992 2012 2035 2039 2047 2059 2081 2128 2130 2131 2139 2168
2171 2172 2246 2263 2285 2336 2359 2366 2376 2403 2452 2494 2531
2535 2562 *2654 *2662 2674 *2677 2680 *2688 *2697 *2708 2713 *2813
2834 *2858 2944 2950 2960 2973 2992 2995 3076 3092 3103 3110 3144
3152 3155 3195 3196 3199 3228 3229 3336 *3366 3376 3413 3450 3531
3541 3556 3572 *3591 *3595 3715 3724 3727 3748 3774 = 130*26

WHATEUER *see* euer
WHATS = 17*3
 Mar. Thanks. What's the matter you dissentious rogues 174
 Him vilde, that was your Garland. What's the matter, 195
 Would feede on one another? What's their seeking? 199
 What's done i'th Capitoll: Who's like to rise, 204
 Mess. Where's *Caius Martius*? | *Mar*. Heere: what's the matter! 239
 Brutus. What's the matter? 1189
 What's like to be their words, We did request it, 1830
 When what's not meet, but what must be, was Law, 1868
 What's in his heart, and that is there which lookes 2294
 *your Fauour is well appear'd by your Tongue. What's 2579
 Why speak'st not? Speake man: What's thy name? 2709
 Auf. Say, what's thy name? 2716
 Thou shew'st a Noble Vessell: What's thy name? 2719
 1 Directitude? What's that? 2868
 Mene. What's the newes? What's the newes? 2999
 Corio. What's the matter? 3296
 *now presently, and swoond for what's to come vpon 3303
 Corio. What's this? your knees to me? | To your Corrected Sonne? 3407
 Sicin. What's the Newes? 3610
WHATSOEUER = 1
 As if that whatsoeuer God, who leades him, 1138
WHEELE = 2
 Mes. Spies of the *Volces* | Held me in chace, that I was forc'd to wheele 624
 Death on the Wheele, or at wilde Horses heeles, 2085
WHELMD = 1
 And Wrath o're-whelm'd my pittie: I request you 845
WHELME = 1
 Corio. Thou wretch, despight ore-whelme thee: 1864
WHEN *l*.79 *98 *282 336 *366 *367 *368 403 404 *423 556 641 642 765
 798 801 825 *953 *968 *980 *1044 1182 1284 1289 1293 1302 1305 1310
 1329 1441 1557 1570 1578 1604 1606 1657 1678 1727 1797 1803 1820
 1868 1971 2044 2053 2097 2136 2275 2282 2288 2330 2442 *2444 2453
 2454 2490 2508 *2536 *2578 *2601 2775 *2869 2872 2926 2948 3056
 3067 *3082 3101 3109 3117 3147 3172 3211 *3276 3519 *3587 *3601
 3680 3697 3716 3738 3815 = 64*19
WHENCE = 4*4
 *whence he return'd, his browes bound with Oake. I tell 375
 The Noble House o'th'*Martians*: from whence came 1641
 *1 *Ser*. What would you haue Friend? whence are you? 2662
 *2 *Ser*. Whence are you sir? Ha's the Porter his eyes in 2666
 Auf. Whence com'st thou? What wouldst y? Thy name? 2708
 1.*Wat*. Stay: whence are you. 3236
 1 From whence? *Mene*. From Rome. 3240
 The booke of his good Acts, whence men haue read 3253
WHENERE *see* ere
WHERE *l*.57 77 103 182 183 269 *366 *373 602 651 653 661 750 751 752
 *753 831 871 883 *1039 1042 1065 1088 1145 1322 1332 *1417 *1430
 1539 1741 1780 *1843 1938 1994 *2006 2067 2077 2161 2439 2479 *2631
 2691 2705 2765 2911 2957 3618 3652 3729 3731 = 41*9
WHEREAT = 1
 2.*Lord*. Thou hast done a deed, whereat | Valour will weepe. 3810
WHEREBY = 1
 Whereby they liue. And though that all at once 147
WHEREFORE = 2*1
 *be many that they haue loued, they know not wherefore: 1213

WHEREFORE *cont.*
Both. Wherefore? Wherefore?	2837

WHEREIN = 7*3
*I should freelier reioyce in that absence wherein	364
Mar. I do beseech you, | By all the Battailes wherein we haue fought,	671
Wherein you see me smear'd, if any feare	688
Wherein thou seest me maskt, for thy Reuenge	735
*Senate ha's Letters from the Generall, wherein hee giues	1031
*He's to make his requests by particulars, wherein euerie	1431
There Mutinies and Reuolts, wherein they shew'd	1823
Wherein this Trunke was fram'd, and in her hand	3372
Wherein I seeme vnnaturall: Desire not t'allay	3439
Wherein you wisht vs parties: Wee'l deliuer you | Of your great danger.	3664

WHEREOF = 1
Whereof we haue ta'ne good, and good store of all,	784

WHEREON = 2
Whereon part do's disdaine with cause, the other	1842
Your Franchises, whereon you stood, confin'd | Into an Augors boare.	3001

WHERES = 2*1
Mess. Where's *Caius Martius*? | *Mar.* Heere: what's the matter!	239
2 Ser. Where's *Cotus*: my M.(aster) cals for him: *Cotus. Exit*	2657
3 Where's that? | *Corio.* I'th City of Kites and crowes.	2695

WHERETO = 2
Whereto we are bound, together with thy victory:	3463
Whereto we are bound: Alacke, or we must loose	3464

WHERE-ERE *see* ere

WHEROF = *1
Men. For Corne at their owne rates, wherof they say	200

WHETHER = 9*3
Whether for East or West: the Dearth is great,	324
Whether 'tis bent: most likely, 'tis for you: | Consider of it.	330
*whether his fall enrag'd him, or how 'twas, hee did so set	426
Whether I blush or no: howbeit, I thanke you,	826
*care whether they loue, or hate him, manifests the true	1216
1.Off. If he did not care whether he had their loue, or	1219
Ile trie whether my old Wit be in request	1977
Volum. My first sonne, | Whether will thou go? Take good *Cominius*	2472
Whether to knocke against the Gates of Rome,	2800
Carry his Honors eeuen: whether 'twas Pride	3128
The happy man; whether detect of iudgement,	3130
Which he was Lord of: or whether Nature,	3132

WHICH *see also* w *1.**40 110 139 160 190 198 *222 *290 293 *337 339 507 *520 652 698 706 775 *797 805 816 *1012 1058 1115 1152 1183 *1225 *1266 1325 1339 1370 *1398 *1411 1448 *1468 1505 1566 1595 1598 1628 1670 *1675 1740 1742 *1761 1764 1771 1825 1834 1856 1858 1860 1917 2001 2019 2037 2127 2144 2153 2159 2179 2183 2211 2221 2294 2325 2345 2417 2483 2546 2635 *2730 2754 *2865 2895 2948 3060 3079 3116 3129 3132 3153 3361 3377 3381 3421 3444 3453 3460 3468 3500 3524 3564 3680 3690 3700 3701 3716 3790 3817 3835 = 84*16

WHILE = 6*1
*vs. If they would yeelde vs but the superfluitie while it	19
While she chats him: the Kitchin *Malkin* pinnes	1126
Of generall Ignorance, it must omit | Reall Necessities, and giue way the while	1845
Mene. Downe with that Sword, Tribunes withdraw | a while.	1943
While I remaine aboue the ground, you shall	2492

WHILE *cont*.

Shew duty as mistaken, all this while, | Betweene the Childe, and
Parent. 3405
Is that you reconcile them: While the Volces 3493
WHILES = 1

We shall be charg'd againe. Whiles we haue strooke 607
WHILEST = 1

*not (looke you sir) shew themselues (as we terme it) his | Friends,
whilest he's in Directitude. 2866
WHILST = 3

Whil'st I with those that haue the spirit, wil haste | To helpe *Cominius*. 584
Volum. Oh stand vp blest! | Whil'st with no softer Cushion then the
Flint 3402
3.*Con*. The People will remaine vncertaine, whil'st 3668
WHIND = 1

He whin'd and roar'd away your Victory, 3766
WHIP = 4

Auf. Wer't thou the *Hector*, | That was the whip of your bragg'd
Progeny, 737
Least you shall chance to whip your Information, 2958
Go whip him fore the peoples eyes: His raising, | Nothing but his
report. 2968
Which will not proue a whip: As many Coxcombes 3060
WHIPT = 1

Bru. Go see this Rumorer whipt, it cannot be, 2951
WHISPER = *1

*Neuer admitted a priuat whisper, no not with such frends | That
thought them sure of you. 3353
WHITE = 1*1

Commit the Warre of White and Damaske 1135
*white o'th'eye to his Discourse. But the bottome of the 2856
WHITHER *see also* whether = *1

*were shee Earthly, no Nobler; whither doe you follow | your Eyes so
fast? 995
WHO *see also* who's *l*.51 78 126 187 189 197 205 327 551 555 764 904
*985 1138 1178 *1212 *1228 1643 1763 1799 1808 2093 2227 2641 2722
2732 2791 2792 2824 2897 2946 2959 3022 3024 3028 3045 3125 3153
3232 *3313 3674 3778 3805 = 40*4
WHOEUER *see* euer

WHOLE = 3*2

Of the whole body, the Belly answer'd. 107
Of the whole Body. But, if you do remember, 141
*my Sonne the whole Name of the Warre: he hath in this 1032
For the whole State; I would put mine Armour on, 2126
*the intreaty and graunt of the whole Table. Hee'l go he 2859
WHOLESOME = *1

*legges: you weare out a good wholesome Forenoone, in 965
WHOLSOME = 1*2

*were wholsome, wee might guesse they releeued vs hu-|manely: 20
*repeale daily any wholsome Act established against 83
Ile leaue you: Pray you speake to em, I pray you | In wholsome manner.
Exit 1450
WHOM *l*.294 *460 834 1109 1149 1253 1304 1866 1905 2504 2554 2940
3174 3256 3356 3491 = 15*1
WHOS = 1

What's done i'th Capitoll: Who's like to rise, 204

WHOSE = 18*3

Against the Roman State, whose course will on	70
To make him worthy, whose offence subdues him,	186
Com. Whose yonder, | That doe's appeare as he were Flead? O Gods,	629
He was a thing of Blood, whose euery motion	1323
Sicin. Go call the people, in whose name my Selfe	1876
Vpon the part o'th' People, in whose power	1922
Before the Tagge returne? whose Rage doth rend	1973
That our renowned Rome, whose gratitude	2028
Those whose great power must try him.	2362
Corio. You common cry of Curs, whose breath I hate,	2408
As reeke a'th'rotten Fennes: whose Loues I prize,	2409
Whose double bosomes seemes to weare one heart,	2639
Whose Houres, whose Bed, whose Meale and Exercise	2640
*Whose Passions, and whose Plots haue broke their sleep	2645
Was to send him: for whose old Loue I haue	3359
Whose repetition will be dogg'd with Curses:	3501
Whose Chronicle thus writ, The man was Noble,	3502
2.*Con*. And patient Fooles, | Whose children he hath slaine, their base	
throats teare	3710

WHY *l*.49 *63 164 444 662 921 *925 *939 *1214 1416 1506 1563 1574 1606 *1718 1730 *1736 *1785 1814 2099 2149 2189 2514 2556 2709 2776 *2838 2840 *2851 *2876 3168 3510 3572 *3620 3788 = 24*11

WIDDOWED = 1

Hath widdowed and vnchilded many a one,	3834

WIDDOWES = 1

'Tis I that made thy Widdowes: Many an heyre	2624

WIDE = 1

To teare with Thunder the wide Cheekes a'th'Ayre,	3508

WIDENS = 1

'Tis for the followers Fortune, widens them,	541

WIDOWES = 1

Such eyes the Widowes in Carioles were,	1084

WIFE = 16*6

Enter Volumnia and Virgilia, mother and wife to Martius:	360
*hearing a cause betweene an Orendge wife, and a Forfet-|seller,	966
*another, his Wife another, and (I thinke) there's one at | home for you.	1006
But oh, thy Wife. | *Corio*. My gracious silence, hayle:	1080
*returne for Conscience sake, to helpe to get thee a Wife.	1419
Your Wife, your Sonne: These Senators, the Nobles,	2164
Commend me to my Wife, Ile returne Consull,	2245
If you had beene the Wife of *Hercules*,	2455
Droope not, Adieu: Farewell my Wife, my Mother,	2458
Come my sweet wife, my deerest Mother, and	2489
*it saide, the fittest time to corrupt a mans Wife, is when	2601
His Mother and his wife, heare nothing from him.	2913
I am one of those: his Mother, Wife, his Childe,	3183
And his Wife, who (as I heare) meane to solicite him	3232
Corio. Wife, Mother, Child, I know not. My affaires | Are Seruanted	
to others: Though I owe	3317
My wife comes formost, then the honour'd mould	3371
Volum. Euen he, your wife, this Ladie, and my selfe, | Are Sutors to	
you.	3431
Making the Mother, wife, and Childe to see,	3456
Thy Wife and Childrens blood: For my selfe, Sonne,	3473
His Wife is in *Corioles*, and his Childe	3536
Stand to me in this cause. Oh Mother! Wife!	3558

WIFE *cont*.

I say your City to his Wife and Mother, 3762
WIL *l.**178 584 *1381 *1499 = 1*3
WILDE = 3

Death on the Wheele, or at wilde Horses heeles, 2085
More then a wilde exposture, to each chance | That starts i'th'way
before thee. 2475
Were in wilde hurry. Heere do we make his Friends 2896
WILL *see also* hee'l, he'l, Ile, they'l, they'le, 'twill, wee'l, wee'le wil,
you'l *l.*64 70 *86 92 130 *178 233 249 *285 299 435 *442 *451 *466 469
*491 570 *592 660 704 716 824 831 889 *922 *926 *990 *1008 *1012
*1043 1099 1116 1145 1150 1152 1167 1185 1208 1361 1390 *1401 *1413
*1414 *1486 *1490 *1491 *1500 1515 1545 1551 1569 1613 1617 1659
1668 1706 1714 1724 1740 1751 1754 1834 1849 1952 1966 1972 2054
2071 2081 2088 2165 2181 2203 2204 2207 2228 2255 2263 2301 2470
2473 2521 2547 *2598 *2603 2608 2679 *2688 2747 *2861 *2864 *2870
3060 3061 3123 3220 3242 3327 *3347 *3366 3368 3442 3444 3501 3514
3523 3529 3562 3565 *3600 3626 3654 3668 3716 3789 3811 = 86*30, 6*2
Euen like a fawning Grey-hound in the Leash, | To let him slip at will. 649
He that ha's but effected his good will, | Hath ouerta'ne mine Act. 768
To curbe the will of the Nobilitie: 1722
Volum. Do your will. *Exit Volumnia* 2248
Cit. And you. | *Corio. Direct me, if it be your will, where great *Auf-*
| *fidius* lies: Is he in *Antium*? 2630
*willingly consented to his Banishment, yet it was against | our will. 3071
Sicin. Yet your good will | Must haue that thankes from Rome, after
the measure | As you intended well. 3202
*so slight. He that hath a will to die by himselfe, feares it 3339
WILLING = 1

Mar. Those are they | That most are willing; if any such be heere, 685
WILLINGLY = *2

*Brutus. Most willingly: but yet my Caution was 1271
*willingly consented to his Banishment, yet it was against | our will. 3071
WILLS = 1*1

*Scicin. It shall be to him then, as our good wills; a | sure destruction. 1168
What Custome wills in all things, should we doo't? 1509
WILT *see also* thou't *l.*2185 2742 2795 = 3
WIN = 4

Lead'st first to win some vantage. 168
Win vpon power, and throw forth greater Theames | For Insurrections
arguing. 234
And did retyre to win our purpose. 664
Our wish, which side should win. For either thou 3468
WINDE = 4

Against the Winde a mile: you soules of Geese, 529
Be free, as is the Winde: deliuer him, *Titus*. 849
And throw't against the Winde. Toth' Market place: 2210
From Rome all season'd Office, and to winde 2343
WINDES = 1

Fillop the Starres: Then, let the mutinous windes 3410
WINDE-SHAKEN = 1

The Oake not to be winde-shaken. *Exit Watch*. 3345
WINDOWES = 1

Stalls, Bulkes, Windowes, are smother'd vp, 1129
WINE = 2*4

Haue we no Wine here? 853
*one that loues a cup of hot Wine, with not a drop of alay- | ing 944

WINE *cont.*

  1 Ser. Wine, Wine, Wine: What seruice is heere? I   2654
  With Wine and Feeding, we haue suppler Soules   3213
WINGS = *1
  *growne from Man to Dragon: He has wings, hee's more | then a
  creeping thing.   3582
WINNE = 1
  To winne a vulgar station: our veyl'd Dames   1134
WIPD = 1
  But with his last Attempt, he wip'd it out: 3503
WIPE = *1
  *of their Feast, and tŏ be executed ere they wipe their lips.   2875
WIPING = 1
  With his mail'd hand, then wiping, forth he goes   397
WISDOMS = *1
  Mar. Fiue Tribunes to defend their vulgar wisdoms   229
WISE = 1*1
  Of this most wise Rebellion, thou goest formost: 166
  Volum. Moe Noble blowes, then euer y wise words.   2530
WISEDOM = *1
  *Insult without all reason: where Gentry, Title, wisedom   1843
WISEDOME = *1
  *the wisedome of their choice, is rather to haue my Hat,   1489
WISH = 13*2
  I would wish me onely he.   252
  Virg. I will wish her speedy strength, and visite her   442
  I wish you much mirth.   476
  Euen to *Calues* wish, not fierce and terrible   559
  Leade their successes, as we wish our owne,   610
  Com. Though I could wish, | You were conducted to a gentle Bath,   680
  Scicin. I wish no better, then haue him hold that pur-|pose, and to put
  it in execution.   1165
  Our purpose to them, and to our Noble Consull | Wish we all Ioy, and
  Honor.   1375
  Corio. I wish I had a cause to seeke him there,   1697
  A Noble life, before a Long, and Wish,   1852
  Why did you wish me milder? Would you haue me   2099
  1 *Sen.* Amen, Amen. | *Mene.* A Noble wish.   2307
  Bru. Rais'd onely, that the weaker sort may wish | Good *Martius* home
  againe.   2980
  Lieu. Yet I wish Sir, | (I meane for your particular) you had not   3104
  Our wish, which side should win. For either thou   3468
WISHES = 1
  Volum. I haue liued, | To see inherited my very Wishes,   1111
WISHT = 2
  Bru. Farewell kinde Neighbours: | We wisht *Coriolanus* had lou'd you as
  we did.   2921
  Wherein you wisht vs parties: Wee'l deliuer you | Of your great danger.   3664
WIT = 2*1
  2.Cit. Thinke you so? Which way do you iudge my | wit would flye.   1411
  3.Cit. Nay your wit will not so soone out as another   1413
  Ile trie whether my old Wit be in request   1977
WITCHCRAFTS = 1
  Lieu. I do not know what Witchcraft's in him: but   3092
WITH *see also* with's = 245*59

WITHALL = 3
Bru. He's poore in no one fault, but stor'd withall. | *Sicin.* Especially in
Pride.   915
Seale what I end withall. This double worship,   1841
Auf. I was mou'd withall.   3552
WITHDRAW = *1
*Mene. Downe with that Sword, Tribunes withdraw | a while.   1943
WITHIN = 12*2
he hath faults (with surplus) to tyre in repetition. | *Showts within.*   46
Mess. Within this mile and halfe.   494
Tullus Auffidious, is he within your Walles?   501
Mar. Within these three houres *Tullus*   732
But then *Auffidius* was within my view,   844
Within Corioles Gates: where he hath wonne,   1065
He heard the Name of Death. *A Noise within.*   1988
Within thine eyes sate twenty thousand deaths   2350
Vnseparable, shall within this houre,   2642
**2 Here sir, I'de haue beaten him like a dogge, but for | disturbing the
Lords within.   2706
**3 Why he is so made on heere within, as if hee were   2851
Within my Age. But reason with the fellow   2956
**Will I lend eare to. Ha? what shout is this? *Shout within*   3366
Make the Sunne dance. Hearke you. *A shout within*   3624
WITHOUT = 6*6
Which without note, here's many else haue done,   805
*Menen. Wondrous: I, I warrant you, and not with-|out his true
purchasing.   1035
**without any further deed, to haue them at all into   1230
*2 Cit. You are neuer without your trickes, you may, | you may.   1420
*1.Cit. Hee ha's done Nobly, and cannot goe without | any honest mans
Voyce.   1524
**Insult without all reason: where Gentry, Title, wisedom   1843
That's sure of death without it: at once plucke out   1854
He throwes without distinction. Giue me leaue,   2065
That wonne you without blowes, despising   2421
*Sicin. And affecting one sole Throne, without assista(n)ce   2932
Bru. The Gods haue well preuented it, and Rome | Sits safe and still,
without him.   2936
Would without lapsing suffer: Nay, sometimes,   3257
WITHS = *1
**of him, Sanctifies himselfe with's hand, and turnes vp the   2855
WITNESSE = 3
Great hurt and Mischiefe: thereto witnesse my   2724
And witnesse of the Malice and Displeasure   2729
And you shall beare | A better witnesse backe then words, which we   3563
WITS = 1*1
**bald; but that our wits are so diuersly Coulord; and true-|ly   1406
With one that wants her Wits. *Exit Tribunes.*   2557
WITTES = *1
**I thinke, if all our wittes were to issue out of one Scull,   1407
WIUES = 5
If you'l stand fast, wee'l beate them to their Wiues,   536
My deere Wiues estimate, her wombes encrease,   2400
Least that thy Wiues with Spits, and Boyes with stones   2627
1 Our selues, our wiues, and children, on our knees,   2918
To see your Wiues dishonour'd to your Noses.   2998

WOLD *l.**55 = *1
WOLFE = 2
  Men. Pray you, who does the Wolfe loue? | *Sicin*. The Lambe.   904
  Deserue such pitty of him, as the Wolfe   3030
WOLLEN = 1
  To call them Wollen Vassailes, things created   2094
WOLUISH *see* wooluish
WOMAN = 3
  When he might act the Woman in the Scene,   1310
  Mene. Well said, Noble woman: 2123
  Virg. Oh heauens! O heauens! | *Corio*. Nay, I prythee woman.   2448
WOMANS = 2
  Corio. Not of a womans tendernesse to be,   3485
  Requires nor Childe, nor womans face to see: | I haue sate too long.   3486
WOMB = *1
  *tender-bodied, and the onely Sonne of my womb; when   367
WOMBE = 1
  (Trust too't, thou shalt not) on thy Mothers wombe | That brought thee
  to this world.   3479
WOMBES = 1
  My deere Wiues estimate, her wombes encrease,   2400
WOMEN = 2*1
  Heart-hardning spectacles. Tell these sad women,   2463
  *easie groanes of old women, the Virginall Palms of your   3279
  How more vnfortunate then all liuing women   3452
WOMENS = 1
  At a few drops of Womens rhewme, which are   3701
WONDER = 1*1
  *wonder, his insolence can brooke to be commanded vn- | der *Cominius*?   291
  In Congregations, to yawne, be still, and wonder,   2096
WONDRING = 1
  That Pages blush'd at him, and men of heart | Look'd wond'ring each
  at others.   3767
WONDROUS = 1*3
  Menen. Either you must | Confesse your selues wondrous Malicious,   88
  *helpes are many, or else your actions would growe won- | drous   932
  *Valer. In troth, there's wondrous things spoke of him.   1034
  *Menen. Wondrous: I, I warrant you, and not with- | out his true
  purchasing.   1035
WONNE = 4*1
  *he wonne Honor, then in the embracements of his Bed,   365
  Within Corioles Gates: where he hath wonne,   1065
  From where he should begin, and end, but will | Lose those he hath
  wonne.   1145
  That wonne you without blowes, despising   2421
  You haue wonne a happy Victory to Rome.   3544
WONT = 3*1
  he was wont to come home wounded? | *Virgil*. Oh no, no, no.   1016
  Corio. I muse my Mother | Do's not approue me further, who was wont   2092
  Resume that Spirit, when you were wont to say,   2454
  *3 Why here's he that was wont to thwacke our Ge- | nerall, *Caius*
  Martius.   2838
WOOD = 1
  Mart. Oh! let me clip ye | In Armes as sound, as when I woo'd in heart;   640
WOOLLEN *see* wollen
WOOLUISH = 1
  Why in this Wooluish tongue should I stand heere,   1506

WOORTH = *1
*you speake best vnto the purpose. It is not woorth the   981
WORD = 14*2
2.*Cit.* One word, good Citizens.   16
2.*Cit.* We haue euer your good word.   177
Val. A my word the Fathers Sonne: Ile sweare 'tis a   420
Virgil. No | At a word Madam; Indeed I must not,   474
('Tis South the City Mils) bring me word thither   891
Scicin. 'Tis right. | *Brutus.* It was his word: 1160
Mene. Heare me one word, 'beseech you Tribunes,   1930
heare me but a word.   1931
I may be heard, I would craue a word or two,   2018
Menen. One word more, one word: 2052
Corio. The word is, Mildely. Pray you let vs go,   2253
Their mercie, at the price of one faire word,   2375
Th'art tyr'd, then in a word, I also am   2751
Each word thou hast spoke, hath weeded from my heart   2760
And would haue sent it. Another word *Menenius,*   3326
WORDS = 12*3
Mar. He that will giue good words to thee, wil flatter   178
Since I heard thence, these are the words, I thinke   321
Brutus. Sir, I hope my words dis-bench'd you not? | *Coriol.* No Sir: yet oft,   1282
When blowes haue made me stay, I fled from words.   1284
Senat. No more words, we beseech you.   1766
Coine words till their decay, against those Meazels   1770
What's like to be their words, We did request it,   1830
Which your heart prompts you, but with such words   2153
Then to take in a Towne with gentle words,   2158
For they haue Pardons, being ask'd, as free, | As words to little purpose.   2190
To banish him that strooke more blowes for Rome | Then thou hast spoken words.   2527
Volum. Moe Noble blowes, then euer y wise words.   2530
*as you haue vttered words in your owne, you should not   3263
And you shall beare | A better witnesse backe then words, which we   3563
To purge himselfe with words. Dispatch.   3657
WORE = 3*1
Bury with those that wore them. These base slaues,   578
Brut. With a prowd heart he wore his humble Weeds: 1550
With what Contempt he wore the humble Weed,   1624
Corio. These eyes are not the same I wore in Rome.   3387
WORKE = 14*1
Now Mars, I prythee make vs quicke in worke,   496
There is *Auffidious.* List what worke he makes | Among'st your clouen Army.   510
My worke hath yet not warm'd me. Fare you well: 590
And made what worke I pleas'd: 'Tis not my blood,   734
Com. If I should tell thee o're this thy dayes Worke,   748
A little of that worthy Worke, perform'd   1252
Here's goodly worke.   1989
Com. Oh you haue made good worke.   2994
*You haue made faire worke I feare me: pray your newes,   3004
Mene. You haue made good worke,   3012
You haue made faire worke.   3018
Mene. You haue made good worke | You and your cry. Shal's to the Capitoll?   3074

WORKE *cont.*

Menen. Why so: you haue made good worke: 3168
Murd'ring Impossibility, to make | What cannot be, slight worke. 3412
At difference in thee: Out of that Ile worke | My selfe a former
Fortune. 3560
WORKS = 1
Men. What work's my Countrimen in hand? 56
WORLD = 17*4
Mar. Were halfe to halfe the world by th'eares, & he 254
Thou mad'st thine enemies shake, as if the World | Were Feauorous,
and did tremble. 562
As to vs, to all the World, That *Caius Martius* 815
How the world goes: that to the pace of it 892
Of no more Soule, nor fitnesse for the World, 1177
The man I speake of, cannot in the World 1300
The common Muck of the World: he couets lesse 1342
Mene. His nature is too noble for the World: 1983
A brand to th'end a'th World. 2041
There is a world elsewhere. 2423
O're the vast world, to seeke a single man, 2482
*Oh World, thy slippery turnes! Friends now fast sworn, 2638
I had fear'd death, of all the Men i'th'World 2738
*2 So did I, Ile be sworne: He is simply the rarest man | i'th'world. 2820
*2 Why then wee shall haue a stirring World againe: 2876
Blush, that the world goes well: who rather had, 2897
Thrusts forth his hornes againe into the world 2947
Menen. I neither care for th'world, nor your General: 3337
And the most noble Mother of the world 3398
(Trust too't, thou shalt not) on thy Mothers wombe | That brought thee
to this world. 3479
Then can our Reasons. There's no man in the world 3515
WORNE = 2
Com. They are worne (Lord Consull) so, 1680
Before you had worne it out. | *Corio.* Let go. 2104
WORSE = 5*1
Cominius, *Martius* your old Enemy | (Who is of Rome worse hated then
of you) 326
The Mouse ne're shunn'd the Cat, as they did budge | From Rascals
worse then they. 657
Mar. Ile fight with none but thee, for I do hate thee | Worse then a
Promise-breaker. 724
'Twere a Concealement worse then a Theft, 772
You adopt your policy: How is it lesse or worse 2145
*particular prosperity, and loue thee no worse then thy old . 3305
WORSHIP = 1
Seale what I end withall. This double worship, 1841
WORSHIPFULL = 1
To gnaw their Garners. Worshipfull Mutiners, 277
WORSHIPPES = *1
*Worshippes haue deliuer'd the matter well, when I finde 953
WORSHIPS = *2
*Godden to your Worships, more of your conuer- |sation 988
*hee wounded, God saue your good Worships? *Martius* 1040
WORST = 2*1
Thou Rascall, that art worst in blood to run, 167
Or what is worst will follow. 2081
*not from another: Let your Generall do his worst. For 3340

WORTH *see also* woorth = 5*2
    *worth all your predecessors, since *Deucalion*, though per-|aduenture   986
    Euer to conquer, and to haue his worth   2291
    Cats, that can iudge as fitly of his worth,   2545
    *Some tricke not worth an Egge, shall grow deere friends   2647
    2 Worth six on him.   2826
    What is that Curt'sie worth? Or those Doues eyes,   3376
    Is worth of Consuls, Senators, Patricians,   3627
WORTHIE = 1*1
    their Bed-fellow: Worthie *Cominius* speake.   1274
    Corio. A match Sir, there's in all two worthie voyces   1471
WORTHIER = *2
    *would incline to the people, there was neuer a worthier | man.   1424
    *More worthier then their Voyces. They know the Corne   1817
WORTHIEST = 2
    Lar. Thou worthiest *Martius*, | Go sound thy Trumpet in the Market
    place,   599
    The worthiest men haue done't?   1437
WORTHILY = 1*1
    *2.*Off*. Hee hath deserued worthily of his Countrey,   1227
    Menen. That's worthily | As any eare can heare. Come, let's not weepe,   2495
WORTHINESSE = 1
    The Consuls worthinesse, so can I name his Faults.   2011
WORTHY *see also* worthie = 20*5
    *2 *Cit*. Worthy *Menenius Agrippa*, one that hath al-|wayes lou'd the
    people.   53
    To make him worthy, whose offence subdues him,   186
    1.*Sen*. Then worthy *Martius*, | Attend vpon *Cominius* to these Warres.   258
    Tit. Lead you on: Follow *Cominius*, we must followe | you, right
    worthy your Priority.   271
    Lar. Worthy Sir, thou bleed'st,   586
    Volum. I, worthy *Menenius*, and with most prosperous | approbation.   1000
    My gentle *Martius*, worthy *Caius*,   1077
    *1.*Off*. No more of him, hee's a worthy man: make | way, they are
    comming.   1237
    A little of that worthy Worke, perform'd   1252
    To ease his Brest with panting. | *Menen*. Worthy man.   1336
    2 *Cit*. You shall ha't worthy Sir.   1470
    Corio. Worthy Voyces.   1529
    That as his worthy deeds did clayme no lesse   1587
    We were elected theirs, *Martius* is worthy | Of present Death.   1923
    Be gone, put not your worthy Rage into your Tongue,   1965
    Mene. You worthy Tribunes.   1996
    What ha's he done to Rome, that's worthy death?   2035
    Supplied with worthy men, plant loue amongs   2304
    *to heart, the Banishment of that worthy *Coriolanus*, that   2591
    And wak'd halfe dead with nothing. Worthy *Martius*,   2784
    Bru. *Caius Martius* was | A worthy Officer i'th'Warre, but Insolent,   2928
    Aedile. Worthy Tribunes, | There is a Slaue whom we haue put in
    prison,   2939
    Mes. Yes worthy Sir, | The Slaues report is seconded, and more   2970
    *2 The worthy Fellow is our General. He's the Rock,   3344
    But worthy Lords, haue you with heede perused | What I haue written
    to you?   3723
WOT = 2
    As 'tis to laugh at 'em. My Mother, you wot well   2465
    1 I thinke he is: but a greater soldier then he, | You wot one.   2822

WOULD *see also* hee'ld, I'de, I'ld, 'twould, wold, you'ld *l*.*18 *19 *27
  *179 190 199 209 226 252 *366 *371 *382 *446 *448 470 531 577 776
  862 885 *906 *932 *989 *1027 1155 1162 1173 *1235 *1269 1343 *1408
  1412 *1418 *1424 1447 1510 1514 1523 1568 1589 1597 1692 1821 1859
  *1888 1904 1934 1962 1984 1990 1991 *1995 2018 2099 2103 2126 2159
  2161 2352 2374 2401 2446 2522 2532 2540 2543 *2544 2559 2561 *2590
  *2662 2739 2754 2786 2814 *2818 2835 *2907 3078 3087 3088 3100 3159
  3164 3190 3228 3229 3257 *3271 3288 3326 3450 3531 3550 3682
  3715 = 71*26
WOULDST *l*.867 1082 *2708 = 2*1
WOUNDED = 3*3

*better report then a Horse-drench. Is he not wounded?	1015
he was wont to come home wounded? | *Virgil*. Oh no, no, no.	1016
Volum. Oh, he is wounded, I thanke the Gods for't.	1018
*hee wounded, God saue your good Worships? *Martius*	1040
where is he wounded?	1042
*When most strooke home, being gentle wounded, craues	2444

WOUNDS = 11*5

Martius. I haue some Wounds vpon me, and they smart	779
Victorie in his Pocket? the wounds become him.	1020
Volum. Hee had, before this last Expedition, twentie | fiue Wounds	
vpon him.	1049
Nor shewing (as the manner is) his Wounds	1158
Coriol. Your Honors pardon: | I had rather haue my Wounds to heale	
againe,	1279
For my Wounds sake, to giue their sufferage:	1358
*his wounds, and tell vs his deeds, we are to put our ton-|gues	1393
*into those wounds, and speake for them: So if he tel	1394
Plague vpon't, I cannot bring | My tongue to such a pace. Looke Sir,	
my wounds,	1439
Corio. Kindly sir, I pray let me ha't: I haue wounds to	1467
*1. You haue receyued many wounds for your Coun-|trey.	1497
Of Wounds, two dozen odde: Battailes thrice six	1520
His Marks of Merit, Wounds receiu'd for's Countrey.	1562
3.*Cit*. Hee said hee had Wounds,	1565
Vpon the wounds his body beares, which shew	2325
Volum. Bastards, and all. | Good man, the Wounds that he does beare	
for Rome!	2537

WRACKD = 1

A paire of Tribunes, that haue wrack'd for Rome,	3169

WRATH = 2*2

*which makes me sweat with wrath. Come on my fellows	520
And Wrath o're-whelm'd my pittie: I request you	845
True Sword to Sword: Ile potche at him some way, | Or Wrath, or Craft	
may get him.	873
*Gods asswage thy wrath, and turne the dregs of it, vpon	3312

WREAKE = 1

A heart of wreake in thee, that wilt reuenge	2742

WREAKLESSE = 1

You graue, but wreaklesse Senators, haue you thus	1786

WRENCH = 1

Wrench vp thy power to th'highest.	736

WRETCH = 2

My Nose that bled, or foyl'd some debile Wretch,	804
Corio. Thou wretch, despight ore-whelme thee:	1864

WRIT = 3

Take this along, I writ it for thy sake,	3325

WRIT *cont*.
  Whose Chronicle thus writ, The man was Noble,   3502
  If you haue writ your Annales true, 'tis there,   3784
WRITE = 1
  Where ere we doe repose vs, we will write   831
WRITES = *1
  Volum. *Titus Lartius* writes, they fought together, but | *Auffidius* got
  off.   1024
WRITING = 1
  He sent in writing after me: what he would not,   3229
WRITTEN = 1
  But worthy Lords, haue you with heede perused | What I haue written
  to you?   3723
WRONG = 1*1
  *home, I euer said we were i'th wrong, when we banish'd | him.   3082
  To do my selfe this wrong: Till at the last   3691
WRONGS = 2
  Thine owne particular wrongs, and stop those maimes   2743
  Still to remember wrongs? Daughter, speake you: 3512
WROUGHT = 1
  Scicin. One thus descended, | That hath beside well in his person
  wrought,   1648
Y = 1*3
  Through our large Temples with y shewes of peace   2305
  Volum. Moe Noble blowes, then euer y wise words.   2530
  Auf. Whence com'st thou? What wouldst y? Thy name?   2708
  Corio. Prepare thy brow to frowne: knowst y me yet?   2720
YARD = 1
  Like Graues i'th holy Church-yard.   2326
YARE = 4*1
  2.*Cit*. Y'are long about it.   133
  And y'are welcome all.   1090
  Volum. Oh y'are well met: 2517
  Com. Y'are goodly things, you Voyces.   3073
  *for such things as you. I can scarse thinke ther's any, y'are   3338
YARNE *see* yearne
YAWNE = 1
  In Congregations, to yawne, be still, and wonder,   2096
YE *l*.*192 640 1885 2059 2109 2310 2485 = 6*2
YEA = 4
  I am wearie, yea, my memorie is tyr'd: 852
  Cannot conclude, but by the yea and no   1844
  Mene. I could my selfe take vp a Brace o'th' best of | them, yea, the
  two Tribunes.   1968
  Say yea to thy desires. A thousand welcomes,   2804
YEARE = *1
  *Mother now, then an eight yeare old horse. The tartnesse   3586
YEARES *see also* yeeres = 2
  For halfe a hundred yeares: Summon the Towne.   492
  Corio. Fare ye well: | Thou hast yeares vpon thee, and thou art too full   2485
YEARNE = *1
  *the yearne she spun in *Vlisses* absence, did but fill *Athica*   447
YEELD = 6
  Your louing motion toward the common Body, | To yeeld what passes
  here.   1261
  Or seeing it, of such Childish friendlinesse, | To yeeld your Voyces?   1575
  Must these haue Voyces, that can yeeld them now,   1716

YEELD *cont*.
  Brut. Aediles seize him. | *All Ple*. Yeeld *Martius*, yeeld.   1928
  Bound with an Oath to yeeld to his conditions: 3230
YEELDE = *1
  *vs. If they would yeelde vs but the superfluitie while it   19
YEELDED = 2
  Yeelded the Towne: he is retyred to Antium.   1686
  I haue yeelded too. Fresh Embasses, and Suites,   3364
YEELDING = 1
  There was a yeelding; this admits no excuse.   3732
YEELDS = 1
  Auf. All places yeelds to him ere he sits downe,   3119
YEERES = 1*1
  *yeeres health; in which time, I will make a Lippe at   1012
  Be singly counter-poys'd. At sixteene yeeres,   1301
YES = 4*3
  I haue the Letter heere: yes, heere it is;   322
  Virgil. Yes certaine, there's a Letter for you, I saw't.   1010
  Volum. Good Ladies let's goe. Yes, yes, yes: The   1030
  Mes. Yes worthy Sir, | The Slaues report is seconded, and more   2970
  Sicin. Yes, mercy, if you report him truly.   3594
YESTERDAY = *1
  *of what he was yesterday. For the other ha's halfe, by   2858
YET = 42*12
  *yet. Suffer vs to famish, and their Store-houses cramm'd   81
  2 *Citizen*. Well, | Ile heare it Sir: yet you must not thinke   94
  Yet I can make my Awdit vp, that all   152
  Yet are they passing Cowardly. But I beseech you,   215
  We neuer yet made doubt but Rome was ready | To answer vs.   333
  *where he would shew most loue. When yet hee was but   366
  Val. You would be another *Penelope*: yet they say, all   446
  Virg. Oh good Madam, there can be none yet.   455
  Mess. They lye in view, but haue not spoke as yet.   488
  Which yet seeme shut, we haue but pin'd with Rushes,   507
  Ere yet the fight be done, packe vp, downe with them.   579
  My worke hath yet not warm'd me. Fare you well: 590
  And Balmes applyed to you, yet dare I neuer   682
  Yet cam'st thou to a Morsell of this Feast, | Hauing fully din'd before.   757
  *that say you are reuerend graue men, yet they lye deadly,   956
  *be intomb'd in an Asses Packe-saddle; yet you must bee   984
  Com. And liue you yet? Oh my sweet Lady, pardon.   1087
  Yet by the faith of men, we haue   1097
  Yet welcome Warriors: 1100
  Brutus. Most willingly: but yet my Caution was   1271
  Brutus. Sir, I hope my words dis-bench'd you not? | *Coriol*. No Sir: yet
  oft,   1282
  Corio. No Sir, 'twas neuer my desire yet to trouble the | poore with
  begging.   1461
  3.*Cit*. Hee's not confirm'd, we may deny him yet.   1612
  Which we disdaine should Tetter vs, yet sought   1771
  And burie all, which yet distinctly raunges | In heapes, and piles of
  Ruine.   1917
  Below the beame of sight; yet will I still | Be thus to them.   2088
  But yet a braine, that leades my vse of Anger | To better vantage.   2121
  Yet were there but this single Plot, to loose   2208
  With Accusations, as I heare more strong | Then are vpon you yet.   2251
  Ile do well yet. Thou old and true *Menenius*,   2459

YET *cont*.

That's yet vnbruis'd: bring me but out at gate.	2488
And for Romes good, Ile tell thee what: yet goe:	2531
Rom. I am a Roman, and my Seruices are as you are, | against 'em.	
Know you me yet.	2574
Corio. If *Tullus* not yet thou know'st me, and seeing	2710
Corio. Prepare thy brow to frowne: knowst y me yet?	2720
Yet *Martius* that was much. Your hand: most welcome. | *Exeunt*	2806
*a Cudgell, and yet my minde gaue my, his cloathes made | a false	
report of him.	2811
*willingly consented to his Banishment, yet it was against | our will.	3071
When first I did embrace him. Yet his Nature	3101
Lieu. Yet I wish Sir, | (I meane for your particular) you had not	3104
As draw his Sword: yet he hath left vndone	3115
Com. Yet one time he did call me by my name:	3161
In this so neuer-needed helpe, yet do not	3188
Sicin. Yet your good will | Must haue that thankes from Rome, after	
the measure | As you intended well.	3202
Mene. Ile vndertak't: | I thinke hee'l heare me. Yet to bite his lip,	3205
Your gates against my force. Yet for I loued thee,	3324
Was my belou'd in Rome: yet thou behold'st.	3328
Which you deny already: yet we will aske,	3444
And yet to change thy Sulphure with a Boult	3509
More bound to's Mother, yet heere he let's me prate	3516
Like him by chance: yet giue vs our dispatch:	3537
*yet your Butterfly was a Grub: this *Martius*, is	3581
A merrier day did neuer yet greet Rome,	3613
Yet he shall haue a Noble Memory. Assist.	3836

YIELDE *see* yeeld, yeelde
YIELDED *see* yeelded
YIELDING *see* yeelding
YIELDS *see* yeelds
YOAKE = 1

Nor yoake with him for Tribune.	1744

YOKE *see* yoake
YOND = 1*3

Corio. Why then should I be Consull? by yond Clouds	1736
Should from yond clowd speake diuine things,	2762
Mene. See you yon'd Coin a'th Capitol, yon'd corner | (stone?	3571

YONDER = 2

Martius. Yonder comes Newes: | A Wager they haue met.	482
Com. Whose yonder, | That doe's appeare as he were Flead? O Gods,	629

YONG = 3

*Enter Coriolanus, Volumnia, Virgilia, Menenius, Cominius, | with the	
yong Nobility of Rome*.	2435
Enter Virgilia, Volumnia, Valeria, yong Martius, | with Attendants.	3369
In supplication Nod: and my yong Boy	3380

YONGER = 1

Thy teares are salter then a yonger mans,	2460

YONGST = 1

And vowes Reuenge as spacious, as betweene | The yong'st and oldest	
thing.	2977

YOU *see also* y'are, you'l, you'ld, you'st = 453*174
YOUL = 10

Men. I will tell you, | If you'l bestow a small (of what you haue little)	130
Bring vp your Army: but (I thinke) you'l finde	346
If you'l stand fast, wee'l beate them to their Wiues,	536

YOUL *cont*.
  Men. You'l marre all, 1449
  And by my troth you haue cause: you'l Sup with me. 2564
  Brut. But is this true sir? | *Com*. I, and you'l looke pale 3019
  2 You'l see your Rome embrac'd with fire, before | You'l speake with
  Coriolanus. 3243
  What peace you'l make, aduise me: For my part, 3556
  Which this mans life did owe you, you'l reioyce 3817
YOULD = 3
  Six of his Labours youl'd haue done, and sau'd 2456
  Corio. I beseech you peace: | Or if you'ld aske, remember this before; 3433
  Mes. Sir, if you'ld saue your life, flye to your House, 3604
YOUNG *see also* yong = 1
  Mene. Helpe *Martius*, helpe: you that be noble, helpe | him young and
  old. 1946
YOUNGER *see* yonger
YOUNGEST *see* yong'st
YOUNGLY = 1
  How youngly he began to serue his Countrey, 1639
YOUR *l*.64 67 68 69 73 75 89 117 135 142 162 169 175 176 177 185 188
  191 194 195 260 269 272 274 278 314 326 336 343 346 351 356 *362 391
  413 416 417 *432 *438 *440 *448 *449 454 *462 501 511 516 639 652
  683 684 *714 720 733 738 743 770 774 788 810 811 812 827 828 855
  *927 *931 *932 *933 *935 *936 *952 *954 *959 *963 *973 *982 *986
  *988 996 *1040 1073 1099 1106 1124 1260 1261 *1273 1276 1279 1285
  1292 1364 1365 *1413 *1420 *1422 1442 1458 1460 1465 *1468 1472
  *1477 *1479 1481 *1497 *1499 *1500 1518 1519 1521 1523 1531 1538
  1555 1560 1569 1570 1571 *1572 1576 1580 1581 1585 1586 1589 1591
  1604 1606 1611 1622 1625 1630 1632 1634 *1635 1651 1653 1654 1657
  1692 1694 1715 *1717 1738 1741 1790 1791 1792 1793 1797 1856 *1888
  1903 *1933 1942 1960 1965 2074 2080 2103 2108 2143 2144 2145 2152
  2153 2154 2156 2159 2164 2198 2248 *2249 2311 2344 2347 2360 *2369
  2403 2412 2413 2414 2416 2417 2418 2419 *2437 2439 2457 2466 2469
  *2516 2518 *2571 *2579 *2602 2617 *2631 2679 *2686 2792 2806 *2906
  2958 *2996 2997 2998 3000 3001 3003 *3004 3013 3016 3025 3038 3045
  3057 3062 3075 3093 3096 3105 3107 3187 3190 3196 3202 3218 *3238
  3243 3246 3248 3249 *3263 3267 *3276 *3277 *3278 *3279 *3282 *3284
  *3292 3294 *3310 3323 3324 3331 *3334 *3337 *3340 *3341 *3342 3352
  3407 3408 3422 3429 3431 3440 3446 3448 3482 3492 3513 3545 *3573
  *3581 3604 3605 3630 3633 3642 3665 *3707 3713 3715 3717 3736 3739
  3741 3752 3760 3761 3762 3766 *3776 3783 3784 3786 3790 3791 3813
  3818 3819 3820 3821 3833 = 244*75
YOURS = 10*1
  And know how we proceede, | *Auf*. Is it not yours? 316
  Lar. My horse to yours, no. | *Mar*. Tis done. | *Lart*. Agreed. 484
  Com. Tak't, 'tis yours: what is't? 840
  Cor. Your Hand, and yours? 1106
  *shew you, which shall bee yours in priuate: your good | voice sir, what
  say you? 1468
  Brut. Not vnlike each way to better yours. 1735
  Mene. If by the Tribunes leaue, | And yours good people, 2016
  I haue a heart as little apt as yours, 2120
  Menen. This but done, | Euen as she speakes, why their hearts were
  yours: 2188
  Volce. You take my part from me sir, I haue the most | cause to be
  glad of yours. 2618
  Volum. This is a poore Epitome of yours, 3420

YOURSELFE *see* selfe, selfe
YOURSELUES *see* selues
YOUST = 1
    Patience awhile; you'st heare the Bellies answer. 132
YOUTH = *2
    *youth with comelinesse pluck'd all gaze his way; when 368
    Hearke, our Drummes | *Are bringing forth our youth: Wee'l breake
    our Walles 504
YSSUED = 1
    Mess. The Cittizens of *Corioles* haue yssued, 614
YSSUES = 1
    And inter-ioyne their yssues. So with me, 2648
& *l.*205 *254 279 *423 *495 897 *1430 *1488 *1615 *1761 *1995 *2503
    *2587 *2857 *2996 *3239 *3385 *3449 *3455 *3538 *3559 *3580
    3648 = 5*19
1 *l.*2673 = 1
1 = 23*17
1CIT = 2*11
1CON = 2*1
1LORD = 3
1OFF = *4
1ROM = 1
1SEN = 6*1
1SENAT = 1
1SOL = 4
1WAT = 1
2 = 18*19
2CIT = 14*5
2CON = 1*1
2LADIES = 1
2LORD = 2
2OFF = *3
2ROM = 1
2SEN = 2
2SENA = 1
2SOL = 1
2WAT = 1
3 *l.*2673 3658 = 2
3 = 10*17
3CIT = 3*3
3CON = 2
3CONSP = 1
3LORD = 1
3ROM = *1
4 *l.*3658 = 1

6

Q1